FAMILY LAW IN NORTHERN IRELAND

Family Law in Northern Ireland

KERRY O'HALLORAN

GILL & MACMILLAN

Gill & Macmillan Ltd
Goldenbridge
Dublin 8
With associated companies throughout the world
© Kerry O'Halloran
0 7171 23189
Index compiled by Tara Levins
Print origination by Carrigboy Typesetting Services
Printed by ColourBooks Ltd, Dublin

All rights reserved. No part of this publication may be reproduced, copied or transmitted in any form or by any means, without written permission of the publishers or else under the terms of any licence permitting limited copying issued by the Irish Copyright Licensing Agency, The Writers' Centre, Parnell Square, Dublin 1.

A catalogue record is available for this book from the British Library.

1 3 5 4 2

This book is dedicated to Elizabeth

Contents

GENERAL INTRODUCTION	xiii
FOREWORD	xv
ACKNOWLEDGMENTS	xvii
TABLE OF CASES	xix
TABLE OF STATUTES	xxxix
TABLE OF STATUTORY INSTRUMENTS AND RULES	lviii
FAMILY LAW: STRUCTURES AND PROCESSES	lxi

Part One: Parents

Introduction	3
Chapter One: Marriage	5
Introduction	5
The Marriage Process	5
Nullity	11
Chapter Two: The Marital Family	25
Introduction	25
Spouses	25
Marital Parenthood	32
The Modern Parental Responsibilities of a Spouse	39
Marital Child	41
Termination of Marriage	43
Chapter Three: The Non-Marital Family	46
Introduction	46
Definitions	47
Cohabitation	52
Cohabitee Parents	55
Abortion	56
Registration	60
Non-Cohabiting Parents	62

Chapter Four: Assisted Parenthood — 63

    Introduction — 63
    The Background — 64
    The Legal Framework in Northern Ireland — 65
    The Law in Practice — 69
    Right to Information — 74

Chapter Five: Guardianship, Parental Responsibilities and the Carer Relationship — 76

    Introduction — 76
    Guardianship: The Concept and the Law — 77
    Guardianship: Jurisdiction and Parties — 78
    Guardianship versus Parenthood — 79
    The Law in Practice — 83
    Parental Responsibility — 86
    The Law Relating to Other Care Relationships after the Children (NI) Order 1995 — 90

Chapter Six: Adoption — 94

    Introduction — 94
    The Jurisdiction, Principles, Parties and Officials of the Adoption Process — 95
    The Authority to Make an Adoption Placement — 102
    The Placement — 115
    The Application — 118
    Decision of the Court — 121
    The Order Granted — 126
    An Adoption Order and Its Consequences — 132

Chapter Seven: Wardship — 135

    Introduction — 135
    Jurisdiction, Principle, Operation, Parties and Administration — 136
    Wardship before the Children (NI) Order 1995 — 144
    Wardship, the Inherent Jurisdiction and the Trusts after the Introduction of the Children (NI) Order 1995 — 154
    Wardship, the Inherent Jurisdiction and Private Applicants after the Children (NI) Order 1995 — 158

Chapter Eight: Marriage Breakdown: Separation — 160

    Introduction — 160
    Judicial Separation — 160
    Separation by Agreement — 163
    Domestic Violence — 164

Chapter Nine: Marriage Breakdown: Divorce 174

    Introduction 174
    The Background to the Present Legislative Framework 174
    The Present Law Governing Divorce 175
    Substantive Law 175
    Procedural Law 185
    Effects of Divorce 193

Chapter Ten: Child Abduction 195

    Introduction 195
    The Background 195
    Prevention 198
    The Criminal Law 200
    The Civil Law and Unlawful Removal within the
        Jurisdictions of the United Kingdom 204
    The Civil Law and the Hague Convention 206
    The Civil Law and the European Convention 213
    Non-Convention Cases 215

Part Two: The Welfare of Children

    Introduction 219

Chapter Eleven: The Children (NI) Order 1995: Principles,
Framework and the Public/Private Divide Procedures 221

    Introduction 221
    Background to the Introduction of the Children (NI) Order 1995 221
    The Family Law Framework and the Welfare Principle 228
    Legislative Change — The Consequences in Terms of Principle
        and Court Procedures 230
    Intervention Thresholds 235

Chapter Twelve: Private Proceedings: Article 8 Orders 243

    Introduction 243
    The Introduction of the Children (NI) Order 1995 243
    The Intervention Threshold 245

Chapter Thirteen: Children in Need and Their Families 263

    Introduction 263
    The Welfare of the Child: A Preventative Approach 264
    The Children (NI) Order 1995: Consensual Statutory Intervention 265
    Children in Need 272

x   *Family Law in Northern Ireland*

*Chapter Fourteen: Child Care and Supervision: Significant Harm,
the Court, the Trusts and the Orders*   284

    Introduction   284
    Intervention: The Legal Routes into Care   285
    The Intervention Threshold   285
    Jurisdiction   287
    Judicial Determination   296
    Public Family Law Orders   298
    Private Family Law Orders   315

*Chapter Fifteen: Child Protection: The Law, the Process and the Orders
Relating to the Abuse of Children*   322

    Introduction   322
    Child Abuse   323
    Child Protection   331

*Chapter Sixteen: Children Being 'Looked After' by a Trust: In
Care and in Accommodation*   358

    Introduction   358
    Being 'Looked After' by a Trust   359
    Placements for a Child Being Looked After by a Trust   363
    Family Placements   365
    Trust Duties in Relation to Children Being Looked After by the Trust   369
    Secure Accommodation   382
    Discharge from Care   385
    After Care   387

Chapter Seventeen: Children, Young Persons and Juvenile Justice   389

    Introduction   389
    The Jurisdiction, Parties and Bodies of the Juvenile Justice System   390
    Juveniles, Offences and Social Policy   394
    Juvenile Offences   397
    Terrorist-Type Offences by Juveniles   402
    Juvenile Offenders — The Disposal Options   403
    Remand   409
    Treatment of Offenders   411

Chapter Eighteen: The Views and Legal Interests of the Child   416

    Introduction   416
    The Views of the Child: The Law, the Parties and the Principle   417
    Public Family Law   424
    Private Family Law   432

Chapter Nineteen: Representing the Views and Legal Interests of the Child	435
Introduction	435
The Law, Jurisdiction of the Courts and the Child as a Party	436
Representation	442
Representation in Private Proceedings	451
Representation in Public Proceedings	455

Part Three: Property and Finance

Introduction	467
Chapter Twenty: Property, Finance and the Marital Family	469
Introduction	469
Matrimonial Property	469
Matrimonial Property	
The Ownership of Property	482
The Matrimonial Home	488
The Matrimonial Home and Beneficial Interests	491
The Matrimonial Home and Legal Interests	498
Mortgages and Charges	502
Chapter Twenty-One: Property, Finance and the Non-Marital Family	505
Introduction	505
Statute Law, Unmarried Persons and Property	505
Equity, Cohabitees and the Family Home	507
Equity, Cohabitees and Ownership of Property Other than the Family Home	513
The Law, Unmarried Parents and the Family Home	514
Finances	517
Chapter Twenty-Two: Family Breakdown: The Child Support Scheme	517
Introduction	519
The Child Support Legislation	519
The Child Support Scheme	523
The Parties to Whom the Child Support Scheme Applies	527
Procedures	531
Applying the Assessment Formula	534
Financial Provision for Children	536

xii *Family Law in Northern Ireland*

Chapter Twenty-Three: Separation: Maintenance	537
Introduction	537
Jurisdiction	537
Maintenance by Private Agreement	538
Maintenance	543
Chapter Twenty-Four: Divorce: Ancillary Relief	550
Introduction	550
Jurisdiction	550
Ancillary Relief	554
Matters to Which the Court Must Have Regard	561
The 'Clean Break'	566
Chapter Twenty-Five: Testate Succession	573
Introduction	573
Wills	573
The Testator	579
The Administration of Wills	582
Chapter Twenty-Six: Intestate Succession	593
Introduction	593
Intestacy	593
The Marital Family	595
The Non-Marital Family	598
Judicial Determination of Claims Brought against an Intestate's Estate	600
Appendix 1	
The Eight Principles of the Honourable Justice MacDermott	604
Appendix 2	
The Changing Context of Private Family Law since 1967	607
Appendix 3	
The Changing Context of Public Family Law since 1967	608
Appendix 4	
Useful Agencies	609
Index	612

General Introduction

The relationship between law and the family has always been complex. It provides a fertile ground for research by political scientists, sociologists and others with an interest in identifying and tracing the influence of particular ideologies, policies and strategies. For lawyers this relationship is increasingly difficult to grasp.

The family has become an uncertain entity. When it can be defined as marital, monogamous and nuclear, the membership and boundaries of a family are readily established, as are the legal relationships within it and between it and other such families. Many households, however, do not conform to this definition. The diffuse relationships which may loosely bind an individual to one or more households, concurrently or consecutively, are not easily made amenable to legal definition. Neither gender nor blood relationships are necessary role determinants for those living in domestic circumstances in the modern family unit. In law such a unit is now often best viewed in terms of its constituent relationships of carers and dependants.

The law itself lacks a hard edge. Each case depends on its individual facts. It is no longer based on a coherent body of principles, its function is not always obvious and cannot be readily established without reference to material other than statutes and case law. The process of determination may involve expert witnesses drawn from a broad range of professions and disciplines. The law in this area is exercised with a discretion not usually available elsewhere, and the outcome of a legal process often lacks the finality of many other types of proceedings.

In a sense, the family is now experiencing less law and more administration. Statutes are becoming more broad-brush statements of principle underpinned by volumes of guidance and regulations. In an increasing range of proceedings, the contact time between parties and the court is greatly outweighed by that spent between the parties and authorised officials. Family law is withdrawing to those matters where the adult parties are unable to reach an accommodation with each other or where the welfare of a child is in jeopardy.

In Northern Ireland, for lawyers and others, the relationship between the family and the law is currently particularly difficult. The volume of legislation on family matters has, in recent years, made this period one of unprecedented change. A swathe of old legislation, long since repealed in England and Wales, has now also been removed from the statute books for Northern Ireland. New law in the form of a range of statutes together with case-law developments (some precedents forged locally, others originating in Great Britain or the European Court of Human Rights) has taken its place. Much legislation has not been fully implemented, more is on the way, and it all largely remains to be fully tested in the courts. The cumulative impact of such change has brought the province's family law into a new alignment with that prevailing in Great Britain and with the principles of international conventions. While this period of concentrated and widespread change has done much to harmonise the family law of these islands, there continue to be areas of difference.

This book does not attempt to explore either the sociological aspects of change in the family or the history of jurisdictional differences in these islands. Many matters of process and administration which it might legitimately have been expected to include are not addressed. It confines itself to setting out the law relating to the family which most frequently demands the attention of busy practitioners. It examines and explains all major areas of family law with reference to local and English case law. It provides a guide to the legislation, to the related court rules and to the Guidance and Regulations in effect in the winter of 1996/7. It does so in three parts which deal sequentially with parenting, the welfare of children and property/finance. In a brief introduction it outlines the structure of the courts, the statutory framework and the legal aid scheme and identifies the main players (Judiciary, Official Solicitor, Registrars, etc.) who at present constitute the 'family law system' in Northern Ireland.

KERRY O'HALLORAN
White Park Bay
Spring 1997

FOREWORD

The Family and Family Law

Well over 2,000 years ago Aristotle declared:

> The family is the association established by nature for the supply of man's everyday wants.

Today this traditional and long-established view of the family and family life is not universally accepted. We are constantly being reminded that more and more marriages are ending in divorce, more and more children are being brought up by a single parent. Whether viewed as being established by nature or by law, the family has never seemed more fragile as it struggles to supply and hold in balance the every day wants of man, woman and child. These social changes, added to an upsurge in relevant legislation, have led to the production of a vast array of books and periodicals dealing with all aspects of what is loosely called 'family law'.

In such circumstances one might ask if this is an opportune time for Dr O'Halloran to launch his book *Family Law in Northern Ireland*. I have no doubt that such a book is called for. Though family law enjoys a similarity of form and substance throughout the United Kingdom, practice in Northern Ireland bears its own characteristics, and practitioners and students do greatly appreciate books on general subjects written from a local perspective.

As I made my way through Dr O'Halloran's book I was amazed at the amount of local material rediscovered by his industry and research. In this context the wardship section is of particular interest and a timely reminder that for many years 'wardship' was a much-used and, I believe, effective tool as judges and practitioners sought to ensure that the best interests of children were properly protected.

Another section of present-day relevance is that dealing with the Children (Northern Ireland) Order 1995. Its application will be a challenge to all involved with the administration of a complex piece of legislation, and Dr O'Halloran's book is likely to be of much assistance and guidance to those who practise in this field. It will be interesting to see if the courts in this jurisdiction approach all issues in the same manner as that currently favoured by the courts in England and Wales.

I believe that this will in fact be a useful textbook. It is pleasantly written and shows how the law has been applied in individual cases; and that is important. In the Family Division judges and practitioners face problems which may be of a common nature, but they must never forget that each case is individual and a decision as to what is in the best interests of a child or what is fair as between the parties to a broken marriage cannot be reached simply by reference to a textbook. The book will seek to make clear what the law is; but the application of the law to individual cases will require judgment and understanding, and the approach of the trial judge will be all important. Understandably neither Dr O'Halloran nor any textbook writer can forecast how judges will resolve every case. That is because decision-making is, within the law, a personal matter.

The eminent American jurist, Justice Benjamin Cardoze, in his lectures at Yale University in 1921 (subsequently published under the title *The Nature of the Judicial Process*) sought to define the subtle influences which affect judicial decision-making. He said:

> There is in each of us a stream of tendency, whether you choose to call it philosophy or not, which gives coherence and direction to thought and action. Judges cannot escape that current any more than other mortals. All their lives, forces which they do not recognise and cannot name, have been tugging at them — inherited instincts, traditional beliefs, acquired convictions; and the result is an outlook on life, a conception of social needs, a sense . . . of 'the total push and pressure of the cosmos' which, when reasons are nicely balanced, must determine where choice shall fall. In this mental background every problem finds its setting. We may try to see things as objectively as we please. Nonetheless, we can never see them with any eyes except our own.

In this jurisdiction judges, I believe, tend to share the view that so-called family values are indeed valuable, and for my part the declaration of Aristotle remains relevant and sensible.

To have the law — Family Law — as it affects practice in Northern Ireland brought together in a manageable volume will be a boon to practitioners in this jurisdiction. They will I am sure share my belief that the layout is sensible and practical. We will be grateful to Dr O'Halloran for what he has done on our behalf.

RT HON LORD JUSTICE MACDERMOTT
Court of Appeal (NI)
Royal Courts of Justice
Belfast
Janauary 1997

Acknowledgments

It is not possible to render a full account of the extensive information, advice and encouragement given so willingly by many busy professionals during the three–four year gestation period of this book. The contribution of some, however, has been too crucial to allow to go unrecorded. The sources of support reflect the different balances held in this book between substantive and procedural law, between the work of lawyers and of other practitioners and between the singular importance of individual cases and the trends disclosed by an overview of statistical data.

The most significant input to the shaping of this book was made by legal practitioners. None contributed more than the Right Honourable Lord Justice MacDermott. The advice he gave at the outset, his willingness thereafter to share selected case material and the personal sacrifice entailed in spending much of the summer recess of 1996 reading and commenting on the material, grounded this project and enabled a certain momentum to be maintained. For all that work, and for contributing the Foreword, the author is sincerely grateful. Mrs Corrine Philpott QC, in her capacity as consultant editor, provided invaluable sound advice and good humour throughout the project. Mr Charles Redpath, Official Solicitor, fastidiously read and commented on most chapters and provided many useful case references and related material. His consistent encouragement and support, and his availability as a sounding board for the author to talk matters through, was always appreciated.

A significant contribution was also made by lawyers further removed from practice. Ms Sheena Grattan, law lecturer at QUB, patiently made time — when in the throes of preparing *Succession Law in NI*, SLS (1996) for publication — to read and comment on the two chapters concerning testate and intestate succession. Mr Niall Small, solicitor and honorary secretary of the Family Law Association (NI), kindly arranged for members of the association to read and comment on some of the chapters dealing with property. Ms Allison Lemon, Supreme Court librarian, assisted with the citing of cases and also helpfully located and supplied transcripts of unreported judgments. Mr GW Johnston, principal secretary to the Lord Chief Justice, advised on the judicial staffing of the Family Division. Mrs Laura McPolin and her colleagues, including Ms Deborah Kerr and Ms Joanne Flood in Court Service, gave advice on matters relating to court structures and court orders. The office of the Registrar General provided extensive statistical information very promptly and efficiently. Ms Miriam Dudley, librarian at the QUB law library, proved to be a constant source of reliable information and guidance.

Many formal and informal contributions were made by professionals based in different practice agencies. Mr Jim Loughrey, director of family and community services in Causeway HSS Trust, provided the support and time necessary to complete this project. Others commented on how, from the perspective of their particular agency, the law is actually applied. Mr John Fenton, principal social worker (child care) of the Northern Health and Social Services Board, commented on the author's interpretation of agency practice and procedures in five chapters concerned with implementation of the Children (NI) Order 1995. Mr Ronnie Williamson, panel manager of the NI Guardian ad Litem Agency, did likewise in relation to two chapters concerning the views of children and their representation in court. Mr Tim Chapman, assistant chief probation officer with the Probation Board (NI), at short notice, made time to read the chapter on juvenile justice and offered valuable advice on agency procedures. Mr Trevor Rea of the DHSS (Policy and Legislation Division), advised on the chapter dealing with child support. Mr Robert McLardy, DHSS (Strategy and Intelligence Group), supplied much of the statistical data relating to children.

Acknowledgment must also be made of the lessons learned from the example set by those whose work in this area stands as a beacon by which others may steer. This author admits to being more than a little influenced, though perhaps less than he should have been, by the works of such others as Bromley, Cretney, Dewar and Hayes/Williams.

A deep debt of gratitude is owed to Gill & Macmillan and particularly to Michael Gill, without whom this project would not have progressed beyond the point of being a mildly interesting concept. Mention must be made of the trust and support provided at the inception of the project by Ms Finola O'Sullivan the commissioning editor, and continued thereafter by her successor Ms Deirdre Greenan. It has been a challenge and a privilege to work with such a professional team.

Finally, a sincere thank-you to my wife Elizabeth and boys Neil and Connor for their endless patience and understanding.

KERRY O'HALLORAN
August 1997

Table of Cases

Northern Ireland

A-MW, In the matter of unrep (1992) 124
Adjudications Officer v Una McMenamin [1993] 11 NIJB 29 525
Allied Irish Banks Ltd v McWilliams and Another [1982] NILR 156 495
AMNH, Re [1994] 4 BNIL 57, 58
APP and LP (Minors), Re unrep (1973) 252

B (An Infant), Re [1946] NI 1 . . . . 37, 152, 238
B 847, In the matter of unrep (1974) 131
B, In Re (A Minor) unrep (1990) 124
B, In Re (A Minor) unrep 14 Nov., 1990 105
BM and BH (Minors), Re unrep (1979) 145
Britannia Building Society v Johnston and Others [1994] 10 BNIL 75 . . . 473, 493
Brown v Brown [1992] 2 BNIL 48 . . . . 182, 192
Bullock, Re [1968] NI 96 577

C v C [1989] 10 NIJB 39 207
Campbell v Campbell [1982] NIJB 18 602
CB and AJB (minors), Re unrep (1983) 38, 145, 151, 205, 238, 420
CDH (A Minor), Re unrep (1980) 145, 212
CH (A Minor), In the matter of unrep (1995) 58, 59, 150
Creeney, Creeney v Smith [1984] NI 397 590
Crozier v Crozier [1993] 10 BNIL 34 . . . . 540, 559

D (Minors), Re unrep (1986) 138
Department of Health and Social Security v Lowry [1993] 10 NIJB 42 525
DPP for Northern Ireland v Lynch [1975] AC 653; [1975] 1 All ER 913 19

E.68, In the matter of unrep (1987) 126
EAW and MW (Infants), Re [1949] NI 1 152
EB and Others (Minors), In Re [1985] 5 NIJB 1 . . . . 108, 113, 125, 455
EHSSB v Warnock [1993] 4 NIJB 5 113

Folio 3540, The Matter of, Co. Tyrone [1991] NI 273 471
Fulton v Kee [1961] NI 1 576

G and S (Minors) unrep (1991) 113
GD and JD (Minors: and Access), Re unrep (1996) 215
Gilliland, Re [1937] NI 156 578
Grieve v Grieve [1993] 6 NIJB 347 577

Hamilton, Re [1982] NI 197 574
Hull v Mullan and Others [1985] NIJB 4 575
Hutchinson v McSorley [1993] 6 NIJB 49 580

ICS and RHS (Minors), Re unrep (1982) 145, 255
Irwin v Brown and Others [1993] 6 NIJB 18 408

JRS (A Minor), Re unrep (1983) 145, 151, 205, 237, 238

K, In the matter of a minor unrep (1993) 60
K (A Minor), Re [1970] NIJB July /Sept. 58, 59
K (A Minor), In the matter of unrep (1993) 16 . . . . 150, 429
K v K (Re LEK, An Infant), unrep (1992) 254
KH and EH (Minors), In Re [1989] 7 NIJB 1 . . . . 110, 122
Knell v Knell [1970] NIJB 58

L (Minors), Re unrep (1981) 145
LEC and NCC (Minors), Re unrep (1983) 252

M (An Infant), In Re unrep (1976) 125
M and M (Minors), In Re unrep (1988) 124
M McC and DH (Minors), Re [1986] 5 NIJB 1 . . . . 109, 138, 149
M v M [1983] 7 BNIL 1 . . . . 542, 557, 571
Martin v Martin [1941] NI 1; [1976] Fam 335; [1976]
    3 All ER 625 . . . . 184, 542, 560, 565
Mason v Mason [1944] NI 134 14
McA P (Minor), Re unrep (1993) 150, 151, 237, 252
McC (A Minor), Re [1985]AC 528 396
McC J v A McC [1982] 14 NIJB 93 570
McC T and B (Minors), Re unrep (1982) 148, 362
McFarlane v McFarlane [1972] NI 59 . . . . 484, 485, 488, 494, 495, 497
McGrillen v Cullen [1991] NILR 53 395
McGuigan A v B and E McGuigan unrep (1996) 588
McReynolds v McReynolds unrep (1985) 183
Megarry v Megarry [1978] 7 NIJB 544
MEMV and MRVV (Minors), Re unrep (1981) 151, 152, 237, 252
MPW and NPW (Minors), Re unrep (1983) 252
Murphy v Murphy [1980] 3 NIJB 580

Table of Cases xxi

Northern Bank Ltd. v Adams unrep (1996) 502
Northern Bank Ltd. v Beattie [1982] NIJB 18 561
Northern Bank Ltd. v Haggerty unrep (1995) 504
Northern Bank v Beattie [1982] NIJB 18 .... 496, 506, 561
Northern Bank v McNeill [1988] 7 BNIL 79 494
Northern Health and Social Services v YB(A Minor) unrep 1986 444
Northern Ireland Child Support Commissioners unrep
   Decision No. CSC6/94 [1994] 6 BNIL 56 526
Northern Ireland Child Support Commissioners unrep
   Decision No. CSC 8/94 [1995] 3 BNIL 57 528

Official Assignee for Bankruptcy for Northern Ireland and Assignee
   of the Property of Helen Beattie v Beattie and Another
   [1992] 12 NIJB 11 500

Patton, McIlveen and Another v Patton [1986] NI 45 .... 588, 590
PB (A Minor), In Re unrep 1986 .... 147, 327, 345, 444
PM, In the matter of (Freeing Application) unrep (1993) 114

R v Brown [1991] NI 290 445
R v Charters [1990] 6 BNIL 70 330
R v Farquhar [1989] 3 NIJB 28 165
R v McDonald [1989] 3 NIJB 28 165
R v Stephenson [1947] NI 110 58
R v Taggart [1989] 3 NIJB 28 165
RASJ and PFJ (Minors), Re unrep (1976) 151, 212, 238
RASJ and PFJ (Minors), Re unrep (1980) 212, 237, 373
RAW and MW (Infants), Re [1949] NI 1 39
Ridgeway v Murray [1981] 7 NIJB 478

S (Otherwise B) v S [1944] NI 134 18
SLH (Minors), Re unrep (1982) 204

T (A Minor), Re unrep (1993) 114, 129, 362
TB, Re (Care Proceedings: Criminal Trial) [1995] 2 FLR 80 297
TC (A Minor), Re unrep (1993) 59, 60
TC (A Minor), Re [1994] 4 BNIL 45 .... 141, 146, 428, 455
TMW and AMW (Minors), In the matter of [1979] 9 NIJB 150, 211
Toner v Toner [1972] NILR 1 .... 478, 483
Tubman v Johnston [1981] NI 53 503

Ulster Bank v McCullough and Others [1985] 11 NIJB 1 576

V and Another, In Re unrep (1981) 200

W (A Ward), Re unrep (1988) 109, 309
Ward v Byham [1956] 1 WLR 496 163
Watters v Watters [1979] 3 NIJB 487
Weir and Others v Davey and Others: Watts v Weir and Others [1993]
   2 NIJB 46 587
Wellesley v Beaufort [1827] 2 Russell 1 36

England and Wales

A & W (Minors) (Residence Order: Leave to Apply) [1992] 2 FLR 154 246
A (A Minor) unrep (1993) 59, 141
A (A Minor), Re (Abduction) [1988] 1 FLR 365 211 (Contact
   Application: Grandparent) The Times, 6 March 1995 .... 254, 374
A (A Minor), Re (Abduction) [1991] FCR 765, [1991] 1 FLR 413 211
A (A Minor), Re (Custody) [1991] 2 FLR 394 .... 42, 237
A (A Minor), Re (Wardship: Medical Treatment) [1992] 3 WLR 785;
   [1992] 4 All ER 627 423
A and Others (Minors), Re (Child Abuse: Guidelines) [1992]
   1 FLR 439 .... 345, 446
A (An Infant), In Re [1963] 1 WLR 34 98
A (A Minor), In Re (Paternity: Refusal of Blood Tests) [1994]
   2 FLR 463 51
A v A (A Minor) (Financial Provision) [1994] 1 FLR 657; [1995]
   1 FLR 345 .... 517, 518, 565
A v A (Family: Unborn Child) [1974] Fam 6; [1974]
   1 All ER 755 .... 250, 552
A v Liverpool City Council [1982] AC 363 .... 138, 148, 153, 154, 227, 299, 303
A v N (Committal: Refusal of Contact) 11 Oct. 1996 256
A, Re (Adoption: Contact Order) [1993] 2 FLR 645 105
A, Re (Adoption: Placement) [1988] 1 WLR 229 103
A, Re (An Infant) [1963] 1 All ER 531; [1963] 1 WLR 231 125
A, Re (Care: Discharge Application by Child) [1995]
   1 FLR 599 .... 385, 460, 461
A, Re (Foreign Access Order: Enforcement) [1996] 1 FLR 561 198
AB, Re (Adoption: Shared Residence Order) [1996] 1 FLR 1 .... 99, 128
AB, Re (Child Abuse: Expert Witnesses) [1995] 1 FLR 191 450
Abbey National Building Society v Cann [1990] 1 All ER 1085 491
Abram (Deceased), Re [1996] 2 FLR 379 590
ACB v JLB 1980 153
AD (A Minor), Re [1993] Fam Law vol. 23, 43, 405 .... 252, 439, 453
Adoption Application (Note), Re [1990] 1 FLR 412 134
Adoption Application, Re (Adoption: Payment) [1987] 2 FLR 291 97
Adoption Application, Re (Payment for Adoption) [1937] 2 All ER 326 69

Adoption Application, Re [1992] 1 FLR 341 .... 69, 112, 125
AG (ex rel Tiley) v London Borough of Wandsworth [1981]
　1 All ER 1162 .... 276, 281
Agar-Ellis, Re [1883] 24 Ch D 317 .... 32, 34, 35, 77
Ali v Ali [1966] 1 All ER 664 11
Allan v Allan [1974] 1 WLR 1171 560
Allsop v Allsop (1980) 124 SJ 710 164
Argyll v Argyll [1965] 2 WLR 790 30
Ashley v Blackman [1988] 2 FLR 278 567
Associated Provincial Picture Houses Ltd v Wednesbury Corporation
　[1948] 1 KB 223 .... 148, 153
Astwood v Astwood (1981) 131 NLJ 990 179
Atkinson v Atkinson [1987] 3 All ER 849; [1995] 2 FLR 569
Attar v Attar (No. 2) [1985] FLR 653 563
AW (Adoption Application), Re [1992] Fam Law 53 125
AZ (A Minor) (Abduction Acquiescence) (no. 2), Re [1993]
　1 FLR 396 212
AZ (A Minor) (Abduction Acquiescence), Re [1993] 1 FLR 682 210

B (A Minor), Re (Abduction) [1994] 2 FLR 249 208
B (A Minor), Re (Access) [1992] 1 FLR 142 255
B (A Minor), Re (Adoption by Parent) [1975] 2 All ER 449 105
B (A Minor), Re (Adoption) [1988] 18 Fam Law 172 126
B (A Minor), Re (Interim Care Order: Criteria) [1993]
　1 FLR 815 .... 295, 308, 310, 334
B (A Minor), Re [1990] 1 FLR 415 50
B (Minors), Re (Care: Contact: Local Authority's Plans) [1993]
　1 FLR 543 .... 299, 376
B (Minors), Re (Disclosure of Evidence) [1993] 1 FLR 191 450
B (Minors), Re (Residence Order) [1992] 3 All ER 867 238
B (Supervision Order: Parental Undertaking) [1996] 1 FLR 676 .... 304, 305
B v B (1982) 3 FLR 299 564
B v B (Custody of Children) [1985] 1 FLR 166 238
B v B (Minors) (Custody, Care and Control) [1991] Fam Law 174;
　[1991] 1 FLR 402 .... 74, 240
B v B (Periodical Payment: Transitional Provisions) [1995]
　1 FLR 868 547
B v B(A Minor) (Residence Order) [1992] 2 FLR 327 247
B v C (Enforcement Arrears) [1995] Fam Law 243 547
B v France [1992] 2 FLR 249 15
B, In Re (A Minor) [1987] 2 FLR 314 140
B, Re (Adoption by Parent) [1975] Fam 127; [1975] All ER 449 124
B, Re (Adoption by Parent) [1990] 2 FLR 383 .... 123, 126, 433
B, Re (Adoption: Child's Welfare) [1995] 2 FLR 895 .... 125, 126

B, Re (Care or Supervision Order) [1996] 2 FLR 693 304
B, Re (Change of Surname) [1981] 1 All ER 100 432
B, Re (Change of Surname) [1996] 1 FLR 791 253
B, Re (Child Sexual Abuse: Standard of Proof) [1995] 1 FLR 904 328
B, Re (MF) (An Infant) [1972] 1 All ER 898 130
Bailey v Tolliday [1983] 4 FLR 542 565
Baindail v Baindail [1946] 1 All ER 342 .... 10, 16
Balfour v Balfour [1919] 2 KB 571 28
Banning Deceased, Banning v Salmon and Others, Re [1984]
  3 All ER 1 588
Barder v Barder (Caluori Intervening) [1987] 2 FLR 480 541
Barking and Dagenham LBC v O and Another [1993] 3 WLR 493 137
Barnes v Barnes [1972] 3 All ER 872 570
Barratt v Barratt [1988] 2 FLR 516 568
Baxter v Baxter [1948] AC 274; [1947] 2 All ER 886 17
Beach v Beach [1995] 2 FLR 160 542
Beales v Beales [1972] Fam 210; [1972] 2 All ER 677 193
Benson v Benson (Deceased) [1996] 1 FLR 692 558
Berry v Berry [1987] 1 FLR 105 533
Bethell (1888), Re 38 Ch D 220 .... 10, 11
Birch v Birch [1992] 1 FLR 564 178
Birmingham City Council v H (no. 2)[1993] 1 FLR 883 .... 242, 378
Birmingham City Council v H [1992] 2 FLR 323 172
Blackwell v Blackwell [1943] 2 All ER 579 471
Boggins v Boggins (1966) 5 CC 102 17
Bradley v Bradley [1973] 1 WLR 1291 180
Bravada, Re [1968] 2 All ER 217 577
Browne (A minor), Re [1852] 2 ICR 151 35
Browne v Browne [1989] 1 FLR 291 562
Buckinghamshire County Council v M [1994] 2 FLR 506 302
Buckland v Buckland [1967] 2 All ER 300 19
Bullock v Bullock [1960] 2 All ER 307 44
Burgess, Burgess v Bottomley, Re (1883) 25 Ch D 243 436
Burnett v George [1992] 1 FLR 525 166
Burns v Burns [1984] 1 All ER 244 512
Butler v Butler (1885) 14 QBD 831 27

C (A Minor), Re (Adopted Child: Contact) [1993] 2 FLR 431 133
C (A Minor), Re (Adoption Application) [1993] Fam Law vol. 22, 538 125
C (A Minor), Re (Irregularity of Practice) [1991] 2 FLR 438
C (A Minor), Re (Wardship: Surrogacy) [1985] FL 846 .... 70, 74
C (A Minor), Re [1988] 1 AER 712h 131
C (An Infant), Re *The Times*, 14 Dec. 1956 142
C (An Infant), Re [1959] Ch 363 138
C v C (A Minor) (Custody Appeal) [1991] 1 FLR 223 240

C v C (Minors) (Child Abduction) [1992] 1 FLR 163	213
C v C (Minors: Custody) [1988] 2 FLR 291	238
C v C [1921] P 399	17
C v C [1942] NZLR 356	20
C v DPP [1995] 1 FLR 933	392
C v K (Inherent Powers: Exclusion Order) [1996] 2 FLR 506	169
C v S (A Minor) (Child Abduction)[1990] 2 FLR 442	197
C v Solihull Metropolitan Borough Council [1993] 1 FLR 290	302, 309, 318
C, In Re (A Minor) (Adoption Order: Condition) [1986] 1 FLR 315	129
C, Re (Adoption: Parties) [1995] 2 FLR 187	98
C, Re (Contact Jurisdiction) [1995] FLR 777	105
C, Re (Expert Evidence: Disclosure: Practice) [1995] 1 FLR 204	457
C, Re (Family Assistance Order) [1996] 1 FLR 424	261, 321
C, Re (Guardian ad Litem: Disclosure of Report) [1996] 1 FLR 61	458
C, Re (Interim Care Order: Assessment) [1996] 2 FLR 708	309
C, Re (Interim Care Order: Residential) [1997] 1 FLR 1	309
C, Re [1993] 1 FLR 832	461
Calderbank v Calderbank [1975] 3 All ER 333	563
Campbell and Cosssans v UK (1982) 4 EHRR 293	326
Campbell v Secretary of State for Social Services (1981) 3 FLR 232	53
Carega Properties v Sharratt [1979] 2 All ER 1084	599
CB v CB[1988] Fam Law 471	568
CD Petitioners [1963] LT (Sh Ct) 7	98
CH, Re (Contact) [1996] 1 FLR 569	71
Chaplin, Re [1950] 2 All ER 155	596
Chard v Chard [1955] 3 All ER 721	44
Cheni v Cheni [1962] 3 All ER 882	10
Cheshire County Council v B [1992] 2 FCR 572	303
Chilton v Chilton [1952] 1 All ER 132	470
Churchard v Churchard [1984] FLR 635	256
Citro, Re (A Bankrupt) and Another [1991] 1 FLR 71	500
Clifford v Clifford [1948] 1 All ER 394	22
Cochrane, Re (1840) 8 Dowl 630	28
Colling, Re [1972] 3 All ER 729	577
Cooke v Head [1972] 2 All ER 38	478, 492, 508
Coombes v Smith [1987] 1 FLR 352	511
Corbett v Corbett [1970] 2 All ER 33	15
Cornick v Cornick [1995] 2 FLR 789	563
Cossey v United Kingdom [1991] 2 FLR 492	15
Costello-Roberts v UK [1994] ECR 1	269, 326
Council of Civil Service Unions v Minister for Civil Defence [1985] AC 374	153
Court v Court [1982] Fam 105 [1981] 2 All ER 531	180
Couser v Couser [1996] 2 FLR 46	577
Coventry Deceased, Re [1980] Ch 461	585, 601

Coventry, Re [1979] 2 WLR 835; [1979] 3 All ER 815 574
Crake v Supplementary Benefits Commisssion (1980) 2 FLR 264 53
Crispin's Will Trusts, Re [1974] 3 All ER 722 596
Croydon London Borough Council v A (no. 3) [1992] 2 FCR 481; [1992]
   2 FLR 350 305
Croydon London Borough Council v A and Others [1992] Fam 169 ..... 260, 319
CT (A Minor), Re (Wardship: Representation) [1993] 2 FLR 278
   Fam Law vol. 233, P 569 .... 137, 448

D (A Minor) v Berkshire County Council (1987) 1 All ER 33 43
D (A Minor), Re (Care or Supervision Order) [1993] 2 FLR 423 .... 293, 303
D (A Minor), Re (Contact: Mother's Hostility) [1993] 2 FLR 1 256
D (A Minor), Re (Removal from the Jurisdiction) [1992] 1 All ER 892 258
D (A Minor), Re *The Times*, 5 Dec. 1986 149
D (A Minor), Re [1976] Fam 185; [1976] 1 ALL ER 326 141
D (A Minor), Re [1987] 1 FLR 422 295
D (An Infant), Re (Adoption: Parent's Consent) [1977]
   1 All ER 145 HL 114, 124
D (An Infant), Re [1959] 1 QB 229; [1958] 3 All ER 716 124
D (Minor), Re (Adoption by Parents) [1973] 3 All ER 1001 114
D (Minor), Re (Adoption by Step-Parent) [1980] 2 FLR 103 126
D v D (1974) 118 SJ 715 539
D v D (Child Abduction Non-Convention Country) [1941] 1 FLR 137 216
D v D (Child Abduction) [1994] 1 FLR 137 216
D v D [1979] 3 All ER 337 22
D v NSPCC [1978] AC 171 337
D v Registrar General [1996] 1 FLR 707 134
D'Altroy's Will Trusts, Re [1968] 1 WLR 1173 24
D, In Re (A Minor) (Adoption Order: Validity) [1991] 2 FLR 66 126
D, Re (Adoption Reports: Confidentiality) [1995] 2 FLR 687 120
D, Re (An Infant) [1972] 1 All ER 898 130
D, Re (no. 2) [1959] 1 QB 229 9
D, Re (Prohibited Steps Order) [1996] 2 FLR 273 172
D, Re (Residence: imposition of conditions) [1996] 2 FLR 281 253
D-E v AG (1845) 1 Rob Eccl 279 17
Dale, Proctor v Dale, Re [1994] Ch 31 581
Dart v Dart [1996] 2 FLR 286 562
Davis v Johnston [1978] 2 WLR 553 515
Day v Day [1988] 1 FLR 278 .... 566, 569
De Lasala v De Lasala [1980] AC 546 540
De Mannneville v De Manneville 1804, 10 Vessey Junior 52 35
Dellow's WT, Re [1964] 1 WLR 451
Dennis v Dennis [1955] 2 All ER 51 176
Dennis v MacDonald [1982] 2 WLR 275 170
Dennis, Re [1981] 2 All ER 140 .... 585, 601

Table of Cases xxvii

Denshaw, Re [1975] 1 WLR 1519; [1975] 3 All ER 726 482
Department of Health and Social Security v Butler [1996] 1 FLR 1 533
Devon County Council v S and Another [1994] 1 FLR 355 .... 158, 173, 321
DH, In Re (A Minor) (Child Abuse) [1994] 1 FLR 679 451
Dinch v Dinch [1987] 1 All ER 818; [1987] 2 FLR 162 541
Diococco v Milne (1983) 4 FLR 247 238
Dixon v Dixon (1974) Fam Law 58 565
DM (A Minor), In Re (Wardship: Jurisdiction) [1986] 2 FRL 102 154
Dobson v North Tyneside Health Authority [1997] 1 FLR 598 575
Downing v Downing (Downing Intervening) [1976] Fam 288 552
DPP v Majewski [1977] AC 443 177
Drake v Whipp [1996] 1 FLR 826 509
Dredge v Dredge [1947] 1 All ER 29 17
Dudgeon v UK (1982) 4 EHRR 149 52
Dufour v Pereira (1769) 1 Dick 420 582
Duke of Somerset, Thynne v St Maur, Re (1877) 34 Ch D 465 .... 436, 458
Duxbury v Duxbury [1987] 1 FLR 7 556
DX (An Infant), In Re [1949] 1 Ch 320 124
Dyson Holdings v Fox [1976] QB 503 599

E (A Minor), Re (Adoption) [1989] 1 FLR 126 114
E (A Minor), Re (Care Order: Contact) [1994] 1 FLR 146 376
E (A Minor), Re (Child Support: Blood Test) [1994] 2 FLR 548 529
E (An Infant), In Re [1964] 1 WLR 51 129
E v C (Maintenance) [1996] 1 FLR 472 533
E v E (Financial Provision) [1990] 2 FLR 233 560
E, Re [1994] Fam Law 483 124
EC, Re (Disclosure of Material) [1996] 2 FLR 725 343
Edgar v Edgar [1980] 3 All ER 887 .... 540, 572
Elsey v Cox (1858) 26 Beav 95 442
Essex County Council v F [1993] 1 FLR 847 354
Essex County Council v R [1993] 2 FLR 826 451
Evans v Evans [1990] 2 All ER 147 568
Evers' Trust, Re [1980] 1 WLR 1327 514
Eves v Eves [1975] 3 All ER 768 509

F (An Infant), Re [1970] 1 All ER 344 124
F (R) (An Infant), Re [1970] 1 QB 358 .... 112, 127
F v F (Duxbury Calculation: Rate of Return) [1996] 1 FLR 833 563
F v F (Protection from Violence: Continuing Cohabitation) [1989]
   2 FLR 451 166
F v F unrep (1996) 206
F v F [1902] 1 Ch 688 35
F v F [1963] 1 All ER 242 62
F v S [1973] Fm 203; [1973] 1 All ER 722 124

F, In Re (In Utero) [1988] 2 All ER 193 141
F, Re (Contact: Child in Care) [1995] 1 FLR 510 377
F, Re (Minor: Paternity Tests) (1992) 2 FC 752 FD 51
Figgis, Re [1969] 1 Ch 123; [1968] 1 All ER 999 .... 480, 488
Fisher v Fisher [1989] 1 FLR 423 563
Ford v Ford [1978] Fam Law 232 19
Freeeman, Re [1984] 3 All ER 906 585
Furnival v Brooke (1883) 49 LT 134 442

G (A Minor), Re (Parental Responsibility Order) [1994] 1 FLR 504 261
G, Re (Adoption: Freeing Order) 1996 2 FLR 398 107
G, Re (Adoption Illegal placement) [1995] 1 FLR 403 103
G (Minors), Re (Interim Care Order) [1993] 2 FLR 839 .... 307, 308, 310
G (Minors), Re (Welfare Report: Disclosure) [1993] 2 FLR 293 450
G (no. 2) (A Minor), Re [1988] 1 FLR 314 328
G (TJ) (An Infant), Re [1963] 1 All ER 20 126
G v G (Joint Residence Orders) [1993] Fam Law vol. 23, 615 253
G v Kirklees Metropolitan Borough Council [1993] 1 FLR 805 249
G, Re [1992] 1 WLR 438 447
Galloway v Galloway (1914) 30 TLR 531 164
Garcia v Garcia [1991] 3 All ER 451; [1991] 1 FLR 256 191
Gardner v Gardner (1877) 2 App Cas 723 62
Gateshead MBC v N [1993] 1 FLR 811 310
Gee v Gee (1863) 12 WR 187 437
George v George [1986] 2 FLR 347 168
Gibson v Austin [1992] 2 FLR 437 .... 164, 490, 515
Gillick v West Norfolk and Wisbech Health Authority
    [1986] AC 13, 32, 40, 59, 126, 150, 239, 418, 420, 421, 422, 429, 434, 577
Gissing v Gissing [1971] AC 886; [1970]
    2 All ER 780 HL 472, 476, 485, 486, 492, 498
Glass v McManus unrep (1996) 506
Gojikovic v Gojikovic [1990] 2 All ER 84 .... 556, 567
Goodchild (Deceased) and Another, Re [1996] 1 FLR 591 ..... 581, 582, 590, 600
Goodman v Gallant [1986] 1 All ER 31 507
Gorman v Gorman [1964] 3 All ER 739 542
Gorman, Re [1990] 2 FLR 284 502
Goshawk v Goshawk (1965) 109 Sol Jo 290 177
Gould v Gould [1970] 1 QB 275, [1969] 3 All ER 728 28
Grant v Edwards[1986] Ch 638, [1987] 1 FLR 87 .... 508, 510

H (A Minor), Re (Care Proceedings: Child's Wishes) [1993]
    1 FLR 440 .... 441, 453
H (A Minor), Re (Contact) [1994] 2 FLR 776 256
H (A Minor), Re (Contact: Enforcement) [1996] 1 FLR 614 256
H (A Minor), Re (Custody: Interim Care and Control) [1991]2 FLR 109 146

H (A Minor), Re (Role of Official Solicitor) [1993] 2 FLR 552 448 453
H (A Minor), Re (Section 37 Direction) [1993] 2 FLR 541 74
H (A Minor), Re (Shared Residence) [1994] 1 FLR 717 253
H (Minors), Re (Access) [1992] 1 FL 148 .... 42, 255
H (Minors), Re (Local Authority: Parental Rights) [1989]
 2 All ER 353; [1989] 1 WLR 551 123
H and Others (Minors), Re (Sexual Abuse: Standard of Proof) [1995]
 1 FLR 643 .... 294, 328
H v H (Financial Provision: Conduct) [1994] 2 FLR 801 562
H v H (Residence Order: Leave to Remove from the Jurisdiction) [1995]
 1 FLR 529 253
H v H and C (Kent CC intervening) (Child Abuse: Evidence) [1989]
 3 All ER 740 329
H v P (Illegitimate Child: Capital Provision) [1939] Fam Law 51 517
H v UK (1987) 10 EHRR 95 222
H, In Re (A Minor) (Adoption: Non Patrial) [1982] Fam Law 121 98
H, In Re (Illegitimate Children: Father: Parental Rights) (no. 2) [1991]
 1 FLR 214 127
H, In Re [1983] 4 FLR 614 130
H, Re (Adoption: Disclosure of Information) [1995] 1 FLR 236 134
H, Re (Adoption: Non Patrial) [1966] 1 FLR 717 125
H, Re (Adoption: Non Patrial) [1996] 2 FLR 187 98
H, Re (Illegitimate Children: Father: Parental Rights) (no. 2) [1991]
 1 FLR 214 261
H, Re (Infants) (Adoption: Parental Agreement) [1977] 2 All ER 339 .... 123, 124
H, Re (Minor: Paternity Tests) [1996] 2 FLR 65 50
H, Re (Prohibited Steps Order) [1995] 1 FLR 638 .... 171, 260
Hagger, Freeman v Ascot, Re[1930] 2 Ch 190 582
Halifax Building Society v Brown [1996] 1 FLR 103 483
Hammond v Mitchell [1991] 1 WLR 1127 .... 508, 509
Hampshire County Council v S [1993] Fam 158; [1993] 1 FLR 559;
 [1993] Fam Law 269 307
Hanlon v Hanlon [1978] 1 WLR 59 .... 559, 567
Harriman v Harriman [1909] p 123 181
Harrington v Gill [1982] 4 FLR 265 603
Harrison v Harrison (1842) 5 Beav 130 437
Harrogate Borough Council v Simpson [1986] 2 FLR 91 599
Harthan v Harthan [1948] 2 All ER 639 17
Hawkesworth v Hawkesworth LRR 6 Ch 542 35
Hedges v Hedges [1991] 1 FLR 196 568
Henry v Archibald (1871) 5 R Eq 559 442
Heseltine v Heseltine [1971] 1 All ER 952 480
Hewer v Bryant [1970] 1 QB 357 42
Hindmarsh v Charleton (1861) 8 HLC 160 577
HL and R v Luffe (1807) 8 East 193 62

Holliday, Re [1981] Ch 405 499
Hopes v Hopes [1949] 2 All ER 920 180
Hopkins, ex p. [1732] 3 Peere Williams 152 36
Horner v Horner [1982] 2 All ER 495 167
Hounslow London Borough Council v A [1993] 1 FLR 419 . . . . 302, 309, 318
Hussain v Hussain [1982] 3 All ER 369 . . . . 15, 16
Hyde v Hyde (1866) LR 1 P&D 130, 133 . . . . 6, 9, 25, 47
Hyman v Hyman [1929] AC 601 HL 539

J (A Minor), Re (Abduction: Custody Rights) [1990] 2 AC 562 209
J (A Minor), Re (Change of Name) [1993] 1 FLR 699 . . . . 290, 456
J (A Minor), Re (Contact) [1994] 1 FLR 6 256
J (Adoption), Re (Confidential Report: Disclosure) (1982) 3 FLR 183 102
J (Minors), Re (Care: Care Plan) [1994] 1 FLR 253 . . . . 302, 308
J, Re (Specific Issues Order; Leave to Apply) [1995] 1 FLR 669 320
J M (A Minor) v Runeckles (1984) 79 Cr App Rep 255 392
J v C [1970] AC 668 . . . . 43, 139, 246
J v J [1955] 2 All ER 617 540
J v S-T (formerly J) *The Independent* 16 Nov. 1996 15
Jackson v Watson & Son [1909] 2 KB 193 31
Jacob v Lucas (1839) 1 Beav 436 437
Jane v Janee (1984) 4 FLR 712 239
Jelly v Iliffe [1981] 2 WLR 801 . . . . 584, 591, 600
JK, Re (Adoption; Transracial Placement) [1991] 2 FLR 340 239
Jones v Jones [1975] 2 All ER 12 565
Jones v Lloyd (1874) LR 18 Eq 265 436
Jones v Maynard [1951] Ch 572; [1951] 1 All ER 802 480
Jones, Re [1981] 1 All ER 1 574

K (A Minor), Re (Removal from the Jurisdiction) [1992] 2 FLR 98 252
K (An Infant), Re [1953] 1 QB 117; [1952] 2 All ER 877 100
K v K (Haringey London BC Intervening) (Child Abuse: Evidence)
    [1989] 3 All ER 740 [1990] Fam 86 329
K v K: Re M-NK and AK (Minors) unrep (1996) 210
K, Re (Adoption) [1997] 1 FLR No. 5 127
K, Re [1966] 1 WLR 1241 138
K, W and H (Minors), Re (Medical Treatment) [1993] 1 FLR 845 . . . . 441, 460
Katz v Katz [1972] 3 All ER 219 179
Kaur v Gill [1988] Fam 110; [1988] 2 All ER 28 489
Kaur v Singh [1972] 1 All ER 292 18
KD, Re (A Minor) (Access: Principles) [1988] 2 FLR 139 373
KD, Re (A Minor) (Ward: Termination of Access) [1988] 1 AC 806 296
KD, Re (A Minor) [1988] 1 All ER 577 222
Kent County Council v C and Another [1993] Fam 57 290
Kent County Court v C [1993] 1 FLR 308 299

Khorasandjan v Bush [1993] 3 All ER 669 166
Kiely v Kiely [1988] 1 FLR 248 556
Kourkey v Lusher (1983) 4 FLR 65 603
Krishnan v Sutton London Borough Council [1969] 3 All ER 1367 283

L (A Minor), Re (Adoption: Parental Agreement) [1987] 1 FLR 400 112
L (A Minor), Re (Adoption: Procedure) [1991]1 FLR 171 123
L (A Minor), Re (*The Times*, 4 July 1987) 138, 140
L v L (Children: Separate Representation) [1994] 1 FLR 890 448
L, Re (Police Investigation: Privilege) [1996] 1 FLR 731 451
L, Re (Sexual Abuse: Standard of Proof) [1996] 1 FLR 116 .... 298, 308, 309, 376
L, Re(Adoption: Disclosure of Information) (1977) 2 FL 431 134
Layton v Martin and Others [1986] 2 FLR 227 513
Leach (Deceased), Re [1985] 2 All ER 754 602
Leadbetter v Leadbetter [1985] FLR 789 563
Leaver v Torres (1899) 43 Sol Jo 778 442
Lempriere v Lange (1879) 12 Ch D 675 442
Lewis v Nobbs (1878) 8 Ch D 591 436
Livesey (formerly Jenkins) v Jenkins [1985] AC 424; [1985] FLR 813 541
Livingstone Stallard v Livingstone Stallard [1974] 2 All ER 766 178
Lloyds Bank v Rosset and Another [1991] 1 AC 107, 130; [1990] 1 All ER
    111, 117 HL 473, 476, 482, 491, 492, 493, 507, 508, 509
LM (A Minor), Re (Wardship: Jurisdiction) [1986] 2 FLR 102 154
London Borough of Sutton v Davies (no. 2) [1995] 1 All ER 65 .... 327, 379
London Borough of Sutton v Davies [1994] 1 FLR 737 269
Lumley v Ravenscroft [1895] 1 QB 683 442
Lyons v Blenkin (1812) Jacob 245 36

M (A Minor), Re (Care Order: Threshold Conditions) [1994] 2 FLR 577 295
M (A Minor), Re (Child Abduction) [1994] 1 FLR 390 .... 212, 213
M (A Minor), Re (Contact: Conditions) [1994] 1 FLR 272
M (A Minor), Re [1980] CLY 1801 96
M (Minors), Re (Sexual Abuse: Evidence) [1993] 1 FLR 822 .... 308, 337
M and C, Re (Minors) (Interim Care Order) [1995] Fam Law 315 308
M and N, Re (Wardship: Publication of Information) [1990] Fam 211 CA ... 159
M and R, Re (Child Abuse: Evidence) [1996] 2 FLR 195 .... 330, 450
M v A (Wardship: Removal from Jurisdiction) [1993] 2 FLR 715 253
M v M (Child: Access) [1973] 2 All ER 81 .... 42, 254, 434
M v M (Minor: Custody Appeal) [1987] 1 WLR 404 433
M v M (Minors) (Removal from the Jurisdiction) [1992] 2 FLR 303 252
M v M (Property Adjustment: Impaired Life Expectancy) [1993] 2 FLR 723 ... 564
M v Westminster City Council [1985]FLR 325 295
M, Re (Abduction: Non-Convention Country) [1995] 1 FLR 89
M, Re (Child's Upbringing) [1996] 2 FLR 441 125
M, Re (Interim Care Order: Assessment) [1996] 2 FLR 464 308

M, Re (Minors) (Access) [1992] Fam Law vol. 22, 152 255
M, Re (Minors) (Care Proceedings: Child's Wishes) [1994]
  1 FLR 749 .... 449, 451, 460
M, Re (Minors) (Disclosure of Evidence) [1994]
  1 FLR 760 .... 162, 172, 421, 450
M, Re (Petition to European Commission of Human Rights)
  [1997] 1 FLR 140
M, Re (Secure Accommodation Order) [1995] FLR 418 384
M, Re [1955] 2 QB 479 39
M, Re [1994] 3 All ER 298 230
Macey v Macey (1981) 3 FLR 7 562
Manchester City Council v F [1993] 1 FLR 419 302
Mc Grath, In Re (Infants) [1893] 1 Ch 143 .... 37, 138
Mc Kenzie v Mc Kenzie [1971] P 33; [1970] 3 All ER 1034 CA 141, 437
Mc Michael v United Kingdom [1995] Fam Law 478 .... 42, 120, 123
Mc Veigh v Beattie [1988] Fam Law vol. 18 p. 222 [1988] 2 All ER 500 51
McBroom Deceased, Re [1992] 2 FLR 49 585
McCartney v McCartney [1981] 1 All ER 597 167
McGowan v McGowan [1948] 2 All ER 1032 470
McHardy and Sons (A Firm) v Warren and Another [1994] 2 FLR 338 483
McLavery v Secretary of State for Social Security (Child Benefit; Child in Care)
  [1996] 2 FLR no. 6 363
McV (Minors), Re unrep (1986) 148
MD and TD (Minors), Re (Time Estimates) [1994] 2 FLR 336 300
Merritt v Merritt [1970] 1 WLR 1211 163
Mesher v Mesher [1980] 1 All ER 126 560
Metha v Metha [1945] 2 ALL ER 690 20
MH v MH [1981] FLR 429 539
Michael v Michael [1986] 2 FLR 389 562
Midland Bank v Cooke and Another [1995]
  2 FLR 915 .... 473, 479, 483, 491, 507, 512
Midland Bank v Dobson [1986] 1 FLR 171 482
Minton v Minton [1979] AC 593 .... 163, 524, 566
Mohamed v Knott [1969] 1 QB 10, 294
Mohammed Arif (An Infant), Re Nirbhai Singh, Re [1968] Ch 643 138
Moody Deceased, Moody v Stevenson [1992] 2 All ER 524 588
Moody v Stevenson [1992] 2 All ER 481 600
Moore v King (1842) 253 577
Morgan v Dillon [1724] 9 Modern 135 36
Morgan v Thorne (1841) 7 M&W 640 437
Morris v Morris [1985] FLR 1176 568
Mossop v Mossop [1988] 2 All ER 202 6
Mouncer v Mouncer [1972] 1 WLR 321 180
Moynihan v Moynihan (nos 1 and 2)[1997] 1 FLR 59 185
MW, Re (Adoption: Surrogacy) [1995] 2 FLR 759 .... 69, 73

N (Minors), Re (Abduction) [1991] FCR 756; [1991] 1 FLR 413 211
N (Minors), Re [1974] 1 All ER 126 33
N, Re (Child Abuse: Evidence) [1996] 2 FLR 2 445
N, Re [1974] 1 All R 126 39
Nachimson v Nachimson (1930) CA 6
Nanda v Nanda [1968] P. 351; [1967] 3 All ER 40 29
Nash v Nash [1940] 1 All ER 206 18
Newham London Borough Council v AG [1993] 1 FLR 643 .... 294, 343
Nixon v Nixon [1969] 1 WLR 1676 483
Northern Banking Company Ltd. v Devlin [1924] IR 90 502
Northrop v Northrop [1968] P 74 544
Nottinghamptonshire County Council v S and Others [1993] 1 FLR 554 295
Nottinghamshire County Council v P (no. 2) [1993] 3 All ER 815;
    2 FLR 134 .... 171, 172, 260, 286, 287, 301, 316, 317, 319
Nottinghamshire County Council v S and Others [1992] 3 WLR 1010 295

O v UK [1988] ECHR 2 FLR 445 222
O'Connor v A and B [1971] 2 All ER 1230 J [1971] 1 WLR 1227 114
O'Donnell v O'Donnell [1975] 2 All ER 829 .... 564, 566
O'Hara, In Re [1900] 2 IR 684 35
O'Neill v O'Neill [1975] 3 All ER 289 178
O, B, W and R v UK ECHR Series A, No, 120–121Series A No. 136-A
    and C-E (1988) 373
O, Re (A Minor) (Care Order: Education: Procedure) [1992]
    2 FLR 7 .... 293, 294, 312
O, Re (A Minor) (Contact: Imposition of Conditions) [1995]
    2 FLR 124 .... 172, 253, 255
O, Re (A Minor) (Medical Treatment) [1993] 2 FLR 149 .... 157, 429
O, Re (Care or Supervision Order) [1996] 2 FLR 755 304
O, Re (Child Abduction: Undertakings) [1994] 2 FLR 349 216
Oakley v Jackson [1914] 1 KB 216 325
Oakley v Walker (1977) 121 Sol Jo 619 31
Official Solicitor v K [1965] AC 201 .... 120, 450
OH v Ford (1988-1989) 167 CLR p. 337 211
Oxfordshire County Council v M [1994] 1 FLR 175 .... 235, 450
Oxfordshire County Council v P [1995] 1 FLR 552 .... 291, 451
Oxfordshire County Council v R [1992] 1 FLR 648 384

P (Minors), Re (Contact with Children in Care) [1993] 2 FLR 156 376
P (Minors), Re (Interim Order)[1993] 2 FLR 742 309
P (Minors), Re (Wardship: Surrogacy) [1987]2 FLR 421 70
P, In Re [1977] Fam 25 98
P, Re (An Infant) (Adoption Parental Consent) [1977] 1 All ER 182 96
P, Re (A Minor) (Custody) (1993) FLR 401 74
P, Re (A Minor) (Education) [1992] 1 FLR 316 .... 236, 421, 424

P, Re (A Minor) [1986] 1 FLR 272 .... 58, 59
P, Re (Emergency Protection Order) [1996] 1 FLR 482 354
PA (An Infant), Re [1959] 1 WLR 1530 102
Pace v Doe [1977] Fam 18; [1977] 1 All ER 176 543
Park, Re [1953] 3 WLR 1012; [1953] 2 All ER 1411 20
Patel v Patel [1988] 2 FLR 179 166
Paul v Constance [1977] 1 All ER 195 514
Pearson v Franklin (Parental Home: Ouster) [1994]
    1 FLRR 246 .... 172, 173, 516
Pettitt v Pettitt [1969] 2 All ER 385 .... 475, 484, 486, 496
Phillips v Peace [1996] 2 FLR 230 536
Place v Searle [1932] 2 KB 497 28
PMK, In Re [1981] 6 NIJB 213
Potter v Potter (1975) 5 Fam Law 161 18
Practice Direction [1986] 2 All ER 832 448
Preston v Preston [1982] Fam 17; [1982] 1 All ER 41 CA 559
Pugh v Pugh [1951] 2 All ER 680 12
Pulford v Pulford [1923] P18 180
Puttick v AG [1973] 3 All ER 463 13

Quoraishi v Quoraishi [1985] FLR 780 CA 11

R (A Minor), Re (Adoption: Parental Agreement) [1978] 1 FLR 391 123
R (A Minor), Re (Blood Transfusion) [1993] 2 FLR 609, 757 157, 320, 428
R (A Minor), Re (Blood Transfusion) [1993] Fam Law vol. 23, 577 137, 258
R (A Minor), Re (Expert's Evidence)(Note)[1991] 1 FLR 291 449
R (A Minor), Re (Wardship: Medical Treatment) [1992] 1 FL 190 40
R (A Minor), Re [1993] 2 FLR 762 42
R (J) v Oxfordshire County Council [1992] 3 All ER 660 444
R and G (Minors), Re (Interim Care or Supervision Orders) [1994]
    1 FLR 793 .... 305, 306
R v B County Council ex p. P [1991] 1 FLR 470 444
R v Bourne [1939] 1 KB 687 57
R v Chief Constable of Kent and Another, ex p. L [1991] Crim LKR 841 404
R v Connor [1908] 2 KB 26 325
R v Cornwall County Council [1992] 1 WLR 427 292
R v Devon County Council, ex p. L [1991] 2 FLR 541 .... 154, 339
R v Harrow London Borough, ex p. D [1989] 3 WLR 1239 339
R v Harrow London Borough, ex p. D [1990] Fam 133 339
R v Hayes [1977] 1 WLR 234 443
R v Hopley (1860) 2 F & F 202 .... 269, 379
R v Hopley (1860) 2 F & F 202 326
R v Howes (1860) 3 EP L 332 42
R v Human Fertilisation and Embryology Authority, ex p. Blood
    [1997] 1 FLR no. 6 71

R v Ireland (1996) unrep 167
R v Jackson [1891] 1 QB 671 .... 29, 165
R v Johnson (1996) unrep 167
R v Kowalski [1988] 1 FLR 447 .... 29, 165
R v Lister (1721) 1 Stra 478 28
R v Moses Soper (1793) 5 Term Rep 278 50
R v Newton and Stango [1958] Crim LR 469 58
R v Norfolk County Council, ex p. M [1989] 2 All ER 359 .... 154, 339
R v North Yorkshire County Council, ex p. M (no. 3)[1989] 2 FLR 82 155
R v North Yorkshire County Council, ex p. M [1989] 1 All ER 143 458
R v Northampton Juvenile Court, ex p. London Borough of Hammersmith
   and Fulham [1985] FLR 193 382
R v Northaven DC, ex p. Smith [1993] 2 FLR 897 281
R v Nottinghamshire County Court ex p. Byers [1985] 1 WLR 403 [1985]
   FLR 695 185
R v Oldham Metropolitan Borough Council, ex p. Garlick and Related
   Appeals [1993] 2 FLR 194 281
R v R (Blood Test: Jurisdiction) [1973] 3 All ER 933 52
R v R [1991] 3 WLR 767 29
R v Rahman (1958) 81 Cr App Rep 349 203
R v Royal Borough of Kingston Upon Thames, ex p. T [1994] 1 FLR 798 276
R v Royal Borough of Kingston Upon Thames, ex p. T [1994] 276
R v Secretary of State for Social Security, ex p. Biggin [1995]
   1 FLR 851 .... 531, 533
R v Secretary of State for Social Security, ex p. Lloyd [1995]
   1 FLR 856 531
R v Senior [1899] 1 QB 283 .... 40, 325
R v Tan [1983] 2 All ER 420 15
R v UK [1988] ECHR 2 FLR 445 222
R v Waltham Forest London Borough, ex p. G [1989] 2 FLR 138 434
R v Wandsworth London Borough, ex p. Hawthorne [1995]
   2 FLR 238 281
R, Re (Adoption) [1966] 3 All ER 13 112
R, Re (Care Orders: Jurisdiction) [195] 1 FLR 712 289
RA (Minors), Re [1974] Fam Law 182 127
Ratcliffe v Ratcliffe [1962] 3 All ER 933 542
Richards v Richards [1984] AC 174; [1983]
   2 All ER 807 .... 162, 169, 173, 489, 490
Rignal (HM Inspector of Taxes) v Andrews 8 BNIL 73 .... 55, 518
Riley v Riley [1986] 2 FLR 429 253
Risk (Otherwise Yerburgh) v Risk [1950] 2 All ER 973 11
Robson v Secretary of State for Social Services (1981) 3 FL 232 53
Rochdale Borough Council v A [1991] 2 FLR 192 .... 324, 446
Roger's Question, Re [1948] 1 All ER 328 483
Royal College of Nursing v DHSS [1981] AC 800 57

S (A Minor), Re (Independent Representation) [1993] 2 FLR 437 290
S (A Minor), Re [1978] QB 120 312
S (J) (A Minor), Re (Care or Supervision) [1993] 2 FLR 919 299
S (Minors), Re (Access) [1990] 2 FLR 166 256
S and B (Minors), Re (Child Abuse: Evidence) [1990] 2 FLR 489 328
S and D, Re (Children: Powers of Court) [1995] 2 FLR 456 287
S and R (Minors), Re (Care Order) [1993] Fam Law 43 294
S and R (Minors), Re (Care Order) [1993] Fam Law 43 294
S v S (Child Abduction) [1992] 2 FLR 311 237
S v S (Custody of Children) 1980) FLR 143 74
S v S (Minors) (Custody) [1992] 1 FCR 158; [1992] Fam Law 148 247
S v S (Otherwise C) [1954] 3 All ER 736 .... 8, 17
S v S [1972] AC 24 529
S v S, W v Official Solicitor [1972] AC 24; [1970] 3 All ER 50
S, In Re [1967] 1 WLR 396 140
S, Re (Abduction: Children: Separate Representation) [1997]
   1 FLR 486 213
S, Re (Care or Supervision Order) [1996] 1 FLR 776 304
S, Re (Contact: Grandparents) [1996] 1 FLR 158 .... 290, 316, 318
S, Re (Gifts by Mental Patients) [1977] 1 FLR 96 579
S, Re (Inherent Jurisdiction: Ouster) [1994] 1 FLR 623 173
Salmon, Re [1986] 3 All ER 532 585
Samson v Samson[1982] 1 WLR 252; [1982] 1 All ER 780 479
Santos v Santos [1972] Fam 247; [1972] 2 All ER 246 .... 29, 182
Savage v Dunningham [1973] 3 WLR 219 483
Scott v Scott [1959] 1 All ER 531 22
Seaford, Re [1968] 1 All ER 482 595
Section (A Minor), Re (Independent Representation) [1993]
   2 FLR 437, 444H 421, 441, 458, 460
Section (A Minor), Re (Independent Representation) [1993] Fam 263
   [1993] 2 FCR 452
Serio v Serio (1993) 4 FLR 756 62
Sharpe, Re [1980] 1 WLR 219 483
Shaw v Fitzgerald [1992] 1 FLR 357 478
Sheldon v Sheldon [1966] 2 WLR 933 17
Simpson v Simpson [1989] Fam Law vol. 19 p. 146 164
Sinclair v Sinclair (1845) 13 M & W 640 437
Sinclair, Re [1985] 1 All ER 1066 581
Singh v Singh [1971] 2 All ER 828 .... 17, 19
Skinner, ex p. 9 Moo 278 35
Smith v Palmer (1840) 3 Beav 10 437
Smith v Smith [1991] 2 All ER 993 566
SN v ST (Maintenance Order: Enforcement) [1995] 1 FLR 868 547
South Glamorgan County Council v W and B[1993] 1 FLR 574 ..... 156, 157
Sowa v Sowa [1951] 1 All ER 687 11

Spence v Dennis [1990] Ch D 625; [1990] 2 All ER 827 48
Spencer v Camacho (1984) 4 FLR 662 168
Springette v Defoe [1992] 2 FLR 437; [1992] Fam Law 489 510
Stanga v Stanga [1954] 2 All ER 16 442
Stocker v Stocker (1966) 1 WLR 190 21
Stockford v Stockford (1982) 3 FLR 58 563
Sutter v Sutter and Jones [1987] 2 FLR 232 .... 561, 568, 569
Sutton v Sutton [1984] 1 All ER 168 539
Szechter v Szechter [1970] 3 All ER 905 19

T (A Minor), Re (Care or Supervision Order) [1994] 1 FLR 103 299
T (A Minor), Re (Care: Order: Conditions) [1994] 2 FLR 423 .... 299, 308
T (A Minor), Re (Guardian ad Litem) [1994] 1 FLR 632 457
T (A Minor), Re (Parental Responsibility: Contact) [1993] 2 FLR 450 261
T (A Minor), Re (Wardship: Representation) *The Times*, 10 May 1993 441
T (A Minor), Re [1995] Supreme Court Practice, News 4 112
T and E, Re (Proceedings: Conflict of Interests) [1995] 1 FLR 581 378
T v Surrey County Council [1994] 4 All ER 577 269
T v T (Consent Order: Procedure to Set Aside) [1996] 2 FLR 640 567
T v W (Contact: Reasons for Refusing Leave) [1996] 2 FLR 473 231
T, Re (Adoption: Contact) [1995] 2 FLR 251 131
T, Re (Child Representation) [1993] 3 WLR 602 447
T, Re (Divorce: Interim Maintenance: Discovery) [1990] 1 FLR 1 555
T, Re (Liver Transplant: Consent) *The Times, The Independent*,
  29 Oct. 1996 157
Talbot v Talbot (1971) 115 Sol Jo 870 16
Tanner v Tanner [1975] 3 All ER 776 511
Taylor's Application, Re [1972] 2 QB 369; [1972] 2 All ER 873 437
TD (A Minor), Re unrep (1985) FD 50
Thomas v Fuller-Brown [1988] 1 FLR 237 512
Thomasset v Thomasset [1894] 295 35
Tinsley v Milligan [1993] 2 FLR 968 .... 475, 513, 592
Turton v Turton [1987] 2 All ER 641 507
Twiname v Twiname [1992] 1 FLR 29 .... 191, 567

Ulrich v Ulrich [1968] 1 WLR 180 478

V (A Minor), Re (Adoption: Consent) [1987] 2 FLR 89 123
V, Re (Care or Supervision Order) [1996] 1 FLR 776 .... 304, 305
Valier v Valier (1925)133 LT 830 20
Van G v Van G (Financial Provision: Millionaire's Defence) [1995]
  1 FLR 328 562
Vaughan v Vaughan [1973] 1 WLR 1159 168
Vervaeke v Smith [1983] 1 AC 145; [1982] 2 All ER 144 20

W (A Minor), Re (Consent to Medical Treatment) [1993] 1 FLR 1 434
W (A Minor), Re (Contact) [1994] 2 FLR 441 .... 256, 421
W (A Minor), Re (Custody) (1982) 4 FLR 492 239
W (A Minor), Re (Inherent Jurisdiction: Consent to Treatment) [1993]
  1 FLR 1 40
W (A Minor), Re (Medical Treatment: Court's Jurisdiction) [1992] 3 WLR 785;
  [1992] 4 All ER 627 .... 137, 156, 423, 429
W (A Minor), Re (Wardship: Jurisdiction) [1985] AC 791 146
W (An Infant), Re [1971] 2 All ER 49 114
W (Minors), Re (Surrogacy) [1991] 1 FLR 385 71
W (Minors), Re (Wardship: Evidence) [1990] 1 FLR 203 .... 329, 444
W v A (Child: Surname) [1981] 1 All ER 100 432
W v K (Proof of Paternity) [1988] 1 FLR 86 62
W v UK [1988] ECHR 2 FLR 445 222
W v W (Child Abduction: Acquiescence) [1993] 1 FLR 682 210
W v W (Child of the Family) [1984] FLR 796 250
W v Wakefield City Council [1995] 1 FLR 170 234
W, B, R v UK (1987) 10 EHRR 29 222
W, Re (Adoption: Parental Agreement) (1993) 4 FLR 614 124
W, Re (Arrangements to place for Adoption) [1995] 1 FLR 163 103
Wagstaff v Wagstaff [1992] 1 FLR 389 562
Wales v Wadham [1977] 1 WLR 199 164
Ward v Laverty (1925) AC 101 139
Ward v Secretary of State for Social Services [1990] 1 FLR 119 23
Watchel v Watchel [1973] 1 All ER 829 564
Watson v Lucas [1980] 1 WLR 1493 599
Wayling v Jones [1995] 2 FLR 1029 .... 475, 509, 591
Wellesley v Wellesley [1828] 2 Bl, NI 124 35
Whiston v Whiston [1995] 2 FL 268 14
Whitby, Re [1944] 1 All ER 299 596
Williams and Glyn's Bank v Boland [1980] 2 All ER 408 491
Williams v Williams [1964] AC 698 .... 177, 179, 574
Wiseman v Simpson [1988] 1 All ER 245 516
WM (A Minor), Re (Non-Patrial) [1997] 1 FLR 132 99
Woolf v Woolf [1899] 1 Ch 343 442
Wooton v Wooton [1984] FLR 871 167

X (A Minor), Re (Adoption Details: Disclosure) [1994] 2 FLR 450 137
X (A Minor), Re [1975] Fam 47; [1975] 1 All ER 697 .... 136, 138, 246
X v X [1958] Crim LR 805 392

Z (A Minor), Re (Freedom of Publication of Information) [1990]
  Fam 211 CA 159
Z v Z [1996] Fam Law 255 256

Table of Statutes

Northern Ireland

Access to Health Records (NI)
    Order 1993 432
Access to Personal Files and
    Medical Reports (NI)
    Order 1991 432
Administration of Estates (NI)
    Act 1955 .... 573, 583, 593,
        594, 597, 598, 599, 600
    s. 18 594
    s. 45 595
    s. 45(1) 596
Administration of Estates (NI)
    Order 1979
    Art. 11 584
Administration of Justice Act
    1969 lxii
Adoption Act 1976 .... 95, 96
Adoption (Hague Convention)
    Act (NI) 1969 97
Adoption of Children Act
    (NI) 1929 94
Adoption (NI) Act 1967 ...... 95, 96,
        98, 107, 115, 367
    Art. 66 120
Adoption (NI) Order 1987 .... 95, 97,
        98, 100, 101, 102, 131, 237
    Art. 2 89
    Art. 2(2) 78, 97, 98, 99
    Art. 4(2)(e) 101
    Art. 9 .... 95, 98, 125, 126,
        246, 433
    Art. 9(a)(i) 125, 126
    Art. 11 .... 102, 117
    Art. 11(1)(b) 104
    Art. 12 .... 110, 128, 129, 133
    Art. 12(3) 387
    Art. 12(5) 97
    Art. 12(6) 105, 129,
        132, 133, 134
    Art. 12(7) 97
    Art. 13 .... 116, 117
    Art. 13(1) 97, 99, 100
    Art. 13(2) 97, 103
    Art. 14(1) 99
    Art. 14(3) 127
    Art. 15(4) 127
    Art. 16 .... 100, 111
    Art. 16(1) 132
    Art. 16(1)(b) 122
    Art. 16(1)(b)(i) 133, 134
    Art. 16(1)(b)(i)(ab) 105, 129
    Art. 16(2)(b) 112
    Art. 16(2) 122
    Art. 16(3) 122
    Art. 16(5) 111
    Art. 16(6) 111
    Art. 17 104
    Art. 17(1) 105
    Art. 17(3) 387
    Art. 17(5) 106
    Art. 17(6) 106
    Art. 18 .... 110, 111, 113
    Art. 19 127
    Art. 20 127
    Art. 22 .... 104, 117, 119
    Art. 22(1) 132
    Art. 22(2) 123
    Art. 24 119
    Art. 24(2) 125
    Art. 27 .... 122, 128, 285
    Art. 28 119
    Art. 29 119

Art. 29(3)	119
Art. 31	127
Art. 32	107
Art. 33	118
Art. 34	118
Art. 35	118
Art. 40	596
Art. 40–2	49
Art. 40–99	129
Art. 42	132
Art. 50	102, 132
Art. 50(1)(c)	133
Art. 50(3)	132
Art. 54	102, 13, 134
Art. 57	125, 132
Art. 59	99
Art. 64(3)	127
Art. 66	101
Art. 66A	101
Pt II	100
Age of Marriage Act (NI) 1951	13
s. 2	12
Age of Majority Act (NI) 1969	97

Births and Death Registration (NI) Order 1976

Art. 14	60
Art. 14(3)	61
Art. 14(3)(b)	61
Art. 14(3)(c)	61
Art. 14(3)(d)	61
Art. 14(3)(e)	61
Art. 14(4)	61
Art. 19A	61
Art. 37(7)	62

Child Abduction (NI) Order 1985	195, 200, 207, 213
Art. 2(2A)	202
Art. 3	200
Art. 3(5)	202
Art. 4	203
Art. 4(3)(b)	203
Art. 5(a)	208
Art. 6	203
Art. 9	214
Art. 10	214
Art. 10(1)(b)	214, 215
Art. 16	214
Art. 16(1)	215
Art. 18	214
Pt I	197
Pt III	202
Child Support (NI) Order 1991	39, 40, 50, 55, 56, 62, 519, 520, 521, 523, 537, 547, 550, 551, 552, 553, 555
Art. 3	522, 530
Art. 3(1)	547
Art. 3(1)(b)	524
Art. 4(1)	530
Art. 4(2)	528, 530
Art. 4(3)	527
Art. 5	520
Art. 5(2)	530
Art. 6	522
Art. 7	56, 523
Art. 7(1)	527
Art. 7(10)	529
Art. 9	532
Art. 9(1)	528
Art. 9(2)	531
Art. 10	529, 546
Art. 10(5)	524
Art. 10(6)(c)	547
Art. 10(7)	547
Art. 10(8)	524, 547
Art. 10(10)	548
Art. 11	529
Art. 11(2)	524
Art. 12(3)	56
Art. 13(1)	531
Art. 15(1)	525
Art. 15(3)	526
Art. 15(4)	526
Art. 18	527, 532
Art. 19	532
Art. 20	525, 527
Art. 20(7)	532
Art. 21	56, 525

Art. 21(1)	532
Art. 22	526, 527
Art. 23(1)	526
Art. 25(1)	526
Art. 25(3)	52
Art. 27A	529
Art. 27(1)	529
Art. 28(1A)	529
Art. 28A–28I	535
Art. 28E(2)	535
Art. 29	532
Art. 29-37	533
Art. 31	533
Art. 33	533
Art. 37	533
Art. 38	534
Art. 38(6)	534
Art. 41	521, 522, 524, 527, 530, 531
Art. 42	526
Sch. 1	534
Sch. 3	526
Sch. 4	526
Sch. 4B	535

Child Support (NI) Order 1991
(Consequential Amendments)
Order (NI) 1994 519

Child Support (NI) Order
1995 .... 519, 537, 547, 550, 555
Art. 10 532

Children (Allocation of
Proceedings) Order (Northern
Ireland) 1996 .... lxii, 233

Art. 3	233
Art. 5	233
Art. 56	233
Art. 166	234
Art. 166(1)	234
Art. 166(2)(a)	234
Art. 166(2)(b)	234
Art. 166(3)	234
Art. 166(5)	234
Art. 166(6)	234
Sch. 1	xxiii
Sch. 7	234

Children and (Juvenile Courts)
Act (NI) 1942 391

Children and Young Persons Act
(Northern Ireland) 1968 ... 37, 40,
107, 147, 148, 225, 227, 228, 263,
266, 271, 285, 312, 332, 335, 341,
358, 363, 372, 387, 389, 390, 391,
394, 395, 396, 399, 403, 536

s. 20	39, 90
s. 25	39
s. 29	39
s. 30	39
s. 37	272
s. 48	391
s. 53	272, 404, 408
s. 53(2)	399
s. 57	443
s. 58	443
s. 58A	443
s. 63	232
s. 64 A(2)	402
s. 69	392
s. 72	405
s. 72(3)	415
s. 73	402
s. 73(i)	409
s. 73(2)	408
s. 73(4)	409
s. 73(5)	409
s. 74	407, 410, 415
s. 74(1)(c)	313, 315
s. 75	410
s. 79	391
s. 93(2)(b)	147, 148
s. 94	399, 408
s. 95	148, 325, 395, 396, 407, 408
s. 103	148, 149, 154, 272, 280, 282, 285, 298, 325
s. 104	285
s. 108(a)	408
s. 132	410
s. 132(4)	411
s. 133	410
s. 137	413

s. 139 413
s. 149(ii)(b) 415
s. 143(6)(b) 408
s. 163 . . . . 272, 397, 398
s. 164 . . . . 272, 398
Pt I 103, 266
Pt III 272
Sch. 2 . . . . xxiii, 232
Sch. 5
para 10(i) 415
para 11(1)(b) 415
Sch. 8
para 5(2) 408
Children and Young Persons
(Protection from Tobacco)
(NI) Order 1991 271
Children (Northern Ireland)
Order 1995 . . . . lxiii, 32, 38,
39, 40, 41, 43, 47, 50, 55, 62, 76, 77,
78, 81, 83, 84, 86, 89, 90, 91, 95, 96,
97, 99, 101, 104, 105, 107, 116, 122,
128, 129, 131, 132, 133, 135, 136,
137, 143, 144, 155, 157, 158, 159,
160, 170, 171, 172, 190, 205, 219,
221, 223, 225, 226, 228, 229, 230,
231, 232, 235, 236, 241, 244, 245,
247, 250, 251, 253, 257, 258, 259,
263, 265, 270, 274, 277, 279, 285,
286, 287, 292, 293, 296, 299, 302,
303, 312, 316, 317, 319, 300, 311,
313, 316, 320, 322, 333, 335, 336,
339, 341, 345, 348, 349, 350, 355,
357, 358, 361, 362, 365, 366, 368,
369, 371, 372, 373, 374, 375, 379,
380, 383, 386, 389, 390, 391, 418,
420, 428, 436, 457, 448, 451, 452,
499, 505, 521, 534, 550, 557
Art. 2 91,
239, 273, 274, 359, 543
Art. 2(1) 111, 246
Art. 2(2) 167, 293, 324,
325, 326, 327, 330
Art. 2(2)(b) 93
Art. 2(6) 359

Art. 3 . . . . 126, 235, 239,
247, 416, 418, 522
Art. 3(1) 245, 296, 424, 453
Art. 3(2) 201, 229,
246, 286, 297
Art. 3(2A) 199
Art. 3(3) . . . 82, 229, 248, 300, 433
Art. 3(3)(a) 212, 371, 417, 422
Art. 3(4) 297
Art. 3(5) 208, 229, 277,
286, 296, 300
Art. 4 . . . . 244, 333, 334, 454
Art. 4(1) 321
Art. 5 . . . . 86, 89, 229
Art. 5(1) 79
Art. 5(2) 520
Art. 5(3) 40, 84, 242, 243
Art. 5(5) 252
Art. 5(6) 253
Art. 5(7) 253
Art. 5(8) 90
Art. 6 . . . . 80, 86
Art. 6(2) 85
Art. 6(5) 89
Art. 6(5)(b) 282
Art. 6(4)(a) 86
Art. 6(4)(b) 50, 86
Art. 7 . . . . 61, 90, 91, 199,
229, 253, 261
Art. 7(1) 87, 89, 105
Art. 7(1)(a) 50, 85
Art. 7(2) 89
Art. 7(4) 520
Art. 8 . . . . xxiii, 55, 62, 74,
78, 79, 81, 91, 93, 124, 128, 137,
144, 156, 157, 162, 171, 172, 199,
201, 205, 219, 230, 241, 246, 248,
249, 250, 251, 255, 259, 260, 303,
304, 316, 317, 318, 341, 342, 363,
367, 376, 381, 418, 441, 453, 544
Art. 8(1) . . 199, 251, 254, 257, 259
Art. 8(3) 311
Art. 8(3)(a) 144
Art. 8(4) 67, 311, 342

Art. 8(4)(b) 162	Art. 15(1) 100
Art. 8(4)(c) 167	Art. 15(4) 100
Art. 9 .... 111, 119, 249, 316, 317, 367	Art. 16 ... 128, 229, 241, 260, 321
	Art. 16(3)(a) 260
Art. 9(b) 241	Art. 17 .... 242, 273, 276
Art. 9(1) 252, 317, 386	Art. 18 ...... 275, 336, 341, 398
Art. 9(2) 252, 316	Art. 18(1) 372
Art. 9(3) 249, 251, 254, 386	Art. 18(1)(b) 277, 286
Art. 9(4) 251	Art. 19 .... 267, 279
Art. 9(5) 171, 172	Art. 19(1) 279
Art. 9(5)(a) 260	Art. 20 .... 106, 267, 280
Art. 9(5)(b) 316	Art. 20(1)b) 268
Art. 10 ...... 105, 315, 381, 434	Art. 20(1)(c) 281
Art. 10(1) 144, 249	Art. 20(1)(5) 280
Art. 10(1)(a) 254	Art. 20(3) 281
Art. 10(1)(b) 251	Art. 21 .... 282, 398, 425, 431
Art. 10(2) 199, 248	Art. 21(6) 283
Art. 10(2)(b) 453	Art. 22 .... 384, 431
Art. 10(4) 56, 199, 248, 251, 254, 258, 259	Art. 22(2) 282, 385
	Art. 22(5) 282, 431
Art. 10(4)(a) 386	Art. 23 .... 281, 357
Art. 10(4)(b) 199	Art. 24 283
Art. 10(5) ... 92, 93, 248, 251, 254	Art. 25 359
Art. 10(5)(b) 367, 386	Art. 26 ... 364, 370, 371, 425, 458
Art. 10(5)(c)(ii) 367, 386	Art. 26(1) 372
Art. 10(8) 248, 367, 441	Art. 26(1)(a) 282
Art. 10(9) 248, 249, 386	Art. 26(2) 287, 367, 374
Art. 11 .... 101, 271	Art. 26(3) 367
Art. 11(1) 246	Art. 26(7) 287
Art. 11(3) 249, 316	Art. 26(8) 287
Art. 11(5) 254	Art. 27 .... 342, 408, 426
Art. 11(6) 257	Art. 27(e) 281
Art. 11(7) 172, 251, 253, 255, 259	Art. 27(f) 281
	Art. 27(2) 365
Art. 12 .... 101, 253, 529	Art. 27(2)(a) 369
Art. 12(1) 88	Art. 27(2)(f) 426
Art. 12(2) 88, 252	Art. 27(5) 304, 369
Art. 12(4) 90, 253	Art. 27(7) 369, 370
Art. 13 .... 199, 253	Art. 27(8) 370
Art. 13(1) 252	Art. 27(8)(a) 373
Art. 13(1)(a) 432	Art. 27(9) 274, 304
Art. 14 (3) 100	Art. 28 .... 365, 366
Art. 14 529	Art. 29 .... 353, 426
Art. 15 .... 262, 516, 529	Art. 29(1) 374

Art. 30 353	Art. 53(1) 56, 299, 373, 376, 377
Art. 31(1) 431	Art. 53(4) 299, 375, 376
Art. 33(1) 430	Art. 53(5) 375
Art. 35 . . . . 388, 432	Art. 53(6)(b)(ii) 375
Art. 35(2) 462	Art. 53(7) 377
Art. 35(5) 387	Art. 54 304
Art. 36(1) 388	Art. 54(1) 430
Art. 37 462	Art. 54A 132
Art. 37(3) 388	Art. 55 . . . . 310, 312
Art. 37(4) 462	Art. 55(5) 310
Art. 39(3)(b) 431	Art. 55(7) 312
Art. 44 . . . . 382, 384, 459	Art. 56 . . . . 128, 144, 241, 261,
Art. 44(1) 382	318, 321, 333, 334
Art. 44(4) 382, 383	Art. 56(1) 306
Art. 44(5) 383	Art. 56(2) 334
Art. 44(6) 383	Art. 56(3) 334
Art. 44(7) 384	Art. 56(4) 334
Art. 45 . . . . 379, 385,	Art. 57 354
408, 426, 462	Art. 57(1) 306
Art. 45(2)(d)(i) 462	Art. 57(3) 316
Art. 45(2)(g) 462	Art. 57(4) 310
Art. 45(3) 381	Art. 57(5) 310
Art. 46 . . . . 229, 276, 312, 381	Art. 57(6) 157, 300, 308, 309
Art. 47 381	Art. 57(7) 308
Art. 49(2) 300, 332, 346, 350	Art. 57(10) 310
Art. 50 . . . . 288, 293, 298, 315, 331	Art. 58 . . . . 306, 385, 386
Art. 50(1) 361	Art. 58(1) 431
Art. 50(1)(a) 551	Art. 58(1)(b) 381, 460
Art. 50(2) 294, 300, 306, 328	Art. 58(2) 304, 431
Art. 50(2)(a) 329	Art. 59(4) 134
Art. 50(2)(b) 294, 329	Art. 60 . . . . 289, 291, 384, 438,
Art. 50(3) 239	439, 455
Art. 50(4) 242	Art. 60(2)(b) 290, 457
Art. 50(6)(7a) 386	Art. 60(3) 460
Art. 51 . . . . 297, 310	Art. 60(4) 460
Art. 51(1) 300	Art. 60(4)(b) 441
Art. 52 . . . . 361, 362	Art. 60(6) 289, 456
Art. 52(3)(b) 363	Art. 60(6)(g) 346
Art. 52(5) 304	Art. 60(7) 289
Art. 52(6) 89, 362	Art. 60(8) 459
Art. 52(7) 363	Art. 60(9) 290
Art. 52(7)(a) 432	Art. 60(11) 290
Art. 52(9) 304	Art. 61 457
Art. 53 . . . . 255, 300, 303,	Art. 62 . . . 331, 345, 347, 348, 430
346, 353, 372, 375, 378	Art. 62(1) 346

Art. 62(1)(a) 324	Art. 66(7) 336, 342
Art. 62(3) 347	Art. 66(8) 287, 300, 341
Art. 62(4) 347	Art. 66(9) 336, 337
Art. 62(7) 351	Art. 66(10) 336
Art. 62(12) 347	Art. 66(11) 336
Art. 63 .... 331, 348	Art. 67(1) 353
Art. 63(1) 349, 430	Art. 67(4) 353
Art. 63(1)(a) 349, 350	Art. 68 .... 204, 354
Art. 63(1)(b) 348, 349, 350	Art. 68(2) 204, 355
Art. 63(1)(c) 349, 350	Art. 69 354
Art. 63(4) 352	Art. 69(3) 355
Art. 63(4)(c) 89	Art. 70 357
Art. 63(5) 89	Art. 71(3) 351
Art. 63(5)(b) 353	Art. 76 .... 372, 381, 427
Art. 63(6) 351	Art. 76(2) 374
Art. 63(6)(b) 430	Art. 92 .... 372, 381
Art. 63(7) 430	Art. 92(1)(c) 427
Art. 63(9) 351	Art. 92(2) 374
Art. 63(13) 353	Art. 92(2)(a) 427
Art. 64 354	Art. 93(a) 427
Art. 64(4) 354	Art. 106(1) 269
Art. 64(5) 354	Art. 107(1)(a) 270
Art. 64(7) 354	Art. 108 270
Art. 64(7)(a) 431	Art. 109 271
Art. 64(8) 354	Art. 110 271
Art. 64(9) 354	Art. 111 271
Art. 64(12) 353	Art. 118 268
Art. 65 .... 204, 333, 335, 356	Art. 120 268
Art. 65(1) 356, 427	Art. 122 268
Art. 65(1)(b) 282, 331	Art. 124 268
Art. 65(4) 336	Art. 125 .... 268, 269
Art. 65(5) 356, 427	Art. 126 269
Art. 65(5)(a) 357	Art. 128 269
Art. 65(5)(b) 357	Art. 129 269
Art. 65(5)(c) 357	Art. 130 268
Art. 65(5)(e) 357	Art. 131 268
Art. 65(6) 336	Art. 132 269
Art. 65(8) 356	Art. 135 272
Art. 65(10) 427	Art. 149 364
Art. 66 .... 331, 333, 334, 335, 336, 350	Art. 155 .... 49, 123, 201
	Art. 155–7 599
Art. 66(1)(a) 333	Art. 155(3)(b) 49
Art. 66(1)(b) 333	Art. 158 48
Art. 66(5) 336	Art. 159 .... 79, 89, 241, 262, 434
Art. 66(6) 349	Art. 159(1) 82, 85

Art. 159(2) 79, 321
Art. 159(4) 79
Art. 159(5) 81, 85
Art. 159(6) 81
Art. 160 .... 89, 434
Art. 160(1) 80, 84
Art. 160(4) 79
Art. 161(1) 82
Art. 162(1) 82
Art. 163(1) 434
Art. 164 232
Art. 164(4) lxiii
Art. 164 (4)(1) lxi
Art. 166 .... 384, 440
Art. 167 288
Art. 167(1) 440, 461
Art. 168 .... 298, 442
Art. 169 443
Art. 169(5)-(8) 443
Art. 170 .... 159, 298
Art. 171 .... 343, 445
Art. 172 ...... 288, 298, 384, 442
Art. 172(3) 456
Art. 173 .... 137, 154, 155, 173, 320
Art. 173(1) 156,
Art. 173(1)(c) 157
Art. 173(2) 320
Art. 173(3) 156, 173, 306
Art. 173(4) 156, 173
Art. 173(5) 136
Art. 179 386
Art. 179(1) 319, 386
Art. 179(2) 253, 254
Art. 179(7) 81
Art. 179(8) 81
Art. 179(10) 254, 257
Art. 179(12) 387
Art. 179(13) 306
Art. 179(14) 236
Art. 179(15) 347
Art. 180 303
Pt II lxiii
Pt III .... lxiii, 243
Pt IV ... 39, 230, 263, 266, 342, 381

Pt V .... lxiii, 40, 284, 285, 288, 292, 298, 300, 332, 343, 358, 418
Pt VI 39, 285, 288, 298, 322, 342, 343, 344, 345
Pt IX 267
Pt X ... xxiii, 40, 85, 266, 269, 270
Pt XI 266, 267, 520
Pt XII 266, 271, 272
Pt XV 287
Pt XVI 287
Sch. 1 .... 262, 517, 548
para 2 .... 61, 144, 368, 516
para 2(2)(c) 536
para 5 516
para 12 548
para 12(2) 548
para 13 549
para 15 536
para 17 .... 92, 368
Sch. 2 .... 275, 277, 304, 535
para 2 .... 279, 388
para 2(1) 462
para 3 .... 274, 275, 535
para 4 .... 274, 275, 462
para 5 .... 278, 323, 331
para 6 .... 171, 277, 350
para 7 .... 274, 277
para 8 .... 277, 232, 331, 398
para 9 277
para 10 277
para 11 277
para 12 279
Sch. 3 .... 305, 386
para 1 304
para 3 305
para 4 .... 302, 305, 430
para 6(1) 306
para 6(4) 306
para 8 304
Sch. 4
para 2 .... 314, 427
para 3 313
para 4 .... 310, 313
para 6 314

Table of Statutes xlvii

para 6(1)	315	Art. 3	418, 443
para 7	334, 431	Art. 5	445
para 8	315	Chronically Sick and Disabled	
para 9	314, 335	Persons (NI) Act 1978	
Sch. 5	271	s. 1	275
Sch. 6	599	s. 2	275
Sch. 7	287	Coroners Act (NI) 1959	
Sch. 8	270	s. 11	574
para 10	252	County Courts (Northern Ireland)	
para 10(3)	431	Order 1980	lxii
para 17	432	Art. 60	127
para 30(3)	408	Art. 61	192
para 33	599	County Courts (Northern Ireland)	
Sch. 9	13	Order 1981	lxii
para 3	190	County Courts (Financial Limits)	
para 8	49	Order (Northern Ireland)	
para 14	48	1993	lxii
para 140(1)	387	Criminal Evidence Act (NI) 1923	
para 143(2)	387	s. 3	26
para 84	60	Criminal Evidence (NI) Order 1988	
para 87	61	Art. 3	401
para 88	62	Art. 4	401
para 89	50	Art. 5	401
para 95	189, 243, 249	Criminal Injuries (NI) Order 1988	
para 102	162	Art. 5(2)	55, 165
para 119	68	Criminal Justice Act (NI) 1966	
para 121	200, 201, 202	s. 9(2)	402, 405
para 121(3)	199	Criminal Justice (NI) Order	
para 121(5)	202	1980	390, 406
para 122	200	Criminal Justice (NI) Order 1986	
para 122(3)	203	Art. 5	415
para 138–167	95	Art. 59(b)	415
para 140	87	Criminal Justice (NI) Order	
para 166	290	1996	389
Sch. 10	250	Criminal Penalties (Increase) Order	
Children (Admissibility of		(NI) 1984	405
Hearsay Evidence) Order			
(NI) 1996	443	Domestic Proceedings (Northern	
Children (Allocation of		Ireland) Order 1980	lxii, lxiii,
Proceedings) Order (Northern			160, 169, 244, 245, 254, 470,
Ireland) 1996	lxiii		488, 520, 538
Children and Young Persons		Art. 3	538, 545
Act (NI) 1950	413	Art. 3–9	32, 161, 545
Children's Evidence (NI)		Art. 4	537, 538, 545
Order 1995	442, 547	Art. 5	546

Art. 8 .... 540, 545, 546
Art. 9 .... 540, 545, 546
Art. 10 .... 146, 162
Art. 10(2) 546
Art. 12 283
Art. 13(2) 545, 546
Art. 16 146
Art. 18 .... 166, 167, 168,
                        169, 481, 515
Art. 19 .... 166, 481
Art. 20 546
Art. 21 481
Art. 21(2) 170
Art. 24 546
Art. 27 546
Art. 30 545
Art. 31 546
Art. 36 547
Art. 37 547

Education and Libraries (NI)
  Order 1972
  Sch. 9
    para 4 396
    para 5 395
    para 7 396
Education and Libraries (NI)
  Order 1986 .... 40, 552
  Art. 26–36 275
  Art. 45 315
  Sch. 13 315
Education and Libraries Boards
  Act (NI) 1972 285
Education (NI) Order 1987 275
Emergency Provisions Act 1973 .. 390
Employment (Miscellaneous
  Provisions) (NI) Order 1990 .. 271

Family Law
  (Miscellaneous Provisions)
  (NI) Order 1984 .... 5, 166,
                        169, 175, 490
  Art. 4–14 162
  Art. 4–13 .... 470, 481
  Art. 3–13 488

Art. 4 .... 246, 471, 488
Art. 13(1) 489
Art. 15(1) 477
Art. 15-17 478
Art. 17 479
Art. 17(7) 479
Art. 20 ..... 54, 162, 170, 481, 516
s. 18 12
Art. 18(1) 133
s. 19 13
s. 20 170
Family Law (Miscellaneous Provisions)
  (NI) Order 1994 ...... 5, 47, 470
  Art. 1 185
  Art. 4 lxiii
  Art. 13 lxiii
Family Law (Matrimonial
  Provisions) (NI) Order 1984
  Art. 20
Family Law (NI) Order
  1993 ...... 5, 7, 11, 12, 166, 175
  Art. 4 12
  Arts 6-11 537
  Art. 13 175
  Art. 14(1) 166
  Art. 15 188
  Art. 96A 554
Family Law (NI) Order 1994 136
Family Law Reform (NI) Order
  1977 .. 43, 47, 50, 83, 123, 142, 599
  Art. 8 .... 21, 51, 529
  Art. 13 .... 21, 529
  Art. 15 .... 50, 78, 89
Family Law Reform (NI) Order 1978
  Art. 15 87
Family Law Reform (NI) Order
  1987 536
Forfeiture (NI) Order 1982 581

Health and Personal Social Services
  (NI) Order 1972 263
  Art. 15 273
Health and Personal Social Services
  (NI) Order 1994 394

Table of Statutes xlix

Health and Social Services (NI)
    Order 1991 394
Health and Personal Social
    Services (Special Agencies)
    (NI) Order 1972 .... 291, 393
    Art. 17(1) 360
Homosexual Offences (NI) Order
    1982 271
Housing(NI) Order 1988 281
Human Tissue Act (NI) 1962 575

Illegitimate Children (Affiliation
    Orders) Act (NI) 1924 44,
                             55, 61, 228
Insolvency (NI) Order 1989 27,
              470, 471, 499, 500, 517
    Art. 209(5) 503
    Art. 302 49
    Art. 309(2)(a) 498
    Art. 309(5) 499

Judgements (Enforcement) Act
    (NI) 1969 495
Judgements (Enforcement) (NI)
    Order 1981
    Art. 46 504
    Art. 52 .... 502, 503
Judicature (Northern Ireland)
    Act 1978 lxi
    s. 26–9 143
    s. 62(4) 186
    s. 75(2) 447, 459

Law Reform (Husband and Wife)
    Act (NI) 1923
    s. 7 26
Law Reform (Husband and Wife)
    Act (NI) 1964 ..... 470, 471, 506
    s. 3 481
Law Reform (Miscellaneous
    Provisions) Act (NI) 1937 27
    s. 9 .... 27, 499
Law Reform (Matrimonial
    Provisions) Act (NI) 1951
    s. 4 544

Legal Aid, Advice and Assistance
    (NI) Order 1981 .... lxiv, 288
    Art. 5 384
Legitimacy Act (NI) 1928 49
    s. 1 .... 42, 48
    s. 2 47
    s. 8 .... 42, 48
    s. 8A 49
Legitimacy Act (NI) 1961 47
Licensing (NI) Order 1990 271

Magistrates' Courts (NI) Order
    1981 519
Marriages Act (NI) 1954 ...... 7, 13
    s. 1 13
    s. 6(1) 13
    Sch. 13
Marriage (Declaration of Law) Act
    (NI) 1944 7
Marriage (Prohibited Degrees of
    Relationship) Act (NI)
    1949 .... 7, 13
Matrimonial and Family Proceedings
    (NI) Order 1984
    Art. 6(4) 553
Matrimonial and Family Proceedings
    (NI) Order 1989 .... 11, 32,
                       47, 313, 537, 545
    Art. 3 184
    Art. 4(2) 22
    Art. 4(3) 23
    Art. 5 556
    Art. 5–11 550
    Art. 6 .... 541, 558, 561, 566
    Art. 6(3) 562
    Art. 10 54
    Art. 12 546
    Art. 11 581
    Art. 13 546
    Art. 31(c) 43
    Art. 31(1) 191
    Art.31(1)(e) 192
    Art. 32 48
    Art. 32(2)(a) 48
    Art. 32(4) 61

Art. 37 11	Art. 14 (b) 18
Art. 37 (1) 16	Art. 14 (c) 19
Art. 41 559	Art. 14 (d) 20
Pt IV lxiii	Art. 14 (e) 21
Sch. 1 559	Art. 14 (f) 21
Sch. 1, para 10 192	Art. 16 (4) 23
Sch. 9, para 171	Art. 17 10
Matrimonial and Family Proceedings	Art. 18 49
(NI) Order 1993 13	Art. 19 160
Matrimonial Causes (NI) Act	Art. 19(3) 161
1939 .... 29, 31, 174	Art. 20 .... 161, 545, 595
Matrimonial Causes (NI)	Art. 20(2) 162
Order 1978 .... lxiii, 5, 6,	Art. 21 44
10, 12, 20, 23, 27, 29, 31, 100,	Art. 23 162
120, 160, 169, 174, 175, 191,	Art. 23-31 550
244, 470, 520, 546, 550, 592	Art. 24 .... 162, 191, 545, 554
Art. 2 551	Art. 25 .... 184, 189, 550,
Art. 3 175	553, 555, 561
Art. 3(2) 161	Art. 25(1) 567
Art. 3(2)(a) 176	Art. 25(1)(a) 567, 568
Art. 3(2)(b) 178	Art. 25(1)(b) 567, 568
Art. 3(2)(c) 180	Art. 25(4) 556
Art. 3(2)(d) 182	Art. 25(7) 556
Art. 3(2)(e) 182	Art. 26 .... 184, 550, 553, 558, 561
Art. 3(4) 175, 188	Art. 26(1)(a) 552, 559
Art. 3(6) 186, 189	Art. 26(1)(b) 560
Art. 4 .... 175, 185	Art. 26(1)(c) 479, 560
Art. 4(1) 177	Art. 26(1)(d) 560
Art. 4(2) 178, 185	Art. 26(4) 560
Art. 4(4) 181	Art. 27 .... 32, 541, 551,
Art. 5 .... 175, 184	559, 561, 567, 568, 570, 571
Art. 6(1) 161	Art. 27A 541, 558, 559
Art. 7 .... 183, 185	Art. 27(1) 246, 571
Art. 7(1) 183, 184	Art. 27(2) 562, 563, 564, 565
Art. 7(2) 183	Art. 27(3) 553, 565
Art. 8 .... 187, 189	Art. 29 .... 543, 545, 552
Art. 11 189	Art. 29(5) 544
Art. 11(2) 189	Art. 31(1) 552
Art. 12 .... 185, 191	Art. 31(3) 552
Art. 12(2) 184	Art. 31(3)(b) 552
Art. 13 (1) (d) 7, 13, 15	Art. 33 557
Art. 13 (1) (e) 7, 15	Art. 33(7) 557
Art. 13 (1) (f) 7	Arts 35A 540
Art. 14 23	Arts 36 539
Art. 14 (a) 17	Arts 36–8 538

Table of National Legislation

Art. 37(2) 541
Art. 38(2) 543
Art. 38(3) 543
Art. 38(4) 543
Art. 39 566
Art. 39(2) 553
Art. 43(1) 161
Art. 43(1)(b)(ii) 454
Art. 44 .... 161, 185,
                    189, 190, 243, 247
Art. 44(1) 190, 244
Art. 44(3) 249
Art. 45 .... 127, 250
Art. 45(1) 205
Art. 46 285
Art. 47 250
Art. 48 186
Art. 48(9) 192
Art. 49 .... 182, 186
Art. 50(2) 16
Art. 55 481
Art. 58 31
Pt III 32
Pt IV 146
Sch. 1, para. 3 9
Sch. 3, para 19 49
Magistrates' Courts (Northern
   Ireland) Order 1981
   Art. 19(1) 66
Mental Health (NI) Order
   1986 .... 21, 23, 383, 409
   Art. 33 275
   Art. 39 275
   Art. 99(1)(e) 579
   Art. 100(a) 579
   Art. 100(b) 579
   Pt II 431

Northern Ireland Guardian ad Litem
   Agency (Establishment and
   Constitution) Order 1995 291

Pensions (NI) Order 1995 ... 19, 557, 565
Police and Criminal Evidence (NI)
   Order 1988

Art. 13 444
Art. 81 445
Art. 81A 445
Art. 81B 445
Police and Criminal Evidence (NI)
   Order 1989 .... 27, 332, 356
   Art. 19(1)(c) 356
   Art. 27(3)(e) 356
   Art. 38(9) 399
   Art. 81(1)(b)(i) 445
   Pt IV 399
   Pt V 399
Probation Act (NI) 1950
   .... 390, 403, 407
Probation Board (NI) Order 1982
Prosecution of Offences (NI)
   Order 1972 391
Protection of Children (NI)
   Order 1978 39
Provision for Family and Dependants
   (NI) Order 1979 590
   Art. 2(1)(a) 588
   Art. 2(2) 591
   Art. 3(1)(a) 588
   Art. 4 .... 581, 589
   Art. 4(1) 592
   Art. 4(1)(6) 588
   Art. 5 588
   Art. 5(1) 589
   Art. 5(2) 589

Rent (NI) Order 1978
   Art. 4 599
   Sch. 1 599

Social Security Administration (NI)
   Act 1992
   s. 34 527
Social Security (NI) Order 1986 ... 40
Summary Jurisdiction (Separation
   and Maintenance) Act
   (NI) 1945 544

Treatment of Offenders Act (NI)
   1968
   s. 7(1)(b) 415

Treatment of Offenders (NI) Order 1976
  Art. 8 406
  Art. 15 396
  Art. 15(1) 396
Treatment of Offenders (NI) Order 1989 .... 390, 407, 408
  Art. 7 415
Trustee Act (NI) 1958
  s. 32 574

Wills and Administration Proceedings (NI) Order 1994 .... 28, 573
  Art. 4 579
  Art. 5 575
  Art. 5(d)(ii) 577
  Art. 8 576
  Art. 11 578
  Art. 12 .... 28, 580
  Art. 12(1)(3) 579
  Art. 13 .... 45, 193, 581
  Art. 14(1)(d) 578
  Art. 29(1) 580

England and Wales

Abortion Act 1967 .. 56, 57, 66, 150, 228
Act for Joint Tenants 1542 ... 471, 506
Administration of Justice Act 1982 573
Administration of Justice Act 1984
  Pt 1 200
Adoption Act 1976 .... 95, 96

Child Abduction Act 1986 196
  s. 25 197
  s. 27 197
  s. 29 197
Child Abduction and Custody Act 1985 213
  Pt 1 206
  Sch. 1 206
Child Care Act 1980 ... 228, 375, 377
Child Support Act 1991 .... 520, 523
Children Act 1908
  s. III 390
Children Act 1989 .. 76, 131, 136, 137, 156, 172, 205, 224, 225, 226, 228, 230, 237, 240, 247, 248, 253, 263, 269, 279, 298, 303, 312, 323, 325, 334, 345, 354, 364, 378, 418, 420, 421, 423, 424, 449, 451, 516, 536, 540
  s. 1(3) 422
  s. 1(5) 208

  s. 8 246
  s. 24 6
  s. 31(2)(a) 329
  s. 31(2)(b) 329
  s. 34 373
  s. 34(2) 377
  s. 38 309
  s. 39(1)(b) 460
  s. 41(8) 459
  s. 98(2) 343, 344
  Sch. 1, para 1(1)(d) 517
  Pt 1 224
  Pt 11 224
Children and Young Persons Act 1963 .... 38, 227, 390
Children and Young Persons Act 1969 .... 228, 391
Children and Young Persons (Amendment) Act 1986 228
Children's Act 1948 .... 38, 227
Children's Act 1975 ... 77, 90, 226, 228
Children's Homes Act 1982 228
Criminal Justice Act 1888
  s. 36 330
Criminal Justice Act 1948
  s. 1(1) 416
  s. 1(2) 416
  s. 2 416

Table of Statutes

Criminal Law Amendment Act 1885
    ss 4–7 39
    s.12 78
Custody of Children Act
    1891 .... 39, 228
Custody of Infants Act
    1873 .... 39, 228

Data Protection Act 1984 432
Domicile and Matrimonial
    Proceedings Act 1973 26

Family Law Act 1986
    s. 56 48
Family Law Act 1996 ...... 175, 199,
    204, 205, 557
    s. 19 .... 205, 206
    s. 19(2)(b) 206
    s. 20 .... 205, 206
Family Law Reform Act 1969
    s. 20 51
Family Law Reform Act 1987
    s. 22 48
    s. 23 51
    s. 28 48
Fatal Accidents
    Art. 5(2) 518
Foster Children Act 1980 228

Guardianship of Infants Act 1839 ... 37
Guardianship of Infants Act 1873 ... 37
Guardianship of Infants Act 1886 ... 32,
    37, 38, 39, 77, 83, 84, 123, 228, 536
    s. 3 78
    s. 5 ...... 37, 84, 99, 152, 205, 242
    s. 5A 61, 78
Guardianship of Infants
    Act 1925 .... 37, 77
    s. 1 37
Guardianship of Infants
    Act 1971 .... 77, 228
Guardianship of Infants
    Act 1973 .... 77, 228
Government of Ireland Act 1920 ... 94

Human Fertilisation and Embryology
    Act 1990 .... 66, 69, 71, 74
    s. 4(1) 71
    s. (8)(c) 66
    s. 12 71
    s. 27 .... 67, 68, 75
    s. 28 68
    s. 28(6) 68
    s. 29 75
    s. 30 .... xxiii, 67, 72, 74
    s. 30(1) 71, 72, 73
    s. 30(1)(5) 73
    s. 30(1)(7) 73
    s. 30(1)(11) 73
    s. 30(2) 72
    s. 30(3) 72
    s. 30(7) 73
    s. 31(1) 75
    s. 31(2) 75
    s. 31(3) 75
    s. 32 75
    s. 34 75
    s. 37 74
    s. 48 66
    s. 50 529
    Sch. 3
    paras 3–71 68
    para 5 71

Income and Corporation Taxes
    Act 1970
    s. 8(1)(a) 55, 518
Infant Life (Preservation) Act 1929
    s. 1(i) 57
Inheritance (Provision for Family
    and Dependants)
    Order 1975 584
Inheritance (Provision for Family
    and Dependants) Order
    1979 .... 584, 585,
    593, 597, 598, 600, 603
    Art. 2 584
    Art. 2(1) 582
    Art. 3(1) 584, 586, 600

Art. 4(1) 601, 602	Northern Ireland Constitution
Art. 5(1) 586, 602	Act 1973 393
Art. 5(2) 586	Northern Ireland Constitution
Art. 12 582	Act 1974 573
Inheritance Tax Act 1984 583	Northern Ireland (Emergency
Intoxicating Substances (Supply)	Provisions) Act 1973 ... 402, 403
Act 1985 271	s. 45 399
	Sch. 4 403
Law of Property Act 1925 498	Northern Ireland (Emergency
s. 175 574	Provisions) Act 1978
Law Reform (Succession)	s. 1(3) 409
Act 1995 594	s. 9(5) 411
Legitimacy Act 1976	s. 10(1) 408
s. 1 48	s. 10(2) 410
Legitimacy Declaration Act	Sch. 4 410
(Ireland) 1868 47	
	Offences Against the Person Act 1861
Marriage Act 1983 7	s. 18 165
Marriage Act 1994	s. 20 165
s. 1 8	s. 42 165
s. 2 8	s. 43 165
Marriage Law (Ireland)	s. 47 165
Amendment Act 1863	s. 56 .... 195, 199
s. 3 7	s. 58 .... 56, 150
Married Women (Maintenance in	s. 59 .... 57, 150
Case of Desertion) Act 1886 ... 544	
Married Woman's Property	Petition Act 1868 67,
Act 1882 470,	471, 498, 501, 561
472, 479, 481, 550, 587	s. 3 .... 471, 503, 506
s. 2(2) 478	s. 4 .... 471, 502, 504, 506
s. 17 .... 32, 470, 471, 475, 476,	s. 5 471
478, 479, 480, 483, 486, 487, 495,	Petition Act 1876 .... 467, 471,
505, 558	498, 501, 506, 561
Matrimonial Causes Act 1973 176,	Prevention of Terrorism
191, 243, 558, 561	(Temporary Provisions)
s. 23(1) 567	Act 1984 399
s. 25 588	Punishment of Incest Act 1908 59
s. 25A 566, 588	s. 1 327
Matrimonial Homes Act	
1983 .... 169, 488	Recognition of Divorces and
s. 1(3) 516	Legal Separation Act 1971
Matrimonial Proceedings	s. 3(1) 192
(Polygamous Marriages) Act 1972	
s. 3 13	Sexual Offences Act 1956 15
Mental Health Act 1983 579	Sexual Offences Act 1967 15

Sunday Observance Act (Ireland)
1695
   s. 7 118
Surrogacy Arrangements Act
1985 .... 66, 69
   s.1 .... 67, 69
   s.1(2)(b) 68
   s. 2 70
   s. 2(1) 70
   s. 2(2) 70
   s. 4(2)(b) 66
   s. 5 66
   s. 36(1) 69
   s. 36(7) 70

Tenures Abolition Act 1660
   s. 8 32
Tenures Abolition (Ireland) Act 1662
   s. 6 78

Venereal Disease Act 1917
   s. 4 21
Wills (Amendment) Act 1852 573
   s. 1 576
Wills (Amendment) Act 1954 573
Wills Act 1837 .... 573, 576,
577, 578, 579
   s. 9 .... 575, 580
   s. 11 .... 574, 579
   s. 15 .... 576, 580
   s. 18 580
   s. 29 575
   s. 33 574
Wills (Soldiers and Sailors) Act
1918 574

Republic of Ireland

Law Reform (Miscellaneous
   Provisions) Act 1970 6

Europe and UN

EC Treaty
   Art. 59 72
   Art. 60 72
   Art. 177 525
European Convention for the
Protection of Human Rights and
Fundamental Freedoms
1950 .... 141, 222, 256, 371
   Art. 3 .... 326, 327
   Art. 6 370
   Art. 6(1) 222
   Art. 8 .... 15, 222, 327, 373
   Art. 12 15
   Art. 51(d) 348
European Convention on Adoption
of Children 1967 222

European Convention on Human
   Rights 1950 222
European Convention on Recognition
and Enforcement of Decisions
Concerning Custody of
Children 1980 198
European Convention on
Restoration of Custody of
children 1980 ... 198, 213, 214, 215
   Art. 7 213
European (Social) Charter
1961 .... 222 (272)

Hague Convention on Civil Aspects of
International Child Abduction
1980 .... 198, 206, 214, 215

Art. 1 213	Art. 5 . . . . 417, 440
Art. 3 . . . . 196, 206	Art. 7 363
Art. 12 . . . . 207, 209, 210	Art. 8 . . . . 363, 440
Art. 13 . . . . 210, 211, 212	Art. 9 433
Art. 18 210	Art. 12 . . . . 417, 438
Art. 21 213	Art. 18 . . . . 265, 273
Hague Convention on Inter-Country Adoption 1993 265	Art. 23 275
Hague Convention on the Recognition of Divorces and Separations 1970 192	Art. 25 . . . . 370, 380
	Art. 37 . . . . 326, 409, 413
	Art. 40 413
United Nations Conventions on the Rights of the Child 1989 . . . 223, 225, 265, 371	UN Declaration on Social and Legal Principles relating to the Protection and Welfare of Children with special reference to Foster placement and Adoption Nationally and Internationally (1986)
Art. 2 433	
Art. 3.3 370	Art. 3 265

Table of Statutory Instruments and Rules

Northern Ireland

Adoption Agencies Regulations
(NI) 1989 .... 97, 100, 118
   Reg. 5 101
   Reg. 5(1) 101
   Reg. 10(3) 96
   Reg. 12 .... 116, 117
   Reg. 15(1)(e) 119

Blood Tests (Evidence of
Paternity) (Amendment)
Regulations (NI) 1990 529

Child Minding and Day-Care
(Applications for Registration)
Regulations (NI) 1996 267
Children (Private Arrangements
for Fostering) Regulations (NI)
1996 269
Children (Secure Accommodation)
Regulations (NI) 1996 ... 382, 383
Child Support (Collection and
Enforcement) Regulations
(NI) 1992 533
Contact with Children Regulations
(NI) 1996 375
   Reg. 2 375
County Courts Rules (Northern
Ireland) 1981 xxii
County Court (Amendment No. 3)
Rules (NI) 1989 .... 100, 101, 118
   Rule 14 118
   Rule 17 120
   Rule 19(1) 121
   Rule 20 121
   Rule 20(1) 121
   Rule 21 119

Crown Court (Amendment No. 2)
Rules (NI) 1989
   Rule 44B 445

Disqualification for Caring for
Children Regulations
(NI) 1996 267

Emergency Protection Orders
(Transfer of Responsibilities)
Regulations (NI) 1996
   Reg. 2 351
   Reg. 3 .... 351, 352
   Reg. 4 352
   Reg. 5 352
Exempted Supervised Activities
Children Regulations
(NI) 1996 267

Family Proceedings Rules
(NI) 1996 .... lvii, 186
   Rule 2.1 23
   Rule 2.1.4 188
   Rule 2.23 188
   Rule 2.26 17
   Rule 2.27 17
   Rule 2.3
   Rule 2.3.2 187
   Rule 2.36 187
   Rule 2.52 189
   Rule 2.53 189
   Rule 2.7 190
   Rule 2.72 540
   Rule 4.11 290
   Rule 4.12 290
   Rule 4.12(4) 459

Rule 4.12(5)	457, 459	Rule 19	446
Rule 4.13	292	Rule 21.(4)(b)	231
Rule 4.14	292	Rule 23	450
Rule 4.15	288	Rule 23(1)	458
Rule 4.17	288	Rule 26	383
Rule 4.19	446	Rule 28	234, 310
Rule 4.23	234, 310		
Rule 4.24	450		
Rule 4.24(1)	458		
Rule 4.4	249		
Rule 6.(3)(1)	452		
Rule 6.5	21		
Appendix 2	186		
Pt III	537		
Rule 1.3	554		
Rule 2.55–2.73	550		
Rule 2.56	551		
Rule 2.7	555		
Rule 2.73	565		
Rule 3.1	543		
Rule 3.2(1)	544		
Rule 3.4	541		
Rule 3.5	541		

Magistrates' Courts (Domestic Proceedings) Rules (NI) 1966

Rule 3(2)	538
Rule 5	540
Rule 10	
Rule 11	
Rule 13	

Matrimonial Causes (Northern Ireland) Rules 1980 lxii

Matrimonial Causes (Amendment) Rules (Northern Ireland) 1989 lxii

Matrimonial Causes (Amendment) Rules (Northern Ireland) 1993 lxii

Matrimonial Causes Rules (NI) 1979 175

Matrimonial Causes Rules (NI) 1981 186

Rule 45	10
Rule 88	16

Matrimonial Causes Rules (NI) 1989 186

Matrimonial Causes Rules (NI) 1993 186

Rule 2.26	
Rule 2.27	
Rule 44	188
Rule 89	188

Matrimonial Charges Regulations (NI) 1989 489

Guardian ad Litem (Panel) Regulations (NI) 1996 ... 290, 291

Land Registration Rules (NI) 1994 489

Magistrates' Courts (Children and Young Persons) Rules (NI) 1969 lxiii

Magistrates' Courts (Children (NI) Order 1995) Rules (NI) 1996

Rule 2(2)	430
Rule 11	290
Rule 12	290, 457
Rule 12(3)	441
Rule 13	292
Rule 14	292
Rule 15	288
Rule 15(2)(d)	290
Rule 17	288

Prison and Young Offender Centre Rules (NI) 1994 414

Rules of the Supreme Court (NI) 1980 143

Order 80 85
Order 98 48
Rules of the Supreme Court (NI)
 (Amendment Act No. 6)
 1989 .... 100, 11
Rule 15 118
Rule 22(1) 119
Rules of the Supreme Court (NI)
 (Amendment Act No. 4)
 1996 48

Rule 2 86
Rules 3 and 3A
Rule 6 101
Rule 18 .... 101, 120

Secure Accommodation (NI)
 Regulations 1996 383
Statutory Rules and Orders for
 Northern Ireland No. 32
 (Training School Rules) 413

England and Wales

Adoption Rules 1984
 Rule 53(2) 121
Arrangements for Placement of
 Children (General)
 Regulations 1996 .... 360, 366
 Reg. 3 371
 Reg. 4 372
 Sch. 1–4 372

Children's Homes Regulations
 1996 364

Child Support (Information,
 Evidence and Disclosure)
 Regulations 1992 532
Child Support (Maintenance
 Assessment Procedure)
 Regulations 1992 531

Foster Placement (Children)
 Regulations 1996 367

Family Law: Structures and Processes

The Courts

Three tiers of courts are available to process family law business: the High Court; the county courts; and the family proceedings courts (Article 164(1) of the 1995 Order).

Where that business arises in the form of proceedings commenced under the Children (NI) Order 1995, a principle of concurrent jurisdiction applies. This confers on each tier the capacity to hear the same proceedings and to make the same orders (with the exception of some proceedings reserved for the High Court or county courts). In addition, under the Children (Allocation of Proceedings) Order (NI) 1996, 'family proceedings' cases may be transferred among the tiers depending on their gravity, importance or complexity. A case may also be transferred in order to consolidate proceedings.

Other forms of family law business remain specific to the jurisdiction of particular courts (e.g. undefended divorce cases are heard in county courts).

I. High Court

The High Court is constituted in three divisions. The Family Division is the most recent and was established by the Judicature (NI) Act 1978.

The Family Division

The Family Division of the High Court continues to exercise its established jurisdiction in relation to family matters. In addition to family proceedings cases allocated upwards to it for reasons such as complexity or heard on appeal from a county court, the High Court continues to have a reserved jurisdiction in relation to proceedings such as contested divorce cases, ancillary proceedings where considerable sums are involved, nullity suits, wardship, declarations of marital status and legitimacy status, child abduction cases under the Hague and European Conventions and contested cases concerning wills and intestacy.

The judges who have served in the Family Division of the High Court (NI) since it was established in 1979, and their terms of office are as follows:

The Honourable Mr Justice Malachy Higgins 1996–
The Honourable Mr Justice John Shiel 1993–96
The Honourable Mr Justice Eoin Higgins 1987–93
The Honourable Mr Justice Brian Hattan 1984–87
The Honourable Mr Justice John MacDermott 1979–84.

An appeal lies from the decision of the High Court to the Court of Appeal.

Under the Administration of Justice Act 1969, in certain cases an appeal may lie directly from the High Court to the House of Lords.

II. County Courts

The county court tier now has two divisions. The 'care centre' deals with both private and public cases while the domestic proceedings courts deal exclusively with private cases. Procedure, in general, is governed by the County Courts (NI) Order 1980, the County Courts (Financial Limits) Order (NI) 1993 and the County Court Rules (NI) 1981, as amended. There are a total of twelve county court judges assisted by thirty-four deputies.

1. Care Centres

Care centres are county courts specially designated by the Children (Allocation of Proceedings) Order (NI) 1996 to hear proceedings commenced under the Children Order (NI) 1995. Under Schedule 2 of the 1996 Order, the following are so designated: Belfast Recorder's Court, Londonderry Recorder's Court and Craigavon County Court. Procedure is governed, in particular, by the Family Proceedings Rules (NI) 1996.

In addition to some family proceedings cases which may have been allocated upwards for reasons such as gravity or complexity or are being heard on appeal from a magistrates' court, the county courts continue to have a reserved jurisdiction for adoption and guardianship proceedings.

2. Domestic Proceedings Court

Domestic proceedings courts are county courts which continue their jurisdiction to hear proceedings arising principally under the Domestic Proceedings (NI) Order 1980, particularly undefended divorce proceedings. Proceedings for ancillary relief in cases of divorce, nullity and judicial separation will be heard here. In cases concerning property and finance, the jurisdiction of the county courts is determined by the size of the sums of money or property values involved.

Cases heard in a domestic proceedings court are determined by a magistrate sitting alone. Procedure is governed, in particular by the County Court Rules (NI) 1981 and also by the Matrimonial Causes (NI) Rules 1980 and the Matrimonial Causes (Amendment) Rules (NI) 1989 and 1993.

An appeal may lie from a decision of a county court to the High Court or, on a point of law only, to the Court of Appeal.

III. Magistrates' Courts

There are a total of twenty-three courts of summary jurisdiction in Northern Ireland. In addition to those magistrates' courts which deal with civil and criminal proceedings concerning adults, there are also two types — the juvenile court and the family proceedings court — which deal with children. In the former, cases are heard by a resident magistrate sitting alone. In the latter, where a case concerns children, the resident magistrate sits with a panel consisting of two lay magistrates, one of whom must be a woman.

IV. *Juvenile Court*

The Juvenile Court (as constituted under Schedule 2 of the Children and Young Persons Act (NI) 1968) retains a residual jurisdiction to hear proceedings other than those commenced under the 1995 Order. Procedure is governed by the Magistrates' Courts (Children and Young Persons) Rules (NI) 1969. This, in effect, is a criminal jurisdiction and the courts will shortly be reconstituted as such under the name 'Youth Courts'.

V. *Family Proceedings Court*

Family proceedings courts are specially constituted courts of summary jurisdiction established by Article 164(4) of the Children (NI) Order 1995 to hear 'family proceedings'. Procedure is governed by the Magistrates' Courts (Children (NI) Order 1995) Rules (NI) 1996. Under Schedule 1 of the Children (Allocation of Proceedings) Order (NI) 1996, seven juvenile courts have been designated as family proceedings courts. One is located in each division of the county court: Londonderry; Ballymena; Omagh; Craigavon; Newry and Mourne; Ards; Belfast and Newtownabbey.

Under Article 8 of the Children (NI) Order 1995 'family proceedings' means proceedings under the inherent jurisdiction of the High Court and under the following provisions:

(a) the 1995 Order — Part II, Part III, Part V (care and supervision) and Part XV (guardians);
(b) the Matrimonial Causes (NI) Order 1978;
(c) the Domestic Proceedings (NI) Order 1980;
(d) Articles 4 and 13 of the Family Law (Miscellaneous Provisions)(NI) Order 1994;
(e) the Adoption Order;
(f) Part IV of the Matrimonial and Family Proceedings (NI) Order 1989;
(g) Section 30 of the Human Fertilisation and Embryology Act 1990.

These proceedings will normally, with one or two exceptions reserved for other courts, commence in family proceedings courts.

Cases which should commence there may be allocated to a higher court depending on the complexity of the case, its likely duration, the availability of court time and the number of expert witnesses who may be involved.

An appeal may lie from a decision taken in a magistrates' court to a county court. An appeal may also lie to the Court of Appeal but only by way of case stated and only on a point of law.

Law Reports

All family proceedings courts are required to file statements of decisions reached, together with a brief summary of the facts and reasoning upon which they were based. At magistrates' court level these do not have to constitute fully reasoned judgments, whereas at the superior court level this is mandatory. Judgments relating to cases heard in the superior courts are normally published in the two official publications for this jurisdiction: the Northern Ireland Law Reports (NILR) and the Northern Ireland Judgments Bulletin (NIJB), commonly known as 'the bluebook'. In addition, the Northern Ireland Legal Quarterly (NILQ) provides a broad academic perspective on legal developments in this jurisdiction and elsewhere.

The reporting of judgments which has been beset with difficulties in recent years broke down completely in 1992/3. The 1992 Law Reports were not published until February 1997; the 1993 NIJB until 1996; and the 1993 NILR until June 1997. Unreported judgments have therefore assumed an unusual significance with the LEXIS information retrieval system and the provision of transcripts by the Supreme Court librarian providing the means whereby practitioners may access such judgments.

Legal Aid, Advice and Assistance

Access to the courts is as essential to applicants and respondents in proceedings relating to the family as in any other branch of law. There are three different forms of legal aid available: legal advice; legal aid; and legal assistance. They are all governed by the Legal Aid, Advice and Assistance (NI) Order 1981.

I. Legal Advice

Commonly known as 'the green form scheme', the idea for legal advice was introduced in 1974 and is a means-tested entitlement to advice and assistance from a solicitor to a value of £86.50. Eligibility is determined by possession of disposable capital of less than £1,000 and disposable income of less than £156 per week. Allowances are made for an applicant's dependants when calculating entitlement. Where an applicant's means exceed these limits, a level of contribution may be fixed on a sliding-scale basis. The solicitor approached to provide the service also bears responsibility for determining eligibility.

The scheme allows for advice to be given, letters written, documents drafted, negotiations conducted and phone calls made. It is not available in certain types of cases such as contested ancillary proceedings. It can be particularly useful in proceedings, such as in undefended divorces where legal aid is not available, but the scheme may be used to prepare documents etc.

II. Legal Assistance by Way of Representation

The green form scheme can be extended to provide 'assistance by way of representation' in certain types of cases including family proceedings. The disposable capital limit is then fixed at £3,000. An assisted party is still restricted to £86.50 worth of a solicitor's time and expertise, unless a successful application for extended assistance is made to the Law Society.

III. *Legal Aid*

Although the statutory legal aid scheme is administered by the Legal Aid Department of the Law Society, it did not become available until 1965 for family law cases in Northern Ireland. It is now granted in many family proceedings such as for injunctions, ancillary relief on divorce and orders relating to the upbringing of children. In particular, free legal aid is available to children, parents and others with parental responsibility in applications for a care order, supervision order, child assessment order, emergency protection order (or for extensions) and for children (who must be given the opportunity to have legal assistance) in secure accommodation. Again, eligibility is means tested. It is also, however, subject to a merits test, i.e. does the applicant have a case worth arguing? It is for the Law Society, not an individual solicitor, to determine eligibility.

A legally aided party will be subject to a 'claw-back' requirement if successful in a financial action. Any such recovered monies are paid into the Legal Aid Fund.

The publication in July 1996 of the Legal Aid White Paper, *Striking the Balance*, has served notice of impending change to the statutory legal aid scheme. Demonstrating an adherence to the purchaser/provider model of service delivery, the paper sets out the principles governing targeting, contracting and eligibility by means of which the Government will reduce and control future spending. There can be little doubt that if, as suggested, the changes include standard fees, increasing the range of those eligible to contribute to costs and more specific targeting, then this will adversely affect access to family proceedings in Northern Ireland.

PART ONE

Parents

Introduction

The twin axis of the relationships between spouses and between parents and their children have always been at the heart of family law. This remains the current position in Northern Ireland. Part One starts with that recognition and is, therefore, almost exclusively concerned with private family law.

Central to that discussion is the fact that the axis have fallen out of alignment. Marriage, marital status and the reciprocal obligations of spouses are no longer viewed as the defining characteristics of family law, integrating its parts and essential to its overall coherence. Whether or not the parents are married to each other is, increasingly, beside the point. Whether a parent is so as a consequence of nature, science or law is similarly of little legal significance. The boundaries of the nuclear family unit may now give way to admit a child of the family, a carer or a person other than a parent but bearing parental responsibilities. The retraction of substantive law is accompanied by an ever-increasing volume and spread of administrative law. Adjudication is giving way to mediation. Adjusting, in a conciliatory and flexible manner, the mutual legal responsibilities of adults living together in domestic circumstances has become the main business occupying the courts. Assigning and/or policing the exercise of parental responsibilities, while determining the relative *locus standi* of the children concerned, is of central importance. Family law is now focused more on function than status.

In that private law context Part One deals, in three sections, with the types of proceedings in which the interests of adults are to the fore in their construction and deconstruction of family units; in the reciprocal roles and obligations of partners, whether marital or non-marital; in the exercise of their parental responsibilities; and in their management of family boundaries. But, in the main, parenthood is the subject, and the focus is on the law relating to the role and responsibilities of a parent.

The first section deals with birth families. Beginning with the status of marriage, it considers the legal incidences differentiating marital and other relationships. It then considers the layer of additional legal responsibilities which parenting brings to both sets of relationships. Most obviously this section focuses on issues relating to legal status (marriage, legitimacy etc.) and issues which flow from the exercise of the parties rights and duties towards each other and towards their children.

The second section deals with acquired families. It takes as its subject the areas of family law such as adoption, wardship and guardianship in which the proceedings are generally initiated by those seeking to either become parents or to undertake the responsibilities of a parent. It considers also, private proceedings initiated against those acting in a parental capacity. The primary criteria for inclusion in this section is that the issues concern the acquisition or exercise of parental responsibilities by adults in respect of children not born to them. It outlines the law in relation to the formal and informal, natural and contrived, processes of becoming a parent. It examines the apportioning and exercising of responsibilities among those who undertake a parental role.

The third section deals with family breakdown. The focus is on the substantive law governing separation and divorce. It also takes into consideration matters such as domestic violence and child abduction which may occur in the context of breakdown. It does not consider contested proceedings concerning the future care arrangements for any children of the family or for the distribution of property and finance. These are dealt with in Parts Two and Three, respectively.

CHAPTER ONE

Marriage

Introduction

The time when family law meant marital family law has long gone. Now there are few legal characteristics of family relationships which do not equally apply to both marital and non-marital family units. Sexual relations between cohabiting couples, the responsibilities of parenthood, the status of children and the ownership of property are all crucial areas of family life where the application of the law no longer significantly differentiates between the parties involved on the basis of whether or not they form part of a marital family. In the very near future, any residual legal distinction may well be open to challenge on the grounds of being incompatible with legislation governing equal opportunities and discriminatory practices. At present in Northern Ireland, marriage and indeed re-marriage is the preferred framework for establishing most families.

This chapter, however, deals with the institution of marriage. It begins with a consideration of the law in relation to pre-marital relationships, the status and obligations of engagement and the possible significance of pre- and post-nuptial contracts. It examines marital capacity and the formalities of marriage within the jurisdiction and the conditions for the recognition of foreign marriages. Of necessity, as a means of defining what constitutes a valid marriage, much material is assembled to demonstrate when it is not so constituted. The law relating to nullity is explained and the history of the distinction between void and voidable marriages is explored in some detail.

The Marriage Process

'Marriage' refers both to the ceremony, which changes the legal status of those undergoing it from single persons to husband and wife, and to the state of their relationship thereafter. The process of becoming married is governed by statutory requirements which if not fully satisfied will render a marriage void or voidable. Litigation is also increasingly being generated by pre-nuptial and by post-nuptial agreements. In Northern Ireland the substantive law of marriage is to be found largely in the Family Law (Miscellaneous Provisions) (NI) Order 1984, the Matrimonial Causes (NI) Order 1978 and the Family Law (NI) Order 1993.

I. Engagements

In this jurisdiction, a marriage is customarily preceded by an engagement. This term refers not only to the act itself and the status of the couple's relationship but also to a time-limited period terminating on marriage. The act of 'engagement' had, under common law, recognition as a contractual agreement which could give rise to an action for 'breach of promise of marriage'.[1] Such actions were prohibited by the Family Law (Miscellaneous Provisions) (NI) Order 1984 following the recommendations of the Law Commission.[2] This legislation did not, however, impose an absolute bar on litigation to recover losses suffered as a consequence of a broken engagement (see further Part III, Chapter 20).

II. Definition

As Lord Penzance declared more than a century ago:

> I conceive that marriage, as understood in Christendom, may . . . be defined as the voluntary union for life of one man and one woman to the exclusion of all others.[3]

This concise and frequently quoted definition, resting on four conditions, has borne the test of time relatively well.

1. Voluntary

As with any contract, the consent of both parties is essential if it is to be binding; the absence of a valid consent has long been recognised as grounds for the annulment of a marriage. The normal contractual components must be satisfied:

(a) capacity, i.e. the parties will not have the requisite capacity if they breach any of the grounds listed under Article 13 of the Matrimonial Causes (NI) Order 1978;
(b) full understanding;
(c) absence of duress;
(d) absence of improper inducement.

2. For Life

Adherence to the Christian model of marriage as a monogamous union, subsisting until death, has ceased to be a legal requirement. The suggestion[4] that this should be interpreted as the required intention of a prospective husband and wife has also failed to endure. A 'marriage of convenience' may be undertaken (e.g. for the purpose of acquiring citizenship or legitimising a child) and may be open to criticism, but if all conditions have been fulfilled it will still be a valid marriage.

---

1 The offended party would be entitled to seek the return of any gifts (ring, furniture, accommodation etc.) given to the prospective spouse in furtherance of their common intent. But the court does not have the same power to make property adjustment orders as it would have in a marital context; see *Mossop v Mossop* [1988] 2 All ER 202.
2 See *Breach of Promise of Marriage* Law Com No. 26, (1969). The Commission's recommendations were enacted rather more promptly across the Irish Sea in the Law Reform (Miscellaneous Provisions) Act 1970.
3 See *Hyde v Hyde* (1866) LR 1 P&D 130, 133.
4 See *Nachimson v Nachimson* [1930] p. 217 CA.

3. One Man and One Woman

The concept of one man and one woman is the stated requirement of Article 13(1)(e) of the Matrimonial Causes (NI) Order 1978.

4. Excluding All Others

It is a requirement of Article 13(1)(d) of the 1978 Order that to contract a valid marriage each party must be unmarried at that time. To sustain that marriage Article 13(1)(f) of the 1978 Order requires that neither party may enter into another marriage while the other party is still alive.

III. Formalities

The rules relating to marriage formalities are to be found in the Marriage (Declaration of Law) Act (NI) 1944 (as amended), the Marriages Act (NI) 1954, the Marriage (Prohibited Degrees of Relationship) Act (NI) 1949 and the Family Law (NI) Order 1993. They illustrate the extent to which the formalities of the modern marriage originate in ecclesiastical law. Although the ceremony may now take a civil or religious form, marriage itself remains subject to standard public law requirements, determined by the law of the parties' country of domicile, such as proof of capacity and registration. There are four main categories of marriage ceremony: civil marriages, marriage in accordance with the rites of the Church of Ireland, marriage in accordance with non-Church of Ireland religious ceremony and Quaker and Jewish marriages.

1. Civil Marriages

(a) Authority to Marry

The couple must first establish their right to be married. This is done by obtaining either a superintendent registrar's certificate, a superintendent registrar's certificate with licence or the Registrar General's licence.[5] In each instance, written notice must be lodged in the Registrar's office, a fee paid and a declaration made of no known impediment to marriage. In addition, the required consents must have been obtained and the residence requirements fulfilled. The traditional obligation on the Registrar's office that notice be given of the intended marriage (twenty-one days notice in the first instance, served publicly; fifteen days in the second, not served publicly) is now subject to the Family Law (NI) Order 1993:

> The requirement in section 3 of the Marriage Law (Ireland) Amendment Act 1863 for notices of certain marriages intended to be contracted in the office of a registrar to be published on 2 consecutive weeks in a newspaper circulating in the district in which such marriage is intended is hereby abolished; and, accordingly, section 41 of the Matrimonial Causes and Marriage Law (Ireland) Amendment Act 1870 is hereby repealed.

---

5 The first is the most common; the second is increasingly being used by couples who wish to avoid the public announcement entailed in the first, though a higher fee is payable; the third results from the Marriage Act 1983 which extends to Northern Ireland the authority of the Registrar General to issue a licence to house-bound or detained persons enabling them to be married at the place where they reside.

The certificate/licence is then issued. This provides authority for the marriage ceremony to take place.

(b) Marriage Ceremony

The marriage ceremony must be performed in an authorised place, most usually the local register office in the area where one party resides.[6] It must entail a declaration of no known lawful impediment to marriage, an exchange of solemn vows in the presence of at least two witnesses and the entry of the couple's signatures in the register of marriages.

2. Religious Marriages

(a) Church of Ireland

(i) Publication of Banns

An essential component of the Church of Ireland marriage formalities is the requirement that the parties 'publish the banns' of their proposed marriage. This involves notice of the marriage being formally entered in a public register and the clergyman for the parish, where the betrothed normally worship, declaring on three successive Sundays the couple's intention to marry. Seven days' advance notice must be given, and the clergyman must be provided with details of each party's name, place and duration of residence and consents. Anyone who objects may register their objection during this period after which, if no objections have been received, the marriage ceremony may take place.

(ii) Licences

There are two kinds of licences, i.e. a 'common licence' and a 'special licence'. The first, which is granted by the bishop, excuses the couple from having to publish banns and from the obligation to provide seven days' advance notice and gives permission for the marriage to be held in the church where one of the parties would normally worship or in the parish where the residence requirements have been met. Before this can be obtained, one party must swear an affidavit to the effect that there are no known impediments to the marriage, the residence requirements are satisfied and the necessary consents are in order. The second, granted by the Archbishop, is only available in exceptional circumstances and gives a blanket permission for the proposed marriage to be held in any church at any time.

(iii) Ceremony

Once one of the above preliminary stages has been completed, the marriage ceremony can go ahead. This will take place in one of the churches where the banns were pub-

---

6   Under the Marriage Act 1994:

   s.1 — a civil marriage need not take place in a register office, instead a local authority may approve, for a fee, sites other than their own register office; s.2 — a couple need no longer be married in the district of residence of one of the parties. Instead a certificate or certificate and licence may be issued in one register office to validate a service held in another.

   The first part of this Act came into effect early in 1995.

lished, within three months of that event, between the hours of eight a.m. and six p.m. A clergyman will officiate in the presence of at least two witnesses.

(b) Non-Church of Ireland

(i) Preliminaries

The parties must comply with the civil requirements (as above) and the certificate issued must state where the ceremony is to be held; this should be the normal place of worship, or other registered building, in the area where one of the parties resides.

(ii) The Ceremony

This must be held under the supervision of a registrar or an 'authorised person' who, in the latter instance, will most usually be a minister or priest in the religion concerned. The ceremony should take place with open doors in the presence of two or more witnesses, and both parties must make a declaration that they know of no lawful impediment to the marriage.

(c) Quaker and Jewish

Those partaking in a Quaker or Jewish marriage ceremony must first obtain authorisation in the form of either a superintendent registrar's certificate (with or without a licence) or the Registrar General's licence. When giving advance notice, a Quaker (or member of the Society of Friends) must make a special declaration, though neither party need in fact be a Quaker to be married in accordance with Quaker rites. Both parties to a Jewish marriage must make a declaration of adherence to the Jewish faith. Neither form of marriage ceremony need take place in a registered building; nor do they require officiating or witnesses. However, in common with all marriages, the parties must sign a register[7] and their signatures must be witnessed.

IV. Foreign Marriages

The essential conditions for the recognition of a valid marriage, as noted by Lord Penzance in *Hyde v Hyde*,[8] apply also to the recognition of marriages conducted in another jurisdiction other than a related jurisdiction.[9] For many years after that ruling it was held that polygamous marriages did not comply with his monogamous

---

7 Note the Government White Paper *Registration: Proposals for Change*, (Cm 939/1990), which suggested changes to the legal requirements regarding registration and the marriage ceremony.
8 Op. cit, see p. 6.
9 Under the Matrimonial Causes (NI) Order 1978, Sched 1, para. 3:

  3.—(1) 'Another jurisdiction' means any country other than Northern Ireland.
   (2) 'Related jurisdiction' means any of the following countries, namely, England and Wales, Scotland, Jersey, Guernsey and the Isle of Man (the reference to Guernsey being treated as including Alderney and Sark).

requirement and, therefore, could not be recognised as valid marriages.[10] However, as Article 17 of the 1978 Order makes clear, it is now beyond doubt that if a couple have full legal capacity according to their *lex domicilii* and satisfy the formalities of the *lex loci celebrationis*, then their marriage will be recognised by the courts in this jurisdiction. So, for example, the Court of Appeal in England had no difficulty in acknowledging the validity of a marriage between a thirteen-year-old Nigerian girl and her twenty-five-year-old husband when, after their marriage in Nigeria, they then became resident in the U.K. As the judge then remarked a polygamous marriages is now 'recognised in this country unless there is some strong reason to the contrary'.[11] (See further Chapter 14.) Rule 45 of the Matrimonial Causes Rules requires the validity of a foreign marriage to be proven by the production of either a marriage certificate (or similar document) or a certified copy of an entry in a marriage register from the country where the marriage took place. Proof of the existence of such a marriage will prevent the re-marriage of either spouse in this jurisdiction during the lifetime of the other.

1. The *Lex Loci Celebrationis*

Whether a marriage is monogamous or polygamous is determined by the place where the marriage ceremony is celebrated.

(a) Monogamous marriages

If a marriage is conducted in a jurisdiction where the law requires that it be monogamous, then, notwithstanding that one or both parties are citizens of a jurisdiction which permits polygamy, that marriage will be monogamous and is incapable of becoming polygamous.[12] The issue is not so much whether a marriage breaches the letter of the law but whether in doing so it presents a serious offence to the public policy of this jurisdiction. A marriage between an uncle and his niece and celebrated in Egypt, which was the couple's place of domicile, was later recognised by a court in England despite clearly falling within the prohibited degrees of relationship. At that time Simon P stated:[13]

> What I believe to be the true test [is] whether the marriage is so offensive to the conscience of the English court that it should refuse to recognise and give effect to the proper foreign law. In deciding that question the court will seek to exercise common sense, good manners and a reasonable tolerance.

(b) Polygamous marriages

If a marriage is conducted in a jurisdiction where the law requires that it be polygamous, then, regardless of the fact that one or both parties may be citizens of a jurisdiction

---

10   See *Re Bethell* (1888) 38 ChD 220.
11   See *Mohamed v Knot* [1969] 1 QB 1, pp 13–14.
12   See *Baindail v Baindail* [1946] 1 All ER 342 CA where the husband, who was a Hindu and domiciled in India, married an English domiciled woman in a registry office in England. The marriage was monogamous as no other form of marriage could be legally conducted in England.
13   See *Cheni v Cheni* [1965] pp 98–9, [1962] 3 All ER 882–883.

where only monogamy is practised, that marriage will be either actually or potentially polygamous. That neither partner takes, nor has the intention of taking, another spouse does not prevent their marriage from being inherently polygamous. So, for example, a marriage which took place in Egypt between a Muslim who was domiciled in that country and a woman who was a citizen of, and domiciled in, England,[14] was held to be polygamous.

2. Potentially polygamous marriages

A marriage is potentially polygamous when one partner may take another spouse but never actually does so. It is the fact that such a partner has contracted to provide for a capacity to marry again, during the continuance of the first marriage, which offends the marriage laws of this jurisdiction. A potentially polygamous marriage is regarded in law as being polygamous and while neither form may be conducted under the marriage law of this jurisdiction both will be recognised as valid marriages if conducted in compliance with the requirements of the parties *lex domicilii*. A marriage which is polygamous, or potentially so, may be converted into a monogamous one by, for example, a change of domicile.[15] Under Article 37 of the Matrimonial and Family Proceedings (NI) Order 1989, a court is not to be prevented from making a declaration as to the validity of a marriage solely because that marriage was polygamous or potentially so in the jurisdiction where it was conducted.

Nullity

Having undergone a ceremony of marriage the presumption[16] arises that the couple are in fact lawfully married. The law of nullity establishes the circumstances in which this is not the case. Insofar as it affects marriages celebrated in this jurisdiction after 18 April 1979, the law is to be found in the Matrimonial Causes (NI) Order 1978 (as amended by the Matrimonial and Family Proceedings (NI) Order 1989) and, to a lesser extent, in the Family Law (NI) Order 1993.

There are two aspects of the law of nullity: void marriages and voidable marriages.

I. Void Marriages

Under the Matrimonial Causes (NI) Order 1978:

---

14 See *Risk (Otherwise Yerburgh) v Risk* [1950] 2 All ER 973; also see *Re Bethell* (1887) 38 Ch D 220 where an English citizen married, in Africa, a member of an African tribe in accordance with tribal rites which recognised only polygamy. The marriage was held to be polygamous.
15 See *Ali v Ali* [1966] 1 All ER 664; but also see *Quoraishi v Quoraishi* [1985] FLR 780 CA where two Muslim doctors, domiciled and married in Bangladesh, later settled in England and where the husband after 15 years of monogamy then married again in Bangladesh. The court in England held that his action justified the desertion of the first wife. The mere promise to make a polygamous marriage monogamous, at some future time, is insufficient. See *Sowa v Sowa* (1961) [1961] 1 All ER 687, CA.
16 It is a presumption which is rarely challenged: in Northern Ireland there were only two petitions for the annulment of marriages in 1993.

(1) A marriage celebrated after the commencement of this Article shall be void on the following grounds only, that is to say —
   (a) that the parties are within the prohibited degrees of relationship;
   (b) that it is not a valid marriage under the provisions of the Age of Marriage Act (NI) 1951 (a) (persons under 16);
   (c) that it is not a valid marriage by reason of non-compliance with any statutory provision or rule of law governing the formation of marriage;
   (d) that at the time of the marriage either party was already lawfully married;
   (e) that the parties are not respectively male and female;
   (f) in the case of a polygamous marriage entered into outside Northern Ireland, that either party was at the time of the marriage domiciled in Northern Ireland.
(2) For the purposes of paragraph (1)(f) a marriage may be polygamous although at its inception neither party has any spouse additional to the other.

A void marriage is one which was so fundamentally flawed from the outset, by reason of a party lacking capacity or because of a procedural defect, that it needs no decree to annul it but may be regarded, in terms of law and religion, as having never taken place. A decree may nevertheless be sought in respect of a marriage which is void *ab initio* in order to obtain legal verification of that fact. The following are the grounds on which such a decree may be acquired.

1. Prohibited Degrees of Relationship

A relationship may be prohibited because of consanguinity (i.e. proximity of relationships derived from blood-links) or affinity (i.e. proximity of relationships derived from marriage). The rules governing both may be found in the Marriage (Prohibited Degrees of Relationship) Act (NI) 1949, as amended by Article 18 of the Family Law (Miscellaneous Provisions) (NI) Order 1984. These rules have been further amended by the provisions of the Family Law (NI) Order 1993. Article 4 relaxes the restrictions on marriages within prohibited degrees of relationships, mainly between 'in-laws', if certain requirements are satisfied. Article 5 enables the parties to an intended marriage within certain degrees of affinity to seek a declaration that the marriage would not be void for that reason. Basically, a man is prohibited from marrying his mother, daughter, grand-daughter, sister, aunt or niece, and a woman is prohibited from marrying her equivalent male relatives. The rules in relation to 'prohibited degrees' are slightly relaxed in relation to adopted persons.

2. Under Age

Under the Age of Marriage Act (NI) 1951, a condition of a valid marriage is that both parties have reached the age of sixteen. This is subject to the *lex domicilii* rule[17] (see

---

17 See *Pugh v Pugh* [1951] 2 All ER 680 where a man, domiciled in England, married a fifteen-year-old girl in Austria. She was domiciled in Hungary, where the law would have permitted such a marriage. The marriage was held to be void as the man, under English law, had no capacity to marry her.

also 'Foreign Marriages' above). The marriage of a person who has reached the age of sixteen but is less than eighteen requires the consent of an adult. The law governing who may give or withhold such consent is to be found in section 1 of, and the Schedule to, the Marriages Act (NI) 1954 as amended by Schedule 9 of the Children (NI) Order 1995 (section 2 of the 1951 Act was repealed by the 1995 Order; 'minor' is defined in section 6(1) of the 1954 Act).

The consents of the following will be necessary: each parent with parental responsibility; each guardian; anyone with a residence order (see page 88); the Trust, if the young person (aged sixteen or seventeen) is the subject of a care order; and the High Court if he or she is a ward. The necessity for consent may be dispensed with if the person or parent in question is absent or incapacitated. Where the subject is *'Gillick competent'* (see page 43), however, then failure to secure consents may not necessarily render the marriage void. Application may be made to the court, under the 1954 Act, in circumstances where consent is refused.

3. Formal Defects

The Marriages Act (NI) 1954 specifically states that certain defects will not render a marriage void. Only if both parties complete proceedings with full knowledge of the defect will it be so. If the defect is one which is not expressly declared in the statute as liable to have that effect, then it will not be construed in that way. *Omnia praesumuntur pro matrimonio* summarises the general approach.

A commonly quoted example of the type of circumstance in which the court will not hold that a marriage has been rendered void by a procedural defect is the case[18] of Astrid Proll, a German national and wanted terrorist, who entered England under a false name and by using a false passport. She then used that false identity when marrying another German national by certificate and licence in a registry office. She later sought a declaration that the marriage was valid as a means of confirming an entitlement to British citizenship and avoiding extradition to Germany. The court held that as she had chosen to proceed by way of licence, the marriage was not rendered void as a consequence of her deceptions. Had she been married by banns the marriage would have been void as the point of publishing banns would have been deliberately negated. She may have breached the law relating to perjury but not that relating to the formalities of marriage.

4. Bigamy

A marriage will be void if either party to it is already validly married to another. The law relating to bigamous marriages is to be found largely in section 13(1)(d) of the Matrimonial Causes (NI) Order 1978 and Article 19 of the Family Law (Miscellaneous Provisions) (NI) Order 1984.[19] Any party who has already been married can only marry

---

18 See *Puttick v AG* [1973] 3 All ER 463.
19 Note that s. 3 of the Matrimonial Proceedings (Polygamous Marriages) Act 1972 has been repealed by the Matrimonial and Family Proceedings (NI) Order 1993.

a second time if the first spouse has died or been divorced or that marriage has been annulled. This is a matter of strict liability; the innocence of one party cannot redeem the flaw. Bigamy is a criminal offence and a bigamist may be debarred on public policy grounds from benefiting from that crime. Such was the *ratio decendi* for the decision reached by the Court of Appeal in *Whiston v Whiston*.[20] The court then upheld a husband's appeal against an award for ancillary relief made against him in favour of his bigamist wife following the annulment of their marriage.

In this jurisdiction the case of *Mason v Mason*[21] graphically illustrates some of the legal complications which can arise. The case centred on a marriage which took place in England in 1932, in respect of which a decree *nisi* was issued in 1934 on the grounds of a failure to consummate due to the incapacity of the 'other party'. In 1935, eleven days before the decree *nisi* was made absolute and while the other party was still alive, the man concerned (the respondent) entered into a ceremony of marriage in Scotland with another woman (the petitioner); both parties were born in London. They set up home together in Northern Ireland and in 1935 the only child of that relationship was born after which the petitioner became an invalid for three years. Eventually, difficulties arose which in 1942 led to the petitioner presenting a petition for a declaration that the ceremony of marriage which she and the respondent had entered into in Scotland was null and void on the grounds that it had been conducted while the respondent was still married to the other party; consequently the latter marriage was bigamous and invalid. At the time of the petition both parties were resident in Northern Ireland but domiciled in England.

The court, after much deliberation, held that the *bona fide* residence of both parties in Northern Ireland was sufficient to found jurisdiction for the court to hear the petition. Andrews LCJ noted that although domicile was necessary to give jurisdiction in dissolution suits, residence was sufficient for nullity. The following were among the issues which then fell for determination: Was the first marriage ever extinguished, given that the respondent had purported to alter his marital status before issue of the decree absolute? Was the second ceremony a valid marriage? Was the respondent a bigamist? What was the legal status of their child?

The primary finding of the court was that the decree absolute in the nullity suit was retrospective in effect. It was noted that before the ecclesiastical courts the rule was 'ever or never' and no distinction was made between void and voidable marriages; if a marriage was annulled it was annulled *ab initio*. In the words of Andrews LCJ:

> No doubt in the case of a voidable marriage its validity might never be questioned, and in such case it would be deemed valid, and never could be regarded as a void marriage; but, once its validity is successfully challenged and it is declared null and void by decree absolute, the invalidity is established retrospectively from the date of the marriage itself.[22]

The respondent could therefore be regarded as unmarried at the time of the ceremony in 1935 and, resulting from that finding, the marriage between the respondent and the

---

20 [1995] 2 FLR 268, vol. 25.
21 [1944] NI 134.
22 Ibid at 162.

plaintiff was valid, their child was a marital child and the plaintiff's petition must be dismissed.

A marriage may be potentially bigamous but never in fact become so. This, for example, was the case[23] where an applicant, who was domiciled in England, had undergone a Moslem marriage (which permitted him but not her to take a second spouse) in Pakistan with a woman domiciled there. He sought to obtain a declaration that the marriage was void on the grounds that it was potentially bigamous. His application failed as the court held that though potentially bigamous the marriage could never in fact become bigamous as neither party had the capacity to marry again: the applicant was prevented by English law from taking a second wife; the wife was prevented by the law of Pakistan from taking a second husband. In Northern Ireland, as in England under the equivalent legislative provision, Article 13(1)(d) of the 1978 Order does not have the consequence of voiding all marriages contracted abroad by persons domiciled here if the law of the country where the marriage was contracted permitted polygamy.

5. Gender

A marriage will be void if the parties fail to comply with the requirement, as stated in Article 13(1)(e) of the 1978 Order, that they be male and female respectively. In Northern Ireland, since the early 1970s, a considerable number of surgically assisted gender change operations have been completed. The question has occasionally arisen as to whether it is legally possible for a person born male, but having undergone such an operation, to then lawfully marry someone born female. The Court of Appeal in England has held[24] that, for the purposes of the Sexual Offences Acts 1956 and 1967, a person retains the gender in which they were born. The European Court of Human Rights has also broadly upheld[25] the position taken by the courts in England and Wales that in law a marriage will only be valid if conducted in respect of a heterosexual relationship.

The leading case in this particularly difficult area of human relationships is that of *Corbett v Corbett*[26] where the male party to a marriage petitioned for a decree of nullity on the grounds that his partner was not female. Ormrod J was then required to make a determination of gender identity in respect of the respondent who, though born male,

---

23 See *Hussain v Hussain* [1982] 3 All ER 369 and the Matrimonial Causes (NI) Order 1978, Art. 13(d).
24 See *R v Tan* [1983] 2 All ER 420 and *J v S–T (formerly J)* (1996) *The Independent*, November 26, CA. Also see Bradley *Transsexuals and the Law* (1987) Fam Law 350 vol. 17, pp 350–353.
25 See *Rees v United Kingdom* (1986) 9 EHRR 56; *Cossey v United Kingdom* [1991] 2 FLR 492; and *B v France* [1992] 2 FLR 249. The plaintiffs contended, unsuccessfully, that the British government was in breach of the following Articles of the Convention for the Protection of Human Rights and Fundamental Freedoms:

Art. 8 — Everyone has the right to respect for his private and family life, his home and his correspondence.

Art. 12 — Men and women of marriageable age have the right to marry and to found a family, according to the national laws governing the exercise of this right.
26 [1970] 2 All ER 33.

had undergone a sex change operation (in the earlier case of *Talbot v Talbot*[27] he had been faced with two persons born female). In his judgment he held that gender was to be determined by applying the three separate biological criteria: chromosomal, gonadal and genital. While accepting that some persons could be male under one test but female under another, he concluded that persons retained the gender with which they were born. In the present case the marriage was held to be void as, despite the effects of surgery, the respondent must in law be considered male and thus without the capacity to 'marry' another male.

6. Polygamy by Person Domiciled in Northern Ireland

A marriage is polygamous if either party to it has the capacity to contract a further marriage, without extinguishing the first, whether or not they actually do so.[28] It is prohibited to enter into such a marriage within this jurisdiction and if conducted such marriage will be void from the outset. A polygamous marriage will nonetheless be recognised as valid within this jurisdiction if it took place elsewhere, was in accordance with the requirements of the *lex loci celebrationis* and neither of the parties were at that time domiciled within this jurisdiction. Under Article 37 of the Matrimonial and Family Proceeding (NI) Order 1989:

> (1) A court shall not be precluded from making any declaration under this Part involving a determination as to the validity of a marriage by reason only that the marriage in question was entered into under a law which permits polygamy.

Under Article 50(2) of the 1978 Order, in the same circumstances, a court is similarly not precluded from granting matrimonial relief. Rule 88 of the Matrimonial Causes Rules governs the proceedings relating to a polygamous marriage commenced under Article 50(2).

II. Voidable Marriages

Under the Matrimonial Causes (NI) Order 1978:

> A marriage celebrated after the commencement of this Article shall be voidable on the following grounds only, that is to say —
>
> (a) that the marriage has not been consummated owing to the incapacity of either party to consummate it;
> (b) that the marriage has not been consummated owing to the wilful refusal of the respondent to consummate it;
> (c) that either party to the marriage did not validly consent to it; whether in consequence of duress, mistake or unsoundness of mind or otherwise;
> (d) that at the time of the marriage either party, though capable of giving a valid consent, was suffering (whether continuously or intermittently) from mental disorder within the meaning of the Mental Health Act (Northern Ireland) 1961 (a) of such a kind or to such an extent as to be unfitted for marriage;

---

27 (1971) 115 Sol Jo 870.
28 See *Baindail v Baindail*, f/n 12; also see *Hussain v Hussain*, f/n 23.

(e) that at the time of the marriage the respondent was suffering from venereal disease in a communicable form;

(f) that at the time of the marriage the respondent was pregnant by some person other than the petitioner.

A voidable marriage is one which subsists until such time as the court grants a decree to annul it.

1. Incapacity to Consummate

By their first act of sexual intercourse following the marriage[29] ceremony the newly-wed spouses consummate their marriage. It is only necessary that the sexual act be, in Dr Lushington's words[30] 'ordinary and complete'. The fact that one or both spouses are infertile, that *coitus interuptus* was practised, that condoms were used or that sexual intercourse was discontinued will not prevent consummation.[31]

A marriage will be rendered voidable, however, if at the time of the petition either spouse has a permanent and incurable[32] physical or psychological incapacity to consummate. Under Article 14(a) of the 1978 Order, as previously under common law, the impotence of the petitioner[33] may be relied upon to ground a petition alleging non-consummation. Although either spouse may petition on the grounds of impotence of self or the other, that impotence does require a high level of proof. Where the cause lies in a physical defect then the necessary evidence is readily available and the respondent must either co-operate with the court in verifying it or show some good cause for non-co-operation. Where the impotence is attributed to psychological causes, however, the petitioner must convince the court that it is not merely due to a reluctance or unwillingness but to an absolute aversion or 'invincible repugnance' to intercourse with the respondent.[34] Rules 2.26 and 2.27 of the Family Proceedings Rules (NI) 1996 detail the requirements for medical examinations in such cases.

---

29 Pre-marital intercourse will not suffice, see *Dredge v Dredge* [1947] 1 All ER 29; even if a child is born to the couple, see *Boggins v Boggins* (1966) 5 CC 102.
30 See *D – E v AG* (1845) 1 Rob Eccl 279.
31 See *Baxter v Baxter* [1948] AC 274, [1947] 2 All ER 886 HL where it was noted that the fact that conception was impossible is irrelevant; sterility must not be confused with impotence. See also *Sheldon v Sheldon* [1966] 2 WLR 933 for authority that once consummated a marriage cannot be annulled because a party refuses to continue sexual intercourse.
32 See *S v S (Otherwise C)* [1954] 3 All ER 736 where it was held that 'incurable' could extend to circumstances which required an operation entailing a high level of risk and the outcome of which was uncertain.
33 See *Harthan v Harthan* [1948] 2 All ER 639 CA. See also *C v C* [1921] P 399 for authority that the impotence must lie in relation to the spouse; the fact that the petitioner may not be impotent in relation to others is irrelevant.
34 See *Singh v Singh* [1971] 2 All ER 828 CA where a Sikh girl underwent an 'arranged marriage', at the behest of her parents, without having met, or even knowing the name of, her bridegroom. The marriage was never consummated. Her petition for a decree of nullity on the grounds of duress was refused because, in the words of Karminski LJ,

> There was no danger to Mrs Singh's life, liberty or limbs. True, she obeyed the wishes of her parents and acted out of a proper sense of duty, but that was insufficient to vitiate the consent she had given to the marriage.

In this jurisdiction the case of *S (Otherwise B) v S*,[35] heard before Andrews LCJ, is relevant. The case concerned a couple who had been married for four years, cohabited for only brief periods during the first three months and had on several occasions attempted unsuccessfully to consummate their marriage. These attempts ended when the respondent, on his own initiative, ceased to occupy the same bedroom as the petitioner whereupon she left him and returned to her mother in Cookstown, where she remained. The respondent neither submitted to medical examination, filed any affidavits made an appearance nor was represented at the hearing. The main issue for the court was the brevity of cohabitation, as Andrews LCJ remarked:

> I do not hesitate to say that if there were no other facts in this case I would have considerable difficulty in holding that the time and opportunity test had been sufficiently complied with to entitle the petitioner to a decree.

However, the collective evidence of the respondent's reluctance in relation to sexual matters and his failure to defend his own case persuaded the court to find in favour of the petitioner.

The fact that the petitioner knew of the respondent's impotence before their marriage is not necessarily a bar to a petition.[36]

2. Wilful Refusal to Consummate

In the words of Jowitt LC, wilful refusal is 'a settled and definite decision come to without just excuse'[37] which, naturally, is available only to one of the spouses and is sufficient to render a marriage voidable under Article 14(b) of the 1978 Order. The necessary ingredients of duration and resolve will become apparent only if the marriage is viewed as a whole over a considerable period of time. A 'just excuse' will provide a good defence. Mere loss of sexual desire, for example, lacks the necessary wilfulness and may be a transient phenomenon.[38] Where a spouse deliberately contrives to avoid consummation, even if the period is relatively short,[39] this may suffice. So, also, where a spouse refuses to seek or accept treatment (which does not entail an undue level of risk) for any physical or psychological cause of non-consummation.[40]

As it is necessary to prove wilful intent, a respondent will have a good defence to a petition for nullity on the grounds of wilful refusal to consummate if he or she can

---

35 [1942] KBD.
36 See *Nash v Nash* [1940] 1 All ER 206, 209.
37 See *Horton v Horton* [1947] 2 All ER 871 HL.
38 See *Potter v Potter* (1975) 5 Fam Law 161 CA.
39 See *Kaur v Singh* [1972] 1 All ER 292, CA where the couple had a pre-marital agreement not to sleep together until married in accordance with their religion and, following completion of a civil marriage ceremony, the husband then refused to make the necessary arrangements for the religious ceremony. In its finding of 'no just excuse' the court relied on the decision of Hewson J in *Jodla v Jodla* [1960] 1 All ER 625 where the facts were quite similar. See also *A v J (Nullity Proceedings)* [1989] 1 FLR 110 where the wife postponed the religious ceremony indefinitely; the husband was granted a decree of nullity.
40 See *S v S (Otherwise C)* [1944] 1 All ER 439.

show that there was not the necessary opportunity. This would clearly be the case if the respondent was imprisoned or hospitalised for a prolonged period. If while so confined, however, the respondent should clearly state a settled resolve never to consummate, then the petitioner is not obliged to wait until the opportunity arises for this resolve to be tested.[41]

3. Invalid Consent

A consent to marriage is only valid if each party making it has the capacity to do so and does so freely, voluntarily and with full understanding. A marriage may be voidable at the petition of either spouse, under Article 14(c) of the 1978 Order, if the consent of petitioner or respondent was invalid due to duress, mistake, unsoundness of mind or otherwise.

(a) Duress

The classic definition of duress in this context is as stated by Sir Jocelyn Simon P:[42]

> In order for the impediment of duress to vitiate an otherwise valid marriage, it must, in my judgment, be proved that the will of one of the parties thereto has been overborne by genuine and reasonably held fear caused by threat of immediate danger (for which the party is not himself responsible), to life, limb or liberty, so that the constraint destroys the reality of consent to ordinary wedlock.

It must be proven that the consent would never have been given if it had not been for the fear induced by the threats of another party. In the case in question, the petitioner successfully passed Sir Simon's test and had her marriage annulled on the grounds of duress. The court was readily convinced that after experiencing fourteen months of imprisonment and interrogation in Poland for 'anti-state activities' and then being sentenced to three years' imprisonment, her decision to enter into a 'marriage of convenience' in order to flee the country was one which was made under duress. There is a fine line to be drawn here between circumstances in which the petitioner's decision was one made under such direct and extreme pressure that his or her capacity for free will was completely subjugated and circumstances in which the decision was coolly made in order to evade a very unpleasant alternative.[43]

The ground of duress is often relied upon by a person seeking to renounce a 'sham marriage' entered into willingly by both parties explicitly for the purpose of indirectly obtaining some social advantage for one of them, most usually citizenship. So, for example, where a young man in Malta entered into a 'shotgun marriage' with a fifteen-year-old girl while under threat of denouncement and probable imprisonment for seduction, the court granted his petition for nullity.[44]

---

41 See *Ford v Ford* [1987] Fam Law 232.
42 See *Szechter v Szechter* [1970] 3 All ER 905, p. 915.
43 See *DPP for Northern Ireland v Lynch* [1975] AC 653, [1975] 1 All ER 913, HL.
44 See *Buckland v Buckland* [1967] 2 All ER 300; also see *Singh v Singh* [1971] 2 All ER 828, CA above at f/n 34.

In fact the leading case in this area is *Vervaeke v Smith*[45] where the parties underwent a marriage ceremony in order to permit the woman, a Belgian prostitute, to gain British citizenship and thereby avoid deportation. It was held, by the House of Lords, that as both parties had fully and freely consented, their marriage was therefore valid and binding on both.

(b) Mistake

The mistake must be either in respect of the identity of the other party or as to the nature of the ceremony. In the first instance, if the person married is not the person whom it was intended to marry, then the marriage will be voidable. In a case[46] where the petitioner sought to have her marriage annulled when it transpired that her spouse was not, as he had claimed to be, a famous boxer of the same name, the petition was refused as she had clearly married the man she intended to marry: the mistake lay in relation to status not to identity.

In the second instance, if one of the parties to a marriage ceremony has entered into it in the belief that it is something other than a marriage ceremony, then the marriage will be voidable. In a case,[47] for example, where the Italian husband, with little understanding of the English language, had undergone a marriage ceremony in an English registry office with an English woman in the belief that he was participating in an engagement ceremony, his nullity petition was granted. Again, where an English woman went through a Hindu marriage ceremony thinking that it was a ceremony of religious conversion, her petition for the annulment of the marriage was granted.[48]

(c) Unsoundness of Mind

If one party to a marriage suffered, at the time of the marriage ceremony, from 'unsoundness of mind', then this will provide grounds for annulment. The relevant test is as stated by Singleton LJ:[49]

> Was the [person] . . . capable of understanding the nature of the contract into which he was entering, or was his mental condition such that he was incapable of understanding it?

Bromley and Lowe suggest[50] that a person suffering from the effects of alcohol or drug abuse at the time of the ceremony may meet the terms of this test.

4. Mental Disorder

A marriage may be voidable at the petition of either spouse, under Article 14(d) of the 1978 Order if, at the time of the ceremony, either the petitioner or the respondent was

---

45 [1983] 1 AC 145, [1982] 2 All ER 144.
46 *C v C* [1942] NZLR 356.
47 See *Valier v Valier* (1925) 133 LT 830.
48 See *Mehta v Mehta* [1945] 2 All ER 690.
49 See *Re Park* [1953] 3 WLR 1012, [1953] 2 All ER 1411.
50 See PM Bromley & NV Lowe, *Bromley's Family Law*, 8th ed., London: Butterworths, 1992, 91.

suffering from mental disorder as defined in the Mental Health (NI) Order 1986. The mental disorder must be of such a kind or extent as to render the person unfit for marriage. This ground assumes that while at the time a person may have had the capacity to give a valid consent, nonetheless he or she was suffering from such a state of mental illness as to be incapable of carrying out the obligations of a spouse. The rules[51] provide that a petitioner cannot proceed under this ground without leave of the Master who may require the appointment of a guardian ad litem for the respondent as a condition of granting leave.

5. Venereal Disease

If a petitioner can prove that at the time of the marriage the respondent was suffering from venereal disease in a communicable form,[52] then, under Article 14(e) of the 1978 Order, a decree of nullity may be granted. It remains an open question as to whether the definition of venereal disease includes the AIDS virus.

6. Pregnancy *per Alium*

Under Article 14(f) of the 1978 Order, a husband petitioner may be granted a decree of nullity if he can prove that at the time of the marriage ceremony his respondent wife was pregnant by another.[53]

7. Bars to Relief

Under the Matrimonial Causes (NI) Order 1978:

(1) The court shall not, in proceedings instituted after the commencement of this Article, grant a decree of nullity on the ground that a marriage is voidable if the respondent satisfies the court —
   (a) that the petitioner, with knowledge that it was open to him to have the marriage avoided, so conducted himself in relation to the respondent as to lead the respondent reasonably to believe that he would not seek to do so; and
   (b) that it would be unjust to the respondent to grant the decree.

(a) Petitioner's Conduct

This statutory bar to a decree being granted to a petitioner rests on the traditional ground of 'approbation', i.e. that the petitioner has, by his conduct, disqualified himself from any entitlement to the relief which the court would otherwise grant. The burden placed on the respondent is to both raise the issue before the court and to then satisfy the grounds. If the possibility of a petition being statute-barred is not raised by the

---

51 Rule 6.5 of the Family Proceedings Rules (NI) 1996.
52 As defined in the Venereal Disease Act 1917, s.4.
53 See *Stocker v Stocker* (1966) 1 WLR 190 where a husband was granted a decree on the grounds of his wife's pregnancy *per alium* when blood tests showed that he was not the father. See also the Family Law Reform (NI) Order 1977, Arts 8–13.

respondent, the court will not do so. Further, if having raised the issue, the respondent is unable to prove that he or she did not earlier condone the conduct now complained of, then the court will not impose the bar. An example of the latter occurred in a case[54] where the husband's petition was refused because the wife was able to prove that his conduct, in seeking a decree on the basis of her wilful refusal to consummate, was inequitable as he had earlier agreed with her to adopt two children. By doing so he could be held to have waived any right to pursue a claim for a decree on that particular ground. If, however, as well as acceding to adoption, he had also stated that he was only doing so in the hope that this would remove a 'psychological block' to consummation, then it would not have been possible to draw the inference that he was waiving a right to petition at a later date on that ground. Arguably, in any case where the respondent can show that the petitioner had married with full knowledge of the existence of the circumstances on which the petition was later grounded (e.g. terminal illness), then, unless the petitioner had specifically addressed this matter at the time of the marriage (and it is difficult to envisage what form such a caveat might take), it must be concluded that the latter accepted the situation and waived any right to later petition on the grounds of predictable dissatisfaction. Again, any undue delay[55] in seeking a decree will also be construed to the disadvantage of the petitioner: the court will hold that, by not taking action earlier, the petitioner may have given the respondent good reason to believe that there was then no dissatisfaction with the matter now complained of.

(b) Injustice to the Respondent

To succeed in imposing the statutory bar, the respondent must not only demonstrate that the petitioner's conduct was such as to nullify his or her eligibility for a decree but must also go on to prove that, if granted, the decree would have an unjust effect on the respondent. Financial hardship resulting, for example, from loss of pension rights in the case of an elderly respondent, might well be considered unjust.

(c) Time

Under the Matrimonial and Family Proceedings (NI) Order 1989, the following provision was added to Article 16:

> 4.—(2) . . . the court shall not grant a decree of nullity by virtue of Article 14 on the grounds mentioned in paragraph (c), (d), (e) or (f) of that Article unless —
> (a) it is satisfied that proceedings were instituted within the period of three years from the date of the marriage, or
> (b) leave for the institution of proceedings after the expiration of that period has been granted under paragraph (4).

A petitioner will be statute barred from seeking a decree of nullity on any ground, except impotence or wilful refusal to consummate unless application is made within

---

54 See *D v D* [1979] 3 All ER 337.
55 But see *Clifford v Clifford* [1948] 1 All ER 394, where the husband brought a petition, on the grounds of his wife's wilful refusal to consummate, twenty-seven years after their marriage; the decree was granted. See also *Scott v Scott* [1959] 1 All ER 531.

three years of the marriage ceremony or unless the court grants leave to apply outside that time period. Under Article 14 of the 1978 Order, as amended by Article 4(3) of the Matrimonial and Family Proceedings (NI) Order 1989, leave will be granted only to petition on the grounds of lack of consent, mental disorder, venereal disease or pregnancy *per alium* if (a) at some time during the three year period the petitioner has suffered from mental disorder within the meaning of the Mental Health (NI) Order 1986; and (b) the court considers that in all the circumstances of the case it would be just to grant such leave.

III. Petitions, Pleadings and Amendment

Under Rule 2.1 of the Family Proceedings Rules (NI) 1996, an application made under Article 16(4) of the 1978 Order for leave to institute proceedings for a decree of nullity more than three years after the date of the marriage may be made by originating summons accompanied by specified supporting documentation.

IV. The Effect of a Decree

Under the Matrimonial Causes (NI) Order 1978:

> The court has jurisdiction to grant a decree of nullity —
> (a) of a marriage which is void; or
> (b) on the petition of a party to the marriage, of a marriage which is voidable.

Whereas a decree has never been necessary under statute or common law to annul a void marriage, it has always been required for a marriage which is merely voidable.

1. Void Marriages

The effect of a nullity decree on a void marriage is a declaration that it never existed. It has a potentially draconian retrospective impact on, for example, the status of a couple's children and/or property dispositions.[56] For this reason a doctrine of estoppel was cultivated whereby the courts recognised that, in certain circumstances, granting a decree would have such inequitable consequences for a respondent that the petitioner should be estopped from claiming a judicial declaration that the marriage was void. A party to a void marriage may remarry with or without a decree of nullity.

2. Voidable Marriages

Under the Matrimonial Causes (NI) Order 1978:

> 18. A decree of nullity granted after the commencement of this Article in respect of a voidable marriage shall operate to annul the marriage only as respects any time after the decree has been made absolute, and the marriage shall, notwithstanding the decree, be treated as if it had existed up to that time.

---

56 See, for example *Ward v Secretary of State for Social Services* [1990] 1 FLR 119.

This provision has the effect of treating a voidable marriage as subsisting until the decree absolute is made.[57] Afterwards all rights under matrimonial statutes will be lost and both parties may remarry.

---

[57] This avoids such previous effects of a decree as automatically rendering illegitimate any children born during the 'marriage' and nullifying any trusts made by the couple — see *Re D'Altroy's Will Trusts* [1968] 1 WLR 1173.

CHAPTER TWO

The Marital Family

Introduction

Marital families are a declining proportion of all families. In this jurisdiction, however, they still provide for the upbringing of the majority of children. Such a family no longer necessarily conforms to the model envisaged by Lord Penzance in *Hyde v Hyde*[1] in that it may well not be established on the premise of the spouses' life-long monogamous union. In this jurisdiction, as in Great Britain and elsewhere, the marital family is now quite often a reconstituted product of elements drawn from other marital and non-marital families. The serial marriages of parents, compounding the relationships of 'child of the marriage' and 'child of the family' and blurring the age-old understanding of 'kith and kin', have taken the development of the concept of 'marital family' well beyond that which could have been foreseen in 1866. The fluidity of many modern marital family boundaries has introduced uncertainty as to the distinction between the nuclear and the extended family and confusion as to the exact standing of such blood relatives as grandfathers and legal relatives such as step-parents.

This chapter, however, deals with the legal effects of marriage, not the sociology of the modern family. It briefly identifies the distinctive legal hallmarks of the marital family. It then considers the effect of the change in legal status conferred by marriage on the relationships between the persons concerned and between them and third parties. It examines the legal relationship between spouses and between spouses and their children. Finally, it considers the growing recognition given to the separateness of a parent and child's legal interests.

As an indication of the changes occurring in Northern Ireland, the number and rate of marriages has been steadily falling. In 1967 there were 10,924 marriages, or 7.3 per 1,000. These figures peaked in 1970 when there were 12,297 marriages, or 8.1 per 1,000, and fell to 9,636, or 6.2 per 1,000, in 1981. For the rest of the 1980s the data show that marriages remained at around 10,000 per annum, or 6.4 per 1,000. By 1994 the number of marriages recorded had slipped to 8,683 or a rate of 5.3 per 1,000.

Spouses

The common-law principle[2] that through marriage the legal identity of the wife was subsumed within that of her husband has been almost completely erased. For most

---

1 (1866) LR 1 P & D 130.
2 As Blackstone has said of this doctrine of unity: 'By marriage, the husband and wife are one person in law; that is, the very being or legal existence of the woman is suspended during the marriage, or at least is incorporated and consolidated into that of the husband; under whose wing, protection, and *cover* she performs everything . . .' *Commentaries*, i 442.

purposes, the husband and wife now have separate legal identities. As separate individuals they may contract with or be sued by each other. Each may contract independently with or be separately sued by third parties. If they act jointly, perhaps to purchase or own property, it is because they choose to do so. The effect of marriage on the modern legal standing of a spouse may be seen by examining the traditional legal characteristics of that relationship.

I. Status

Marriage confers a legal status on the couple concerned which distinguishes their joint legal standing from those who are not married. It also adjusts their legal relationship in respect of each other. Such traditional aspects of marital status which survive illustrate the previously protected and subordinate position of the wife relative to that of her husband in civil and criminal law.

1. Marital Name

Perhaps no consequence of marriage symbolised its traditional legal effect on the parties concerned as much as the wife's taking the surname of her husband. An implied loss of her independent identity accompanied her acquisition of his name. There was an inference that she was being absorbed into his family, to become a component and procreator in its history. This mirrored the legal realities.

In fact there is not and never has been any requirement in law that a husband and wife share the same surname. That the practice nonetheless became so firmly established serves to emphasise the absolute authority that was vested by marriage in the husband at the expense of the wife. There was a weight of social expectation that the latter would be content for her identity to be assimilated within that of her husband.

The custom whereby the wife assumes her husband's surname, while still the norm, is not as prevalent as tradition dictated. Many wives now retain their pre-marital name for business purposes and some couples find the merging of their surnames an acceptable compromise.

2. Domicile

On marriage, a wife's place of domicile was in law thereafter treated as being that of her husband. This remained the case until the coming into effect of the Domicile and Matrimonial Proceedings Act 1973. A married woman then acquired the right to retain her domicile of origin or acquire a domicile of choice, where either was different from that of her husband. The residence or habitual residence of a wife has, in law, never been determined by that of her husband. They may hold or acquire different citizenship.

3. Criminal Law

The presumption (under the Criminal Evidence Act (NI) 1923, section 3, and the Law Reform (Husband and Wife) Act (NI) 1964, section 7) that a woman who commits an offence in the presence of her husband does so while acting under his coercion and therefore without the necessary *mens rea* to be criminally liable has been abolished.

The law is now to be found largely in the Police and Criminal Evidence (NI) Order 1989. However, certain traces of a wife's special place in the criminal law still survive.

In the above instance, for example, while there is no longer the presumption of coercion, it may still, in such circumstances, be pleaded by a wife as a good defence. Further, where spouses are jointly charged with a criminal offence (except in relation to certain offences against children) neither may be compelled to give evidence against the other if either is liable to be convicted. The previous blanket immunity which was granted to one spouse to excuse him or her from testifying against the other has, however, been abolished. The law now recognises that each spouse has the capacity to give evidence and to commit a crime against the other.

4. Bankruptcy

One of the earliest legislative acknowledgments of a wife's independent legal standing occurred with the introduction of the Law Reform (Miscellaneous Provisions) Act (NI) 1937. Section 9 rendered a wife as liable to the effects of the law relating to bankruptcy as if she were unmarried. The Insolvency (NI) Order 1989 has since introduced special rules in relation to claims between spouses in circumstances where one has been declared bankrupt and where the rights of the innocent spouse in the matrimonial home may be in jeopardy.

5. Contract

The common-law rule that a wife, having no contractual capacity, could only enter into contracts while acting as her husband's agent has been abolished. This rule enabled a wife's debts to be imputed to her husband and, initially, prevented her from contracting with her husband.[3] In one respect, however, the agency rule continues in effect and differentiates the position of married and unmarried women. The broad rule of agency of necessity was abolished by the Matrimonial Causes (NI) Order 1978:

> Any rule of law or equity conferring on a wife authority, as agent of necessity of her husband, to pledge his credit or borrow money on his credit is hereby abrogated.

The law continues, however, to afford a married woman this defence in certain circumstances. If, while still residing with her husband, she enters into arrangements for the supply of such necessities as food and clothing for herself or for their dependant children, then she may subsequently plead this defence in response to a charge of incurring debt in respect of those goods. If the husband condoned such purchasing by his wife in the past, it will be presumed that she has his authority to continue to do so. The husband may avoid responsibility as principal if he can show that his wife has previously contracted independently with that tradesperson or that he has clearly stated to the tradesperson that his wife does not have his authority to pledge his credit.

Again, while either spouse may now contract or sue for breach of contract in respect of each other or so act independently of each other in respect of third parties, there is at least one circumstance in which the law continues to favour the position of the

---

3 Eventually this was corrected by statute; see *Butler v Butler* (1885) 14 QBD 831.

married woman to that of the unmarried. There is a presumption that spouses, when making arrangements with each other in respect of matters in which as husband and wife they have a joint interest, do not intend to establish a contractual relationship. This principle was reaffirmed in the leading case of *Balfour v Balfour*[4] where it was held that a husband's agreement to pay his wife a monthly allowance while he was abroad was unenforceable. It had been entered into while they were still living together in the marital home and could be construed as forming a part of normal household management. If the spouses are still living together, the law will infer a presumption that they did not intend to establish contractual relationships between each other.

6. Wills

One of the legal effects of marriage is to render null and void any will previously made by either party, unless clearly made in contemplation of that particular marriage. An exception to this rule is to be found in the Wills and Administration Proceedings (NI) Order 1994 which provides, in Article 12, that where the testator's intention in making the gift is that it should take effect after a particular marriage, then it will not be nullified by the marriage (see further Chapter Twenty-five).

II. Consortium

Consortium is a term which implies a breadth, duration and proximity of companionship of which sexual relations may, but need not, form a part. It refers to the expectation that after marriage a couple will 'live together as husband and wife'. This is a traditional legal characteristic of the marital relationship which continues to distinguish it from non-marital relationships.

1. The Right to Consortium

Like most legal aspects of the marital relationship, consortium was initially understood to vest rights in the husband and reciprocal duties in his wife.[5] Now, however, in the words of Scrutton LJ:[6]

> It seems to be clear that at the present day a husband has a right to the consortium of his wife, and the wife to the consortium of her husband.

In keeping with modern principles governing equal opportunities and anti-discriminatory practices, each spouse now has equal and reciprocal rights in respect of the other which neither may press to the disadvantage of the other.

(a) Co-habitation

The law has always required that a couple, entering into a marriage, should have the intention of living together as husband and wife. This intention may not be capable of

---

4 [1919] 2 KB 571 CA. See also *Gould v Gould* [1970] 1 QB 275, [1969] 3 All ER 728.
5 See, for example *R v Lister* (1721) 1 Stra 478 and *Re Cochrane* (1840) 8 Dowl 630.
6 See *Place v Searle* [1932] 2 KB 497, 512 CA.

being met in the immediate future, as where one party is in prison, but when marrying, both parties should fully intend to co-habit. Paradoxically, where the parties are living apart they will not necessarily be treated as ceasing to co-habit. The test to be applied[7] is whether they have the intention to share a home when circumstances permit.

Normally, the parties give effect to this intention by setting up and thereafter sharing life in their marital home. Neither party may force a right to co-habit upon the other.[8]

(b) Sexual Relations

Consummation by sexual intercourse is an essential and explicit ingredient of a valid marriage, and consortium refers to the implied right of both parties to mutual sexual relations for the duration of their marriage. This right is subject to the condition that it be exercised reasonably, which will not be the case if either uses coercion, forces the other to engage in perverted practices or inflicts actual bodily harm. Either extreme of insisting on unreasonably frequent sexual relations or forbidding such relations may constitute grounds for divorce. In the latter case, the traditional right of a spouse to petition the court for 'restitution of conjugal rights', as embodied in the Matrimonial Causes (NI) Act 1939, was abolished by Matrimonial Causes (NI) Order 1978:

> After the commencement of this Article no person shall be entitled to petition the court for restitution of conjugal rights.

The sexual conduct of one spouse in relation to the other may give rise to criminal proceedings. A husband, for example, will be guilty of a criminal offence if he forces his wife to submit to indecent forms of sexual practice.[9] Further, in the leading case of *R v R*,[10] the House of Lords broke new ground with their decision that a husband could be guilty of raping his wife. Dismissing his appeal, the court held that the ancient common-law rule to the effect that a husband cannot be guilty of rape on his lawful wife was no longer valid. Modern marriage is a partnership of equals in which the

---

7 A test formulated by the Court of Appeal in *Santos v Santos* [1972] Fam 247, [1972] 2 All ER 246 CA.
8 See *R v Jackson* [1891] 1 QB 671 CA where the court finally laid to rest the claim that a husband might be justified in enforcing his right to his wife's consortium, in this case by having her abducted, brought to his home and confined there. See also *Nanda v Nanda* [1968] P 351, [1967] 3 All ER 401 where the court granted a husband an injunction to prevent his wife from installing herself in the flat where he resided with his mistress.
9 See *R v Kowalski* [1988] 1 FLR 447.
10 [1991] 3 WLR 767. The history to this decision may be seen as dating back to the Criminal Law Revision Committee and its *Fifteenth Report on Sexual Offences* (1984) which recommended against abolishing the concept of marital rape. This was endorsed by the Law Commission in its *Draft Criminal Code* (1989). However, the Commission subsequently recommended removing a husband's traditional exemption from being chargeable with the offence of raping his wife. See also Law Commission: Working Paper No. 116, *Rape Within Marriage* (1990); and No. 205 *Rape Within Marriages* (1992).

proposition[11] that by her marriage a wife irrevocably consents to sexual intercourse with her husband regardless of the circumstances can have no place.[12]

(c) Marital Confidences

A married couple are bound by a mutual duty of marital confidentiality. That is to say, each has a duty not to disclose to a third party matters which the other imparted in confidence during the course of their marriage. This duty is not limited to matters pertaining to the marriage (e.g. sexual habits, housekeeping skills, etc.) but extends to include any material which one spouse imparts, or which comes to light, and the other knows is confidential. As Ungoed-Thomas said:[13]

> There could hardly be anything more intimate or confidential than is involved in that relationship, or than in the mutual trust and confidences which are shared between husband and wife. The confidential nature of the relationship is of its very essence and so obviously and necessarily implicit in it that there is no need for it to be expressed.

In that case the plaintiff was granted an injunction restraining her ex-husband from publishing in a Sunday newspaper any further information regarding her private life which she had disclosed to him in confidence while they were married. The fact that she had previously committed much the same breach of confidence and therefore 'did not have clean hands' in relation to the matter before the court was not seen as providing her ex-husband with a sufficient defence.

2. Loss of Consortium

The spouses' mutual rights to consortium, being an incident of their marital relationship, will subsist for the duration of that relationship. A spouse will lose the right to or be relieved from the obligation of consortium when that relationship breaks down. This will be the case if: they have resolved to live apart; one has obtained a decree of separation; one has committed adultery or has otherwise behaved in a way which gives grounds for their partner to commence divorce proceedings; such proceedings are underway and a decree *nisi* has been issued.

3. Actions for Loss of Consortium

(a) Sexual Relations

When the law recognised the almost proprietary rights of a husband to the services of his wife,[14] it also provided him with the means for suing third parties where they were

---

11 As stated by Sir Matthew Hale in his *History of the Pleas of the Crown* (1736).
12 See P. R. Ghandi and J. A. James, *Marital Rape and Retrospectivity — the Human Rights Dimension at Strasbourg; CR v UK and SW v UK*, Child and Family Law Quarterly, Vol. 9, No. 1, 1997.
13 See *Argyll v Argyll* [1965] 2 WLR 790.
14 For example, the writ of trespass *vi et armis de uxore rapta et abducta* was available only at the suit of a husband.

responsible for the loss of those services. The common-law form of this remedy was the action for criminal conversation. This was abolished and replaced by a statutory action available to a husband for damages against anyone found guilty of adultery with his wife. The most recent statutory form of this traditional remedy was to be found in the Matrimonial Causes (NI) Act 1939, which was repealed by the Matrimonial Causes (NI) Order 1978:

> After the commencement of this Article, no person shall be entitled to petition the court for, or include in a petition a claim for, damages from any other person on the ground of adultery with the wife of the first-mentioned person.

Since then the law has not recognised any right of a spouse to claim damages from a third party for enticing, harbouring (Article 58 of the 1978 Order) or having sexual relations with the partner of that spouse.

(b) Resulting from a Breach of Contract

Where a spouse suffers injury or death as a consequence of a breach of a contractual duty owed to him or her by a third party, then the partner of that spouse may well succeed in an action against the third party for loss of consortium.[15]

(c) Resulting from a Tort

If one spouse should suffer injury or death as a result of a third party's tortious conduct (e.g. causing a traffic accident[16]), then the partner may have grounds to recover damages against that third party for loss of his spouse's consortium.

Whether the action is in contract or tort, to succeed the plaintiff will have to show that the loss of consortium was a fairly direct result of the defendant's breach of a duty owed to the spouse.

III. Property

Marriage, as such, does not confer any rights to property. Persons bring into marriage their separate ownership of property. Thereafter, they retain and may add to their independent property rights. Some rights, however, they may acquire and hold jointly either in law, through normal contract arrangements, or in equity, through one party's having established a beneficial interest under an implied trust in property acquired by the other.

Although it is important to examine the respective legal position of a husband and wife in relation to property, it is clear that the law is mostly concerned about their respective rights at the point of marital breakdown. The law relating to property disputes

---

15 See, for example *Jackson v Watson & Sons* [1909] 2 KB 193, CA where the court held that the plaintiff was entitled to damages for loss of consortium against the defendant who had sold defective goods to the plaintiff's wife causing her death.
16 See, for example *Oakley v Walker* (1977) 121 Sol Jo 619 where it was held that the plaintiff could recover damages because his wife left him as a consequence of the injuries he suffered from an accident caused by the defendant's negligence.

between spouses in the context of proceedings for the termination of their marriage is largely governed by Part III of the Matrimonial Causes (NI) Order 1978 together with section 17 of the Married Woman's Property Act 1882; it is dealt with in Part Three of this book. The law relating to property disputes between spouses and third parties, occurring for example in the context of proceedings for bankruptcy, is similarly to be found in Part Three.

IV. Support

The common-law duty which required a husband to maintain his wife has been replaced by the mutual duty of both spouses to support each other. This is now a statutory duty which may be enforced through proceedings for breach of a voluntary maintenance agreement or under Article 27 of the Matrimonial Causes (NI) Order 1978 or under Articles 3–9 of the Domestic Proceedings (NI) Order 1980 (as amended by the Matrimonial and Family Proceedings (NI) Order 1989). A spouse may also seek financial support from the State. The duty to support a spouse terminates on divorce; though a court may determine otherwise.

For the law relating to financial disputes, see Part Three of this book.

V. Taxation

The modern principle that marriage should, for most purposes, be treated in law as a divisible unit and the parties to it as holding autonomous legal interests is now also reflected in the law as it relates to taxation. From 6 April 1990 spouses have been assessed and taxed independently; each on his or her own income; each receiving their own personal allowance.

Marital Parenthood

The parental responsibility of a spouse towards the children of his or her marriage continues until such children reach adulthood, whether or not the marriage continues. Traditionally, these responsibilities have been seen in terms of the rights and duties of parents in respect of their children and the latter's welfare interests. In fact, the history of the law as it relates to the welfare interests of children has for centuries been a history of paternal rights.[17]

I. Parental Rights

The one hundred years which separate the decisions taken in *Re Agar-Ellis*[18] and in *Gillick v West Norfolk and Wisbech Area Health Authority and the DHSS*[19] have

---

17   The first statutory acknowledgment of a paternal right to custody is made in s 8 of the Tenures Abolition Act 1660. Not until the Guardianship of Infants Act 1886 was any statutory recognition given to the principle of the welfare of the child. While the 1886 Act was substantially amended in England and Wales by three subsequent pieces of guardianship legislation, it remained intact in NI until wholly repealed by the Children (NI) Order 1995.
18   [1883] 24 CH D 317.
19   [1986] AC 112, HL.

witnessed a quiet revolution in the relative legal standing of parents and their children in proceedings concerning the latter's welfare. The former case is a reference point for the law's recognition of a father's exclusive rights to determine matters affecting his children, within an autonomous marital family unit. The latter provides a marker of equal significance for the law's recognition of a 'mature minor's' emerging right to take unilateral decisions on such matters, within or without a marital unit, and in relation to matters defined as falling within public or private family law.

1. Nature of Parental Rights

The legal construct 'parental rights/duties' may be seen as an umbrella term for a number of legal concepts which interweave the triangular relationship between parents, their children and third parties. That it is an imprecise term has been noted by Ormrod J:[20]

> If one were asked to define what are the rights of a parent apropos his child or her child I for one would find it very difficult. Most of them are rights to apply for orders, or rights to apply for consent or withhold consent to marriage, and limited things of that kind. There are plenty of obligations, but when it comes to rights it is by no means easy.

The principal concepts to be found under the umbrella of parental rights and duties, from which the others are largely derived, are 'custody', 'guardianship' and 'care, protection and control'.

(a) Custody

The Law Commission found that in the common law the term 'custody' had two meanings:

> In one sense, it has been held to mean the 'bundle of powers' exercisable by parents over their children, including not merely physical control but also such matters as the control of education and of the choice of religion, the power to withhold consent to marriage, and the power to administer the child's property. In another, and narrower sense, 'custody' means the power of physical control over a child.[21]

Both parents were usually equally eligible to hold such rights and, in respect of the children of their marriage, would normally do so jointly.

(b) Guardianship

The concept of guardianship is one rooted in a sense of the duties owed by a parent to his or her child. Of medieval origins, it may in fact have been a source of feudal abuse by guardians more interested in protecting the property than the person of a ward. In

---

20 See *Re N (Minors)* [1974] 1 All ER 126. Its vagueness was also remarked upon by Eekelaar: ... a loose way of describing the conglomeration of rights, powers, liberties and (perhaps) duties which a parent has with respect to his child 89 *Law Quarterly Review*, 1973: P 210. Maidment, however, from an examination of the common law was able to identify sixteen rights and four duties as constituting the legal aspects of the parent/child relationship (1984 p. 23).
21 See *Family Law Review of Child Law Guardianship and Custody* (Law Com no. 172, 1985, p. 12).

theory, however, the concept remained grounded on duties owed to a child and not on rights vested in a guardian. The common law recognised a basic distinction between guardianship by nature and guardianship by nurture, and as explained by Bowen LJ:[22]

> The strict common law gave to the father the guardianship of his children during the age of nurture and until the age of discretion. . . . But for a great number of years the term 'guardian by nature' has not been confined, so far as the father is concerned, to the case of the heirs apparent, but has been used on the contrary to denote that sort of guardianship which the ordinary law of nature entrusts to the father, until the age of infancy has completely passed and gone.

Under the common law, custody of a legitimate child always vested exclusively in the father, so the concept of guardianship came to be used as a convenient means for legally entrusting to his wife or other third party, in his absence, the exercise of his parental duties to protect and maintain. On his death, the absolute right of the father at common law to the custody of his legitimate children may either have transferred to the testamentary guardian previously appointed by him or the mother would become guardian by nature and nurture.

(c) Care, Protection and Control

The concepts of care, protection and control represent the duty owed to children by their parents or, failing their parents, by the State to provide for their physical needs and safeguard them from any foreseeable injury. The standards statutorily implied may have changed since the Poor Laws but the principle behind the concept remains the same. This may be seen as the legitimate entitlement of a child to an adequate standard of physical care and to protection from an abusive, exploitive or neglectful parent — an entitlement which warrants enforcement or coercive removal of care responsibility by the State. The relatively modern concept of 'control' owes its origins to the doctrine of parental rights and is an acknowledgment that the recipient of parental care has a corresponding duty to the provider not to obstruct or make impossible the provision of such care by their own wilful behaviour. All three concepts reflect a public interest in the internal affairs of the family, an interest which has grown as the autonomy and cohesion of the family unit has faded (see also Chapter Twelve).

2. History of Parental Rights

Initially the courts were solely interested in the circumstances whereby a father could be held to have forfeited his rights by particularly reprehensible behaviour. That is to say, the courts were concerned more with applying sanctions against a father, in order to defend socially approved standards of behaviour, than with protecting or promoting the welfare of his child in pursuance of any recognition of the latter's separate legal interests. However, it was out of such concerns that eventually a positive affirmation of the separate legal interests of a child was to grow.

---

22   See *Re Agar-Ellis*, f/n 18.

This initial approach of the common law was reflected clearly by the judgment of Lord Ellenborough for the Court of King's Bench:[23]

> We draw no inference to the disadvantage of the father. But he is the person by law entitled to the custody of his child. If he abuses that right to the detriment of the child, the court will protect the child. But there is no pretence that the child has been injured from want of nurture or in any other respect. Thus he having a legal right to the custody of his child and not having abused that right is entitled to have it restored to him.

At common law the *prima facie* right of a father to the custody of his legitimate child was almost absolute. He had the right to determine questions relating to the education and religious training of his child.[24] His right to control and to custody of his legitimate children was subject to the paramount consideration of their welfare[25] and absolute as against the mother.[26] The welfare interests of his child could only be legally acknowledged after it had been shown that his conduct was such that he should be disentitled from this right.

II. Welfare of the Child

The concept of welfare may be seen as the thin end of a legal wedge, representing a public interest in the quality of parenting arrangements and, as such, warranting State intervention in the affairs of a family.

1. Nature of Child Welfare

The concept of child welfare endemically pervades both public and private family law as they relate to children. It often appears in the form of a synonym for 'welfare', being statutorily referred to in terms such as 'best interests', 'well-being' and 'to the advantage of'. It also frequently appears in an obverse statutory form as a prohibition against practices such as the sale of cigarettes or alcohol to minors. Sometimes it is in itself the purpose, directing the thrust of legislative intent and, as in child care legislation, is the objective around which a set of statutory provisions has been built. At other times its statutory significance is more incidental when it becomes, as in the criminal law, merely a factor to be judicially taken into account when giving judgment. Then, in addition to statute law, there is also the significance attached to this concept in wardship proceedings where, in matters affecting custody and upbringing, it is always the consideration of paramount importance (see also Chapter Seven).

---

23 See *De Manneville v De Manneville* 1804, 10 Vessey Junior 52. The sort of abuses justifying, at common law, the removal of a parental right to custody were as stated by Bowen LJ in *Re Agar-Ellis*, f/n 18: '... grave moral turpitude', or as in *Wellesley v Wellesley* [1828] 2 Bl, NS 124: '... abdication of paternal authority'.
24 See *Re Browne, a minor* [1852] 2 ICR 151 and *Hawkesworth v Hawkesworth* LR 6 Ch 542 and *In re O'Hara* [1900] 2 IR 684 and *F v F* [1902] 1 Ch 688 and *Re Agar-Ellis*, f/n 18.
25 See *Thomasset v Thomasset* [1894] P 295, CA.
26 See *Ex parte Skinner* 9 Moo 278.

2. History of the Principle of the Welfare of the Child

From time immemorial Chancery had supervised the conduct of guardians in relation to their wards.[27] From the principle of trust underpinning 'guardianship in socage' and that of a parental duty to care which grounded 'guardianship by nurture', Chancery developed firm expectations that a guardian would use his position of trust for the benefit of a child. This link between a father's right of custody and his duties as a guardian was alluded to by King LC:[28]

> The father is entitled to the custody of his own children during their infancy, not only as guardian by nurture, but by nature. . . .

In the eyes of Chancery any abuse of trust,[29] amounting to '. . . any misbehaviour or ill-usage of the person of the ward', could lead the Court to 'remove the person out of his custody'. The eventual extension of this jurisdiction to include the conduct of parents was a natural one to which Chancery was able to bring a ready-formed body of principle. As Lord Eldon LC declared:[30]

> It is certain that the court will interfere against the acts of a guardian, if acting in a manner inconsistent with his duty; and it is equally clear that the court will control a parent if acting in a manner in which he should not.

In this way the judiciary in Chancery formed the bare bones for the future evolution of the welfare principle: a guardian, even if a parent, held a position of trust in relation to a child; the exercise of rights inherent in such a position was conditional upon first fulfilling a basic duty of care owed by a 'guardian' to a 'ward'; failure to fulfil the duties of a guardian would justify removal of rights, even from a parent.

III. Parental Rights and the Welfare of the Child in Northern Ireland

The characteristic feature which to some extent distinguishes the development of parental rights and the welfare of the child in Northern Ireland is that the statutory framework defining and giving effect to them has always followed closely, but at some distance, behind that of England and Wales. This lack of legislative contemporaneity did not improve with direct rule. As a consequence, it has often been the case that for some purposes the relative legal standing of parent and child in Northern Ireland is as it had been some years earlier in England and Wales.

---

27 See *Latey Report*, (Cmnd 3342, para.192 1967).
28 See *ex parte Hopkins* [1732] 3 Peere Williams 152, 153.
29 Such as occurred in *Morgan v Dillon* [1724] 9 Modern 135, 141.
30 See *Lyons v Blenkin* (1821) Jacob 245, 253. That Chancery was allowing itself to be used to remedy deficiencies in the common-law capacity to focus on parental rights was noted by the same judge in *Wellesley v Beaufort* [1827] 2 Russell 1, 23:
> The courts of law can enforce the rights of the father, but they are not equal to the office of enforcing the duties of the father. Those duties have been acknowledged in this his Majesty's Court for centuries past.

1. Private Family Law

The Guardianship of Infants Act 1886 was the first statute to give recognition to the principle of the welfare of the child and to its determining significance in any private family law dispute regarding the future upbringing of a child. Section 5 of this Act required the courts to consider three separate factors when responding to an application from a parent on such a matter: '... the welfare of the child, the conduct of the parties, and the wishes of the mother as well as of the father'. This Act had immediate effect throughout the UK and, unlike the rest of the UK, continued to function as the basic building block of private family law in Northern Ireland well into the second half of the twentieth century. Its judicial consequences were quickly apparent in this jurisdiction when, as Lindley LJ stated:[31]

> The dominant matter for the consideration of the Court is the welfare of the child. But the welfare of a child is not to be measured by money only, nor by physical comfort only. The word welfare must be taken in its widest sense. The moral and religious welfare of the child must be considered as well as its physical well-being. Nor can the ties of affection be disregarded.

However, the legislative intent to provide a principle upon which a mother could ground a challenge to a father's right to custody was unsuccessful. Subsequent case law left intact the common-law *prima facie* right of the father to the custody of his legitimate child as well as his rights to determine religion and education and to appoint a testamentary guardian. This was eventually countered, in England and Wales, by the Guardianship of Infants Act 1925 which reduced the three factors of section 5 to simply the welfare principle. In this jurisdiction, however, its survival was confirmed by the decision in *Re B (An Infant)*[32] which reverberated throughout the subsequent decades of marital custody disputes. This was a case where a married couple separated by mutual consent. Their only child, an eleven-year-old boy, remained with his father. The boy's mother removed him without the father's knowledge or permission. She then issued a writ of *habeas corpus* claiming custody and the matter came before the court on a motion to make absolute the conditional writ of *habeas corpus*. The court (Black J and Lord MacDermott) found that there was nothing in the conduct or wishes of either parent to indicate which should be preferred. It then went on to consider the extent, if any, to which the father's superior rights had been abrogated by section 5 of the 1886 Act and noted, in the words of Lord MacDermott:[33]

> While the Act of 1886 went further than its predecessors of 1839 and 1873 its effect on the common law position was different only in degree. I do not think it has abolished the father's former rights root and branch.... There is still a residue of common law rights in the father.

Awarding custody to the father, the court ruled that in Northern Ireland, in the absence of any provision equivalent to section 1 of the Guardianship of Infants Act 1925 (which

---

31 See *In re McGrath (Infants)* [1893] 1 Ch 143, 148.
32 [1946] NI 1.
33 Ibid.

placed both parents on an equal footing), the common-law presumption favouring the father had survived. As MacDermott LJ (son of the aforementioned) stated in the course of many judgments[34] made in private family law cases heard by him throughout the 1970s and 80s:

> If the welfare of the child is equally assured irrespective of which parent obtains custody, there exists, in Northern Ireland at least, a sufficient residue of the father's common law right to custody to tip the balance in his favour.

Subsequent guardianship legislation in Great Britain continued to amend the 1886 Act in favour of the welfare principle and to further equate the rights of both spouses, but these statutes were never extended to include Northern Ireland.

2. Public Family Law

'The child is not the child of the State' as has been noted by the DHSS.[35] However, the duty of care owed to children has always been a contentious interface, separating the right of the family to privately manage its own affairs from the right of the State to insist that any individual exercise of this right conforms to a standard that is accepted as reasonable throughout that society. Intervention, accordingly, is not for the purpose of asserting the State's view as to how a family might best optimise the welfare interests of a child. It is tied, instead, to specific conduct by parents or others which is held to constitute a threat to a minimum threshold of care owed in a general sense to all children.

The Children and Young Persons Act (NI) 1968 basically represented an amalgam of the public family law provisions concerning children as previously stated for England and Wales in the Children's Act 1948 Act and in the Children and Young Persons Act 1963. Like its predecessors it legislated against certain practices which might endanger the threshold of care, such as the employment of underaged children; non-attendance at school; unapproved child-minding arrangements. It also legislated for the maintenance of a socially acceptable threshold of parental care, protection and control by entrusting the Health and Social Services Boards (now Trusts) with specific duties and certain general powers to prevent a breach of that threshold by an abuse or default, respectively, of parental rights. In short, in public family law the statutory grounds for State intervention in the affairs of a family have been focused more on the rights of parents than on the needs of their children.

Now, there is a growing range of public and private legislation in which welfare has no direct role (e.g. divorce, housing, education) or where it has a lesser role (e.g. adoption and juvenile justice). Only where legislation has been given family proceedings status for the purposes of the Children (NI) Order 1995 has welfare been upgraded to paramountcy status.

---

34 See *Re RAW and MW (Infants)* [1949] NI 1. By 1983, however, MacDermott LJ was treating this principle as an anachronism: 'In practice, however, I would doubt if today a full analysis of the ingredients which make up the concept of welfare will often achieve such a finely balanced conclusion' (In *Re CB and AJB (Minors)*, unreported (1983)).
35 See *Review of Child Care Law* (1985, para. 2.13).

3. Criminal Law

The legislative concern to provide for the protection of children in circumstances of abuse or neglect at the hands of their parents or third parties has long been evident in the criminal law. The far-reaching changes introduced by the 1995 Order to the civil law (repealing the Custody of Infants Act 1873, the Guardianship of Infants Act 1886, the Custody of Children Act 1891) as they affect children have tended to distract attention from the fact that much of the relevant criminal law is now very dated. The law relating to crimes against children is still to be found in sections 4–7 of the Criminal Law Amendment Act 1885, sections 27, 42 and 60 of the Offences against the Persons Act 1861, the Punishment of Incest Act 1908, sections 20–25, 29 and 30 of the Children and Young Persons Act (NI) 1968 and the Protection of Children (NI) Order 1978.

The Modern Parental Responsibilities of a Spouse

The rights and duties of marital parents in respect of the children of their marriage have not undergone any significant redefinition as a consequence of the 1995 Order. However, the civil authority governing the modern parental responsibilities of a spouse is now to be found in that Order and in such other legislation as the Child Support (NI) Order 1991, not in the common law.

I. 'Parent' Defined

'Parent' has been defined in law as meaning both the mother and father of a legitimate child and the unmarried mother of an illegitimate child.[36] This definition excludes such others as a step-father[37] and an unmarried father. The latter may, however, acquire 'parent' status.

II. Duties and Rights

The rights and duties held by a marital parent in respect of his or her child have not materially changed as a consequence of their displacement by an alternative concept of 'parental responsibility' under the 1995 Order.

1. Duties

The duties traditionally borne by a parent are now to be found largely in the Children (NI) Order 1995, Parts IV and VI.

(a) Physical Care

The primary responsibility of those with parental responsibility is to provide a home for the child in question or to determine where he or she shall live.

---

36 See *Re M* [1955] 2 QB 479.
37 See *Re N* [1974] 1 All ER 126.

(b) Protection

A fundamental parental duty is that of affording adequate protection to the child. This duty is enforced by the provisions of Part V of the 1995 Order.

(c) Control

The duty to exercise parental control, so as to protect the legal interests of third parties from the consequences of an unruly child's behaviour, continues to be governed by the Children and Young Persons Act (NI) 1968.

(d) Maintenance

The statutory duty requiring a parent to maintain his or her child is to be found mainly in the Child Support (NI) Order 1991 and also in the provisions of the Social Security (NI) Order 1986 and those of the 1995 Order.

(e) Education

Any person bearing parental responsibility for a child of school age is required to ensure that he or she receives a proper full-time education as provided for under the Education and Libraries (NI) Order 1986.

(f) Medical Treatment

Any person with parental responsibility, or having the care of a child, has a duty to obtain essential medical treatment[38] in an emergency. A child may give or withhold consent to treatment if aged sixteen or more or if *Gillick* competent (see page 43).

2. Rights

The rights traditionally borne by a parent are largely to be found in case law, as modified by the 1995 Order.

(a) Possession

The right to physical possession is a traditional characteristic of parenting which has been affected by the 1995 Order. Article 5(3) specifically repeals the common-law presumption vesting custody of a marital child in the father and defines parental responsibility as permitting a person to have duties for, without possession of, a child.

---

[38] This parental duty has been upheld by the courts since at least *R v Senior* [1899] 1 QB 283 where an otherwise excellent father failed to provide medical aid for his nine-month-old child, who subsequently died, because he believed that medical treatment was sinful. The father was found guilty of wilful neglect because, although he had no evil intent, he had deliberately chosen an unreasonable course of action which caused the death of his child (see further Chap 15). See *Re R (A Minor)(Wardship: Medical Treatment)* [1992] 1 FLR 190 where Donaldson LJ held that a parent retained the right to consent to treatment even though the child was of age and understanding and had refused her consent. Also, see *Re W (A Minor)(Inherent Jurisdiction: Consent to Treatment)* [1993] 1 FLR 1 CA.

(b) Religious Upbringing

A parent or a person with parental responsibility has the right to determine a child's religious upbringing. It is a right retained by a parent even in circumstances where his or her other rights are curtailed by a care order or by an adoption order. It is not, however, a right which may be exercised by a parent or person with parental responsibility so as to force a child to abandon his or her religious beliefs.

(c) Chastise

A parent, a person with parental responsibility or someone with the care of a child (such as a registered child-minder) may chastise a child; this, however, must be for the purposes of admonition rather than punishment and not of a degree such as would breach the significant harm threshold.

(d) Appoint Guardian

Any parent with parental responsibility may appoint someone to act as guardian to the child in the event of that parent's death.

(e) Consents

A parent has the right to give or withhold consent to such matters affecting their child as any proposed medical treatment; adoption or freeing for adoption; removal from the jurisdiction; or, if the child is between the ages of sixteen and eighteen, to the proposed marriage of that child.

(f) Contact

The traditional right of a parent to maintain contact with his or her child has to some extent now been overcome by case-law developments.

(g) Represent Legal Interests

A parent has always been held to have the right to represent his or her child in legal proceedings by acting as the child's next friend or guardian ad litem, unless disqualified by evidence of impropriety (see further Chapters 15 and 16). This right has now been curtailed by provisions in the 1995 Order which give a child full party status for the purposes of certain proceedings and thereby allow his or her interests to be represented separately from those of the parent/s.

(For parental responsibilities, see also Chapter Five (the law) and Chapter Eleven (the concept).)

Marital Child

Distinguishing a child's legal interests from those of his or her parents, particularly in private proceedings, has always been a fraught and complicated area of family law. This is less so where the distinction to be made is between a child's interests and those of a third party. In the context of proceedings where an offence involving a child is known or alleged to have been committed, the legal issues at least are usually relatively uncomplicated and will dictate the separation of a child's interests from those of any first or third parties. Where the child is of an age and understanding to express views[39] on the issues raised, these will have a bearing on the judicial task of separating the different sets of legal interests.[40]

A marital child is one born to his parents and of their marriage. Such a child is recognised in law as legitimate and, if not born so, may subsequently be legitimated under the terms of sections 1 or 8 of the Legitimacy Act (NI) 1928. As a consequence of legislative change[41] and judicial precedent,[42] this status has become a good deal less significant in recent years. However, it still exists, and therefore the legal standing of legitimate ('marital') children may still be distinguished from that of illegitimate ('non-marital' or 'extra-marital') children. This is the case, for example, in respect of citizenship, certain dispositions of property, succession rights to a title of honour and the parental responsibilities of a child's father. The domicile of origin of a legitimate child is that of the child's father.

The Separateness of a Child's Legal Interests

In recent years the courts have had to adjudicate on the separateness of the interests of parents and children where the latter have been either too young to express any views or are insufficiently mature to have their legal competence recognised when doing so.

1. Very Young Children

In relation to babies, the courts have always held to the view[43] that the younger the child the greater the weight to be attached to preserving the 'psychological bond' between mother and child as a factor in determining the welfare interests of that child, the inference being that the welfare of a young child is not readily separable from the legal interests of the mother. This approach has had and continues to have a virtually

---

39 This has not always been the case: see *R v Howes*, 1860 3 El, L El. 332, when Cockburn LCJ, in deciding whether or not a father should recover custody of a teenage daughter, thought the views of the fifteen-year-old daughter to be dangerously precocious and might lead to 'irreparable injury'.

40 See *Hewer v Bryant* [1970] 1 QB 357, 369 where the court recognised a gradual displacement of parental rights by an adolescent's right of self-determination. Also see: *M v M (Child: Access)* [1973] 2 All ER 81 where the court established that a right of access between parent and child attached more to the latter than the former; *Re H (Minors) (Access)* [1992] 1 FLR 148 where the court held that the test was not what positive advantages would the child gain by a resumption of contact? but rather did any cogent reason exist for denying a child the opportunity to have contact with a parent?; and *Re R (A Minor) (Contact)* [1993] 2 FLR 762 where Butler-Sloss LJ emphasised that the companionship of a parent is so important for a child that it gives rise to a basic right in a child to such companionship.

41 For example, the repeal of the Illegitimate Children (Affiliation Orders) Act (NI) 1924.

42 See, for example, the decision of the ECHR *in McMichael v United Kingdom* [1995] Fam Law, vol. 25, 478.

43 See Bowlby et al. However, as is often stressed (see, for example the deliberation of Butler-Sloss LJ in *Re A (A Minor: Custody)* [1991] 2 FLR 394) this view has never attained the status of a presumption favouring maternal care for a young child.

determining effect on contested private family law proceedings. In relation to a foetus, the courts have recognised[44] that a mother owes a duty of care to her unborn child, albeit one that is not actionable until after birth. The significance of this landmark decision, in terms of the light it sheds on judicial rationale for distinguishing between the welfare of the child and the legal interests of the mother, is difficult to judge. It may, perhaps, be seen as a logical extension of the judicial view that the younger the child the more fused are mother/child interests; the greater, therefore, is the maternal obligation to safeguard her own well-being, as only by doing so will her child's interests be protected.

2. Adolescents

The two landmark decisions which have contributed most in shaping the modern role of the child in proceedings affecting his or her welfare are *J v C*[45] and *Gillick v West Norfolk and Wisbech Area Health Authority*.[46] The first firmly established that a child's welfare must be judicially treated as the factor of paramount importance in any case affecting the care, custody or upbringing of that child. The second held that the decision of a 'mature minor' with the mental capacity to understand the nature and effects of the proposed treatment could prevail over the contrary views of a parent and be binding on a third party. In legal terms, the distance between these two cases is enormous. *J v C* marks, perhaps, the apotheosis of a welfare jurisprudence in which the child is objectified to become merely the recipient of a welfare allocation made in accordance with a standardised judicial formula. The *Gillick* ruling may be seen as the first step away from the objectification of the child within a paternalistic welfare philosophy and towards welfare as a matter capable of subjective interpretation and of justifying action, as a right, by the child concerned.[47]

Termination of Marriage

Marital life will end with the grant of certain court decrees or on the death of either spouse. Marriage, however, or its legal effect, in some respects endures beyond the formal ending of marital life.

I. Termination by Decree

The granting of a decree absolute in divorce proceedings or of a decree for dissolution in annulment proceedings terminates a marriage. A petitioner may obtain a declaration, under Article 31(c) of the Matrimonial and Family Proceedings (NI) Order 1989, that his or her marriage did not subsist on a certain date, but this merely provides legal recognition of the status of a marriage, it does not alter that status.

---

44 See *D (A Minor) v Berkshire County Council* (1987) 1 All ER 33.
45 [1970] AC 668 HL.
46 [1986] 1 AC 112 HL.
47 One effect of the Family Law Reform (NI) Order 1977 is that children over the age of sixteen are, like adults, assumed to be competent unless there is reason to believe otherwise; neither may any order may be made nor extended under the 1995 Order in respect of a young person who has reached that age.

II. Termination on Death

The death of either party terminates the marriage. There are circumstances, however, where in the absence of proof of death, statute has provided a means whereby death may be presumed in law to have occurred.

III. Presumption of Death

Under Article 21 of the Matrimonial Causes (NI) Order 1978:

> (1) Any married person who alleges that reasonable grounds exist for supposing that the other party to the marriage is dead may present a petition to the High Court to have it presumed that the other party is dead and to have the marriage dissolved, and the High Court may, if satisfied that such reasonable grounds exist, grant a decree of presumption of death and dissolution of the marriage.

The type of circumstances in which a person may wish to make such a petition occurs most usually when a deserted spouse wishes to re-marry. If that person has had no contact with the missing spouse for many years and has no information to indicate that he or she is still alive, then the High Court may be petitioned to obtain a decree of presumption of death in respect of the spouse. Under the same article, this presumption will be substantiated where

> (2) In any proceedings under this Article the fact that for a period of seven years or more the other party to the marriage has been continually absent from the petitioner and the petitioner has no reason to believe that the other party has been living within that time shall be evidence that the other party is dead until the contrary is proved.

In such circumstances the petitioner will be entitled to a decree of presumption of death and dissolution of the marriage. A decree may be granted before the expiry of the seven-year period, though the burden of proof on the petitioner to produce the evidence necessary to convince the court and avoid reliance on the presumption is that much greater.

Where the petitioner is relying on the presumption, the court has held that before a decree can be granted the petitioner must first establish a bona fide belief[48] that the missing spouse is dead, that persons who could be expected to have been in contact with the missing spouse have not heard from him or her[49] and that all appropriate enquiries have been made. The courts have held[50] that where the police have failed to execute a warrant for the arrest of a husband, whose maintenance payments were in arrears, there was sufficient proof that he could not be found; consequently, his wife was justified in presuming him dead and marrying another. Once granted, the decree irrevocably dissolves the marriage. Should the missing spouse reappear and the petitioner have remarried, the latter will not be guilty of bigamy.

---

[48] See *Thompson v Thompson* [1956] 1 All ER 603.
[49] See *Chard v Chard* [1955] 3 All ER 721.
[50] See *Bullock v Bullock* [1960] 2 All ER 307.

IV. Termination of Marital Life but Continuation of its Legal Effects

Once acquired, the status of married person will in some respects survive the termination of his or her marriage. For some purposes a once-married person and a never-married person have a different standing in law.

1. Death

A widow or widower does not revert wholly to their pre-marital legal status. In law, for the purposes of rights of inheritance and entitlement to pensions, such a person is not treated as though the marriage had never taken place. Should a spouse have died intestate, for example, then the surviving widow/er will have an enforceable legal right to a share in the deceased's estate. Even if the deceased died testate, leaving perhaps the matrimonial home to someone other than the surviving spouse, the latter may well have a defensible equitable claim to a share in the estate.

2. Dissolution

In contrast, the rights of inheritance of a former spouse die with the granting of the decree of dissolution. Under Article 13 of the Wills and Administration Proceedings (NI) Order 1994, any gift made in the will of a person to a former spouse of that person in respect of whom a decree *nisi* has been granted is rendered null and void (see further Part Three).

CHAPTER THREE

The Non-Marital Family

Introduction

In law the definition of 'marital family' is quite readily understood. The same cannot be said of the 'non-marital', or extra-marital family.[1] Some of the relationships encompassed by this term do not come within the definition of marital status because the parties cannot meet the necessary legal requirements; their relationship may not be heterosexual; one or both may not satisfy such capacity criteria as age, domicile, consent or being unmarried; or perhaps the couple are within the 'prohibited degrees' of relationship. For the majority of cases, however, and for present purposes, the term 'non-marital family' refers to a parent or parents who choose to be excluded from marital status and to the child or children of such parent or parents.

The law governing the distinctions between parent, parenthood, parenting and parentage have never before been so complex nor associated with so much uncertainty for the adults and children involved. The many ways in which parenthood may now be achieved through medical assistance, the attributes of parenting which may be delegated to or assumed by third parties and the implications of such developments for our understanding of parentage in the context of the law governing hereditary succession are explored in other chapters. This chapter deals with the law as it affects the relationships between members of a non-marital family and between them and third parties. Beginning with a definition of the legal standing of each of the parties involved in such a family, it then considers the cohabitee relationship and finally examines the roles and responsibilities of non-marital parents.

An indication of the growth in the numbers of non-marital families can be seen by comparing the figures for the United Kingdom and for Northern Ireland. In the United Kingdom, according to data collated by the Office of Population Census and Surveys, by 1991 a total of 10 per cent of all children aged two or below lived with unmarried cohabiting couples. The cohabiting rate for non-married women aged between eighteen and forty-nine rose from 11 per cent in 1979 to 22 per cent in 1993.

In Northern Ireland, the number and rate of illegitimate births have multiplied in the past three decades. In 1967 some 1,205 births (or 3.6 per 1,000 live births) were

---

1   In addition to the many permutations of married and unmarried persons living together in heterosexual relationships for varying periods of time, there are now increasing numbers of homosexual couples, some with children conceived by means of in vitro fertilisation or gamete intra-fallopian transfer or acquired by surrogacy arrangements, whose households arguably also come within the definition of 'family'. Again, there are a wide variety of households established on a non-sexual basis, sibling groups and other groups of friends or relatives which, if they include children and parents, would also conform to a broad understanding of 'family'.

registered as 'illegitimate'. Thereafter, the lowest point reached was in 1974, when the figures were 1,296 and 4.8, respectively, and the highest in 1992 when there were 5,603 such births, representing a rate of 21.9 per 1,000 of all live births that year. In 1995, while the rate reached 23.1 the number was somewhat reduced at 5,503.

Definitions

The legal status of the parties to a non-marital relationship or those constituting a non-marital family unit has traditionally[2] been a matter of central importance.

I. Unmarried Mother

The most distinctive legal characteristic of an unmarried mother is that parental responsibility for her child or children vests exclusively in her unless and until others subsequently also acquire responsibility by way of statutorily prescribed procedures.

II. Non-Marital Child

A child born of a non-marital relationship is in law an illegitimate child. Under common law such a child, being *filius nullius,* had no legal relationship with anyone. He or she had no rights, for example, to maintenance or to inherit property; nor did anyone owe such a child any duty, for example, to protect him/her from harm. Statute law, however, has intervened to displace most common-law inequities and remove many of the effects of illegitimacy.

1. Illegitimacy

The legal significance of the distinction traditionally made between legitimate and illegitimate children has been steadily eroded. This trend has been evident in such legislation as the Legitimacy Act (NI)1961, the Family Law Reform (NI) Order 1977, the Family Law (Miscellaneous Provisions) (NI) Order 1984 and the Matrimonial and Family Proceedings (NI) Order 1989. It has now been consolidated by the Children (NI) Order 1995.

The judiciary have defended the presumption in common law that where a child's parents were married to each other at the time of conception or at the time of birth that child is legitimate; a high level of proof has been required to displace it.[3] In addition, legislators have introduced provisions extending ligitimacy to children born in circumstances not conforming wholly to the model marital union as envisaged by Lord Penzance.[4] Various statutory measures have, in recent years, had the effect of narrowing the definition of illegitimacy.[5] The domicile of origin of an illegitimate child is that of the child's mother.

---

2   See, for example, M Hayes, *Law Commission Working Paper No. 74: Illegitimacy* (1980) 43 MLR 299.
3   See *Second Report on Illegitimacy* (Law Comm No. 157, para. 2.1).
4   See *Hyde v Hyde* (1866) LR 1 P&D 130, 133 (op. cit Chap 1).
5   The Legitimacy Declaration Act (Ireland) 1868 (declarations as to legitimacy and validity of marriage) and the Legitimacy Act (NI) 1928, section 2 (declarations as to legitimation) were repealed by the Matrimonial and Family Proceedings (NI) Order 1989.

2. Legitimation

Under Article 32 of the Matrimonial and Family Proceedings (NI) Order 1989:[6]

> (5) In this Article—
> 'legitimated person' means a person legitimated or recognised as legitimated—
> (a) under section 1 or 8 of the Legitimacy Act (Northern Ireland) 1928; or
> (b) by a legitimation (whether or not by virtue of the subsequent marriage of his parents) recognised by the law of Northern Ireland and effected under the law of another country.

Under section 1 of the Legitimacy Act (NI) 1928, a child born illegitimate may subsequently be legitimated by the marriage, to each other, of both parents.

3. Declarations

Under Article 32(2)(a) of the Matrimonial and Family Proceedings (NI) Order 1989 (as amended by Article 155(3)(b) of the Children (NI) Order 1995, which is given effect to by Schedule 9, para 171),[7] any person may apply to the court for a declaration that he has become a legitimated person.

Declarations as to parentage, legitimacy or legitimation are now addressed by Rules 3 and 3A of the Rules of the Supreme Court (NI) (Amendment No 4) 1996 (amending Order 98 of the Rules of the Supreme Court (NI) 1980)). These state the particulars to be specified in a petition and make reference to required supporting documentation. They also require an applicant to be domiciled in Northern Ireland or to have been habitually resident in the jurisdiction for the twelve-month period ending on the date of application.

4. Children of Void Marriages

The Legitimacy Act (NI) 1961 has been amended by the Children (NI) Order 1995, Schedule 9, para 14,[8] to enable a child born of a void marriage to be treated as the legitimate child of his parents in certain circumstances, i.e. if at the time of the 'insemination resulting in the birth or, where there was no such insemination, the child's conception' or 'at the time of the celebration of the marriage if later' both or either of the parents reasonably believed that the marriage was valid. The courts in England have recently held[9] that where a child was born before his or her parents entered into a void marriage, then he or she could not be regarded as legitimate for the purposes of these provisions.

---

6 As amended by the Children (NI) Order 1995, Schedule 9, para. 171.
7 The equivalent provisions in England and Wales are the Family Law Act 1986, s. 56 as amended by the Family Law Reform Act 1987, s. 22.
8 The equivalent law in England and Wales is to be found in the Legitimacy Act 1976, s. 1 as amended by the Family Law Reform Act 1987, s. 28.
9 See *Re Spence, Spence v Dennis* [1990] Ch 652, [1990] 2 All ER 827 CA.

5. Children of Voidable Marriages

Under Article 18 of the Matrimonial Causes (NI) Order 1978 reinforced by Schedule 3, paragraph 19, a voidable marriage 'is to be treated as if it had existed' up until the granting of the decree of annulment. This has the effect of permitting any children born after the marriage but before the decree and any legitimated by the marriage to be treated as legitimate.

6. Children Born Overseas

If a child was regarded as legitimate by the law of the country of birth, then he or she will be so regarded in this jurisdiction.

7. Children Adopted

The Children (NI) Order 1995, Schedule 9, para 8, inserts the following provision into the Legitimacy Act (NI) 1928:

> 8A.—(1) Article 40 of the Adoption (NI) Order 1987 does not prevent an adopted child being legitimated under section 1 or 8 if either parent is the sole adoptive parent.
>
> (2) Where an adopted child (with a sole adoptive parent) is legitimated—
>
> (a) paragraph (2) of Article 40 shall not apply after the legitimation to the natural relationship with the other natural parent; and
> (b) revocation of the adoption order in consequence of the legitimation shall not affect Articles 40 to 42 as they apply to any instrument made before the date of legitimation.

This is expressly governed by Article 155 of the 1995 Order:

> (1) In this Order and in any statutory provision or any instrument passed or made after the commencement of this Article, references (however expressed) to any relationship between two persons shall be construed without regard to whether or not the father and mother of either of them or the father and mother of any person through whom the relationship is deduced, have or had been married to each other at any time.

8. Current Distinctive Characteristics of Legal Standing

Despite the ameliorative effect of judicial and legislative intervention in recent years there still remain some respects in which a non-marital child is disadvantaged in comparison with his or her marital counterpart. For the purposes of determining citizenship and as regards succession rights to a title of honour, the mother of a non-marital child is regarded as being the sole parent.

III. Unmarried Father

Under common law a father had no rights in respect of his illegitimate child.[10] Prior to the introduction of the Children (NI) Order 1995 he could acquire rights only by applying for a custody order under Article 15 of the Family Law Reform (NI) Order 1977 or by making application in wardship.[11] Now, particularly as a result of the combined effect of the 1995 Order and the Child Support (NI) Order 1991, such a father will not avoid his duty to maintain a non-marital child. However, his position in regard to legal rights remains virtually unaltered. Unless he instigates certain legal proceedings an unmarried father will not have any rights in respect of his child.[12]

IV. Paternity

The renewed vigour with which legislators are now providing the means whereby unmarried fathers can acquire or be ascribed parental responsibility has been matched by the advances in scientific techniques for ascertaining paternity.

1. Proof of Paternity

Under the provisions of the Family Law Reform (NI) Order 1977, as amended by the Children (NI) Order 1995, Schedule 9, para. 89, in any civil proceedings where the court is required to make a determination as to paternity, the court may, on application from a party to the proceedings, direct that blood tests be conducted to ascertain whether a named man could or could not be the father of the child in question. The House of Lords has advised[13] that the court should have recourse to blood tests in any case where to do so cannot be shown to be detrimental to a child's best interests. This may be necessary in a case where, for example, a putative father is seeking to prove paternity in the context of proceedings under Article 7(1)(a) of the 1995 Order for a parental responsibility order. In *Re H (Paternity: Blood Test)*[14] the Court of Appeal adopted the House of Lords' detriment test where a putative father sought a judicial direction for blood tests to be conducted in order to prove that he, not the husband (who had had a vasectomy some years earlier), was the father of a married woman's baby. The mother, who acknowledged her affair with the applicant at the time of conception, was reconciled with her husband and implacably opposed to blood tests and to any possibility of future contact between the applicant and the child. However, holding that the wishes of the mother was not the most important factor, the court ruled that tests should be conducted.

---

10 For example, he had no right to custody, see *R v Moses Soper* (1793) 5 Term Rep 278. See also *Re B (A Minor)* [1990] 1 FLR 415 where the Court of Appeal held that an unmarried father had no right to be named as a party to adoption proceedings.
11 See the judgment of Sheldon J in *Re TD (A Minor)* (unreported) (1985) FD for confirmation of the exclusion of statutory rights for a putative father and his opinion that this was the legislative intent.
12 An exception exists under Article 6(4)(b) of the 1995 Order, which provides for 'any rights which, in the event of the child's death, he (or any other person) may have in relation to the child's property'.
13 See *S v S, W v Official Solicitor* [1972] AC 24, [1970] 3 All ER 107 HL.
14 [1996] 2 FLR 65.

The court cannot compel a person to give a blood sample and the results of any such test are not conclusive proof of paternity; being exclusionary in its effect, it can only determine whether or not a man *could* be the father.

The best interests test may also be applied to dismiss a mother's application for a blood test to disprove a husband's paternity. This was the outcome when, during the course of divorce proceedings, a husband sought contact arrangements with 'a child of the family' but was faced with his wife's challenge that he was not the father and therefore should not have contact. The Court of Appeal[15] endorsed the finding of the judge at first instance that such action would be prejudicial to the welfare interests of the child.

2. Refusal to Provide Samples

Under Articles 8–13 of the Family Law Reform (NI) Order 1977,[16] the court has the power to draw its own conclusions if a putative father declines to submit to tests for the purposes of establishing paternity.[17] These tests include blood samples and DNA 'fingerprinting'.[18] Judicial interpretation of a defendant's refusal to co-operate with such tests was demonstrated in a recent English case.[19] The court at first instance had accepted the defendant's denial of paternity and his refusal to submit to a blood test on the ground, as he contended, that the mother was having intercourse with two other men at the relevant time and he should not now be placed in jeopardy by such testing when this was not required of either of the other men. In allowing the mother's appeal the Court of Appeal held that

1. parentage is to be established on a balance of probability;
2. the court has the power to draw such inferences from the fact that a person fails to comply with a blood test direction as seem appropriate in the circumstances (reliance is not to be placed on cases relating to corroboration decided under the old affiliation law);[20]
3. genetic testing has now advanced to the point where paternity can be determined with almost conclusive certainty and the court will therefore be justified in drawing the inference that any man not availing of the opportunity to resolve a paternity issue and not producing very cogent reasons for such an avoidance is the child's father.

---

15 See *O v L (Blood Tests)* [1995] 2 FLR 930.
16 The equivalent law in England and Wales is to be found in the Family Law Reform Act 1969, s. 20, as amended by the Family Law Reform Act 1987, s. 23.
17 See Regulation 2(1) of the Blood Tests (Evidence of Paternity) Regulations (NI) 1978 (as amended in 1990).
18 See *Re F (Minor: Paternity Tests)* (1992) 2 FCR 725 FD.
19 See *In re A (A Minor)(Paternity: Refusal of Blood Test)* [1994] 2 FLR 463.
20 See, for example, *McVeigh v Beattie* [1988] Fam Law, vol. 18, p. 222, [1988] 2 All ER 500 where the court took the view that it could justifiably conclude that such a refusal provides corroboration for the mother's evidence that he is the father of the child. This judgment is now seen as confusing and perhaps misleading.

Where an application for a blood test is opposed, then the proceedings should be transferred to the High Court if not already being heard there.[21]

Cohabitation

The term 'cohabitation' generally refers to the heterosexual relationship[22] of two persons, neither of whom is or has been married, who set up home and thereafter live together, to all intents and purposes as man and wife; they may or may not have children. The number of persons in this jurisdiction who choose to establish families on this basis instead of opting for the status of marriage is increasing annually. Traditionally, the law has negatively discriminated between marital and non-marital families in relation to the *locus standii* of respective family members, particularly as regards their relations with third parties, so as to protect the status and institution of marriage. More recently, however, following enquiries conducted by the Law Commission[23] and other bodies and under the influence of principles and case law emanating from the European Convention on Human Rights, many of the legal disadvantages of belonging to a non-marital family have been removed.

I. Rationale

For tax purposes and other financial reasons, many couples find it preferable to set up home on a non-marital basis. Other couples have no alternative as one or both are married to another. The main rationale, however, is that for many people there would appear to be no longer any good enough reason to change from their independent legal status. The removal of preferential treatment given by law and statutory bodies to married persons and the fading of the social stigma previously associated with non-marital relationships have adversely affected the incentive to exchange non-marital for marital status.

II. The Cohabitee Relationship

Exclusion from marital status has the consequence of also excluding the cohabitee relationship, to a large extent, from the statutory framework which gives recognition to and protects the rights of family members in respect of each other and in relation to third parties. As mentioned above this is steadily becoming less so, as individual statutes have gradually extended particular provisions, such as those dealing with violence in the home, from a marital to a non-marital context. Some of the legal indices of a marital relationship, however, have not transferred to that of cohabitees.

---

21 See *R v R (Blood Test: Jurisdiction)* [1973] 3 All ER 933.
22 See *Dudgeon v United Kingdom* (1982) 4 EHRR 149 in which the plaintiff successfully challenged the law governing homosexual relationships in this jurisdiction. The ruling of the ECHR led directly to the law being changed to permit such a relationship, between consenting adults, in private.
23 See *Illegitimacy* Law Com no. 118, (1982) and *Illegitimacy* (Law Com no. 157, 1986).

1. Intent

There are occasions when to satisfy a statutory requirement it is necessary to prove that a person is a cohabitee. Unlike the position with married couples, there is no *prima facie* evidence in the form of a certificate available to prove the fact and nature of a cohabitee relationship. Evidence will be needed to demonstrate that the couple do not have a casual, temporary or platonic relationship, that it is heterosexual and that it extends to making shared arrangements for housekeeping etc.

Perhaps the best evidence of an intention to cohabit would be the existence of a cohabitation or 'living together' contract. Such contracts are now not uncommon and, if properly set out and attested, can provide a useful statement of mutual expectations, responsibilities and financial arrangements. Like any other contract, one day this may need to be enforced in court.[24]

2. 'Living Together as Husband and Wife'

Intention often has to be deduced retrospectively from conduct. Where questions arise as to whether or not a couple had intended to establish a cohabitee relationship, then evidence of their intent may be adduced from arrangements they have made. So, for example, it has been held that a man who had moved into an ill woman's house did so with the intention of providing nursing care,[25] that a severely disabled couple moved into the same house with the intention of sharing household duties and expenses,[26] and that where a couple had made application for a joint tenancy they were held to have had the intention of living together as husband and wife.[27] If the evidence points to the couple holding themselves out as being a husband and wife by, for example, sharing the same surname, then this will usually be conclusive.

3. Continuity and Duration of Relationship

Cohabitation implies a settled domestic way of life.[28] Any assessment of such necessitates establishing the continuity and duration of the relationship. Intermittent domestic arrangements, for example where a couple only cohabit during holiday periods or only during term time, do not provide sufficient evidence of a stable, durable mutual commitment. The length of time a relationship has subsisted is an important factor in determining intent to cohabit. In fact, for some statutory purposes a stated minimum period is an essential part of the criteria for defining cohabitation.

III. Support

There is no duty to maintain in a cohabitee relationship; neither partner is under any legal obligation to financially support the other. Should that relationship be terminated,

---

24 See Pawlowski *Cohabitation Contracts — are they Legal?*, NLJ 1125 (1996).
25 See *Crake v Supplementary Benefits Commission* (1980) 2 FLR 264.
26 See *Robson v Secretary of State for Social Services* (1981) 3 FLR 232.
27 See *Campbell v Secretary of State for Social Services* (1983) 4 FLR 138.
28 See Parry *The Law Relating to Cohabitation*, Sweet & Maxwell, London (1993), for a fuller exposition.

there is similarly no duty on either to provide for the other. However, there are now some circumstances in which legislation provides that a cohabiting couple are to be treated as though they are mutually sharing expenses in the same way as a married couple.

Assessment by Statutory Bodies for Benefit/Service Entitlement

(a) Income support

For the purposes of determining entitlement to the statutory benefit of income support, a cohabiting couple are treated jointly, as if married, the outcome being that the aggregated award will be less than the total if each had been separately assessed. The official justification of this basis for assessment is that as both types of couples benefit in the same way from shared utilities and general overhead costs, so it would be illogical to assess each cohabitee separately and it would also be inequitable to married couples. DHSS officials are always very alert to the possibility that persons may be cohabiting, and where this is suspected they will be rigorous in their efforts to prove it by uncovering evidence that the couple are living together as man and wife. Persons initially assessed separately but later found to have been cohabiting will be liable not only for a reduction in future benefits but also for some repayment of past benefits.

(b) Public Housing

The same approach is evident in NIHE assessments of entitlement to tenancy of public housing. A cohabiting couple acting as joint applicants will not be disadvantaged by their status, particularly if they have children. Separate applicants later found to be cohabiting, however, will be liable to rent adjustments similar in effect to those imposed in relation to the income support benefit, the loss of one tenancy and the possible compulsory transfer to designated family accommodation.

IV. Domestic Violence

The legislative protection afforded a cohabitee against the violent actions of a partner is not the same as that afforded to a marital couple[29] (see further Chapter Eight).

V. Property

The legislative provisions affording some recognition of claims by a spouse to property acquired by his/her partner during the course of marriage do not extend the same recognition to cohabitees. The law governing the position of the latter is to be found in Chapter Twenty-one.

VI. Succession

A cohabitee has no statutory rights of succession, nor does he or she enjoy the same right as a spouse to occupy the matrimonial home in the event of the death or bankruptcy of a partner. The relevant law is to be found in Chapter Twenty-five.

---

29   See the Family Law (Miscellaneous Provisions) (NI) Order 1984, Article 20.

VII. Tax and Social Security Assessments

The court has held[30] that the reference to 'wife' in section 8(1)(a) of the Income and Corporation Taxes Act 1970 does not include a 'common law wife', the definition of 'wife' is to be restricted to its statutory meaning within the Marriage Acts (see further Chapter Twenty-one).

VIII. Compensation

A cohabitee's right to compensation as a consequence of the injury or death of a partner is governed by the Criminal Injuries (NI) Order 1988, Article 5(2) and the Fatal Accidents legislation (see further Chapter Twenty-one).

Cohabitee Parents

The parents of a child are the mother and the father of that child. Both cohabitees are treated as being 'parents' for the purposes of the Children (NI) Order 1995, whether or not the father has acquired parental responsibility. Both, therefore, are recognised as parents for the purposes of proceedings for Article 8 orders and for proceedings to obtain care, supervision and emergency protection orders.

I. Unmarried Mother

The rule is that parental responsibility for a non-marital child vests exclusively in the child's unmarried mother unless and until the father acquires such responsibility.

1. Genetic Parent

At common law and by statute the natural mother has long been recognised as being, at birth, the sole parent of an illegitimate child.

2. Non-Genetic Parent

The advance of medical science in recent years has complicated the simple legal rules for establishing parentage. It is now quite possible for the woman genetically related to the child and the non-related bearer of that child to be different persons (see further Chapter Six).

II. Unmarried Father

The law's main interest in unmarried fathers has traditionally been to hold them accountable for the maintenance of their children. Arguably, the Child Support (NI) Order 1991 is evidence that this continues to be the case.[31] An alternative view may

---

30 See *Rignal (HM Inspector of Taxes) v Andrews* [1990] 8 BNIL 73.
31 Note, the Illegitimate Children (Affiliation Orders) Act (NI) 1924 has now been repealed by Article 158 of the Children (NI) Order 1995.

be that the concept of parental responsibility is an acknowledgment that the law is now also concerned with providing an opportunity for a fuller recognition of the rights as well as the duties of such a parent. For an unmarried father, acquiring parental responsibility transforms his legal standing in respect of his child. Most importantly, perhaps, he will have the right to consent or withhold consent to the proposed adoption of that child.[32]

Unmarried Father without Parental Responsibility

Until such time as the appropriate legal process is completed, an unmarried father will not have parental responsibility. Among the number of considerable disadvantages which result from this position is that his agreement is not required for the adoption of his child nor would he be entitled to remove the child from accommodation provided under Article 21. However, even though he has not been vested with parental responsibility, he is still recognised as a 'parent' for the purposes of the 1995 Order and as such has the right under Article 10(4) to apply to the court for an order, under Article 53(1), for reasonable contact with any child of his who may be in care and to apply to the court to be appointed as guardian or for a residence order (see Part Three for the law relating to the maintenance obligations of an unmarried father under the Child Support (NI) Order 1991 and under maintenance agreements).

There are occasions when the court will consider it appropriate for a father to be granted parental responsibility so as to enable him to participate as a full party in proceedings which have been brought for the purpose of depriving him of those same responsibilities.[33]

Abortion

In this jurisdiction, the law relating to abortion is problematic.

I. Legislation

The absence of any equivalent to the Abortion Act 1967, which governs such matters in England and Wales, has left the lawfulness of abortion in Northern Ireland to be determined in accordance with the provisions of the Offences against the Persons Act 1861, section 58 of which provides:

> Every woman, being with child, who, with intent to procure her own miscarriage, shall unlawfully administer to herself any poison or other noxious thing, or shall unlawfully use any instrument or other means whatsoever with the like intent, and

---

32 This is a right denied by Article 12(3) to any non-parent who on being granted a residence order will be vested with parental responsibilities subsumed within that order rather than by a separate Article 7 order.
33 See *Re H (Illegitimate Children: Parental Rights)(no. 2)* [1991] 1 FLR 214 where the court, in the course of freeing order proceedings, found sufficient evidence of contact and attachment between a father and his child to award him parental responsibilities but then went on to grant the application.

whosoever, with intent to procure the miscarriage of any woman whether she be or be not with child, shall unlawfully administer to her or cause to be taken by her any poison or other noxious thing, or unlawfully use any instrument or other means whatsoever with the like intent, shall be guilty of felony, and being convicted thereof shall be liable to be kept in penal servitude for life.

Section 59 provides:

> Whosoever shall unlawfully supply or procure any poison or other noxious thing, or any instrument or thing whatsoever, knowing that the same is intended to be unlawfully used or employed with intent to procure the miscarriage of any woman, whether she be or be not with child, shall be guilty of a misdemeanour, and being convicted thereof shall be liable to be kept in penal servitude.

In this jurisdiction, MacDermott LJ, quoting with approval the comment of Diplock LJ[34] that the law relating to abortion in England prior to the 1967 Act had been 'unsatisfactory and uncertain' has said[35] of the situation here:

> That continues to be the position in NI, a position which in the best interests not only of the medical and legal professions but more importantly of the public at large ought to be remedied. The Abortion Act 1967 may have its faults but it presents a much more coherent and understandable position than that which continues to prevail in this jurisdiction (at p. 3–4).

'Unlawfully'

In the leading case of *R v Bourne*[36] Macnaghten J considered the meaning of the word 'unlawfully' in the above provisions and formed the view that it was qualified in two respects only. The first derives from the caveat contained in section 1(i) of the Infant Life (Preservation) Act 1929 which in this jurisdiction is replicated by section 25(i) of the Criminal Justice Act (NI) 1945:

> ... [A]ny person who, with intent to destroy the life of a child then capable of being born alive, by any wilful act causes a child to die before it has an existence independent of its mother, shall be guilty of felony, to wit, of child destruction, and shall be liable on conviction thereof on indictment to penal servitude for life: Provided that no person shall be found guilty of an offence under this section unless it is proved that the act which caused the death of the child was not done in good faith for the purpose only of preserving the life of the mother.

The learned judge was quite clear as to the circumstances when 'unlawfully' was properly construed:

> Some there may be, for all I know, who hold the view that the fact that a woman desires the operation to be performed is a sufficient justification for it. Well, that is

---

34 In *Royal College of Nursing v DHSS* [1981] AC 800, 826.
35 In *Re AMNH*, unreported (1994).
36 [1939] 1 KB 687.

not the law: a desire of a woman to be relieved of her pregnancy is no justification at all for performing the operation. On the other hand there are people who, from what are said to be religious reasons, object to the operation being performed under any circumstances. That is not the law either.[37]

Secondly, it was qualified to the extent that where a probability existed that if continued the pregnancy might 'make the woman a physical or mental wreck' then abortion would come within the protection afforded by the words 'preserving the life of the mother'. The Macnaghten dicta, qualified by a subsequent ruling[38] which firmly extended the interpretation of 'life of the mother' to encompass her physical and mental health, remains the law in Northern Ireland.

Case Law in Northern Ireland

In this jurisdiction, there are very few reported cases. In *R v Stephenson*,[39] proceedings for murder were brought against a chemist in Belfast for procuring a miscarriage which resulted in the death of a young woman. In *Knell v Knell*,[40] in the context of matrimonial proceedings, the court considered the position of a pregnant woman who had attempted suicide. It was not, however, until the early 1990s, when the High Court was required to determine three cases in fairly quick succession, that the law relating to abortion attracted concentrated judicial and academic[41] scrutiny.

1. Consent

The above English case law, together with guidance given by Butler-Sloss J (as she then was),[42] were taken into consideration by Shiel J in *Re K (A Minor)*,[43] by MacDermott LJ in *Re AMNH*,[44] and subsequently by Shiel J in *In the Matter of CH (A Minor)*.[45] The Northern Ireland cases were similar in that a Health and Social Services Board (now Trust) was the applicant and the preliminary issue was the incapacity of the young women concerned to give a valid consent: in the first case, because the fourteen-year-old was a minor; in the second, because the twenty-four-year-old was severely mentally handicapped; in the third, because she was receiving psychiatric treatment. In all cases the High Court accepted that the incapacity of the subjects and the inability of the applicants to give the required consent made it appropriate for the court to do so if this should be judged lawful and necessary.

---

37 At p. 691.
38 See *R v Newton and Stungo* [1958] Crim LR 469.
39 [1947] NI 110
40 [1970] NIJB
41 See T McGleenan, *Bourne Again? Abortion Law in Northern Ireland after Re K and Re A* (1994) 45 NILQ (no. 4) 389–94.
42 In *Re P (A Minor)* [1986] 1 FLR 272.
43 [1970] NIJB July/Sept.
44 [1994] 4 BNIL.
45 Unreported (1995).

2. Lawful

In giving judgment in respect of the young woman aged twenty-four with an IQ of sixty-one who was ten weeks pregnant and 'very upset at being pregnant and wanted it terminated', MacDermott LJ said of the phrase 'for the purpose of preserving the life of the mother' that it[46]

> ... does not relate only to some life threatening situation. Life in this context means the physical and mental health or well-being of the mother and the doctor's act is lawful while the continuance of the pregnancy would adversely affect the mental and physical health of the mother. The adverse effect must however be a real and serious one and it will always be a question of fact and degree whether the perceived effect of non-termination is sufficiently grave to warrant terminating the unborn child.

On hearing evidence from a consultant gynaecologist, a consultant psychiatrist, a psychiatrist and a general medical practitioner, MacDermott LJ concluded that on the facts of the case the proposed abortion would be lawful.

In considering the circumstances of the two girls, both considered to be '*Gillick* competent' (see page 43), Shiel J[47] received evidence of their steadfast resolve to have their pregnancies terminated and of threats to attempt suicide if denied abortions. He concluded that continuance of the pregnancies would adversely affect the mental health of both minors and therefore abortion was lawful and, in the circumstances, necessary (see further Chapter Seven).

3. Judicial and Medical Decisions

The role of the court is to rule on whether the proposed action would, in all the circumstances of the case, be lawful. Shiel J, in the most recently decided case, was at pains to stress the limited brief of the court. Noting that the Trust had sought 'an order directing that the minor undergo such medical and surgical treatment as might be necessary to terminate her pregnancy', he emphasised that as a matter of law, this was precisely what the court was not prepared to do:

> I wish to make it clear that this court, while granting permission for the minor's pregnancy to be terminated, does not give any *direction* that this be done.[48]

The role of the court is to clear the legal obstacles. Decisions relating to medical matters must be taken by the parties concerned. The words of Johnson J,[49] as quoted with approval by MacDermott LJ[50] in relation to cases of 'brain-stem death', seem equally applicable to the aforementioned abortion cases.

---

46 See f/ns 43 and 44.
47 See f/n 45.
48 *In the Matter of CH (A Minor)* unreported (1993), p. 11.
49 In *Re A (A Minor)* unreported (1993).
50 In *Re TC (A Minor)* unreported (1994) BNIL.

The function of the court in this delicate jurisdiction is to assist by clarifying the position and not to usurp the discretion of the doctors to do what they think is best in the difficult circumstances in which they are placed.

The difference with abortion cases, however, is that the court is also required not to usurp the discretion of the *Gillick* competent minor nor that of the treatment centre in England.

4. Abortion Operations within the Jurisdiction

Once it is determined that a proposed abortion is lawful and that a valid consent can be given to the relevant medical practitioner, then it remains only to request the latter to carry out the termination. Within the jurisdiction this final hurdle has, at times, proved to be insurmountable. As was asserted by a senior consultant during the course of the *In Re K*[51] hearing,

> No consultant will be found in this jurisdiction who will be prepared to carry out the operation to terminate the minor's pregnancy because of her mother's objection thereto and their perceived uncertainty concerning the present state of the law relating to abortion in Northern Ireland.

This assertion associates consultant objections with the issue of consent and not with any issue of lawfulness. The readiness of consultants to perform abortions *per se* is evidenced by the considerable number of such operations carried out within the jurisdiction every year, on request, in circumstances where foetal abnormality is suspected (as Mr McGleenan points out[52]). Where the necessary consent is forthcoming within the immediate context of a confidential doctor/patient relationship, an issue of lawfulness such as might require recourse to the courts does not seem to arise. The non-availability of first-party consent is the impediment to consultant decision-making which triggers court involvement and, even when judicially removed, is perceived by consultants to be a continuing obstacle preventing the performance of an operation judged necessary on health grounds. This seems incongruous (a) because of consultant readiness to allow the same operation to be carried out by colleagues in England, despite the additional risks entailed (in terms of factors such as time, travel and the strange environment) to the health of the subject and (b) because of consultant readiness to accept and act on judicial removal of the consent impediment in circumstances such as those illustrated by the case of *In re TC (A Minor)*[53] (see further Chapter Seven).

Registration

The Births and Deaths Registration (NI) Order 1976, Article 14, as substituted by the Children (NI) Order 1995, Schedule 9, paragraph 84, makes provision for the registration of fathers where the parents are unmarried. There are several different circumstances where the name of an unmarried father may be entered on the Register of Birth.

---

51 Unreported (1993).
52 Op. cit.
53 Unreported (1993).

I. Registration Methods

The name of the unmarried father may be entered on the Register at the time of a child's birth.

1. By Request of Both Parents

Under Article 14(3)(a), where both mother and father jointly request the registrar to do so and both sign the Register the name of the unmarried father will be entered on the Register.

2. By Parental Declaration

Under Article 14(3)(b) and (c), the father's name will be entered if the request is made by either parent and the father has made a statutory declaration of paternity which has been acknowledged by the mother.

3. By Parental Agreement and Declaration

Under Article 14(3)(d), the father's name will be entered if either parent makes the request in circumstances where they have completed and produced a parental responsibility agreement accompanied by a declaration in the prescribed form that the agreement has not been brought to an end by an order of the court.

4. By Court Order and Declaration

Under Article 14(3)(e), the father's name will be entered at the request of either parent who produces a certified copy of an order made under either Article 7 of the 1995 Order or paragraph 2 of Schedule 1 of the 1995 Order or under any similar preceding statutory provision. (As listed in Article 14(4) these are: an order under section 5A of the Guardianship of Infants Act 1886 giving that person custody of the child or under the Illegitimate Children (Affiliation Orders) Act (NI) 1924 adjudging that person to be the putative father of the child.) This must be accompanied by a declaration in the prescribed form that such an order has not been brought to an end or discharged by the court.

II. Re-registration

In situations where the father's name was not entered on the Register at the time of the child's birth, provision is made for this entry to be made later.

1. By Parental Agreement or Court Order

The Births and Deaths Registration (NI) Order 1976, Article 19A, as inserted by the Children (NI) Order 1995, Schedule 9, paragraph 87, applies where, subsequent to registration, the child's parents make parental agreements with each other or appropriate court orders are obtained. Where, in such circumstances, the Registrar General receives notification (under Article 32(4) of the Matrimonial and Family Proceedings (NI) Order

1989) that a declaration has been made in respect of the parentage of a registered child, then, if satisfied that the birth should be re-registered, he or she may authorise the father's name to be added to the Register.

2. Qualified Applicant

The Births and Deaths Registration (NI) Order 1976, Article 37(7), as amended by the Children (NI) Order 1995, Schedule 9, paragraph 88, provides for a number of specific circumstances where again the Register may be altered to take account of a change in a child's status.

Non-Cohabiting Parents

The distinction between 'parent' and 'parenting' is particularly fraught where the adults concerned are not living together.

III. The Single-Parent Family

By far the majority of non-marital family units consist of mothers and their children.[54] The Children (NI) Order 1995 protects the position of such mothers by vesting parental responsibility solely in an unmarried mother to the exclusion of the father. Such a mother may further protect her position by applying for any Article 8 order. Protection for her financial position is available under the Child Support (NI) Order 1991 (see Chapter 22) or by way of maintenance agreement.

IV. Married Woman and Unmarried Father

There is a common-law presumption that a child born to a married woman during her marriage is the legitimate child of that woman and of her husband.[55] The burden of rebutting this presumption falls on the husband, or on any man claiming paternity. A high standard of proof is required.[56] Blood tests may be ordered where a husband is seeking to establish that he is not the father of his wife's child and that she has therefore committed adultery.[57]

---

54 See *Report of the Committee on One-Parent Families* (the Finer Report) (Cmnd 5629, 1974). Parenting in such circumstances is a vulnerable activity carrying a possibility of coercive Trust intervention (see Gibbons et al in *Operating the Child Protection System* (1995), HMSO, who found that 36 per cent of all cases on Child Protection Registers involved single-parent families.
55 See, for example, *Gardner v Gardner* (1877) 2 App Cas 723 HL and *R v Luffe* (1807) 8 East 193.
56 See, for example, *Serio v Serio* (1983) 4 FLR 756 and *W v K (Proof of Paternity)* [1988] 1 FLR 86.
57 See, for example, *F v F* [1968] 1 All ER 242.

CHAPTER FOUR

Assisted Parenthood

Introduction

In the space of a few brief decades, the United Kingdom, in keeping with other modern western societies, has reversed its parenting dilemma of too many unwanted babies for too few prospective parents. An equation, once redressed by the benign transportation[1] from these shores of hundreds of thousands of children, is now counterbalanced by the adoption of overseas children[2] and by medically assisted parenthood. Whether the law is coping any better than formerly, with the moral complexities of adjusting the supply of children in relation to the demand of actual and prospective parents, is a matter outside the scope of this book.

Over the past fifteen years or so, some tens of thousands of children in the United Kingdom have been born as the result of artificial means of reproduction. New methods of assisted conception have had the incidental consequence of making possible new parenting arrangements and have transformed the traditional definition of parent. In England and Wales some of the resulting issues have appeared before the courts, generated specific legislation and attracted academic interest. In this jurisdiction, where very many couples have benefited from medically assisted means of reproduction, these developments have been accompanied by neither case law, legislation specific to the province nor much academic interest. Given the province's history of legal initiative in matters relating to sex and morals (e.g. abortion and homosexuality), it is perhaps not surprising that this should be so. As the advances of medical science and the related legislation are, however, directly applicable to Northern Ireland, there is a need for a book such as this to take into account the implications arising for family law practitioners in the province. Indeed, it is important to stress that this is a matter of more than esoteric interest. Given the number of children in Northern Ireland born through reliance on assisted parenthood, the fact that relevant British legislation applies also to the province, the background influence of the European Convention on Human Rights and the UN Convention on the Rights of the Child and that of the European Court of Human Rights, this subject area must, of necessity, become of increasing interest to practitioners in Northern Ireland

This chapter does no more than briefly outline the statutory law and accompanying case law which have application throughout the United Kingdom but, so far, have had little practical relevance for the courts in Northern Ireland.

---

1 See, for example, Bean & Melville, *Lost Children of the Empire*, London: Unwin Hyman (1989).
2 See, for example, D Ngabonziza, *Inter-country adoption: in whose best interests?*, Adoption & Fostering, Vol. 2, no. 1 (1988).

The Background

The common law regarded any child, other than one born to a married couple and of their marriage, as *filius nullius*, or no-one's child. For all legal purposes he or she was regarded as illegitimate unless and until there was either an adoption or the marriage (to each other) of the parents. This, initially, continued to be the approach of the law to children born as a result of medically assisted conceptions.

I. Medicine

Advances in medical science have led to the development of a variety of different techniques for assisting human conception.

1. Artificial Insemination by Donor (AID)

Assisted conception by reliance on the implanting of donor-supplied sperm in the cervix, vagina or womb of a recipient is perhaps the most traditional medical response to childless couples, where the problem lies in male infertility. It remains the method most frequently relied upon, with some 1,700 children being born as a result of AID treatment every year in the UK. Where the difficulty lies with the woman and the donation is in fact from the husband, not from an anonymous source, the treatment is referred to as AIH.

2. In Vitro Fertilisation (IVF)

In vitro fertilisation refers to the medical technique whereby eggs, fertilised by partner- or donor-supplied sperm, are either implanted in the recipient or are nurtured until the growth of a viable embryo, which is then implanted. This form of treatment originated in the pioneering work of Dr Patrick Steptoe. Its medical significance lies in its reliance on the transfer of eggs.

3. Gamete Intra-Fallopian Transfer (GIFT)

Gamete intra-fallopian transfer relies on the implanting of unfertilised eggs and sperm in the fallopian tube of the recipient.

II. Surrogacy

The term 'surrogacy' usually refers to a birth which would not have occurred had it not been for third-party intervention. In this case, however, it comes about in the context of an arrangement of social convenience rather than of medical treatment. The involvement of the third party is not necessarily governed by professional rules of engagement.

The arrangement whereby a woman contracts, for altruistic or mercenary reasons, to be impregnated with the sperm, fertilised eggs or embryo provided by another party or parties, and then conceives, carries to full-term and delivers to that party a baby, has come to be known as 'surrogacy'. It is an arrangement which is usually associated with couples whose childlessness is due to the woman's inability to produce eggs. The recipient, or commissioning parent, thereafter undertakes full parental responsibility, most usually by way of adoption. The birth mother thereafter ceases her involvement. The commercial potential for such arrangements has been fully developed in countries such as the USA.

III. Ethics

The advances made by medical science in the field of human reproduction have, not surprisingly, been accompanied by profound ethical dilemmas. Genetic engineering, including the cloning of human beings, has become a scientific possibility. The choice factor, in relation to the decision to become a parent and the genetic make-up of the child, previously matters solely within the control of the couple concerned, has now come to be amenable to medical adjustment. The area of choice has been broadened — to break the genetic link between parent and child; to bring the possibility of parenthood to lesbian and gay couples; to potentially disrupt the lateral network of nuclear and extended family relationships; and to disrupt also the hierarchical generational structure of families.

IV. Law

The advances of science have thrown into considerable disarray the formerly simple legal rules for establishing parentage. The Law Commission considered[3] some of the issues arising and recommended that paternity should in law be ascribed to the birth mother's husband. The Warnock Committee[4] was then set up to broadly examine matters relating to artificially induced methods of human reproduction and to make recommendations on the legal implications arising for all parties. The Warnock recommendations were accepted, incorporated in a White Paper[5] and eventually resulted in the legislation which now governs the complex field of assisted parenthood.

The Legal Framework in Northern Ireland

There are no orders in council relating to assisted parenthood nor are there court judgments, reported or unreported, to show that the courts of this jurisdiction have ever had to determine any of the associated legal issues. In an unusual precedent, however, the two pieces of legislation which state the entire relevant law for Great Britain also have application to this jurisdiction. The resulting law applies in relation to children born as a consequence of assisted parenthood, and to the respective legal status of the parties involved, regardless of whether a child was born as a result of a private surrogacy arrangement, medical treatment or a combination of the two.

---

3 See the Law Commission Working Papers No. 74 'Illegitimacy' (1979) and No. 91 *Guardianship* (1985) HMSO.
4 See *Inquiry into Human Fertilisation and Embryology* (Cmnd 9314, 1984).
5 *Human Fertilisation and Embryology: A Framework for Legislation* (Cmm 259, 1987). See also *Legislation on Human Infertility Services and Embryology Research: A Consultation Paper* (Cmmd 46, 1986).

I. The Legislation

The Surrogacy Arrangements Act 1985 and the Human Fertilisation and Embryology Act 1990 are inter-related statutes which combine to form the statutory framework for the law as it relates to assisted parenthood in Northern Ireland. Each statute, however, to some extent also represents a distinctively different legal approach to the issues involved. There is a clearly discernible legislative intent to discourage private enterprise in the methods of assisted reproduction and in the making of arrangements to that end; this is mainly embodied in the 1985 Act. It is also apparent that when the provisions move from dealing with the means of acquiring parenthood to the reality of being a parent, then an approach of pragmatic realism is applied; this is mainly evident in the 1990 Act.

1. The Surrogacy Arrangements Act 1985

Under section 5 of the Surrogacy Arrangements Act 1985:

> (2) This Act is extended to Northern Ireland.

The provisions thereby applied to this jurisdiction, by this final section of a brief piece of legislation, in effect also bring with them the related case law principles. The main concern of the Act is to prohibit the development of any form of organised commercial practice in relation to surrogacy.

2. The Human Fertilisation and Embryology Act 1990

Under section 48 of the Human Fertilisation and Embryology Act 1990:

> (1) This Act (except section 37) extends to Northern Ireland.

The exempted section deals with matters pertaining to the Abortion Act 1967, a statute which has no application to this jurisdiction. The 1990 Act is more comprehensive than its predecessor and seeks to address the particular legal issues associated with assisted parenthood whether arising from surrogacy or otherwise.

II. The Court

1. Jurisdiction

Any person commencing proceedings under the 1985 Act, in respect of an alleged offence, is required by section 4(2)(b) to have the prior consent of the DPP. Under Article 19(1) of the Magistrates' Courts (NI) Order 1981, such proceedings must be brought within six months of the alleged offence.

Proceedings commenced under the 1990 Act must be heard in the High Court or in a county court. This is apparent from section (8)(c) which states that in this jurisdiction 'the court', for the purposes of this provision, 'means the High Court or any county court within whose division the child is'.

2. Family Proceedings

Family proceedings for the purpose of the Children (NI) Order 1995, Article 8(4), include proceedings taken under:

> (g) section 30 of the Human Fertilisation and Embryology Act 1990.

In such proceedings, therefore, the court is required to apply the paramountcy principle, the no-delay principle and the no-order presumption. Where the proceedings are contested, the court must apply the welfare checklist. It is also free to make any Article 8 order in addition to or instead of the order sought.

3. Specified Proceedings

Applications for an order under section 30 of the 1990 Act are designated as 'special proceedings' under the court rules. The child is therefore automatically made a party to the proceedings and the court is required to appoint a guardian ad litem unless satisfied that such an appointment is unnecessary.

III. *The Parties*

Legislators have had difficulties in coming to grips with the traditionally simple concepts of 'mother' and 'father'. The outcome is that while in this context the legal definition of 'mother' now rests on the fact of pregnancy, the carrying of a foetus to full term and the act of giving birth, that of 'father' rests, with less certainty, on a combination of his status in relation to the mother and his responsibility for fertilisation.

1. Mother

Under section 27 of the 1990 Act:

> (1) The woman who is carrying or has carried a child as a result of placing in her of an embryo or of sperm and eggs, and no other woman, is to be treated as the mother of the child.

This provision brings firm, legal clarity to an otherwise less than certain state of affairs. Regardless of whether she has any genetic link with the child, the birth mother is the *de jure* mother. The fact that the actual 'placing' occurred in another United Kingdom jurisdiction or in a jurisdiction other than the United Kingdom is irrelevant. Much of this statute remains to be implemented.

From this reference point other legal relationships are construed.

2. Surrogate Mother

Under the 1985 Act, section 1:

> (2) 'Surrogate mother' means a woman who carries a child in pursuance of an arrangement—

(a) made before she began to carry the child, and
(b) made with a view to any child carried in pursuance of it being handed over to, and the parental rights being exercised (so far as practicable) by, another person or other persons.

This provision allows for the special position of commissioning parents in a surrogacy arrangement and provides an exception to the definition of 'mother' given in Article 27 of the 1990 Act (another exception is a mother who becomes so as a consequence of an adoption order). Provided certain conditions are met, the linking of maternal status to the act of giving birth can be broken.

Article 119 of the 1995 Order, Schedule 9, amends the Surrogacy Arrangements Act 1985 as follows:

> In section 1(2)(b) (meaning of 'surrogate mother', etc.) for 'the parental rights being exercised' substitute 'parental responsibility being met'.

3. Father

Under section 28 of the 1990 Act:

> (2) If—
> (a) at the time of the placing in her of the embryo or the sperm and eggs or of her insemination, the woman was a party to a marriage, and
> (b) the creation of the embryo carried by her was not brought about with the sperm of the other party to the marriage, then, subject to subsection (5) below, the other party to the marriage shall be treated as the father of the child unless it is shown that he did not consent to the placing in her of the embryo or the sperm and eggs or to her insemination (as the case may be).

This provision endorses the common-law principle[6] that where a child is born to a married woman the husband of that woman is presumed to be the father of her child. This presumption applies whether or not there is any genetic link between husband and child. It also provides for specific circumstances where the presumption may be rebutted.

If, at the time of placing, the husband of the birth mother stated that the arrangement did not have his approval, and his non-involvement in the process comes within the terms of section 2(b), then he is not to be regarded in law as the child's father.

4. Donor Father

Under section 28(6) of the 1990 Act, if sperm has been provided by an anonymous (i.e. in accordance with the licensing requirements of the 1990 Act, Schedule 3) or deceased donor, then such a man cannot be regarded as the father and the child is in law fatherless.

---

6 This principle is sometimes expressed as *Pater est quem nuptiae demonstrant*.

The Law in Practice

Again, it should be pointed out that to date there has not been any litigation in this field in the province.

I. Proceedings under the Surrogacy Arrangements Act 1985

The legislative intent with regard to possible third-party involvement in surrogacy arrangements is a natural extension of its approach towards the same issue in the context of adoption, i.e. to prohibit any such involvement for purposes of commercial gain and to prevent arrangements from acquiring any of the trappings of a business enterprise. Under the 1985 Act, the only way in which the commissioning parent could displace the *locus standi* of the birth parent in relation to the child was through adoption, proceedings which were often threatened by the issue of payments made by the applicants to the birth parent.[7]

Where the contractual arrangement broke down, which was not infrequently, the courts had little option but to declare the birth mother as *de facto* the legal mother. This was not wholly satisfactory as almost always the only genetic link to the child lay with the commissioning parents. The 1990 Act was introduced to provide some recognition for *the locus standi* of a genetically linked commissioning parent.

1. The Surrogacy Arrangement

Under section 1 of the 1985 Act:

> (3) An arrangement is a surrogacy arrangement if, were a woman to whom the arrangement relates to carry a child in pursuance of it, she would be a surrogate mother.
>
> (4) In determining whether an arrangement is made with such a view as is mentioned in subsection (2) above regard may be had to the circumstances as a whole (and, in particular, where there is a promise or understanding that any payment will or may be made to the woman or for her benefit in respect of the carrying of any child in pursuance of the arrangement, to that promise or understanding).

The 1990 Act amends that as of 1985 by inserting section 36(1), a clause which provides that 'no surrogacy arrangement is enforceable by or against any of the parties making it'. Neither part of the contractual arrangement is legally enforceable. The birth mother need not surrender the child, the commissioning couple may refuse to make the agreed payment. Where the issue arises, the courts will always favour a birth mother with current parenting responsibility retaining care of her child.

---

7 See, for example, *Re Adoption Application (Payment for Adoption)* [1987] 2 All ER 826 and *Re An Adoption Application* [1992] 1 FLR 341. See also *Re MW (Adoption: Surrogacy)* [1995] 2 FLR 759.

2. Commercial Surrogacy

Under section 2 of the 1985 Act:

> (1) No person shall on a commercial basis do any of the following acts in the United Kingdom, that is—
> - (a) initiate or take part in any negotiations with a view to the making of a surrogacy arrangement,
> - (b) offer or agree to negotiate the making of a surrogacy arrangement, or
> - (c) compile any information with a view to its use in making, or negotiating the making of, surrogacy arrangements; and no person shall in the United Kingdom knowingly cause another to do any of those acts on a commercial basis.

This provision makes it an offence to initiate or to be involved in the advertising of surrogacy services or the negotiating of surrogacy arrangements on a commercial basis. The commercial complexities were first highlighted by the so-called 'Baby Cotton' case[8] where Kim Cotton, an English woman, was commissioned by an American agency to act as a surrogate mother on behalf of an American couple. The involvement of an agency acting for commercial gain by advertising or contracting for surrogacy arrangements is now a criminal offence under the 1985 Act. However, persons who would otherwise be in breach of any of the activities prohibited under section 2(1) are exempted under section 2(2) from prosecution, if acting in a private capacity with a view to becoming either a surrogate mother or a commissioning parent. Moreover, where a surrogate mother has received money or other benefits from the commissioning parents (whether or not for the purpose of defraying reasonable expenses), the court is empowered under section 36(7) to authorise such payments retrospectively.

II. The Child of a Surrogacy Arrangement

The parties are not bound by the terms of a surrogacy arrangement and neither are the courts when it comes to determining the respective rights of the parties in relation to the resulting child. The court will look to the child's best interests.

1. *Locus Standi* of the Birth Parent

The presumption that a birth mother is the lawful parent of the child will not be rebutted by evidence of an agreement nor by evidence of alternative material advantages offered by commissioning parents. The court will seek to protect and sustain an existing satisfactory, caring relationship. For example, in wardship proceedings, the court refused to order the transfer of twins aged five months from the birth mother to a commissioning couple, despite evidence that the latter could offer a more secure and materially more advantageous upbringing.[9]

---

8 See *Re C (A Minor)(Wardship: Surrogacy)* [1985] FLR 846.
9 See *Re P (Minors)(Wardship: Surrogacy)* [1987] 2 FLR 421.

Not only will the law regard the birth mother as the child's *prima facie* parent, whether genetically linked or not, but if married then her husband will be treated similarly and he will be presumed to have all the normal contact rights of a biological father.[10]

2. *Locus Standi* of the Commissioning Parent

Where the commissioning parents, rather than the birth parent, provided the total post-natal care for twins, the court, again in wardship proceedings, has directed that the status quo be maintained, the former being directed to apply for a section 30 order within 28 days of the 1990 Act coming into effect.[11]

III. Proceedings under the Human Fertilisation and Embryology Act 1990

The legislation regarding proceedings under the Human Fertilisation and Embryology Act 1990 is mainly concerned with disputes on the 'ownership' of children born as a result of assisted parenthood, whichever methods are employed. It enables the court to make an order declaring that the commissioning parents are, in law, the parents of any such child.

1. Treatment

Under Schedule 3, paragraph 5 of the 1990 Act:

> (1) A person's gametes must not be used for the purpose of treatment services unless there is an effective consent by that person to their being so used and they are used in accordance with the terms of the consent.
>
> (2) A person's gametes must not be received for use for those purposes unless there is an effective consent by that person to their being so used.

This necessity for donor consent lay at the heart of a difficult and well-publicised case[12] which recently received considerable judicial attention. The applicant, Mrs Blood, sought the release of her late husband's sperm, removed on her instructions while he was in a coma and stored by the Infertility Research Trust, for use by her in treatment to artificially assist pregnancy. The Human Fertilisation and Embryology Authority (HFEA) refused to comply because there was not, and could never be, an 'effective consent' from the donor. HFEA claimed their hands were tied by specific statutory provisions, including the above section 4(1) which prohibits the use of sperm for treatment purposes unless authorised by licence; and section 12 (in conjunction with Schedule 3, paragraph 3) which prohibits the granting of a licence except where a proper consent, preceded by counselling, has been obtained from the donor. In the High Court and subsequently in judicial review, the HFEA decision was upheld: Mrs

---

10 See, *Re CH (Contact)* [1996] 1 FLR 569, FD.
11 See *Re W (Minors)(Surrogacy)* [1991] 1 FLR 385.
12 See *R v Human Fertilisation and Embryology Authority ex parte Blood* [1997] 1 FLR no. 6.

Blood was denied the use of the sperm within the jurisdiction and denied permission to export it for treatment abroad. The Court of Appeal, however, took the view that the law could only be ascertained by interpreting the provision of the 1990 Act in conjunction with relevant EC legislation. The court found that under Articles 59 and 60 of the EC Treaty Mrs Blood has the right to receive treatment in another member State and that HFEA's refusal to permit export was preventing her enjoyment of that right. The court held that HFEA had been remiss not to take cognisance of the EC legislation and directed that body to reconsider its decision.

This Court of Appeal initiative, to explicitly test UK legislation against the EC Treaty and so secure an advantage for a UK citizen, may well serve as a reference point for further case law in other areas.

2. The Order

Under section 30(1) of the 1990 Act:

> The court may make an order providing for a child to be treated in law as the child of the parties to a marriage (referred to in this section as 'the husband' and 'the wife').

A section 30 order is an order ascribing the legal status of parent to both parties of a marriage in respect of a child acquired by them and genetically linked to one or both of them as a consequence of assisted parenthood.

(a) The Genetically Linked Child

Under section 30(1) of the 1990 Act a child born of a surrogate arrangement may be the subject of an order under this provision if:

> (b) the gametes of the husband or the wife, or both, were used to bring about the creation of the embryo.

A condition precedent to the granting of an order under this provision is the existence of a genetic link between child and applicant. This requires two separate matters to be proven: that the wife did not give birth to the child; and that the birth mother did so as a consequence of the implanting of 'the gametes of the husband or the wife or both'. The latter will not be proven by evidence that impregnation occurred as a consequence of sexual intercourse between birth parent and commissioning husband. The burden of proof is on the applicants to provide the evidence necessary to demonstrate the existence of a genetic link between one or both of them and the child concerned.

(b) The Applicants

Under section 30(1) of the 1990 Act the application for an order must be made by 'the parties to a marriage (referred to in this section as 'the husband' and 'the wife')', and section 30(2) requires that it be made within six months of the child's birth. An unmarried couple are clearly ineligible for a section 30 order. Under Article 30(3) the child's home must be with the husband and wife at the time of the application and of the making of the order and one or both of them must be domiciled within the United

Kingdom, Channel Islands or Isle of Man. Both husband and wife must have reached the age of eighteen at the time of the order. Under Article 30(7) the husband and wife are required to satisfy the court that no money or other benefit (other than for expenses reasonably incurred) has been given or received by them in connection with the surrogacy arrangement, delivery of the child or making of the order 'unless authorised by the court'.

(c) The Birth Parents

Under section 30(1) of the 1990 Act where

   (a) the child has been carried by a woman other than the wife as the result of the placing in her of an embryo or sperm and eggs or her artificial insemination,

sub-section 5 requires the consent of that woman to the making of the order. Where the 'placing' that occurred is rendered immaterial by sub-section 11, the consent of the father of the child is also required. Both must consent freely, unconditionally and with full understanding of what is involved if a section 30 order is to be made. However, under sub-section 7 the court will dispense with the need for the consent of either party if he or she cannot be found or is incapable of giving agreement, and any agreement given by the birth mother, if given within six weeks of the birth, will be invalid.

(d) The Effects of the Order

The order declares that in law the child is the child of the commissioning parents and of their marriage; the woman who gave birth is not to be regarded as the mother.

(e) Alternative Orders

Adoption Order

Adoption proceedings have often provided the legal sequel to surrogacy arrangements. Where the consent of the birth mother is not available, where the applicants are a married couple but neither is genetically linked to the child or where an applicant is unmarried but is part of a settled secure domestic arrangement closely approximating a marital relationship, adoption is then an appropriate statutory option offering the applicants the best prospect of legal security for their relationship with the child.

One such case,[13] however, recently illustrated the difficulties typically associated with adoption in this context. The applicants were a commissioning couple who had from the outset agreed with the birth mother that the surrogacy arrangement would conclude with their adopting the child with her consent. From impregnation with the commissioning father's sperm to handing over of the child, all terms of this arrangement were complied with, including payments to the birth mother and the latter's consent to adoption. However, although post-natal relationships between the parties were initially good, with contact between birth mother and child, they quickly broke down and her consent was withdrawn. The birth mother conducted a high-profile media campaign against the commissioning parents before adoption proceedings commenced.

---

13   See *Re MW (Adoption: Surrogacy)* [1995] 2 FLR 759.

The court held that the parties had been in breach of adoption law by making a direct placement with the commissioning mother, a non-relative (the commissioning father, being genetically linked to the child, was a relative for these purposes), and by making illegal payments. These breaches did not bar the court from determining the application on its merits. This fell to be decided on the basis of whether the birth mother's consent could be dispensed with on the grounds of unreasonableness. On the basis that removal from the present secure, caring environment would be detrimental to the child's welfare interests, the court ruled that consent could be dispensed with. The court also took into account the fact that the mother had previously given her consent in the context of a formal legal agreement. Further, because of her publicity campaign which had brought distress to the adopters and public exposure for the child, the court ruled that the birth mother should have no further contact with the child.

Article 8 Order

Where the eligibility criteria for a section 30 order or for an adoption order cannot be met and in any dispute over the upbringing of children, the commissioning parents may choose to initiate proceedings for an Article 8 order; or the court may of its own motion, in any family proceedings, decide to make such an order instead of the one sought. Proceedings initiated by lesbian couples concerning the custody, care or upbringing of children have from time to time been heard by the courts,[14] more often in the context of parenting than parenthood relationships. Such issues are now being heard in proceedings for residence orders. Occasionally a case involves a surrogate mother.

In one case[15] the High Court heard an application for a residence order, in respect of an eight-month-old baby girl, made by a lesbian couple in a stable relationship and with the consent of the child's mother. The court issued a section 37 direction (equivalent to Article 56) requiring the Trust's counterpart to conduct an investigation which should in particular consider any emotional or other difficulties the child was likely to face; the availability of counselling or psychiatric services should these be necessary; and the relative advantages or otherwise of removing the child. As a result of the ensuing social worker's report, Scott Baker J stated on behalf of the court that 'the fact that the applicants were lesbians did not appear (*sic*) that the placement was any less likely to succeed'.

Right to Information

The Human Fertilisation and Embryology Act 1990 requires information to be recorded regarding births resulting from methods of assisted parenthood governed by the Act. It also provides for limited rights of access to that information.

---

14 See, for example, *S v S (Custody of Children)* (1980) FLR 143; *Re P (A Minor)(Custody)* (1983) FLR 401; *Re C (A Minor)(Wardship: Surrogacy)* [1985] FLR 846; *C v C (A Minor)(Custody: Appeal)* [1991] 1 FLR 223; *B v B (Minors)(Custody, Care and Control)* [1991] Fam Law 174. Also, see Fiona L. Tasker and Susan Golombok, *Children Raised by Lesbian Mothers; The Empirical Evidence* [1991] vol. 21, Fam Law 184.
15 See *Re H (A Minor)(Section 37 Direction)* [1993] 2 FLR 541.

I. Duty to Record Information

Under the 1990 Act, Article 31(1) and (2), the Human Fertilisation and Embryology Authority is required to keep a register containing information relating to

 (a) the provision of treatment services for any identifiable individual, or
 (b) the keeping or use of the gametes of any identifiable individual or of an embryo taken from any identifiable woman, or if it shows that any identifiable individual was, or may have been, born in consequence of treatment services.

II. Right of Access to Recorded Information

The Human Fertilisation and Embryology Act 1990 places a duty on certain agencies to respond to *bona fide* enquiries.

1. The Authority

Under the 1990 Act, Article 31(3), a person who has reached the age of eighteen and has been offered counselling has the right[17] to require the Human Fertilisation and Embryology Authority to disclose information relating to his or her birth and genetic origins as recorded in the register.

2. The Registrar General

Under the 1990 Act, Article 32, where a claim is made before the Registrar General that a man is not the father of a child, the Registrar General may require the Authority to disclose any information which has a bearing on the matter.

3. The Court

Under the 1990 Act, Article 34, where in any proceedings a court needs to rule on the issue of whether or not a person is a parent of a particular child by virtue of sections 27 to 29, on application by one of the parties, it may require the Authority to disclose any relevant information.

---

16 As recommended by the Warnock Committee, f/n 4, para 4.21.

CHAPTER FIVE

Guardianship, Parental Responsibilities and the Carer Relationship

Introduction

Legal guardianship has been well described by Dr S Cretney as a formula used to attribute powers over the upbringing of a child to a particular individual or individuals.[1] It is a formula developed from judicial recognition of the legal attributes of parenting. There is a sense, therefore, in which guardianship is an office deriving from the status and functions of a parent, which may be held naturally by the parent or be transferred and held by others. The authority for such a transfer, the range of authorised care relationships and the differing degree to which each type is vested with the office of guardianship is a rapidly expanding area of modern family law and the subject of this chapter.

Guardianship has its origins at the heart of private family law. Given the more complex relationships now associated with the modern role of the family in society, particularly those resulting from second and third marriages, it was to be expected that the private law of guardianship would require revision. The proliferation of care relationships in the domain of public family law, however, would itself have provided sufficient cause for review. The increased litigation as to the rights and duties of baby-sitters, child-minders, foster-parents, playgroup organisers, teachers, supervisors in crèche and nursery school facilities etc. brought its own pressure on the law to formulate a coherent approach accommodating such different types of care responsibility. The work of the Law Commission[2] sought to address this need. The Children (NI) Order 1995 integrated the Commission's recommendations within a comprehensive treatment of public and private family law.

This chapter examines the origins and core components of guardianship and the range of other care relationships which it has engendered. It then considers the law now governing them as stated in the 1995 Order and as interpreted by the courts in England acting under the equivalent provisions of the Children Act 1989.

It is interesting to note the statistical trends in the use of orders in the last several years. In Northern Ireland, the number of guardianship orders being made annually has steadily increased in recent years. In 1992 some eighty-seven orders were made, 108 in 1993, 156 in 1994 and 180 in 1995. The relative significance of this increase may best be appreciated when set against the fourteen orders issued in 1985.

---

1 See SM Cretney, *Principles of Family Law*, London: Sweet & Maxwell, 4th ed., 1984, 296.
2 See Law Commission, *Family Law, Review of Child Law: Guardianship*, Working Paper 91 (1985).

Guardianship: The Concept and the Law

Under the common law, a parent was regarded as being the natural guardian of a legitimate child.[3] As guardian, the parent was viewed as being inherently vested with the duty to provide for and protect any child of his or her marriage. On the death of the parent, the guardianship duties could be transferred to another person by appointment of the court or by the will or deed of the deceased.

A guardianship appointment confers a *de jure* duty of care on a named adult in respect of a specific child. This distinguishes it from a number of other *de facto* care relationships, such as child-minding and foster care, which are non-specific in terms of the parties and are not individually endorsed by a grant of authority.

I. Concept

Guardianship, as the Law Commission pointed out,[4] is the oldest of the concepts associated with legal responsibilities for children and 'the way it has developed helps to explain the origins of wardship, custody and the present status of parents'. It originated as a legal device to safeguard a family's property and ensure that wealth and estates passed from generation to generation within the same family. It subsequently became the means for maintaining the authority of a father over the upbringing of his children — by testamentary direction he could determine matters such as their religious upbringing from beyond the grave. It is an elastic concept and, unlike others associated with rights in respect of children, has also been applied across a disparate range of legislation including adoption, mental health and education.

II. *The Statutory Law of Guardianship*

Throughout the centuries, guardianship has evolved in a piece-meal fashion in response to the pressures of the day and, as has been observed,[5] 'no part of our ... law was more disjointed and incomplete'. It is an amalgam of common law, equity and statute law which, in this jurisdiction, last found statutory expression in the Guardianship of Infants Act 1886. It was thus never updated by the Guardianship of Infants Act 1925 nor by the Guardianship of Minors Act 1971. It was not consolidated as in England and Wales by the Guardianship of Infants Act 1973. Nor was it exposed to the challenge of 'custodianship' as introduced by the Children Act 1975. A legislative initiative to modernise this area of law was abandoned when the draft Guardianship (NI) Order 1985 was withdrawn. In Northern Ireland the statutory law of guardianship remained as stated by the 1886 Act until the introduction of the 1995 Order.

1. The Court Appointment of Guardians

The absence of any consolidating legislation meant that the 1886 Act remained the primary but not the sole source of statutory authority for the appointment of guardians

---

3 See, for example, *Re Agar-Ellis* [1883] 24 CH D 317.
4 F/n 2, para 1.28.
5 See Sir Frederick Pollock and Frederick William Maitland, *The History of English Law*, vol. 11, 2nd ed, Cambridge, 1898, reissued 1968, 443.

in Northern Ireland. Under section 5A of that Act (as amended by Article 15 of the Family Law Reform (NI) Order 1977), the father of an illegitimate child who obtained custody by virtue of a court order, or any person appointed under sections 3 or 6, would be a 'guardian' and would be recognised as such by the court for the purposes of adoption proceedings under Article 2(2) of the Adoption (NI) Order 1987. A guardian could also be appointed under section 12 of the Criminal Law Amendment Act 1885 or section 6 of the Tenures Abolition Act (Ireland) 1662.

By the mid 1990s, although some guardians were still being appointed by orders made under the 1886 Act,[6] the majority were appointed by the High Court in wardship proceedings.[7]

2. The Private Appointment of Guardians

Private guardianship appointments were only valid if made by will or deed. The guardianship appointment automatically took effect on the death of the appointing parent and the appointee was known as a 'testamentary guardian'. If there was a surviving parent, the guardian shared authority and responsibilities with that parent. Custody of the child vested in the guardian as it would in a natural parent although in practice, because the former was acting as a trustee, he or she would be subject to the expressed wishes of testator or court in respect of matters such as the child's religious or educational upbringing.

3. Reasons for Legislative Change

As the Law Commission pointed out,[8] 'the notion of parental guardianship confuses the separate legal concepts of parenthood and guardianship'. One reason for legislative change was to end the legal construction of guardianship as an incidence of parental rights, which carried with it the assumption that a parent, most usually the father, could exercise such rights through the appointment of a guardian after death.

In Northern Ireland, the presumption that the custody of legitimate children vested in their fathers to the exclusion of mothers was, by the end of the twentieth century, an offensive anachronism. His right to appoint a testamentary guardian in respect of their children, which not only did not extend to her but would take effect even if she survived him, was equally anomalous.

The 1995 Order has removed the concept of guardianship and reframed the related statutory law.

Guardianship: Jurisdiction and Parties

The essential characteristics of guardianship under the 1995 Order are as stated in the Guidance and Regulations:

---

6 In 1985, for example, a total of fourteen orders were made affecting twenty children.
7 In 1985 some 169 wardship orders were issued affecting 224 children.
8 F/n 2, para 3.2.

All guardians will be non-parents, apart from those exceptional cases in which an unmarried father is appointed guardian instead of being given parental responsibility under Article 7. A guardian must be an 'individual', i.e. a person rather than a Trust or voluntary organisation. Once the appointment takes effect, the guardian will have the same parental responsibility as a natural parent (Articles 159(4) and 160(4)).[9]

In particular a Trust cannot be appointed guardian.[10]

Guardianship versus Parenthood

Under Article 5(1) of the 1995 Order, parental responsibility is held to be vested equally and permanently in both spouses if they were married to each other at the time of the child's birth. All other persons may, at best, only attain the status of guardian. This definition of parenthood and the separation of the status of parent from that of guardian is of central importance to the 1995 Order.

It brings to an end the interpretation of 'guardian' as essentially derived from, and fundamentally a constituent part of, parenthood. As has been said:[11]

> ... the concepts of parenthood and guardianship are now legally distinct: parents are no longer regarded as guardians and apart from exceptional cases in which an unmarried father is appointed guardian instead of being given parental responsibility ... no guardians will be parents.

As guardianship proceedings are defined as family proceedings for the purposes of the 1995 Order, they are also governed by the paramountcy principle.

I. Jurisdiction

The authority to appoint a guardian lies with a parent and with the High Court or a county court; unlike the position in England and Wales, the magistrates' courts in Northern Ireland do not have jurisdiction to make guardianship orders. Because guardianship proceedings are family proceedings for the purposes of the 1995 Order, the court does have the power instead to:

(a) require the relevant Trust to carry out investigations as to the child's circumstances and submit a report to the court on any matters having a bearing on the child's welfare;
(b) make any Article 8 order; or
(c) make an order for financial assistance. However, under Article 159(2), the corollary is also true. The court may, in the course of any other family proceedings, determine that the paramountcy principle indicates the issue of a guardianship order, rather than the order sought, notwithstanding that no application has been made for it.

1. The Appointment of a Guardian by the Court

Under the Children (NI) Order 1995, Article 159:

---

9 The Children (NI) Order 1995, Regulations and Guidance, vol. 1, para 3.1.
10 See, for example, *Re SH (Care Order: Orphan)* [1995] 1 FLR 746.
11 See *FM Bromley's Family Law*, London, Butterworths, 8th ed., 1992, 395.

> (1) Where an application with respect to a child is made by any individual, the High Court or a county court may by order appoint that individual to be the child's guardian if—
>
>> (a) the child has no parent with parental responsibility for him; or
>> (b) a residence order has been made with respect to the child in favour of a parent or guardian of his who has died while the order was in force.

The court may make such an appointment either on application or of its own motion in any family proceedings. Under paragraph 27 of Schedule 8 of the 1995 Order, any existing guardianship appointments are continued for the purposes of Article 6 of the Order.

2. The Appointment of a Guardian by a Parent

Under the Children (NI) Order 1995, Article 160:

> (1) A parent who has parental responsibility for his child may appoint another individual to be the child's guardian in the event of his [the parent's] death.

This appointment may be made by someone already appointed as guardian to the child. The parent or guardian may appoint more than one person as guardian or may add a further appointment subsequently. The provision requires the appointment to be made by will or deed or by means of some other such properly attested legal document, i.e. no special document is needed.

3. The Date an Appointment Takes Effect

Unlike the position formerly, an appointment no longer automatically takes effect on the death of the appointer. Only if, at that time, there is no other parent with parental responsibility and no other person in favour of whom a residence order relating to the child has been made will the appointment take effect. There is now a presumption that such a parent or person will assume parental responsibility. In either of the alternative circumstances the appointment will be deferred until the death of the aforementioned parent or person.

II. The Effect of a Guardianship Appointment

A guardianship appointment creates a legal relationship between the child and the person appointed by the court or the person appointed by either or both parents. Under paragraph 4 of Articles 159 and 160, the effect of this relationship is to vest parental responsibility for the child in the guardian.

The Role of a Guardian

(a) The Responsibilities

Under Article 6 of the 1995 Order, the guardian assumes the role of the parent in relation to 'all the rights, duties, powers, responsibilities and authority which by law a parent has in relation to the child and his property'. The role of the guardian is to 'stand in the shoes of the parent' and bear the responsibilities of that parent towards the child in the manner of that parent. Like a parent, a guardian will be liable to criminal charges for any neglect, ill-treatment or failure to educate the child. Again, like a parent, if parental responsibility is shared between a number of guardians, or between a parent and a guardian, then each has an equal and independent right of action and right of access to the court to resolve disputes. In a sense, guardianship is unique in that it does not divest a parent of authority, but rather it is a trust relationship which empowers an appointed person to act for the parent.

(b) The Limitations

There are limits on the extent to which a guardian 'stands in the shoes of the parent'. A guardian is not expected to shoulder the full private family law responsibilities of a parent. The public sector provides a 'guardianship allowance' to defray maintenance expenses, and special provision is also made in the Child Support (NI) Order 1991 for guardians; nor is he permitted to benefit from his appointment by, for example, inheriting the property of the child in the event of the latter pre-deceasing him. A guardian has no rights of succession. The appointment will not have the effect of conferring on the child the citizenship of the guardian.

Among the attributes of parental authority which vest in a guardian, but not in the holder of a residence order, are the right to consent or withhold consent to adoption and the right to appoint a testamentary guardian.

Before the introduction of the 1995 Order it was common practice in both the High Court and county court to appoint a guardian to look after damages received by a child — often the entire estate possessed by that child. After the 1995 Order this power to appoint a guardian of the fortune or estate of any child has been retained by rules made under Article 159(5) and (6).

III. Termination, Revocation and Disclaimer of a Guardianship Appointment

In common with other trust relationships, but unlike parental relationships, a guardian can be removed from office.

1. Termination

Under Article 179(7) and (8), guardianship (in common with all other orders relating to children) will terminate on the subject's death or eighteenth birthday; whether it will do so on the marriage of the subject is uncertain. The same consequence will ensue in the event of the guardian dying before the child and without having appointed a successor. Under Article 163 of the 1995 Order, guardianship may be terminated by the court on the application of any person with parental responsibility for the child. This article also provides for termination by the subject (but only with leave of the court) and termination on the initiative of the court in any family proceedings if it should consider this to be desirable. Where the court orders a termination of one appointment, it may then appoint another guardian if this is necessary in light of the paramount interests of the child or it may make any Article 8 order.

Actual or threatened misconduct by a guardian has, in the past, provided sufficient reason for the court to terminate a guardianship.[12] A guardian's long abandonment of his rights has been held to be such that it would not be in the child's interests to permit a resumption of the guardianship.[13] It has also been held that a guardian's change of religion from Protestant to Catholic provided sufficient cause to terminate the guardianship of a Protestant child, even though no attempt was made to influence the child.[14]

2. Revocation

Under Article 161(1) of the 1995 Order, an appointment revokes any earlier guardianship appointment, including one made in an unrevoked will or codicil, 'unless it is clear that the purpose of the later appointment is to appoint an additional guardian'. Under paragraph 2 of the same Article, an appointment will be revoked by a written, signed and dated document, properly attested. It will also be revoked if the appointing parent/guardian intentionally destroys the operative document or authorises and supervises its destruction.

3. Disclaimer

Under Article 162(1) of the 1995 Order, the person concerned has a right to disclaim an appointment. This must be done 'by an instrument in writing signed by him and made within a reasonable time of his first knowing that the appointment has taken effect'. Provision is also made for the possible mandatory registration of such disclaimers in the future.

IV. The Parties

The parties in a guardianship are the appointer or testator, the appointee or applicant, and the child.

1. The Appointer

The circumstances in which a person or the court may make a guardianship appointment are as stated above in Article 159(1). The court may exercise its power of appointment in favour of an individual but not a body. It may make an appointment even though the child already has a guardian, is the subject of a residence order in favour of a non-parent or has an unmarried father, still alive, but without parental responsibility.

2. The Applicant

Under Article 159(1) of the 1995 Order, an application to be appointed guardian 'may be made by any individual', therefore not by a body. It is clear from this provision that

---

12 See, for example, in *Beaufort v Berty* (1721) 1 P Wms 703, 704–5 and *Re X* [1899] 1 Ch 526, 531 CA.
13 See *Andrews v Salt* (1873) 8 Ch App 622.
14 See *F v F* [1902] 1 Ch 688.

the individual making the application, and subsequently appearing before the court, must be the person intending to be the guardian. It is not necessary to obtain the leave of the court before making an application. Once these family proceedings are underway, it is, of course, open to the court to appoint someone other than the applicant as guardian.

3. The Child

The subject must be under the age of eighteen. The marital status of that person is not addressed by the 1995 Order. It is uncertain whether a court would be prepared to make a guardianship order in respect of a married minor.

The Law in Practice

The 1995 Order has given a new and more straightforward definition of guardianship. This, in turn, serves to make for a sharper distinction between it and other legally recognised care relationships.

Guardianship

1. The 1886 Act

It would be a mistake to regard the 1886 Act as merely an enduring anachronism impeding, or not helping, judicial efforts to achieve a just decision in custody and access cases. It has provided the judiciary with a statutory basis, not otherwise available, for the recognition of paternal rights. Indeed, as stated by the Official Solicitor:

> Speaking generally, it appears to me that the 1886 Act has most often been used to provide for access by putative fathers to their children.[15]

For example, the case of *In the Matter of B (A Minor)*,[16] concerned an appeal heard by Girvan J from a ruling made by the master dismissing the appellant's application for an access order. The parties were a young unmarried couple whose four-year-old daughter was the result of a brief and volatile relationship. Both parties had since formed other relationships. In considering whether the father had sufficient interest in and commitment to the child to warrant an access order, the court noted that he had never shown any interest during pregnancy, in fact had encouraged abortion; at times he had disclaimed paternity; he had had no contact with her since birth; and he had never made any financial contribution towards her upkeep. The court also noted that at all times the child had been competently cared for by her mother who was now implacably opposed to any paternal access.

It was the view of the court that the appellant's capacity to keep up and develop a relationship with his daughter was at best doubtful and that his

---

15 An observation made by CWG Redpath, Official Solicitor for Northern Ireland in correspondence with the author.
16 Recorded under the heading *In the Matter of B (An Infant) and In the Matter of the Guardianship of Infants Act 1886 As Amended by Article 15 Part IV of the Family Law Reform (NI) Order 1977*, unreported (1995).

> ... involvement with the child is always going to be relatively limited and shallow. It is difficult to imagine any circumstances in which he would be involved in taking any significant decisions in relation to upbringing . . . .

However, the court also acknowledged that

> ... the child has a right to know the truth and the court must recognise that to leave this wholly to the mother is to allow her to put an unwelcome duty on one side for as long as possible.

Accordingly, the court held that the father should be denied an access order but, instead, adjourned the application for two years with provision that in the interim

- the child should be made a party and the Official Solicitor invited to act for her in the capacity of guardian ad litem;
- the Official Solicitor should instruct a child psychiatrist to assess all parties and assist the mother to tell the child about the facts of her parentage;
- the psychiatrist should have discretion to advise the child of these facts in the event of the mother's refusal to co-operate;
- the psychiatrist should also advise the court as to the appropriateness or otherwise of paternal access; and
- both parents should seek counselling from Trust social workers as regards their respective responsibilities towards their daughter.

Under the aegis of the 1886 Act, as amended, the court was thus able to fully consider a prospective access right for an unmarried father in inauspicious circumstances and where no other statutory proceedings were available.

2. The 1995 Order

The principal overall effect of the 1995 Order on the law relating to guardianship has been to confine its role to that of providing the means to fill the gap left by a deceased parent. A guardian is now vested with parental responsibility which provides him or her with virtually the same authority and obligations in relation to the child as the parent would have had.

(a) The Married Father

One immediate effect of the 1995 Order was to repeal the whole of the 1886 Act. This extinguished a particularly archaic rule of law and the debates about its significance which have distracted several generations of lawyers. Article 5(3) of the 1995 Order abolished the rule of law, perpetuated by section 5 of the 1886 Act, that a father is the natural guardian of his legitimate child.

(b) The Unmarried Father

Under Article 160(1) of the 1995 Order, the mother of a non-marital child may appoint the father to be the child's guardian in the event of her pre-deceasing him. If, in that event, she has not appointed him guardian, he can then make an application, under

Article 159(1), for the court to do so. Alternatively, he may apply to the court under Article 7(1)(a) for an order granting him parental responsibility. However, where he is alive but has neither applied for parental responsibility nor made an agreement with the mother, then the court will be free to appoint someone else as the child's guardian.

(c) Parents with Parental Responsibility

The claim of a surviving spouse in relation to children of the marriage will, because he or she retains parental responsibility, have precedence over that of any guardian appointed by the deceased spouse. The appointment of such a guardian will be held in abeyance until the death of that surviving spouse. Only if the deceased had obtained an exclusive custody order or residence order will there then be a presumption favouring the claims of the guardian.

(d) Divorced Parents

Where the parents are divorced and the one with care and possession of the children wishes to ensure that in the event of his or her death the other does not remove them, then a guardianship appointment could be made in favour of a third party (perhaps the grandparents on that side of the family). This will have the effect of placing the guardians on the same legal footing as the surviving parent who, of course, retains parental responsibility. They will then be able to resist any threatened peremptory removal by that parent at least until the matter is brought before the court. This, in fact, was more or less what occurred in a case[17] where the Court of Appeal in England, overturning a decision favouring a surviving divorcee, ordered that the children remain with the appointed guardians pending an assessment by a social worker.

(e) Property

Under Article 6(2) of the 1995 Order, the meaning of 'parental responsibility' is extended to include 'the rights, powers and duties which a guardian of the child's estate [appointed, before the commencement of Part XV (guardians), to act generally] would have had in relation to the child and his property'. Paragraph 3 of the same Article includes 'in particular, the right of the guardian to receive or recover in his own name, for the benefit of the child, property of whatever description and wherever situated which the child is entitled to receive or recover'.

Under Article 159(5) of the 1995 Order, authority was provided to amend Order 80 of the Rules of the Supreme Court (NI) 1980 and allow the Official Solicitor or some other person to be appointed guardian of the fortune or estate of a child. Such an appointment must cease when the child reaches eighteen and the consent of any person with parental responsibility must be obtained where possible unless it is dispensable. The circumstances justifying such an appointment are:

 (a) where money is paid into court on behalf of the child in accordance with directions given under rule 10 (control of money recovered by person under disability);

---

17 See *Re H (A Minor)(Custody: Interim Care and Control)* [1991] 2 FLR 109.

(b) where a court or tribunal outside NI notifies the court that it has ordered or intends to order that money be paid to the child;
(c) where the child is absolutely entitled to the proceeds of a pension fund; or
(d) where such an appointment seems desirable to the court.[18]

Parental Responsibility

The Law

The law relating to parental responsibility is now to be found in the Children (NI) Order 1995.

1. Meaning

Under Article 6 of the 1995 Order:

> (1) In this Order 'parental responsibility' means all the rights, duties, powers, responsibilities and authority which by law a parent of a child has in relation to the child and his property.

The legislative intent is to replace 'rights' and 'duties' with 'responsibilities' and so indicate a philosophical change in the law from a proprietal to an accountable approach towards the *locus standi* of a parent in relation to the upbringing of his or her child. However, as is evident from the terminology relied upon in the above definition, to some degree the partialising of 'responsibilities' will continue to be in terms of specific 'rights' and 'duties' as identified and interpreted in previous case law. The philosophy has indeed changed, but this change is likely to be outlived by some of the terminology and case law which preceded it.

The responsibilities of a parent may be held by someone other than the parent of the child concerned. Parental responsibility, as explained in the Regulations,

> is therefore concerned with bringing the child up, caring for him and making decisions about him, but does not affect the relationship of parent and child for other purposes. Thus whether or not a parent has parental responsibility for a child does not affect any obligation towards the child, such as a statutory duty to maintain him (Article 6(4)(a)), nor does it affect succession rights (Article 6(4)(b)).[19]

Any person with parental responsibility may act independently of any other person or persons with parental responsibility. For further detail on the concept of parental responsibilities, see Chapter Eleven.

2. Acquisition

Under Article 5 of the 1995 Order:

---

18 The Rules of the Supreme Court (NI) (Amendment no. 4), 1966, Rule 2.
19 Children (NI) Order 1995, Guidance and Regulations, vol. 1, para 3.1.

(2) Where a child's father and mother were not married to each other at the time of his birth —
- (a) the mother shall have parental responsibility for the child;
- (b) the father shall not have parental responsibility for the child, unless he acquires it in accordance with the provisions of this Order.

Where parental responsibility is acquired by married parents, by virtue of their status as such, then under Schedule 9, paragraph 140, it cannot thereafter be lost except by the making of an adoption order or freeing order.

(a) By an Unmarried Mother

The automatic vesting, under Article 5(2)(a) of the 1995 Order, of full parental responsibility solely in an unmarried mother on the birth of her child, was a provision which generated considerable debate when first formulated in England and Wales.[20]

(b) By an Unmarried Father

The fact that an unmarried father does not acquire parental responsibility on the birth of his child was a matter which arose for consideration before the European Court of Human Rights in *McMichael v UK*.[21] The plaintiff then argued that such non-acquisition constituted discrimination against him contrary to Article 14 of the European Convention of Human Rights 1950 which provides that the enjoyment of rights under the Convention shall be 'secured without discrimination on any ground'. The Court held that the plaintiff had not been discriminated against because a 'meritorious' unmarried father had available to him a legal process whereby he could be awarded parental responsibility. In this jurisdiction, a similar plaintiff would have had recourse under Article 15 of the Family Law Reform (NI) Order 1978 but now has a choice of several different routes.

(i) By Marriage

An unmarried father may simply marry the mother of his child, which will have the effect of automatically and retrospectively legitimating that child, i.e. in law the child will thereafter be treated as though born of and after the marriage. Provision is made for this under Article 32(2)(a) of the Matrimonial and Family Proceedings (NI) Order 1989 (as amended by Article 155(3)(b) of the Children (NI) Order 1995 (see above)).

(ii) By Court Order

Under Article 7(1) of the 1995 Order,

(a) the court may, on the application of the father, order that he shall have parental responsibility for the child.[22]

---

20 See the Law Commission (1979) which initially proposed that unmarried parents should be equally vested with parental responsibility on birth of their child.
21 [1995] Fam Law, vol 25, 478. This was not the primary issue before the court (see further Chapter Thirteen).
22 See *Re H (A Minor)(Contact and Parental Responsibility)* [1993] 1 FCR 85.

The court may only respond to the father's application; it has no power to make that order under its own volition. The court may not withhold an order until the father demonstrates his parental commitment by paying maintenance for the children.[23] Parental responsibility should only be conferred by the court when a father has shown commitment and some attachment to the child and where the 'no order' presumption can be rebutted.

(iii) By Residence Order

If the father has applied for and been granted a residence order, then, under Article 12(1), the court must also issue a separate Article 7 order (which is not the case where the residence order is granted to a non-parent — see Article 12(2)).

In determining whether to grant an unmarried father's application for a parental responsibility order, the court is not obliged to apply the checklist criteria under Article 3(3), though the factors listed will have a relevance to the decision. It must, however, apply the paramountcy principle, the 'no order' presumption and the 'no delay' principle. The court should not allow its judgment to be influenced by considerations of enforceability,[24] nor should it be swayed by the understandable apprehensions of an unmarried mother. In *Re P (A Minor)*,[25] a case where the mother contested an application on the grounds that if granted it would licence the father to interfere in the day-to-day upbringing of their child, the court held that her anxieties were based on a misunderstanding of the effects of the order. If granted, the order would not enable a non-caring parent to intervene in the caring parent's normal day-to-day management of their child's affairs. Any threat of such action could be countered by an application for either an Article 8 order or for the discharge of the parental responsibility order. Despite mutual parental animosity, the court ruled that the father had demonstrated an attachment to his daughter and was therefore entitled to parental responsibility for her. The test to be applied is as stated by Balcombe LJ:[26]

> In considering whether to make an order under section 4 of the 1987 Act, the court will have to take into account a number of factors, of which the following will undoubtedly be material (although there may well be others, as the list is not intended to be exhaustive):
>
> (1) the degree of commitment which the father has shown towards the child;
> (2) the degree of attachment which exists between the father and the child;
> (3) the reasons of the father for applying for the order.

An unmarried father can apply under this provision to share parental responsibilities for his child with the mother even if she herself is married.

---

23 See *Re H (Parental Responsibility Order: Maintenance)* [1996] 1 FLR 867.
24 See *Re C (Minors)(Parental Rights)* [1992] 2 All ER 86 CA where the Court of Appeal ruled that the father had shown sufficient commitment to justify a parental responsibility order despite the fact that the implacable opposition of a step-father would make it impossible for the father to contact the child. Also, see *Re G (A Minor) (Parental Responsibility)* [1994] 2 FCR 1037.
25 See *Re P (A Minor)(Parental Responsibility Order)* [1994] 1 FLR 484.
26 See *Re H (Minors)(Illegitimate Children: Parental Rights)(no. 2)* [1991] 1 FLR 214, 218.

(iv) By Agreement

Under Article 7(1) of the 1995 Order:

> (b) the father and mother may by agreement ('a parental responsibility agreement') provide for the father to have parental responsibility for the child.

Such an agreement will have exactly the same legal standing as a court order.[27] It will have no effect at all, however, unless the parties strictly adhere to the procedure outlined by the Department of Finance and Personnel in regulations governed by Article 7(2). Once properly made, the agreement must then be registered.

An agreement made by an unmarried couple may be rescinded by the court on application by one of the parties.[28]

(v) By Being Appointed Guardian

Although Article 15 of the Family Law Reform (NI) Order 1977 has now been repealed by the Children (NI) Order 1995, an unmarried father may be appointed 'guardian' in accordance with Articles 159 or 160. He will then be automatically vested with parental responsibility and be included within the definition of 'guardian' for the purposes of Article 2 of the Adoption (NI) Order 1987.

(c) By Others

Parental responsibility will automatically be acquired by a successful applicant for a residence order. This, as stated above, will impart less extensive powers than those conferred on an unmarried father, as also where a Trust acquires parental responsibility subsumed within a care order. Under Article 52(6) of the 1995 Order, specific restrictions are then placed upon the powers thereby available to it. Where a Trust, or any person, acquires an emergency protection order, parental responsibility (within the limits set by Article 63(4)(c) and (5)) is also thereby acquired.

3. Temporarily Delegated to Others

Under Article 5 of the 1995 Order:

> (8) A person who has parental responsibility for a child may not surrender or transfer any part of that responsibility to another but may arrange for some or all of it to be met by one or more persons acting on his behalf.

This provision allows informal arrangements to be made whereby responsibility may be shared with another person. The person with care of the child but without full parental responsibility is required, under Article 6(5), to do 'what is reasonable in all the circumstances of the case for the purpose of safeguarding or promoting the child's

---

27 This procedure was introduced contrary to the advice of the Law Commission in *Illegitimacy* (Law Comm No. 118, 1982).
28 See *Re P (Terminating Parental Responsibility)* [1995] 1 FLR 1048 in which the application was brought by a mother to terminate a father's parental responsibility in respect of their child.

welfare'. This would include taking decisions such as to remove a child in need of protection to a safe place and to authorise treatment in the event of an accident.

The act of delegation will not affect the continuing liability of the delegator for ensuring the safety and well-being of the child concerned. As noted in the Regulations,

> ... whilst the Children's Order permits parents to delegate responsibility on a temporary basis, for example, to a baby-sitter, it will be the parent's duty to ensure that the arrangements made for temporary care of the child are satisfactory. Failure to do so may render a parent guilty of an offence (of cruelty, neglect etc) under section 20 of the Children and Young Persons Act (NI) 1968.[29]

4. Loss

Under Article 7 of the 1995 Order:

> (4) Subject to Article 12(4) (residence orders and parental responsibility), an order under paragraph (1)(a), or a parental responsibility agreement, may only be brought to an end by an order of the court made on the application —
>
> (a) of any person who has parental responsibility for the child; or
> (b) with leave of the court, of the child himself.

This prohibition against any termination of parental responsibility except by court order, is reinforced by Article 5(8) which prohibits a person vested with parental responsibility from surrendering or transferring it. Clearly, the applicant need not be a parent of the child. In considering an application for termination, the court is required to apply the paramountcy principle and the 'no order' presumption.

The Law Relating to Other Care Relationships after the Children (NI) Order 1995

In the context of an increased rate of family breakdown and disrupted parenting arrangements, the courts have developed a sympathetic approach towards the non-parental applicant who wishes to secure the care relationship that he/she has been providing for a child. As Simon LJ has said,[30]

> Volunteers to perform a social duty primarily imposed on others who are unwilling themselves to perform such duty acquire thereby a right to be considered; and once they actually enter upon the performance of responsibilities towards the child, acquire thereby a further right to be considered.

In England and Wales the introduction of custodianship orders under the Children Act 1975 gave the judiciary access to a statutory means of protecting and providing on-going security for established care relationships. In Northern Ireland, however, not

---

29 Children (NI) Order 1995, Guidance and Regulations, vol. 1, para 3.13.
30 See *O'Connor v A and B* [1971] 1 WLR 1227, 1236.

until Article 8 orders were introduced by the Children (NI) Order 1995 did such specific statutory powers become available to the judiciary.

Care by a Relative

Under Article 2 of the 1995 Order:

> ...'relative' in relation to a child, means a grandparent, brother, sister, uncle or aunt (whether of the full blood or half blood or by affinity), or step-parent.

Arguably, one reason for this definition is to mark a legislative distinction between the *locus standi* of those entitled to be heard by the court on a matter affecting the welfare of a child and those not so entitled, though there are no provisions explicitly to this effect. It also serves to place the respective rights of all those mentioned on an equal footing.

In general the courts now look more favourably on arrangements which keep responsibility for the care of a child within the family, albeit the extended family, rather than arrangements which require Trust involvement. In recent years, the legislators have strongly indicated that adoption proceedings are not always the most appropriate means of achieving this; this view has been endorsed more fully by the judiciary in England and Wales than in Northern Ireland. The 1995 Order has consolidated the legislative approach by statements of principle requiring the courts and Trusts to give preference to family-based care and through the Article 8 range of intermediate orders which enable the judiciary to give new security to carers and child. Together these are intended to provide private applicants and the Trusts with an incentive to view family-based care as a readily accessible and statutorily protected alternative to adoption proceedings.

1. Grandparents and Other Relatives

Under the Domestic Proceedings (NI) Order 1980, Article 16, grandparents were singled out as having a particular right to apply, in the course of proceedings, for an access order. This specific statutory recognition given to the special position of a grandparent in a child's network of psychologically significant relationships was furthered in this jurisdiction by the judiciary in wardship. However, it was repealed by the Children (NI) Order 1995. It thus seems somewhat unlikely that, as stated in the Guidance and Regulations, 'their position should, on the whole, be better than under the previous law'.[31]

Now, grandparents, in common with all others defined as 'relatives', are entitled to apply for residence and contact orders under the 1995 Order (see also Chapter 12). The court recognises that a residence order gives a grandparent *locus standi* in relation to the child enabling them to better manage matters such as arrangements for the child's health, schooling and daycare.[32] Where the child has lived with them for a minimum of three years, and they have the consent of anyone with parental responsibility, then

---

31 The Children (NI) Order 1995, Regulations and Guidance, vol. 1, para 5.34.
32 See *B v B (A Minor) (Residence Order)* [1992] 2 FLR 327.

under Article 10(5) of the 1995 Order the application may be made without leave of the court; leave must otherwise be obtained. A grandparent with a residence order is entitled to apply to their local Trust for a financial allowance. Under Schedule 1, para 17 of the 1995 Order a Trust has a discretionary power to make such payments in support of placements authorised by a residence order; except where the placement is with a parent or step-parent.

In private family law proceedings, an application by a grandparent for a residence order will stand a greater chance of success if supported by a natural parent and, conversely, will be more likely to fail if contested by such a parent. Where the evidence demonstrates that contact would be in the child's best interests, even where the child is in care, then the court will need to be dissuaded from making an order.[33] Where there is parental hostility to such contact, in the context of a well-established relationship between child and grandparent, then the court must consider whether compelling the parent would place the child at risk of significant harm;[34] if not, then applying the paramountcy principle will determine the matter.[35]

On the other hand, if the contest lies between a grandparent and a non-relative, the presumption in favour of family care will work to the advantage of the former. However, where the grandparent is competing with another non-parental relative, the age difference between applicant and child may be crucial, and may weigh against the grandparent.

As the 'win-or-lose' effect of matrimonial proceedings often resulted in the severing of a child's relationship with one set of grandparents, the courts have been particularly sympathetic to the latter's claims for rights of custody or access. This has not, however, extended to the point of recognising a presumption[36] favouring a contact order where a grandparent has been granted leave to apply (see further Chapter 7). However, the courts in England have been prepared to find that a grandparent with biological links to a child has, *ipso facto*, a stronger claim than a step-parent to an order protecting their relationship with that child.[37] The courts have also shown great wariness in their approach to grandparent applications which may merely amount to a fallback strategy for a parent; the former must be prepared to show how their position is different from and better than that of the latter.[38]

2. Step-Parents

The law relating to the legal position of step-parents has been ambivalent. A step-parent has long been denied recognition as coming within the legal definition of parent.[39] The fact that they have lacked legal rights in respect of their spouses children, despite

---

33 See *Re F and R (A Minor)(Section 8 Order: Grandparent's Application)* [1995] 1 FLR 524 and *Re M (Care: Contact: Grandmother's Application for Leave)* [1995] 2 FLR 86.
34 See *Re D (A Minor)(Contact: Mother's Hostility)* [1993] 2 FLR 1 and *Re W (A Minor) (Contact)* [1994] 2 FLR 441.
35 See *Re S (Contact: Grandparents)* [1996] 1 FLR 158.
36 See *Re A (Section 8 Order: Grandparent Application)* [1995] 2 FLR 153.
37 See dictum of Butler-Sloss in *Re H (A Minor)(Contact)* [1994] 2 FLR 776.
38 See *Re M (Minors)(Sexual Abuse: Evidence)* [1993] 1 FLR 822.
39 See *Re N* [1974] 12 All ER 126.

voluntarily undertaking maintenance and other responsibilities, has often been the subject of judicial concern. However, legislative unease about the use of adoption by a step-parent to acquire with a spouse joint exclusive custodial rights to the latter's children of a previous marriage has been apparent in the adoption legislation of both jurisdictions in recent years (see Chapter Six). The Article 8 orders were created with the circumstances of step-parents very much in mind.

Residence orders are seen as offering an enduring degree of status, protection and security commensurate to the care responsibilities of a step-parent and not necessarily foreclosing a child's relationships with the 'other side of the family'. Where a child is 'a child of the family', as defined by Article 2(2)(b) of the 1995 Order, then a step-parent is entitled under Article 10(5), without leave, to apply for a residence or contact order and, with leave, to apply for a specific issue or prohibited steps order. The effects of such orders are the same as for any carer (see Chapter Twelve).

CHAPTER SIX

Adoption

Introduction

Legislation establishing the State of Northern Ireland and establishing adoption in that State entered the statute books in the same decade.[1] Thereafter, dependency on Westminster has always been a particular feature of the law of adoption in Northern Ireland.

In the sixty-year period since its legislative introduction, there have been vast changes in the social context which defines the legal role of adoption. The traditional inviolability of the nuclear marital family has succumbed to pressures from within (modern methods of birth control, ease of divorce etc.) and from without (increasing intrusion from state organised services). Such changes have combined to alter the reasons why children become available for adoption in Northern Ireland, have greatly reduced the proportion of third party adoptions and have prompted a steady growth in inter-country adoptions.

That adoption now serves a range of very different social functions from those which it was initially designed to meet can be seen from a brief examination of statistical trends. Some 17,800 children have been adopted in Northern Ireland since the Adoption of Children Act (NI) 1929 first introduced a legal means of making this possible. From a peak of 554 orders in 1970, the annual total of adoptions declined rapidly to a level of 155 in 1995. That stark statistic reveals the most distinctive feature of modern adoption — simply that it is ceasing to function in its traditional legal role[2] of 'providing homes for children who need them' with third-party applicants.

The nature of the change in adopters and adopted is evident from a closer look at the statistical data. In relation to adopters, for example, in 1974, of the 332 orders granted, 211 were to third-party applicants, 89 to parents and 26 to relatives; in 1984, of the 253 orders the distribution was 128, 110 and 15, respectively, and by 1994, the 119 applications received were distributed 49, 66 and 4 respectively. Then, in relation to the children being adopted: of the 270/2 orders made in the period 1988/9, only six or seven were in respect of children from overseas; by 1992 of the 161 adoption applications received, twelve were in respect of such children (ten were from Romania, one from India and one from Brazil). Moreover, practitioner experience is that orders are now being made in respect of children who are much more likely to be legitimate, abused, older and/or suffering from a disability than was the case formerly. The inescapable logic of these trends is that adoption in Northern Ireland — as a consensual

---

1 The Government of Ireland Act 1920 and the Adoption of Children Act (NI) 1929.
2 See the *Houghton Committee Report of the Departmental Committee on the Adoption of Children* (1972) where the view is expressed that 'The child is the focal point in adoption; providing homes for children who need them is its primary purpose'.

process for securing homes for indigenous healthy babies with unrelated applicants — is dying out.

This chapter examines and explains the law of adoption as governed by the Adoption (NI) Order 1987 and amended by Schedule 9, paragraphs 138–167, of the Children (NI) Order 1995. In doing so it outlines the adoption process and the role and functions of various agencies and officials within it.

The Jurisdiction, Principles, Parties and Officials of the Adoption Process

I. The Jurisdiction

Under the Adoption (NI) Order 1987, jurisdiction is restricted to the High Court and the county courts. Unlike the position in England and Wales, the magistrates' courts in Northern Ireland do not have jurisdiction to hear adoption applications. In the less typical case where the child is not in Northern Ireland and the application is for either an adoption order or for an order freeing the child, then the 'authorised court' is the High Court. The latter will also be the appropriate venue when the case concerns both adoption and wardship applications. The issue of the jurisdictional dividing line between the High Court and the county courts has been considered by the Court of Appeal for England and Wales. It then determined[3] that the county court was more appropriate than the High Court as the issues, which concerned two Chilean children, were not particularly complex. The High Court may direct that proceedings initiated there be transferred to an 'authorised' county court.

Under the Children (NI) Order 1995, however, adoption falls within the definition of family proceedings. It is therefore amenable to vertical and horizontal transfer at judicial discretion in the same way as any other form of such proceedings. The range of alternative public and private orders available under the 1995 Order have equal relevance to adoption applications. Indeed, in contrast to the position under the 1967 Act when applications were usually made to the High Court and could result only in success or failure, they now may also result in the issue of an adoption order subject to contact conditions or a quite different order (such as a residence order), and this may be issued by a court other than the one to which application was made.

There is a right of appeal to the Court of Appeal and from there to the House of Lords from an order of the county court making, or refusing to make, an order for the adoption or for the freeing of a child. If it is to be compatible with the child's welfare interests, such a right should be exercised as soon as reasonably possible, preferably within six weeks.

II. The Principles

Under Article 9 of the 1987 Order:

---

3 See *In Re N and L (Minors)(Adoption: Transfer of Actions)* [1987] 2 All ER 732.

(1) In deciding on any course of action in relation to the adoption of a child, a court or adoption agency shall regard the welfare of the child as the most important consideration and shall—

    (a) have regard to all circumstances, full consideration being given to—

        (i) the need to be satisfied that adoption, or adoption by a particular person or persons, will be in the best interests of the child; and

        (ii) the need to safeguard and promote the welfare of the child throughout his childhood; and

        (iii) the importance of providing the child with a stable and harmonious home; and

    (b) so far as is practicable, first ascertain the wishes and feelings of the child regarding the decision and give due consideration to them, having regard to his age and understanding.

This statement of the welfare principle is of central importance to the 1987 Order. Acknowledgment of its significance is made in Regulation 10(3) of the Adoption Agencies Regulations (NI) 1989 by the instruction that an adoption panel should 'have regard to the duties imposed upon the adoption agency by Article 9' when making its recommendations.

1. Definition of the Principle

A number of the component parts of this statement of the welfare principle have been the subject of judicial consideration. The opening directive that it is binding on both the court and an adoption agency 'in deciding on any course of action in relation to the adoption of a child' in effect means that it governs the entire public dimension of the adoption process. However, it is unlikely that the substitution of 'course of action' for 'any decision' (the latter being the wording used in the equivalent provision of the 1976 Act) will impact the well-established precedent[4] to the effect that 'any decision' does not apply to the issue of dispensing with agreement. The welfare principle will continue to be excluded from determining the issue of dispensing with parental agreement; though remaining relevant to it.

2. Effect of the Children (NI) Order 1995 on the Principle

There is, clearly, something of a philosophical conflict between the exclusiveness of an adoption order, with its presumption of severing all ties between a child and his or her family of origin and the sharing of parental responsibility ethos underpinning the orders introduced under the Children (NI) Order 1995. However, for now the conflict exists largely on a philosophical level and adoption law remains relatively intact.[5]

---

4 See the ruling of the House of Lords in *Re M (A Minor)* [1980] CLY 1801 endorsing the judicial approach in *Re P (An Infant)(Adoption: Parental Consent)* [1977] 1 All ER 182, CA.

5 In due course the findings of the *Review of Adoption Law: Report to Ministers of an Interdepartmental Working Group* (DoH, 1992) and the subsequent White Paper *Adoption: the Future* (Cm 2288) should result in changes to adoption law which will address the problem of harmonising the role of the welfare principle in child care and adoption.

The fact that under the Children (NI) Order 1995 adoption proceedings are family proceedings means, for example, that the 'no-order' presumption applies, though this may be open to a slightly different interpretation than the Article 9 direction that 'the order if made be for the welfare of the child concerned'. The 'no-delay' rule similarly applies.

3. Future Developments

The draft Adoption Bill issued in 1996, following the White Paper of 1993, promises to introduce the paramountcy principle to adoption law in England and Wales, to be followed, presumably, by its eventual incorporation into adoption law in this jurisdiction. As the implications of this development will not be felt for some time in the law being examined at present, it is not proposed to do more than note the prospect of radical change to one of the more central principles in the law of adoption. In addition, the recent ministerial announcement that the government intends to introduce new regulations to govern agency criteria for the selection and approval of adopters and placement of children, is likely to be followed in due course by ammendments to the same effect to the 1989 Adoption Agencies Regulations.

III. The Parties

A natural parent or parents, their child and a person or couple wishing to undertake full and permanent responsibility for the care of that child are the primary participants in any adoption process.

1. The Child

To be eligible for adoption a child must first be born,[6] be more than nineteen weeks old[7] but less than eighteen years of age[8] and, if related to the applicant, have been in the care of that person for at least thirteen consecutive weeks prior to the order being made. In third party applications the child must be at least twelve months old and have been with the applicants for at least the twelve month period immediately preceding the order.[9] The 1987 Order imposes the traditional requirement that the child is not and never has been married.[10] Further, the fact that the child has previously been adopted is not a bar to his or her subsequent adoption.[11]

To be available for adoption a child must be resident in Northern Ireland, though neither domicile nor citizenship is necessary.[12] A number of children have been adopted

---

6   It is not possible to adopt a foetus. However, as was apparent in *Re Adoption Application (Adoption: Payment)* [1987] 2 FLR 291, it is possible to contract in respect of a foetus to be carried to full-term by a surrogate mother on behalf of a sperm donor in order that she may eventually be in a position to commence adoption proceedings.
7   Article 13(1) of the 1987 Order.
8   This condition is incorporated into Article 2(2) of the 1987 Order as a consequence of the Age of Majority Act (NI) 1969.
9   Article 13(2) of the 1987 Order.
10 See Article 12(5) of the 1987 Order.
11 See Article 12(7) of the 1987 Order.
12 Subject to the limitations imposed by the Adoption (Hague Convention) Act (NI) 1969.

having first acquired residential status by being brought into the jurisdiction for the purposes of adoption. Traditionally, such children have originated in the Republic of Ireland, though more recently there has been a steady trickle of children entering the adoption process from much further afield.

To be adopted it must be shown that this would be in the particular child's best interests.[13] Thus it must be demonstrated that the child's circumstances satisfy not only the above eligibility and availability criteria but also welfare criteria. The comparative material advantages[14] offered by the prospective adopters would not satisfy welfare criteria, neither would reasons such as legitimation,[15] immigration[16] or simply the wish to change a child's name.[17] Though welfare is insufficient in itself, the granting of the proposed adoption order must, in the words of Davies LJ,[18] demonstrably further the welfare interests of a child by offering '... material and financial prospects, education, general surroundings, happiness, stability of home and the like'.

2. The Natural Parents: The Mother

For the purposes of the statutory law of adoption 'natural parents' are defined as the father and mother jointly of a legitimate child and the mother of an illegitimate child.[19]

The role of unmarried mothers in the adoption process has, paradoxically, declined in recent years, despite the fact that they have greatly increased in number during the same period. The annual fall in the proportion of non-marital children entering the adoption process has, for some years, been a characteristic of adoption in Northern Ireland. This has been due to factors such as the reduction in the number of unwanted pregnancies as a result of improved and more accessible methods of birth control, the fact that improved benefits now enable more single mothers to retain care responsibility for their children and the fading of the social stigma traditionally associated with unmarried parenthood.

3. The Natural Parents: The Father

The role statutorily assigned to a putative father in the adoption process has recently become marginally more significant. Such a person was not recognised as a parent of an illegitimate child within the terms of the 1987 Order any more than he was under the terms of the 1967 Act.[20] However, this must now be read subject to Article 155 of

---

13 Article 9 of the 1987 Order.
14 See *Re D (no 2)* [1959] 1 QB 229.
15 See *CD Petitioners* [1963] SLT (Sh Ct) 7.
16 See *In re A (An Infant)* [1963] 1 WLR 34. Also see *In re H (A Minor)(Adoption: Non-Patrial)* [1982] Fam Law 121 and *Re H (Adoption: Non-Patrial)* [1996] 2 FLR 187 where adoption orders were granted in respect of immigrants despite contrary advice from the Secretary of State and Home Office respectively.
17 See, for example, *In re D (Minors)* [1973] Fam 209.
18 See *In re P* [1977] Fam 25 CA.
19 Article 2(2) of the 1987 Order.
20 The basis of his non-standing in such proceedings was established by the decision in *Re M* [1955] 2 QB 479, and subsequently endorsed in judgments such as that of Sheldon J in *Re TD (A Minor)* (1985) FD.

the 1995 Order which prevents any distinction in law being made between parents who are married to each other and parents who are not. Under Article 2(2) of the 1987 Order, a putative father was recognised as a 'guardian' if he had acquired custody under section 5 of the Guardianship of Infants Act 1886.[21] Now, he will have *locus standi* if he has acquired a parental responsibility order or made an agreement to that effect with the mother under Article 7 of the 1995 Order. However, if such a father fails to obtain parental responsibility, his position is no better after the 1995 Order than it was before.[22]

In this jurisdiction, as a matter of practice, a putative father was usually automatically treated as a party to adoption proceedings. More recently, however, he has had to make an *ex parte* application to show why he should be joined as a party.

4. The Adopters

The eligibility of adopters is determined by their ability to satisfy a set of statutory criteria. Their suitability is largely determined by criteria set by the adoption agencies. The bearing of such criteria on the standing of the applicants differs according to whether they are first- or third-party applicants.

A third-party application (i.e. from those who are 'strangers' in relation to the child) cannot be from more than one person unless they are married to each other.[23] In the case of an application from one spouse, there must be evidence that the consent of the other is available. The effect of Article 14(1) of the 1987 Order (as amended by the 1995 Order) is that lack of consent by one partner would not necessarily pose a barrier to an application from the other in the case of an unmarried but cohabiting couple.[24] Indeed, the courts in England have made such orders, sometimes coupling the adoption order with a residence order made in favour of the adopter and the co-habitee.[25] The same Article imposes a minimum age requirement of twenty-one years (except where the husband or wife is the natural parent of the child, in which case the parent must be at least eighteen) and stipulates that at least one of the applicants be domiciled in either the United Kingdom, Isle of Man or the Channel Isles. Other basic statutory criteria include proof that the applicants had care and possession of the child for not less than the thirteen-week period immediately preceding the hearing[26] (an amendment introduced by the Children (NI) Order 1995 provides that '... in determining with what person, or where, a child has his home, any absence of the child at a hospital or at a school providing accommodation for him shall be disregarded'), no evidence of unauthorised payments having been made[27] and the consent of every parent or guardian of the child

---

21 The 1886 Act has been repealed in its entirety by the 1995 Order.
22 See the Court of Appeal ruling in *Re C (Adoption: Parties)* [1995] 2 FLR 483.
23 However, adoption by unmarried couples would seem to contravene Article 6(1) of the European Adoption Convention.
24 Also, note *Re WM (Adoption: Non-Patrial)* [1997] 1 FLR 132 where an adoption order was granted despite the fact that the applicants had separated.
25 See, for example, *Re AB (Adoption: Shared Residence Order)* [1996] 1 FLR 27.
26 Article 13(1) of the 1987 Order.
27 Article 59 of the 1987 Order. However, as in *Re WM* (op. cit.), the fact that illegal payments have been made does not pose a bar to the making of an adoption order.

has either been obtained or is dispensable.[28] The suitability criteria set by the agencies will include reference to religion, maximum age, quality of relationships and lifestyle.

Article 15(1) removes the prohibition under the 1967 Act against applications, except in special circumstances, from single males in respect of female children, whether or not related.

A first-party application (i.e. from a parent or relative of the child) is now the most common form of adoption in Northern Ireland.[29] The consent of an adopting natural mother, herself a minor, will be valid for the purposes of the 1987 Order.[30]

IV. The Officials and Administration of the Adoption Process

The roles and functions of different officials and bodies are governed by the 1987 Order, the accompanying Adoption Agencies Regulations (NI) 1989, the Rules of the Supreme Court (NI) (Amendment no. 6) 1989 and the County Court (Amendment no. 3) Rules (NI) 1989.

1. Bodies

The role of the Department of Health and Social Services (DHSS) is prescribed by Part II of the 1987 Order. This requires the DHSS to administer a system of registration, regulation and inspection in respect of adoption agencies and to ensure that they provide a localised and accessible adoption service throughout the province. It is also responsible for monitoring the programme and practice of each individual registered adoption agency in accordance with the requirements of the Adoption Agencies Regulations.

The role of the Health and Social Services Boards (or 'Trusts') as outlined in the 1987 Order rests on four planks: their contribution to forming and maintaining a local adoption service; linking adoption to their other child-care services; managing their own work as registered adoption agencies; and carrying out certain supervisory duties in relation to placements. The adoption service requirement, as stated in Article 3(1), entails each Board/Trust providing within its area, or ensuring that voluntary agencies provide, services (including, for example, residential, assessment and counselling services) appropriate to the needs of all parties to an adoption. The 1987 Order also places supervisory duties on the Board/Trusts in respect of 'protected' children in addition to the duties they bear as adoption agencies in relation to establishing Adoption Panels and facilitating guardians ad litem.

A registered adoption society, now known as an adoption agency, has been defined as a '. . . body of persons whose functions consist of, or include the making of, arrangements for the adoption of children'.[31] The role and functions of this body are outlined in the 1987 Order and are further detailed in the Adoption Agencies

---

28 Article 16 of the 1987 Order.
29 This is so despite the fact that Articles 14(3) and 15(4) required the court to dismiss such applications where it considered that they would be better dealt with under Article 45 of the Matrimonial Causes (NI) Order 1978. Both Articles were repealed by the 1995 Order.
30 See *Re K (An Infant)* [1953] 1 QB 117, [1952] 2 All ER 877 CA.
31 JF Josling & A Levy, *Adoption of Children:* 10th ed., London: Longman 1985, 23.

Regulations (NI) 1989 which require that such bodies be registered by the DHSS. At present, in addition to the four Boards/Trusts, only two voluntary bodies are so registered: the Catholic Family Care Society and the Church of Ireland Adoption Society for Northern Ireland. The Children (NI) Order 1995 extends the definition of adoption agency to include '. . . for the purposes of Articles 11 and 12 adoption agencies in England and Wales and Scotland.' The voluntary agencies must apply for re-registration every three years, at which point the onus is on each to show that it is making, and will continue to make, an effective contribution to local adoption services. The 1987 Order requires that, to be registered, an agency must possess an adoption programme, a number of suitably qualified staff and a sound fiscal and management policy. It also requires, under Article 4(2)(e), that an agency should have available to it '. . . competent medical, legal and social work advice'. The Regulations are a complex body of rules concerned with regulating professional standards of practice in relation to the assessment of adopters, promoting the welfare of a child, managing of placements and overseeing post-adoption work.

The role of an Adoption Panel is addressed by Regulation 5 of the Adoption Agencies Regulations (NI) 1989. This requires each agency to set up at least one such Panel to which must be referred any question as to whether adoption is in the best interests of a particular child, whether a prospective adopter should be approved as an adoptive parent and whether the home of a particular approved prospective adopter would provide a suitable placement for a particular child. This Panel is not a decision-making body. Its function is restricted to making recommendations to the agency. However, the latter is prevented by the Regulations from taking decisions in the areas listed above without first inviting recommendations from the Panel. According to Regulation 5(1) an Adoption Panel composed of a maximum of ten members must include a social worker, a person holding an executive management position in the agency, a medical adviser, an independent member and a chairman who need not be a member of the agency but must be experienced in adoption work.

2. The Officials

A guardian ad litem (GAL)[32] must, under Article 66 of the 1987 Order, be appointed in relation to any application for an adoption order, for one seeking to obtain or revoke a freeing order or for an application for adoption by a person domiciled outside Northern Ireland. Under Article 66A, inserted by the Children (NI) Order 1995, this official must be selected from a panel of persons approved to act as GALs. The GAL Panel is managed by the Northern Ireland Guardian ad Litem Agency, established by the DHSS to service the courts with independent professional social work advice in adoption cases under the Adoption (NI) Order 1987 (and also in specified proceedings under the Children (NI) Order 1995). Once appointed, the GAL is required to carry out an exhaustive investigation into all the circumstances of the proposed adoption, interview all applicants and respondents including, where feasible, the child and ensure

---

32 The details of this official's duties are outlined in Rules 5 and 17 of the County Court (Amendment no. 3) Rules (NI) 1989 and Rules 6 and 18 of the Rules of the Supreme Court (NI) (Amendment no. 6) 1989.

that any factor having a bearing on the welfare of the child is brought to the attention of the court. In so doing it will be necessary to verify the findings of the other bodies and officials involved. The GAL will also be expected to locate and interview any man reputed to be the father of a non-marital child, unless he or she is satisfied that good reason exists to believe that this would not be in the child's best interests. It has been held that this official has no right to a private hearing[33] and that his or her report is confidential to the court.[34] However, it has also been held that where a decision against the applicants has been based on information supplied to the judge but not to the applicants, then this could be grounds for an appeal.[35]

The question of whether or not a natural parent has sufficient grounds to oppose an adoption is a matter for judicial consideration and not one on which a GAL should offer an opinion.

The responsibilities of the Registrar General are in effect tied to a post-adoption role. This official is obliged, by Article 50 of the 1987 Order, to maintain an Adopted Children Register, keep an index of this in the General Register Office and ensure that records are kept which provide a link between an entry in the Register of Births marked 'adopted' and the corresponding entry in the Adopted Children Register. This allows for the collection of information sufficient to identify the child, the adopters and the date and place in respect of every adoption order issued. Article 54 governs the role of the Registrar General in disclosure proceedings and requires him to provide on request a copy of a birth certificate to those entitled.

The Authority to Make an Adoption Placement

One objective of the 1987 Order was to end the possibility (as graphically expressed by the Houghton Committee) of a parent, or someone acting on a parent's behalf, giving a child to a casual acquaintance such as someone met in a launderette.[36] This objective is addressed specifically by Article 11 but is also reinforced by other provisions. Whether an adoption placement is made with or without parental agreement and whether made by an adoption agency or by or with the authority of a parent, there are certain standard preliminary requirements.

I. Placements made with Parental Agreement

Placements to which there is parental agreement may be made either by a parent or with parental authority, under Article 13(2), by authority of the High Court or by an adoption agency.

1. Placements made with Parental Authority

Under Article 11 of the 1987 Order:

---

33 See *Re B (A Minor)(Adoption by Parent)* [1975] 2 All ER 449.
34 See *Re P A (An Infant)* [1959] 1 WLR 1530.
35 See *Re J (Adoption)(Confidential Report: Disclosure)* (1982) 3 FLR 183.
36 See *Houghton Committee Report*, f/n 2, para 81.

(1) A person other than an adoption agency shall not make arrangements for the adoption of a child, or place a child for adoption, unless:

   (a) he is a parent of the child and the proposed adopter, or one of the proposed adopters is a relative of the child; or
   (b) he is acting in pursuance of an order of the High Court.

This provision prohibits the practice of either a parent making a 'direct' adoption placement of his or her child with a 'stranger' or authorising a third party to do so. However, it leaves open the possibility of a parent either placing or making an arrangement to place a child with a parent or relative of that child. In that respect it differs from the equivalent prohibition in section 11 of the Adoption Act 1976 which prohibits all such placements. Thus, in this jurisdiction, a direct parental placement will remain particularly vulnerable in the event of a retraction of parental consent. For, in the words of Fitz-Gibbon LJ:

> ... the surrender of a child to an adopted parent, as an act of prudence or of necessity, under the pressure of present inability to maintain it, being an act done in the interests of the child, cannot be regarded as abandonment or desertion, or even as unmindfulness of parental duty ... [37]

Where a mother with learning difficulties authorises a non-relative to approach an adoption agency on her behalf in order to make placement arrangements in respect of her child, that intermediary will not be guilty of infringing Article 11 nor will a care order be necessary to legitimise the placement.[38] A placement which has been made in breach of Article 11 is an illegal adoption placement and cannot be retrospectively legalised.[39] However, this in itself will not prevent the court from making an adoption order. Only the High Court should have jurisdiction to consider private applications where a breach of Article 11 has occurred.

This provision, in conjunction with Part I of the Children and Young Persons Act (NI) 1968, has governed the placement arrangements for children of foreign nationality adopted within this jurisdiction.[40] As yet, there is no specific statutory authority to regulate inter-country adoption arrangements. They are processed in accordance with Home Office guidelines as set out in the leaflet RON 117. The Hague Convention on inter-country adoption, which was signed by 75 nations in 1993, will provide the legal framework for regulating such placements when the government introduces the necessary legislation. In the meantime adoption applications in relation to children of foreign nationality continue, in this jurisdiction, to be dealt with in wardship.

2. Placements made under Article 13(2)

Under Article 13(2) of the 1987 Order:

---

37 See *In re O'Hara* [1900] 2 IR 233 at p. 224.
38 See *Re W (Arrangements to Place for Adoption)* [1995] 1 FLR 163.
39 See *Re G (Adoption: Illegal Placement)* [1995] 1 FLR 403. Also, see *Re WM (Adoption: Non-patrial)* [1997] 1 FLR 13.
40 Such a placement does not occur, as in *Re A (Adoption: Placement)* [1988] 1 WLR 229, until there has been physical contact between child and prospective adopters.

(2) Where paragraph (1) does not apply, an adoption order shall not be made unless the child is at least 12 months old and at all times during the preceding 13 weeks had his home with the applicants or one of them.

This provision does not provide authority for an adoption placement to be made. However, because it anticipates the possibility of an adoption placement arising or being made other than by or within the child's family or by an adoption agency, it may occasionally be found to be relevant in situations where long-term care has been provided for a child placed with parental consent. It is subject to the standard requirement in Article 22 that all non-agency placements be notified to the appropriate Board/Trust three months before the hearing. It carries within it the implication that circumstances of parental agreement, absence or at least no contest will prevail at the hearing.

3. Placements made with the Authority of the High Court

Under Article 11(1)(b) of the 1987 Order, a person will be 'acting in pursuance of an order of the High Court' when making an adoption placement of a ward as directed by the judiciary exercising their powers under the wardship jurisdiction.

Wardship has always been primarily a private family law jurisdiction. In recent years the controversy over its role in public family law has tended to divert attention from the fact that the High Court continues to grant wardship orders in respect of children who are not the subject of statutory child-care orders. Subsequently, applications may be made to the High Court for permission to place some of these children for adoption. Where any such application is contested, the matter is referred to the freeing procedures. Where an application to place for adoption is uncontested, authority to proceed comes from the wardship jurisdiction. Some nine or ten adoption placements of wards occur in this way every year.

4. Placements Made by an Adoption Agency: The Freeing Process

Under Article 17 of the 1987 Order, as amended by the Children (NI) Order 1995:

> (1) ... where, on the joint application of the parents or guardian of the child and an adoption agency, an authorised court is satisfied in the case of each parent or guardian that he freely, and with full understanding of what is involved, agrees—
> (a) generally, and
> (b) either unconditionally or subject only to a condition with respect to the religious persuasion in which the child is to be brought up, to the making of an adoption order, the court shall make an order declaring the child free for adoption.

This provision reflects the primary legislative intent behind the introduction of 'freeing' to the adoption process: to provide a means whereby a natural mother may take an early decision to voluntarily relinquish her child for adoption and be spared any further legal involvement in that process. It also allows the mother to be constructively involved, if that is thought appropriate, in the transferral phase until the child is settled. However, for certain reasons this order has not quite fulfilled expectations.

(a) Unconditional Consent

The stipulation in Article 17(1), prior to its above amendment, was that each parent or guardian give an unconditional consent. This meant that they thereby waived their rights under Article 16(1)(b)(i)(ab) to attach a 'condition with respect to the religious persuasion in which the child is to be brought up'. They also had to forego any possibility of the court exercising its powers under Article 12(6) whereby 'an adoption order may contain such terms and conditions as the court thinks fit'. So, for example, there could be no possibility of the court attaching a condition to the adoption order imposing access or contact conditions in favour of the consenting parent. This presented a considerable disincentive to some parents, but it has now been corrected. Case law may now follow the precedent established in England[41] where a court granted a freeing order subject to a contact condition in favour of the mother permitting a 1^1/$_2$ hour monthly visit.

(b) The Putative Father

It is clear from Article 17(6) of the 1987 Order that where a natural mother is applying jointly with an adoption agency for a freeing order in respect of her non-marital child, then, before such an order can be granted, the court must first satisfy itself that 'all reasonable steps have been taken' to identify the putative father, serve notice on him of the hearing and give him the opportunity to intercede in the proceedings. If he has been identified and located, under the amendment to this Article introduced by the Children (NI) Order 1995:

> (6) Before making an adoption order or an order under paragraph (1) in the case of a child whose father does not have parental responsibility for him, the court shall satisfy itself in relation to any person claiming to be the father that—
>
>   (a) he has no intention of applying for—
>
>   (i) an order under Article 7(1) of the Children (NI) Order 1995, or
>
>   (ii) a residence order under Article 10 of that Order, or
>
>   (b) if he did make any such application, it would be likely to be refused.

In this jurisdiction, where the mother is before the court as an applicant and the court is satisfied that the identity of the father is a matter which is plainly within her knowledge, disclosure will be insisted upon.[42]

(c) The Unmarried Mother

The availability of freeing orders is largely due to the legislative assumption that there will always be a number of natural mothers who will approach an adoption agency with the resolute and settled conviction that her child should be adopted. There are

---

41 See *Re A (A Minor) (Adoption: Contact Order)* [1993] 2 FLR 645. Also, see *Re C (Contact Jurisdiction)* [1995] 1 FLR 777.

42 This was the effect of the ruling made by Higgins J in *In re B (A Minor)*, unreported (14 November 1990).

two problems with this assumption. First, the size of such a group is probably a good deal smaller than may have been anticipated by the legislators. This arises because the proportion of single mothers choosing to allow the adoption of their children has been steadily declining in this jurisdiction as elsewhere in the United Kingdom as welfare benefits and other support facilities increase and the associated social stigma fades. Also, within such a group of single mothers the proportion who are completely free to act without the potential legal involvement of the children's fathers is declining as the courts, in line with decisions taken by the European Court of Human Rights in recent years, have begun to give more recognition to the interests of unmarried fathers. Second, the Board/Trusts have always viewed the prospect of acting on the early decision of an unmarried mother to relinquish her child for adoption as carrying a very high level of risk to all parties. Indeed, there have been cases in Northern Ireland where mothers have changed their minds while waiting for the court to hear their applications for freeing orders. Faced with a risk factor which is much the same whether the process is for a freeing order or for a full adoption order and given the time it can take to obtain either, it is perhaps understandable that a Board/Trust might be hesitant to commit itself to a two-staged rather than a one-staged process.

(d) Cumbersome Process

The legislative intent that freeing orders should provide a natural mother with the means whereby she can legally disengage early and cleanly from the adoption process has been subverted by the machinery for giving effect to that process. First, there is the fact that, for whatever reason, the freeing procedure actually takes much longer than was intended or foreseen. It can take as long to get a freeing order as it would to obtain, directly, a full adoption order. Second, despite the intention to give the natural mother an opportunity to make an early clean legal break from the adoption process, in practice she is also being involved at the final stage in the application for an adoption order. As a matter of routine she is then served with a copy of the Notice of Hearing. Finally, for reasons associated with a general sense of uncertainty about the freeing procedures among the professionals involved, for some years all applications were made only to the High Court when they could have been more expeditiously processed through the county courts.

(e) Declaration of No Further Involvement

Under Article 17(5) of the 1987 Order, each parent must be given the opportunity to make '... a declaration that he prefers not to be involved in future questions concerning the adoption of the child'. As this is a matter of choice, the natural parent may elect not to make this declaration, and in that situation she has on-going rights of notification regarding her child's placement until an adoption order is made. In the event of no declaration being made and the child remaining unadopted one year later, then Article 20, as amended by the Children (NI) Order 1995, gives the parent the right to apply for a revocation of the freeing order. A revocation has the effect of extinguishing the parental responsibility vested in the agency, returning that responsibility to the parents and reviving any previous parental responsibility agreement, order or appointment of guardian. In *Re G (Adoption: Freeing Order)*[43] the Court of Appeal in England ruled that when revoking a freeing order it was not possible to make an interim care order. The freeing order is either revoked, in which case the parent is fully vested with all responsibility, or not revoked, in which case the child is left 'in a sort of freed for adoption limbo potentially for the rest of his life'. Such risks are a disincentive for an agency looking to the freeing process as a means of effecting an early clean break.

(f) No Revocation and No Adoption Order

Under Article 32 of the 1987 Order, in the event of an adoption placement never being made or of an adoption application failing, all parental responsibilities vested by the freeing order in the agency remained so vested for the duration of the subject's childhood, unless displaced by an eventual adoption order. However, the Children (NI) Order 1995 has replaced Article 32 with a provision which allows protection for the child in existing care arrangements, i.e. the Board/Trust will now seldom resume full parental responsibilities. For an adoption agency the risk of such complications can act as a real deterrent to becoming involved as an applicant for a freeing order.

These are the main reasons why the freeing order with parental agreement has failed to fulfil legislative expectations. Together they explain why it is that adoption agencies, particularly the Board/Trusts, approach freeing orders with some hesitancy. The equal failure of the freeing order without parental agreement, however, has been due more to judicial hesitancy. The draft Adoption Bill 1996, which embodies provisions previously addressed in the consultation paper *Adoption — A Service for Children*, promises to remove freeing orders and replace them with placement orders.

II. Placements Made without Parental Agreement but with Authority from the Wardship Jurisdiction

In Northern Ireland the wardship jurisdiction has, over the past twenty years, played an important role in forming the principles and developing the procedures which have enabled many children to enter the adoption process who may not otherwise have done so (see Chapter Seven). Until the introduction of the Children (NI) Order 1995, many adoption orders continued to be made in respect of children who were wards of court.

1. Adoption of a Ward without Parental Consent prior to the Introduction of the 1987 Order

Under the Adoption (NI) Act 1967, there was no statutory power available to permit the adoption placement of a child in the care of a Board/Trust without the prior consent of that child's parents. Whereas the parents had their rights abridged by the issue of an FPO or PRO under the Children and Young Persons Act (NI) 1968 in favour of a Board/Trust, they retained the power to veto any initiative by the latter to place their child for adoption. Given that a three-month placement formed a minimum eligibility requirement for every adoption applicant, the Board/Trusts were faced with a significant problem in relation to the increasing numbers of children committed to long-term care.

---

43 [1996] 2 FLR 398.

This statutory gap was bridged by the willingness of the High Court judiciary to make available the authority of wardship to supplement the Trusts' statutory powers. The latter availed of it by either opting to seek a wardship order instead of a statutory order, from the outset, in respect of a child whose circumstances were unusual and for whom it wished to keep open the adoption option or by seeking a wardship order in respect of a child already subject to a statutory care order for whom it considered adoption to be appropriate.

Applications by the Board/Trusts to the wardship jurisdiction for authority to make non-consensual adoption placements were heard by a judiciary who were concerned that a distinction be drawn between the grounds justifying that agency's removal of a child in pursuance of its care and protection duties and those which might permit an adoption placement. Although the High Court was prepared to allow the paramountcy principle of wardship to open the door to the Trusts, it was not prepared to allow that principle to determine whether or not adoption should be facilitated. Instead, the court imported and applied the case-law principles emerging as a consequence of freeing applications in England and Wales under the Adoption Act 1976.

The guiding principle was stated by Hutton J:[44]

> If the only test to be applied was the welfare of the child, and the court did not have to consider whether it was entitled to dispense with the consent of the natural parents, it is very probable that I would be satisfied that these children should be placed for adoption and subsequently adopted . . . but that is not the test and I desire to emphasise this for the guidance of the Board in this and other cases. If the only test was the welfare of the child and the wishes of the natural parents could be disregarded, then there would be some cases where a child, taken into care for a short time because of the illness of his parents or some other family emergency, could be taken away permanently from humble and poor parents of low intelligence, and perhaps with a criminal record, and placed with adoptive parents in much better economic circumstances who could provide the child with greater material care and intellectual stimulation, a more stable background and a brighter future.

The decision then taken was to reject an application from the NHSSB for permission to make non-consensual adoption placements of wards because the learned judge did not consider that the NHSSB had proved parental 'unreasonableness' to the degree necessary to sustain an eventual adoption application. Instead, he instructed the NHSSB to commence a phased return of the children to parental care and the introduction of a rehabilitation programme.

The effect of this ruling was to make it clear that in cases where a Trust was seeking the authority of the court to make non-consensual adoption placements, the onus on that body was to prove not merely that the proposed placement would be in the welfare interests of the child but that the parents, through their fault or default in relation to that child, had provided the grounds upon which an adoption applicant could subsequently rely to permanently disqualify the parents from resuming care responsibility.

---

44 See the leading case of *In re EB and Others (Minors)* [1985] 5 NIJB 1. Note that the draft Adoption Bill 1996 will in fact make the welfare test the determinant of both placement and of the making of an adoption order.

The grounds justifying the exercise of its care and protection powers would be insufficient to justify a Trust making a non-consensual adoption placement. Subsequent case law illustrates the difficulties sometimes faced by these bodies as they sought to meet this double test.[45]

2. Non-Consensual Adoption Placements: The 'Reasonableness' Test before the Introduction of Freeing

The primary statutory ground relied upon for making freeing orders under the 1976 Act was that the parent was acting unreasonably in withholding his or her consent and therefore there was a need to dispense with that consent. This became the accepted test for determining whether, in similar circumstances, the powers of wardship should be exercised to authorise adoption placements in this jurisdiction.

The above ruling by Hutton J (as he then was), which basically rested on a finding that it was the judgment of the social worker rather than that of the parent which was 'unreasonable', was later endorsed by his converse decision in a similar case. He explained the court's dilemma in the following terms:

> The reason why the Board (EHSSB) has brought the present application that the two children should be confirmed as wards of court is because the Board considers that the mother will never be able to give proper care, protection and guidance to them, and therefore the Board seeks the leave of the Judge of the Family Division of the High Court to place the two children for adoption[,] it being apparent that the mother will not give her consent to adoption.
>
> There is a clear line of authority that the High Court should not exercise its jurisdiction in wardship where an order has been made by a magistrate's court which adequately protects the child and that the High Court should not intervene where any further question arising in relation to the safety or welfare of the child can properly be dealt with by the magistrates' court.

He then acknowledged that the magistrates' court did not (unlike its counterpart in England) have available to it the authority necessary to give effect to the EHSSB's reasonable plans to safeguard and promote the children's welfare. He decided[46] that even though the children were subject only to statutory care orders, the EHSSB should place them for adoption, notwithstanding parental opposition, because it seemed probable that the grounds of section 5(1) of the 1967 Act could be subsequently satisfied.

The same approach is discernible in the ruling[47] of Higgins J who, having adjourned the hearing for three months to test whether parental care was viable, decided, on the

---

45 It might be added that there was a perverse logic to the second strand of this test as the courts in Northern Ireland, unlike those of England and Wales, had available to them the sweeping discretionary powers of section 5(1)(e) of the 1967 Act which could always have been deployed in favour of adoption applicants. That the judiciary chose instead to follow English case-law principles demonstrates the strength of their conviction that the rights of a natural parent should not be nullified by a well-intentioned Board decision that the welfare of a child would be best assured through the making of an adoption placement.
46 See *Re M McC and DH (Minors)* [1986] 5 NIJB 1.
47 See *Re W (A Ward)*, unreported (1988).

evidence of the foster-parents and social workers involved, that the parent could not cope and her consent was therefore being withheld unreasonably and could be dispensed with. Again[48] at an initial wardship hearing to determine whether the children who were the subject of FPOs should be placed by the EHSSB for adoption, Higgins J found that the intellectually impaired mother ' . . . has shown an utter lack of insight into the needs and problems of her children and into her own deficiencies as a mother'. He therefore ruled that in the circumstances she was withholding her consent unreasonably and this could be dispensed with.

These cases are representative of the many others which came before the High Court in wardship proceedings before the introduction of freeing orders in 1989. They all reveal the same source of tension between social services social workers and judiciary. The former most usually present the court with evidence of a child's welfare having been impaired by the parental fault or default which occasioned the child's removal, the risk which would accompany any attempted return and the predicted welfare advantages of making the planned adoption placement. The judiciary counter with a request for evidence demonstrating current and comprehensive parental failure, in relation to the child concerned, sufficient to enable a prospective adopter to subsequently disqualify the parents from eligibility to resume care responsibility and thereby satisfy the 'unreasonableness' test. Producing such evidence often entailed attempting a rehabilitation programme to assess current parenting competence. Where this had not already been initiated by the social workers it would usually then be required by the judiciary.

III. Placements Made without Parental Agreement but with Authority from the Statutory Jurisdiction: The Freeing Process

In this jurisdiction there has not been much enthusiasm for freeing orders.[49]

Freeing without parental consent occurs when a Trust as sole applicant makes what is almost always a contested application in respect of a child in its care, either on a voluntary or a statutory basis. In such cases the child is seldom a baby but is usually under five years of age. Both forms are subject to the requirement in Article 12 of the 1987 Order that the applicant must satisfy the court that the order, if granted, would be compatible with the child's welfare interests.

IV. Non-Consensual Adoption Agency Placements: The Availability of Freeing Orders

Under Article 18 of the 1987 Order:

---

48 See *In the matter of KH and EH (Minors)* [1989] 7 NIJB 1.
49 In the first fifteen months of the existence of the 1987 Order only one freeing order was granted. Thereafter the annual number of applications speaks for itself: in 1991, twelve applications were made; in 1992, fifteen; ten were made in 1993; ten in 1994; and seven in 1995. Of that total of fifty-five accepted applications, by the end of 1995 only forty-nine had resulted in the issue of freeing orders, four had been withdrawn and the remainder were still pending.

(1) Where, on an application by an adoption agency, an authorised court is satisfied in the case of each parent or guardian of a child that his agreement to the making of an adoption order should be dispensed with on a ground specified in Article 16(2)[,] the court shall make an order declaring the child free for adoption.

(2) No application shall be made under paragraph (1) unless—
   (a) the child is in the care of the adoption agency; and
   (b) the child is already placed for adoption or the court is satisfied that it is likely that the child will be placed for adoption.

For an adoption agency there are now fewer advantages in making an Article 18 application for a freeing order than existed prior to the introduction of the 1995 Order. First, the drawbacks to the use of the freeing procedure with parental agreement (as listed at 4(a)–(f) above) are equally troublesome when an agency is acting without that agreement. The circumstances as illustrated by *Re G* do, of course, present serious difficulties for a Trust which will invariably have had a care order in effect in respect of the child prior to commencing freeing proceedings. It is clear from the judgment that parental revocation of a freeing order will not operate to revive a care order: the claims of public law are thereby extinguished and the welfare of the child becomes wholly a matter of private parental responsibility. The Trust is prohibited from both applying itself for a revocation of the freeing order and from seeking to attach any conditions to a parental application. Second, whereas it was possible to make such an application in respect of a child in care on a voluntary basis,[50] this is now prohibited. The repeal of Article 16(5) and (6) of the 1987 Order by the 1995 Order, in conjunction with Article 2(1) of the latter, has had the effect of ending any possibility of the freeing process being used in respect of any child who is not the subject of a statutory care order. However, if made before placement, a freeing application still affords the opportunity to rely on fairly immediate evidence as to parental inadequacy or abuse.

Before making application, however, an agency must be sure that it can meet certain basic requirements. A preliminary issue for the court will be whether the order if granted would satisfy the 'best interests' test of Article 9. There is also a clear expectation that the child concerned is either already placed with prospective adopters or is about to be so placed.

V. Placements Made without Parental Agreement: The Judicial Determinants after the Introduction of the Freeing Process

Under Article 16 of the 1987 Order, parental agreement to making an adoption placement is dispensable only if certain grounds can be satisfied, that is,

(2) . . . that the parent or guardian—
   (a) cannot be found or is incapable of giving agreement;
   (b) is withholding his consent unreasonably;

---

50 Research in England and Wales has shown that a high percentage of freeing orders (approx. 33 per cent in one study) was made in relation to children in care with parental consent.

(c) has persistently failed without reasonable cause to discharge the parental duties in relation to the child;
(d) has abandoned or neglected the child;
(e) has persistently ill-treated the child;
(f) has seriously ill-treated the child (subject to paragraph . . .)

As the final two grounds are explicitly related to child care, the last being new to adoption law, it may be assumed that the legislative intent was to provide a limited degree of synchronisation between the use of statutory authority to remove parental rights under child-care legislation and its use to dispense with parental consent for adoption, i.e. that to a limited degree the same evidence of parental fault/default could satisfy both sets of grounds. However, as in England and Wales under the same provisions, there is strong evidence of a judicial reluctance to utilise these grounds. In both jurisdictions the dispensing of parental consent, after the introduction of freeing, continues to rest largely on well-established precepts.

1. Cannot Be Found or Is Incapable of Giving Agreement

A person 'cannot be found' only if evidence is produced which demonstrates that all reasonable steps have been taken to ascertain his or her whereabouts. Such evidence might take the form of producing a recorded delivery letter, posted to the last-known address and marked 'not known', statements from all known relatives and advertisements placed in local papers.[51] A person is 'incapable of giving agreement' if it is impossible to communicate with him or her, perhaps due to mental illness[52] or political exile.[53] This ground is seldom relied upon.

2. Is Withholding His Consent Unreasonably

For some years prior to the availability of freeing orders in this jurisdiction, parental 'unreasonableness' has been the customary basis for Trust applications for judicial authority to make non-consensual adoption placements. Under Article 16(2)(b) of the

---

51 In *Re F (R) (An Infant)* [1970] 1 QB 385 a mother's appeal against the granting of an order some five months earlier and the ruling that her consent be dispensed with was upheld because she was able to prove that the applicants knew her father's address and of his contact with her yet had not bothered to approach him. See also *Re T (A Minor)* [1995] Supreme Court Practice, News 4, a step-adoption, where the adopting mother had claimed not to know the whereabouts of her former husband (the child's father). An adoption order had been made and six years later the father applied for leave to appeal out of time against the order, on the grounds that it had been made without his agreement or knowledge. The Court of Appeal required the relevant county court to re-examine the mother's claim, indicating that if it didn't stand up the father's application could well be granted.
52 However, see *Re L (A Minor)(Adoption: Parental Agreement)* [1987] 1 FLR 400. There is an argument for holding that this provision does not apply to mental illness for the simple reason that the parent concerned could find his or her agreement being dispensed with on the basis of inability to understand the proceedings.
53 See *Re R (Adoption)* [1966] 3 All ER 613; also *Re An Adoption Application* [1992] 1 FLR 341.

1987 Order, this continues to be the most frequently used ground. The test is whether a reasonable person in the parent's position, being mindful of the child's best interests, would be justified in withholding agreement. But, as MacDermott LJ once observed:

> ... the mere fact that an adoption will be for the welfare of the child does not itself necessarily show that a parent's refusal to consent to that adoption is unreasonable.[54]

The main problem in relying on this ground in circumstances where the child is either in a placement with prospective adopters or has been placed in foster care or residential care pending an adoption placement is providing recent evidence of bad parenting to prove to the court that the parents are being unreasonable in withholding consent. The onus is on the applying agency to demonstrate not a history or a prospect of bad parenting, but that this is a current and on-going state of affairs. One way for the agency to do so is for it to provide the court with evidence of very recent efforts to rehabilitate the child concerned with the parents. In this jurisdiction, where appropriate, the courts have placed a firm onus on the applying agency to show that they have made every effort to return the child to safe parental care. As the following cases illustrate, the courts have treated with great caution Board/Trust applications for judicial authority to make non-consensual adoption placements of children in care.

In the case of *In re G and S (Minors)*,[55] which was one of the first to be heard in relation to freeing orders, Higgins J emphasised that the judicial approach adopted in the wardship jurisdiction would be maintained. Declaring that 'I do not propose to depart from the practice as laid down by Hutton J (as he then was) in *In Re EB and Others* [1985] 5 NIJB 1', he then went on to say 'it is only necessary that the application under Article 18 by each Board is one which might reasonably succeed'.

Later, in the leading case of *EHSSB v Warnock*,[56] Higgins J ruled on an application for a freeing order brought by the EHSSB in respect of one of three siblings, two of whom were wards of court. Following three consecutive assessment and training programmes carried out with the parents during 1987–88, the learned judge had no difficulty in finding that 'Mr and Mrs W even with help from Social Services staff are not capable of providing a satisfactory level of care for either A–M or G. I think it is very unlikely that Mr and Mrs W would ever be capable of providing satisfactory care for either child. ... That being so, I am satisfied that it is in the interests of the welfare of both A–M and G that they should be adopted'. Despite such an unequivocal finding, the judge, in an unusually long judgment extensively reviewing English precedents, was unable to accede to the EHSSB's request in relation to the child G. His reasoning seemed to rest on uncertainty as to whether his view of what constituted unreasonableness in the present case was necessarily the only view capable of being supported by the facts. However, his decision was promptly reversed by the Court of Appeal in a judgment which commented that he had been too searching in the proofs he required to substantiate the grounds of unreasonableness.

---

54   See *Re W (An Infant)* [1971] AC 682 at p. 706.
55   Unreported (1991).
56   [1993] NIJB 4, 52–3.

However, evidence of an agency's rehabilitative efforts is not always a prerequisite for commencing proceedings on this ground. The parent's conduct may speak for itself. For example, in *Re T (A Minor)*,[57] Higgins J, after an exhaustive nine-day hearing, granted the EHSSB a freeing order in respect of a three-year-old girl with cystic fibrosis in the care of foster parents (who were the prospective adopters) for the preceding two years. The respondents were the child's unmarried natural parents. The father did not contest the proceedings, nor attend or play any part in them; he stated that he wanted nothing to do with the child. The mother had a very poor record of visiting the child, who had been very ill in hospital for the thirteen months following her birth. She had also failed to demonstrate any realistic understanding of her daughter's condition or the necessary motivation and commitment to care adequately for her. Given that the mother had not shown much interest, let alone taken advantage of opportunities to care for her child while the latter was in hospital, Higgins J considered that he could make the order sought without first requiring the EHSSB to provide a rehabilitative programme.

In the matter of *PM (Freeing Application)*,[58] Higgins J again rested his decision on well-established principles when he found that the marital parents of a child, aged three-and-a-half years, were being unreasonable in withholding their consent to an application by the EHSSB for a freeing order in respect of that child. He reiterated the point frequently made in such cases that 'the welfare of the child was not *per se* the test'. In this case the determining fact was that the mother 'could not be trusted to provide care for the child' by appreciating that her child needed protection from the attentions of her elderly husband who had been convicted of child-abuse offences.

In these and other freeing cases the judiciary in this jurisdiction consistently rely on the principles laid down by their colleagues in England and Wales.[59] In interpreting and applying such principles the judiciary rely on the same indicators of reasonableness as are applied when hearing an application for an adoption order. The observation of Balcombe LJ[60] is also instructive — the mother 'may have been wrong, she may have been mistaken, but she was not unreasonable'.

3. Has Persistently Failed without Reasonable Cause to Discharge the Parental Duties in Relation to the Child

The failure to discharge parental duties must be of such long standing duration that the child's welfare would be relatively unimpaired if the relationship were to be discontinued.[61] This ground is seldom relied upon.

---

57 Unreported (1993).
58 Unreported (1993) at 12.
59 See *Re W (An Infant)* [1971] 2 All ER 49, HL *O'Connor v A and B* [1971] 2 All ER 1230, [1971] 1 WLR 1227, and also *Re D (An Infant)(Adoption: Parent's Consent)* [1977] 1 All ER 145, HL.
60 See *Re E (A Minor)(Adoption)* [1989] 1 FLR 126, 133.
61 See *Re D (Minors)(Adoption by Parent)* [1973] 3 All ER 1001.

4. Has Abandoned or Neglected the Child

In this context the terms 'abandoned' and 'neglected' are confined to extreme instances of parental fault. The ground is seldom used.

5. Has Persistently Ill-Treated the Child

It is the recurring nature over a period of time, rather than the severity, of the ill-treatment which is important. Again this ground is of marginal significance.

6. Has Seriously Ill-Treated the Child and the Child's Rehabilitation within the Household of the Parent or Guardian Is Unlikely

Although one incident of ill-treatment would be sufficient, provided it caused grievous harm, it must be accompanied by little prospect of the child being restored to family life in the home of the parent or guardian. Parental fault may not in itself be sufficient reason for not attempting rehabilitation. This is the one new ground added by the 1987 Order to those previously available under the 1967 Act. It is seldom used.

The Placement

The statutory requirements governing the period from the making of the placement to the hearing differ according to whether the placement was made privately or by an adoption agency.

I. Private Placements

Private placements may take the form of a direct placement made within the jurisdiction by a natural parent to a relative or outside the jurisdiction by a natural parent to a 'stranger'. Most often it simply refers to the practice whereby a parent, who has retained care responsibility for a child, applies jointly with a new spouse to adopt that child.

Made Directly

If the placement is to be made between a natural parent and a relative, then, whether or not it is intended for adoption purposes, there is no requirement to serve advance notice and obtain the consent of a Board/Trust. When the placement is for the purpose of adoption, it is important to ensure that the recipient falls within the definition of relative. However, most usually a 'family' adoption results from one natural parent simply retaining care and possession after a breakdown in joint parenting arrangements and the child is never actually 'placed' before an adoption application is made. This is quite similar to the circumstances typical of 'foreign' adoptions where, because the placement occurs outside the jurisdiction, it, as in a family adoption, only becomes susceptible to professional scrutiny at a time chosen by the prospective adopters.

II. Agency Placements

Agency placements may be made by an adoption agency or they may arise from placements made by a Board/Trust in pursuance of its statutory child-care duties.

1. Made by an Adoption Agency

An agency placement may be made by an adoption agency acting after, if not on, the recommendation of its adoption panel. It must be preceded by the offer of an adoption service to all parties and a counselling service to the natural parents. As a further preliminary requirement, Regulation 12 of the Adoption Agencies Regulations (NI) 1989 calls for notification to be served on the prospective adopters (giving them information on the child and procedural details and advising them as to any benefit entitlement, allowances, access arrangements or religious upbringing condition), to which they must make a formal response, stating whether they want the placement to proceed. The child must also be informed (where feasible he or she should be advised as to the facts of the planned placement) as well as the natural parents (but only in circumstances where a freeing order has been made) and other parties (such as the relevant doctor and health visitor). In all placements made by at adoption agency, as a minimum, all matters covered by Regulation 12(2)(a–d) of the 1989 Regulations must be completed.

2. Made by a Trust

A placement by a Board/Trust may occur in respect of a child, subject to a care order or a wardship order, who has been placed with foster parents by a Trust. At the initiative of the foster parents this may now be transformed into an adoption placement either within three years if supported by the Board/Trust (following amendments introduced by the 1995 Order) or after that period, even if opposed by that body (see further Chapter Sixteen, page 367).

In this context, it is relevant to note a particularly important change introduced by the Children (NI) Order 1995. Trust discretion to decide unilaterally the possibility of parental access to a child in care, and thereafter the frequency of any such access, has been terminated. Previously, the absence of a right to parental access together with the ruling in *Liverpool* (see page 299) left the Trusts free to facilitate the transformation of care placements into possible adoption placements by terminating a child's links with his or her family of origin. Since the 1995 Order the decision as to whether parents have contact with their children in care, and the frequency of any such contact, is to be made by the court (when making the care order or later on application) and not a Board/Trust.

III. Placement Supervision

Under Article 13 of the 1987 Order, the distinction between agency adoption placements and all other forms of placement continues to have significance until the applications are made. The main professional responsibilities are those associated with supervision duties which fall into two categories. First, there are those duties placed on an agency in respect of placements it has made or, in the case of a Trust, those placements for which it has acquired responsibility. Second, there are those duties placed on a Trust in respect of placements brought to its attention under the notification requirement of Article 22 of the 1987 Order. In addition there is the added difference between a placement made by an adoption agency in respect of a child voluntarily relinquished by a mother for that purpose and one where the child is the subject of a care order. In the former case, the parental rights of access to the child and to request the return of the child are exercisable at her discretion. In the latter case, that discretion is exercisable by the relevant Trust.

1. Supervision of Adoption Agency Placements

Under Regulation 12(2)(f) of the 1989 Regulations, once the placement has been made the agency is required to notify the natural parents accordingly, including the father of a non-marital child, if this is thought to be in the interests of the child. Regulation 12(2)(g) requires the first agency visit to be made within a week of placement. Thereafter, the agency must visit as often as is necessary to ensure the child's wellbeing, must offer such advice and assistance as may be necessary and must maintain written records of visits as evidential material to show how the child is adjusting.

Under Article 13 of the 1987 Order:

> (1) ... an adoption order shall not be made unless the child is at least 19 weeks old and at all times during the preceding 13 weeks had his home with the applicants or one of them.

This is to allow sufficient time for the supervising social worker to make an assessment of how the child is settling with the family and to generally form a view about the long-term viability of the placement.

2. Supervision of Non-Agency Placements

Under Article 22 of the 1987 Order, as amended by the Children (NI) Order 1995:

> (1) An adoption order shall not be made in respect of a child who was not placed with the applicant by an adoption agency unless the applicant has, at least three months before the date of the order, served notice on the Board within whose area he has his home of his intention to apply for the adoption order.
>
> (1A) An application for such an adoption order shall not be made unless the person wishing to make the application has, within the period of two years preceding the making of the application, given notice as mentioned in paragraph (1).
>
> (2) On receipt of such a notice the Board shall investigate the matter and submit to the court a report of its investigation and shall assist the court in any manner the court may direct.

This notification requirement applies to all family placements and to all other non-agency placements.

Article 11 of the 1987 order then requires a Trust to assess the suitability of the applicant, all matters relating to the child's welfare and the circumstances whereby the child was placed. If the notification is in respect of a child known to be in the care of another Trust, then that body must be informed within seven days. The notification also serves to trigger the provisions of Article 33, as amended by the Children (NI) Order 1995, which make the subject of any such placement a 'protected child' until

- the grant or refusal of an adoption order
- withdrawal of the application
- the end of a two-year period from the time of serving notice if no application is lodged
- the making of a residence order, a care order or a supervision order
- the appointment of a guardian
- the child reaches the age of 18
- the child marries

A 'protected child' is one whose well-being is entrusted, by Article 34, to a Board/Trust social worker. That person is authorised to inspect the premises, is required to visit and offer advice and may be empowered under Article 35 to remove the child to a place of safety (even on a Sunday[62]) or admit such a child into care.

Children placed by an adoption agency are not regarded as 'protected'. The onus to supervise and ensure the well-being of such children falls on the agency making the placement.

The Application

The lodging of an application marks a turning point in the adoption process. Decision-making then ceases to be largely a discretionary matter governed by the Adoption Agencies Regulations (NI) 1989. Instead it becomes a matter formally governed by the Rules of the Supreme Court (NI) (Amendment no. 6) 1989 and by the County Court (Amendment no. 3) Rules (NI) 1989 and structured by specific time constraints.

Lodging an Application

Rules 14 of the County Court Rules and 15 of the Supreme Court Rules govern the lodging of an application for an adoption order which is by way of petition in the former and originating summons in the latter, accompanied in either case by the appropriate fee. If confidentiality is important, an applicant may request a serial number at this stage. The parties to an adoption application are the applicants, certain bodies and persons and a number of possible participants at the discretion of the court. The respondents include each parent or guardian, the child in the High Court and any Trust or adoption agency which has borne placement responsibilities.

1. Applicant Duties

Detailed medical reports must be submitted in respect of each third-party applicant and child. In 'placement' cases the agency concerned will already be in possession of

---

62 See section 7 of The Sunday Observance Act (Ireland) 1695, disapplied by Article 35(2) of the 1987 Order.

such evidence, but all other third-party applicants will have to make the necessary arrangements and traditionally they have been left to bear their own costs. First-party applicants are not required to provide evidence of good health as the court takes the common-sense view that in any event they will continue to care for the children.

Every applicant must complete a minimum period of care and possession immediately prior to the hearing. This is thirteen weeks in the case of agency placements, twelve months if placed by parents, twelve months in the case of Trust placements with foster-parents who apply with the approval of that body and five years if such approval is withheld. All applicants must also, in accordance with Regulation 15(1)(e) of the 1989 Regulations, facilitate the visits of the GAL appointed to complete a report for submission to the court on all matters affecting the welfare of the child.

2. Agency/Trust Duties

A social worker from either the adoption agency responsible for making the placement or from the local Board/Trust in respect of family placements will regularly visit the home of the applicants. In either case the primary duties are to ensure the protection and retention of the child in the placement and to provide a report to the court. A social worker will also continue supportive visits to the natural parents.

Protecting the child in the placement is a high priority for an agency or Trust during this stage. Under Article 28 of the 1987 Order, it is prohibited to remove the subject of an application for an adoption order in two sets of circumstances: (1) where the placement occurred with parental consent or (2) where consent is withheld, the child is in the care of an adoption agency and that agency is applying for a freeing order. In addition, the 'protected children' procedures prohibit any unauthorised removal of a child in respect of whom notification has been made to a Board/Trust in accordance with Article 22. The 'five-year rule' introduced by Article 29, as amended by the Children (NI) Order 1995, prevents the removal of the subject of an adoption application in circumstances where that subject has been in the care of the applicant for the preceding five years except with the latter's consent, with the leave of the court, under statutory authority or on the arrest of the child. Under Article 29(3) this rule is explicitly extended to foster-parents.

Completing and submitting the court report is also a priority concern at this stage. The adoption agency responsible for placement has, under Article 24 of the 1987 Order together with either Rule 22(1) of the Supreme Court Rules or Rule 21(2) of the County Court Rules, a maximum period of six weeks from receipt of the Notice of Hearing to submit its report. This report should advise on the suitability of the applicants and on any other maters relevant to the operation of Article 9. A Board/Trust which has been notified of a non-agency placement is similarly bound by Article 22(2) together with either Rule 22(2) of the Supreme Court Rules or Rule 21(2) of the County Court Rules. The format of this report should be as outlined in Form 249B of the Supreme Court Rules and Appendix G to the County Court Rules. It requires comprehensive information on the ability of the applicants to safeguard and promote the welfare of the child throughout childhood and on the wishes of the child in this respect. Ideally, this report should be submitted along with the applicant's petition or summons.

3. GAL Duties

Under Article 66 of the 1987 Order, the court must appoint a GAL in relation to every application for an adoption order. The court ensures that the GAL is provided with a copy of the court report completed by the Trust social worker, together with a copy of the original application, the accompanying documentation and, where appropriate, a copy of the statement of facts. The basic duty of this official is to safeguard the interests of the child concerned. In so doing he or she is directed by Rule 18 of the Supreme Court Rules or Rule 17 of the County Court Rules to investigate all circumstances relating to any agreement given or withheld and to ensure that in the former case it was given freely, unconditionally and with full understanding and in the latter that this was a reasoned choice made in full knowledge of all available options. This may involve ensuring that every effort has been made to locate the father of a non-marital child and address any issues relating to agreement. It will certainly involve visits to the applicant's home to establish at first hand whether the child's current and prospective welfare is assured there. According to the age of the child, the GAL may also need to be satisfied that he or she understands and has given a reasoned response to the adoption proposal. The GAL must also investigate all matters relating to the summons or petition or arising from the accompanying documentation, complete and submit to the court a full report drawing attention to matters considered significant and advise the court as to whether the child should be present at the hearing.

4. Reports: Confidentiality

The vexed issue of access to a GAL's report has recently been examined by the House of Lords.[63] This was a contested adoption application in which the father and stepmother sought to dispense with the natural mother's consent, on the grounds that it was being unreasonably withheld. The GAL had a number of interviews with the mother and children, some of the content of which was entered in his report. The wishes and feelings of the children were recorded in two sections of the report and the issue facing the court was whether these sections could be disclosed to the mother in accordance with her request. The decision of the court at first instance to veto disclosure was endorsed by the Court of Appeal, but the appeal was upheld by the House of Lords. In giving judgment, the House took into account existing case law,[64] the differential in significance of disclosure in the context of proceedings in adoption, wardship and, under the 1989 Act, the lack of any similar differential in relation to the reports of a GAL, adoption agency or social services social worker. Because of its importance, the ruling given by the House is set out in full as follows:

> (1) It was a fundamental principle of fairness that a party was entitled to the disclosure of all materials which might be taken into account by a court when reaching a decision adverse to that party. That principle applied with particular force to adoption proceedings.

---

[63] See *Re D (Adoption Reports: Confidentiality)* [1995] 2 FLR 687.
[64] In particular: *Official Solicitor v K* [1965] AC 201; *Re B (A Minor)(Disclosure of Evidence)* [1993] 1 All ER 931 and *McMichael v United Kingdom* [1995] Fam Law, vol. 25, 478.

(2) When deciding whether to direct that notwithstanding rule 53(2) of the Adoption Rules 1984 a party referred to in a confidential report supplied by an adoption agency, a local authority, a reporting officer or a guardian ad litem should not be entitled to inspect that part of the report referring to him or her, the court should first consider whether disclosure of the material would involve a real possibility of harm to the child.

(3) If it would, the court should next consider whether the overall interests of the child would benefit from non-disclosure, weighing the interests of the child in having the material properly tested against the magnitude of the risk that harm would occur and the gravity of that harm.

(4) If the court was satisfied that the interests of the child pointed towards non-disclosure, the next and final step was for the court to weigh that consideration against the interests of the parent or other party in having an opportunity to see and respond to the material. In the latter regard the court should take into account the importance of the material to the issue in the case.

(5) Non-disclosure should be the exception and not the rule. The court should be rigorous in its examination of the risk and the gravity of the feared harm to the child and should order non-disclosure only where the case for doing so was compelling.

(6) In the present case the judge had erred in approaching the question of disclosure in the manner of a pure discretion and in giving no weight to the strong presumption in favour of disclosure in adoption proceedings.

This House of Lords ruling must now be treated as the most binding authority on matters regarding disclosure of 'confidential' material contained in reports submitted to the court in issues affecting the welfare of children.

5. Court Duties

To the Master or the Chief Clerk in the High Court or in a county court, respectively, falls the duty to ensure that all parties are notified, documentary evidence is submitted, the GAL appointed and his or her report submitted so as to enable a judicial hearing to be held on the merits of an adoption application.

Within fourteen days of being notified by the GAL that his or her report has been lodged, the applicants, in accordance with Rule 20(1) of the Supreme Court Rules and Rule 19(1) of the County Court Rules, must apply to the Master or the Chief Clerk as appropriate for the date of the hearing to be confirmed. This official then confirms the date and time, notifies the applicant and the GAL accordingly and serves notice on all parties. Anyone wishing to lodge an objection to the making of an adoption order must complete Form 12A (Rule 20 of the Supreme Court Rules) and has fourteen days in which to do so. The Trust or agency, as may be, must lodge three copies of the social worker's report in the court within six weeks of receiving the Notice of Hearing.

Decision of the Court

There are three factors which determine the outcome of an adoption hearing: the agreement of the natural parents, the eligibility/suitability of the applicants and the welfare of the child.

I. Parental Agreement

Unless a freeing order has been granted or consent is being withheld, the court must ensure not only that the tests of welfare and eligibility/suitability can be satisfied but also that the agreement of each parent or guardian is available within the terms of Article 16(1)(b) of the 1987 Order. Under Article 16(3) such agreement is invalid if given within six weeks following the birth, though it may be given at any time thereafter, up to or even during the hearing. A 'parent' for the purposes of this provision does not include the father of a non-marital child and his consent will not be necessary unless he has acquired parental responsibility under the Children (NI) Order 1995. If a freeing order is not in effect a parent can still withdraw consent up to the time of hearing, but (as per Article 27 of the 1987 Order) may not remove the child. Article 16 permits parental consent to be given subject to a condition as to the child's religious upbringing.

Where parental agreement is being withheld, it may be dispensed with only if one of the grounds of Article 16(2) can be satisfied. Where it has already been dispensed with by way of the freeing process, it still arises for consideration at this stage. However, as the late Higgins J once ruled,[65] this may be simplified by applying the *res judicata* principle. At the adoption hearing he acknowledged that he was then obliged to 'consider afresh whether or not Miss H's consent should be dispensed with and whether or not adoption is in the best interests of the children'. However, he explained, 'to decide these matters I am entitled to rely on the testimony and the reports which I received, and the findings which I made, at the earlier hearing. None of the parties need call again the witnesses, who had given evidence previously, for the purpose of proving what had been proven already.'

Where parental agreement is being withheld and has not been previously dispensed with by way of the freeing process, then the court will at this stage consider the same issues in light of the same grounds as listed in Article 16(2) (see 'The Freeing Process' above). The characteristic legal issues which are otherwise likely to be present in relation to the typical non-parental application envisaged by Article 16(2) are those concerning the status of the parent whose agreement is being withheld and the particular relevance of certain grounds for dispensing with the necessity for that agreement.

1. Status of the Parent

The natural mother of a non-marital child who wished to relinquish that child to a voluntary adoption society formed the primary set of needs around which the adoption process was initially constructed (though in fact in Northern Ireland a great many such babies were placed directly by their unmarried mothers). Now such a mother is likely to want to continue carrying care responsibility for her child but parental fault or default will cause her reluctant involvement with the adoption process. When such circumstances occur, the judiciary will now place a heavy burden of proof upon her to show that she has made the arrangements necessary to secure a stable home environment

---

65 See *In the matter of KH and EH (Minors)* [1989] 7 NIJB 1.

for her child. Many such mothers are very young, a factor which will not weigh in their favour as the standards of reasonableness required in relation to any proposed arrangements are those appropriate to a mature, reflective parent able to give objective consideration to a child's best interests.[66]

A putative father does not have parental responsibility and is therefore not accorded the same legal standing as a marital father in adoption proceedings.[67] However, there have been some recent legislative efforts to improve his position. Articles 17(6) and 22(2) of the 1987 Order require the court to be furnished with reports relating to the natural parents according to the format as outlined in Appendix G to the Supreme Court Rules or Form 249B of the County Court Rules which require information 'where appropriate' on such a father. However, the Court of Appeal has held[68] that determining what constituted 'appropriate' was a matter for the discretion of the agency concerned. Again, although the Family Law Reform (NI) Order 1977 inserted an amendment to the Guardianship of Infants Act 1886 enabling the father of a non-marital child to apply for custody, this has been judicially countered by a decision[69] which held that such a custodial father would merely have a right to be heard by the court. However, his position has strengthened somewhat in recent years as a result of rulings made by the European Court of Human Rights[70] and as a consequence of Article 155 of the Children (NI) Order 1995 (see 'Parties' above).

2. Aspects of the Statutory Grounds

At this stage certain aspects of the grounds of 'unreasonableness' seem to attract particular judicial attention when considering whether parental consent can be dispensed with, i.e. the vacillating parent, the passage of time, the nature of parental conduct and parental motivation.

Case law[71] in England and Wales indicates that the courts are placing a heavier onus on the parent who withdraws agreement, as opposed to one who withholds it, to show that it was the second decision which was reasonable. A corollary to this is that the courts are also requiring the professionals involved to prove that they have thoroughly assessed the feasibility of a resumption of parental care.[72] The longer the period of time a child has spent away from the direct care of a non-consenting parent and the longer the child has spent with the applicants, the heavier the onus on the parent to demonstrate that he or she is being reasonable in withholding agreement to the appli-

---

66 See the Court of Appeal decisions in both *Re V (A Minor)(Adoption: Consent)* [1987] 2 FLR 89 and *Re R (A Minor)(Adoption: Parental Agreement)* [1987] 1 FLR 391 where the court held that young mothers were being unreasonable in withholding consent when their conduct was viewed objectively.
67 See, for example *Re C (Adoption: Parties)* [1995] 2 FLR 483 where the court held that such a father did not have to be made a respondent to an adoption or freeing application.
68 See in *Re L (A Minor)(Adoption: Procedure)* [1991] 1 FLR 171.
69 See *Re H (Minors) (Local Authority: Parental Rights)* [1989] 2 All ER 353, [1989] 1 WLR 551 CA.
70 See *McMichael v United Kingdom* [1995] Fam Law, vol. 25, 478.
71 See, for example, *Re H (Infants)(Adoption: Parental Agreement)* [1977] 2 All ER 339 CA.
72 See, for example, *Re B (Adoption: Parental Agreement)* [1990] 2 FLR 383.

cation.[73] This approach was endorsed by Higgins J in a case[74] where he granted an application contested by marital parents in respect of their three-and-a-half-year-old daughter whom they had not seen for almost three years.

The more grievous the parental conduct, the stronger the onus on such a parent to prove that he or she is being reasonable in withholding consent.[75] However, the courts will not view homosexuality or lesbianism as evidence of parental misconduct,[76] nor will past conduct be the sole determinant of an applicant's suitability.[77] The motivation of the non-custodial and non-consenting parent must be above reproach.[78] It is not enough that such a parent is motivated by a sense of grievance.

II. Eligibility/Suitability of the Applicants

It is seldom that matters affecting the eligibility of adopters would be at issue at this final stage of the adoption process. An unmarried mother may adopt her own child.[79] An unmarried father may also do so.[80] However, the fact that a mother of an illegitimate child, when applying jointly with her husband to adopt her child, should deny that child's father the opportunity to be informed of the application by refusing to disclose his identity to the court was held[81] by Higgins J to breach her eligibility to have her application considered by the court. There has been little evidence of suitability criteria being applied by the judiciary to refer uncontested step-parent applications to marital proceedings, despite the warning in the Haughton Report that an adoption order in such circumstances might prejudice rather than benefit the welfare of the child concerned (paragraphs 97 and 103). Where such applications are contested, however, there is evidence in this jurisdiction of suitability criteria having a crucial bearing on the outcome.[82] The *Haughton Report* also took the view that adoption by grandparents was not, as a rule, desirable (paragraphs 111–14). This reservation rests on the significance of age differentials between adopter and adopted and echoes the warning given by Vaisey J that 'they should be regarded as exceptional and made with great caution'.[83] It may well be that the availability of Article 8 orders under the Children (NI) Order 1995 will serve to significantly raise the suitability threshold for step-parent applicants. The court may, perhaps following advice from the GAL, decide that an application under Article 8 for a residence order would be more appropriate.

---

73 See *In re H (Infants) (Adoption: Parental Consent)* [1977] 2 All ER 339, 34 OCA.
74 See *In the matter of A–MW*, unreported (1992).
75 See *Re F (An Infant)* [1970] 1 All ER 344.
76 See, for example, *Re D (An Infant) (Parent's Consent)* [1977] 1 All ER 145. Also see *Re E* [1994] Fam Law 483 where a mother was held to be unreasonable to object to the placement of her child with an adopter who was single and a lesbian.
77 See, for example, *Re W (Adoption: Parental Agreement)* (1983) 4 FLR 614.
78 See, for example, *In re B (A Minor)(Adoption by Parent)* [1975] Fam 127, [1975] All ER 449.
79 See *Re D (An Infant)* [1959] 1 QB 229, [1958] 3 All ER 716.
80 See *F v S* [1973] Fam 203 at 207, [1973] 1 All ER 722, 725 CA.
81 See *In re B (A Minor)*, unreported (1990).
82 See, for example, *In re M and M (Minors)*, unreported (1988).
83 See *In re DX (An Infant)* [1949] 1 Ch 320 at p. 321.

Inter-country adoptions have given rise to eligibility issues. These most often occur in relation to the prohibition on unauthorised payments[84] and proof of consents. The former represents the traditional legal abhorrence of 'trafficking' in children and is made a criminal offence under Article 57. Any suggestion of improper payments (e.g. direct or indirect payments to the child's mother) may under Article 24(2), if proven, prevent the court from making an adoption order. The latter refers to the difficulty in establishing, across geographical, cultural and language barriers, the legal status of parent and child and confirming that any consent given was done so freely and with full understanding of the consequences.[85]

III. Welfare of the Child

Welfare may be interpreted as benefit, but this is not necessarily confined to benefits of a material nature, as removal of the stigma of illegitimacy has itself been considered a benefit. In the words of Josling,[86] 'the main benefit of adoption will be to give the child the social, legal and psychological benefits of belonging to a family'. Welfare is an important factor to be taken into account in all adoption applications. It will, however, be insufficient in itself to justify an order. Where an application is clearly compatible with a child's welfare, the order sought may still be refused as when, for example, its purpose is to circumvent immigration policy.[87]

Under the first part of Article 9 of the 1987 Order, certain directions are given for applying the welfare principle. For example Article 9(a)(i) requires that the order, if made, 'will be in the best interests of the child'. In contested cases, however, the legal and social work professions often seem to approach the significance of a child's best interests from different positions. The social worker seeks to extend the paramountcy principle into the adoption process and so permanently place a child's best interests beyond the reach of those who previously threatened them. The judiciary have to respect the fact that in adoption 'welfare is not *per se* the test'. This difference of approach was most notably addressed[88] by Hutton LCJ. It was apparent also, for example, in a case[89] where a Trust appealed against the making of an adoption order in respect of a child it had placed with the adopters. The grounds of the appeal rested on the husband's frank disclosure that since the placement he himself had 'developed symptoms of anaemia which have necessitated an intensive course of treatment the outcome of which is uncertain'. The Board/Trust's case that this development jeopardised the child's best interests was dismissed by the Court of Appeal in a judgment

---

84 See *Re an Adoption Application* [1992] 1 FLR 341; *Re AW (Adoption Application)* [1992] Fam Law 539; and *Re C (A Minor)(Adoption Application)* [1993] Fam Law, vol. 22, 538.
85 See, for example, *Re B (Adoption: Child's Welfare)* [1995] 2 FLR 895 and *Re M (Child's Upbringing)* [1996] 2 FLR 441.
86 Josling and Levy, *Adoption of Children*, 10th ed., London: Longman 1985, 5.
87 See *Re A (An Infant)* [1963] 1 All ER 531, [1963] 1 WLR 231; *Re R (Adoption)* [1963] 3 All ER 613, [1967] 1 WLR 34. However, see also, *Re H (Adoption: Non-Patrial)* [1966] 1 FLR 717 where the adoption was allowed despite breach of immigration rules.
88 In *In re EB*, at f/n 44.
89 See *In re M (An Infant)*, unreported (1976).

where Lowry LCJ made reference to the difficulties 'of ensuring ... in this uncertain life that a child shall have the advantage of both parents whether natural or adoptive'. More recently, however, the judiciary can be seen[90] attaching greater significance to welfare relative to other factors but, as was emphasised in a recent English case,[91] adoption remains unaffected by the paramountcy principle.

Under the same part of Article 9 there is also an explicit requirement to consider whether the adoption order, if made, would promote the welfare of the child 'throughout his childhood'. This adds a prospective dimension to the welfare test. So, for example, where the Court of Appeal upheld[92] an adoption order granted six days before the mentally handicapped subject attained his eighteenth birthday, it was held that in such circumstances the welfare consideration should extend beyond childhood. The similar requirement in the same Article to take into account whether the applicants can offer 'a stable and harmonious home' has the effect of raising a presumption in favour of adoption for long-term care arrangements such as those provided by step-parents and foster-parents.

Under the second part of Article 9 there is a requirement to '. . . ascertain the wishes and feelings of the child . . . having regard to his age and understanding'. This has been held to refer to once-off decisions, for example, to place for adoption, to change his/her name and to parental access. Following the *Gillick* ruling and the Children Act 1989, a certain amount of English case law has built up around the weighting given to a child's views (see further Chapters 15 and 16). For example, the decision of a court[93] to dispense with parental agreement was significantly influenced by an eleven-year-old boy's views on adoption. This judicial approach has been endorsed by an official recommendation[94] that the court should not be allowed to make an adoption order in relation to a child aged twelve years or over, unless that child's consent has either been obtained or has been dispensed with. It is probable that the above provision will consolidate similar practice already established here in the wardship jurisdiction.

The Order Granted

The outcome of an adoption application may be either of the statutory options available under the 1987 Order. However, since the introduction of the Children (NI) Order 1995, other permutations have become possible.

1. No Order

Under Article 9(a)(i) of the 1987 Order, the court cannot grant an adoption order unless satisfied that to do so would be in the best interests of the child. Under Article 3 of the

---

90 As in *In the matter of E.68*, unreported (1987).
91 See *Re B (Adoption: Child's Welfare)* [1995] 1 FLR 895.
92 See *In re D (A Minor)(Adoption Order: Validity)* [1991] 2 FLR 66.
93 See *Re B (Minor) (Adoption: Parental Agreement)* [1990] 2 FLR 383. See also *Re G (TJ) (An Infant)* [1963] 1 All ER 20 CA; *Re D (Minors) (Adoption by Step-Parent)* [1980] 2 FLR 103, and *Re B (A Minor) (Adoption)* [1988] 18 Fam Law 172.
94 See Interdepartmental Group, DoH, *Review of Adoption Law*, para 3 (1992).

Children (NI) Order 1995, the 'no order' presumption applies as this is a form of family proceedings. An application may fail on other counts, but even if successful on all other criteria, it must fail if it does not also satisfy these aspects of the welfare test.

1. Application on Foot of a Freeing Order

Articles 19 and 20 of the 1987 Order, as amended by the Children (NI) Order 1995, apply in circumstances where a child has been freed for adoption. Both extend certain rights to the natural parents. Article 19 requires the relevant adoption agency, in circumstances where a freeing order was obtained without parental agreement, to inform the 'former parent', within two weeks of the first anniversary of that order, whether an adoption order has been made and if not whether the child has been placed for adoption; this requirement may apply to the father of an illegitimate child.[95] In the event of neither an adoption order nor an adoption placement having been made, Article 20 gives the 'former parent' the right to apply for a revocation of the freeing order and return of the child. Should the 'former parent' be successful, all parental rights and duties will revert to that person and to his or her spouse if they were married to each other at the time of the child's birth.

2. Application for an Adoption Order

Article 31 of the 1987 Order applies where an application is withdrawn by either the prospective adopters or by the adoption agency or where it has been refused by the court. It requires all parties to be notified of such events and the child to be returned to the adoption agency within seven days.

3. Appeals

Under Article 64(3) of the 1987 Order, any person aggrieved as a result of a decision of a county court has a right of appeal to the Court of Appeal as per Article 60 of the County Courts (NI) Order 1980. This right is one that should be promptly exercised, usually within six weeks, as time is of the essence. Successful applications have been made to have an adoption order set aside. Although very rare, such an application may succeed on the grounds of a failure of natural justice (as in, for example, *Re K (Adoption)*[96] or because of a procedural irregularity (as was the case in *Re F(R) (An Infant)*[97] and *Re RA (Minors)*).[98] A final right of appeal will lie to the House of Lords.

II. *Different Order*

Under Articles 14(3) and 15(4) of the 1987 Order, the court was required to dismiss an application if it considered the matter would be better dealt with under Article 45 of the Matrimonial Causes (NI) Order 1978. The continued steep rise in the proportion

---

95 See In *re H (Illegitimate Children: Father: Parental Rights)(no. 2)* [1991] 1 FLR 214.
96 [1997] 1 FLR No. 5.
97 [1970] 1 QB 385.
98 [1974] Fam Law 182.

of step-parent adoptions in this jurisdiction indicated a judicial reluctance to apply such an appropriateness test and this has now been repealed by the 1995 Order. Similarly, the power of the court under Article 27 of the 1987 Order, when rejecting an adoption application, to direct that the child be instead placed under the supervision or committed into the care of the Board, has also been repealed.

III. Article 8 Orders

1. As an Option for a Cohabitee

As mentioned earlier, where a couple are unmarried, only one of them may make an adoption application. A recent case[99] in England concerned a couple who wished to adopt a five-year-old child whom they had been fostering for three years. An adoption order was granted to the father, despite opposition from the child's mother, and a shared residence order was granted to both foster parents. The adoption order was appropriate as it placed the child on the same legal footing as the couple's other two children and gave the adopted child the same surname. The residence order gave the foster parent, who was the primary carer, a secure legal relationship with the child.

2. As a Judicial Option

The above judicial options must now be read subject to the special rules introduced by the Children (NI) Order 1995. Adoption proceedings are defined as family proceedings for the purposes of this Order and the court is therefore entitled, instead of granting an adoption order, to make any of the orders available under Article 8 order (e.g. residence order) which may be more appropriate where the prospective adopter already has, in relation to the child, the status of step-parent, relative or foster-parent (see Chapter 10). The court also has the option of making an order under Article 16 or of directing the local Board/Trust to conduct an investigation into the child's circumstances under Article 56.

3. As a Third-Party Option

Third parties may now apply, or seek leave to apply, for Article 8 orders in the course of adoption proceedings. This would allow a third party, such as a grandparent, to make application for a contact order during the adoption proceedings. Even after an adoption order (or a freeing order) has been granted, a member of the child's family of origin would be entitled to seek the leave of the court to apply for an Article 8 order. The court may itself, of its own motion, make an Article 8 order in respect of an adopted child.

IV. Full Adoption Order

Under Article 12 of the 1987 Order, as amended by the Children (NI) Order 1995:

(1) An adoption order is an order giving parental responsibility for a child to the adopters...

---

99 See *Re AB (Adoption: Shared Residence Order)* [1996] 1 FLR 1.

Under Articles 40–49 of the 1987 Order, the effects of granting a full adoption order on the parties concerned — in terms of consanguinity, property rights, insurance and pension rights — are spelt out. Broadly, all existing rights and duties of the natural parents, guardian or any other party are extinguished and all rights and duties appropriate to the parents of a legitimate child vest in the adopters

V. Conditional Adoption Order

Under Article 12 of the 1987 Order:

> (6) An adoption order may contain such terms and conditions as the court thinks fit.

The orthodox view is that attaching a condition to an adoption order is contrary to the spirit of adoption. As Roskill LJ has said,[100]

> ... the court must be extremely careful to see that it is not imposing terms and conditions which are fundamentally inconsistent with the principles which underline the making of an adoption order.

This view is changing. The new flexibility permitted by the Children (NI) Order 1995 together with the tacit encouragement offered in a recent White Paper[101] to the practice of facilitating more 'open' adoptions and the concern expressed about step-adoptions may well lead to conditional adoption orders becoming common in the future.

1. Adoption Subject to a Condition in Relation to Religious Upbringing

The power of the court to make a conditional order under Article 12(6) may be exercised so as to give effect to the parental right as expressed in Article 16(1)(b)(i) when giving consent to do so:

> (ab) either unconditionally or subject only to a condition with respect to the religious persuasion in which the child is to be brought up.

This provision is restricted to consensual adoptions. However, the right to determine religious upbringing has long been recognised in the common law as inherently vesting in a natural parent. The late Higgins J, therefore, was able to consider in *Re T (A Minor)*[102] the issue of a natural mother's insistence on a Roman Catholic upbringing for her child as a factor in the reasonableness of her refusal to consent to adoption where the prospective adopters were Protestant and proposed to bring up the child in that religion. This was a case[103] where the three-year-old child suffered from cystic fibrosis and had spent the previous two years in the care of the prospective adopters. Higgins J took the following view:

---

100 See *In Re C (A Minor)(Adoption Order: Condition)* [1986] 1 FLR 315.
101 See *Adoption: The Future* (Cmnd 2288).
102 Unreported (1993).
103 Higgins J relied on the judgment of Wilberforce J in *In re E (An Infant)* [1964] 1 WLR 51.

> If [T] was a normal, healthy child, I would consider that effect should be given to her mother's religious wishes, which I regard as genuine, and I would not be prepared to authorise adoption, unless and until the Board undertook that steps would be taken to approve Roman Catholic adoptive parents.

In the circumstances, however, he regarded the mother's 'religious preferences as less important in this situation than [her daughter's] happiness, health, security and stability'. If, as seems to have been the case, this ruling is giving a determinative weighting to the benefits of attained psychological bonding as opposed to possible future religious belief as factors constituting the welfare of the child for the purposes of such proceedings, then it is an important statement of the law with general application to care arrangements for children in this jurisdiction.

2. Adoption Subject to a Condition of Contact with Family of Origin

Adoption severs all legal relationships between the child concerned and his natural parent and, normally, all links which may exist with members of the family of origin. The final and irrevocable nature of the order naturally calls for the court to pause and reflect whether such a legal severing of the blood-link is a price worth paying to secure a child's future welfare. Where a relationship already exists between the child and a natural parent or sibling, which may constitute a psychological bond and thus in itself be a determining factor of such welfare, then the courts have demonstrated great caution before reaching a decision. In the past the existence of such a meaningful bond has often been judicially viewed as vitiating the welfare ground for an adoption order; adoption and continued contact being seen as mutually exclusive.[104] In the future this either/or approach is unlikely to survive.

The judicial dilemma in third-party applications was illustrated in England by the not untypical case of *In re H*[105] which concerned an adoption application by foster-parents in respect of a ten-year-old boy. The judge at first instance decided to dispense with the mother's consent despite evidence that she had maintained a regular pattern of visits to her son over a number of years. The Court of Appeal reversed that decision and ordered a re-hearing on the ground that the judge had erred by not taking into account the desirability that the boy should retain contact with his mother. Purchas LJ[106] commented:

> Where a boy of the age of ten knows who his mother is, it is at least of some importance that he should retain contact, provided that such contact does not threaten his sense of security in the foster home or in any other way cause a disturbance to him.

---

104 As expressed by Salmon LJ in *Re B (MF)(An Infant); (Re D (An Infant))* [1972] 1 All ER 898:
> As a rule, it is highly undesirable that after an adoption order is made there should be any contact between the child or children and their natural parents . . . it is desirable in normal circumstances for there to be a complete break (p. 900).

105 [1983] 4 FLR 614.
106 *Ibid* at 627.

The two factors which have now come to determine whether a contact condition (or any other condition) should be attached to an adoption order are the welfare of the child and enforceability. In this jurisdiction, judicial regard for the first factor can be traced back to the judgment of MacDermott J[107] where he stated:

> Exceptional cases however do arise where the welfare of a child can be enhanced by preserving contact between him and one or both of his parents.

In that case he then went on to offer guidelines as to the circumstances which would, in his view, merit attaching an access condition to an adoption order. Both factors arose for consideration in a leading English case[108] where the condition sought and granted was for sibling access. It was then held that a distinction could be meaningfully drawn between the legal standing of a parent and a sibling as regards the legitimacy of their respective claims that an access condition would be to the benefit of the child concerned. While the former would have had every opportunity to bring their claim before the court at the time the substantive issue of consent was being determined, the latter would not. It was also pointed out that the court making the adoption order had the power to

> retain jurisdiction to continue and, as and when appropriate, to supervise and regulate access between M and C during the continuance of the adoption order . . .

The House of Lords went on to suggest that the involvement of the Official Solicitor and the court welfare officer would facilitate the setting-up of access arrangements which could ultimately 'if all else fails, be enforceable by committal proceedings, as with any other order of the court'. However, because of difficulties with enforcement, the likelihood is that an access condition will usually only be attached with the consent of the adopters. Where they strongly object the court is likely to defer to their wishes.[109]

In recent years, the introduction of contact orders under the Children Act 1989 together with the rather sudden acceptance of the philosophy of 'openness' (related, perhaps, to a rapid rise in the number of first-party applicants) has, in England and Wales, led to a proliferation of adoption orders being made subject to a contact condition. Similarly in this jurisdiction, now that adoption proceedings are defined as family proceedings for the purposes of the Children (NI) Order 1995, the court has the power to attach such conditions or directions to adoption orders as it should see fit: which, in effect, is likely to render redundant the equivalent power in the Adoption (NI) Order 1987. In adoption, as throughout the body of family law, it is proving impossible to contain the influence of the welfare principle.

---

107 See *In the matter of B 847*, unreported (1974).
108 See *Re C (A Minor)* [1988] 1 AER 712h.
109 See *Re T (Adoption: Contact)* [1995] 2 FLR 251 where the court granted the adopters' appeal against the contact condition (for annual contact with natural mother) attached to their adoption order.

VI. Partial Orders

There used to be two forms of partial orders: interim and provisional.

Under Article 26 of the 1987 Order, where the terms of Article 16(1) and Article 22(1) are satisfied, the court may postpone making a decision in respect of an application and instead grant an order vesting legal custody of the child in the applicants for a probationary period, or for successive periods, not exceeding two years. The purpose of such an interim order is not simply to examine the suitability of the applicants but is intended to provide an opportunity to examine all factors relating to the application. Interim orders are now very seldom made and the use of provisional orders has been discontinued.

An Adoption Order and Its Consequences

For all three parties the consequences of an adoption order are that the legal relationships among them are irreversibly altered. Thereafter each is treated as though the child had been born into the adopters' family. These consequences are largely governed by Articles 50–54 of the 1987 Order and the adjustments introduced by the Children (NI) Order 1995.

I. Consequences for the Child

Under Article 40 of the 1987 Order, it is stated that an adopted child is to be treated in law as if he or she is not the child of anyone other than the adopters. Article 40(4) prevents the child's legal status from being anything other than legitimate. Because the child's status is defined by the adopters, so also, for the duration of childhood, are all matters of residence, domicile and nationality.

The succession rights of an adopted child have been addressed by Article 42 of the 1987 Order which stops short of completely abolishing a distinction which the law has traditionally made between the inheritance rights of a parent's natural and adopted children. The effect of the Order, however, is to create a presumption that any reference to 'children' in a will or settlement, whenever made, was intended to include any adopted child.

The rights of access, which a court may have acknowledged in respect of the subject of an adoption application, will have been given effect by the attachment of a condition under Article 12(6) of the 1987 Order or, perhaps, by the attachment of a contact order following the introduction of the Children (NI) Order 1995.

Disclosure of Information to Child

The right to information about the fact and circumstances of his or her adoption, the means for accessing that information and the availability of related counselling services have been provided to an adopted person by Article 54 of the 1987 Order. This has been amended by the Children (NI) Order 1995 to provide, under Article 54A, for the setting-up and maintenance of an 'Adoption Contact Register' in which is to be recorded information relating to desired contact between adopted persons and members of their family of origin. Article 50(3) confines the right of access to information about an adopted person by prohibiting public inspection and search of the registers, books and records maintained under Article 50(1)(c). Any adopted person under the age of eighteen and intending to be married may now apply to the Registrar General for a declaration that the intended spouse is not within the prohibited degrees of relationship for the purposes of Article 18(1) of the Family Law (Miscellaneous Provisions) (NI) Order 1984. Any adopted person having reached the age of eighteen may apply to the Registrar General for a copy of his or her original birth certificate and has a right of access to information relating to the circumstances of his or her adoption.

II. Consequences for the Natural Parents

Under Article 12 of the 1987 Order, as amended by the Children (NI) Order 1995:

> (3) The making of an adoption order operates to extinguish—
>
> (a) the parental responsibility which any person has for the child immediately before the making of the order;
> (b) any order of a court under the Children (NI) Order 1995;
> (c) any duty arising by virtue of an agreement or the order of a court to make payments, so far as the payments are in respect of the child's maintenance or upbringing for any period after the making of an order.

It therefore removes not only all inherently vesting parental rights or duties but also all other statutory orders affecting them which may have been in existence at the time of adoption. So, a prior adoption order, custody or care order or an order which provided for maintenance, access/contact or parental contribution would automatically be cancelled. The only possible rights which may be retained by a natural parent and accommodated within an adoption order are a condition under Article 16(1)(b)(i) of the 1987 Order as to the preferred religious upbringing of the child and under Article 12(6) as to possible access/contact, if judicially sanctioned.

The rights of a natural parent must now, however, also be read subject to the provisions of the 1995 Order. Under this Order there exists the potential opportunity for a natural parent to make application for an Article 8 order, even after the adoption of the child. However, as such a person would no longer be a 'parent', leave to apply will need to be obtained in advance from the court.[110]

Disclosure of Information to Natural Parents

Natural parents now have the right to advise the Registrar General of their wish to have their names entered in the Contact Register, thereby indicating a wish for contact with their children in the event of enquiries being made by the latter when they have attained the age of eighteen.

The approach of the courts towards natural parents seeking disclosure of identifying information in respect of an adopted child has been one of fairly consistent refusal. For example, where a putative father and alleged rapist sought disclosure of files from a social services department relating to the adoption of the child of his victim so that

---

110 See *Re C (A Minor) (Adopted Child: Contact)* [1993] 2 FLR 431.

the child could be traced and blood-tests conducted to establish possible paternity, this was rejected on grounds of confidentiality.[111] Recently, the courts seem to have relaxed this approach at least to the extent of requiring an applicant parent to show good reason, not necessarily exceptional circumstances, to justify disclosure.[112] Strong emotional curiousity on the part of a natural parent has, however, been held to be insufficient.[113]

III. Consequences for the Adopters

All rights and duties inherently vesting in natural parents are transferred to and vested in the adopters by the granting of an adoption order. However, in some respects the legal standing of adopters will be different from that of the natural parents. Under Article 59(4), as amended by the Children (NI) Order 1995, for example, there is provision for

> ... a scheme for the payment by the agency of adoption allowances to persons who have adopted or intend to adopt a child where arrangements for the adoption were made, or are to be made, by that agency . . . .

This provision offers the possibility of an entitlement to continued financial support for adopters on the basis of their status as such, an entitlement which is over and above anything due to natural parents. There are, on the other hand, the possible restrictions on their freedom to exercise parental rights imposed under Articles 12(6) and 16(1)(b)(i) of the 1987 Order which, together with the eventual effect of the disclosure provisions of Article 54, serve to differentiate their legal standing from that of natural parents.

---

111 See *Re H (Adoption: Disclosure of Information)* [1995] 1 FLR 236. However, in *Re an Adoption Application (Note)* [1990] 1 FLR 412, the court was prepared to order disclosure to the Attorney-General in a similar case.
112 See *D v Registrar General* [1996] 1 FLR 707.
113 See *Re L (Adoption: Disclosure of Information)* (1997) 2 FLR 431.

CHAPTER SEVEN

Wardship

Introduction

The Children (NI) Order 1995 has undone the authority of Dr S Cretney's trenchant assertion[1] that 'the outstanding characteristic of the wardship jurisdiction is that no limit has ever been set to it'. Legislative unease at the extent to which a combination of judicial discretion and Health and Social Services Board (or Trust) child-care pressures permitted wardship to undermine carefully constructed (if often outdated) statutory boundaries has been responsible for the severe restrictions now placed upon it. The 1995 Order marks a turning point for the role of wardship in the family law of Northern Ireland.

In Northern Ireland, from the early 1980s, the annual number of wardship orders made has shown a rapid rate of increase. In 1982 only 55 orders were made, 136 in 1986, 184 in 1992, increasing to 235 in 1995. The explanation for this is evident in the source of applications. The orders made in favour of Trusts (or Health and Social Services Boards) during roughly the same period were as follows: in 1983 they were awarded a total of 46 orders, 95 in 1992 and 154 in 1995. The overall numerical increase in wardship applications is attributable to a general escalation in rates of family breakdown. This in turn has resulted in a high proportion of complex custody and access cases in private family law and of similarly complicated child-care cases in public law: both types have required High Court expertise and the flexibility of wardship proceedings. While there is no reason to predict any future decline in the annual number of untenable parenting arrangements requiring judicial resolution, there is every reason to predict that the proportion in wardship proceedings on the foot of applications made by Trusts will now sharply decline as a consequence of the Children (NI) Order 1995.

This chapter begins by explaining the remit and organisation of the wardship jurisdiction. It then examines the contribution made by the wardship jurisdiction to the development of an indigenous body of jurisprudence founded on the principle of the welfare of the child. This is considered in conjunction with the relevant statutory framework, first in relation to private family law, then in relation to the public child care responsibilities of the Trusts. Those case-law principles established during the twenty–twenty-five-year period before the introduction of the 1995 Order, which are likely to endure as reference points under that Order, are noted and analysed. The distinctive characteristics of wardship are examined, its achievements in remedying statutory deficiencies are assessed and emerging trends are identified. The chapter concludes by examining the bearing of the 1995 Order on the probable future role for

---

1 See SM Cretney, *Principles of Family Law*, London: Sweet & Maxwell, 1979.

wardship in Northern Ireland. Guidance is sought from the case law generated in England and Wales as a consequence of judicial interpretation of equivalent provisions under the 1989 Act. The potential implications arising from the distinction which may be made between wardship and the inherent jurisdiction of the High Court are also considered.

Jurisdiction, Principle, Operation, Parties and Administration

Prior to the introduction of the 1995 Order the High Court, when exercising its wardship jurisdiction was held to be activating its inherent powers as *parens patriae* over the person and property of minors, i.e. wardship and the inherent powers were seen as coterminous. However, the effect of the 1995 Order in conjunction with the Family Law (NI) Order 1994 has been to restrict severely the traditional scope of wardship. The newly drawn boundaries between the wardship and statutory jurisdictions have yet to be fully explored, but one significant development is the emerging distinction to be drawn between the jurisdiction of the High Court when exercising its wardship powers and when exercising its inherent powers other than wardship. The future non-statutory role of the High Court in family law in Northern Ireland may rest on this distinction.

I. *Jurisdiction*

Under Article 173(5) of the Children (NI) Order 1995 the wardship jurisdiction continues to be restricted exclusively to the High Court. This is unlike the position in England and Wales where since 1986 the wardship jurisdiction has been also exercisable by the county courts, except as regards decisions to ward or to de-ward a child.

1. Authority of the Court

The basis of wardship is rooted in the allegiance that a subject owes to his sovereign and in the feudal paternalistic obligation assumed by the latter as *parens patriae* to protect the person and property of minors.[2] This obligation was delegated to the Lord Chancellor, subsequently to the Court of Chancery and ultimately to the Family Division of the High Court.

The authority of the Court when exercising the wardship jurisdiction is not quite the same as that vested in a parent. In some respects its scope is not so extensive. Authority for the adoption of a ward, for example, will not necessarily rest on its consent. However, when exercising its inherent and unlimited *parens patriae* jurisdiction (which encompasses wardship), its authority is more extensive than that of a parent. It may, for example, prohibit the publishing of information[3] concerning a ward, override

---

2 See N Lowe & R White, *Wards of Court*, London: Butterworths 1979 for a history of wardship.
3 See, for example, in *Re X (A Minor)* [1975] 1 All ER 697 CA 47 where it was held that in the particular circumstances of the case the interests of the ward should not prevail over the interests of freedom of publication. Note, also, that the court's inherent powers are buttressed by the Administration of Justice Act, section 12, which makes it a contempt of court to publish

the refusal of a parent or mature minor to consent to medical treatment,[4] override legal or professional privilege to obtain evidence[5] or attach a direction to an adoption order[6] requiring the Registrar General not to divulge certain information. Therefore, regardless of whether parental responsibility is vested in a Trust by a care order, in the court by a wardship order or remains with the parent or with a mature minor, the High Court may, if leave is granted, exercise its inherent jurisdiction to determine issues which neither the Trust nor the parent have the authority to decide. Since the Children Act 1989 came into effect, this has occurred in England and Wales in a small number of cases concerning children subject to care orders, usually regarding issues of consent to medical treatment.

2. Statutory Restrictions on the Use of Wardship

The crucial restriction imposed by Article 173 of the Children (NI) Order 1995 is intended to prevent wardship from being available in public family law at the suit of a Trust (wardship and care orders are mutually exclusive). The range and flexibility of orders under Article 8 of the 1995 Order are intended to counter the attractions of wardship in private family law as an alternative to statutory proceedings.[7] As Waite LJ stated,[8] when referring to the effect of the 1989 Act on the use of wardship in private law matters,

> ... the courts' undoubted discretion to allow wardship proceedings to go forward in a suitable case is subject to their clear duty, in loyalty to the scheme and purpose of the Children Act legislation, to permit recourse to wardship only when it becomes apparent to the judge in any particular case that the question which the court is determining in regard to the minor's upbringing or property cannot be resolved under the statutory procedures ...

He went on to express the view that there has to be a special justification for giving a child 'the status — an exceptional status under the modern law as it must now be applied — of a ward of court'. Following the introduction of the 1995 Order, wardship is now envisaged as a residuary jurisdiction in both public and private law.

3. Judicial Restrictions on the Use of Wardship

Apart from the restrictions imposed by the 1995 Order, access to the wardship jurisdiction has also been limited by the self-imposed restrictions of the High Court.

---

any report of a wardship hearing and the Children (NI) Order 1995, Article 170, which prohibits publicity identifying a child or the address of his or her school.
4 See *Re W (A Minor)(Medical Treatment: Court's Jurisdiction)* [1992] 3 WLR 785, [1992] 4 All ER 627.
5 See *Barking and Dagenham LBC v O and Another* [1993] 3 WLR 493.
6 See *Re X (A Minor)(Adoption Details: Disclosure)* [1994] 2 FLR 450.
7 See *Re CT (A Minor)(Wardship: Representation)* [1993] 2 FLR 278 and *Re R (A Minor): Blood Transfusion)* [1993] Fam Law, vol. 23, 577 for judicial views on the effect of restrictions imposed by the 1989 Act on access to wardship in private and public law respectively.
8 In *Re CT (A Minor)(Wardship: Representation)* [1993] 2 FLR 278 Fam Law, vol. 23, P 569.

First, it has set definite limits to exclude certain classes of applicants such as diplomats[9] and their families as well as children of other nationalities who have been refused a right of entry by immigration authorities.[10] Second, in relation to those not so excluded, it employs its prerogative discretion to determine in each case whether the circumstances disclose a further and adequate justification for it to exercise its jurisdiction. This power of discretion has so far been used to restrict the use of wardship from having any application to the following circumstances:

(a) reviewing the merits of a properly made decision taken by the appropriate public servants in accordance with their statutorily defined duties,[11] e.g. decisions of immigration officials and Trust social workers;
(b) appealing against a decision properly taken[12] in a magistrates' court;
(c) overriding certain rights of equal social importance, for example, the right to publish[13] and the right of a parent to reasonably withhold consent to the adoption of her child.[14]

The costs of initiating in the High Court what are usually lengthy proceedings, involving many parties and witnesses, will also act as a rationing device.

II. The Principle

The guiding principle of wardship is that in any matter affecting the upbringing or property of a minor the welfare of that minor must be treated as the factor of paramount importance.

1. Definition of Paramountcy

Paramountcy, traditionally the distinguishing feature of wardship, was explained a century ago by Lindly LJ:[15]

---

9 See *In Re C (An Infant)* [1959] Ch 363 where Harman J ruled that a father was entitled under his shield of diplomatic immunity to reject the paternal jurisdiction of the Crown.
10 See, for example, *Re Mohammed Arif (An Infant), Re Nirbhai Singh* [1968] Ch 643. In this jurisdiction wardship has been used to protect the position of a child from Romania, pending an adoption application, after the child's visa (issued for the purpose of permitting medical treatment) had expired.
11 See *A v Liverpool City Council* [1982] AC 363.
12 See in *Re K* [1966] 1 WLR 1241, 1242 E. See also the decision of Hutton J in *Re D (Minors)*, unreported (1986) where he ruled that 'the law is clear that the High Court should not exercise its wardship jurisdiction where the question as to the custody of, and access to, a child is already properly before a magistrate's court'.
13 See *Re X (A Minor)* [1975] Fam 47, where it was held that in the particular circumstances of the case the interests of the ward should not prevail over the interests of freedom of publication. But see also *Re L (A Minor)* (The Times, July 4, 1987).
14 See the judgment of Hutton J in *Re M McC and DH (Minors)* [1986] 5 NIJB 1 where he ruled that the Board must not seek to avail of the paramountcy principle in wardship proceedings as a means of overruling reasonably withheld parental consent.
15 See *In re McGrath (Infants)* [1893] 1 Ch 143, 148.

> The dominant matter for the consideration of the Court is the welfare of the child. But the welfare of a child is not to be measured by money only, nor by physical comfort only. The word welfare must be taken in its widest sense. The moral and religious welfare of the child must be considered as well as its physical well-being. Nor can the ties of affection be disregarded.

The mandatory priority given by the paramountcy principle to identifying, safeguarding and promoting the welfare of the child has, until recently, distinguished wardship from the statutory jurisdiction. It was in a Northern Ireland case,[16] heard on appeal by the House of Lords, that this principle first gained judicial recognition. As Viscount Cave then stated:

> It is the welfare of the children, which, according to rules which are now well accepted, forms the paramount consideration in these cases.

2. Role of Paramountcy

The part to be played by the principle of paramountcy was most notably explained by Lord MacDermott in what has long continued to be the leading case[17] in this area:

> ... when all the relevant facts, claims and wishes of parents, risks, choices, and other circumstances are taken into account and weighed, the course to be followed is that which is most in the interests of the child's welfare.

This principle has long governed wardship. It has indicated the need for such proceedings because an issue could not otherwise be heard, or be given the same priority, within the framework of statutory law. It has relaxed the formal court strictures to make wardship more accessible, non-adversarial and more thorough than statutory proceedings. Finally, it has provided the measure for ultimately determining issues of custody and upbringing.

III. The Effect of a Wardship Order

The full powers of the High Court are applied to protect the subject of a wardship application and freeze the prevailing circumstances from the moment the originating summons is issued. Thereafter, for a period of twenty-one days or until an order is made, no person may take any action which might disturb the status quo in relation to the child without prior court approval. To ensure the protection of its wards, the court is entitled to call upon the RUC, in the absence of a tipstaff, to take whatever action may be necessary. The RUC may, in turn, call upon the co-operation of harbour and airport officials, the Passport Office, the DHSS and the Ministry of Defence and, if the judge so directs, full publicity may be sought. Any person interfering with the court's authority over its ward may be guilty of contempt. The penalty imposed for contempt

---

16 See *Ward v Laverty* (1925) [1925] AC 101 at p. 108.
17 See *J v C* [1970] AC 668, 710–11; 1 All ER 788, 809, HL.

can be a fine, sequestration of assets, or imprisonment, though the primary concern of the court is securing the protection of the ward and restoring its own authority rather than the punishment of offenders.

1. The Order

A wardship order, which is only one of the court's inherent powers, vests the custody of the child in the High Court. It is the only inherent power to do so. The order normally includes a direction that care and control of the ward be entrusted to one of the parties to the proceedings or that the child be committed to the care of a Trust. A direction may contain conditions, for example, as to residence, maintenance, removal from the jurisdiction, access/contact, education, medical treatment, religious upbringing or disposal of property. The absence of any such direction means that the existing status quo regarding the child's circumstances should be maintained; it does not imply that the person or body entrusted with care responsibility is free to initiate any change in those circumstances.

2. 'Important Steps' in a Ward's Life

As Cross LJ has said,[18] once a wardship order has been issued, then 'no important step in the child's life can be taken without the court's consent'. There has never been a definitive assessment of what might or might not constitute an 'important step'. The steps that have so far been regarded as important by the court include:

(a) the traditional injunction against marrying or removing a ward from the jurisdiction, which lies against the ward as well as against all third parties;
(b) adoption of a ward, or a placement by the Trust for that purpose, or even a change of surname by deed poll;
(c) a psychiatric examination, blood test, sterilisation,[19] abortion or any planned, significant and non-therapeutic form of medical treatment;
(d) enlistment in the armed forces; and
(e) the publication of information relating to a ward which was disclosed during the course of wardship proceedings.[20]

One important step, recently determined[21] not to require the court's consent, is the petitioning of the European Commission of Human Rights to allege that decisions of

---

18 See *In re S* [1967] 1 WLR 396, 407.
19 See *In re B (A Minor)* [1987] 2 FLR 314. Th decision of the House of Lords was that a seventeen-year-old mentally handicapped, epileptic girl with a mental age of five should be sterilised in accordance with the wishes of the mother, despite the opposition of the Official Solicitor acting as guardian of the child.
20 See *Re L (A Minor)* (The Times, July 4, 1987) where it was held that there was no total prohibition on the publishing of information relating to a ward. The freedom of the press would only be restricted in such cases when the information concerned court proceedings known to be private, and the scope of the restriction must be clearly and precisely defined.
21 See *Re M (Petition to European Commission of Human Rights)* [1997] 1 FLR where it was held that leave of the court was not required.

the court constitute a violation of the ward's rights under the Convention for the Protection of Human Rights and Fundamental Freedoms.

IV. *The Parties*

Anyone who can show an interest in matters affecting the welfare of a child may initiate wardship proceedings or be later joined as a party to such proceedings.

1. The Applicant

Any person or body who can show an interest may make application to the wardship jurisdiction. The applicant need not be a relative but could, for example, be a professional,[22] a statutory or voluntary body or someone who has simply undertaken care responsibility for a child. Usually, the applicant is a parent, relative or guardian, though it is possible that a minor may be both applicant and subject in the same proceedings[23] (as per the *McKenzie* principle).

2. The Subject

To be the subject of a wardship application a minor must have been born,[24] as it has been held that there is no jurisdiction to make an unborn child a ward of court. That it is less certain whether the jurisdiction lies in respect of a minor who is dead is apparent from contrasting the approach taken in England by Johnson J in *Re A (A Minor)*[25] with that taken in Northern Ireland by MacDermott LJ in *Re TC (A Minor)*.[26] Both cases concerned children whom the judiciary accepted as 'brain-stem dead'. In the former Johnson J stated:

> Holding, as I do, that he is now dead, it is not possible for me to exercise the inherent jurisdiction of the court over him as a child, nor is it possible for him to become a ward of court by the issue of an originating summons in wardship (p. 5).

In the latter MacDermott LJ, while taking notice of Johnson J's judgment and accepting 'much of the good sense of his exposition', went on to say:

> I remain, however, to be satisfied that where, as in this case, the wardship order antedated by some months the diagnosis of 'brain-stem death', the order is terminated. Where a child is a ward of court the Court is concerned with its welfare as long as it remains a ward. Death, in the usual sense, of course, terminates a wardship and

---

22 See, for example, *Re D (A Minor)* [1976] Fam 185, [1976] 1 All ER 326 where the application to prevent the proposed sterilisation of a child was made by an educational psychologist.
23 See *McKenzie v McKenzie* [1971] P 33 CA where the plaintiff was assisted by a learned 'next friend' who assisted in presenting the case by taking notes and giving advice. Now, under the Children (NI) Order 1995 there are circumstances in which an application may be made by the child concerned.
24 See *In re F (In Utero)* [1988] 2 All ER 193 CA.
25 Unreported (1993).
26 [1994] 4 BNIL 45.

though medically and in law 'brain-stem death' is accepted as death I think that it is preferable that where wardship is involved an application should be brought ...

For Johnson J the fact of death ousted the inherent jurisdiction, prevented the exercise of wardship powers but permitted him to make a declaration, which he did, to authorise doctors to use their discretion in relation to disconnecting the child's ventilator. For MacDermott LJ the fact that the child was already a ward gave the court jurisdiction which, despite the death of the subject, was exercised using inherent rather than wardship powers to the same effect.

The child must be less than eighteen years of age[27] and come within the jurisdiction of the courts though he or she need not necessarily be a resident national.[28] A minor who is a British subject domiciled within the jurisdiction will be entitled to seek the protection of wardship even if resident abroad, as will a minor of foreign nationality who is normally resident in Northern Ireland. Indeed, merely being in transit through the jurisdiction will render the minor amenable to wardship.[29]

3. The Defendant

The defendant will normally be the person or persons, body or institution against whom the plaintiff wishes to enforce the wardship order. Normally the child is not named as defendant, but this could occur if, for example, both parents are agreed on a need to restrain the child from associating with unsuitable persons or if at any time during the proceedings it became apparent that the child's best interests would be served by he or she being named as a defendant and represented accordingly. Where the minor has formed an undesirable association with another person, then that person should be named as a defendant.

V. Administration

Wardship proceedings are High Court proceedings. This means that they are expensive, usually lengthy and are processed in accordance with the full formality of that court.

1. Officials

The judge, who is available on a twenty-four-hour basis, presides over wardship proceedings. All contested hearings or those involving a point of law are heard before him or her, usually in chambers. The judge's role at such time has been best explained by MacDermott LJ:[30]

---

27 Only a person under the age of eighteen may be made a ward; see the Family Law Reform (NI) Order 1977.
28 The test is allegiance rather than residence; see N Lowe and R White, *Wards of Court*, London: Kluwer Law Publications 1986.
29 See *Re C (An Infant)* (The Times, Dec 14, 1956), where an application was heard in respect of an infant en route from the USA to the USSR but physically present in England at the time of application.
30 From the address of MacDermott LJ on the occasion of a conference on the law of custody and access held by QUB in 1982.

> Firstly, I find from my experience that it is helpful that the hearing should be as informal as reasonable decorum allows . . . . Secondly, the hearing should concentrate on the factors which relate to the child . . . . Thirdly, the parents should be allowed to develop their evidence freely.

The judge is assisted by a registrar who is a Master of the High Court. The Master normally conducts the initial hearing, decides whether to refer to the judge for a full hearing or for determination of particular legal issues and it is he or she who will be personally responsible for the management of the ward's affairs thereafter. The Master is, in turn, assisted by the staff of the Office of Care and Protection.

Because wardship proceedings are family proceedings for the purposes of the 1995 Order, a guardian ad litem (GAL) will, therefore, be appointed in all public family law applications. The Official Solicitor may, at the court's discretion, be appointed as GAL in private proceedings or, on occasion, be appointed subsequently as guardian of the ward's estate. In Northern Ireland he or she has only rarely been involved in wardship proceedings, mainly where there is a clear conflict between the interests of a child and those of other parties. His function is 'to give the child a voice in proceedings', by representing the child's views, defending the child's legal interests, instructing specialist consultants, negotiating with overseas officials and generally being a solicitor to his client the child, while reporting to the court.[31]

2. Procedure

Procedure is governed by sections 26–29 of the Judicature Act (NI) 1978 and Order 90 of the Supreme Court Rules (NI) 1980. In addition, one Practice Direction has been issued. The usual procedure is as outlined below.

(a) An application, by way of originating summons under section 26 of the Judicature Act (NI) 1978, is lodged by a petitioner with the Office of Care and Protection and copies served on the defendants who must make an appearance within fourteen days; and the Trust is duly notified that such application has been made.

(b) Within twenty-one days of the summons being issued, the plaintiff must make application to the Office, and the Office must, within that period, set a suitable date for an initial hearing of the matters alleged in the summons.

(c) Unless there has been an emergency application heard directly by the judge, in the normal course of events the Master conducts an initial hearing at which he or she identifies the legal issues, directs who should be parties to the proceedings, makes arrangements for the filing of evidence, appoints the Official Solicitor if this should be appropriate and concludes by adjourning the proceedings either for a second hearing before himself or herself, for judicial determination of particular legal issues or for a full judicial hearing.

(d) The result of a full hearing before the judge may be a confirmation of the initial application, in which case the child will be made a ward of court, or the application

---

31 See N Turner, (former Official Solicitor for England and Wales), *Adoption and Fostering*, British Agencies for Adoption and Fostering, London 1977.

may be dismissed, or an alternative order may be made. Under Article 8(3)(a) of the Children (NI) Order 1995, wardship proceedings are now family proceedings which opens up the possibility of the court making an Article 8 order (Article 10(1)), an order directing a Trust to investigate the child's circumstances (Article 56), an order for financial provision for the child (Schedule 1, para 2 of the 1995 Order) or an order appointing a guardian (Article 7).

(e) If the outcome results in a confirmation of the wardship order, this has the effect of vesting the custody of the child in the High Court and entrusting responsibility for daily care and control to one of the parties, subject to the supervision of the Master.

(f) An appeal from any decision or order made by the Master will lie to the judge, and from him or her to the Court of Appeal and thence, with leave, to the House of Lords.

(g) Finally, wardship terminates at the expiration of the twenty-one-day period following issue of the originating summons or if the plaintiff fails to make application for a hearing within that period. It will also terminate upon the ward attaining the age of eighteen, upon the order of the court acting on its own initiative or in response to an application to de-ward.

Wardship before the Children (NI) Order 1995

From the 1970s through to the mid-1990s the wardship jurisdiction played a pivotal role in developing the law and practice relating to the custody, care and upbringing of children in Northern Ireland.

I. The Role of Wardship in Relation to Private Family Law

Long before the wardship jurisdiction in Northern Ireland came to be associated with care and protection issues in proceedings brought by the Health and Social Services Boards (or Trusts), it had earned a reputation for using its powers where those of the statutory processes were unavailable or inappropriate to assist parental applicants negotiate equitable arrangements for the upbringing of their children. By 1995 the majority of wardship applications were private. The wardship jurisdiction also provided a forum where the legal interests of persons (such as an unmarried father or grandparent) who would have had difficulty in finding representation in statutory proceedings could be taken into account when determining matters of custody or access. Finally, it offered a 'court of last resort' when a particularly difficult or urgent issue arose in relation to the welfare of a child.

1. Wardship as a Forum for Resolving Issues of Custody or Access

A well-established characteristic of wardship in Northern Ireland, unlike England, has been its availability to spouses to resolve issues relating to the custody or upbringing of their children after the breakdown of the marriage but before the initiation of statutory proceedings. Indeed, MacDermott J once characterised as immoral the contemporary practice in England of admitting wardship applications on such issues only on condition that matrimonial proceedings have or will be commenced. The majority of the cases appearing in the wardship jurisdiction during the 1970s and early 1980s were private proceedings, following marital breakdown, brought by spouses who wished to avoid adversarial and acrimonious statutory proceedings. In responding to such applications the judiciary firmly applied the paramountcy principle.[32]

In the course of processing many quite ordinary custody and access disputes, the judiciary in the wardship jurisdiction were able to use the paramountcy principle to transcend many of the restrictions which made a conciliatory approach to securing a child's welfare so difficult to achieve in statutory proceedings.

For example, in *Re P McA (A Minor)*,[33] MacDermott J was able to set aside the issue of parental fault when considering the matter of custody arrangements for a two-year-old boy. As he then said of the mother:

> She has in the past acted stupidly, perhaps irresponsibly. I am however, satisfied that she genuinely loves the child. . . . I have no doubt that the child should be with his mother.

This approach was extended to 'tug-of-love' cases where the fact that a parent had been guilty of kidnapping a child did not disqualify him or her from being regarded by the court as the best person to carry care responsibility for that child.[34] In *Re JRS (A Minor)*,[35] MacDermott J stated that

> . . . these cases concerning the welfare of a child are decided not according to the so-called principle of the unimpeachable parent but by regard to the welfare of the child.

In *Re CDH (A Minor)*,[36] the kidnapping father was awarded care and control, and in *Re L (Minors)*,[37] the same learned judge pointed out that, in wardship, considerations of the child's welfare must prevail over the court's traditional concern that no person should benefit from wrong-doing:

> It would be easy to say that the law's delays should not work to the disadvantage of the mother and that therefore the children must be returned. . . . [H]owever . . . the guilt or innocence of a parent is not the decisive point, much less the consequences of the law's delays. It is the welfare of the child which is important.

The same approach was applied to the traditional *prima facie* right of a father to the custody of his legitimate child and was also employed to override the tradition of

---

32 This was very apparent, for example, in *Re CB and AJB (Minors)*, unreported (1983), where MacDermott J in dealing with an access dispute remarked: 'Access is of course a right of the child supposedly being for its benefit'. He asserted this right in *Re BM and BH (Minors)*, unreported (1979), when the care and control of two children were awarded separately to each parent with an order directing no reciprocal access because of strained parental relationships. Again, in *Re ICS and RHS (Minors)*, unreported (1982), not only was the application for care and control from the grandparents refused, but in view of their bitter attitudes, they were specifically denied access.
33 Unreported (1983).
34 See, for example, in *Re CB and JB (Minors)*, unreported (1983), where a kidnapping mother was awarded care and control.
35 Unreported (1983).
36 Unreported (1980).
37 Unreported (1981).

upholding the principle of comity between jurisdictions (see further Chapter Ten). One attraction of pursuing such issues in wardship rather than in a statutory context was that because the process whereby the High Court supervises its wards remains constantly open, care and access arrangements could be swiftly and informally considered, reviewed and adjusted as necessary on a continuing basis. Any unauthorised action by either party could be speedily handled by the High Court's use of its prerogative powers to safeguard the welfare of its wards.

2. Wardship as a Forum for Taking into Account the Interests of Non-Statutory Parties

Under Part IV of the Matrimonial Causes (NI) Order 1978 and Article 10 of the Domestic Proceedings (NI) Order 1980, only natural parents or parents by marriage were entitled to be applicants in statutory custody proceedings. Therefore, when the father of a non-marital child wished, for example, to claim custody or to challenge the proposed adoption of the latter by the mother and her spouse, then the wardship jurisdiction was available to give him *locus standi* in such proceedings. This was also the case when such a challenge came from a grandparent, sibling, other relative or foster-parent who wished to protect his or her relationship with a child. In fact, grandparents often had recourse to wardship in order to bring their claims for custody or access before the court or to challenge decisions taken in respect of a child in care.[38] Wardship was the only form of proceedings which they could initiate. They could, however, apply for an access order under Article 16 of the Domestic Proceedings Order 1980 or seek leave to be joined as a party to care proceedings once these had been commenced.

3. Wardship as the 'Court of Last Resort'

There have and always will be unusual cases which require the time, detailed examination and involvement of many parties and expert witnesses for which only the High Court can reasonably hope to provide. One such case was *Re TC (A Minor)*,[39] which concerned a child born on 12 December 1991 with spina bifida and hydrocephalus. The child had been maintained on a ventilator since 23 November 1993. The hospital trust sought permission to disconnect the ventilator which was sustaining the life of the two-year-old severely brain damaged child. Having received evidence that the child suffered from 'brain stem death' and considered relevant English case law, MacDermott LJ concluded:

> I hold that it would be wholly contrary to the interests of TC for her to be subjected to what would seem to me to be the continuing indignity to which she is presently but properly subjected. I consider that the nursing and medical staff of this hospital have done all that could be done for the welfare and well-being of this child. TC may now be separated from the ventilation which supports her existence — not life — when the medical staff at the hospital consider it proper to do so.

---

38 See, for example, the 'Dropping Well Case': *Re W (A Minor)(Wardship: Jurisdiction)* [1985] AC 791 *and Re H (A Minor)(Custody: Interim Care and Control)* [1991] 2 FLR 109.
39 [1994] 4 BNIL p. 45.

II. The Role of Wardship in Relation to Public Family Law

The contribution made by the wardship jurisdiction to securing the welfare of children placed at risk by abusing or neglecting parents in the last fifteen years or so of the 1968 Act would be difficult to overestimate. The considerable difference between the child-care legislation of Northern Ireland and that of the rest of the United Kingdom ensured that the role played by wardship in compensating for the statutory deficit in the powers necessary to secure the welfare of children was of greater significance in this jurisdiction.

1. Wardship as a Means of Supplementing the Trust's Committal to Care Powers

The orders available to a Trust under the terms of the Children and Young Persons Act (NI) 1968 were not always appropriate to the circumstances which exposed a child to risk. If appropriate, such orders were sometimes not available, due perhaps to lack of time or insufficient evidence. Applying to the wardship jurisdiction instead of initiating care proceedings was at times the only option open to a Trust seeking to secure a child's welfare.

A situation which arose with some frequency was the birth of a child to a mother who had been convicted of serious offences in relation to other children. The Trust, unwilling to expose the baby to the risk of similar abuse or neglect, would wish to remove the child. However, statutory intervention was only possible under section 93(2)(b) of the 1968 Act *after* 'the lack of care, protection or guidance' made future suffering likely. The *probability* of harm provided insufficient grounds for removing a newly born baby from a mother who had not yet had the opportunity to demonstrate abuse or neglect towards the child. Many wardship orders were sought and obtained in respect of such young babies. Allied to this was the problem of a child already in a place designated as 'safe' such as a hospital or foster home[40] but threatened with removal by an abusive or neglectful parent. The only relevant statutory powers were those of a place of safety order (PSO), which, given the child's location, was inappropriate. Again, in such circumstances, the Trusts had no choice but to resort to wardship.

Certain classes of case also presented the Trusts with particular problems and were more likely to result in the initiation of wardship than statutory proceedings. Cases where a Trust's allegation of sexual abuse of a young child was being strenuously denied by a parent perpetrator[41] were quite commonly heard in wardship. The reason for this was to do with the difficulty in providing evidence of sufficient quality to satisfy the narrowly defined statutory grounds combined with Trust hesitancy to carry the responsibility of returning a child to an abusing environment. By sharing their concerns about the causes of a threat to a child's welfare with the wardship judiciary, a Trust was thereby also able to share the responsibility for on-going protection of that child's welfare.

Finally, there were the occasional situations where a Trust needed to rely on wardship to urgently secure the welfare of a child, following the failure of statutory

---

40 Strictly speaking, the child or young person should be brought to a position outside the precincts of such a place before a PSO could be served in respect of him or her.
41 See, for example, *In re PB (A Minor)*, unreported (1986).

proceedings. This, for example, occurred in *Re McV (Minors)*,[42] when, following the dismissal of its application to secure fit person orders (FPOs) in a magistrates' court, the Trust's immediate application to the wardship jurisdiction was granted in order to allow it time to prepare an appeal through the normal statutory procedures.

2. Wardship as a Means of Supplementing the Trust's Powers in Respect of Children Already Subject to Care Orders

A Trust's powers in respect of a child in its care, under the terms of the Children and Young Persons Act (NI) 1968, were exercisable at its discretion. Unless it infringed the *Wednesbury Rules*,[43] a Trust's decision-making would be shielded from court scrutiny by the *Liverpool* (see page 299) ruling. There were limitations, however, and these were imposed by the degree of authority vesting in a Trust as a consequence of a child being admitted into its care under section 103 of the 1968 Act or being committed under section 95 of that Act. In addition, the occasional urgent, difficult or complex problem arose in respect of which a Trust needed both the advice and the protection of the High Court. Each of these areas generated Trust applications to the wardship jurisdiction.

An illustration of such a difficult problem (given the political/cultural context) arose in regard to the future care arrangements of four children from the same family but of different parentage, different religions and subject to FPOs. Mrs B, the mother of nine children, had been brought up as a Roman Catholic and three of her children were being reared by her mother in that faith. Her two youngest were the subjects of supervision orders in favour of the EHSSB and were being reared at home with her 'husband' (their marriage was apparently void) and herself. The family lived in a Protestant area and considered itself to be Protestant. The case[44] concerned the remaining four children: a girl, born in 1969, who was illegitimate; a boy, born in 1971, a child of Mrs B's marriage; and two boys, born in 1976 and 1977, sons of Mr B. The case concerned these four children who were all the subject of FPOs and who had been placed, with parental consent, in St Joseph's Children's Home, the only place which could then accommodate them. Among the parental rights not transferred to the EHSSB under an FPO was the right to determine religious upbringing. When Mr B refused to visit his children because he disliked the Roman Catholic atmosphere, the EHSSB

---

42 Unreported (1986).
43 See *Associated Provincial Picture Houses Ltd v Wednesbury Corporation* [1948] 1 KB 223 and the principle stated therein by Lord Greene:
> The court is entitled to investigate the action of the local authority with a view to seeing whether they have taken into account or conversely, have refused to take into account or neglected to take into account matters which they ought to take into account. Once that question is answered in favour of the local authority it may still be possible to say that although the local authority have kept within the four corners of the matters which they ought to consider they have nonetheless come to a conclusion so unreasonable that no reasonable authority could ever come to it. In such a case again, I think the Court can interfere.

This principle was quoted with approval in the *Liverpool* case (see f/n 11).
44 See *Re McC T and B (Minors)*, unreported (1982).

then rightly considered itself to be compromised and the four children were made wards of court on application by the EHSSB so that the latter could be judicially advised as to the appropriate decisions to be taken. MacDermott J, as he then was, determined that all four should be moved to a non-Roman Catholic children's home (where four places had become available). He further ruled that the two youngest children should be brought up as Protestants, in accordance with their parents' wishes. In relation to the older two, however, as he did not 'ascertain any evidence of deep-seated religious conviction' he therefore declined to make any ruling on religious upbringing.

An admission to care under section 103 of the 1968 Act placed the Trust in a *loco parentis* relationship to the admitted child; all authority was retained by the parents. The Trust, having no statutory powers to prevent a parent from removing the child from care and no statutory orders being appropriate to such a situation, was sometimes forced to resort to wardship.

A committal to care under a fit person order, place of safety order or parental rights order also at times placed the Trust in a situation where it had a deficit of authority, and parental consent was necessary but unavailable, for certain courses of action. Most frequently this occurred when parental consent was refused for a Trust to place a child in care for adoption. In *Re M McC and DH (Minors)*,[45] for example, Hutton J granted a Trust's wardship application so as to free two small children from the unreasonable veto of a natural parent to a proposed adoption placement. This case was typical of many on the same issue brought by Trusts in the wardship jurisdiction because of a lack of statutory authority (see also Chapter Six). Other rights retained by parents such as the right to consent to the administering of anaesthetic also resulted in Trust wardship applications.

In its management of a child committed to its care, a Trust would occasionally be faced with a particularly worrying problem. Then, by following the advice of Sheldon J in *Re LH (A Minor)(Wardship)*,[46]

> ... they were entitled to seek the assistance of the High Court ... where it was thought that the problem would be best solved by the wide powers available to the courts in wardship proceedings.

One such case was *In Re DR (A Minor)*,[47] where a child was warded on being found to be suffering from methadone withdrawal symptoms at birth. The Trust brought the application[48] on the grounds that the child's condition showed that its 'health or proper development', within the terms of section 93(2)(b) of the 1968 Act, was being prevented or neglected. As this could only have been incurred while *en ventre sa mere* (unborn), there was, therefore, a continuing state of affairs justifying Trust intervention because of the likelihood of future harm unless protective measures were taken.

---

45 [1986] 5 NIJB 1.
46 Unreported (1986).
47 Unreported (1987).
48 Following the similar case of *Re D (A Minor)* The Times, Dec 5, 1986 decided by the House of Lords.

Two cases concerning consent for the termination of pregnancies of young and disturbed adolescents in care have also, in recent years, been heard in wardship. They were *In the matter of K (A Minor)*[49] and *In the matter of CH (A Minor)*,[50] both heard by Sheil J. The first involved a fourteen-year-old who was the subject of an FPO and resident in a children's home. She was thirteen weeks pregnant and requested an abortion to which her mother contested. The second concerned a girl aged sixteen, in care and resident on a similar basis, who was twelve weeks pregnant and whose wish for an abortion was accepted by her parent and the putative father. There being no statutory authority available to permit abortion in Northern Ireland, the Trusts warded the minors with a view to seeking this authority from the wardship jurisdiction. Indeed, in the absence of any equivalent to the Abortion Act 1967, the relevant statutory provisions governing this issue are to be found in the Offences against the Person Act 1861, sections 58 and 59. Having received evidence that both minors were '*Gillick* competent', were steadfast in their desire for a termination and threatened suicide if their wishes were obstructed and following evidence from Trust staff, doctors and psychiatrists as to the minors' mental health, the court decided, in the light of established English case law, to give permission for the pregnancies to be terminated and for appropriate travel arrangements to be made (see also Chapter Three).

III. The Role of Wardship in Relation to the Welfare Interests of the Child

The most significant contribution made by the wardship jurisdiction to the law relating to the custody, care and upbringing of children in Northern Ireland has been the extent to which it has reached behind the statutory references to child welfare, 'best interests', 'for the good of' etc. and injected some specific indicators of what in particular may be held to constitute the substance of 'welfare'. In doing so it has also proved to be an effective judicial means of countering conservative legislative principles.

1. Age and Gender of Child

There is no legislative requirement that a child's age or gender should play any part in the determination of custody proceedings in respect of that child. The judiciary in Northern Ireland, however, in keeping with the practice of their colleagues elsewhere in the United Kingdom, developed certain rules of thumb to guide decision-making on such matters. In this jurisdiction these rules were first applied in wardship cases before gaining more generalised judicial credence in cases of contested custody.

One such rule was that the younger the child the stronger the presumption that maternal rather than paternal care was to be preferred. This was apparent, for example, in *In the matter of TMW and AMW (Minors)*[51] where MacDermott J, in awarding custody of two girls, aged seven and three, concluded that 'these two girls should remain together and are too young to separate from their mother'. That this rule applied regardless of the child's gender is evident from his decision in cases such as *Re P McA*

---

49 Unreported (1993).
50 Unreported (1995).
51 [1979] 9 NIJB.

(Minor),[52] where, when awarding the care and control of a three-year-old boy to his mother, he commented, 'I have no doubt that the child should be with his mother . . . during his tender formative years.'

This was offset by another such rule to the effect that the older the child the stronger the presumption that he or she should be cared for by the parent of corresponding gender. The bearing of this factor on custody issues was apparent in cases such as in *Re JRS (A Minor)*,[53] where, in relation to an eleven-year-old boy, MacDermott J stated:

> I feel strongly that J is at a stage when he needs to be in a home in which there is a man. He needs guidance and discipline and preferably of a sensible and practical nature. I have no doubt that his father will supply these needs more readily than his mother.

This ruling echoed previous unreported judgments by the same judge,[54] where again gender affinity was a key factor in the award of custody to a contesting parent.

The extent to which these rules of thumb may be compatible with the dictates of the paramountcy principle has been open to contention.

2. The Importance of Keeping Siblings Together

The importance of keeping siblings together has been acknowledged by MacDermott J.[55] In *Re MEMV and MRVV (Minors)*,[56] he stressed:

> Additionally, I am strongly of the opinion that young children should be brought up together. That is the way of nature and self-protectively children draw closer to each other as parents drift apart.

3. The Importance of Keeping Children in a Familiar Environment

The importance of keeping children in a familiar environment is a principle which, in this jurisdiction, has guided judicial decision-making in a number of cases such as in *In re RASJ and PFJ (Minors)*[57] (see further Chapter Ten).

4. The Opinion of the Child

As MacDermott J stated in *Re CB and AJB (Minors)*:[58]

> The older a child gets the greater weight which can be given to its wishes . . . These girls are twelve and ten and quite mature . . . of an age to express a meaningful opinion and I bear it in mind.

---

52 Unreported (1983).
53 Unreported (1983).
54 See, for example, such cases as *Re RASJ and PFJ (Minors)*, unreported (1976) and *Re BM and BH (Minors)*, unreported (1979).
55 See, for example, in *Re RASJ and PFJ (Minors)*, unreported (1976), where he stated that 'the courts look favourably on an arrangement which keeps the children of a family united'.
56 Unreported (1981).
57 Unreported (1976).
58 Unreported (1983).

The case law of the wardship jurisdiction reveals a consistent judicial concern to establish a direct relationship with the children who come before the court. In recent years this has been accompanied by a judicial willingness to solicit and give more weight to their opinions.

5. Regard for the Children's Future Welfare

A characteristic of the wardship in this jurisdiction is that, unlike statutory law, wardship has not been tied to past or present circumstances but has had the capacity to consider also the likely bearing of future probabilities. Throughout the judgments, decisions are taken with reference to such projected welfare considerations as the ages, career potential and domestic relationship of the prospective custodians. In the words of MacDermott J in *Re MEMV and MRVV (Minors)*:[59]

> The welfare of the child is my sole concern ... one is concerned with the welfare of a child next week, next month, next year and on into the foreseeable future. Chopping and changing do no child any good.

6. Presumption of Paternal Right to Custody

A singular anachronism in the family law of Northern Ireland has been the survival of the *prima facie* right of a father to the custody of his legitimate child. The letter, if not the practice, of the law continued this common-law presumption, as embodied in section 5 of the Guardianship of Infants Act 1886, that custody vests in the father until a court orders otherwise. Judicial initiative in wardship proceedings sought to correct legislative omission, as when MacDermott J ruled[60] that, 'In having regard to the conduct of the parents under section 5 of the Act of 1886 the Court should consider the spouses as of equal status and ignore the inequality of their rights at common law.' However, MacDermott J was, some years later, still able to state:[61]

> If the welfare of the child is equally assured irrespective of which parent obtains custody, there exists, in Northern Ireland at least, a sufficient residue of the father's common law right to custody to tip the balance in his favour.

Testimony to the prolonged life of this principle in the private family law of Northern Ireland is available in the very many unreported judgments from the wardship jurisdiction throughout the 1970s and 1980s which bear a reference to it.[62]

7. Conduct of the Parties

The doctrine of the unimpeachable parent no longer plays a role in determining custody disputes. This has been due, at least in part, to the role played by the judiciary in wardship. As MacDermott J[63] has remarked:

---

59 Unreported (1981).
60 See *In Re B (An Infant)* [1946] NI 1, 8.
61 See *Re EAW and MW (Infants)* [1949] NI 1.
62 See appendix 1 for a full statement of the eight principles of the MacDermott J. which governed the determination of many private family law wardship cases during this period.
63 See appendix 1, 'The 8 Principles'.

Even if a parent's conduct is blameworthy, he or she may be preferred to the innocent parent if the court is satisfied that the future welfare of the child will be best secured by that course being taken.

Parental fitness for custody may, however, be lost through conduct such as incest.[64]

IV. The Role of Wardship in Relation to Judicial Review

The judicial review procedure is not available simply as a means of appealing a decision unfavourable to the applicant; it must raise a point of principle. The action must be brought within three months, and in order to avoid frivolous, vexatious or hopeless actions, applicants must first obtain leave of the court. The order sought is almost always either a *certiorari* to quash the defective decision and/or a *mandamus* directing the body to comply with its statutory duty.

1. Grounds for Judicial Review

The grounds for judicial review are usually held to be those which would fit within the scope of the *Wednesbury* principle. Diplock LJ has suggested[65] that there are three separate and distinct reasons which would ground a judicial review. First, 'illegality', i.e. where there was an error of law in reaching the relevant decision. Second, 'procedural impropriety', i.e. where the relevant rules have not been complied with. Finally, 'irrationality', i.e. where a decision 'is so outrageous in its defiance of logic or of accepted standards that no sensible person who had applied his mind to the question to be decided could have arrived at it'.

2. Judicial Review and Wards

In wardship the custody of a ward vests in the High Court. Therefore, of necessity, the judiciary have had to maintain a close involvement in all decisions taken in respect of its wards. This involvement has obviated the need for judicial review in regard to Trust management of wards as the court is a party to all significant Trust decisions.

3. Judicial Review and Children in Care

Trust decision-making in respect of children who are not wards but who have been made the subject of care orders are exempted from judicial scrutiny by the *Liverpool* decision[66] which held that the statutory responsibilities of the Trust's English counterparts should not be circumvented by applications to the wardship jurisdiction. However, the protection offered by the *Liverpool* ruling (see page 299) is lost if the decisions of a Trust should fall within the *Wednesbury* rules.

In England the practice of reviewing the latter in the High Court is well established. There have been many applications, usually by parents or foster-parents, for judicial

---

64 See, for example, *ACB v JLB* 1980.
65 See *In Council of Civil Service Unions v Minister for Civil Defence* [1985] AC 374.
66 See *A v Liverpool City Council* [1982] AC 363, [1981] FLR 222.

review of decisions.[67] In Northern Ireland the judicial review procedure has been initiated on at least two occasions, both of which concerned Trusts' interpretation of the adoption procedure. One was in 1989 when Higgins J had cause to examine the source of authority for a decision taken by the adoption panel of the EHSSB. This concerned the right of the EHSSB to 'fetter its discretion' by imposing an age limit on, admittedly excellent, prospective adopters which had the effect of rendering them ineligible to adopt the disabled child, in care under section 103 of the 1968 Act, for whom they had been providing care almost since birth. As the applicants withdrew on the second day of the hearing, no conclusion was reached. The second case concerned the authority of an agency's adoption panel to reject an independent assessment report recommending the approval of a couple who wished to be registered as approved adopters. The outcome is unknown.

4. Judicial Review and the Wardship Jurisdiction

For some years it was accepted that the wardship jurisdiction was the proper place for reviewing decisions taken by statutory bodies affecting the custody, care or upbringing of children, which were deficient by *Wednesbury* standards. A number of cases were so reviewed by the High Court judiciary in England. However, it was eventually determined[68] that this should be discontinued as the wardship jurisdiction was not an appropriate forum for judicial review. This practice has been followed in Northern Ireland.

Wardship, the Inherent Jurisdiction and the Trusts after the Introduction of the Children (NI) Order 1995

Under the Children (NI) Order 1995, Article 173:

> (1) The court shall not exercise its inherent jurisdiction with respect to children—
>
> (a) so as to require a child to be placed in the care of, or put under the supervision of, a Board or Health and Social Services trust;
> (b) so as to require a child to be accommodated by or on behalf of a Board or Health and Social Services trust;
> (c) so as to make a child who is the subject of a care order a ward of court; or
> (d) for the purpose of conferring on any Board or Health and Social Services trust power to determine any question which has arisen, or which may arise, in connection with any aspect of parental responsibility for a child.

---

67 For example, in *R v Norfolk County Council ex parte M* [1989] 2 All ER 359, where the complainant queried the decision to place a child on an agency's Child Protection Register and *R v Devon County Council, ex parte L* [1991] 2 FLR 541, where a social worker had informed the applicant's partner that he was suspected of sexual abuse.
68 See *In Re DM (A Minor)(Wardship: Jurisdiction)* [1986] 2 FRL 102 and *Re LM (Minors) (Wardship: Jurisdiction)* [1986] 2 FLR 205.

The legislative intent in this provision is to prevent future overlap between the statutory and wardship jurisdictions by barring the door to any continuation of the Trusts' use of wardship as an alternative to the statutory jurisdiction and by prohibiting the judicial practice of committing wards into the statutory care of the Trusts. The jurisdictions of wardship and statutory child care have now been made mutually exclusive. The 1995 Order has simplified the legal routes into care (see Chapter Twelve) and linked them to the common bench-mark of 'significant harm', this provision seeks to ensure that wardship is not available as an alternative means of effecting state intervention in family affairs.

I. Restrictions on Access to the Wardship Jurisdiction

As intended, the 1995 Order, in particular the above provision, has radically affected the availability of wardship both to the Boards and to private applicants.

1. Preventing Trust Use of Wardship

As Ewbank J has observed[69] the High Court has an inherent power to make a child a ward of court, but a Trust will be denied access to the wardship jurisdiction when this is for the purpose of having a child committed to care or placed under supervision, having a child, already the subject of a care order, made a ward so as to allow a course of action not available under the terms of the care order or requiring accommodation to be provided for a child. Furthermore, because wardship proceedings are now defined as family proceedings for the purposes of the Children (NI) Order 1995, the High Court is restricted in the exercise of its powers in respect of wards to those which are necessary to give effect to 'parental responsibility'. It would seem that any power in excess of this quotient will now be unavailable to the judiciary when acting to protect the interests of its wards. This constriction of wardship to conformity with other family proceedings, which have in turn now been invested with the powers formerly associated with wardship, will largely remove its attractiveness to the Trusts.

2. Preventing Access to Wardship to Challenge Trust Decisions

Under the Children (NI) Order 1995, wardship and the statutory child care provided by the Trusts have been rendered incompatible. This has the effect of removing any possibility of a person using wardship to challenge Trust decision-making in respect of a child in care.

II. Trust Access to the Inherent Jurisdiction

Under the Children (NI) Order 1995, Article 173, a Trust may apply to the inherent jurisdiction only with leave of the court and:

> (3) The court may only grant leave if it is satisfied that—
> (a) the result which the authority wishes to achieve could not be achieved through the making of any order of a kind to which paragraph (4) applies; and

---

69   See *R v North Yorkshire County Council, ex parte M (no. 3)* [1989] 2 FLR 82.

(b) there is reasonable cause to believe that if the court's inherent jurisdiction is not exercised with respect to the child he is likely to suffer significant harm.

(4) This paragraph applies to any order—
(a) made otherwise than in the exercise of the court's inherent jurisdiction; and
(b) which the authority is entitled to apply for (assuming, in the case of any application which may only be made with leave, that leave is granted).

This provision prohibits a court from granting leave for a Trust to apply to the wardship jurisdiction except in situations where it is convinced that there is no statutory procedure available to the Trust, which it would be entitled to avail of, to safeguard a child who will be left in or at risk of significant harm unless the powers of that jurisdiction are exercised. In England, since the 1989 Act, leave has been granted in a number of cases[70] concerning the medical treatment of wards, where the issue was one which held particularly grave consequences for a child's welfare, for the matter to be heard in the wardship/inherent jurisdiction of the High Court. Where a child is already subject to a care order, a Trust will be unable to resort to wardship, as this is now statute barred by Article 173 (1) of the 1995 Order; nor will Article 8 orders be possible.

1. Remit of the Inherent Jurisdiction

The inherent jurisdiction rather than the wardship jurisdiction of the High Court will be available to the Trusts in respect of children where complex problems arise and leave of the court is obtained. If leave is granted and the inherent jurisdiction exercised, then, because proceedings in the inherent jurisdiction are defined as family proceedings for the purpose of the 1995 Order, the court will have power to make any Article 8 order, except in respect of a child in care. However, the inherent jurisdiction exceeds the scope of family proceedings, as it exceeds wardship, and is not limited to determining matters which fall within the definition of 'parental responsibility'. Arguably, in any circumstance where a Trust is seeking access to powers in excess of those necessary to give effect to parental responsibility it will now have to apply to the court's inherent jurisdiction.

A Trust will have a power, under Article 173(3) and (4) of the 1995 Order, to gain access to the inherent jurisdiction of the High Court to resolve an issue concerning a child in care. The leading case on this matter is *Re W (A Minor)(Medical Treatment: Court's Jurisdiction)*[71] which considered an application made by a Trust's English counterpart under the equivalent provision of the 1989 Act. Then, the application was made, in respect of a sixteen-year-old anorexic girl in care, for permission to arrange medical treatment and for this to be provided without her consent if necessary. The Court of Appeal unanimously gave its consent, holding that it had authority to do so under the court's unlimited inherent *parens patriae* jurisdiction. It further held that the authority of those holding 'parental responsibility' for a child would be insufficient to

---

[70] See, for example, *South Glamorgan County Council v W and B* [1993] 1 FLR 574.
[71] [1992] 3 WLR 785, [1992] 4 All ER 627.

override the decision of a *'Gillick* competent' child and that its authority when exercising this jurisdiction exceeded that which came within the definition of 'parental responsibility'. It was decided that the High Court's inherent jurisdiction may apply regardless of whether or not the child in question was a ward. (For the law relating to the parental duty to ensure treatment, see Chapters Two and Fifteen.)

Much the same *ratio decendi* is discernible in *South Glamorgan County Council v W and B*,[72] where it was necessary for a Trust's counterpart to override the refusal of a fifteen-year-old, the subject of an interim care order, to have a psychiatric assessment and, if necessary, treatment. In what could prove to be a decision with significant precedent potential, the court held that the Trust's counterpart was entitled to invoke the inherent jurisdiction to supplement the statutory powers available to it, thereby achieving a result which legislative intent had specifically sought to prohibit.

Both these decisions would seem largely to undo the effect of two provisions in the 1995 Order: Article 57(6) which enables the subject of an interim care order, if of sufficient understanding, to refuse to submit to a psychiatric assessment; and Article 173(1)(c) which prevents a Trust from making the subject of a care order a ward of court. Only time will reveal whether they will come to be seen as the thin end of a wedge which, for some purposes, return the Trust's use of wardship/inherent jurisdiction to the pre-1995 position.

A Trust may also, in fact, have a duty to apply to the inherent jurisdiction in circumstances where the use of its statutory powers of coercive intervention are inappropriate. This is the implication which emerges from the judgment of Johnson J in *Re O (A Minor)(Medical Treatment)*[73] *(See also Re R (A Minor)(Blood Transfusion)*[74] where he ruled that the inherent jurisdiction was the most appropriate forum to authorise a blood transfusion for a child, against the wishes of the child's parents who were Jehovah Witnesses and caring, committed and capable people.[75] Such applications are most often made in respect of children whose need for urgent medical treatment is opposed by their parents. As the outcome of *Re T (Liver Transplant: Consent)*[76] illustrates, once a matter is admitted to the inherent jurisdiction the role of the paramountcy principle may then be difficult to predict. In that case leave was granted for an application to be brought by a Trust's counterpart, supported by the Official Solicitor who had been appointed GAL, in respect of a baby suffering from a life threatening liver defect whose parents were opposed to treatment. At the substantive hearing expert evidence from the staff of three hospitals indicated that with a transplant the prognosis for recovery was good, without it the child would die within eighteen months. The parents, unmarried but in a stable relationship, who were both health care professionals with experience in the care of sick children, maintained that it was not in their child's best interests to suffer the further pain and distress of a major operation.

---

72   [1993] 1 FLR 574.
73   [1993] 2 FLR 149.
74   [1993] 2 FLR 757.
75   However, more recently the practice in England has been to use specific issue orders to deal with less controversial issues such as blood transfusions.
76   (1996) *The Times, The Independent*, October 29, CA.

The decision of the court to order the operation went on appeal to the Court of Appeal which held that it was not in the child's best interests to order the caring, well-informed parents to facilitate an operation with which they so profoundly disagreed. It was a matter best left to the judgment of the parents. The significance of this decision lies in the judicial assimilation of the interests of a very dependent baby and those of a devoted caring mother. It also poses serious questions for the role of GAL. Again, where the Trust does not wish to have powers conferred on it but instead considers that the court should take certain steps for which the Trust does not have the necessary statutory authority, recourse to the inherent jurisdiction may be necessary. This was found to be a justifiable course of action in *Devon County Council v S and Another*[77] where the court was invited to use the powers available to it in the exercise of its inherent jurisdiction to achieve an objective beyond the statutory powers of a Trust's counterpart, to bar a father who was a convicted sex offender from having contact with his children.

It is clear that there will still be circumstances in which, if a Trust is to discharge its duty to safeguard the welfare of a child in its care, it will have to make application to the inherent jurisdiction of the High Court.

2. Limits of the Inherent Jurisdiction

Where a child is already subject to a care order and a Trust needs authority to make decisions which lie outside the powers invested in it by virtue of it holding 'parental responsibility', it will have to seek that additional authority from the court. However, the only Article 8 order the court can make is a residence order in favour of a party other than the Trust. This it is unlikely to do, as its effect will be to discharge the care order and terminate the Trust's principal statutory duties in respect of the child. It cannot make a wardship order as this is now statute barred. The only source of such authority is the inherent *parens patriae* jurisdiction of the High Court. This jurisdiction is unlimited. A difference between an order made by the High Court in the exercise of its wardship jurisdiction as opposed to its inherent jurisdiction is that in the former, but not in the latter, custody of the child vests in the court.

Wardship, the Inherent Jurisdiction and Private Applicants after the Children (NI) Order 1995

The 1995 Order does not prevent private applicants from gaining access to the wardship jurisdiction or to the inherent jurisdiction of the High Court. Unlike the Trusts, private individuals are not statute barred from making application to the wardship jurisdiction as an alternative to statutory proceedings.

I. Restrictions on the Use of Wardship

Wardship is an expensive way to gain remedies which are now, in most cases, available in the magistrates' court and the county court. One of the more important achievements

---

77 [1994] 1 FLR 355.

of the 1995 Order has been to make generally accessible those legal powers which were formerly exclusive to wardship. The situations which previously prompted relatives, foster parents and unmarried fathers to seek wardship orders may well now be met more quickly and cheaply by residence orders. There will seldom be circumstances when the remedy sought by a private applicant is now not available in the statutory jurisdiction.

II. Reasons for Continued Use of Wardship

There will always be the unusual or particularly complex case, perhaps requiring the involvement of many parties or drawing on the skills of many expert witnesses, for which the flexibility, thoroughness and on-going management provided by wardship will offer a more appropriate framework for resolution than statutory proceedings. Wardship provides a useful safety net to protect the welfare of children who might slip through the fairly comprehensive provisions of the 1995 Order.

In addition, there are certain powers such as protection from publicity[78] which may on occasion require recourse to wardship. Although this is most usually initiated by parents or guardians seeking injunctions to prevent unwelcome media attention being focused on their children, it may also be imposed by the court against the wishes of a parent.[79] However, Article 170 of the 1995 Order now provides a statutory power to prohibit any publicity identifying a child or his or her school, and this should remove the necessity to resort to wardship for this purpose. The emergency 'stop and hold' powers, which can be used at times of kidnapping or 'tug of love' cases to direct the RUC and officials at harbours and airports, are also likely to continue to attract applications to wardship.

---

[78] This was the case in *Re M and N (Minors)(Wardship: Publication of Information)* [1990] Fam 211 CA.
[79] See *Re Z (A Minor)(Freedom of Publication)* [1996] 1 FLR 191.

CHAPTER EIGHT

Marriage Breakdown: Separation

Introduction

The breakdown of a marriage can lead to separation rather than divorce. One or both parties may decide to initiate proceedings which stop short of terminating their legal status as spouses.

In Northern Ireland, in 1991, a total of 3,188 separation orders were issued by the magistrates' courts under the Domestic Proceedings (NI) Order 1980. In 1992 the figure was 3,023.

This chapter deals with separation proceedings brought for the limited purpose of enforcing certain specific rights. It also examines the law relating to domestic violence. Excluding petitions for divorce, it is this area which generates the most work for the courts in relation to marriage breakdown. Where children are concerned, as in divorce proceedings, the law relating to their future care arrangements is now consolidated under the Children (NI) Order 1995 and reference must be made to Part II of this book. Where property, maintenance and the matrimonial home are concerned, the law is to be found in Part III.

Judicial Separation

Spouses may achieve a formal separation either by way of judicial separation or by a separation agreement. Usually these options are chosen because religious principles, time or the prospect of financial hardship prevents divorce proceedings. Alternatively, one party may simply wish to deal with a particular aspect of their marriage, such as care arrangements for the children or maintenance, while denying the other the freedom to re-marry. Judicial separation has been the subject of review[1] by the Law Commission.

I. Judicial Separation: Eligibility

The court must be satisfied that the parties have been married for a minimum period of two years. The Matrimonial Causes (NI) Order 1978, Article 19(2), exempts the petitioner from the necessity of proving that the marriage has in fact broken down irretrievably. The special procedure applies in the same way as it does in divorce (see Chapter Nine).

---

1 See the Law Commission, Report No. 192 *Ground for Divorce*, 1990, paras 4.2 – 4.19, where it is recommended that judicial separations be retained and re-named 'separation orders'.

1. Grounds

Under the 1978 Order, Article 19, a petition for a decree of judicial separation must be grounded on one of the five facts stated in Article 3(2) (see further Chapter Nine); if proven, the same ground may later be relied upon in divorce proceedings.

2. Reconciliation and Conciliation

Article 19(3) applies the requirement in Articles 8 and 9 that if at any stage it appears to the court 'that there is a reasonable possibility of a reconciliation between the parties to the marriage', then the proceedings should be adjourned 'to enable attempts to be made to effect such a reconciliation'.

Article 43(1) of the 1978 Order requires the court, when considering an application for a decree of judicial separation in a case involving children, to refer to 'a suitably qualified person' the possibility of conciliating the parties to the marriage.

II. The Order and its Effects

Under Article 20 of the 1978 Order, a decree terminates certain legal incidences of marriage but not the marriage itself: neither party is free to re-marry. The granting of a decree has no effect on the right of either party to subsequently commence divorce proceedings (see the 1978 Order, Article 6(1)). A decree may be rescinded.

1. Duty to Cohabit

Under Article 20,

> (1) Where the court grants a decree of judicial separation it shall no longer be obligatory for the petitioner to cohabit with the respondent.

One consequence of terminating the petitioner's obligation to cohabit with the respondent is, of course, the removal of any possibility of either party thereafter relying on the fact of desertion in subsequent divorce proceedings.

2. Duty to Support

The decree will contain such directions regarding the payment of maintenance as the court deems appropriate (see further Chapter Twenty-two). Under Articles 3–9 of the Domestic Proceedings (NI) Order 1980, the court has powers to make orders for financial provision on behalf of a separated applicant and children of that family.

3. Parental Responsibilities

The restriction imposed by Article 44 of the 1978 Order has been significantly affected by the Children (NI) Order 1995.[2] The court is still prevented from making a decree

---

2 Article 43(1)(ii) of the 1978 Order has now been repealed by the 1995 Order. The repealed provision required the court to seek a report from 'a suitably qualified person' on 'the children and the suitability of any arrangements which have been made, or are proposed by either

of judicial separation unless, by order, it declares itself satisfied that there are no children of the family or the arrangements that have been made for the welfare of the children are satisfactory, are the best that can be made in the circumstances or it is impracticable for the party or parties appearing before the court to make any such arrangements for the children. If the court is able to make such a finding, it may then issue an order to that effect and need not be concerned about the possible bearing of the provisions available under the 1995 Order. If, however, issues do arise concerning the upbringing of children, then, as proceedings for judicial separation are family proceedings for the purposes of the 1995 Order,[3] the court will be obliged to resolve those issues within the context of that Order (see also Chapter Nine). The court's powers in respect of parental responsibilities for any 'children of the family' are as outlined in Chapter Twelve.

During the course of proceedings for a decree, the court may grant injunctions.

1. The Matrimonial Home

A petition for judicial separation will usually also be accompanied by an application for 'ancillary relief' which will include an application for property adjustment. The main piece of property of interest to both spouses will be the matrimonial home. The law governing disputes in respect of the family home is to be found in the Family Law (Miscellaneous Provisions)(NI) Order 1984, Articles 4–14 and 20; the principle in *Richards v Richards*[4] applies[5] (see further Chapter Twenty-three).

5. Other Property and Finance

The powers of the court under the 1978 Order, Articles 23 and 24, to make orders adjusting the parties' rights in respect of financial provision, the matrimonial home and other property and assets are the same as in divorce proceedings (see further Chapters Twenty, Twenty-two and Twenty-three). As the marriage has not been terminated, the pension rights of a dependant spouse continue unaffected.

6. Rights of Inheritance

If either spouse should die intestate while a decree of separation is in effect, then the survivor will have no rights of inheritance in respect of the deceased's estate. The effect of Article 20(2) of the 1978 Order is that the law treats the parties as though they had pre-deceased each other. If a spouse should die testate, then any gift left to his or her

---

party to be made for their welfare'. This provision, which had mandatory application in all cases where children were involved, had no counterpart in the equivalent legislation of England and Wales and was considered by the judiciary in this jurisdiction to provide a very useful means of ensuring a professional scrutiny of child welfare matters.
3 See Article 8(4)(b) of the 1995 Order. Note also that Sch. 9, para 102 of the 1995 Order repeals Art. 10 of the Domestic Proceedings (NI) Order 1980 which dealt with the powers of the court to make orders in respect of the custody of and access to children. Instead, the court is referred to the Art. 8 orders in the 1995 Order.
4 [1984] AC 174, [1983] 2 All ER 807, HL.
5 See also *Re M (Minors)(Disclosure of Evidence)* [1994] 1 FLR 760.

spouse will, unlike the position following divorce, take effect as though the proceedings had not occurred (see further Chapter Twenty-four).

Separation by Agreement

In recent years the courts have come to look more favourably on arrangements freely entered into by spouses which set out the terms on which they agree to separate. As the legislative intent to remove fault as the basis for sanctioning marriage dissolution has progressed, so the courts have sought to reduce opportunities for spouses to engage in bitter adversarial contest. A conciliatory approach to the settlement of affairs, particularly where children are involved, is now valued as being in the best interests of both parties[6] and of the courts in the light of the commonplace nature and volume of matrimonial proceedings. This is balanced by the principle that the court reserves the right to review and adjust any maintenance agreement or care arrangement made between the parties for any children.

I. Contractual Agreement

There is a presumption that if spouses jointly make arrangements dealing with the management of aspects of their family life, they are merely making domestic arrangements. For a separation by agreement to be recognised and enforced by the court, there must be clear evidence that it goes beyond a domestic arrangement. The agreement must comply with the basic principles of contract law. When it does, the usual remedies of damages, specific performance and injunction will be available in respect of any breach.

1. Evidence of Contractual Intent

The separation agreement should be in writing but may be oral (though if a maintenance agreement, it will not be statutorily enforceable), and the contractual intent of the spouses must be evident — in the former instance, on the face of the document. Where the spouses have in fact separated and the document deals with financial matters, the court will usually be prepared to find that they had the necessary intention to create a legally binding contract.[7] Such agreements should be made by deed. The matters usually dealt with in separation agreements are cohabitation, maintenance, distribution of finances and property and care arrangements for any children of the marriage.

2. Evidence of Consideration

If the agreement is not by deed it should clearly show the nature of the consideration which supports it. This may well take the form of financial arrangements made on behalf of the other in lieu of that other undertaking direct care responsibility for any children of their marriage.[8]

---

6 See, for example, *Minton v Minton* [1979] AC 593, 608 where Scarman LJ said: 'the law now encourages spouses to avoid bitterness after family breakdown and to settle their money and property problems.'
7 See *Merritt v Merritt* [1970] 1 WLR 1211.
8 See *Ward v Byham* [1956] 1 WLR 496.

3. Evidence of Consent

As with any contract, evidence of fraud,[9] duress, undue influence[10] or innocent misrepresentation[11] will render a separation agreement voidable, while mistake[12] will render it void. Similarly, a withdrawal of consent will discharge the agreement. This may occur with consent of both parties, on resumption of cohabitation or by the breach or repudiation of the agreement by one party.

II. Maintenance Agreements, the Parties and the Court

A separation agreement most usually incorporates the parties' arrangements regarding maintenance. However, a maintenance agreement may exist as a separate and distinct entity. In either case, even if the agreement is a properly drawn-up legal document, attesting to the contractual intent of the parties, the agreed maintenance arrangements may still have to give way to the principle that the court reserves to itself the right to be the final arbiter of what constitutes a just and equitable financial arrangement between the parties. The law governing such matters is to be found in Chapter Twenty-three.

Domestic Violence

The violence inflicted by one member of a household on another is generically termed 'domestic violence'. It takes many forms and is prevalent in all age groups, racial groups and social classes. In recent years this term has been found to have application to circumstances where the perpetrator is a young adult son or daughter of the victim. It would also seem appropriate to those situations where an elderly housebound parent or step-parent is physically abused, bullied or intimidated until refuge is sought in a home for the elderly. Occasionally the male partner is the one abused.[13] Most often, however, it is held to mean either parental abuse of small children or, more usually, the physical abuse of a female by her male partner.[14] The legislation governing domestic violence is an unhappy alliance of bodies of quite different statute law (property, crime, tort and family), administered by courts whose different jurisdictions provide a confusing range of powers. It has long been recognised as unsatisfactory and proposals for reform[15] are under consideration.

---

9 See *Allsop v Allsop* (1980) 124 SJ 710.
10 See *Simpson v Simpson* [1989] Fam Law, vol. 19, pp 146, 436.
11 See *Wales v Wadham* [1977] 1 WLR 199.
12 See *Galloway v Galloway* (1914) 30 TLR 531.
13 See, for example, *Gibson v Austin* [1992] 2 FLR 437.
14 See E Pizzey, *Scream Quietly or the Neighbours Will Hear*, Harmondsworth: Penguin Books 1974. Also see J McKiernan and M McWilliams, *Bringing it Out into the Open: Domestic Violence in NI*, Belfast, HMSO (1993).
15 See *Report of the Select Committee on Violence in Marriage* HC 553 (1974–5); Law Commission Working Papers: no. 113; no. 116, *Rape Within Marriage* (1989); no. 207, *Domestic Violence and Occupation of the Family Home*. See also G Hague, E Malos and W Dear *against Domestic Violence: Inter-Agency Initiatives* (Working Paper 127) Bristol University (1995).

I. Criminal Proceedings

An assault is a crime. The fact that an assault is perpetrated within the confines of a family home and, possibly, within a marital relationship, will no longer protect the assailant from a criminal prosecution.[16] The public interest in preventing or at least detecting violent conduct will no longer tolerate exceptions being made for such conduct when it occurs in the privacy of a family home. The police will now intervene in what were previously regarded as 'domestic matters' on request from the victim or a member of the general public, and the DPP's office will then advise as to whether the incident is sufficiently grave to warrant prosecution under the Offences against the Person Act 1861. A prosecution may be brought for offences ranging from common assault (section 42), aggravated assault (section 43), assault occasioning actual bodily harm (section 47), grievous bodily harm (section 18) through to unlawful wounding, manslaughter or murder (section 20). Should proceedings ensue and a conviction be obtained, then the victim may well be entitled to make a claim under the Criminal Injuries (NI) Order 1988, Article 5(2).

Marital Rape

The common-law rule which for centuries held that there was no such offence as marital rape has now been extinguished. The dictum of Sir Matthew Hale[17] that a man could not be guilty of such an offence against his wife because 'by their mutual matrimonial consent and contract the wife hath given up herself in this kind unto her husband which she cannot retract' finally succumbed to the decision in *R v R (Rape: Marital Exemption)*[18] The House of Lords then took the view that the common law was capable of change in the light of changing social, economic and cultural developments, and accordingly, it was now no longer acceptable that a wife should be held to have given an irrevocable consent to intercourse with her husband, regardless of the circumstances.

In this context the guidance given by the Court of Appeal on sentences for rape should be noted.[19] In the course of its judgment in *R v McDonald, R v Taggart* and *R v Farquhar*,[20] the court stated the principle that in this jurisdiction the starting point for sentencing a person pleading guilty to a charge of rape, or found guilty of rape, should be seven years (as opposed to five in England and Wales).

II. Tort Proceedings

In keeping with the general trend over recent years for judicial initiative to compensate for legislative omission, the law of tort has been utilised to provide remedies for victims of domestic violence who would otherwise be unable to find relief in the courts. As

---

16 See, for example, *R v Jackson* [1891] 1 QB 671, CA; *R v Kowalski* [1988] 1 FLR 447 where a husband was found guilty of sexually assaulting his wife; and also see *R v R (Rape: Marital Exemption)* [1991] 4 All ER 481.
17 See Hale, *History of the Pleas of the Crown* 1736, 629.
18 See f/n 16.
19 See, for example, *R v McDonald* [1989] NIJB 28.
20 [1989] 3 NIJB 28.

the available proceedings are designed for and almost wholly used by marital couples, those in other forms of relationship (sibling, homosexual, lesbian etc.) and living in domestic circumstances who suffer violence are generally excluded from the legal protection available to spouses. Usually, the law of tort is resorted to by a victim who is seeking damages rather than protection in respect of violence suffered at the hands of a partner. The plaintiff has had to rest his or her claim on such esoteric grounds as private nuisance and trespass to the person, usually having also to prove property rights if seeking an injunction to restrain a defendant from further violence. However, in England, after some hesitation,[21] judicial recognition has recently been given to the tort of harassment. In the important decision of *Khorasandjian v Bush*,[22] the Court of Appeal ruled that the eighteen-year-old unmarried plaintiff, who had never cohabited with the defendant, had a claim in tort for harassment because of the latter's persistent phone calls to the home where she lived with her parents. The significance of such a finding is that the Court of Appeal was then able to uphold the injunction to restrain the defendant, granted in the court of first instance, despite the absence of any property rights vesting in the plaintiff.

III. Matrimonial Proceedings

1. The Personal Protection Order

Under the Domestic Proceedings (NI) 1980, Articles 18 and 19 (as amended by the Family Law (Matrimonial Proceedings) (NI) Order 1984 and the Family Law (NI) Order 1993), application may be made to a magistrates' court for a personal protection order and, if necessary, also for an exclusion order. The Rules permit applications to be made orally before a Justice of the Peace or Clerk of Petty Sessions and on an *ex parte* basis.[23] Where the applicant makes a statement to the clerk either orally or in writing that there is imminent danger of physical injury to the applicant or to a child of the family, then the clerk must bring the matter before the court or resident magistrate as soon as practicable.[24] The clerk is required to ensure that notice of the making of an order is served personally on the respondent unless this is not practicable, when it may be served by post or through an intermediary, and a copy must also be served on the relevant police station.[25]

Breach of either order is a criminal offence under Article 14(1) of the Family Law (NI) Order 1993.

(a) The Parties

A spouse, but not a casual cohabitee,[26] suffering from domestic violence will be the applicant in proceedings for a personal protection order instigated under the Domestic

---

21 See, for example, *Patel v Patel* [1988] 2 FLR 179 where the Court of Appeal held that there was no tort of harassment; also *Burnett v George* [1992] 1 FLR 525 where the Court of Appeal held that where the harassment caused an impairment of health then it was actionable.
22 [1993] 3 All ER 669.
23 The Magistrates' Courts (Domestic Proceedings) Rules (NI) 1966, Rule 10.
24 The Magistrates' Courts (Domestic Proceedings) Rules (NI) 1966, Rule 11.
25 The Magistrates' Courts (Domestic Proceedings) Rules (NI) 1966, Rule 13.
26 See *F v F (Protection from Violence: Continuing Cohabitation)* [1989] 2 FLR 451.

Proceedings (NI) Order 1980, Article 18. The person against whom an order is sought will be the respondent in any such proceedings.

Applications made under this Order are treated as 'family proceedings' for the purposes of the Children (NI) Order 1995 (see Article 8(4)(c) of the 1995 Order). According to Article 2(2) of the 1995 Order, the term

> 'child of the family', in relation to the parties to a marriage, means—
> (a) a child of both those parties;
> (b) any other child, not being a child who is placed with those parties as foster parents by an authority or a voluntary organisation, who has been treated by both of those parties as a child of their family.

If violence or the threat of it is directed towards a child, the latter must fall within the definition of 'child of the family'. Almost any child who has his or her home with the parties will meet this definition. However, a step-child, being treated by the respondent as not a child of the family and suffering physical abuse at the hands of that person, will not be entitled to the protection afforded by this order.

(b) The Grounds

Under the Domestic Proceedings (NI) Order 1980:

> 18.—(1) Where on an application made by a party to a marriage the court is satisfied—
> (a) that the other party to the marriage ('the respondent') has used, or threatened to use, violence against the applicant or a child of the family, and
> (b) that it is necessary for the protection of the applicant or a child of the family that an order under this paragraph should be made, the court may make an order (a 'personal protection order') restraining the respondent from molesting the applicant or a child of the family or both.

The court must be satisfied that, in relation to the applicant or a child of the family, the respondent has used or threatened to use violence and an order is necessary for their protection. The violence must be of a physical[27] rather than solely of a psychological nature and need not be caused by the defendant's wilful intent.[28] Malicious phone calls may constitute an assault.[29]

A determination that violence, or the threat of it, has been used by the respondent against the applicant or a child of the family is insufficient for the court to grant the order sought. In addition, it must also establish that the order is 'necessary' for the protection of the parties concerned.[30]

---

27 See *Horner v Horner* [1982] 2 All ER 495 where the offending conduct took the form of upsetting notes.
28 See *Wooton v Wooten* [1984] FLR 871 where the violence occurred during the defendant's epileptic fits.
29 See *R v Ireland* and also *R v Johnson* (1996) CA, unreported, *The Times*, May 22.
30 See *McCartney v McCartney* [1981] 1 All ER 597 where although the violence occurred four months prior to the hearing the court, on appeal, held that there was a continuing threat, which was objectively verifiable and warranted an order.

(c) The Powers

Under Article 18(1)(b) the effect of this order is to restrain the respondent from 'molesting the applicant or a child of the family or both'. This extends to a prohibition against inciting, procuring or assisting anyone else to molest the applicant and/or any child of the family. The Court of Appeal for England and Wales has held[31] that, under the equivalent provision for that jurisdiction,[32] although a defendant has not been violent, he may nonetheless have been guilty of molesting his wife. The court considered that pestering the respondent amounted to molestation, as would any action which may cause trouble to, vex, annoy or inconvenience the applicant. Subsequently, in that jurisdiction, molestation has also been held to include activities such as riffling through a respondent's handbag,[33] writing abusive letters and shouting obscenities.[34]

2. The Exclusion Order

An exclusion order, obtained in the magistrates' courts under the 1980 Order, has the effect of legally barring the subject from entering a specified premises and/or area.

(a) The Grounds

Under the Domestic Proceedings (NI) Order 1980:

> 18.—(2) Where on an application made by a party to a marriage the court is satisfied—
>
> (a) either of the fact mentioned in paragraph (1)(a) or that the respondent has molested the applicant or a child of the family in contravention of a personal protection order; and
>
> (b) that it is necessary for the protection of the applicant or a child of the family that an order under this paragraph should be made, the court may make an order (an 'exclusion order').

The court requires proof that, in relation to the applicant and/or to a child of the family, the respondent's conduct satisfies the grounds for a personal protection order or is in breach of such an order and that an exclusion order is necessary for their protection.

(b) The Powers

Under Article 18 of the 1980 Order:

> (4) An exclusion order giving the applicant the exclusive use of the matrimonial home under paragraph (2)(i) shall operate to—
>
> (a) require the respondent forthwith to leave the matrimonial home;
>
> (b) prohibit him from entering it (subject to any temporary provision in the order for enabling him to remove personal effects or other goods of a specified kind);

---

31 See *Vaughan v Vaughan* [1973] 1 WLR 1159.
32 The Domestic Proceedings and Magistrates' Courts Act 1978, section 16(2).
33 See *Spencer v Camacho* (1984) 4 FLR 662.
34 See *George v George* [1986] 2 FLR 347.

(c) require him to permit the applicant to enter it (together with any child of whom the applicant has actual custody) and have peaceful use and enjoyment of it and (subject to any exceptions specified in the order) any goods in it;
(d) restrain him from disposing of any estate he has in it ('disposing' for this purpose including any dealing mentioned in paragraphs (a) to (f) of section 45(3) of the Interpretation Act (NI) 1954);
(e) prohibit him from damaging it or interfering with any services in it;
(f) prohibit him from removing any goods from it (subject to any exceptions specified in the order) or from disposing of, damaging or destroying any goods in it; and shall so operate in relation to any person claiming through the respondent as it operates in relation to the respondent.

In addition to, or instead of, permitting the applicant exclusive use of the matrimonial home, an exclusion order may also exclude the respondent from the area in which that home is situated, from any other specified premises in which the applicant or a child of the family is living and from any area in which such premises are situated. In circumstances where parental abuse has occurred, or is suspected, and inquiries by the Health and Social Services Board (or Trust) and police are underway, a preferable alternative to Trust removal of the child concerned may be an application by the non-abusing parent for a short-term ouster injunction. Alternatively, application could be made to the magistrates' court for an exclusion order under Article 18 of the 1980 Order (see also Chapter Fifteen).

3. The Family Law (Miscellaneous Provisions) (NI) (Order) 1984 and 'Ouster' Orders

The interface between property law and family law in relation to domestic violence became less certain with the decision of the House of Lords[35] that the law governing the right to occupy the matrimonial home was to be found not in the 1978 Act (or 1980 Order) but in the Matrimonial Homes Act 1983 (as incorporated in the Family Law (Miscellaneous Provisions)(NI)(Order)1984). The House ruled that an order to oust a spouse from the matrimonial home should be made under the latter legislation. It also held that when considering such an application equal weighting must be given to the conduct of the spouses, needs and financial resources, needs of the children and all the circumstances of the case. An order which so drastically interferes with the rights of a property owner must be utilised cautiously (see further Part Three).

4. The Court Orders and the Cohabitee Applicant

The law does not extend to cohabitees the same protection from domestic violence that it provides for spouses. Despite recommendations to that effect in a recent report

---

35 See *Richards v Richards* [1984] 1 AC 174. Also see *C v K (Inherent Powers: Exclusion Order)* [1996] 2 FLR 506 where the court declined to grant an exclusion order against a person with a proprietary interest in the property in question.

from the Office of Law Reform,[36] the subsequent Family Homes and Domestic Violence Bill was withdrawn by the Government before submission to parliament. There continues to be strong resistance to the introduction of legislative provisions which, by treating marital and non-marital couples in the same way, may also serve to undermine the institution of marriage. To this general rule there are now some exceptions.

The stipulation that the court must be satisfied as to an applicant's marital status, before it can rule on whether or not it has jurisdiction, has been to some extent relaxed by the Family Law (Miscellaneous Provisions)(NI) Order 1984, Article 20. Where a cohabiting couple are living as husband and wife in the same household, the court may treat them as such for the purposes of issuing personal protection orders and exclusion orders. Eligibility is determined by evidence of an enduring cohabiting relationship. A casual, brief or intermittent relationship, even where the couple are cohabiting, will not suffice. Under the Children (NI) Order 1995 the court will similarly treat marital and non-marital couples equally for the purposes of family proceedings where the upbringing of children is concerned.

Where the parties are registered as co-owners and one is forced to leave because of the other's violence, the court may hold the remaining party liable for the costs of the other's accommodation and require payment of 'occupation rent' to that other.[37]

5. The Emergency Procedure

The emergency procedure may be instigated when a statement, either orally or in writing, is made by the applicant to a justice of the peace. Under Article 21(2) of the 1980 Order, this must declare that there is an 'imminent danger of physical injury' to the applicant or child. This statement is then brought before the court or a resident magistrate forthwith (they are most usually made on an *ex parte* basis), where a determination is made as to whether an interim personal protection order and/or an exclusion order is to be issued.

6. The Duration and Enforcement of the Orders

An interim personal protection order and an exclusion order take effect from the time they are made unless otherwise stated; an emergency order will not do so until served on the respondent. Personal protection orders continue in effect indefinitely unless the court sets a time limit. Exclusion orders expire six months after date of issue but may then be extended for a further maximum period of six months. An emergency order will expire five weeks from date of issue unless an application for a full order is brought before then.

A breach of either order, or a reasonable suspicion of a breach, is a criminal offence and will justify the respondent's arrest by a police constable acting without the necessity of a warrant.

---

36 See Office of Law Reform, Consultation Paper — *Domestic Violence and the Occupation of the Family Home* (May 1995).
37 See *Dennis v MacDonald* [1982] 2 WLR 275.

IV. Other Family Proceedings

The Children (NI) Order 1995 has introduced a number of alternative proceedings for excluding an offender or suspected offender from the matrimonial home.

1. Voluntary Exclusion

The 1995 Order, Schedule 2, paragraph 6, provides that in situations where it appears to a Trust that 'a child who is living on particular premises is suffering, or is likely to suffer, ill-treatment at the hands of another person who is living on those premises', then, if that person is willing, it may assist him or her to obtain alternative accommodation.

2. Compulsory Exclusion

The court may, on its own initiative, in any family proceedings, use its discretionary powers to direct that a perpetrator of violence be prevented from entering a victim's home.

3. Article 8 Orders

Recent case law in England and Wales provides some interesting illustrations of ways in which Article 8 orders may be employed to protect a mother from domestic violence.

(a) Prohibited Steps

A prohibited steps order, or injunction, has long been one of the prerogative powers which have characterised the authority of the High Court when exercising its wardship jurisdiction (see further Chapter Seven). Under Article 8 of the 1995 Order, it is now available to all courts.

On its own motion or in response to a petition, and in any family proceedings, the court may issue a prohibited steps order to prevent an abuser from making contact with, or otherwise harassing, a victim. The use of this order is, however, subject to some restrictions. Under Article 9(5) of the 1995 Order, the court is prevented from making a prohibited steps order with the aim of achieving a result which could either be better achieved by making a residence or contact order or which the High Court is now barred by Article 173 from trying to achieve through the exercise of its inherent jurisdiction. Further, there is good authority[38] for the view that should a Trust, as applicant, wish to avail of this order to ensure protection for a mother and children, it must be re-directed to Part V proceedings.

However, recent decisions of the Court of Appeal in England have important implications also for this jurisdiction.[39] In the first it was held that a judge could make a prohibited steps order against a former cohabitee, identified as a child abuser, to prohibit him from having any contact with his victims, even though the subject was

---

38 See *Nottinghamshire County Council v P (no 2)* [1993] 2 FLR 134.
39 See *Re H (Prohibited Steps Order)* [1995] 1 FLR 638.

not a party to the proceedings. Such an order would not contravene Article 9(5), where the perpetrator is no longer cohabiting, as a (no) contact order would then be inappropriate. Moreover, it would not have been possible to issue a prohibited steps order in favour of the mother, as to do so would be to seek to achieve a result achievable by a (no) contact order which falls within the Article 9(5) embargo. An application for a prohibited steps order by a Trust in such circumstances would be wholly appropriate. In the second,[40] the court upheld on appeal against the making of a PSO which prevented a father from staying overnight when visiting his children in the matrimonial home at weekends.

The factors differentiating the legal position of the subject of proceedings in both cases were that in the second the man had a right of occupation, was not known to pose a threat to the children and consequently a PSO would represent an improper denial of his property rights.

(b) Residence Order with Conditions

Under Article 11(7) of the 1995 Order, the court has the power to attach conditions to any Article 8 order giving directions as to how that order is to be carried into effect. Of its own motion or in response to a petition, and in any family proceedings, the court may therefore attach a condition to a residence order directing that an abuser be barred from entering the residence in question.

Recent case law in England and Wales has clarified the restrictions on the court when exercising its power under the equivalent provision in the 1989 Act (i.e. section 11(7)). Although the Court of Appeal has ruled[41] that the powers conferred by this provision give the court a wide discretionary power which is not subject to limitation, it is nonetheless clear that it cannot impose a condition that might defeat the purpose of the order. Any such condition must not be inconsistent with a residence order;[42] nor seek to oust a parent from the family home;[43] and cannot be used to override proprietary rights.[44]

4. The Inherent Jurisdiction

The Law Commission[45] has drawn attention to a lacuna in the law in relation to the availability of short-term ouster provisions for the protection of children under the Children Act 1989, a lacuna which is equally evident in the 1995 Order. The absence of any appropriate statutory power enabling a Trust's counterpart to evict or bar a child abuser from his victim's home has greatly exercised the judiciary in England. As Butler-Sloss LJ has said,[46] 'The courts do not have power under the Children Act to exclude a parent from the home for the protection of a child . . . .'

---

40 See *Re D (Prohibited Steps Order)* [1996] 2 FLR 273.
41 See *Re O (Contact: Imposition of Conditions)* [1995] 2 FLR 124.
42 See *Birmingham City Council v H* [1992] 2 FLR 323.
43 See *Nottinghamshire County Council v P (no. 2)* [1993] 2 FLR 134.
44 See *Pearson v Franklin (Parental Home: Ouster)* [1994] 1 FLR 246.
45 See, Report No. 207, *Domestic Violence and Occupation of the Family Home* (1992).
46 See *Re M (Minors) (Disclosure of Evidence)* [1994] 1 FLR 760, 765G.

To some extent, the inherent jurisdiction of the High Court has again been made available to make good a legislative omission. The extent of its availability has been set by the decision of the House of Lords in *Richards*[47] (see Part Three). It was then held that the inherent jurisdiction should be used solely as ancillary to other proceedings and only where no statutory relief existed. Thorpe J has suggested[48] that such proceedings would include decisions relating to former spouses or former cohabitees, where the inherent jurisdiction could be utilised to exclude a parent if this was in the welfare interests of a child. In a case[49] which may have fitted into this category, Connell J held that a Trust's counterpart was justified in making application under provisions equivalent to Article 173(3) and (4) of the 1995 Order, for an injunction to exclude an abusing father from the matrimonial home. He granted leave to apply to the inherent jurisdiction because he considered that the father's continued presence would endanger the welfare of the children, that it was not in their interests to be removed from maternal care and because no statutory proceedings existed which could achieve this result (see also Chapter Seven).

---

47   *Richards v Richards* [1984] 1 AC 174.
48   In *Pearson v Franklin*, f/n 44.
49   See *Re S (Inherent Jurisdiction: Ouster)* [1994] 1 FLR 623; see also *Devon County Council v S and Another* [1994] 1 FLR 355 where Thorpe J granted a Trust's counterpart leave to apply to the inherent jurisdiction for an injunction to prevent a mother of three young children from inviting a paedophile to their home.

CHAPTER NINE

Marriage Breakdown: Divorce

Introduction

Divorce law has two basic objectives. First, it permits and facilitates the dignified dissolution of those marriages where the breakdown in the marital relationship is irretrievable. Second, it deals with the arrangements to be made for the future support and upbringing of any children and for the distribution of any capital assets and income between the parties. While the law does nothing to hinder parties from ending their relationship, it insists that certain requirements are met before they formally change their marital status.

This chapter deals with the circumstances in which and the procedures whereby the law in Northern Ireland presently gives effect to these objectives and permits the dissolution of marriage. It deals with matters of property and finance only insofar as these form part of a settlement agreed between the parties (see Chapter Twenty-three for disputed proceedings).

The importance of these issues is indicated by the increasing number of divorces. Currently, one in three marriages in the United Kingdom ends in divorce. This is the highest incidence of divorce in Europe. In Northern Ireland the annual number of divorces has been steadily climbing: 174 in 1967; 382 in 1974; 896 in 1980; 1,552 in 1984; 1,818 in 1989; reaching 2,319 and affecting approximately 3,000 children in 1993. Of the 2,716 divorce petitions filed in that year, 846 were from husbands and 1,870 from wives. The 1991 census for Northern Ireland recorded 11,302 persons registered as divorced. This area of family law is, therefore, one of growing significance for the province's lawyers and social workers.

The Background to the Present Legislative Framework

Divorce has been available in the narrowly defined ecclesiastical form of *mensa et thoro* since the middle ages. This freed the parties from the obligation to continue sharing 'bed and board' but did not free them to re-marry. Divorce subsequently also became available as a civil process to those with sufficient money and influence through private acts of Parliament. Divorce as a judicial process was not available in this jurisdiction until its introduction exclusively as a remedy for a party who could prove a partner's adultery (the traditional ecclesiastic offence) by the Matrimonial Causes and Marriage Law (Ireland) Amendment Act 1870. The grounds for divorce were broadened by the Matrimonial Causes Act (NI) 1939 to include also desertion, cruelty and incurable insanity. It was only with the introduction of the Matrimonial Causes (NI) Order 1978 that the grounds for divorce ceased to be solely offence based. Until recently the development of divorce legislation has always been Westminster led, with the introduction of provisions facilitating ease of access to divorce consistently meeting with considerable resistance from conservative and religious groups.

As always in this jurisdiction, family law legislation has closely followed, in terms of content if not in time, that already established in England and Wales. Certain reports[1] published in the latter jurisdiction have done much to shape the divorce law there. These have been supplemented by two reports from the Law Society's Family Sub-Committee[2] together with a report of the Matrimonial Causes Procedure Committee.[3] The research findings of some academics and the discussion documents published by certain special interest groups,[4] also helped to direct the course of legislative change.

The Present Law Governing Divorce

In Northern Ireland the law governing divorce rests largely on the provisions of the Matrimonial Causes (NI) Order 1978 and the accompanying Matrimonial Causes Rules (NI) 1979. This foundation has since been reinforced by the Family Law (Miscellaneous Provisions)(NI) Order 1984, the Matrimonial and Family Proceedings (NI) Order 1989 and the Family Law (NI) Order 1993 (Article 13 replacing Article 3(4) of the 1978 Order). The effects of this body of legislation may be best viewed through the usual perspectives of substantive and procedural law.

Substantive Law

Substantive law is relatively straightforward in proceedings where there is no contest on matters concerning children, property or finance. The remaining legal issue is then whether the grounds can be satisfied. The Family Law Act 1996, by removing the fact-based grounds, has gone a stage further to leave divorce as a right to be simply asserted in England and Wales after a fifteen-month waiting period.

I. Grounds for Divorce (Articles 3 and 4 of the Matrimonial Causes (NI) Order 1978)

The only ground available for divorce is as stated in Article 3 of the 1978 Order:

> (1) Subject to Article 5, a petition for divorce may be presented to the court by either party on the ground that the marriage has broken down irretrievably.

To satisfy this ground it must first be established that breakdown has occurred. This can only be achieved by producing evidence to prove one of the five separate facts

---

1 These reports include, most notably, those compiled by the Law Commission: Cmnd. 3123, *Reform of the Grounds of Divorce – The Field of Choice* (1966), Report No. 170, *Facing the Future – A Discussion Paper on the Ground for Divorce* (1988) and Report No. 192, *Family Law – The Ground for Divorce* (1990).
2 See *A Better Way Out* (1979) and *A Better Way Out Revisited* (1982).
3 See *The Booth Report* (1985).
4 See, in particular, the report *Putting Asunder* (1966) by the Church of England.

listed in section (2) and examined below. The court must then go on to make a finding that the breakdown is such that the marriage cannot be retrieved. A feature of modern divorce law is the increasing reluctance of the courts to hold that by clearing the first hurdle an applicant has necessarily also cleared the second. The converse is equally true;[5] the fact of demonstrable irretrievability will not in itself permit a divorce. A decree *nisi* will only be granted if both conditions are satisfied separately.

1. Adultery

Article 3(2)(a) of the 1978 Order requires an applicant to prove

> that since the date of the marriage, the respondent has committed adultery.

This is the traditional ground and for a period was the only ground for divorce. There are several different aspects to the provision, its judicial definition and current legal significance. The onus on the applicant is to provide proof that, on the balance of probability, the respondent voluntarily had sexual intercourse with someone of the opposite sex other than the spouse during the course of the marriage. This provision should be read in conjunction with the Matrimonial Causes Act 1973, section 1(2).

(a) Heterosexual Intercourse

As a ground for divorce, evidence of full heterosexual intercourse is required.[6] Impregnation by means of a clinical transfer of donor sperm will not meet this test. It must also violate the essential contractual basis of a marital relationship. Evidence of lesbian or homosexual conduct, therefore, will not in legal terms be seen as constituting adulterous behaviour.

(b) A Single Act May Be Sufficient

A distinguishing feature of Article 3(2) of the 1978 Order is that unlike its counterpart, section 1(2)(a) of the Matrimonial Causes Act 1973, it makes no reference to an additional requirement that the applicant finds it intolerable to live with the respondent. Indeed, adultery need not have been the *cause* of the marital breakdown. Provided it occurred at some point during the course of the marriage, adultery can be used to ground divorce proceedings. Being free of the onus to also prove intolerableness, the applicant can rely simply on the bare fact of adultery, i.e. a single act will suffice. In this respect it perhaps accentuates a problem associated with the corresponding fault-based grounds of the 1973 Act — it attracts petitioner reliance not because the fault in question is the real cause of relationship breakdown, but because one or both spouses decided that it would expedite the process of obtaining a divorce. The alternative requires waiting for a minimum period of two years.

---

5 See *Buffery v Buffery* [1988] 2 FLR 365.
6 See *Dennis v Dennis* [1955] 2 ALL ER 51 where it was held that intercourse need not amount to full penetration.

(c) With Respondent's Consent

As it must be voluntary, any evidence that the respondent did not fully consent would rebut the allegation. This would be the case where the respondent was able to prove coercion or rape. It would also have that effect if evidence existed to prove that the applicant was, at the operative time, incapable of giving consent due perhaps to mental illness or extreme drunkenness. In the former instance, the judicial approach was established in the leading case of *Williams v Williams*[7] where the House of Lords ruled that the fact of the respondent's mental illness did not *per se* provide an adequate defence to a petition pursued under this heading. In the latter instance incapacity at time of intercourse may be construed as resulting from an earlier decision, or willingness, to allow that situation to arise. Such circumstances are governed by the rule[8] that self-induced intoxication would not afford a defence in circumstances where conduct did not require specific intent to constitute a crime. A respondent's self-induced intoxication (carrying with it an implied willingness to accept the consequences) should be distinguished from intoxication induced by excusable circumstances.[9] The firm approach recently taken by the courts in so called 'date-rape' cases is likely to place a heavy onus on any respondent in this context who relies on incapacity to refute an allegation of consensual intercourse.

(d) During the Course of the Marriage

The evidence must not only prove that a spouse consented to penetrative sexual intercourse with a member of the opposite sex, but also that this occurred during the course of the marriage. Reliance on evidence that the respondent behaved in this way before the marriage will not assist an applicant to meet this requirement. Neither will it avail an applicant to claim that such behaviour rendered the marriage breakdown irretrievable.

The fact that a spouse has already been cited as co-respondent in a previous successful divorce action may be adduced as *prima facie* evidence of adulterous conduct.

(e) The Marriage Has Irretrievably Broken Down

Having proven adultery, and thus cleared the first hurdle, an applicant must then convince the court that the marriage has irretrievably broken down. Evidence that the applicant knew of the adulterous behaviour at the time and (perhaps by not intervening then or by explicitly forgiving later) could be said to have treated the marriage as retrievable may prevent clearance of the second hurdle. Article 4(1) of this Order particularly removes the right of a petitioner to rely on adultery for this purpose if it can be shown that he or she, having full knowledge of the adulterous conduct, nevertheless continued to reside with the respondent for a period or periods totalling

---

7   [1964] AC 698.
8   See *DPP v Majewski* [1977] AC 443 where the House of Lords formulated this rule.
9   As stated in *Goshawk v Goshawk* (1965) 109 Sol Jo 290 (where the volition comes from those circumstances and the consequences may not be foreseen).

six months. Article 4(2) has a similar effect where it can be shown the behaviour occurred with the connivance of the petitioner.

2. Unreasonableness and a Respondent's Behaviour

Article 3(2)(b) of the 1978 Order requires an applicant to prove

> that the respondent behaved in such a way that the applicant cannot be reasonably expected to live with the respondent.

This provision is the one most commonly relied upon.

(a) Subjective Test of Reasonableness

The behaviour is to be judged subjectively according to its effect on the particular sensitivities of the petitioner. The courts' approach to this provision was summarised by Dunn J:[10]

> Would any right-thinking person come to the conclusion that *this* husband has behaved in such a way that *this* wife cannot reasonably be expected to live with him, taking into account the whole of the circumstances and the characters and personalities of the parties?

As he then also stated, for the behaviour to be found unreasonable, it must amount to more than that which would be attributable to the normal wear and tear of marriage. In that case it did so because the wife 'was subjected to a constant atmosphere of criticism, disapproval and boorish behaviour on the part of her husband'.

The importance of the subjective test was stressed most recently in a case[11] which overturned an earlier county court decision based on an objective appraisal of the facts.

Although the behaviour in question cannot be judged in isolation and must always be interpreted in the overall context of the circumstances, characters and personalities of the parties, it nevertheless is in itself the primary issue. As elsewhere in family law, this element has now been purged of its previous connotations of culpability. Reasonableness of conduct has been statutorily substituted for culpability. The type of conduct which the courts have found sufficient to justify a petitioner's claim that he or she could not reasonably be expected to continue living with a respondent has included a non-adulterous association with a person of the opposite sex, violence, persistent abusive criticism and, through acts of vindictiveness, the engineering of the petitioner's departure from the marital home.

(b) Actual Behaviour

The fact that a couple no longer have anything in common and are unable to communicate or that half the couple is bored with the marriage have been found insufficient

---

10 See *Livingstone Stallard v Livingstone Stallard* [1974] 2 All ER 766 and later applied by the Court of Appeal in *O'Neill v O'Neill* [1975] 3 All ER 289, 295.
11 See the decision by the Court of Appeal in *Birch v Birch* [1992] 1 FLR 564.

to satisfy this statutory requirement. Incompatibility, in terms of values or lifestyles, has, however, been found sufficient.[12] A mere attitude or state of mind by a respondent will invariably be inadequate; actual behaviour is necessary. This may, however, take the form of a wilful act of omission rather than one of commission. So, while positive behaviour such as obsessional conduct, drunkenness or sexual deviance have all been found sufficient to satisfy this requirement, so also has such negative behaviour as refusal to engage in sexual intercourse. Also, for a respondent's conduct to amount to 'behaviour' within the meaning of this provision, it must have an on-going dimension; it is unlikely that a once-off, unrepresentative piece of aberrant conduct would be found sufficient to warrant terminating the marriage. The court will view the behaviour in the context of the whole marriage and ask whether it was of such significance as to terminally damage the basis of the marriage.

(c) The Effect Rather Than Cause of the Behaviour Is All Important

Intent on the part of the respondent is no longer a vital ingredient to sustain a claim by the applicant under this heading. The *mens rea* requirement ceased to be essential with the de-criminalising of the grounds for divorce, though usually evidence of an element of wilfulness by the respondent will be required. As in other areas of family law, it is now the *effect* not the *cause* of the behaviour which is crucial. Mental illness on the part of the respondent will not therefore excuse behaviour found to be justifiably intolerable to the applicant; though whether it can be found to be so will always depend on the particular circumstances, as a degree of tolerance for an ill spouse is expected.[13] This approach has been followed more recently by, for example, Baker P in a case[14] where an applicant was granted a decree on evidence that her husband was a manic depressive whose treatment of her caused her acute embarrassment and anxiety. Judicial interpretation of the significance of behaviour in that case was as follows.

> Behaviour is something more than a mere state of affairs or a state of mind, such as for example a repugnance to sexual intercourse, or a feeling that the wife is not reciprocating the husband's love, or not being as demonstrative as he thinks she should be. Behaviour in this context is action or conduct by one which affects the other. Such conduct may either take the form of acts or omissions or may be a course of conduct, and, in my view, it must have some reference to the marriage.

(d) Without Applicant's Consent

As with adultery, an applicant will fail under this heading if it can be shown that he or she earlier connived in, tolerated or forgave the respondent for the conduct now complained of. However, if a claim rests on other more recent conduct, the earlier instances can also be relied upon to reinforce the applicant's case. Under Article 4(3) a petitioner will not succeed if it can be shown that, despite the behaviour complained

---

12 As, for example, in *Astwood v Astwood* (1981) 131 NLJ 990.
13 In fact, this has been the case since the ruling of the House of Lords in *Williams v Williams* [1964] AC 698 [1963] 2 All ER 994, HL.
14 See *Katz v Katz* [1972] 3 All ER 219.

of, the couple continued to live together for a period or periods exceeding a total of six months from the last instance of such conduct. The longer the period from the offending behaviour[15] until the petition, the heavier the onus on the petitioner to prove that he or she cannot go on living with the respondent; again, this is best evidenced by applying the separate households test.

3. Desertion

Article 3(2)(c) of the 1978 Order requires an applicant to prove

> that the respondent has deserted the petitioner for a continuous period of at least two years immediately preceding the presentation of the petition.

As Bromley has pointed out,[16] this definition of desertion requires four separate elements to be satisfied:

(a) that the spouses are living apart;
(b) that it is the respondent's intention to permanently continue to do so;
(c) that this is occurring without the applicant's consent;
(d) that the respondent has no reasonable cause for so doing.

When all four are established, desertion is proven. However, only if it can be further shown that all four subsisted, continuously, for at least two full years prior to the application will the terms of this provision have been met. Any resumption of cohabitation, with the mutual intention to live together as husband and wife, will undo the desertion. The fact of desertion is now seldom relied upon to ground a divorce petition as this has been largely displaced by reliance on the fact of two years of separation.

(a) Living Apart

The first element will be satisfied by evidence that the spouses are living independently of each other, even if doing so under the same roof because, as Merrivale P has stated,[17] 'desertion is not the withdrawal from a place, but from a state of things'. The test[18] is — are the spouses living as two households or as one? This test was satisfied in a case[19] where, though continuing to live under the same roof, neither spouse performed any marital duties or engaged jointly in any aspect of family life. In practice, given the real problems presented by the present housing situation and the necessity of coping with everyday care arrangements where children are involved, the 'living apart' test can be very difficult to satisfy.[20]

---

15 As in *Bradley v Bradley* [1973] 1 WLR 1291 and *Court v Court* [1982] Fam 105; [1981] 2 All ER 531.
16 See PM Bromley and NV Lowe *Family Law*, 8th ed., London: Butterworth (1992), p. 200.
17 See *Pulford v Pulford* [1923] P 18, 21.
18 As stated in *Mouncer v Mouncer* [1972] 1 WLR 321.
19 See *Naylor v Naylor* [1962] 2 All ER 129.
20 For example, in *Hopes v Hopes* [1949] 2 All ER 920 the test was not satisfied because the spouses continued to share meals and maintained a semblance of family life.

Intent is not essential to establish the bare fact of separation. The separation may be a consequence of circumstances over which the respondent had no control such as hospitalisation, lack of marital accommodation or imprisonment. Separation in itself therefore does not constitute desertion.

(b) Respondent's Intent

The second element is the ingredient which transforms a separating spouse into a deserting one — the respondent's intent to cease living as a spouse. The separation must be voluntary and with the intention of remaining apart. If involuntary or without that intention, then the separation is only converted into desertion when both factors change. A plea of mental illness may assist a respondent to claim incapacity in respect of either or both factors. By so doing a respondent can avoid a charge that the initial separation constituted desertion or, even if it did, that before the expiration of the two-year period the onset of illness prevented an informed choice to alter that situation.

(c) Without Applicant's Consent

The third element is an absence of consent on the part of the applicant to the respondent's act of desertion. Evidence of any agreement to the departure of a spouse will nullify a claim of desertion, though that agreement must be shown to have been full and mutual as in the words of Buckley LJ:[21]

> Desertion does not necessarily involve that the wife desires her husband to remain with her. She may be thankful that he has gone, but he may nevertheless have deserted her.

The usual evidence of a lack of capacity due, for example, to duress, deceit, mistake or mental illness may be adduced to prove an absence of consent. The fact that a deserting party became incapable, during the period of desertion, of maintaining the necessary intent to continue the desertion is addressed by Article 4(4) of the 1978 Order. This allows the court to construe the period of desertion as having continued despite that inability. The existence of a matrimonial order acknowledging the fact of separation will render a charge of desertion impossible to sustain. Again, what began as a voluntary separation may continue as desertion when consent is withdrawn if all other factors are present. The reverse is, of course, equally true.

(d) Without Justifiable Cause

The fourth element is that the deserting spouse must not have had justifiable cause to leave the marital home. If the behaviour of one spouse causes a breakdown in the marital relationship, this may give rise to what is termed 'constructive desertion'. This occurs where it can be shown that the behaviour of one spouse was such that the other was forced to leave the marital home, in which case the former is held to be the deserting spouse. Whether the behaviour in question was sufficiently grave to warrant

---

[21] See *Harriman v Harriman* [1909] P 123, 148 CA.

the applicant's departure will be determined in accordance with the same principles as applied to desertion *per se*. A deserted spouse in such circumstances who later becomes the applicant in divorce proceedings will seldom need to rely on a charge of constructive desertion, as the behaviour of the spouse which caused the separation will provide sufficient grounds for the action. In this jurisdiction the added complications arising from the domicile and residence requirements of Article 49 of the 1978 Order have also had a part to play in marginalising the use made of constructive desertion.

4. Living Apart for Two Years

Article 3(2)(d) of the 1978 Order requires an applicant to prove

> that the parties to the marriage have lived apart for a continuous period of at least two years immediately preceding the presentation of the petition (hereafter in this Order referred to as 'two years' separation') and the respondent consents to a decree being granted.

In the context of marital relationships this provision marks a turning point in the balance traditionally struck between the private and public interests in family law matters. It represents an almost total concession by the State to the private right of a marital couple to jointly agree to the removal of the legal foundation upon which their family has been built, subject only to the condition of a two-year waiting period. It rests on two specific requirements: proof of 'living apart' for two years and proof of the respondent's consent.

(a) Living Apart

Living apart requires evidence that each spouse is in effect maintaining a separate household. It will not be demonstrated simply by proving that they are living apart.[22]

(b) Consent of Respondent

The second provision requires the respondent to give explicit consent to the decree. This must be a full and informed consent[23] which may be withdrawn at any point prior to the granting of the decree but only with considerable difficulty afterwards. An inability or incapacity to give consent, due for example to not being informed or mental illness respectively, will prevent reliance on this provision.

5. Living Apart for Five Years

Article 3(2)(e) of the 1978 Order requires an applicant to prove

---

22 The Court of Appeal in *Santos v Santos* [1972] 21 All ER 246 ruled that it will only be proven by evidence that consortium between the spouses has ended; though this may result from a decision taken by one spouse even if not communicated to the other.
23 See *Brown v Brown* [1992] 2 BNIL 48 where the Court of Appeal in this jurisdiction ruled that the respondent can make the consent conditional upon not having to pay the costs of the divorce.

that the parties to the marriage have lived apart for a continuous period of at least five years immediately preceding the presentation of the petition (hereafter in this Order referred to as 'five years' separation').

The only proof required is in respect of the period of separation. The fact that neither the respondent's conduct or consent is relevant makes this the most radical departure from the doctrine of culpability which previously underpinned divorce law in this and the neighbouring jurisdiction. Its significance was noted in *McReynolds v McReynolds*,[24] the leading case in this jurisdiction on what constitutes sufficient grounds to contest a petition in such circumstances. It was then observed that in order to balance this advantage given to a petitioner, the legislators had introduced a unique defence unavailable to a respondent in any other form of divorce proceedings. Under Article 7(1) a respondent may resist the granting of a decree grounded on this fact by claiming that if granted it would result in grave financial or other hardship, and Article 7(2) requires the court to dismiss a petition where it finds that such hardship would otherwise ensue.

The facts of this case may be briefly stated. After twenty-five years of marriage, the last thirteen years of which the parties had been separated, the petitioner sought a divorce under this heading. He, an officer in the RUC, proposed to continue existing maintenance payments of £70 per month in respect of his wife and two children. The respondent resisted the petition on the ground that she would suffer grave financial hardship as a consequence of being denied future entitlement to a widow's pension and to the services resulting from their participation in the BUPA health scheme. During the course of the initial hearing before O'Donnell LJ, the petitioner offered to offset any possible hardship by lodging the sum of £16,000 in a trust fund for the respondent within six months of the decree absolute being granted and by increasing his maintenance payments to £155 per month. This offer was made to expedite proceedings, as the petitioner wished to secure a divorce before the impending birth of his child by his co-habitee for the past thirteen years, a motive which attracted judicial sympathy. Ultimately, O'Donnell LJ set a date, before the expected birth, by which the sum of £16,000 was to be lodged in court if proceedings for the grant of a decree *nisi* were to continue. When that date passed without the lodgment being made, the petition was dismissed.

The subsequent Court of Appeal hearing found that the trial judge at first instance had appeared to subject the plaintiff's offers primarily to the test of a reasonable ultimate financial solution for the respondent rather than to the test of whether the granting of a dissolution would prove likely to result in grave financial hardship for her, attached undue importance to the lodgment being made before the expected birth but also, by implication, in signifying his willingness to pronounce a decree on the basis of the plaintiff's offer, the trial judge had accepted that the dissolution of the marriage would not cause the respondent undue financial hardship. The Court of Appeal, therefore, found that the respondent had not discharged the burden of proof cast on her by Article 7 merely by relying on the fact that the plaintiff had failed to take a certain course of action by a certain date and that the 'decree *nisi* ought not to have been refused by reason of grave financial hardship'.

---

24 Unreported (1985).

In the course of delivering judgment on behalf of the Court of Appeal, Lowry LCJ drew attention to the additional clause in Article 7(1) which requires a court, following a finding of grave financial hardship, to also be satisfied that 'it would in all the circumstances be wrong to dissolve the marriage'. The crucial importance he attached to this caveat is apparent from his comment:

> One could have a case of grave financial hardship where it would still be right to dissolve the marriage. That, however, is not the point at issue in the present case, where we have reached the conclusion that the respondent cannot be said to have proved grave financial hardship; even where a decree *nisi* has been granted she has her remedies under Articles 12(2), 25 and 26.

It has been held[25] that an applicant cannot claim that a decree based solely on this ground, as opposed to being based on the respondent's conduct, should be rejected as it presents an affront to the former's conscience.

II. Time as a Bar to Petitioner

Whether defended or not, Article 5 of the Matrimonial Causes (NI) Order 1978 as amended by Article 3 of the Matrimonial and Family Proceedings (NI) Order 1989 prevents any court in Northern Ireland from hearing a divorce petition within the first two years of a marriage. The effect of a time bar was considered in a case[26] where an application was made for leave to present a divorce petition within the three-year period (as it was then) stipulated in Article 5 of the 1978 Order on the grounds of the respondent's promiscuous conduct. There was evidence that the applicant had caught the respondent in *flagrante delicto* during an act of adultery and that there was a tendency on the respondent's part to familiarity with other men. There was evidence also that the applicant had suffered from a lack of concentration, sleeplessness and diarrhoea and also that these physical symptoms could have been stress related. The court held that this was not a case of exceptional depravity on the part of the respondent, but that the applicant had suffered exceptional hardship within the meaning of Article 5.

MacDermott J, in giving judgment, quoted the observations of Murphy LJ in *Martin v Martin*[27] as being of continuing relevance:

> We have been informed that there has been as of yet no reported decision on the meaning of the phrase 'exceptional hardship' or 'exceptional depravity'. An exhaustive definition of either phrase could not be accepted, but I entirely agree with the LCJ that on the facts of this case the plaintiff has failed to establish that it is a case of 'exceptional hardship' suffered by her or of 'exceptional depravity' on the part of the respondent.
>
> In every case in which a petitioner proves that he or she has been subjected to such cruelty as would entitle a judge to pronounce a decree of divorce, the petitioner must

---

25 In *Grenfell v Grenfell* [1978] 1 All ER 561.
26 See *In Re PMK* [1981] NI 211.
27 [1941] NI 1, 14.

have experienced 'hardship' to some extent. The use of 'exceptional' in section 5 indicates hardship 'out of the ordinary course'. It is impossible to define the quantum of hardship which would constitute 'exceptional hardship', but it can be said that the adjective indicates that the judge must be satisfied that the petitioner has suffered greater hardship than that ordinarily associated with those cases in which petitioners successfully establish their claims for divorces on the ground of cruelty.

It was held that although the Act permitted the submission of a petition within three years if 'the case was one of exceptional hardship', this was not such a case. (See also section 1 of the 1984 Act).

Under Article 4 of the 1978 Order, time will also bar a petitioner from relying on the fact of adultery where it can be shown that the petitioner and respondent have since lived together for a period or periods exceeding six months.

III. Connivance as a Bar to Petitioner

Under Article 4(2) of the 1978 Order, where a petitioner is alleging adultery and the respondent proves that this was committed with the connivance of the petitioner, then the court may dismiss the petition. Where a decree has been made which subsequently is shown to have been obtained by fraud then it will be set aside and declared null and void. A recent and well publicised case in England,[28] concerning a deceased peer of the realm, so concluded when evidence was produced to prove that: he had not been domiciled in the UK at the time of proceedings, so the court had no jurisdiction; he had fraudulently claimed that his only child, of the marriage in question, had died; and he had intercepted all court papers addressed to his wife, in particular he had signed and returned the acknowledgment of service which had never been served upon her.

IV. Other Bars to Relief

Where a petitioner is relying on the fact of five years' separation (as seen above), a respondent may successfully oppose, under Article 7 of the 1978 Order, the granting of a decree on the ground that if granted it would result in grave financial or other hardship to the respondent. Under Article 12 the court is not permitted to issue a decree absolute in circumstances where a petitioner has neither made nor proposes to make adequate financial arrangements for the respondent. Under Article 44 it is similarly restricted from doing so in circumstances where the inadequate arrangements are in respect of children of the family.

Procedural Law

In England and Wales almost all divorce petitions are now undefended and are therefore dealt with by what has come to be known as the 'special procedure'. As Latey J has explained,[29] the objectives of this procedure are to promote 'simplicity, speed and

---

28 See *Moynihan v Moynihan (nos 1 and 2)* [1997] 1 FLR 59.
29 See *R v Nottinghamshire County Court ex parte Byers* [1985] 1 WLR 403, [1985] FLR 695.

economy'. In effect it has meant that instead of all petitions being judicially heard and determined, those which are undefended are presented to a Registrar who, if satisfied that all requirements have been met, then so advises the judge who in turn pronounces the decree. In Northern Ireland, however, the 'special procedure' does not apply. Instead, even though largely undefended, all cases continue to be presented to, heard and determined by a judge sitting without a jury (subject to section 62(4) of the Judicature (NI) Act 1978). How this occurs is dependent upon the jurisdiction of the courts and the domicile or residence of the parties.

Under Article 48 of the 1978 Order and Rule 2.30 of the Family Proceedings Rules (NI) 1996, the High Court and any designated 'county court sitting for any division as a Divorce County Court' will have jurisdiction to entertain a divorce petition where either of the parties is domiciled in Northern Ireland when proceedings are commenced or has been habitually resident in Northern Ireland for the twelve-month period immediately preceding the commencement of such proceedings. Whether a petition is heard by the High Court or by such a designated county court will depend mainly on whether it is defended. Currently nearly all divorces in Northern Ireland are undefended because of the inevitability of eventual success and also because of the expense entailed in contesting an action for which legal aid is seldom available. Under Rule 2.32 of the Family Proceedings Rules (NI) 1996, a case may also be transferred to the High Court 'if, having regard to all the circumstances including the difficulty or importance of the cause or of any issue arising therein, the court thinks it desirable' or to another county court on grounds of general convenience. Under Article 49 of the 1978 Order, divorce proceedings may be commenced if either party is domiciled in Northern Ireland at the time of application or has been habitually resident there for the twelve months immediately preceding the application.

The law relating to contested arrangements in respect of property and finance or in respect of children may be found in Parts Three and Two, respectively.

I. *The Two Stages of Divorce Proceedings*

The formal requirements governing divorce procedure are to be found in the Matrimonial Causes Rules (NI) 1981 as amended in 1989 and 1993. These have now been further amended by the Family Proceedings Rules (NI) 1996.

Article 3(6) of the 1978 Order states that a divorce decree may only be granted by first obtaining a decree *nisi* and by then applying for and obtaining a decree absolute.

1. Petition Is Drawn Up

A petition, stating the fact on which the applicant intends to rely to prove the alleged irretrievable breakdown of the marriage, is drawn up. The petition must contain the information required by Appendix 2 of the Family Proceedings Rules (NI) 1996. It should include:

- the names and addresses of both parties and of any children of the family, if these are aged sixteen years or less or are in full-time education;
- the occupations of the parties and particulars relating to the date, place, etc. of their marriage;

- the details relating to the marriage breakdown, any claim to ancillary relief in the form of property or maintenance adjustment or any custody arrangements which the applicant would wish the court to consider.

Where there are children, as described above, Rule 2.3.(2) of the 1996 Rules requires a full statement (Form M4) of proposed arrangements for them.

2. Petition Is Lodged

Once completed the petition is filed in the Matrimonial Office, accompanied by the required supporting documentation (e.g. a notice in Form M5 and M6 addressed to the respondent and any co-respondent) including the marriage certificate and a statement of arrangements to be made for any children under the age of sixteen or in full-time education. In England and Wales, unlike this jurisdiction, a completed reconciliation certificate is also necessary in which the petitioner certifies that arrangements for accessing a reconciliation service have been availed of, or at least have been made available. This certificate testifies to the effort made to prevent the marriage ending in divorce and, in the former jurisdiction, is a pre-requisite to the initiation of divorce proceedings. In this jurisdiction the only requirement is, as stated in Article 8 of the 1978 Order, that at any time during the course of the proceedings 'if it appears to the court that there is a reasonable possibility of reconciliation' an adjournment may be declared to facilitate this possibility (see p. 189 for conciliation services).

The petition must be accompanied by the appropriate fee or a statement of entitlement to free legal aid. A petitioner who intends to rely on legal aid may well be advised to first avail of reconciliation services as the Legal Aid Board would seem to be gradually elevating the significance of attendance at such services to the status of eligibility criteria in divorce cases.

3. Notice Is Served

The court then serves a copy of the petition on the respondent. This is sent together with two other forms — a Notice of Proceedings, which explains the effect of the petition and provides procedural guidance, and an Acknowledgment of Service (Form M6), which requires the respondent, within fourteen days, to confirm receipt of the petition and to indicate whether it will be contested or whether ancillary relief will be sought. The respondent may, under Rule 2.36 of the 1996 Rules, file a reply to the petitioner's statement regarding arrangements for the children, a copy of which will then be sent to the petitioner. Supplemental petitions and petitions amended after service may be filed with leave of the court.

4. Petitioner Seeks Directions

Following return of the Acknowledgment of Service the petitioner applies to the court for directions.

If the respondent has indicated a wish to contest the petition this must be indicated by a statement to that effect on the returned Form M6, supported by a cross petition, stating his or her answer to the matters alleged by the petitioner. This has to be forwarded to the court within twenty-one days of receipt of the Notice of Proceedings. Where, in such cases, the answer is to a petition filed in a divorce county court, the Master is required to transfer the case to the High Court, unless the answer contained no more than a simple denial and no notice is given of an intention to rebut the facts stated in the petition. If the case subsequently becomes undefended, it may then be returned to the initial court.[30]

5. Certificate of Readiness

When the parties are ready to proceed, a certificate of readiness (Form M8) is filed and the cause is listed for trial.

Following an exchange of pleadings a full hearing then takes place in open court with each party calling witnesses and being subject to examination and cross-examination.

6. Oral Testimony

The petitioner must still give oral testimony in support of his or her petition. However, as stated in Article 3(4) of the 1978 Order, this may be averted 'in any particular case where the court for special reasons orders that such testimony be dispensed with'. The related procedures, set out in Rule 44 of the Matrimonial Causes Rules (see also Rule 89), requires counsel or the solicitor to apply on summons and affidavit to the Master giving reasons for oral testimony to be dispensed with. If leave is granted, a petition is filed accompanied by a supporting affidavit affirming the facts stated therein. If the judge accepts that the case is one in which it would be proper to dispense with oral testimony, the decree *nisi* will be granted in the usual way. Since 1984 there have been six cases where oral testimony was dispensed with for reasons such as distance (wife living in Germany or wife in Australia), chronic illness (party suffering from cancer), mental illness (party suffering from claustrophobia) and physical disability (petitioner deaf and dumb).

Article 15 of the Family Law (NI) Order 1993 disapplies the requirement under Article 3(4) of the 1978 Order for the petitioner to give oral testimony:

(a) in any case where the petitioner alleges two years' separation and the respondent consents to a decree being granted; or
(b) in any case where the petitioner alleges five years' separation; or
(c) in any other.

However, this provision has not yet come into effect. When it does, if the respondent has indicated that he or she will not be contesting the petition, the petitioner will merely submit an affidavit and a completed standard form questionnaire providing evidence to support the fact relied upon to ground the petition. The hearing will then be held in chambers and be subject to reporting restrictions.

---

30 The Family Proceedings Rules (NI) 1996, Rules 2.14 and 2.23, respectively.

7. Decree *Nisi* Granted

If satisfied, from the papers submitted (in undefended cases) or from proof of the fact relied upon (in contested cases), that the marriage has irretrievably broken down, the judge then issues a certificate to that effect and sets a date for the granting of the decree *nisi*.

Both parties are duly notified of the date when this decree is to be read out in open court and are free, but not obliged, to attend if they so wish.

8. Decree Absolute Granted

The procedure is governed by Rules 2.52 and 2.53 of the Family Proceedings Rules (NI) 1996. The decree absolute is granted by the court in response to either an application, under Article 3(6) of the 1978 Order, from the petitioner submitted not less than six weeks after the issue of the decree *nisi*, or an application made, under Article 11(2) of that Order, by the respondent at least three months after that event. The reason for this interval is to allow time for an aggrieved respondent to lodge an appeal for possible intervention by the Crown Solicitor and, as stated in Article 11 of the 1978 Order, for anyone else to show cause why the divorce should not be finalised.

There are some circumstances in which the court will accept applications to abridge the time allowed for granting a decree absolute. If the petitioner has failed to apply for a decree absolute three months or more after being granted a decree *nisi,* the respondent may apply to the court requesting that action be taken to settle the matter. Under Article 11 the court may respond by making the decree absolute, by rescinding the decree, by directing further enquiries or by taking such other action as it sees fit.

Before granting the decree absolute the court is required by Article 44 of the 1978 Order to satisfy itself that appropriate arrangements have been made for any children of the marriage. Under the 1995 Order, Schedule 9, paragraph 95, the making of the decree absolute may only be postponed where the court needs more time to give further consideration to the case and there are exceptional circumstances which make such a postponement desirable in the interests of the child concerned. Under Article 25 of the 1978 Order the court has a discretionary power to consider also the adequacy of any financial arrangements made in respect of the respondent. The law relating to the issues arising when these matters are contested between the parties is dealt with in Parts Two and Three.

II. Conciliation/Mediation

The aims of reconciliation are to restore a marriage that has broken down, and evidence that this has been attempted is a necessary component of divorce proceedings if the irretrievable nature of the breakdown is to be proven. It is specifically addressed by Article 8 of the Matrimonial Causes (NI) Order 1978. The aims of conciliation or mediation, however, are more modest and practical; the court will always, in general terms, advise the parties that services exist which may help them to resolve or come to terms with difficulties without having to resort to further litigation. Where a petition for divorce (or for nullity or judicial separation) is presented and there are children of the family to whom Article 44 of the 1978 Order applies, the Master must refer the case to the local Trust with a view to the involvement of a suitably qualified person who will consider the possibility of conciliating the parties to the marriage.[31]

In Northern Ireland conciliation services are provided by Relate and the Family Mediation Service and have a particular relevance to the post-decree *nisi* stage in preparing the parties to reach agreement on arrangements in respect of any children and as regards financial and property matters.

III. Agreed Arrangements in Respect of Children

The *Royal Commission on Marriage and Divorce*[32] advocated an interventionist approach towards ensuring the welfare interests of children when marital proceedings instituted by their parents arise for judicial determination. It recommended that a strict duty be placed on the judiciary in divorce cases to satisfy themselves that appropriate arrangements were made for all children affected by their parents' divorce. This recommendation found legislative acknowledgment in Article 44 of the 1978 Order with application to such arrangements arising in both divorce and separation proceedings. The Children (NI) Order 1995, however, has amended this provision.[33]

The Role of the Courts

Article 44 of the 1978 Order, as amended,[34] now requires the court to examine the proposed arrangements and, in the light of the facts disclosed, to decide whether this gives rise to an interventionist duty. Whereas formerly the judicial onus was to approve all such arrangements before granting a decree, now the onus is to investigate them and then decide whether some call for further action. If judicial investigations do reveal that the arrangements are not wholly satisfactory, it is now a matter of judicial discretion as to whether the decree is deferred until the parties have rectified their plans for the children. Under Article 44, as amended, the court may

> (2) ... direct that the decree of divorce or nullity is not made absolute, or that the decree of judicial separation is not to be granted, until the court directs otherwise.

The procedure for judicial compliance with Article 44 is set out in Rule 2.3 of the Family Proceedings Rules (NI) 1996. Where there are no children or where the court is satisfied that it need not exercise any of its powers under the Children (NI) Order 1995 nor give any direction under Article 44(1) of the 1978 Order in respect of them, the judge may issue a certificate to that effect. Where the court is not so satisfied, the judge may give one or more of the following directions:

---

31 The Family Proceedings Rules (NI) 1996, Rule 2.7.
32 See *The Morton Report* (1956) which concluded that the most suitable arrangements were not always being made for children (para 366) because nobody was 'specifically charged to look after the child's interests' (para 367).
33 In keeping with which the more restrained approach to public intervention in family affairs as recommended in *The Booth Report* (1985).
34 By the Children (NI) Order 1995, Schedule 9, para 93.

(a) that the parties, or any of them, shall file further evidence relating to the arrangements for the children (and the direction shall specify the matters to be dealt with in the further evidence);
(b) that a welfare report on the children, or any of them, be prepared;
(c) that the parties, or any of them, shall attend before him at the date, time and place specified in the direction.

Most often such judicial certification is issued and the decree made.

The law relating to the issues arising where care arrangements for the children are being disputed is considered in Part Two (see Chapter Twelve).

IV. Agreed Arrangements in Respect of Property and Finance

Under Article 24 of the Matrimonial Causes (NI) Order 1978, maintenance pending suit may be made available to a spouse to forestall hardship prior to and during divorce proceedings. This terminates on the granting of the decree absolute (see further Chapter Twenty-three).

Although the distribution of property and finances is often the most hotly contested and expensive aspect of divorce proceedings, many couples make their own private amicable arrangements. However, an agreement as to the distribution of assets and income reached privately between the spouses, prior to the granting of the decree absolute, does not present a complete bar to future proceedings, neither does the fact that a 'clean break' agreement was reached at the time of divorce[35] (again, see Chapter Twenty-three).

V. Special Protection in Separation Cases

Where the respondents are presumed to be without fault, as in all cases grounded on either of the separation facts, then the Matrimonial Causes (NI) Order 1978 places a special onus on the court to satisfy itself that the arrangements made by the parties in respect of their children and finances are adequate. Under Article 12 the court is prevented from making a decree absolute unless and until it has so determined. It has been held[36] (under the equivalent provision in the Matrimonial Causes Act 1973) that this provision may be utilised to delay the granting of a divorce absolute until such time as the court is satisfied that appropriate financial provision has been made for the child. This finding was upheld by the Court of Appeal which confirmed that the provision could be employed retrospectively, as in this case, to force a petitioner to make good his past failure to meet maintenance obligations in respect of a child.

VI. Foreign Divorces

Under Article 31(1) of the Matrimonial and Family Proceedings (NI) Order 1989, any person may apply to the court for

---

35 See, for example, in *Twiname v Twiname* [1992] 1 FLR 29 where a wife was held to have a claim against her ex-husband's assets fifteen years after the agreed divorce settlement.
36 See *Garcia v Garcia* [1991] 3 ALL ER 451, [1992] 1 FLR 256.

(d) a declaration that the validity of a divorce, annulment or legal separation obtained in any country outside Northern Ireland in respect of the marriage is entitled to recognition in Northern Ireland.

An application for a declaration to the opposite effect may be made under Article 31(1)(e).

A declaration of validity will be granted if the conditions as set out in section 3(1) of the Recognition of Divorces and Legal Separations Act 1971 can be met.[37] To satisfy these conditions at the time the proceedings were commenced it is necessary that:

- one spouse was habitually resident in the country, or was a national of the country, in the jurisdiction of which a valid divorce was granted,
- both spouses were domiciled in the jurisdiction where the decree was granted,
- one was domiciled in the jurisdiction and the decree was recognised under the law of the other's domicile,
- neither was domiciled in the jurisdiction where the decree was made but that decree was recognised by the jurisdictions in which they were then domiciled.

Any finding of fact made by the foreign court, for the purposes of such proceedings, will be regarded as conclusive provided both spouses took part in those proceedings. The actual grounds on which the decree was made are of no legal significance to the issue of whether it is recognisable under the law of this jurisdiction.

VII. Appeals

Under Article 48(9) of the Matrimonial Causes (NI) Order 1978 an appeal will lie from the granting or dismissal of any decree or order made by the divorce county court to the Court of Appeal. This is addressed more fully in Schedule 1, paragraph 10, of the 1989 Order which states:

> Without prejudice to Article 61 of the County Courts (NI) Order cases stated, rules of court shall make provision for an appeal to the Court of Appeal from any order made by a divorce county court in the exercise of the jurisdiction conferred by this Schedule, or from the dismissal of any application for such an order, upon a point of law, a question of fact or the admission or rejection of any evidence.

Conditional Consent

In this jurisdiction, the petitioner in *Brown v Brown*[38] appealed against an order as to costs following the granting of his former wife's application for a decree *nisi*. The relevant facts rested on his response as respondent to the questions in the Acknowledgement of Service (Form 5 as prescribed by the Matrimonial Causes Rules (NI) 1979). He had replied as follows:

---

37 This legislation came into effect on 1st Jan 1972 as a consequence of Great Britain signing the Hague Convention on the Recognition of Divorces and Separations 1970.
38 [1992] 2 BNIL 48.

6. Do you consent to a decree being granted?
Yes, provided no claim is made against me for costs . . .
9. Even if you do not intend to defend the case, do you object to paying the costs of the proceedings? If so, on what grounds?
Yes, my consent is conditional on no claim for costs.

The county court judge granted the decree *nisi* and ordered the respondent to pay half the costs incurred, even though the petitioner had made no application for costs.

The Court of Appeal allowed the appeal. It ruled that the consent was a conditional one and was effective only if that condition was completely and exactly fulfilled. Such a conditional consent was legally valid.[39] The decree *nisi* was affirmed as were all parts of the order made by the judge at first instance, save for the part relating to costs.

VIII. Legal Aid

The policy regarding the use of legal aid in divorce cases in Northern Ireland follows that established in the jurisdiction of England and Wales. This, as has been stated,[40]

> . . . is to avoid defended suits in relation to the decree unless there are reasons why the suit should be defended in the interests of either party, and to ensure that normally the award of a decree will not compromise decisions over issues relating to the custody of, access to, and maintenance of children, and the other ancillary matters.

Another facet of the policy regarding legal aid in such cases is the recent linkage being made by the Legal Aid Board between eligibility for aid and willingness to attend conciliation counselling. Resistance to the latter may result in denial of legal aid.

Effects of Divorce

I. Re-marriage

Most obviously, the granting of a decree absolute has the legal effect of dissolving the parties' marriage and leaves both parties free to re-marry.

II. Wills

The basic principle regarding wills is that, unless a contrary intention is evident on the face of a will, a former spouse should not gain from a will made before the divorce. Under Article 13 of the Wills and Administration Proceedings (NI) Order 1994, any gift made in the will of a person, in respect of whom a decree *nisi* has been granted, to a former spouse of that person is rendered null and void. The appointment of a former spouse to act as the testator's executor also lapses. However, the fact of their divorce will not otherwise affect a will made by either party during marriage (see further Chapter Twenty-five).

---

39 See *Beales v Beales* [1972] Fam 210, [1972] 2 All ER 677.
40 See *The Legal Aid Handbook* 1990.

III. Pensions

The rule has been that divorce terminates all rights of a former spouse to the benefits of any pension plan in which he or she stood to gain solely as the spouse of the main beneficiary. As most occupational pensions are of this nature, divorce has very real long-term financial consequences for a former dependant spouse. However, this situation has now been altered by the Pensions (NI) Order 1995 (see further Chapter Twenty-four).

CHAPTER TEN

Child Abduction

Introduction

The abduction of children is a growing problem. This chapter examines the different forms it may take and the related domestic civil and criminal law. As it is increasingly a problem with an extra-territorial dimension, most consideration is given to the law as framed by international Conventions.

It is interesting to note that the number of child abduction cases coming to court in this jurisdiction has been relatively insignificant. In 1992 there were three such cases and there have been four every year since. Current indications are that this trend is changing with cases now appearing in the High Court fairly frequently.

The Background

Abduction occurs when a child is unlawfully removed and/or detained. A child may be abducted either within the jurisdiction, to another jurisdiction or into this jurisdiction. Under the Child Abduction (NI) Order 1985, child abduction is a criminal offence which replaces the offence of child stealing under section 56 of the Offences against the Person Act 1861. The 1985 Order provides for two new offences: one to deal with the abduction of a child from the United Kingdom by a parent or other person connected with the child, the other to deal with the abduction of a child from the lawful control of another person not connected with the child. In certain circumstances, the abduction of a child may also be a criminal offence under common law.

I. The Domestic Context

Abduction may be readily understood in legal terms as the offence of unlawfully taking away and retaining a child. This definition serves to obscure our understanding of a phenomenon which in practice consists of two very different types of activity.

1. Within the 'Family'

The modern problem of abduction has come to be associated with 'tug-of-love' cases where one loving parent unlawfully 'snatches' his or her own child from the home provided by the other equally loving parent, an offence often committed by unmarried fathers. Both adult parties need not necessarily be the child's parents: one could, for example, be a grandparent, step-parent, older sibling or someone else 'connected with' the child. The abducting party is, however, usually well motivated if misguided and has no intention of causing harm to the child. The increase in this type of activity corresponds to the increasing impermanence of the average modern nuclear family unit.

2. By a 'Stranger'

Abduction, unfortunately, also refers to another more sinister and more ancient offence: the kidnapping of a child by a stranger or non-relative who does so with the intention of causing harm. This harm may take the form of extortion whereby the victim is detained until the parents or guardians pay a 'ransom' for his or her safe return. Increasingly, there are also cases of children being abducted within the jurisdiction for the purpose of sale to childless couples elsewhere. More often the abduction is by a stranger for sadistic purposes and results in the death of the abducted child.

II. Unlawful Removal and Habitual Residence

While the offence of child abduction is committed by the unlawful removal of a child from a person or body vested with parental responsibility, the question of which court should determine the resulting issues of future care and upbringing turns on identifying the place where the child concerned was habitually resident. This preliminary legal question is of crucial significance and is relevant as much to abduction within the United Kingdom (Part I of the 1986 Act) as to abduction between the United Kingdom and other countries (Article 3 of the Hague Convention).

The Concept of 'Habitual Residence'

The Law Commission[1] made the following observations regarding 'habitual residence' as a test for jurisdiction:

> 41. ... 'Habitual residence' is an expression which is now commonly used in international conventions, including the Hague Convention on Recognition. It has already found a place in our legislation and has been used by the courts in their discussion of problems of jurisdiction and recognition. There would be advantages for the future, and confusion might be avoided, if a uniform test were adopted throughout the field of family law as far as possible, provided that the test connotes the kind of residential connection with a country which we regard as necessary to establish matrimonial jurisdiction.
>
> 42. We think that 'habitual residence' connotes this kind of connection. It is clearly distinguishable from domicile, a necessary element of which is a particular intention as to the future. Such an intention is not needed to establish 'habitual residence'; it can be provided by evidence of a course of conduct which tends to show substantial links between a person and his country of residence.
>
> The meaning of 'habitual residence' seems to us to be similar to that of ordinary residence. To be habitual, a residence must be more than transient or casual; once established, however, it is not necessarily broken by a temporary absence. It has to be conceded that whatever term is used for the purpose of matrimonial jurisdiction, it will lack sharp definition and give rise to difficult cases.

---

1 In its report *Jurisdiction in Matrimonial Cases* (Law Com no. 48, 1972).

The guidance offered more recently by the House of Lords[2] is very much in keeping with the observations of the Law Commission and now stands as the most authoritative statement on this matter.

> The expression 'habitually resident' is not a term of art; whether a person is habitually resident in a particular country is a question of fact; there is a significant difference between a person ceasing to be habitually resident in one country and becoming habitually resident in another, and a person may cease to be habitually resident in one country in a single day if he leaves it with a settled intention not to return, but cannot become habitually resident in a new country unless he has a settled intention to remain there and an 'appreciable amount of time has elapsed; during the appreciable period of time the person will have ceased to be habitually resident in his former country, but will not have become habitually resident in another, i.e. will not be habitually resident in any country; where a young child is in the sole custody of one parent, the child's habitual residence will be the same as that parent's.

Chapter IV of Part I of the 1986 Act provides the rules which govern the determination of 'habitual residence' by a court in Northern Ireland. An order made by a court in any of the United Kingdom jurisdictions under section 25 of the 1986 Act may be registered under section 27 in any of its other jurisdictions and must then be recognised and enforced under section 29 by the relevant court.

III. The International Context

The phenomenon of child abduction has, in recent years, shown an increasing lack of regard for national frontiers. In response to this problem and the consequent undermining of the principle of comity between nations, two international conventions have been introduced.

1. The Hague Convention

In October 1980 the Hague Convention on the Civil Aspects of International Child Abduction was signed at The Hague. This Convention requires member states to ensure the prompt return of a child unlawfully removed from one Member State and retained in another, whether or not the rights of custody in respect of that child are the subject of a court order. In this way the Hague Convention sought to end the practice of 'forum shopping' which by the 1980s had become a serious international problem. A parent, having 'snatched' his or her child from lawful custody in one jurisdiction and removed him or her to a chosen other, could then with some hope of success claim that the courts of the latter had a right to re-open the issue of custody and, if it saw fit, make an order in favour of the parent presently caring for the child and amenable to the court.[3]

---

2 See *C v S (A Minor)(Abduction)* [1990] 2 FLR 442, 454A–D (per Lord Brandon).
3 See further C Sachs *Child Abduction — The Hague Convention and Recent Case-law*, (Sept 1993) Fam Law. pp 585–86.

2. The European Convention

In May 1980 the European Convention on Recognition and Enforcement of Decisions Concerning Custody of Children and on Restoration of Custody of Children was signed in Luxembourg. This Convention requires the reciprocal enforcement of court orders, regarding custody or access arrangements for children between Member States.

3. The Policy of the Convention

This has been well expressed by Waite LJ as follows:[4]

> Although the Hague Convention and the European Convention are different treaties to which effect is given by different parts of the Child Abduction and Custody Act 1985, the underlying policy is the same. It is to settle the lives of children. The Hague Convention seeks to do that by avoiding the disruption suffered when a child is abducted from the jurisdiction of habitual residence. The European Convention seeks to spare children the unsettling effect of a potential conflict of orders for custody or contact in different jurisdictions.

4. Administration of Convention Procedures

Both Conventions make provision for the setting up of a 'Central Authority' in each signatory state. In this jurisdiction the functions of the 'Central Authority' are discharged by the Northern Ireland Courts Service. To this body is assigned responsibility for implementing all steps necessary to secure, expeditiously, the common Convention objectives of receiving applications from signatory states in respect of abducted children, collecting all relevant information, tracing the child, instigating and overseeing appropriate legal procedures and generally taking all possible steps to ensure the safe return of the children concerned.

Where a case falls within the remit of either Convention the welfare of the child concerned will have a limited bearing on the outcome of proceedings. In non-Convention cases, however, where the issue is likely to be heard in wardship proceedings, the welfare principle must be given a paramount weighting in determining the outcome.

The Lord Chancellor's Department has established a Child Abduction Unit which functions as the Central Authority for England and Wales and for which the Official Solicitor has responsibility. The Central Authority for Scotland lies with the Scottish Courts Administration.

Prevention

The law relating to child abduction deals with the remedies and procedures available to an applicant after the event. There are also, however, measures which may be taken to forestall the need for recourse to such law.

---

4 See *Re A (Foreign Access Order: Enforcement)* [1996] 1 FLR 561 at p. 567.

I. Under the Children (NI) Order 1995

An applicant who fears the possible unauthorised removal of a child may take preventative action under this statute. Any person may, under Article 10(2), make application for one of the following Article 8 orders with leave of the court and any parent or guardian of the child may do so, under Article 10(4), without such leave.

1. Prohibited Steps Order (PSO)

Under Article 8(1) of the 1995 Order, a PSO may be issued prohibiting any specified 'step which could be taken by a parent in meeting his parental responsibility for a child', such as removal from the jurisdiction, from being taken 'without the consent of the court'. Under Article 10(4)(b) a person in whose favour a residence order is in force in respect of the child concerned may make application without court leave.

2. Residence Order (RO)

Under Article 8(1) of the 1995 Order, an RO may be issued 'settling the arrangements to be made as to the person with whom a child is to live'. One of the automatic effects of an RO, as stated in Article 13, is to prevent the removal of the child concerned from the jurisdiction; the provision is qualified by Article 3(2A) of the 1985 Order (as inserted by Schedule 9, paragraph 121(3) of the 1995 Order) permitting such a removal for a maximum period of one month (see also Chapter Twelve). An application may, in exceptional circumstances, be made *ex parte*.

3. Parental Responsibility Order (PRO)

Under Article 7 of the 1995 Order, an unmarried father may apply for a PRO in respect of the child concerned. Such a father should do so if he wishes to be in a position to resist the mother's plans to remove their child from the jurisdiction. The order, if granted, may be buttressed by a further order preventing any unauthorised removal. A successful application for an RO would, of course, achieve both purposes.

II. Under the Family Law Act 1986

A parent or person with whom the child concerned is living may make application under the provisions of this Act for an order requiring the surrender of that child's passport in circumstances where the applicant has reasonable cause to believe that an unauthorised attempt may be made to remove the child from the jurisdiction. The order, if granted, will prevent removal of the child from any part of the United Kingdom.

III. Wardship

Wardship, the traditional legal means of preventing an unauthorised removal of a child from the jurisdiction (see further Chapter Seven), has ostensibly been rendered redundant by the availability of specific issue and prohibited steps orders. However, in unusual or urgent circumstances, it may be necessary to seek the direct intervention of the High Court and its prerogative powers by initiating wardship proceedings. This will instantly prohibit any unauthorised removal.

However, wardship may not always work to the advantage of the applicant as, unlike proceedings under the Conventions or under the 1985 Order, the High Court will apply the paramountcy principle. The case of *In re V and Another*[5] concerned two 'lectors' of QUB, one of Spanish nationality and the other French, who had married in 1971. In 1979 they separated and the mother was awarded custody. She became increasingly unhappy living in Belfast and made known her intention to return, with the children, to France. The father applied to have the children made wards of court and to be granted care and control.

In giving judgment, MacDermott J held that the first and paramount consideration for the court was the welfare of the children, which included their moral and religious welfare, their physical well-being and ties of affection. He stated that there is no rule of law that a mother is entitled to the custody of her children but as a factor of their welfare the presence of the mother must receive considerable weight. He considered that it would be wrong to divide the children between the parents. He further considered that if the mother were to remain in Belfast she would grow increasingly unhappy; this would be harmful to the children and outweigh any advantage from having their father near to hand. Accordingly, the wardship order was confirmed and the mother was given leave to remove the children from the jurisdiction.

IV. Effect of a Court Order

In some circumstances it is essential to have a court order if action is to be taken to prevent an unauthorised removal or to retrieve the child concerned. The provisions of the European Convention and the corresponding powers under the 1985 Order are inoperable on behalf of any applicant who does not have a court order in respect of the child. Authority to call on the assistance of police and port authorities is also dependent on proof of 'custody rights'.

The Criminal Law

The Child Abduction (NI) Order 1985 corresponds to the Child Abduction Act 1984, Part 1. It repeals the Offences against the Person Act 1861, section 56 and restricts prosecutions for the common-law offence of kidnapping. The 1985 Order, as amended by the Children (NI) Order 1995, Schedule 9, paragraphs 121 and 122, now provides the statutory law relating to the criminal offence of child abduction, except where the child concerned is in care, etc.

I. Offence Committed by a Person Connected with a Child

Under the Child Abduction (NI) Order 1985, Article 3:

---

5 Unreported (1981).

(1) Subject to paragraphs (3) and (7), a person connected with a child under the age of sixteen commits an offence if he takes or sends the child out of the United Kingdom without the appropriate consent.

The relevant terms are further defined as follows:

(2) For the purposes of this Order
(a) a person shall be regarded as taking a child if he causes or induces the child to accompany him or any other person or causes the child to be taken;
(b) a person shall be regarded as sending a child if he causes the child to be sent; and
(c) a person shall be regarded as detaining a child if he causes the child to be detained or induces the child to remain with him or any other person and
(d) references to a child's parents and to a child whose parents were (or were not) married to each other at the time of his birth shall be construed in accordance with Article 155 of the Children (NI) Order 1995 (which extends their meaning).

Thus the offence of child abduction is committed if a 'person connected with the child' under the age of sixteen 'takes or sends that child out of the United Kingdom' without the 'appropriate consent'. Attempting to abduct is also an offence.

A distinction is made between offences: by a person 'connected with a child' and by 'other persons'. The former will be committed only if the child is removed from the jurisdiction of the United Kingdom. The latter will be committed by any unauthorised removal. Any person reasonably suspected of attempting an unauthorised removal of a child from the jurisdiction is liable to arrest without warrant. The police may effect an arrest following implementation of 'an all ports alert' procedure whereby all harbours and airports are circulated with a 'stop and detain' list of suspected abducted children and their abductors.

The rationale for the distinction lies in the fact that provision is made in the 1995 Order for parents, or for others connected with the child concerned, to seek redress for their grievances by making application for an appropriate Article 8 order under that legislation. Only when such a parent or person connected with the child clearly demonstrates his or her rejection of any intention to use the proper channels within the civil law will he or she be held to be within the reach of the criminal law.

1. A 'Person Connected with the Child'

The person who so 'takes or sends that child' is an offender if he or she comes within the definition of Article 3(2), as amended by the Children (NI) Order 1995, Schedule 9, paragraph 121:

(a) he is a parent of the child; or
(b) in the case of a child whose parents were not married to each other at the time of his birth, there are reasonable grounds for believing that he is the father of the child; or
(c) he is a guardian of the child; or

(d) he is a person in whose favour a residence order is in force with respect to the child; or
(e) he has custody of the child.

2. 'Appropriate Consent'

Under Article 3(5) of the 1985 Order, as inserted by the 1995 Order, Schedule 9, paragraph 121(5), 'appropriate consent' means the consent of each of the following: the child's mother, father (if he has parental responsibility), any guardian, any person in whom a residence order is vested in respect of the child, any person with custody of the child, or, where a person whose consent is required holds authority by virtue of a court order, the leave of the court granted under any provision of Part III of the 1995 Order, or where any person has custody leave of the court which awarded that order.

II. Defence to a Charge of Child Abduction Committed by a Person Connected with the Child

The defences available under the 1985 Order have been affected by amendments made by the Children (NI) Order 1995.

1. A Person Vested with a Residence Order

Under the Child Abduction (NI) Order 1985, Article 2(2A), as inserted by the Children (NI) Order 1995, Schedule 9, paragraph 121,

> (2A) A person does not commit an offence under this Article by taking or sending a child out of the United Kingdom without obtaining the appropriate consent if —
> (a) he is a person in whose favour there is a residence order in force with respect to the child, and
> (b) he takes or sends him out of the United Kingdom for a period of less than one month.

This defence is not available where the person concerned is acting in breach of an order made under Part III of the 1995 Order.

2. Consent

Under the Child Abduction (NI) Order 1985, Article 3,

> (3) A person does not commit an offence under this Article by doing anything without the consent of another person whose consent is required under the foregoing provisions if—
> (a) he does it in the belief that the other person—
>   (i) has consented; or
>   (ii) would consent if he was aware of all the relevant circumstances; or
> (b) he has taken all reasonable steps to communicate with the other person but has been unable to communicate with him; or
> (c) the other person has unreasonably refused to consent.

The latter defence is not available where the person refusing consent has either custody of or a residence order in relation to the child. Nor is it available where the person 'taking or sending the child out of the United Kingdom is, by so acting, in breach of an order made by a court in the United Kingdom'.

III. Offence Committed by Other Persons

Under the Child Abduction (NI) Order 1985, Article 4, an 'other person' commits the offence of child abduction if

> (1) ... without lawful authority or reasonable excuse, he takes or detains a child under the age of sixteen —
> (a) so as to remove him from the lawful control of any person having lawful control of the child; or
> (b) so as to keep him out of the lawful control of any person entitled to lawful control of the child.

Again, an attempt to abduct is also an offence.

1. 'Lawful Authority'

Persons 'connected with the child', most notably the child's unmarried mother or the married parents (if married to each other at the time of the child's birth), will have the requisite authority whereas an unmarried father will not unless he has parental responsibility. The latter is, however, provided with a statutory defence under Article 4(3)(b), as inserted by the 1995 Order, Schedule 9, paragraph 122(3), if 'at the time of the alleged offence, he believed, on reasonable grounds, that he was the child's father'.

2. 'Reasonable Excuse'

An 'other person' is provided with a statutory defence under Article 4(3)(b), as inserted by the 1995 Order, Schedule 9, paragraph 122(3), if 'at the time of the alleged offence, he believed that the child had attained the age of sixteen'.

IV. Offence of Kidnapping

Under the Child Abduction (NI) Order 1985, Article 6, the common-law offence of kidnapping will no longer attract prosecution, except with the consent of the DPP, if committed in respect of a child 'under the age of sixteen' and by a 'person connected with the child'.

The corollary is, therefore, that kidnapping may still warrant criminal proceedings either where the child victim is aged sixteen or more and the perpetrator is an 'other person' as defined above or where the child is under that age, the perpetrator is a parent or someone else with parental responsibility and the DPP has consented.[6]

---

6 See, for example, *R v Rahman* (1985) 81 Cr App Rep 349.

V. Abduction of Children in Care

Under the Children (NI) Order 1995, Article 68:

> (1) A person shall be guilty of an offence if, knowingly and without lawful authority or reasonable excuse, he —
> (a) takes a child to whom this Article applies away from the responsible person;
> (b) keeps such a child away from the responsible person; or
> (c) induces, assists or incites such a child to run away or stay away from the responsible person.

For the purposes of this provision, the 'responsible person' is defined in Article 68(2) as 'any person who for the time being has care of him by virtue of the care order, the emergency protection order, or Article 65, as the case may be'. While anyone unlawfully taking away such a child will be committing the crime of abduction, it is probable that the legislative intent is directed more towards those who may be tempted to harbour a child who has absconded from care.

The Civil Law and Unlawful Removal within the Jurisdictions of the United Kingdom

The removal of a child by a parent, contrary to the terms of a custody order, from one jurisdiction to another within the UK was a considerable problem in the late 1970s and early 1980s. It was accompanied by considerable judicial contention as to which court should deal with the issue of the return or otherwise of the child, i.e. whether it should be the court initially seised of the matter which had made the relevant custody order or the court of the jurisdiction within which the child was presently located. It was in response to the resulting legal uncertainty and judicial inconsistency that the Law Commission recommendations were made[7] resulting in the introduction of the Family Law Act 1986.

I. Abduction into Northern Ireland from elsewhere in the United Kingdom and the Role of Wardship

In Northern Ireland, before the introduction of the 1986 Act, cases concerning children 'kidnapped' by a parent outside the jurisdiction and then brought within it were considered by the judiciary in wardship proceedings. The preliminary issue facing the High Court in relation to these so-called 'tug-of-love' cases was always whether or not the court should open proceedings in respect of a matter on which another court within the UK had already made an order. Judicial determination of this issue was unpredictable. In *Re SLH (Minors)*,[8] for example, MacDermott J ruled that as a matter

---

[7] See *Custody of Children — Jurisdiction and Enforcement within the UK*, (Law Comm no. 138).
[8] Unreported (1982).

of public policy the English child of a serviceman based in England, already the subject of an English custody order, who had been brought on holiday to Northern Ireland by his mother and then warded on her application, should be returned to England and the legal issues resolved by the courts already seised of them. A year later, however, the same judge came to the opposite conclusion in two similar cases. In *Re JRS (A Minor)*,[9] MacDermott J decided to exercise the wardship jurisdiction in relation to an English girl of English parents who was the subject of an English order. So, also, in *Re CB and AJB (Minors)*,[10] where he stated:

> ... having regard to the mother's existing involvement in the English courts — should I not let the issue of custody be resolved there? ... I think this is a case where I should decide the issue in dispute — and the children's best interests will not be best served by the Court's passing the case back and forth.

Both these judgments were subsequently confirmed by the Court of Appeal.

II. Abduction into Northern Ireland from elsewhere in the United Kingdom after the Family Law Act 1986

The Family Law Act 1986, Part I, chapters III and IV, apply to Northern Ireland (and to Scotland). Under this statute, an order relating to the custody of a child under the age of sixteen made by a court in one of the three constituent jurisdictions of the United Kingdom (England and Wales, Scotland and Northern Ireland) may be enforced by a court in either of the other two jurisdictions as though initially made there. This legislation restores both internal comity between the United Kingdom jurisdictions and the appropriateness of statutory proceedings as the framework for determining such issues. As amended by the Children Act 1989, it also provides that an Article 8 order granted in one UK jurisdiction may 'follow the child' to any other UK jurisdiction by being registered in and then enforced by the appropriate court.

The conditions under which the courts in Northern Ireland may exercise the powers provided by the 1986 Act are as stated in section 19:

> (1) A court in Northern Ireland shall not have jurisdiction to make a Part 1 order within section 1(1)(e) of this Act, other than under Article 45(1) of the Matrimonial Causes (NI) Order 1978 unless the condition in section 20 of this Act is satisfied.
> (2) The High Court in Northern Ireland shall have jurisdiction to make a Part 1 order within section 1(1)(e) of this Act if, and only if:
>   (a) the condition in section 20 of this Act is satisfied; or
>   (b) the ward is present in Northern Ireland on the relative date (within the meaning of section 20(6) of this Act) and the court considers that the immediate exercise of its powers is necessary for his protection.

A Part 1 order is a reference to an order made either under section 5 of the Guardianship of Infants Act 1886 (now repealed by the Children (NI) Order 1995) or by the High

---

9 Unreported (1983).
10 Unreported (1983).

Court in the exercise of its wardship jurisdiction (except where care or care and control is then immediately vested in a Board/Trust). A section 20 condition is a requirement that the child concerned is either habitually resident in Northern Ireland or is present in Northern Ireland and is not habitually resident elsewhere in the UK.

Higgins J gave full consideration to these conditions in the case of *F v F*[11] which concerned three children (aged nine, seven and eleven) summarily removed from the matrimonial home in England in September 1995 by their father to this jurisdiction where, in November, they were made wards of court by the Master who appointed the Director of the SHSSB their guardian with entailed care and control responsibilities. In January 1996, following the mother's instruction of a solicitor in England, the matter came for hearing before Higgins J on the initial question of whether the courts of England or of Northern Ireland would provide the most appropriate forum for resolving the parents' custody dispute. This turned on the central issue of habitual residence. On the facts Higgins J found that: prior to their removal the children had been habitually resident in England; their removal to Northern Ireland did not change their habitual residence because it did not have the mother's consent (she could not be held to have abandoned her responsibilities) and because the father did not have the requisite intention to settle permanently in this jurisdiction (he had not terminated his employment in England); all parties therefore remained habitually resident in England. As the section 20 condition could not be satisfied the judge ruled that the court had no jurisdiction under section 19. He also ruled that there was no need for the court to exercise its inherent jurisdiction, so provided for under section 19(2)(b), as the mother did not present any risk which would require the immediate protection of the children. He concluded that the wardship order made by the Master should be discharged and advised that 'the appointee and the respondent may, if they so wish, proceed with any applications they consider necessary in the jurisdiction in which the children are habitually resident'.

The Civil Law and the Hague Convention

The obligations of the United Kingdom under the Hague Convention are given effect by the Child Abduction and Custody Act 1985, Part 1; the Convention is itself set out in Schedule 1 of the Act. Many countries (approximately forty) across the world are now signatories to this Convention. Because the 1985 Act embodies international commitments on the part of the United Kingdom, it therefore represents and applies equally to the law in Northern Ireland. The basic objective of the Hague Convention is to expedite the return to his or her country of origin of any child wrongfully removed from a person with rights of custody in that country. It also provides for rights of access.

I. Wrongful Removal or Detention

Under Article 3 of the Hague Convention, the removal or retention of a child is to be considered wrongful where

---

11 Unreported (1996).

(a) it is in breach of rights of custody attributed to a person, an institution or any other body, either jointly or alone, under the law of the State in which the child was habitually resident immediately before the removal or retention; and

(b) at the time of removal or retention those rights were actually exercised, either jointly or alone, or would have been so exercised but for the removal or retention.

The rights of custody mentioned in sub-paragraph (a) above may arise in particular by operation of law, by reason of a judicial or administrative decision or by reason of an agreement having legal effect under the law of that State.

Any such proven 'breach of rights of custody' under Article 3 in respect of a child removed from another jurisdiction will bring the matter within the definition of 'convention case'. This in turn will require implementation of the Article 12 directive that the child be returned forthwith to the originating jurisdiction.

II. 'Habitual Residence'

In Northern Ireland, Higgins J gave consideration to the practical application of the concept of habitual residence in $C \ v \ C$[12] where as a preliminary issue the court had to determine whether two children were in fact 'habitually resident' in the country from which the applicant alleged they were wrongfully removed.

Briefly, the facts were as follows. An Australian woman, while in Belfast, met a local man whom she married and by whom she had two children. The family emigrated to Australia where they lived in three successive homes and where forty-five days later the husband declared the marriage to be over. For some weeks he sought a reconciliation before bringing the children, with his wife's permission, to visit her parents in Queensland; from there, and without his wife's permission, he brought the children back to Belfast. The wife then made application under the Child Abduction and Custody Act 1985 for the return of the children whom she alleged were wrongfully removed from her custody in Australia. On the preliminary issue Higgins J found that the children had been habitually resident in Australia; in particular he ruled as follows.

(1) The adjective 'habitual' indicated a quality of residence rather than its length and involved two features, that the residence was adopted voluntarily and for settled purposes. It was not helpful to define residence by reference to domicile.

(2) In deciding the habitual residence of a child too young to decide for himself where to live, the court was able to look, not only at what had happened to the child, but also at the actions and intentions of the child's parents which had a bearing on the children's residence and the quality of that residence.

(3) When the family left for Australia, the intention of the parents was to remain there presumably indefinitely. The children ceased to be habitually resident in Belfast on their departure from Northern Ireland. Notwithstanding the shortness of time spent by the children in Australia and the lack of an established home, the children were habitually resident there before their removal.

---

12 [1989] 10 NIJB 39.

Higgins J was satisfied that on the evidence of the preparations made prior to departure for Australia the children ceased to be 'habitually resident' in Belfast on the date of their departure. Even forty-five days after their arrival in Australia, it was still the couple's intention to remain there. Given the parents' settled intent, their stay was more than casual or transitory, the children had therefore acquired an 'habitual residence' in Australia.

III. Rights of Custody

The rights of custody must be determined in accordance with the domestic laws of the country where the child was habitually resident immediately prior to his or her removal. Under Article 5(a),

> rights of custody shall include rights relating to the care of the person of the child and, in particular, the right to determine the child's place of residence.

1. Court Order in Existence

In a case where there has been a breach of a 'live' order determining custody made by a court of the originating jurisdiction, there is no issue. That order will be regarded as binding on the courts of the destination jurisdiction. The child will be returned to the originating jurisdiction.

2. No Court Order in Existence

Where a child is removed from the originating jurisdiction in circumstances where, at the time of removal, no court order in relation to the custody of that child had been made, the legal issues are more complex. Such circumstances may arise after a marital relationship has broken down but before contested divorce proceedings come before a court or after the determination of uncontested proceedings where in this and some other jurisdictions (i.e. under the 1995 Order, Article 3(5), and under the 1989 Act, section 1(5)) no order will have been made or it may be that no legal ties existed between the parents or adult parties involved.

It is the latter type of circumstance where the parents of the child are unmarried or are not married to each other that has generated most of the more interesting case-law in England and Wales.

The Court of Appeal, for example, recently determined[13] that 'rights of custody' would be held to vest in an unmarried father, notwithstanding the absence of a court order to that effect. This was a case which concerned the child of unmarried parents living in Australia. The mother, a heroin addict, left the six-year-old boy with the father (who undertook primary care responsibility) and her mother while she returned to live in England. Some sixteen months later the grandmother took the child to England, ostensibly for the purpose of visiting the mother, after signing affidavits testifying that she would return the child to the father within six months. On arrival in England, the grandmother instead made the child a ward of court and refused to return him. At the hearing it was accepted that there was no court order in effect in relation to custody

---

13 See *Re B (A Minor)(Abduction)* [1994] 2 FLR 249.

rights either at the time the child was removed from the originating jurisdiction nor subsequently. Nor did the courts in Australia recognise any such rights as inherently vesting in an unmarried father. Nonetheless, the Court of Appeal was persuaded that 'rights of custody' under the Convention encompassed 'rights' which a parent carer could be said to have acquired by virtue of voluntarily undertaking sole responsibility for the child. This ruling is one which leans towards giving effect to the broad spirit of Convention principles rather than towards a narrow legalistic interpretation of actual Convention provisions.

The decision in *Re B* must be distinguished from an earlier decision of the House of Lords[14] which also concerned unmarried parents living in Australia, the removal of a child to England (by the mother) before the making of a custody order and the right of the father in Australia to the return of his child. Their lordships then decided that the father had no such right because the removal of the child from the originating jurisdiction had not been unlawful due to the fact that the mother was entitled, as the parent with sole custody rights under Australian law, to do so, the father had no right, inherently, by court order or otherwise to refuse her permission and as the mother had left with the 'settled intention' of making a home for herself and child permanently in England, she had therefore acquired the status of 'resident' in England before the issue of the Australian custody order.

The difference between these two decisions is interesting. It would seem that 'unlawful removal' will extinguish an abducting grandmother's right to retain the child where a faultless unmarried father was providing adequate care, even where the latter has had no custody rights conferred on him by the originating jurisdiction but will not prevail against an abducting mother where the father, even with such custody rights, has not been bearing exclusive parental responsibilities. The courts will favour and seek to preserve the primary care relationship.

IV. Procedures under the Hague Convention

The central thrust of the Hague Convention is that the courts of a signatory state should expedite the return of a child to the originating jurisdiction rather than examine the relative merits of the parties conflicting claims to custody.

1. 'Central Authority'

The Convention requires every signatory state to establish a 'Central Authority' which must receive applications, collate information and institute proceedings; legal aid is granted automatically. The office of the Lord Chancellor functions in this capacity.

2. Application

The application is lodged with the 'Central Authority'. Under Article 12 an applicant commencing Convention proceedings must do so within twelve months. However, proceedings may be brought later 'unless it is demonstrated that the child is now settled in its new environment'.

---

14   See *Re J (A Minor)(Abduction: Custody Rights)* [1990] 2 AC 562.

V. Order Made: Prompt Return of Child

A case is a 'Convention case' for the purposes of the Hague Convention where the court in the destination jurisdiction is satisfied that, according to the law of the originating jurisdiction, the removal or retention of the child was 'wrongful'. Provided that the application was brought before the court within twelve months of the child's removal, under Article 12, it must direct the child's return, forthwith, to the originating jurisdiction.

IV. Order Not Made: Exceptions to the Hague Convention

The prescriptive approach of Article 12 is mitigated by exceptions permitted under Article 13. If the grounds for one of the exceptions (see below) are satisfied, the court will rule that, according to the law of the originating jurisdiction, the removal or retention of the child was not 'wrongful'. The court then has discretion to claim, rather than automatically cede, jurisdiction on the issue of whether the child should return. Under Article 18, it may choose to nonetheless order the child's return. Should it, however, decide to take jurisdiction, the court will determine the issue of disposition on the basis of the child's welfare.

Exceptions to Prompt Return

(a) Not Providing Care at Time of Unlawful Removal

Under Article 13, the court need not order the child's return in circumstances where

> the person, institution or other body having care of the person of the child was not actually exercising the custody rights at the time of removal or retention,

This is very seldom relied upon.

(b) Consent to or Acquiescence in Unlawful Removal

Again, under Article 13, the court need not order the child's return in circumstances where those with care responsibility at the time of the unlawful removal

> had consented to or subsequently acquiesced in the removal or retention.

Delay in bringing proceedings may be construed as having 'acquiesced in the removal or retention'. So, in this jurisdiction Higgins J held that a father had acquiesced when, for 10 months after learning of his wife's intention not to return his child, he failed to bring proceedings.[15] A similar finding was made by the Court of Appeal in a case where a distinction was drawn between 'removal' and 'retention'. A father was held to have acquiesced in the retention of his child when he decided to leave his child with a maternal aunt for the time being.[16]

Higgins J gave a fuller consideration to the meaning and significance of 'acquiescence' when, in August 1996, he heard a case[17] concerning an application for

---

15 See *W v W (Child Abduction: Acquiescence)* [1993] 2 FLR 211.
16 See *Re AZ (A Minor)(Abduction: Acquiescence)* [1993] 1 FLR 682.
17 See *K v K: Re M-NK* and *AK (Minors)*, unreported (1996).

the return to the island of Spestes in Greece of the applicant's two daughters (aged seven and five) removed in June 1995 by their mother, the wife of the applicant, who was the respondent. The judge acknowledged that

> where the conduct of a parent over a particular period of time is consistent with him accepting as a temporary expedient, a situation forced upon him without notice and which he is, perhaps due to distance or some other reason, unable to change at once, a Court should be slow to infer acquiescence or consent.

However, as a matter of fact, he found that the applicant had acquiesced to the retention of the children in Northern Ireland, in clear and compelling terms, during the course of a meeting with the respondent held in the presence of a retired solicitor. Once acquiescence or consent is established then, in the term used by Dean J in Australia[18] and Balcombe LJ in England,[19] 'the door is unlocked' and the court is freed from its strict mandatory duty under Article 12 of the Convention to ensure the prompt and summary return of children wrongfully removed or retained in another jurisdiction. Instead, the court is able to exercise its discretion. In so doing, Higgins J ruled that 'the children's best interests are best served by them remaining in this jurisdiction with their mother'. He also made them wards of court.

(c) Welfare Considerations

Article 13 provides that an exception may also be made to the mandatory court order for the child's return in circumstances where

> there is a grave risk that his or her return would expose the child to physical or psychological harm or otherwise place the child in an intolerable situation.

This provision rests on two alternative grounds. The proposed return must either expose the child to 'grave risk' of physical or psychological harm or place the child in an intolerable situation.

The first is often relied upon in terms of a claim that to break the present bond between carer and child would cause the latter serious psychological harm; it must be grounded on evidence that the 'grave risk' is of a substantial nature.[20] In the second, the 'grave risk' must be such that the child's well-being would be seriously compromised.[21]

The change affected by this provision to the judicial approach in this jurisdiction to such issues may be illustrated by reference to cases which preceded it. So, for example, in *In the matter of TMW and AMW (Minors)*,[22] the mother, a native of Northern Ireland, retained her children within the jurisdiction against the wishes of her Canadian husband. The children, aged three and seven, had always lived in Canada. The court held that the welfare of the children required that they remain with their

---

18 See *OH v Ford* (1988–1989) 167 CLR 316 at pp 337–8.
19 See *Re A (Minors) (Abduction: Acquiesence)* CA [1992] 2 FLR 14 at p. 21.
20 See, for example, *Re A (A Minor: Abduction)* [1988] 1 FLR 365.
21 See, for example, *Re N (Minors: Abduction)* [1991] FCR 765, [1991] 1 FLR 413.
22 [1979] 9 NIJB.

mother. In *CDH (A Minor)*,[23] a four-year-old boy was removed from South Africa by his father to the paternal grandmother's home in Belfast on 18 November 1979. There then followed a ten-month delay before a wardship application was heard by MacDermott J. It was held that a return to South Africa with his mother would disturb his considerable potential since he had put down roots in Northern Ireland and had 'bonded' with his father. In the case of *In re RASJ and PFJ (Minors)*,[24] the same judge in wardship proceedings said:

> I have no doubt that these two boys (aged ten and seven) should remain in Northern Ireland. They are happy here, they are doing well at school, their friends are here, they have spent their formative years here ... it would be wrong to uproot these boys.

It may be doubted whether the first two cases would meet the Article 13 test. There can be no question of the courts any longer applying the paramountcy principle when determining applications under the Hague Convention.[25]

However, once acquiescence has been established the courts have a greater degree of discretion and are free to give greater weight to considerations of the child's welfare. As Scott LJ has said:[26]

> The interest of the children although not the paramount consideration, must, in my opinion, always be taken into account and will always be important.

The courts have treated claims under this heading with some scepticism.

(a) Objections from Child

In keeping with the modern legal approach of ascertaining and taking into account the wishes of children (where age and understanding permit) when decisions are taken affecting their welfare, Article 13 further provides that:

> [t]he judicial or administrative authority may also refuse to order the return of the child if it finds that the child objects to being returned and has attained an age and degree of maturity at which it is appropriate to take account of its views.

However, the weighting given to the child's wishes in this context is not the same as in circumstances where Article 3(3)(a) of the 1995 Order applies. The courts are wary about the potential for domestic legal principles to subvert the point of the convention which is to restore the right of the originating jurisdiction to determine the substantive issue.

This exception to the 'prompt return' rule is open to challenge on the grounds that the child will be susceptible to undue influence from the abductor. Where the child clearly expresses an early opposition to the prospect of a return to the originating jurisdiction, the court will be more readily convinced that the objection is the product

---

23 Unreported (1980).
24 Unreported (1976).
25 See, for example, *Re M (A Minor)(Child Abduction)* [1994] 1 FLR 390.
26 See *Re A (Minors) (Abduction: Acquiescence)(no. 2)* [1993] 1 FLR 396.

of a settled and genuine resolve rather than a response to the influence of the abductor.[27] Moreover, the older the child and/or the more reasoned the arguments presented, the stronger the likelihood of the court acceding to his or her wishes.

V. The Hague Convention and Rights of Access

Article 1 of the Hague Convention states:

> The objects of the present Convention are . . .
> (b) to ensure that rights . . . of access under the law of one Contracting State are effectively respected in the other Contracting States.

However, nowhere in the Convention nor in the 1985 Act is any specific provision made for court enforcement of such rights of access. The only reference to a procedure for implementation is made in Article 21 which provides that

> . . . an application to make arrangements for organising or securing the effective exercise of rights of access may be presented to the Central Authorities of Contracting States in the same way as an application for the return of a child.

The High Court in England has determined that the Convention does confer authority for it to make orders concerning access and that proceedings under the Convention offer a more appropriate route to do so than proceedings in wardship.[28]

The Civil Law and the European Convention

The European Convention is implemented by the Child Abduction and Custody Act 1985, Part II. Being restricted to Europe and to cases where a court order has already been made, it is less frequently used than the Hague Convention. Again, because it represents the United Kingdom's international obligations, the 1985 Act applies to and on behalf of all the constituent jurisdictions of the United Kingdom. The duty is as stated in Article 7 of the Convention:

> A decision relating to custody given in a Contracting State shall be recognised and, where it is enforceable in the State of origin, made enforceable in every other Contracting State.

I. Application to the Destination Jurisdiction

Where a child, the subject of a custody order made by the courts of one Member State, is believed to have been unlawfully removed to another Member State, under Article 5, on application the latter is required:

---

27 See, for example, *Re M (A Minor) (Child Abduction)* [1994] 1 FLR 390. Also see *Re S (Abduction: Children: Separate Representation)* [1997] 1 FLR 486 where two children aged fourteen and twelve successfully applied for leave to seek residence and prohibited steps orders, following maternal abduction to England, so as to forestall pre-emptory return to foster care in New Zealand.
28 See *C v C (Minors)(Child Abduction)* [1992] 1 FLR 163.

(a) to discover the whereabouts of the child;
(b) to avoid, in particular by any necessary provisional measures, prejudice to the interests of the child or of the applicant;
(c) to secure the recognition or enforcement of the decision;
(d) to secure the delivery of the child to the applicant where enforcement is granted;
(e) to inform the requesting authority of the measures taken and their results.

The application is made in accordance with the provisions of the Child Abduction (NI) Order 1985, Article 16. Not until an application is received, accompanied by details of the relevant court order, will the authorities in the destination jurisdiction be under any duty to act.

II. Registration of Custody Order Made in the Originating Jurisdiction

The first duty to arise is the obligation to register in the destination jurisdiction the decision taken, in respect of the custody of the child concerned, by the court of the originating jurisdiction. Article 8 requires registration where an application is made within six months of an unauthorised removal, although in the UK exceptions to this requirement are permitted. In any case where Northern Ireland happens to be the destination jurisdiction, the duty to register is imposed by Article 16.

1. Duty to Enforce Order

Article 18 requires the court and the relevant authorities in Northern Ireland to treat and enforce the registered order as if it had been made in this jurisdiction.

2. Retrospective Effect

Unlike the Hague Convention, the European Convention may be applied to unauthorised removals which occurred prior to its implementation.

3. Exceptions

(a) Change of Circumstances and Welfare

Not all orders must necessarily be registered nor if so registered will they necessarily impose an enforcement duty. Both Articles 9 and 10 allow for exceptions in certain circumstances. In particular Article 10(1)(b) exempts destination jurisdictions from registration or enforcement duties

> if it is found that by reason of a change in the circumstances including the passage of time but not including a mere change in the residence of the child after an improper removal, the effects of the original decision are manifestly no longer in accordance with the welfare of the child.

However, there is a heavy onus on any party seeking to rely on this provision to produce evidence swiftly and convincingly that the change of circumstance is of such a nature and degree as to clearly demonstrate that a return to the originating jurisdiction would be incompatible with the child's welfare interests. Because the entire thrust of the Convention and the 1985 Order is to negate the advantage attained by the abductor and expedite the return of the child, the burden of proof on the party seeking to rely on Article 10(1)(b) is exceptionally onerous.

In *Re GD and JD (Minors: and Access)*,[29] Higgins J was invited by the respondent to refuse to recognise, register and enforce an order issued in the Republic of Ireland on grounds which rested mainly on Article 10(1)(b). This was a case where, in 1985, the applicant and father of two children was sentenced in the Republic of Ireland to life imprisonment for murder. At about the same time his wife, the respondent, began an affair with another man, returned with him (and the two children) to her home town of Newry where, after her divorce in 1992, they married.

Throughout the period of imprisonment the father vigorously sought regular access visits from his children to whom he frequently wrote and consistently professed his love and affection. However, over a period of twelve years his contact with the children was negligible, most of his correspondence failed to reach them and they grew to regard their step-father as their father. In 1993 he applied, under section 16(1) of the Child Abduction and Custody Act 1985, for an access order granted in his favour by Trim District Court in 1986 to be registered in the High Court in Northern Ireland. Having interviewed the children and heard their wishes for no further contact with their father, Higgins J concluded that the grounds specified in Article 10(1)(b) were satisfied because:

> The likely effect of directing them against their wishes to submit to contact and the instability and upset that would probably cause in their upbringing at home and in their schooling are relevant considerations. When all those matters are weighed against any benefit they may gain from contact with the applicant, albeit their natural father, I do not consider ordering access would be in their best interests.

The application to register was duly refused.

(b) The Child's Views

Exemptions under Article 10(1)(b) are subject to the pre-condition that the court or relevant authorities first

> ascertain the child's views unless this is impracticable having regard in particular to his age and understanding.

Again, there is no evidence of the courts being prepared to attach a domestic law weighting to such views.

Non-Convention Cases

Many countries are not Member States for the purposes of either Convention. When the issue of the proposed repatriation of an abducted child occurs in a non-Convention

---

29 Unreported (1996).

context, the question arises as to whether the responsibility for determination lies with the courts of the originating or of the destination jurisdiction. In the event of Northern Ireland being both the destination jurisdiction and having such responsibility, the questions to be answered are — should the court simply return the child and allow all other issues to be determined in the originating jurisdiction?, should the court apply Convention principles (even though not bound by them) to decide that question?, should the court accept its *forum conveniens* status and determine the substantive issues of custody/parental responsibility?

I. General Principles

Where a child has been abducted into the jurisdiction from a non-Convention country, the accepted practice has been to apply the same general criteria (subject to the exception noted below) as would be applied to determine a Convention case.[30] This means that the courts will generally accede to a request for the prompt return of the child. In order to build in some safeguards for the child, the court will often also seek undertakings from the lawful custodian in the originating jurisdiction as to the exact nature of the provision intended to be made for the child on his or her return.[31] Where such undertakings are given before a court in the originating jurisdiction and a copy formally forwarded to the court conducting the hearing, the latter will be in a more confident position to expedite the child's return.[32]

II. Paramountcy

A non-Convention case is a domestic case. The Court of Appeal in England has in recent years advised that non-Convention cases should be determined in accordance with domestic law principles. The paramountcy principle must, therefore, prevail in issues regarding the upbringing of children. As Balcombe LJ has said,[33]

> I should stress that, in a non-Convention case, the welfare of the children remains the paramount consideration, and the principles of the Convention are applicable only to the extent that they indicate what is normally in the interests of the children.

---

30 See the ruling in *D v D (Child Abduction: Non-Convention Country)* [1941] 1 FLR 137, CA (Greece).
31 See, for example, *Re O (Child Abduction: Undertakings)* [1994] 2 FLR 349.
32 See, for example, *Re M (Abduction: Non-Convention Country)* [1995] 1 FLR 89 and E Harte *Child Abduction — Undertakings*, (January 1995), Fam Law pp 38–9.
33 See *D v D (Child Abduction)* [1994] 1 FLR 137, 144.

PART TWO

The Welfare of Children

Introduction

In no area of family law has the increase in new legislation and in the amount of litigation been so sudden, comprehensive and challenging to such a broad range of professionals as in the law relating to children. In no part of the United Kingdom has the scale of legislative change in that area of law been so radical as in Northern Ireland. It is significant that it should be in relation to children that family law first experiences the legislative overhaul necessary to achieve a new harmonisation of principle and process, of public and private sectors and of court level and function. With matters of status and ownership diminishing as the key reference points of family law, the welfare of children has emerged as the matter of paramount importance.

Part Two deals, in nine chapters, with proceedings in which the interests of children are to the fore. The legal issues tend to arise mainly in the context of a breakdown in parenting arrangements. The resulting proceedings or processes are mostly, but not exclusively, concerned with public family law. The welfare of children is the subject and the focus is on the law relating to identifying, safeguarding and promoting that welfare.

Chapter Eleven deals with the Children (NI) Order 1995, the provisions of which largely govern the matters considered throughout this part of the book. It begins by considering the background to the introduction of the 1995 Order and then identifies and explains the core principles. It outlines the organisation and key processes of the family proceedings court. In this way it provides a basic foundation for subsequent chapters dealing with private and public family law and, in particular, with state intervention whether occurring in a consensual, coercive or 'in care' fashion.

Chapter Twelve deals with contested arrangements for the care of children occurring in private family law. It identifies and explains the proceedings available to those parents who invite court intervention, usually in the context of divorce or judicial separation, to determine future family-based care arrangements for their children. The central concern is with contested arrangements for the upbringing of children: where that contest lies between the parents or between them and other family members. It sets out and explains the law relating to the use of Article 8 orders.

Chapter Thirteen begins the examination of public family law with the processes of consensual Trust intervention in parental care. This is intervention which proceeds on the basis of a partnership established between the Trust and parents with the objective of improving and sustaining family based care arrangements for vulnerable children. The chapter sets out and explains the powers and duties of a Trust in relation to children in need and their families.

The fourth and largest subdivision, Chapters fourteen to seventeen, deals with the processes of coercive Trust intervention in parental care. This is intervention based on the public interest in safeguarding and promoting the welfare interests of children placed at risk by the fault or default of their parents. The central concern is with contested arrangements for the future upbringing of children: where that contest lies between Trust and parents. It focuses on the legal incidences of failed parenting. It outlines the various orders providing for the care and supervision, the protection and control of children. It considers also the arrangements which may be made by Trusts for children who are in care, being accommodated or are being discharged into the community.

Finally, Chapter Eighteen and Nineteen deal with the law relating to the ascertainment and representation of children's interests. It considers when and how the voice of a child is heard during the course of contested proceedings, whether of private or public law, and to what effect. The role and responsibilities of those who may or must be heard by the court in this context are also examined.

CHAPTER ELEVEN

The Children (NI) Order 1995: Principles, Framework and the Public/Private Divide

Introduction

The Children (NI) Order 1995 has laid down a new synthesis of principles, procedures, court orders and court administration in the civil law relating to children. For most purposes, the 1995 Order consolidates the public and private sectors of family law insofar as these affect the care and upbringing of children in Northern Ireland. The principle of the welfare of the child provided the main tool for shaping this legislation. The concept of parental responsibilities functioned as the natural counterbalance to that principle. Other principles were also at work and important new structures and processes were developed, but primarily, the 1995 Order can be seen as being built on a foundation created by a radical juxtaposition of child welfare and parental responsibilities.

This chapter briefly explores the more immediate background to the introduction of the 1995 Order. The main forces responsible for effecting legislative change are identified. The key concepts and strategic principles bridging the public and private areas of family law under the new legislation are examined. Mostly, however, this chapter broadly explains the new framework, processes and intervention thresholds which, in relation to both public and private family law, now form the basis for identifying and resolving most issues affecting the welfare of children. In so doing, it provides the conceptual key to the subsequent chapters which focus on the practical application of the law in public and in private proceedings.

Background to the Introduction of the Children (NI) Order 1995

The need for legislative change to the triangle of legal relationships among parents, children and the state had its origins in the pressure resulting from certain trends in modern parenting arrangements during the last quarter of the twentieth century (see also Part One and Appendices). The volume of work and complexity of problems contained therein prompted the setting up of consultative bodies to review the appropriateness of family law functions.

I. Forces for Legislative Change Generated outside the United Kingdom

The drive to achieve greater coherence in the principles, structures and procedures of family law in the United Kingdom was, arguably, led and shaped by developments in Strasbourg and the United Nations. The Children (NI) Order 1995 may come to be seen as a means for achieving harmonisation with family law developments in Europe as much as harmonisation within the United Kingdom. In Great Britain the more immediate impetus for change came from a growing public and professional concern about social work practice as demonstrated in a series of highly publicised cases involving abused and endangered children. The same momentum was also largely responsible for change in Northern Ireland. Here, however, there were also some indigenous factors at work.

1. Strasbourg

A considerable body of legislation with a bearing on the legal interests of children in the United Kingdom has been quietly consolidating in Europe. The more significant of its components include: the Convention on Human Rights 1950; the European Charter 1961; the European Convention on the Adoption of Children 1967; the European Convention on the Legal Status of Children Born out of Wedlock 1975; the European Custody Convention 1980 (ratified by the United Kingdom on 21 April 1986 by the Child Abduction and Custody Act 1985).

The European Convention on Human Rights 1950, which the United Kingdom failed to incorporate into its domestic law, has exercised a steadily growing influence on the legislators and judiciary of Great Britain: particularly so since 1966, from which date British subjects became entitled to complain to the European Court of Human Rights for infringements to their rights under the Convention for the Protection of Human Rights and Fundamental Freedoms. Article 6(1), for example, specifies that in the determination of a person's 'civil rights and obligations or any criminal charge against him, everyone is entitled to a fair and public hearing within a reasonable time ...'. This principle formed the basis of the plaintiff's case in *H v UK*.[1] The court there found that the period of two years and seven months which it had taken a parent to pursue her claim for contact with her daughter — from the first application in wardship/adoption proceedings to the rejection of her leave to appeal to the House of Lords — constituted 'excessive delay' and thus breached Article 6(1). The court also found that the applicant's rights under Article 8 — which specifies that 'everyone has the right to respect for his private and family life, his home and his correspondence' — had been breached. Again, in *W, B, R v UK*,[2] the parents were seeking access to their children in care at a time when the local authority had wide discretion to terminate such access. The court held that the termination of contact procedures violated Article 8, the parents being insufficiently involved in the decision-making process. This Article, because it addresses the basic and reciprocal legal rights of parents and child within the nuclear family, generated considerable interest in the English courts.[3]

---

1 (1987) 10 EHRR 95.
2 (1987) 10 EHRR 29.
3 In fact the House of Lords referred at length to Convention provisions before reaching a decision on access in *Re KD (A Minor)* [1988] 1 All ER 577. In a succession of cases (e.g. *R v UK, O v UK* and *W v UK* [1988] ECHR 2 FLR 445), the European Court of Human Rights ruled that decisions taken by the British judiciary were in breach of the Convention.

The influence of continental Europe on the forming of the more basic concepts underpinning the Children (NI) Order 1995 has not been fully recognised. Fifteen years earlier, in 1979, the Parliamentary Assembly to the Committee of Ministers to the Council of Ministers recommended steps to create a European Charter on the rights of the child 'which should among other considerations take account of "the new concept of parental responsibility"'. In 1984 they further recommended that parental responsibilities be defined 'as a collection of duties and powers which aim at insuring the moral and material welfare of the child, in particular by taking care of the person of the child, by maintaining personal relationships with him and by providing for his education, his maintenance, his legal representation and the administration of his property'. This recommendation takes account of the views of children by stating that when decisions are to be taken relating to parental responsibilities and applying to the legal interests of children, then the children 'should be consulted if their degree of maturity with regard to the decision so permits'. In 1988, at a conference in Lisbon, the European Ministers of Justice upheld a resolution on the principle that the interests of the child should be paramount. In 1990 the Parliamentary Assembly made a recommendation to the Committee of Ministers on the rights of children. Such initiatives reveal the extent to which some of the foundations of the 1995 Order were laid outside these islands.

2. United Nations

In 1989 the United Nations issued its Convention on the Rights of the Child. The United Kingdom became a signatory to this Convention on 19 April 1990, ratified it on 16 December 1991 with an effective date of 15 January 1992.[4]

II. Forces for Legislative Change Generated in England and Wales

The acceptance of the need for a comprehensive reform of the law relating to children grew from increasing practitioner (and indeed consumer) dissatisfaction with the logistical problems involved in negotiating the pre-1989 legal system. The law was to be sought across a disparate range of statutes. The courts provided separate sets of proceedings in different types of courts to deal with aspects of what was most often one complex problem. The court orders were available in two very separate blocks of family law despite the common nature of many issues, and the authority they conferred was either too narrow and specific or too all embracing. On top of this there was the inescapable fact that the number of children whose needs or deeds required judicial attention was increasing at a rate which would lead to unacceptable delays if their welfare was to be adequately safeguarded. This need to streamline the way in which the legal system responded to problems affecting children was made more acute by other more direct pressures.

---

4 *The United Kingdom's First Report to the UN Committee on the Rights of the Child HMSO* (1994) provides many illustrations of the extent to which recent developments in public and private family law as they affect children have been shaped by extra-territorial influences.

1. Child Abuse Cases and the Media

One of the more powerful forces for legislative change in child care law had its roots in a growing public disquiet centred on the conduct of social workers in child abuse situations. On the one hand they were criticised for what was perceived to be heavy-handed intervention in family affairs prior to a judicial hearing. A succession of unfortunate cases in the neighbouring island (e.g. the misguided intervention of social workers in Cleveland, Rochdale and the Orkneys) had been the focus of much media attention and eventual public enquiries.[5] On the other hand, ironically, a perceived lack of sufficiently assertive social work intervention was equally problematic. Again, a series of cases involving the deaths of children[6] were attributed to the failure of social workers to act promptly and decisively in giving effect to the powers vested in them by court order and were the subject of much-publicised public enquiries.[7] In all, during the fifteen-year period 1972–87, there were thirty-four public enquiries into deaths of children known to social workers. Whether associated with too much or too little social work intervention, child abuse had become a matter of great public concern by the mid-1980s.

2. Review of Child Care Law by the Inter-Departmental Committee

The House of Commons Social Services Committee recommended that a working party be established by the DHSS to review child care law. This was duly set up in July 1984 with the brief to frame proposals for changes to child care law which would provide a framework for developing the best child care practice and meet more effectively the needs of children and their families. The review was solely concerned with aspects of public family law governing statutory child-care matters. The findings were published as a consultative document[8] and formed the basis for a subsequent Government White Paper.[9] Both papers exercised a formative influence in determining the content of the Children Act 1989.

3. Review of Private Family Law by the Law Commission

The Law Commission's review formed part of a staged but comprehensive examination of all aspects of private family law governing the care and custody of children in England and Wales. This was on-going throughout the period of the Inter-Departmental Committee review. Between 1985–7 the Committee issued a series of papers; the last[10] made a particularly strong contribution to the formulation of principles and content in Parts 1 and 11 of the 1989 Act.

---

5 See, for example, the *Report of the Enquiry into Child Abuse in Cleveland 1987* (Cmnd 412, 1987).
6 See, for example, the deaths of Jasmine Beckford and Tyra Henry.
7 As in, *A Child in Mind: Protection of Children in a Responsible Society: Report of the Commission of Enquiry into the Circumstances Surrounding the Death of Kimberley Carlile*, London Borough of Greenwich (1989).
8 See the *Review of Child Care Law* (1985).
9 See *The Law on Child Care and Family Services* (Cmnd 62, 1987).
10 See *Review of Child Law: Guardianship and Custody* (Law Com no. 172 1988).

4. Case Law on the Wishes of a Child

The House of Lords in *Gillick v West Norfolk and Wisbech*[11] ruled that in some circumstances a doctor could prescribe contraceptives for a child under sixteen years of age without consulting the parents of that child. This decision gave rise to the so-called 'mature minor' rule which is to the general effect that where children are of sufficient age and understanding then their opinions should be sought, respected and may be decisive in any matter affecting their welfare. This judicial acknowledgement that a child or young person should have at least a say in decisions affecting them was of widespread application but had no statutory recognition in statutory child care law (see further Chapters One, Eighteen and Nineteen) and little in private family law. It was a principle which, in conjunction with the thrust of the UN Declaration, presented a common thread for binding together the two sectors of family law.

III. Forces for Legislative Change Generated in Northern Ireland

While it has to be admitted that the introduction of the Children (NI) Order 1995 was a Westminster-led process, nonetheless much the same set of precipitating factors which paved the way for the Children Act 1989 were also present in Northern Ireland.

1. Child Abuse Cases and the Media

In this jurisdiction there had not been the same level of reportage of child abuse cases as in England and Wales;[12] which is not to say that the prevalence of such cases was any the less. Here, public disquiet emanated from the revelations of child abuse perpetrated by residential social workers, principally in Kincora. The realisation that for twenty years some children, entrusted to the care of the Health and Social Services Boards (or Trusts), had been systematically abused by social workers in nine children's homes,[13] coupled with media portrayal of professional ineffectiveness in child abuse cases in England, gave rise to a similar public scepticism about social workers' use of authority in this jurisdiction.

2. Review of Public Family Law

The *Black Report*[14] recorded deficiencies in the professional staffing and training arrangements for social workers as well as detailing the inadequacies of existing childcare law. This committee drew attention to the problem of a serious deficit in the statutory powers available to social workers in Northern Ireland relative to their counterparts in the neighbouring jurisdiction.[15] By way of preparation for legislative change to the Children and Young Persons Act (NI) 1968, the Department of Health

---

11 [1985] 3 All ER 402.
12 The *Abuse of Trust Report*, DHSS (1993), being one of few exceptions.
13 See *Report of the Committee of Inquiry into Children's Homes and Hostels*, HMSO, 1986.
14 See *Report of the Children and Young Persons Review Group, Legislation and Services for Young Persons in Northern Ireland*, HMSO, 1979.
15 Among the main recommendations made in the *Black Report* were the following:

and Social Services (NI) issued a number of consultative papers in the latter half of the 1980s. The purpose of the first series[16] was to make suggestions for the re-alignment of the law in this jurisdiction, on matters relating to children in care, to match that prevailing in Great Britain. It also sought to take into account recent European Court of Human Rights case law. The following year a second series[17] was issued which dealt with day care arrangements and the employment of children. A final paper[18] gave further support for the *Black Report's* recommendations for change. This paper also proposed that any new legislation incorporate the changes to the status of illegitimacy which already formed part of the 1989 Act and endorsed the principle that, in this jurisdiction, such legislation should be on substantially the same lines as the 1989 Act.

3. Review of Private Family Law

In this jurisdiction there was no counterpart to the comprehensive review of private family law conducted in England and Wales. Instead, efforts were directed towards updating the statutory provisions relating to guardianship while also using the opportunity presented by the preparations for a new enactment to graft on provisions drawn from contemporary British child care legislation, most notably from the Children Act 1975. This initiative collapsed with the withdrawal of the proposed Guardianship (NI) Order 1985.[19] Partial change to private family law was abandoned in favour of more comprehensive change along the lines of the 1989 Act.

4. Use of Wardship in Private and in Public Family Law Matters

In private family law there has been an established practice of utilising the flexible and conciliatory nature of the powers available in the wardship jurisdiction as an

---

(a) The services for children should be better co-ordinated and should focus on preventing harm.
(b) That proceedings in respect of children in need of care should be separated from proceedings dealing with children who had committed offences.
(c) Training school orders should no longer be available in respect of children subject to care proceedings.
(d) A guardian ad litem should be appointed to represent the interests of a child in any case where such interests may be in conflict with those of a parent.
(e) The circumstances of every child in care should be reviewed every six months, including a review of the necessity to continue the care order.
(f) Every care order should be subject to a court review at least every three years.

16 See *Access to Children in Care; Contributions towards the Maintenance of Children in Care; and the Use of Secure Accommodation for Children in Care.*
17 See the *Regulation of Child Minding; Group Care and Care and Maintenance of Children; and the Employment of Children.*
18 See the *Consultation Paper on Proposed Changes to Some Aspects of the Law Relating to Children in Northern Ireland* (1989)
19 The proposed guardianship legislation was to serve as a vehicle to carry a mix of other provisions (e.g. relating to 'custodianship', the 'paramountcy' principle, access rights for grandparents, the concept of 'legal custody' and the status of illegitimacy).

alternative to statutory proceedings where the issues concern the future care arrangements for children following marital breakdown. This practice was distinctive to Northern Ireland and was most prevalent in the 1970s and early 1980s. In England and Wales the parties, in similar circumstances, were required to first seek redress through statutory proceedings.

In public family law, the last years of the 1968 Act were also years of steadily increasing recourse to wardship by the Health and Social Services Boards (see Chapter Seven and Appendices). The urgency and complexity of modern child care cases had become such that they could no longer be readily processed through statutory provisions which remained 'essentially a mixture of the Westminster Children's Act 1948 and the Children and Young Persons Act 1963'.[20] The discretionary powers of the wardship jurisdiction had allowed the Boards to avoid the restrictive technical grounds of the 1968 Act and permitted the judiciary to take almost any action they deemed necessary to safeguard the welfare of a child. The former resorted to wardship to secure either a more effective alternative or a supplement to their statutory powers. The latter granted wardship orders only when convinced that the 1968 Act did not provide the Boards with sufficient powers to appropriately secure the welfare of the children concerned. In effect this practice of using the powers of wardship alongside those of the 1968 Act to deal with certain child care issues was steadily consolidating into a dual approach by the legal system to such matters, one approach attaching a significantly greater weight to the welfare of the child than the other. There was increasing concern that this practice would lead to great uncertainty in the application of the law to child care matters (see also Chapter Seven).

The use of wardship by the Boards was also inequitable as parents did not enjoy an equal right of access to that jurisdiction. This inequity, compounded by the relative immunity from judicial scrutiny enjoyed by the social services as a result of the ruling in *Liverpool*,[21] caused considerable professional concern and frequent parental applications for judicial review. A reduction in such discretionary powers of social workers at the point of initial intervention in family affairs was among the primary objectives of the 1995 Order.

In relation to the use of wardship in both public and private family law matters, it was ultimately held that, notwithstanding the much greater flexibility offered by wardship in reaching a solution favouring the welfare of a child, where Parliament had provided a statutory procedure then it must be used. However, this period gave the High Court judiciary, other lawyers and social workers an opportunity to experience the many points of similarity between public and private aspects of family law when dealing with issues concerning the welfare interests of a child (see also Chapters Seven and Twelve).

---

20   See G Kelley, *Decision Making in Child Care in Northern Ireland*, Social Work and Social Service Review, vol. 1 pp 77–90.
21   See *A v Liverpool City Council* [1982] AC 363; [1981] 2 All ER 385, HL where the House of Lords ruled that the exercise of powers entrusted by Parliament to statutory bodies was not amenable to judicial review; the court cannot take decisions on matters affecting the welfare of children when statute has assigned responsibility for such decisions to social service departments (excepting *Wednesbury*-type circumstances).

The Family Law Framework and the Welfare Principle

The provisions of the Children (NI) Order 1995 and its counterpart — the Children Act 1989 — are substantially the same. Like the 1989 Act, the 1995 Order does not make a completely fresh start in establishing the law relating to children. Many statutes, much case law and some common-law rules continue in effect and will carry over into the new era enough of the principles and practice previously established to ensure a sense of continuity. For example, here as in England, the Children and Young Persons Act (1968 and 1969, respectively), though amended, will remain on the statute books.

I. Legislative Context

The introduction of the 1995 Order was, in a sense, of greater significance than that of its counterpart because of the very different legislative context within which each had to fit. The 1995 Order had first to sweep aside a residue of late Victorian legislation which had long ceased to have effect in the neighbouring jurisdiction.

1. Private Family Law

Apart from statutes only partially repealed, the 1995 Order removed the following in their entirety from the statute book: the Custody of Infants Act 1873, the Guardianship of Infants Act 1886, the Custody of Children Act 1891 and the Illegitimate Children (Affiliation Orders) Act (NI) 1924. Many more recent statutes suffered partial repeal. Moreover, certain other legal anachronisms such as the *prima facie* right of a father to the custody of his legitimate child (perpetuated by the 1886 Act) and vestiges of the law relating to illegitimacy remained in force until repealed by the 1995 Order. Again, unlike its English counterpart, the 1995 Order did not have to be considered in relation to an intermediate body of legislation. For example, there was no equivalent in Northern Ireland to either the Guardianship of Minors Act 1971 or to the Guardianship Act 1973.

2. Public Family Law

The introduction of the 1995 Order was not preceded by any equivalent to the raft of legislation which in recent decades had done much to alter the responsibilities of the social services counterparts in England and Wales. There was no equivalent, for example, to the Abortion Act 1967, the Children Act 1975, the Child Care Act 1980, the Foster Children Act 1980, the Children's Homes Act 1982 and the Children and Young Persons (Amendment) Act 1986. Many other provisions which had long been operational across the Irish Sea (e.g. adoption registers and regional adoption allowance scheme) were not so in Northern Ireland until the 1995 Order placed equivalent duties on the Boards.

The introduction of the 1995 Order thus marked a much greater step forward in the evolution of family law in this jurisdiction than did that of the 1989 Act in England and Wales.

II. The Principle of the Welfare of the Child

1. Prior to the Introduction of the 1995 Order

As the law and the practice governing parental responsibilities in Northern Ireland became increasingly complex and related legislative provisions less appropriate, compared to equivalent developments across the Irish Sea, so the High Court extended the reach of its wardship jurisdiction to apply the paramountcy principle further into the statutory arena. Matters traditionally regarded as confined to the statutory heartland of private family law (e.g. consents in adoption proceedings and custody/access issues in matrimonial proceedings) or of public family law (e.g. child sexual abuse) were regularly becoming subject to judicial examination in wardship proceedings. Throughout the 1980s and early 1990s the escalating rate of recourse to wardship by the Boards testifies to the inadequacy of the 1968 Act as the means for safeguarding the welfare of children in public family law matters.[22] The welfare interests of a child licensed an ever-broadening and more generalised interventionist ethic.

2. After the Introduction of the 1995 Order

The introduction of the Children (NI) Order 1995 sought to restore some coherence throughout family law to the principles and practice of state intervention on matters affecting the welfare and upbringing of children. The judicial duty to make the child's welfare 'the court's paramount consideration' now governs all family proceedings including those instigated to transfer responsibility for the care of a child from parent to Board (or 'Trust'). This consideration is also apparent in some specific provisions which serve to reinforce the role of the welfare principle in public as much as in private family law proceedings.[23]

3. Principle and Policy

Underpinning the new relationship in the 1995 Order among parents, their child and the State is a policy which may be expressed in general terms to the effect that the welfare of a child is best assured by maintaining him or her within the family of origin, and state intervention, when necessary, should primarily be to further this end. This is supported by specific statutory provisions which specify a presumption of non-intervention,[24] require Trust social workers and others to provide assistance to vulnerable families[25] and formulate a doctrine of parental responsibility[26] to replace

---

22 In 1983 they were awarded a total of 46 orders, 95 in 1992, and 154 in 1995.
23 Article 3(2), for example, requires the court to 'have regard to the general principle that any delay in determining the question is likely to prejudice the welfare of the child'. Article 3(3) provides a checklist of specific considerations to which the court is to have regard when assessing the welfare interests of a child.
24 Under Article 3(5), the court is required to apply the no-order presumption.
25 Under Article 16, the court may grant a family assistance order requiring a Trust to provide specific support; see also Art. 46.
26 See Articles 5–7.

traditional concepts of rights and duties (see also Chapters Thirteen and Fourteen). Part 1V of the 1995 Order in particular lends weight to a new legislative thrust to forge a partnership between vulnerable families and Trusts by requiring the latter to be pro-active in undertaking a range of family support duties.

Legislative Change — The Consequences in Terms of Principle and Court Procedures

I. Bridging of Public and Private Family Law

The 1995 Order, like its 1989 counterpart, brings together for civil purposes most provisions of public and private family law affecting the welfare and upbringing of children. This it does through reliance on unifying principles and on a common set of court orders.

1. Unifying Principles

Strategic use of the principles of 'parental responsibility' and the 'paramount welfare interests of the child' are the most obvious of the elements which are used to bind together, in the 1995 Order, certain public and private dimensions of child-care law. Thus, for example, the 'checklist' criteria for determining the application of the welfare principle is mandatory not only in proceedings brought by the Trusts (i.e. public family law matters) but also in contested parental proceedings (i.e. private family law). Other principles, such as the presumption favouring non-intervention, no-delay, the limiting of litigation and the requirement that the wishes and feelings of a child be ascertained and taken into account on any matter affecting the future of that child, also apply equally to proceedings initiated by parent or by Trust under this legislation. Again, the concept of a new 'partnership' between the state and parents and provision for mediatory rather than exclusively adversarial mechanisms to resolve conflicts of interest between them pervade the 1995 Order.

2. Common Set of Court Orders

Article 8 orders are available to the court in both public and private family law proceedings commenced or continued under the 1995 Order. Primarily intended for use in private proceedings, they can also be issued in the context of public proceedings when instead of granting a care or supervision order to a Trust applicant the court may, for example, issue a residence order in favour of a parent or relative.[27] However, commonality in the judicial use of court orders in public and private proceedings is not even-handed: the court may not, of its own motion, issue a care or supervision order in private proceedings; it may only require a Trust to investigate and report on the need or otherwise for such an order.

Though weighted in one direction, this interchangeability of court orders across both public and private proceedings represents a clear repudiation of the assumption

---

27 See *Re M* [1994] 3 All ER 298.

made by the Law Commission[28] that these sets of proceedings were, and should be treated as being, inherently separate.

3. Role of the Guardian Ad Litem

Formerly, the role and duties of the guardian ad litem were confined to the private family law proceedings of adoption. A particularly significant development introduced to this jurisdiction by the 1995 Order is the requirement that this official now plays a role in most public family law proceedings. Again, it may be anticipated that the widespread involvement of guardians in identifying, safeguarding and representing the welfare interests of children will assist with the legislative intent to introduce greater consistency in court management of welfare-related issues (see further Chapter Nineteen for operational aspects of the role of a GAL).

4. Application for Directions

Both public and private proceedings commenced in any court under the 1995 Order will be preceded by a preliminary court hearing. This new forum is where matters such as the following are determined: the appropriate court, the timetable for proceedings and the individual stages, the appointment of a guardian ad litem (if necessary) or solicitor, the preparation and submission of any reports and decisions taken in respect of the attendance or otherwise of the child concerned, the presentation of evidence (particularly that of expert witnesses) and the involvement of witnesses in contested proceedings. All parties will be served with notice and must attend directions appointments or hearings unless the court directs otherwise. Again, this should promote greater consistency and efficiency in the overall management of the means whereby the courts respond to issues affecting the welfare of children. Experience in England and Wales, however, indicates that in fact this measure is having quite the opposite effect.

5. Recorded Findings

The Rules require that at the conclusion of all family proceedings, including those conducted by magistrates, the court must state its findings of fact and it must give the reasons for the decision it reached.[29] At the magistrates' court level this is not required

---

28 In the words of the Commission,
 . . . orders which confer responsibilities for children on public authorities on the ground that care and control is not being adequately provided by a parent . . . are different in kind from disputes between parents or other relatives as to who is to look after the child in question. Moreover, the structure of existing child care law . . . differs substantially from the structure of the law applying in custody proceedings and could not easily be assimilated even if that course were to prove on further examination to be desirable (*Report on the Custody of Children — Jurisdiction and Enforcement within the UK,* Law Com no. 138, para 3.5 HMSO 1985).

29 Rule 21.(4)(b) of the Magistrates Courts (Children (NI) Order 1995) Rules (NI) 1996. Note that in *T v W (Contact: Reasons for Refusing Leave)* [1996] 2 FLR 473 the High Court ruled that the magistrates' total failure to give any reason for their decision vitiated that decision.

to be a fully reasoned judgment. Again, this requirement is one which is intended to promote greater consistency in court room decision making relating to the welfare of children.

II. Unified System of Courts and Procedures

The 1995 Order provides for the introduction of a concurrent system of jurisdiction covering magistrates' courts, county courts and the High Court. This arrangement allows all proceedings relating to a child to be consolidated and heard together and cases to be allocated to courts on the basis of case complexity or gravity. The infrastructure necessary to facilitate ease of access to the appropriate court, promote greater uniformity in the use of orders, permit flexibility but encourage consistency in court procedures and to generally systematise the application of the civil law to the welfare needs of children has thus been put in place.

1. Court Organisation

The introduction of the 1995 Order has brought with it changes in the way courts are organised. The statutory duty to protect a child's welfare from being impaired by avoidable delay necessitates effective management of the processes which ensure that cases are heard expeditiously by the appropriate courts. This is monitored by two committees established by the Court Service (NI) and the DHSS: the Children Order Advisory Committee (COAC) which advises the Secretary of State and the Lord Chancellor on case management and flow within the court system; and the Family Court Business Committees (FCBC), one for each of the three 'care centres'. The role the FCBC is defined in the Guidance and Regulations as being to:

- ensure proper practical arrangements for allocation and transfer;
- promote administrative consistency between tiers of courts;
- ensure that the GAL service is aware of the needs of the court; and
- standardise practice.[30]

(a) Magistrates' Court

The care jurisdiction of the juvenile court (as constituted under the Children and Young Persons Act (NI) 1968, section 63 and Schedule 2) has been expanded to accommodate all proceedings commenced under the 1995 Order and, as stated in Article 164,

> (4) . . . when sitting for the purpose of exercising any jurisdiction conferred by or under this Order may be known as a family proceedings court.

Family proceedings courts are staffed by specially trained magistrates. There is now a clear separation between the juvenile court's family proceedings jurisdiction and its criminal jurisdiction.

---

30 Children (NI) Order 1995, Guidance and Regulation, vol. 6, para 4.11.

(b) County Courts

County courts can deal with all family matters though more complex, serious or lengthy proceedings can be transferred to the High Court. Some are designated as 'care centres' and 'family hearing centres' and are staffed by specially trained judiciary.

(c) High Court

The Family Division of the High Court can hear cases transferred from family hearing centres or from family proceedings courts. Judicial discretion to accept wardship applications from the Trusts (formerly Boards) as an alternative to the latter commencing statutory proceedings has been ended. There is a right of appeal from a decision of a juvenile court or a county court sitting in family proceedings to the High Court and from there to the Court of Appeal.

2. Allocation and Transfer of Proceedings

The allocation and transfer of proceedings are governed by the Children (Allocation of Proceedings) Order (NI) 1996.

(a) Allocation

Article 3 of the above 1996 Order imposes a requirement that all public family law cases concerning children must generally commence in the magistrates' family proceedings court for the area in which the child ordinarily resides or for where the incident occurred if the child was visiting that area. Care proceedings may commence in a higher court (which must be a care centre) if they are the consequence of a direction given by such a court under Article 56 or where other proceedings are pending in another court. Many other types of cases will be self-regulating as, for example, divorce cases involving children which of necessity will commence and continue in a designated county court.

(b) Transfer

Article 5 of the above 1996 Order states that a public law case may be transferred from a family proceedings court to a care centre upon application by a party or on the court's own motion where it considers that the proceedings are exceptionally grave, important or complex: in particular,

(a) because of complicated or conflicting evidence about the child's physical or moral well-being or about other matters relating to the child's welfare;
(b) because of the number of parties;
(c) because of a conflict of law with another jurisdiction;
(d) because of some novel or difficult point of law; or
(e) because of some question of general public interest.

Any such question of transfer is subject to the no-delay principle.[31]

---

31 See, Dame Margaret Booth, *Avoiding Delay in Children Act Cases*, report to the Lord Chancellor (1996). Among the important matters addressed in her report is that the case transfer system is underused and misused.

Private proceedings are subject to vertical and lateral transfers as circumstances dictate. A transfer may occur between courts on the same tier on the grounds of facilitating equitable distribution of workloads or between tiers on the grounds of complexity of the issues involved or in either direction in order to consolidate proceedings. In England Wall J has recently stressed[32] that all proceedings involving the same children (even if spread across both public and private family law) should, where practicable, be consolidated and heard together. Also, in that jurisdiction, the higher courts have advised that certain types of cases should be liable to automatic vertical transfer from magistrates' court.

III. Unified System of Appeals

The right of appeal is addressed under Article 166, Schedule 7, and in the Rules.[33]

1. From Magistrates' Court to County Court

Under Article 166(3), an appeal will lie to the county court from most decisions taken in the magistrates' court.

Exceptions to this general rule are decisions relating to the making or the refusal to make an Emergency Protection Order or in respect of any extension, discharge or direction attached to such an order (Article 64(9)), the declining of jurisdiction in favour of another court (Article 166(5)) and the making of interim orders for periodical payments under Schedule 1 (Article 166(6)).

2. From Magistrate's Court to High Court

Under Article 166(2)(a), an appeal will not lie from a decision taken in the magistrates' court to the Family Division of the High Court.

3. From County Court to High Court

Under Article 166(1), an appeal lies to the Family Division of the High Court against any order granted or refused by a county court. An exception to this rule is where the county court is a divorce court exercising jurisdiction under the Matrimonial Causes (NI) Order 1978 in the same proceedings (Article 166(2)(b)).

4. From County Court or High Court to Court of Appeal

No provision is made under the 1995 Order for any right of appeal from the county court or High Court to the Court of Appeal. The normal rules governing appeals in family cases therefore apply.

---

32 See *W v Wakefield City Council* [1995] 1 FLR 170.
33 Rule 28 of the Magistrates' Courts (Children (NI) Order 1995) Rules (NI) 1996; Rule 4.23 of the Family Proceedings Rules (NI) 1996.

Intervention Thresholds

I. The Children (NI) Order 1995 and the Principle of the Welfare of the Child

In all family proceedings, whether initiated in a public or private family law context, the same rules will now apply to define some aspects of the welfare principle in relation to the threshold for intervention by judiciary and/or Trust in the affairs of a family. These are the new weightings given to the principle of the welfare of the child together with other related principles and the checklist criteria. Because of their statutory application to all family proceedings, they are given general consideration in this chapter. Their more specific judicial application in relation to private and to public areas of family law and the particular court orders which may result are considered in more detail later.

1. The Paramountcy Principle

Article 3 of the 1995 Order states:

> (1) Where a court determines any question with respect to —
> (a) the upbringing of a child; or
> (b) the administration of a child's property or the application of any income arising from it, the child's welfare shall be the court's paramount consideration.

This case-law principle now governs judicial determination of all issues affecting a child's upbringing and ends the uncertainty associated with the fine distinctions previously made between different statutory definitions of the welfare test; the wardship approach has now been comprehensively endorsed. As Sir Stephen Bown P has said:

> [T]he proceedings under the Children Act are not adversarial, although an adversarial approach is frequently adopted by various of the parties. However, as far as the court is concerned, its duty is to investigate and seek to achieve a result which is in the interests of the welfare of the child.... Children's cases ... fall into a special category where the court is bound to undertake all necessary steps to arrive at an appropriate result in the paramount interests of the welfare of the child.[34]

2. The No-Delay Principle

Article 3 of the 1995 Order states:

> (2) In any proceedings in which any question with respect to the upbringing of a child arises, the court shall have regard to the general principle that any delay in determining the question is likely to prejudice the welfare of the child.

This is the first legislative statement of a principle which addresses a matter that, for some years now, has been the focus of growing concern to the judiciary and child-care practitioners both within and without the United Kingdom.[35] In a number of UK

---

[34] See *Oxfordshire County Council v M* [1994] 1 FLR 175.
[35] See, for example, *H and O v UK,* Series A, no. 120, where the European Court of Human Rights ruled that by the undue delay in its litigation process, the United Kingdom was in breach of Articles 6 and 8 of the Human Rights Convention.

cases in recent years, judicial dismay has been expressed at some inordinate, and perhaps deliberately orchestrated, delays which have prejudiced the outcome of proceedings.[36] A child's 'sense of time' is not the same as that of adults and psychological damage may be caused to a child by the anxiety of protracted proceedings. Indeed, it has been claimed[37] that a child's welfare interests are better served by a wrong decision taken swiftly than the right one taken after a lengthy delay.

3. The No-Order Presumption

Article 3 of the 1995 Order states:

> Where a court is considering whether or not to make one or more orders under this Order with respect to a child, it shall not make the order unless it considers that doing so would be better for the child than making no order at all.

This statement is an important declaration of principle which crystallises the minimal intervention ethic underpinning the 1995 Order. It applies equally to public and to private family law proceedings brought under the 1995 Order. The legislative intent is to replace the 'winners and losers' approach to contested care and custody issues with one which presumes that the parties should be able to make their own arrangements outside the court. Once the matter comes before the court, the presumption will necessitate judicial scrutiny of any proposed arrangements for children to establish whether authority should be exercised by court rather than family. Only if decision-making by others is not possible and/or if it is necessary to use authority to secure a child's welfare interests will the court intervene by issuing an order. The onus is then on the judiciary to clearly show why it would not be best for the child if no order was made.

4. The Limiting of Litigation Principle

Article 179(14) of the 1995 Order states:

> On disposing of any application for an order under this Order, the court may (whether or not it makes any other order in response to the application) order that no application for an order under this Order of any specified kind may be made with respect to the child concerned by any person named in the order without leave of the court.

This enables the court to prevent further and unnecessary litigation on a matter upon which it has made a ruling.

5. The Checklist of Considerations

The checklist must be judicially considered in all public family law cases (though see Chapter Fifteen for application to Part VI proceedings) and in private proceedings

---

36 As documented by the Law Com Report no. 172, para 4.55.
37 See *Re P (A Minor)(Education)* [1992] 1 FLR 316 CA.

where the parties are contesting the future arrangements for children. As well as indicating the sort of outcomes the orders should strive to achieve, the legislative intent is that the checklist will promote greater consistency in judicial decisions, practitioner assessments and in the overall coherence of family law.

(a) The Ascertainable Wishes and Feelings of the Child Concerned (Considered in Light of Age and Understanding)

The judicial importance attached to ascertaining the wishes and feeling of the child was made clear when, in considering the equivalent provision of the 1989 Act, it was held that the court should always elicit and respect the views of a child, which it may not be able to act on but which may tip the balance in a difficult case.[38] However, following the ruling in *Gillick*, much will depend on the maturity of the child concerned; and the possible bearing of decrees of the European Convention must also be borne in mind (see also Chapter Sixteen).

This provision gives the child the right to be heard by the court, a right which the latter may direct should be exercised by granting the child full party status with the commensurate freedom to represent his or her own interests. It is very similar to a provision in the Adoption (NI) Order 1987 and echoes established judicial practice in the wardship jurisdiction.

(b) The Child's Physical, Emotional and Educational Needs

The statutory requirement that the court should have regard to the child's physical and educational needs continues the law's concern that these, the basic common-law duties of a guardian, must be attended to. The judiciary have consistently singled out these attributes of good guardianship as constituting criteria for granting or removing custody. The similar requirement in respect of emotional needs merely endorses well-established judicial practice and lends statutory weight to the approach developed in this jurisdiction in wardship cases which tended to favour maternal care for very young children and paternal for older boys.[39] This approach has received further endorsement in rulings[40] made more recently by Butler-Sloss LJ under the equivalent provision in the 1989 Act where she acknowledged the importance of maternal care for very small children, particularly the importance of maintaining the bonding relationship. However, this does not amount to a legal presumption favouring such care arrangements.

When considering a child's emotional needs, judicial weight will be given to the significance of sibling as well as parental relationships. Again, judicial practice in this jurisdiction in wardship cases has traditionally recognised the importance of preserving sibling relationships when determining future care arrangement for a child.[41] Its

---

38 See, for example, *S v S (Child Abduction)* [1992] 2 FLR 311, where the court respected the wishes of a nine-year-old child.
39 See, for example, *Re P McA (A Minor)*, unreported (1983); and *Re JRS (A Minor)*, unreported (1983).
40 See *Re S (A Minor) (Custody)* [1991 2 FLR 388, 390, CA; and *Re A (A Minor) (Custody)* [1991] 2 FLR 394, 400 CA.
41 See, for example, *Re RASJ and PFJ (Minors)*, unreported (1976); and *Re MEMV and MRVV (Minors)*, unreported (1981), where this factor was of crucial significance.

importance in the neighbouring jurisdiction was underlined in a case where Purchas LJ commented '... brothers and sisters should wherever possible be brought up together'.[42]

(c) The Likely Effect on the Child of Any Change in Circumstances

The strength of a child's attachment to persons, places and things has only in recent years come to be judicially recognised as playing a crucial part in contributing to any child's psychological development. The early acknowledgement of trauma caused by disrupting the ties between a young child and a caring parent has now been extended to include an awareness that a risk of similar trauma exists where the ties are to siblings, grandparents or other relatives and perhaps friends. The dilemma this poses for the court is apparent in the observation made many years ago in this jurisdiction by Black J who advised that when considering a minor's welfare the court

> ... must not only address itself to the child's present comfort and happiness but must also look forward and try to consider what is ultimately in the best interests of the child.[43]

In more recent years the courts have tended to favour the parent best positioned to maintain the status quo, and this was a key ingredient of the judicial thinking underpinning such judicial decisions in this jurisdiction as *Re RASJ and PFJ (Minors)*.[44] It was also well established in England where, as Ormrod LJ has observed,[45]

> ... it is generally accepted by those who are professionally concerned with children that, particularly in the early years, continuity of care is a most important part of a child's sense of security and that disruption of established bonds are to be avoided whenever it is possible to do so.

This principle received further endorsement in a fairly recent Court of Appeal decision[46] and now ensures that in by far the majority of contested parenting arrangements the mother retains care responsibility. However, it cannot be regarded as amounting to a legal presumption, and the courts have, on occasion, granted an order to a 'snatching' parent despite the entailed trauma to the child resulting from being abruptly uprooted from a familiar environment.[47]

(d) The Child's Age, Sex, Background and Any Other Characteristics Which the Court Considers Relevant

The age and gender considerations which have been as evident in the wardship rulings in this jurisdiction as in the case law of England and Wales[48] have now been given

---

42 See *C v C (Minors: Custody)* [1988] 2 FLR 291, 302, CA.
43 See *Re B (An Infant)* [1946] NI 1, p. 4.
44 Unreported (1976).
45 See *Dicocco v Milne* (1983) 4 FLR 247, 259 CA.
46 See *Re B (Minors)(Residence Order)* [1992] 3 All ER 867.
47 See, for example, *Re CB and JB (Minors)*, unreported (1983); and *Re JRS (A Minor)*, unreported (1983).
48 See, for example, *B v B (Custody of Children)* [1985] FLR 166 CA.

explicit statutory approval. Their modern significance has undoubtedly been given considerable weight by the judgment in the *Gillick* case and the influence of the European Convention. However, it has to be said that this provision is likely to be judicially regarded as representing tacit legislative support for the established practice of awarding primary care responsibility for very young children and older girls to their mothers, where feasible, and older boys to their fathers. Cumming Bruce LJ, for example,[49] was acknowledging the judicial weight given to these considerations when he commented '. . . if all . . . factors are nicely balanced, then probably it is right for a child of tender years to be brought up by his or her natural mother'.

In the neighbouring jurisdiction the 'background' factor acknowledges the difficulties that have been caused there by 'mixed-race' placements made by statutory and voluntary agencies in England and Wales for fostering and adoption purposes.[50] It is unlikely to cause much change to existing practice in this jurisdiction where agencies and judiciary are long accustomed to taking into account such background features as religion when making orders relating to children. By also including a reference to any other characteristics considered relevant, the legislators have again sought to build in some of the discretionary flexibility which has characterised judicial use of wardship and enabled creative decisions to be taken in respect of children's welfare interests.

(e) Any Harm Which the Child Has Suffered or Is at Risk of Suffering

Article 2 of the 1995 Order defines 'harm' as 'ill-treatment or the impairment of health or development and the question of whether harm is significant shall be determined in accordance with Article 50(3)'. The latter, not very helpfully, suggests that

> [w]here the question of whether harm suffered by a child is significant turns on the child's health or development, his health or development shall be compared with that which could reasonably be expected of a similar child.

Article 2 offers further definitions: 'ill-treatment' is held to include 'sexual abuse and forms of ill-treatment which are not physical' while 'development' is the 'physical, intellectual, emotional, social or behavioural development'.

In addition to its application in a public family law context (see Chapter Fourteen) 'harm' clearly has a bearing on private issues where there is evidence to show that a child has suffered or may be at risk of suffering undue emotional stress or an impairment of his or her physical, intellectual, social or behavioural development. In the past the courts have had opportunities to consider the significance of 'harm' in relation to children if custody is granted to a parent who, being a Jehovah's Witness, might refuse consent for a blood-transfusion.[51] Such evidence will play a critical role in determining an application for a residence order.

The court may consider that the harm, or the risk of it, should be alleviated by means of a family assistance order. Alternatively, where that 'harm' appears to be 'significant',

---

49 See *Re W (A Minor)(Custody)* (1982) 4 FLR, 492, 504 CA.
50 See, for example, *Re JK (Adoption: Transracial Placement)* [1991] 2 FLR 340.
51 See *Jane v Jane* (1984) 4 FLR 712.

the court may well choose to direct the relevant Trust to undertake an investigation of the child's circumstances which in turn could lead to the issue of a care order or of a supervision order.

Previously wardship was the only satisfactory means of securing the welfare of an unharmed but vulnerable child, but now the court may be asked to make a statutory order on the basis of an assessment of predicted risk. This type of situation has in the past often appeared before the courts in cases where immature, inexperienced and perhaps unsupported mothers have been in contest with Trusts in relation to arrangements for the welfare of their children. In future this statutory measure rather than wardship will be available to a court enabling it to make an early decision before predictable harm to a child demonstrates parental incapacity and rehabilitation is proven to be unrealistic.

(f) How Capable of Meeting the Child's Needs Is Each Parent and Any Other Person in Relation to Whom the Court Considers the Question to Be Relevant

It is probable that in framing this provision the legislators had in mind the contention generated in recent years by the influence of the principle of non-discrimination on judicial and social work practice in relation to arrangements for the custody and placement of children. The extent to which ideology may obscure an objective assessment of the parenting abilities of, for example, a very young mother, a lesbian or homosexual person, an older person, a couple of mixed race or perhaps a member of a minority religious group has caused considerable professional and political debate and resulting media interest.

However, it is in relation to the sexual orientation of the parent that this consideration has most notably exercised the judiciary in England and Wales. Two relatively recent cases, both involving lesbian mothers, have fallen to be determined in the light of the equivalent provision under the 1989 Act. In *C v C (A Minor)(Custody: Appeal)*,[52] the Court of Appeal overturned the decision of a county court to grant custody to a lesbian mother because it considered that the judge at first instance had not taken fully into account the significance of the mother's lesbianism; i.e. it was a real factor with a bearing on the welfare of the child concerned and could not be simply discounted. However, on being remitted for a re-hearing to the High Court the lesbian mother was then granted custody. In *B v B (Minors) (Custody, Care and Control)*,[53] the court consulted expert opinion on the issue of whether being reared by a lesbian mother was likely to impair a child's welfare by blurring the latter's sexual identity or by causing the child to be stigmatised. On being advised that neither was necessarily the case and having assessed the mother as loving and mindful of her child's psychological needs, the court granted her custody.

This provision also directs the court to assess the parenting abilities of any other person who may have a direct care role in relation to the child. Given the transient relationships to which many children are now exposed, this provision should afford an important protection in situations where the caring and long-standing relationship of a parent or grandparent may be in danger of being legally displaced by a new cohabitee.

---

52 [1991] 1 FLR 223.
53 [1991] 1 FLR 402.

(g) The Range of Powers Available to the Court under This Order in the Proceedings in Question

The 1995 Order enables the court to look beyond the wishes of the parties, if necessary, to find the court order most compatible with the welfare interests of the child concerned. In doing so, it may also look beyond the above checklist of considerations as this is not intended to be a definitive list. The court may of its own initiative make any of the following orders which are available under the 1995 Order: any Article 8 order, an Article 16 family assistance order (in exceptional circumstances and with the consent of every person, other than the child, named in the order), an Article 159 order on application appointing a guardian for the child or under Article 56 it may issue a direction to the local Trust requiring it to undertake an investigation of the child's circumstances (where a question arises as to the child's welfare and the court believes that a care or supervision order may be necessary). The court may choose to exercise its authority in a way neither requested nor foreseen by the parties. However, it should only do so after ensuring that the judicial alternative is understood and broadly acceptable to the parties; if there is no consensus in favour of the advantages it offers, then it may well fail to achieve its objective.

It is this provision which now provides judicial access to public family law orders in private proceedings, though the responsibility for determining the appropriateness of a care or supervision order is now a matter for Trust assessment not judicial discretion. Again it seems to reflect a legislative intent to provide the judiciary with the range of discretionary authority which would previously only have been available to them in wardship proceedings.

II. The Children (NI) Order 1995 and the Concept of Parental Responsibilities

The 1995 Order has replaced the concepts of 'parental rights' and 'parental duties', which for centuries have formed the basic constructs of family law in the United Kingdom, with the composite term 'parental responsibilities'. The change signals a profound difference of approach from a proprietal frame of reference to one which implies that parental use of authority is valid only if employed for the benefit of the child. It also suggests that such responsibilities are exclusively an attribute of parenthood which may be temporarily met by other persons or bodies but can never be wholly shed by a 'parent' to whom, by definition, they must continue to attach (see Chapter Five for the law relating to parental responsibilities). Only those attributes which have a functional bearing upon the nurture needs of the child, rather than those traditionally associated with the status of parent, are now held to comprise such responsibilities. The reframing of this concept allows it to now play a more consistent role in both public and private family law.

1. The Child to Whom Parental Responsibilities Are Owed

The definition of 'child' in the 1995 Order is restricted to mean a person below the age of sixteen years for the purposes of making an Article 8 order,[54] below seventeen when

---

54 See Article 9(b).

making a care or supervision order[55] and is otherwise to mean a person below the age of eighteen years. A child will be a 'child of the family' when in the care of a person who has parental responsibility for him or her or in the care of any other person with whom he or she has been living[56] and, for the purposes of any proceedings, is the child who is the subject of those proceedings.[57] Parental responsibility cannot be borne by any person or body in respect of a foetus. Nor, in all probability, does the term apply in respect of a married person below the age of eighteen years (see also Chapters One and Fifteen).

2. Nature of Parental Responsibilities

The exact nature of such responsibilities will clearly depend on the age and circumstances of the child concerned. Broadly speaking, however, 'the effect of having parental responsibility is to empower a person to take most decisions in the child's life.[58] Bromley, more specifically, suggests that this composite term comprises at least the following separate areas of responsibility relating to providing a home; having contact; determining and providing for education; determining religion, discipline, consent to treatment, marriage, adoption, emigration and change of surname; vetoing the issue of a passport; taking the child outside the jurisdiction; administering property, protection and maintenance; representing the child in legal proceedings, burial or cremation; and appointing a guardian for the child.[59]

3. Entitlement to Bear Parental Responsibilities

More than one person may bear parental responsibility in respect of the same child at the same time. Having parental responsibility does not entitle the bearer to act in any way which is incompatible with a court order made under this Order in respect of the child.

Article 5(3) specifically abolishes the common-law rule, preserved in Northern Ireland by section 5 of the Guardianship of Infants Act 1886, that a father is presumed to be the natural guardian of his legitimate child.

4. Loss, Transfer, Sharing or Termination of Parental Responsibilities

The mother does not lose parental responsibility merely because the father has it or because he later acquires it. Nor do either or both parents lose it when the court grants a care order to a Trust. Where more than one person bears parental responsibility for the same child, either may act independently of the other in giving effect to that responsibility.

Parental responsibility may only be lost on the death or adoption of the child, by order of the court (or cessation of a court order) or by the child attaining the age of majority (see further Chapter Five for application of the law relating to parental responsibilities).

---

55 See Article 50(4).
56 See Article 17.
57 See *Birmingham City Council v H (No 2)* [1993] 1 FLR 883.
58 See *Introduction to the Children Act,* DoH, 1989, para 2.4.
59 See PM Bromley and NV Lowe *Family Law,* 8th ed, London: Butterworth (1992) 301. See Chapter 1 of this book for judicial interpretation of the role and responsibility of a parent.

CHAPTER TWELVE

Private Proceedings: Article 8 Orders

Introduction

This chapter deals with private family law proceedings commenced under Part III of the Children (NI) Order 1995. Its main focus is on the rules and the orders for allocating parental responsibilities in the context of matrimonial proceedings. It also deals with such matters arising between unmarried parents. As these are not processed exclusively through statutory proceedings, consideration is similarly given to examining how the wardship jurisdiction responds to private family law issues regarding care arrangements for children.

The Introduction of the Children (NI) Order 1995

Under the 1995 Order arrangements for the future care of a child, arising at the initiative of a parent, are determined in accordance with principles which differ in some important respects from those that formerly applied. A range of new orders now consolidate the judicial response to such contests whether occurring in the context of divorce, separation or nullity and whether initiated in the High Court, county court or magistrates' court. These legislative changes are in accordance with the recommendations of the Law Commission[1] as subsequently canvassed by the Office of Law Reform and the DHSS (NI).[2] The resultant law differs only marginally from the corresponding provisions now governing the same matters in England and Wales.

I. *The Law Governing Contested Arrangements for Children Arising in the Context of Divorce, Separation or Nullity Proceedings*

The law is now stated in Article 44 of the Matrimonial Causes (NI) Order 1978, as amended by paragraph 95 of Schedule 9 of the 1995 Order. It exactly replicates the corresponding amended provision in the Matrimonial Causes Act 1973. Article 5(3) of the 1995 Order brings these two pieces of matrimonial legislation even closer by removing the anomalous rule of law that in Northern Ireland had perpetuated the Victorian principle by which the father was held to be the natural guardian of his legitimate child.[3] The law is now given effect by the issue of Article 8 orders. In this

---

1 See *Report on Guardianship and Custody* (Law Com no. 172, 1988).
2 See Part 11 of the *Joint Consultation Paper on Proposed Changes to Some Aspects of the Law Relating to Children in Northern Ireland* (1989).
3 See Article 5:

    (3) The rule of law that a father is the natural guardian of his legitimate child is abolished.

jurisdiction these are most likely to be made in the context of proceedings arising under the Domestic Proceedings (NI) Order 1980 (following a judicial request for a social work report under Article 4 of the 1995 Order) rather than in the context of divorce proceedings (which are usually uncontested).

Under Article 44(1) of the 1978 Act, as amended by the 1995 Order, and in keeping with the new minimalist approach to judicial intervention, the judiciary in this jurisdiction are now bound to do no more than consider

(a) whether there are any children of the family to whom this Article applies; and
(b) where there are any such children, whether (in the light of the arrangements which have been made, or are proposed to be made, for their upbringing and welfare) it should exercise any of its powers under the Children (Northern Ireland) Order 1995 with respect to any of them.

Only in 'exceptional circumstances' will the court delay the granting of a decree absolute. The previous legislative provision required the judiciary to 'positively vet' all actual or proposed arrangements for children. The making of a decree absolute was conditional upon judicial satisfaction with such arrangements. This survived in diluted form under the 1978 Order but has now been abandoned. The link is broken between the private right of parents to obtain an order dissolving the legal basis of their spousal relationship (or settling the terms of their separation) and the duty of the court to ensure that the exercise of that right is compatible with the public interest in adequate care arrangements being made for the future welfare of any children concerned.

In most instances the separation of the two will be demonstrated by the court determining a divorce application without examining the parties on the detail of proposed care arrangements. Later, in fresh proceedings, most typically for residence orders, one of the parties may bring this matter before the court. In that small minority of cases where there is clear conflict regarding proposed care arrangements, the court will issue an Article 4 direction to the local Trust.

II. *The Law Governing Uncontested Arrangements for Children Arising in the Context of Divorce, Separation or Nullity Proceedings*

Under Article 4 of the 1995 Order:

(1) A court considering any question with respect to a child under this Order may ask an authority to arrange for a suitably qualified person to report to the court on such matters relating to the welfare of that child as are required to be dealt with in the report.

In any family proceedings (including contested divorce proceedings), where the court considers the arrangements to be questionable, an Article 4 direction may be issued to the local Trust. For example, it may do so in private applications for maintenance under the Domestic Proceedings (NI) Order 1980 for contact or for a wardship order.

However, the 1995 Order introduces significant changes to uncontested private family law proceedings. First, it greatly reduces the proportion of parental applications which involve professional scrutiny of child welfare considerations. Second, in theory it should also reduce the proportion of such applications which result in orders being made: the assumption that an application requires an order has been displaced by a presumption of no order (though this is not borne out by experience under the 1989 Act). Third, any order issued will not divest a parent of his or her parental responsibilities. Fourth, instead of issuing a single order the court may well elect to make a package of different orders. Finally, whether contested or not, an application for a private order can no longer result in the making of a public care order on the court's own motion.

The Intervention Threshold

I. The Principles to Be Applied by the Court in Private Family Law Proceedings

The most important principle introduced by the 1995 Order is that when determining any issue affecting the upbringing of a child, the court must, as stated in Article 3(1), regard the welfare of that child as the paramount consideration. Other significant factors arising in the context of contested proceedings are that the welfare interests of a child are to be ascertained by reference to a stated checklist of considerations; the concept of parental responsibilities rather than parental rights will guide judicial determination of any such contest; no parent is to lose or be wholly absolved of future responsibility for a child, other than by way of a third party adoption; at any time, more than one person may hold parental responsibility in respect of a child; an order shall not be made in respect of a child unless it would be better for the court to make the order than to make no order at all; and any order must be made with the minimum of delay.

However, the introduction of the 1995 Order, although arguably the most important single piece of family law legislation in the history of the province, does not negate all that went before it. In making decisions affecting the welfare of a child, the judiciary will continue to rely on established case-law precedents, particularly those forged in the wardship jurisdiction, insofar as they prove compatible with the principles and overall philosophy of the new 1995 Order. Previously established case law will continue to guide the future judicial determination of contested custody arrangements.

1. The Paramountcy Principle: Private Law

The paramountcy principle is essentially a principle of private family law. In Northern Ireland its statutory role was initially limited to the determination of custody issues arising under the Domestic Proceedings (NI) Order 1980. For many years, however, it had also been judicially applied in wardship proceedings to decide almost all matters relating to the custody, upbringing and property of a child (though not for dispensing with the need for a parent's consent for the adoption of a child; see further, Chapters Six and Seven). Indeed, though in this jurisdiction it became noteworthy as a result of being applied in wardship proceedings brought by Health and Social Services Boards, it is a principle which has its roots as a rule for governing disputes between parents regarding the custody and access arrangements for their children.

In determining such private family law matters arising in the wardship jurisdiction, the paramountcy principle laid the case-law foundations for Article 3(1) of the 1995

Order which now requires the principle to be applied by the court in determining any question relating to the upbringing of a child, the administration of a child's property or the application of any income arising from it. There are, however, some exceptions to this general rule.

Paramountcy Case Law in a Private Family Law Context

The initial definition given by Lord MacDermott, in what continues to be the leading case in this field, bears repeating. As he then explained, the paramountcy principle referred to

> a process whereby, when all the relevant facts, claims and wishes of parents, risks, choices and other circumstances are taken into account and weighed, the course to be followed is that which is most in the interests of the child's welfare.[4]

From being one among many factors to be judicially considered in family proceedings, 'welfare' has now been elevated to become the primary objective of such proceedings. Case law also points to the fact that paramountcy requires welfare to be the first matter to be ruled upon; only when the matter of how best to secure a child's welfare has been determined can other issues then be addressed.

However, prior to the introduction of the 1989 Act, the courts had ruled that matters such as the following were not subject to this principle: the publication of information harmful to a ward,[5] the exclusion of a spouse from the marital home and the imposing of a blood-test to establish paternity. Subsequently, it has also been held[6] that the principle does not apply to the issue of whether leave should be granted to allow application to be made for a 'section 8' order under section 10 of the 1989 Act. The principle is expressly excluded by Article 2(1) of the 1995 Order from having any bearing on applications for maintenance for a child. It is excluded also from having such a bearing on matters falling within the scope of Article 9 of the Adoption (NI) Order 1987, Article 27(1) of the Matrimonial Causes (NI) Order 1978 and Article 4 of the Family Law (Miscellaneous Provisions)(NI) Order 1984.

2. The No-Delay Principle: Private Law

In addition to the general no-delay duty (see Chapter Eleven) imposed on the court by Article 3(2) of the 1995 Order, there is also a further requirement under Article 11(1) that the court should, when considering any question in relation to the making of an Article 8 order,

(a) draw up a timetable with a view to determining the question without delay; and
(b) give such directions as it considers appropriate for the purpose of ensuring, so far as is reasonably practicable, that that timetable is adhered to.

---

4 See *J v C* [1970] AC 668 [1969] 1 All ER 788, HL.
5 See, for example, *Re X (A Minor)* [1975] Fam 47 [1975] 1 All ER 697, CA.
6 See, *Re A & W (Minors)(Residence Order: Leave to Apply)* [1992] 2 FLR 154.

This is a principle of general application[7] with a bearing on any proceedings concerning a child's upbringing, whether or not instigated under the 1995 Order.

However, the courts recognise that there are some circumstances in which a delay is in a child's best interests.[8]

3. The No-Order Presumption: Private Law

The no-order presumption is as stated in Article 3 of the 1995 Order (see also Chapter Eleven). By presuming that the parties should be free to make their own arrangements regarding the future care of their children, the no-order presumption marks an important fresh start in the law relating to family breakdown. Previously, the issuing of custody and access orders had come to be regarded as an integral 'part of the court package', automatically assimilated into divorce proceedings. As noted in the Guidance and Regulations:[9]

> The operation of this principle will be particularly noticeable in divorce and judicial separation proceedings since Article 44 of the Matrimonial Causes (NI) Order 1978 no longer requires the court to make a declaration that the arrangements proposed for the children are 'satisfactory' or 'the best that can be devised in the circumstances' before granting a decree. The parties still have to provide information to the court about the proposed arrangements but the court is no longer required in every case to approve those arrangements. Instead the duty of the court is limited to considering whether it should exercise any of its powers under the Children Order.

Where there is a dispute between the parties in respect of some aspect of a child's upbringing, it is probable that the court will be readily persuaded that the presumption can be rebutted.

The new approach was demonstrated in a case in England[10] where the applicant applied for a residence order in respect of her eleven-year-old grand-daughter who was already living with her. The judge at first instance decided that this principle should apply as it was not apparent how the desired order would improve the situation. However, the Court of Appeal reversed that decision and granted the residence order on the grounds that by doing so the grandmother would then be empowered to take everyday parental responsibility for matters such as negotiating with teachers and consenting to medical treatment while the girl would feel that her home with the grandmother was more secure and protected by the court.

---

7 Again, a principle not borne out by practice under the 1989 Act where there are significant delays: twenty-six weeks for a hearing in the magistrates' courts, forty-two in the county courts and forty-nine in the High Court.
8 See, for example, *S v S (Minors) (Custody)* [1992] 1 FCR 158, [1992] Fam Law 148 CA, when, despite the equivalent directive under the 1989 Act, it was nonetheless decided to defer making a permanent order until such time as the children concerned had time to adjust and settle down in their 'volatile family situation'.
9 Children (NI) Order 1995, Guidance and Regulations, vol. 1, para 5.47.
10 See *B v B (A Minor)(Residence Order)* [1992] 2 FLR 327.

4. The Checklist of Considerations

The checklist of considerations must be judicially weighed in all contested applications for Article 8 orders or for variation or discharge of such orders. There is no requirement that it be so considered in any uncontested private family law proceedings. As well as indicating the sort of outcomes the orders should strive to achieve, the purpose of the checklist is to promote greater consistency in judicial decisions, practitioner assessments and in the overall coherence of family law. In uncontested private proceedings, for example an adoption application, the court is not obliged to refer to the checklist and therefore is not under a duty to consider alternative orders. The checklist criteria are as stated in Article 3(3) of the 1995 Order and replicate equivalent provisions of the 1989 Act (see Chapter Eleven for case law).

II. The Parties

1. The Applicants

Private family law orders in relation to contested arrangements for children are now available under the 1995 Order and may be sought in three different types of situations.

(a) Without Leave of the Court

Under Article 10(4) of the 1995 Order the following are entitled to apply for any Article 8 order without first obtaining leave of the court:

    (a) any parent or guardian of the child;
    (b) any person in whose favour a residence order is in force with respect to the child.

Under Article 10(5) there are those who may apply only for a residence or contact order: any party to a marriage (whether or not subsisting) in relation to whom the child is a child of the family; or any person with whom the child has lived for a period of at least three years. This category also includes: those who make application with the consent of a person in whose favour a residence order has been made in respect of the child concerned; the Trust in whose favour a care order has been made; or any and every person with parental responsibility for such a child.

(b) With Leave of the Court

Under Article 10(2) the court may make an Article 8 order with respect to any child on the application of a person who

    (b) has obtained the leave of the court to make the application.

Where the child is the applicant, then, under Article 10(8), in determining whether or not to grant leave, the court may only do so when satisfied that the child 'has sufficient understanding to make the application' (see also Chapter Eighteen). Where the applicant is a person other than the child concerned, then, under Article 10(9), the court is required to have particular regard to

(a) the nature of the proposed application for the Article 8 order;
(b) the applicant's connection with the child;
(c) any risk there might be of that proposed application disrupting the child's life to such an extent that he would be harmed by it; and
(d) where the child is being looked after by an authority —
   (i) the authority's plans for the child's future; and
   (ii) the wishes and feelings of the child's parents.

That Article 10(9) does not present a finite checklist of factors was emphasised in *Re A (A Minor)(Residence Order: Leave to Apply)*.[11] The court may also, for example, take into account matters specified in the Article 9 checklist. It may not, however, apply the paramountcy principle. An Article 10(9) applicant must demonstrate a sufficiently strong case to make the chance of success, if leave is granted, reasonable.[12] Rule 4.4 of the Family Proceedings Rules (NI) 1996 details the procedure for seeking leave of the court.

(c) By Intercession of the Court

Under Article 10(1) in any family proceedings in which a question arises with respect to the welfare of any child, the court may make an Article 8 order with respect to the child if

(b) the court considers that the order should be made even though no such application has been made.

Under Article 11(3) it may make such an order at any stage during the course of family proceedings even though not in a position to finalise them. It may even do so in respect of a child in care, though this is restricted to the making of a residence order.

Article 9(3) prohibits any person who is, or has been within the previous six months, a foster parent employed by a Trust from applying for any Article 8 order unless that person has the consent of the Trust, is a relative of the child in question or the child has lived with him or her for the immediately preceding three years.

2. The Children Amenable

As before, the proceedings apply in respect of any child either of the parties or treated as one of the family.

(a) Age of the Child

Article 44(3) of the Matrimonial Causes (NI) Order 1978 (as amended by paragraph 95 of Schedule 9 of the 1995 Order) states that the proceedings will apply to

(a) any child of the family who has not attained the age of sixteen at the date when the court considers the case in accordance with the requirements of this Article; and

---

11 [1993] 1 FLR 425.
12 See *G v Kirklees Metropolitan Borough Council* [1993] 1 FLR 805 (per Booth J).

(b) any child of the family who has attained that age at that date and in relation to whom the court directs that this Article shall apply.

In the latter case the court might, for example, direct that the provision will apply in respect of an older but disabled child.

(b) Child of the Parties

Most obviously, such a child is one born to both spouses during the course of their marriage. The natural child of either spouse or one adopted by either or both who has lived with them in the family home also meet this definition. Conversely, a child of either spouse who has been adopted into another family, as opposed to being placed by them in a private foster care arrangement, can no longer be regarded as a child of the parties.

(c) Child of the Family

The term 'child of the family' remains largely unchanged by the 1995 Order except that, in relation to children in the care of a Trust and fostered with a family, it is now interpreted as applying to children who are 'placed' rather than 'boarded-out'. The relevance of case law which previously defined its boundaries remains equally applicable. So, for example, an unborn child would not be included within this definition. This was the effect of the ruling in a case[13] where a pregnant wife left her husband within a week of their marriage and it was proven that he was not the father of the resultant child. Bagnall J held that there was no sense in which the deserted spouse could be regarded as having treated the then unborn child as a child of the family. The duration of the marriage may be very short, as in a case[14] where it lasted a fortnight, yet still allow children to fall within the definition. However, there must be proof that the family unit actually existed before a child can be regarded as having been treated as a member of it.

III. The Article 8 Orders

Articles 45–47 of the Matrimonial Causes (NI) Order 1978 have been repealed by Schedule 10 of the 1995 Order. In Northern Ireland, as in England and Wales, the power of the court to commit a child into care of its own motion has been removed. In any proceedings for divorce, separation or nullity which give rise to contested arrangements regarding the future of children, the judiciary are now referred to the 1995 Order for orders to determine future arrangements. Similarly, in any circumstances where wardship proceedings have been commenced and such arrangements are the subject of parental dispute, the judiciary are now required to refer to the 1995 Order.

In private family law disputes the main orders now available to deal with arrangements for the upbringing of children are those listed in Article 8 of the 1995 Order. Each Article 8 order may be made for a specific or for an unlimited period of time and

---

13 See *A v A (Family: Unborn Child)* [1974] 1 All ER 755.
14 See *W v W (Child of the Family)* [1984] FLR 796 CA.

will otherwise end on the child's sixteenth birthday unless exceptional circumstances require an extension. Unlike their predecessors these orders are intended to be flexible, and Article 11(7) allows for conditions to be attached or to be supplemented by additional judicial directions and for their duration to be specified. Under Article 10(1)(b) the court may make any Article 8 order, during the course of any family proceedings on its own motion. As stated in the Guidance and Regulations:[15]

> The court will also have the power, when making any Article 8 order, to include directions about how it is to be carried into effect, to impose conditions to be complied with (i) by any person in whose favour the order is made or (ii) a parent or (iii) a non-parent with parental responsibility or (iv) a person with whom the child is living, to specify the period of which the order, or any provision contained in it, will have effect, and to make such incidental, supplemental or consequential provision as the court thinks fit.

This is to enable the new orders to be as flexible as possible and so reduce the need to resort to wardship.

Instead of an Article 8 order the court may make a family assessment order, an order appointing a guardian or an order directing the relevant Trust to carry out an investigation of the child's circumstances.

1. Residence Order (RO)

Article 8(1) of the 1995 Order states that

> 'residence order' means an order settling the arrangements to be made as to the person with whom a child is to live.

This gives parental responsibility for a child, most often accompanied by actual physical possession, to a named person or persons; it replaces the previous custody order. A RO may contain directions as to how it is to be put into effect and/or be subject to conditions.

(a) Applicants/Eligibility

A RO is most usually made in favour of one person: a parent. Under Article 10(4) and (5) a parent or guardian may apply as of right for a RO. Under Article 9(3) and (4), all others require leave of the court. A Trust foster parent may also apply but, depending on duration of care, will require Trust permission before seeking leave of the court. An order can be made out to two or more persons, none of whom may be a parent.[16] Thus grandparents, foster-parents, uncles and aunts or any combination of same, whether living together or not, may be eligible for such an order. Article 11 states that

---

15 Children (NI) Order 1995, Guidance and Regulations, vol 1, para 2.22.
16 See, for example, *A v A* [1994] 1 FLR 669 where a residence order was used to achieve a sharing of parental responsibilities. Also see Baker and Townsend, *Post-Divorce Parenting — Rethinking Shared Residence*, Child and Family Law Quarterly, Vol. 8, No. 3, pp 217–227 (1996).

(4) Where a residence order is made in favour of two or more persons who do not themselves all live together, the order may specify the periods during which the child is to live in the different households concerned.

Significantly, a RO may also be made in favour of a child applicant.[17] Article 9(1) of the 1995 Order enables the court to make a RO in respect of a child in the care of a Trust (the RO thereby discharging any other order: Schedule 8, para 10) but the latter is prohibited by Article 9(2) from being either an applicant or recipient in respect of such an order.

(b) Effects

Under Article 12(2) the making of a RO automatically vests parental responsibility in the person named in the order. Its primary effect is to decide where a child is to live and it is most usually made in favour of one person: a parent. However, a RO does not vest parental responsibility exclusively in the bearer. As between first parties where one parent is granted a RO, both will nonetheless retain full parental responsibility and with it the capacity to make most decisions independently of each other in regard to the child concerned. As between first and third parties Article 12(2) provides that a parent or guardian with parental responsibility will not lose it on the making of a RO in favour of a non-parent. Finally, Article 5(5) provides that in any circumstance a person with parental responsibility will not lose it merely because a RO has been granted to another.

The hallmark of a RO is that it authorises more than one person to hold parental responsibility for a named child at the same time.

(c) Some Limitations

The scope of authority vested by a RO is not coterminous with its predecessor the custody order. In particular, Article 13(1) prevents the child's removal from the jurisdiction, though the courts may be prepared to recognise exceptional circumstances when this is permissible.[18] The assumption implicit in an observation (admittedly in a wardship case) made by Lowry LCJ in private law proceedings may thus now be redundant:

> Sometimes in the past, as it seems to me, the courts have flinched from solutions which allow children to leave the jurisdiction and therefore, though workable and in the children's interest, involve the court in abandoning control of the destinies of minors for whose welfare it has been responsible. Such reluctance is not altogether logical and should never be decisive.[19]

---

17   See *Re AD (A Minor)* [1993] Fam Law, vol. 23, 405.
18   See *Re K (A Minor) (Removal from the Jurisdiction)* [1992] 2 FLR 98 and *M v M (Minors) (Removal from the Jurisdiction)* [1992] 2 FLR 303 CA.
19   See *Re MEMV and MRVV (Minors)*, unreported (1981) CA. See also the following cases where the High Court in this jurisdiction gave leave in wardship proceedings for children to be permanently removed to other countries: *Re APP and LP (Minors)*, unreported (1973); *Re P McA (Minors)*, unreported (1983); *Re MPW and NPW (Minors)*, unreported (1983) and *Re LEC and NCC (Minors)*, unreported (1983).

The Court of Appeal in England has, more recently, held[20] that the law governing this matter remains the same as before the introduction of the 1989 Act. The court confirmed the views earlier expressed by Bracewell J[21] that while the welfare test must now be satisfied by reference to the checklist, it is not necessary to methodically apply and satisfy each item on that list.

Article 13 also prevents any change being made to the child's surname. This particular prohibition has been judicially endorsed by the decision in *Re B (Change of Surname)*.[22]

In keeping with the principle of parental responsibility, a RO does not vest authority exclusively in the named party. The other parent continues to hold and share with the named party all responsibilities in respect of the child except for those which are covered by the order. Article 12 directs that where any court is making a RO in favour of a father who does not yet have parental responsibility, the court shall then also make an order under Article 7 of the 1995 Order giving him that responsibility; where the person vested with a RO is not a parent or guardian, then under Article 12(4) that person shall have parental responsibility for the duration of the order and thereafter until revoked. Each parent retains the right to act independently of the other and the right to delegate his or her responsibility to another, e.g. a child minder. As noted in the Guidance and Regulations[23]:

> The only restrictions on this are that neither parent may act independently in matters where the consent of more than one person is expressly required by statute (Article 5(6)), nor may either parent act in a way that is incompatible with any order made in respect of the child (Article 5(7)).

(d) Conditions

Under Article 11(7) the court may attach conditions to a RO.[24] These may be in relation to matters such as blood transfusions, medical treatment or as regards specific living arrangements. In respect of the latter, if the court issues a joint RO, it may specify the periods the child is to spend in each household. It may also specify the duration of the order. The use of shared ROs has proved contentious under the 1989 Act.[25]

Under Article 179(2) the making of a RO in respect of a child already the subject of a care order discharges that care order.

---

20   See *H v H (Residence Order: Leave to Remove from the Jurisdiction)* [1995] 1 FLR 529.
21   See *M v A (Wardship: Removal from Jurisdiction)* [1993] 2 FLR 715.
22   [1996] 1 FLR 791.
23   Children (NI) Order 1995, Guidance and Regulations, vol. 1, para 5.7.
24   See *Re O (Contact: Imposition of Conditions)* [1995] 2 FLR 124, the leading case on the court's power to attach conditions. See also, *Re D (Residence: Imposition of Conditions)* [1996] 2 FLR 281.
25   See, in particular, *A v A (Minors)(Shared Residence Order)* [1994] 1 FLR 669; also see *Re H (A Minor)(Shared Residence)* [1994] 1 FLR 717 and *G v G (Joint Residence Orders)* [1993] Fam Law, vol. 23, 615. For evidence that judicial disapproval of shared residence predates the 1989 Act, see *Riley v Riley* [1986] 2 FLR 429.

(e) Duration

Article 11(5) provides that a RO shall cease to have effect if the parent in whose favour it was made lives together with the other parent for a continuous period of six months or more. Under Article 179(10) it will cease when the child concerned attains the age of sixteen (eighteen in exceptional circumstances). It will be discharged by the issue of a care order (Article 179(2)).

2. Contact Order

A contact order recognises the authority of Article 8(1) of the European Convention on Human Rights and Fundamental Freedoms which states that 'Everyone has the right to respect for his private and family life, his home and his correspondence'.

(a) Definition

Article 8(1) of the 1995 Order states that

> 'contact order' means an order requiring the person with whom a child lives, or is to live, to allow the child to visit or stay with the person named in the order, or for that person and the child to otherwise have contact with each other.

It also, however, has its roots in the decision in *M v M (Child: Access)*[26] where the court held that access is essentially a right of the child rather than of the parent. This decision has had a consistently influential bearing on judicial decision-making in this jurisdiction. As MacDermott LJ once remarked:

> Custody and access arrangements are for the benefit of the child — they are not awards or prizes or compensations given out by the court to separated parents.[27]

(b) Applicants/Eligibility

Under Article 10(4) and (5) any parent or guardian or any other person who has a RO in respect of the child concerned may apply as of right for a contact order. Under Article 9(3) others must first seek leave of the court. A Trust foster-parent, unless a relative, or unless the child has been living with him or her for the preceding three years, can apply for leave only with the consent of the Trust. The court may make a contact order during the course of any family proceedings. A Trust cannot apply.

In the case of grandparent applicants, there is a requirement under Article 10(1)(a) that leave of the court be obtained before application is made, in contrast to the position under the Domestic Proceedings (NI) Order 1980. Having granted leave, however, the courts will not recognise any presumption entitling a grandparent to contact: the applicant must demonstrate good reason.[28] Indeed, in this jurisdiction, the courts have demonstrated a cautious wariness in relation to the dangers of licensing contact arrangements which may expose a child to acrimonious tensions between grandparents

---

26 [1973] 2 All ER 81.
27 See *K v K (Re LEK, An Infant)*, unreported (1992) at 3.
28 See *Re A (A Minor) (Contact Application: Grandparent)*, The Times, March 6, 1995, CA.

and a natural parent. As MacDermott J said when refusing grandparents their application for care and control and then making an order denying them any rights of contact:

> I am satisfied that contact would not benefit the children. This is a conclusion that no one wishes to reach — I do not reach it lightly. I reach it because I have no doubt whatsoever that by reason of past behaviour, present tensions and the absence of any foreseeable chance of reconciliation or conciliation the only conclusion which will secure the best interests of the children is to grant care and control to the father and make no order for access.[29]

(c) Effect

Like its predecessor the access order, a contact order vests rights in a named adult; it allows defined contact or communication between the child and a named person or persons. That person need not be a parent or relative and more than one contact order may be in effect at the same time in respect of the same child. Contact may take the form of communication by letter or phone instead of or as well as a person-to-person meeting.[30] It may allow for overnight stays, specify visiting arrangements and provide for 'reasonable contact' or contact at such intervals as determined by the court. Under Article 11(7) of the 1995 Order, the court may attach conditions or make such directions as it thinks fit.

A contact order made under Article 8 is not the same as a contact order made under Article 53. The former is a positive order which enables contact between a child and a named person; the latter limits, removes or re-defines such contact. An Article 8 contact order cannot be made in respect of a child who is the subject of a care order.

(d) The Child's Best Interests

Case law has continued the presumption that in fact the inherent right is that of the child to maintain relationships.[31] The courts have demonstrated great caution towards any parental initiative intended to deprive the other parent of contact. So, for example, the Court of Appeal considered that even 'eccentric, bizarre behaviour' should not deprive a father of contact with his children unless this behaviour presented a risk of harm.[32] However, as Balcombe LJ has observed[33] the essential point is not whether contact is beneficial for the child but whether there exists any good reason why the child should not have access.

As before under the introduction of the 1995 Order, disputes relating to contact continue to present the courts with the most litigated and hotly contested problems in

---

29 See *Re ICS and RHS (Minors)*, unreported (1982).
30 See *Re O (A Minor) (Contact: Imposition of Conditions)* [1995] 2 FLR 124 where the contact was in the form of school reports; and *Re M (A Minor)(Contact: Conditions)* [1994] 1 FLR 272 where permission was given for contact by post between an unmarried father in prison and his two-year-old son.
31 This principle has been recognised in such recent cases as *Re H (Minors)(Access)* [1992] 1 FLR 148 CA and *Re O* supra.
32 See *Re B (Minors: Access)* [1992] 1 FLR 142.
33 See *Re M (Minors)(Access)* [1992] Fam Law vol. 22, 152.

the law as it relates to children. These problems are exacerbated when one of the parties refuses to comply with the order.

(e) Contact Refused by Parent

The parent with a RO or custody who flatly refuses to comply with contact arrangements agreed by the court presents the latter with an impossible problem in terms of fulfilling the objectives of a contact order. As Ormrod LJ observed[34] when ruling out enforcement by imprisonment:

> These cases are exceedingly intractable. They can only be dealt with by tact not force. Force is bound to fail.

Such cases are governed by the rule that access between child and parent is presumed to be in the welfare interests of the child concerned. As Balcombe LJ has stated[35] the test to be applied is 'are there any cogent reasons why a child should be denied the opportunity of access to his natural father'. Where the conditions are satisfied and contact is found to be in the child's interests, then it would seem the court must make the order.[36] The principle is that though a parent may ultimately frustrate the court's intentions, he or she cannot be permitted to foreclose the court's duty to make an order giving effect to the child's best interests. However, there is a very fine line to be drawn between the parent who is plainly and simply obstructing the court and the parent who by doing so is also prejudicing the welfare of the child to the point where an order would be counterproductive. For example, a mother's implacable hostility, fuelled by the attitudes of her mother and her second husband, was such that the court considered it to be futile to make an order which would only place the child concerned under considerable pressure.[37] This view was questioned by the Court of Appeal but was ultimately allowed to prevail. The test to be applied is — are the feelings of the non-complying parent of such a nature and intensity and so expressed that there is a real risk they would cause significant emotional upset to the child concerned?

Among the measures which the court may take to buttress a contact order in the face of parental hostility are the use of specific issue orders and prohibited steps orders, the attachment of conditions to a RO and authority for a court officer, constable or Trust social worker to undertake and supervise contact arrangements.

Ultimately, however, and despite the reservations expressed above by Ormrod LJ, the court may be prepared to institute committal proceedings for contempt where a

---

34 See *Churchard v Churchard* [1984] FLR 635, 638 F – H, CA.
35 See *Re D (A Minor)(Contact: Mother's Hostility)* [1993] 2 FLR 1.
36 As in *Re W (A Minor)(Contact)* [1994] 2 FLR 441, *Re H (A Minor)(Contact)* [1994] 2 FLR 776 and *Re H (Contact: Enforcement)* [1996] 1 FLR 614.
37 See *Re J (A Minor)(Contact)* [1994] 1 FLR 6. Also see, *Re S (Minors: Access)* [1990] 2 FLR 166, where the judge refused to make an order because the mother's implacable hostility would render it unworkable.

parent persistently refuses to comply with the terms of a contact order. The paramountcy principle would have no bearing on such proceedings.[38]

(f) Contact Refused by Child

The child who refuses to comply with the court's contact arrangements presents a double problem. First, is the refusal a genuine, reasoned or felt response emanating solely from the child or has it been produced as a result of pressure or prejudice from the child's carer? Second, will the child's welfare be best furthered in the long term by continuing, re-adjusting or severing the contact? The Court of Appeal has recently ruled[39] that the following test should be applied: Is the fundamental emotional need of every child to have an enduring relationship with both parents outweighed in this case by the depth of harm which the child will be at risk of suffering as a consequence of the court making the contact order? In this way the court has raised a presumption of contact, underpinned by the welfare principle, evidenced by a basic tenet of developmental psychology[40] which can only be displaced by evidence that such contact will breach the significant harm threshold.

(g) Contact Order: Duration

Article 11(6) provides that a contact order shall cease to have effect if the parent in whose favour it was made lives together with the other parent for a continuous period of six months or more. Under Article 179(10) it will cease when the child concerned attains the age of sixteen (eighteen in exceptional circumstances). The court may specify when the order, or any provision it may contain, is to cease. A care order discharges a contact order.

3. Specific Issue Order (SIO)

A specific issue order enables the parties, usually parents, to appear before the court to seek direction in relation to a specific aspect of parental responsibility.

(a) Definition

Article 8(1) of the 1995 Order states that

> 'specific issue order' means an order giving directions for the purpose of determining a specific question which has arisen, or which may arise, in connection with any aspect of parental responsibility for a child.

As stated in the Guidance and Regulations:[41]

---

38 See *Z v Z* [1996] Fam Law 255 and *A v N (Committal: Refusal of Contact)*, 11 October 1996, CA. For further discussion on this most difficult subject see C Smart and B Neale *Arguments Against Violence — Must Contact Be Enforced* in Fam Law, vol. 27, 1997, pp 332–6.
39 See *Re M (Contact: Welfare Test)* [1995] 1 FLR 274 CA.
40 See, for example, J Bowlby, *Attachment and Loss*, in vol. 1, 'Attachment' Harmondsworth, Penguin (1971).
41 Children (NI) Order 1995, Guidance and Regulations, vol. 1, para 4.18.

The aim, however, is not to give one parent or the other a general 'right' to make decisions about a particular aspect of the child's upbringing, for example his education or medical treatment, but rather to enable a particular dispute over such a matter to be resolved by the court, including the giving of detailed directions where necessary.

(b) Applicants/Eligibility

Under Article 10(4) a parent or guardian may apply as of right as may any person who has a RO in respect of the child concerned. All others, including the child, may only do so with leave of the court.

(c) Effect

The order made directs that the named party or parties behave in a specified manner in regard to the issue raised; it replaces the flexible powers previously available to the judiciary in wardship proceedings with a narrower discretionary power which may be applied to any specific difficulty between the parties. It may be made in conjunction with contact or residence orders and may be made instead of the latter where its comprehensive authority is unnecessary to resolve a limited area of contention. The court may attach conditions.

(d) Appropriate Use

A SIO, like a prohibited steps order, is confined to dealing with issues which relate to aspects of parental responsibility. Most commonly, such issues have concerned a child's education[42] or his or her return to the jurisdiction.[43] An extreme example of an aspect of parental responsibility which has in the past from time to time required judicial action in wardship proceedings occurs when a child needs urgent medical treatment against parental wishes.

As pointed out in the Guidance and Regulations:[44]

> Trusts will, like anyone else, be able to apply for specific issue and prohibited steps orders, provided they first obtain the court's leave. . . . This will enable them to resolve certain issues which at present can only be resolved by making the child a ward of court, such as whether or not he should have a particular operation. This may arise where a child is accommodated voluntarily by the Trust, is felt to be in need of a particular course of treatment urgently and the parents cannot be contacted. If, in all the circumstances of the case, the decision is likely to cause controversy at some future date, the Trust should seek an Article 8 specific issue order. Trusts will not, however, be able to do this if the child is subject to a care order, as the only Article order which may be made in such cases is a residence order.

That it will now be appropriate for the court to use this order is evident from the ruling in *Re R (A Minor) (Blood Transfusion)*.[45]

---

42 As in *Re P (A Minor)(Education)* [1992] 1 FLR 316 CA.
43 As in *Re D (A Minor)(Removal from the Jurisdiction)* [1992] 1 All ER 892 CA.
44 Children (NI) Order 1995, Guidance and Regulations, vol. 1, para 4.20.
45 [1993] Fam Law, vol. 23, 577.

4. Prohibited Steps Order (PSO)

A PSO replaces the prerogative powers previously available to the judiciary in wardship proceedings.

(a) Definition

Article 8(1) of the 1995 Order states that

> 'prohibited steps order' means an order that no step which could be taken by a parent in meeting his parental responsibility for a child, and which is of a kind specified in the order, shall be taken by any person without the consent of the court.

It may be made *ex parte*.

(b) Applicants/Eligibility

Under Article 10(4) a parent or guardian may apply as of right as may any person who has a RO in respect of the child concerned. All others, including the child, may only do so with leave of the court.

(c) Effects

A PSO enables the court to place a veto against the exercise of specific aspects of parental responsibility, such as a threatened removal of the child in question from the jurisdiction,[46] from a particular school or to prohibit a specific medical operation. It replaces the traditional use of wardship to restrain contact between children and undesirable third parties and as stated in the Guidance and Regulations:[47]

> The purpose of the prohibited steps order, however, is to impose a specific restriction on the exercise of parental responsibility instead of the vague requirement in wardship that no 'important step' be taken in respect of the child without the court's consent. It could, for example, be used to prohibit a child's removal from the country where no residence order has been made and therefore no automatic restriction on removal applies or to prevent the child's removal from his home before the court has had time to decide what order, if any, should be made.

While the issue in question must relate to an aspect of parental responsibility, the order can be made against any person whether or not they are vested with such responsibility. It may, therefore, be made against an unmarried father or a former cohabitee to restrain that person from contacting the applicant. Under Article 11(7) the court may attach conditions to a PSO.

(d) Limitations

A PSO cannot be made in respect of a child in care. Unlike the range of powers available in wardship, a PSO, in common with all Article 8 orders, may have to be

---

46 This in fact was the type of activity instanced as the rationale for such an order by the Law Commission (no. 172, para 4.20).
47 Children (NI) Order 1995, Guidance and Regulations, vol. 1, para 4.16.

buttressed by a separate application for an injunction where the offending matter or behaviour cannot be construed as strictly parental. Where the authority required is to prevent parents from contacting each other,[48] then an injunction rather than a PSO is appropriate. When one parent wishes to bar the other from his or her home, then, as was pointed out by Sir Stephen Brown,[49] 'it is very doubtful whether a PSO could in any circumstances be used to "oust" a father from the matrimonial home'.

Under Article 9(5)(a) neither a PSO nor a SIO may be made where the objective is one which may be achieved by making a RO or a contact order. The Court of Appeal[50] recently had cause to examine the relative merits of a contact order and a PSO as the means for providing a mother with the authority necessary to prevent a former cohabitee from contacting children in respect of whom he was judged to considered to pose a risk. Butler-Sloss LJ, giving judgment for the court, held that a PSO would be more appropriate as liability for a breach would then lie against the cohabitee whereas under a contact order it would lie against the mother.

IV. Other Orders Available to the Court in Private Proceedings

A flexibility of response is available to the court in private proceedings. Although it may no longer direct that a child be committed to care, there are a number of orders other than or, in some instances, in addition to Article 8 orders which it may make.

1. Family Assistance Order (FAO)

Article 16 of the 1995 Order states that

> (1) Where, in any family proceedings, the court has power to make an order under this Part with respect to any child, it may (whether or not it makes such an order) make an order requiring an authority to make a suitably qualified person available, to advise, assist and (where appropriate) befriend any person named in the order.

The persons who may be named in the order are, as stated in the Guidance and Regulations,[51]

> (a) any parent or guardian of the child;
> (b) any person with whom the child is living or in whose favour a contact order is in force with respect to the child;
> (c) the child himself.

Instead or as well as making an Article 8 order, the court may elect to make this minimal interventionist order. A FAO is of a 'hybrid' type in that it is equally applicable to private and public family law matters. Article 16(3)(a) requires the court to be satisfied

---

48 As in *Croydon London Borough Council v A and Others* [1992] Fam 169.
49 See *Nottingham County Council v P* [1993] 3 All ER 815, 825b CA.
50 See *Re H (Prohibited Steps Order)* [1995] 1 FLR 638 CA.
51 Children (NI) Order 1995, Guidance and Regulations, vol. 1, para 2.50.

that the circumstances are exceptional and that it has the consent of all parties (excluding that of the child) before it can make such an order. Under Article 16(4) the order may require any person named in it to take specified steps to keep the relevant officer informed of any change of address and permit that officer to visit. It continues in effect for a maximum period of six months, unless the court specifies a shorter period. It also suffers from the considerable disadvantage of being unenforceable in the face of a Trust plea of inadequate resources.[52]

2. Parental Responsibility Order (PRO)

Article 7 of the 1995 Order states that

> (1) Where a child's father and mother were not married to each other at the time of his birth —
> (a) the court may, on the application of the father, order that he shall have parental responsibility for the child.

This order provides the means whereby an unmarried father who is unable or unwilling to acquire parental responsibility for his child by making a voluntary agreement with the mother may be vested with such responsibility by the court. Where a father has been previously convicted of violence against the mother and of cruel behaviour towards the child, then the court[53] will refuse his application for this order. The court has decided[54] that where the following tests were satisfied, then it would *prima facie* be in the child's best interests for a PRO to be made: (a) the degree of commitment which the father had shown to the child; (b) the degree of attachment which existed between them; and (c) the father's reasons for applying for the order.[55]

The order lasts until terminated by the court on the application of any person with parental responsibility for the child or, with the leave of the court, the application of the child concerned (see also Chapter Four).

3. Order Directing an Investigation of the Child's Circumstances

Article 56 of the 1995 Order states that

> (1) Where, in any family proceedings in which a question arises with respect to the welfare of any child, it appears to the court that it may be appropriate for a care or a supervision order to be made with respect to him, the court may direct the appropriate authority to undertake an investigation of the child's circumstances.

As a 'hybrid' type of order with equal application to private and to public family law issues, this type of order is more commonly associated with the latter (see further Chapter Twelve).

---

52 See, for example, *Re C (Family Assistance Order)* [1996] 1 FLR 424.
53 As in *Re T (A Minor)(Parental Responsibility: Contact)* [1993] 2 FLR 450.
54 See *Re H (Illegitimate Children: Father: Parental Rights)(No 2)* [1991] 1 FLR 214.
55 This approach was later endorsed by the court in *Re G (A Minor)(Parental Responsibility Order)* [1994] 1 FLR 504.

4. Order Appointing a Guardian for the Child

Article 159 of the 1995 Order states that

> (1) Where an application with respect to a child is made by any individual, the High Court or a county court may by order appoint that individual to be the child's guardian if —
> (a) the child has no parent with parental responsibility for him; or
> (b) a residence order has been made with respect to the child in favour of a parent or guardian of his who has died while the order was in force.

This order may also be made by the court of its own initiative in any family proceedings. Again, this is a hybrid type of order which may be made in the course of either private or public family law proceedings (see also Chapter Eight).

5. Orders for Financial Relief with Respect to Children

Article 15 and Schedule 1 of the 1995 Order enable the court to make orders for the financial relief of children who are the subject of residential orders; though not in favour of a parent or step-parent.

CHAPTER THIRTEEN

Children in Need and Their Families

Introduction

This chapter deals with consensual state intervention in the affairs of the family, for the purposes of supporting vulnerable parenting arrangements, as governed by Part 1V of the Children (NI) Order 1995. Such intervention did not begin in Northern Ireland with the 1995 Order. Under both the Children and Young Persons Act (NI) 1968 and the Health and Personal Social Services (NI) Order 1972, there were provisions which laid such responsibilities on the Health and Social Services Boards (now 'Trusts'). As always, it remains difficult to disentangle the welfare of the child from parental incapacity. Before the introduction of the 1995 Order, the *Black Report*[1] offered the most authoritative indigenous testimony to such difficulties. Now, the net effect of the 'no-order' presumption and the principle that a child's welfare is best assured by arrangements which allow for that child to be brought up and cared for within his or her family of origin is to place a firm legislative onus on a Trust to direct assistance towards child and parent. The legislative intent is to further the welfare of a child by measures which assist the coping capacity of the parent.

This chapter identifies and explains Trust responsibilities to provide support for children in need and their families, as statutorily defined by the 1995 Order. In particular it examines the judicial and agency interpretation of support responsibilities under the equivalent provisions of the Children Act 1989 in England and Wales.

Statistical Data in Relation to Children in Need

It has been noted[2] that Northern Ireland has the largest average household size with a greater proportion of households containing children than in the United Kingdom as a whole. It continues to have one of the youngest populations in western Europe with 24.2 per cent aged under 15 years. Northern Ireland also has had the worst record on child-care provision in the EC (children aged up to four are twenty-five per cent less likely to attend playgroups than are children in the rest of the United Kingdom and the EC). Only two to six per 1,000 children in Northern Ireland will be provided with day care, while in Scandinavian countries day care and playgroups are provided for seventy-five to eighty per cent of young children.

However, evidence of improvement in recent years is presented in the DHSS annual report for 1995 which states:

---

1 See *Report of the Children and Young Persons Review Group*, HMSO, 1979.
2 See *Proposal for a Draft Children (NI) Order, a Response* SACHR, 1993.

Day care, which includes playgroups, childminding, and day nurseries is generally provided by voluntary organisations, community groups and private organisations and is the main form of family support in Northern Ireland. The greatest increase in the level of day care has been in day nursery provision, which has trebled in the past 5 years. There has been a 57 per cent increase in the number of registered childminders over the same period.[3]

The Welfare of the Child: A Preventative Approach

In Northern Ireland the importance of the link between deprivation and child-care problems was highlighted by the committee led by Sir Harold Black which was set up in 1976 to review and make recommendations in respect of the related law. The work and findings of the committee, though spanning almost three years, concluded in a submission that did little more than fully endorse the findings of its English predecessor the *Houghton Report*.[4] However, the *Black Report* continues to offer the only relatively recent compilation of evidence relating to indigenous child-care needs and remains an authoritative assessment of the preventative role of the law in that context.

Prevention

The Black Committee had no doubt as to what needed to be done to address the needs of children and their families in Northern Ireland:

> The approach which we recommend lays emphasis on prevention. Where problems do occur, early and accurate identification of the specific difficulties is desirable followed by co-ordinated, flexible and effective action. We advocate a comprehensive and integrated approach to the provision of help and support for children whose personality, background or circumstances leave them ill-equipped to cope with the demands and pressures of society. . . . [W]e are conscious that help for children in need can most appropriately and effectively be provided within a family setting. But the family may need support and must be able to look for this to the wider community, which has a direct responsibility for the future of its children.[5]

This important statement of principle is followed by more particular recommendations for directing assistance.[6]

---

3 See *Annual Report of the Chief Inspector, Social Services Inspectorate, NI,* 1995, p 60, DHSS.
4 See *Report of the Departmental Committee on the Adoption of Children,* HMSO 1972.
5 F/n 1, para 3.3
6 In respect of the structural causes of child welfare needs, the committee suggests that: 'Better housing, better recreational facilities, increased employment opportunities, adequate family income, education in family planning will all create a supportive framework within which the relationships of the family can develop' (para 3.5). Asserting that 'In the majority of cases it will be in the child's best interests to attempt to prevent the disintegration of the family unit', they urge that 'the various agencies concerned should take all possible steps to identify the needs of the child' and 'appropriate support' should be provided to help a family 'through periods of temporary strain and crisis' (para 3.6). The committee goes on to make specific recommendations for channelling assistance through health visitors, schools, an extended

Influence of Extra-Jurisdictional Developments in Child-Care Policy and Law

The United Kingdom is not a signatory to the European Convention for the Protection of Human Rights and Fundamental Freedoms (1953; Cmnd 8969). It has yet to ratify the UN Declaration on Social and Legal Principles relating to the Protection and Welfare of Children with special reference to Foster Placement and Adoption Nationally and Internationally (1986). Article 3 of this Declaration states that 'the first priority for a child is to be cared for by his or her own parents'. Nor has it yet ratified the 1993 Hague Convention on Inter-Country Adoption. Their influence has, nonetheless, contributed to shaping the development of family law within these islands. Following a number of cases in which the Court of Human Rights has ruled against the United Kingdom as being in breach of the former Convention, the House of Lords and Westminster are now paying close attention to Convention principles when interpreting or framing family law provisions.

The United Nations Convention on the Rights of the Child (1989), which received UK ratification in 1991, is also exercising an increasing influence on our legal system. In particular this Convention, which ascribes primary responsibility to the parents for the upbringing and the development of the child, requires that 'State Parties shall render appropriate assistance to parents and legal guardians in the performance of their child-rearing responsibilities' and 'ensure that children of working parents have the right to benefit from child care services and facilities for which they are eligible'(Article 18). It further requires State Parties to 'recognise the right of every child to a standard of living adequate for the child's physical, mental, spiritual, moral and social development' (Article 27). This is now becoming a benchmark document against which present and potential UK family law legislation must be tested.

The Children (NI) Order 1995: Consensual Statutory Intervention

The 1995 Order sets out a range of provisions intended to place on a Trust the responsibility and authority to support vulnerable parenting arrangements and safeguard a child's relationships with the members of his or her family of origin. They give effect to three principles which are fundamental to this statute. First, the legislative intent is now to preserve the legal integrity and privacy of the family unit wherever possible; this is to be achieved by restricting coercive intervention to circumstances where a Trust can convince the court that evidence exists to overcome the 'no-order' presumption and to satisfy the 'significant harm' test. Second, the legislative thrust is for parents and the Trust to work in partnership to secure the welfare interests of children; in the furtherance of this aim, the Trust is to make certain support services available to parents. Finally, specific importance is attached to maintaining a child's links with the members of his or her family of origin; to this end a duty is placed on a Trust to promote the up-bringing of children by their families and to promote contact between a child and his or her parents in circumstances where a child is being accommodated by that agency.

---

day care service for the under five's, local community groups, and new professional networks established to co-ordinate and focus care provision for children in need.

However, these principles are given effect through two different sets of provisions. There are those which are 'universalist' in nature in that they have a broad application to all children and essentially continue the responsibility of a Health and Social Services Board under the Children and Young Persons Act (NI) 1968 to maintain an overview of service spread and related standards and to ensure the protection of children in certain circumstances. Then there are those provisions which, by placing new, specific duties on a Trust in relation to the support requirements of vulnerable family units, positively discriminate in favour of 'children in need'. The latter provisions are to be found in Part IV and Schedule 2 of the 1995 Order while the former are to be found also in Parts X, XI, XII.

The general public service brief of a Trust, as provided for in Part I of the 1968 Act in respect of all children within its area, is to some extent continued under the 1995 Order. What has not been continued is the approach to service provision which required Boards to ensure the creation and growth of a platform of local preventative services. The general statutory duty is now restricted to those who meet the definition 'children in need'. This approach is very much in keeping with the more restrained interventionist ethic which characterises this legislation.

Recent research conducted by David Utting[7] offers a discouraging assessment of the effectiveness of consensual state intervention, following implementation of the same family support provisions on the other side of the Irish Sea. Preventative services continue to be concentrated on parents whose children are on the child protection registers rather than those identified as vulnerable due, for example, to marital stress or material deprivation. There was little evidence that the anticipated partnership between statutory and voluntary agencies had generated any effective strategies for targeting localised preventative services towards vulnerable families. Given the traditional reliance on the voluntary sector in Northern Ireland, it is probable that such preventative work will largely be left to such agencies while the Trusts continue to direct resources almost exclusively at those families where the needs require a protectionist form of intervention.

The Broad Support Responsibilities of a Trust

The Children (NI) Order 1995 outlines a Trust's preventative responsibilities in respect of children who, without support, might become 'children in need'. These may be seen as establishing a minimum baseline from which a Trust may ratchet up the deployment of its consensual and coercive intervention resources. They consist of certain powers which are employed at a Trust's discretion to alleviate the difficulties of those whose circumstances are not so extreme as to satisfy the 'children in need' test. They consist, also, of certain duties which a Trust owes in general to the children resident in its area. Both largely take the form of registration and monitoring responsibilities in respect of privately run care facilities for children.

---

[7] See *Family and Parenthood: Supporting Families, Preventing Breakdown*, Rowntree Foundation (1995).

Child Minding and Day Care

As was observed in the *Black Report*:[8]

> Without the provision of adequate day care arrangements for the under five's there is a grave danger that a number of children will continue to suffer neglect . . . and to experience some form of social, emotional or intellectual impairment.

By the early 1990s the existence of considerable numbers of unregistered child-minding and playgroup facilities was being widely reported.

The law governing child minding and day care is now to be found in Part IX and Part XI, respectively, of the 1995 Order. Further detail is available in the Child Minding and Day-Care (Applications for Registration) Regulations (NI) 1996, the Disqualification for Caring for Children Regulations (NI) 1996 and the Exempted Supervised Activities (Children) Regulations (NI) 1996.

1. Definition

Under Article 119:

> (1) For the purposes of this Part a person acts as a child minder if
> (a) he looks after one or more children under the age of eight (whether for reward or not); and
> (b) the period, or the total of the periods, which he spends so looking after children in any day exceeds two hours.

Such a person is defined as a child minder if he or she is looking after a child or children in respect of whom he or she is neither the parent, relative, an authorised foster parent nor a person who has parental responsibility. Where a child is being looked after on premises other than 'domestic premises' (as defined by Article 118(2)) for more than six days in a year, then the person looking after the child must be registered as providing day care. Any person intending to provide such a service must apply in advance to the local Trust for registration. If such a person is providing care for a continuous period of less than four hours a day, then he or she must be registered as providing sessional day care. If the care period is for four hours or more in any one day, then the person must be registered as providing full day care.

2. Duties of a Trust

The protection afforded a parent who privately places a child with such persons is governed by Articles 19 and 20 of the 1995 Order and provided by the system of registration, certification, notification and inspection as implemented through duties placed on the Trusts under Part XI (Articles 118–32) of the 1995 Order and under the Child Minding and Day-Care Regulations 1996 (including a duty to review under

---

8   See f/n 1, para 3.29.

Article 20(1)(b)). Article 118 outlines the duty to register and thereafter inspect (see also Article 130) any domestic premises which are used for child-minding purposes within a Trust's area. As Article 120 makes clear, it is the place as much as the person which must be registered, and therefore, where a person provides day care in more than one place, separate registration is required for each place. Article 125 details the requirements to be met by child minders if they are to be registered by their local Trust. These include provisions relating to the total number of children, the number within each age group, the safety of the premises, the keeping of records and the equipment to be provided. The powers and responsibilities of the Trusts in relation to the inspection of registered premises and the working arrangements within are set out in Article 131.

3. Requirements for Registration

It is the service per se, rather than the service as it affects an individual child, which is the subject of these provisions. So, the person providing care for more than two hours in a day, even if no individual child is being looked after for more than one hour and no charge is made, will come within these statutory controls.

In determining whether the service meets the criteria for registration, a Trust will assess separately the fitness of the care provider and the fitness of the premises.

Whether a person is fit to provide a child-minding or day-care service will be determined according to the advice of the DHSS in the Children (NI) Order 1995 Guidance and Regulations, volume 2, *Family Support: Day Care and Education for Young Children* 1996. In making an assessment a Trust will have regard to such matters as previous experience, qualifications and training, ability to provide warm and consistent care, multi-cultural awareness, capacity to treat each child as an individual, physical health, attitudes and the existence of any criminal record involving the abuse of children. These criteria must be applied not only to every applicant seeking registration but also to all persons living or working on the premises to be registered.

Whether premises are fit for the purpose of child minding or day care will also be determined in accordance with the advice provided by the DHSS under the above mentioned Guidance and Regulations. In making its assessment a Trust will have regard to such matters as the suitability of the premises in the light of its facilities, situation, construction and size.

4. Refusal of Registration and De-Registration

Article 122 of the 1995 Order disqualifies certain persons from being registered as either a child minder or day-care provider. The reasons for disqualification relate to prescribed offences, orders and requirements made under this or other provisions. Without the written consent of a Trust, any disqualified person is prohibited from providing, or having a financial involvement in the provision of, child-minding and day-care services.

Under Article 124 an application for registration will be refused if the applicant, or any person living in or employed on the premises to be registered and who may be involved in caring for children, is 'not fit to look after children under the age of twelve' or, in certain circumstances, is 'not fit to be in the proximity of children under the age of twelve'. Breach of this requirement may ground an action for negligence.[9] Under paragraph (5) a Trust may also refuse registration if the premises to be used for child minding or for day care 'are not fit to be used for looking after children under the age of twelve, whether because of their condition, or the condition of any equipment used on the premises or for any reason connected with their situation, construction or size'. In a recent case[10] in London, which received considerable media attention, registration was refused to a Mrs Davis, a graduate with primary school teaching experience and child-minding experience, because she refused to comply with the 'no-smacking' requirement in the Guidance on the Children Act 1989. In this case the parent had given permission and smacking was viewed as not constituting a breach of Article 3 of the Convention ('inhuman and degrading punishment').[11] As Wilson J observed, in relation to the status of the Guidance, it '. . . is not intended to be applied so strictly that, if an application for registration is in conflict with part of it, there should automatically be a finding of unfitness.'

Under Article 128 registration may be cancelled at the discretion of a Trust if the care is seriously inadequate having regard to the needs of a child, on contravention of a stipulated requirement or on failure to pay the annual fee within the prescribed time. Emergency protection may be provided under Article 129. Failure to carry out repairs, to make alterations or additions as previously instructed will also justify a cancellation. Powers of enforcement are provided by Article 132.

Fourteen days' notice must be given by a Trust of any intention to refuse or cancel any registration, and this notice must state the reasons for such action. A person aggrieved has a right of appeal.

5. Consequences of Registration

The certificate issued by a Trust following a successful application for registration may, under Articles 125 and 126, impose any condition the Trust thinks fit in respect of matters such as the maximum number of children, security and equipment, record keeping and staffing. Once registered, the premises for child minding or day care may be entered by Trust officials at any time under the inspection powers available in Article 130. Inspection may be made of the building, the care of the children, staffing arrangements, records and any other matters stipulated on the certificate of registration.

Private Arrangements for Fostering Children

Part X, Articles 106–17, of the 1995 Order deal with the responsibilities of a Trust in relation to private arrangements for fostering children. Further detail is given in the Children (Private Arrangements for Fostering) Regulations (NI) 1996.

Under Article 106(1) of the 1995 Order a 'privately fostered child' means a child who is cared for and provided with accommodation by someone other than

---

9 See *T v Surrey County Council* [1994] 4 All ER 577.
10 See *London Borough of Sutton v Davies* [1994] 1 FLR 737.
11 See also *Costello-Roberts v UK* [1994] ECR1 and *R v Hopley* (1860) 2 F & F 202.

(a) a parent of his;
(b) a person who is not a parent of his but who has parental responsibility for him; or
(c) a relative of his.

Article 106(1) defines the term 'foster a child privately' somewhat unhelpfully as meaning to 'look after the child in circumstances in which he is a privately fostered child'.

1. Child

For the purposes of this provision 'a child means a person under the age of sixteen, or, if he is disabled, under the age of eighteen'. Under Article 107(1)(a) to meet the definition the child must be cared for and accommodated for a period of at least twenty-eight days. These and the other provisions of Part X of the 1995 Order dealing with private arrangements for fostering children are subject to further re-definition under Schedule 8, the effect of which is to harden the distinction between domestic and fostering arrangements. So, a child will fall outside the definition if he or she is:

1. being looked after by a Trust; or
2. lives in accommodation provided by a voluntary organisation; or is
3. in a school in which he receives full-time education;
4. in a hospital, nursing or mental nursing home; or
5. is subject to a supervision order.

Again, a child will not be regarded as privately fostered if he or she is living in the same premises as a parent, a person having parental responsibility or a relative who has assumed care responsibility.

2. Private Fostering

As stated in the Guidance and Regulations,

> [p]rivate fostering is the arrangement usually made between the parent and the private foster parent, who becomes responsible for caring for the child in such a way as to promote and safeguard his welfare.[12]

The responsibility for ensuring that the arrangements made do in fact safeguard and promote the welfare of the child concerned rests with the parent.

3. Trust Powers and Duties

Under Article 108 a Trust is required to satisfy itself that the welfare of any child privately fostered in its area is being 'satisfactorily safeguarded and promoted' and that those providing care are appropriately advised. However, as stated in the Guidance and Regulations,

---

12 The Children (NI) Order 1995, Guidance and Regulations, vol. 3, para 13.3.

[a] Trust does not approve or register private foster parents. A proper balance, therefore, needs to be maintained between parental responsibilities and statutory duties towards private foster children.[13]

It must investigate the suitability of any arrangement prior to placement and is required to carry out inspectoral visits thereafter. Article 111 enables a Trust to stipulate requirements in respect of the number, age and sex of the children who may be privately fostered and it may require special equipment and medication to be available. Further, Schedule 5 of the 1995 Order includes private foster parents within its strictures relating to limits on the number of foster children and the related complaints procedures.

Under Articles 109 and 110 a Trust may disqualify and prohibit respectively certain persons from being private foster parents. It may set requirements in respect of same and address ancillary matters regarding notification, appeals, advertising, insurance and the committal of offences.

4. Responsibilities of Parents and Carers

In respect of any proposed private fostering arrangement, the persons making the arrangement, making the placement and receiving the child must all serve advance notice of their intentions on the local Trust; except in emergencies. Also, parents, or those with parental responsibility, must similarly serve notice. This requirement applies where they have knowledge of any such proposed arrangement regardless of whether they are involved in making it.

The General Protection Responsibilities of a Trust and Others towards Children and Young Persons

Part XII of the 1995 Order sets out the law regarding the employment of children and deals with the Trusts' related protection responsibilities. The law imposing a duty on others to protect children in certain circumstances is to be found across a range of legislation such as the Children and Young Persons (Protection from Tobacco)(NI) Order 1991 which prohibits the sale of tobacco to children, the Licensing (NI) Order 1990 which prohibits the purchase of alcohol by minors, the Intoxicating Substances (Supply) Act 1985 which aims to prevent the sale of solvents to children and the Homosexual Offences (NI) Order 1982 which seeks to protect underage boys from sexual abuse by men.

Children and Employment

The Employment (Miscellaneous Provisions)(NI) Order 1990 removed from the 1968 Act the universalist protective measures designed to regulate the circumstances in which young persons, as opposed to children, could be employed.[14] Part XII of the

---

13 The Children (NI) Order 1995, Guidance and Regulations, vol. 3, para 13.4.
14 As was stated in the *Black Report*: 'There is nothing inherently wrong with children aged between thirteen and sixteen working to some extent while they are at school and to a greater extent during school holidays' (para 4.53). The caveat to this approach is, as stated

1995 Order gives effect to the approach of the Black committee and extends the Order's general non-interventionist ethic into the area of employment. The absolute prohibition against the employment of children is tightly confined by Article 135 which states:

(1) No child shall be employed —
    (a) so long as he is under the age of 13 years; or
    (b) before the close of school hours on any day on which he is required to attend school; or
    (c) before seven o'clock in the morning or after seven o'clock in the evening on any day; or
    (d) for more than two hours on any day on which he is required to attend school.

These prohibitive provisions virtually repeat those contained in section 37 of the 1968 Act. Article 135 prevents the employment of children in any occupation likely to be injurious to their life, limbs, health or education and from engaging in any street trading. Other restrictions specified in the 1968 Act also continue to effect the range of employment opportunities for children. For example, section 37 also prohibits the employment of a child for more than two hours on a Sunday.

The employment of children is, however, subject to certain conditions. The first of these rests on the definition of 'child' under Article 133 as 'a person who is not over school-leaving age' which in turn means 'the upper limit of school-leaving age'. This implies that it is the actual age at which a particular child is entitled to leave school, rather than a standard application of the sixteen-year rule, which is all important. In effect this will vary from fifteen years and eight months to sixteen years and seven months.

The restrictions on the employment of children in the performing arts are the subject of considerably detailed provisions in both Part XII of this Order and Part III of the 1968 Act. Basically, before children can be so employed a licence will have to obtained from the relevant ELB.

Children in Need

I. *The Consensual Intervention Threshold*

The concept of 'children in need' sets the threshold for consensual intervention by a Trust in family affairs on child welfare grounds just as 'significant harm' does in respect of coercive intervention. It is a concept rooted in a philosophy which sees the vulnerable family as entitled to support services from the State and it underpins both a statutory onus on a Trust to be proactive in seeking out such children and a statutory duty to target sufficient resources to maintain them, where practicable, in their families. This is markedly different from the blanket responsibility, which rested lightly on a Board under the Children and Young Persons Act (NI) 1968 (sections 53, 103, 163 and 164)

---

    in Article 7(3) of the European Social Charter, that 'persons who are still subject to compulsory education shall not be employed in such work as would deprive them of the full benefit of their education'.

and the Health and Personal Social Services (NI) Order 1972 (Article 15) to prevent child-care proceedings by reacting with services of advice and assistance to eligible claimants. The legislative intent is that in future the role of a Trust, in relation to its preventative responsibilities, should be to develop a needs-led rather than a demand-led approach to service provision. This approach is very much in keeping with that advocated in Article 18 of the UN Convention which emphasises the desirability of state intervention being in the form of partnership with parents so as to enable them to give effect to their parental responsibilities.

1. Definition of 'Children in Need'

Article 17 of the 1995 Order states

> For the purposes of this Part a child shall be taken to be in need if —
> (a) he is unlikely to achieve or maintain, or to have the opportunity of achieving or maintaining, a reasonable standard of health or development without the provision for him of services by an authority under this Part'
> (b) his health or development is likely to be significantly impaired, or further impaired, without the provision for him of such services; or
> (c) he is disabled, and 'family' in relation to such a child, includes any person who has parental responsibility for the child and any other person with whom he has been living.

This provision reflects a legislative intent to incorporate a number of not wholly compatible objectives. For example, a primary objective would seem to be to lay inclusive service responsibilities on a Trust; so certain categories of need are explicitly stated as giving use to a Trust duty. At the same time it is apparent that there is a wish to avoid granting reciprocal service entitlement rights to those who may meet this definition; so there is a lack of specificity in defining eligibility criteria.

(a) Children 'Unlikely to Achieve or Maintain . . . a Reasonable Standard of Health or Development'

Under Article 2 of the 1995 Order 'health' is to be interpreted as meaning 'physical or mental health' and 'development' as 'physical, intellectual, emotional, social or behavioural development'. The significance of the word 'unlikely' is that it clearly imports a requirement that a Trust act in a preventative fashion to forestall the prospect of a child becoming a 'child in need'. The legislative intent is to prompt the Trusts to correct the approach they have adopted in recent years towards their preventative and protective duties. In order to redress the balance previously struck in favour of resource investment for the latter at the expense of the former (on the grounds that in the long-run this may prove to be a more cost effective form of intervention), a firm duty is now placed on the Trusts to ensure the early identification of children in need, including the disabled and, by providing services appropriate to their health and development, to promote the upbringing of such children by their families.

The problem with this provision is that its lack of specificity may allow its intent to be subverted by the pressures on the cash-limited Trusts to continue giving child protection the highest priority. Experience in England and Wales indicates that this provision is being interpreted as a licence to lower the 'significant harm' threshold, thus allowing agency resources to be targeted at those already within the ambit of coercive intervention, rather than as an obligation to prevent private vulnerable parenting arrangements from becoming matters of public concern. This is apparent, for example, in Table 3.1 of the annual Children Act Report (1992) which shows that in the first year of the Children Act the local authorities were directing resources towards families for whom they already had some level of responsibility rather than towards those whose vulnerability was indicated only by difficulties such as rent arrears, disconnected services or school attendance problems. As Dingwall has observed, there is a tendency towards 'diagnostic inflation' in child protection cases in order to access resources.

(b) Children Whose 'Health or Development Is Likely to Be Significantly Impaired'

Again, the 'likelihood' factor implies that a duty rests on the Trusts to invest resources in a preventative strategy. However, the degree of risk necessary to constitute a likelihood and the extent to which an 'impairment' may need to deteriorate before this becomes 'significant' are both open to question. It may be that a Trust could offer a good defence for not investing preventative resources by claiming that its interpretation of a situation did not lead it to believe that, relative to other situations already within its child protection remit, the level of risk or the significance of probable impairment warranted a diverting of funds.

(c) Children Who Are 'Disabled'[15]

Under Article 2 of the 1995 Order 'disabled' means 'blind, deaf or dumb or suffering from mental disorder of any kind or substantially or permanently handicapped by illness, injury or congenital deformity or such other disability as may be prescribed' (other relevant provisions in the Order are: Article 27(9), Schedule 2, paragraphs 3, 4 and 7).

As stated in the Guidance and Regulations:

> Trusts should ensure that work with children with a disability is carried out with particular regard to the following:
>
> - the welfare of the child should be safeguarded and promoted by those providing services;
> - a primary aim should be to promote access for all children to the same range of services;
> - children with a disability are children first;
> - recognition of the importance of parents and families in children's lives;
> - partnership between parents and Trusts and other agencies;
> - the views of children and parents should be sought and taken into account.[16]

The inclusion of children who are disabled within the general definition of 'children in need' is an important landmark in the development of the law relating to children

---

15 See Monteith, McCrystal and Iwaniec *Children and Young People with Disabilities in NI*, Centre for Child Care Research, QUB (1997) for a useful overview of needs and services.
16 The Children (NI) Order 1995, Guidance and Regulations, vol. 5, para 1.5.

in Northern Ireland. For the first time it has not been seen necessary to make separate legislative provision for the disabled. This reflects an acceptance of the principle that for children a recognition of what they share in common by virtue of their childhood is of greater importance than that which may, for whatever reason, separate them.[17] Legislating specifically for the difference between 'normal' and disabled children and then between disabled children on the basis of disability type (i.e. learning disability and physical disability) is now seen as an inappropriate form of discrimination which can be associated with a degree of stigma and is unacceptable in a modern pluralist culture.[18] However, differentiating between children on the basis of the gravity of their needs within the same legislation is seen as acceptable. To that extent this provision does positively discriminate in favour of 'children in need'.

Schedule 2(3) of the 1995 Order requires every Trust to open and maintain a register of disabled children in its area; computers may be used for this purpose.

2. Identification of Children in Need

Schedule 2 of the 1995 Order states that

> 1. Every authority shall take reasonable steps to identify the extent to which there are children in need within the authority's area.

Schedule 2(4) empowers a Trust to assess, for the purposes of this Order, the needs of any child appearing to be a 'child in need' at the same as any assessment is being made under any other statutory provision. The directive 'shall take reasonable steps' emphasises the obligation on the Trusts to be proactive rather than reactive in the delivery of its preventative services.

II. The Duties of a Trust

1. General Duty

Article 18 of the 1995 Order states:

> (1) It shall be the general duty of every authority (in addition to the other duties placed on them by this Part)
>> (a) to safeguard and promote the welfare of children within the authority's area who are in need; and
>> (b) so far as is consistent with that duty, to promote the upbringing of such children by their families, by providing a range and level of personal social services appropriate to those children's needs.

---

17 It also reflects the principles embodied in Article 23 of the United Nations Convention on the Rights of the Child (1989).
18 Separate legislation continues to make additional provision for children with 'special needs': see the Chronically Sick and Disabled Persons (NI) Act 1978, sections 1 and 2; the Mental Health Order 1986, Articles 33 and 39; the Education and Libraries (NI) Order 1986, Articles 26–36; the Education (NI) Order 1987; and, in due course, the Disability Discrimination Act 1996. For a full picture of the law as it relates to the needs of disabled children in Northern Ireland, reference must also be made to this legislation.

The use of the word 'general' is intended to indicate that the duty on a Trust is to plan and deliver services broadly appropriate to the needs which vulnerable children as a group would have in common. Its effect is to statutorily over-rule the decision in *AG (ex rel Tiley) v London Borough of Wandsworth*[19] which determined that a Trust's counterpart across the Irish Sea would be expected to anticipate the consequences of its actions for the welfare of a particular child. In that case the agency was held to be liable to a claimant who, having met the agency specified eligibility criteria, had nonetheless been denied the corresponding service. The agency's plea of insufficient finance was found to be an inadequate defence. However, enforceability continues to be problematic.[20]

(a) Towards Children in Need

A 'child in need' may on occasion also be a 'child at risk of significant harm', while the reverse is always the case. Such an overlap of thresholds may occur in situations where it comes to the attention of a Trust that a child particularly susceptible to harm (perhaps due to 'special needs') is exposed to a level of stress which, though insufficient to require protection for an 'average' child, carries a significant level of risk for that child. An assessment by a Trust social worker of a breakdown in parenting arrangements occurring in a public or private context may reveal no statutory duty of coercive intervention but may alert the Trust to the presence of a particularly vulnerable child for whom the 'family' requires support services.

(b) To Promote Upbringing within Families

'Family', as defined in Article 17, includes any person who has parental responsibility for the child and any other person with whom the child has been living, whether or not a relative. It will not extend to include a person — relative or friend — no matter how close the relationship unless the child has in fact also been living with them. This very wide definition will apply to situations where direct care responsibility for a child has been borne for some time by a carer such as a neighbour, foster parent or by a relative such as a grand-parent. Any service which serves to safeguard and promote the welfare of a child may be provided to the 'family' as a whole or to any member of it.

(c) Range and Level of Appropriate Services

The duty is one to which it is the collective responsibility of the constituent parts of a Trust to respond; because any or all of its services may be required, a multi-disciplinary team approach is required. This is also likely to have important consequences for entitlement in other areas, i.e. success or failure in meeting the terms of the definition will trigger an entitlement to all or none of the spectrum of such related public services as housing, phones and benefits. Under Article 46 of the Order a number of agencies are directed to co-operate with a Trust requesting assistance for any child in need:

---

19 [1981] 1 All ER 1162.
20 See, for example, *R v Royal Borough of Kingston Upon Thames, ex parte T* [1994] 1 FLR 798.

(2) A body whose help is so requested shall comply with the request if it is compatible with that body's own statutory or other duties and obligations and does not unduly prejudice the discharge of any of its functions.

(3) The bodies are —
  (a) any Board;
  (b) any education and library board;
  (c) any Health and Social Services trust or special agency;
  (d) any district council;
  (e) the Northern Ireland Housing Executive; and
  (f) such other persons as the Department may direct for the purposes of this Article.

For these reasons full implementation of the 1995 Order will only be successful if it is accompanied by a Trust child-care policy and strategy which sets a priority on the management of integrated teams of health and social service professionals accompanied by systems for co-ordinating its service provision with those of such other public service agencies as listed above.

2. Particular Duties

(a) Assistance

Assistance may be provided as a cash grant, a loan or as a grant of 'necessities' and may be subject to such conditions as a Trust shall see fit to make. Further, as outlined in Schedule 2 of the 1995 Order, more specific assistance may be offered.

(b) Family Centre Facilities

Under Schedule 2(10) of the 1995 Order a Trust has a general duty to provide such family centres as it considers appropriate within its area for a child, parents of that child or person with parental responsibilities or who may be caring for that child. The facilities offered by such a family centre should include occupational, social, cultural or recreational activities, advice, guidance or counselling or accommodation while receiving advice, guidance or counselling.

In relation to disabled children Schedule 2(7) requires a Trust to provide services to minimise the effects of their disabilities and to maximise opportunities to lead as normal lives as possible.

(c) Avoidance of Coercive Intervention

The directive in Article 18(1)(b) — that a Trust should seek to 'promote the upbringing of such children by their families' — is an important statement of principle which serves to reinforce the 'no-order' presumption embodied in Article 3(5). It is further addressed by a directive in Schedule 2(8) requiring every Trust to 'take reasonable steps' to reduce the need to bring proceedings in respect of children, encourage them not to commit criminal offences and avoid the need to place them in secure accommodation.

(d) Prevention of Neglect and Abuse

The preventative duties of a Trust are specifically addressed by Schedule 2(5) of the 1995 Order which requires that

> (1) Every authority shall take reasonable steps, through the provision of services under Part IV, to prevent children within the authority's area suffering ill-treatment or neglect.

A duty is also placed on any Trust to notify the relevant Trust when it believes that a child within its area but living or proposing to live elsewhere is likely to suffer harm.

(e) Provision for Children to Remain at Home

Schedule 2(9) places a duty on a Trust to provide the following services, as appropriate, in respect of children in need who are living with their families:

(a) advice, guidance and counselling;
(b) occupational, social, cultural or recreational activities;
(c) home help (which may include laundry facilities);
(d) facilities for, or assistance with, travelling to and from home for the purpose of taking advantage of any other service provided under this Order or of any similar service;
(e) assistance to enable the child concerned and his family to have a holiday.

This is the first explicit legislative statement of the services considered appropriate to the role of a Trust in the context of consensual intervention. It indicates the extent of public investment which is now considered reasonable in order to reinforce the coping capacity of vulnerable families.

(f) Maintenance of the Family Home

Where a child in need is not living with his or her family and is not being looked after by a Trust, then the latter is required under Schedule 2(11) to take such steps as are reasonably practicable to enable the child to live with that family or promote contact between them if, in the opinion of the Trust, this is necessary to safeguard or promote the child's welfare.

(g) Provision for Alternative Accommodation for Member of Household Posing a Risk to a Child

Schedule 2(6) of the 1995 Order gives a Trust a discretionary power to provide financial assistance to enable a person who may be causing a child to suffer, or who may do so in the future, to find alternative accommodation away from that child. This provision acknowledges the long-standing sense of grievance attached to the practice whereby, in order to afford future protection to a child at risk of abuse from a member of the household, the child was removed from the home. The fact that this is a discretionary responsibility and is not linked to a Trust power to apply for an exclusion order in respect of such a suspected abuser has attracted criticism.

(h) Publishing Information on Services

Under Schedule 2(2) of the 1995 Order every Trust is required to publish information about the support services it has a duty to provide for children in need and their families. It is also permitted to do so in respect of such services provided by other agencies, particularly by voluntary organisations, which it has a power to provide. Every Trust is specifically directed to 'take such steps as are reasonably practicable to ensure that those who might benefit from the services receive the information relevant to them'.

(i) Duty in Respect of Child's Racial Affiliation

Under Schedule 2(12) every Trust making arrangements for day care or for the recruitment of foster parents shall 'have regard to the different racial groups to which children within the Trust's area who are in need belong'. Significantly, this provision makes no concession to any difference between groups attributable to religion as opposed to race.

III. Specific Support Services

1. Day Care

Day care is defined by Article 19(1) of the 1995 Order as

> . . . any form of care or supervised activity provided for children during the day (whether or not it is provided on a regular basis).

In this context 'supervised activity' means an activity supervised by a responsible person. A Trust's basic preventative strategy will rest on the range of services it has available to help and support those children in need resident in its area and their families. Usually this involves providing direct financial assistance, or it may involve a Trust paying for places with child minders, playgroups or family centres.

In relation to pre-school children, Article 19 places on a Trust a strict duty to provide appropriate day care for children in need within their area who are under the age of five and not at school, but only a power to provide day care for other children of that age who are not in need. In relation to school-aged children the duty similarly placed is to provide day care outside school hours and during school holidays for those in need and attending school while it may also do so for those who are attending school but are not in need. The responsibility for actually making day care arrangements remains with the parents. It should be noted that under the 1995 Order, day-care provisions are required for children aged twelve and under, whereas under the 1989 Act the comparable age is eight.

As stated in the Guidance and Regulations:

> It is unreasonable to expect children aged twelve to be wholly responsible for themselves and parents will have to make arrangements for someone else to look after them when or if they are unable to do so. For children aged over twelve it is generally accepted that parents, while encouraging a child's growing independence, need to ensure that their children are not unnecessarily exposed to risk of harm or injury.[21]

---

21 The Children (NI) Order 1995, Guidance and Regulations, vol. 2, para 4.8.

A Trust is required to have regard to any local day-care services provided by an ELB or other body or person when exercising its functions under this provision. This Article also empowers a Trust to provide such facilities as training, advice, guidance and counselling for persons caring or accompanying children in day-care settings.

Article 20 makes elaborate provision for reviews and review procedures in relation to day-care services. These must include registered child-minding services and other day-care services provided by registered persons. Every Trust must conduct a comprehensive review of day-care services provided in its area in respect of children under the age of twelve. The responsibility for making day-care arrangements remains with the parents. The review should take account of services provided in schools, hospitals and other such establishments which are exempt from the registration requirements; the Trusts are themselves exempted from registration requirements. It should be conducted in conjunction with the appropriate ELB and district councils within one year of the 1995 Order taking effect and at three-year intervals thereafter. The results of each review, including information about any proposals affecting the day-care services, must then be published as soon as is reasonably practicable.

2. Accommodation

The new provisions relating to accommodation replace the Trusts' powers under section 103 of the 1968 Act and restore the initial basis of the voluntary admission to care service. It is one of the most tangible expressions of the new partnership between parents and a Trust.

(a) The Duty

The duty now placed on a Trust, as stated in Article 21 of the 1995 Order, is that

> (1) Every authority shall provide accommodation for any child in need within the authority's area who appears to the authority to require accommodation as a result of —
>
> > (a) there being no person who has parental responsibility for him;
> > (b) his being lost or having been abandoned; or
> > (c) the person who has been caring for him being prevented (whether or not permanently, and for whatever reason) from providing him with suitable accommodation or care.

Further:

> (3) Every authority shall provide accommodation for any child in need within the authority's area who has reached the age of sixteen and whose welfare the authority considers is likely to be seriously prejudiced if the authority does not provide him with accommodation.

Because this duty rests so unequivocally on the voluntary consent of all parties, an objection from a parent or from someone with parental responsibility will relieve a Trust of its obligation to provide accommodation. A discretionary power exists under Article 21(5) enabling a Trust to provide accommodation for a person between the ages of sixteen and twenty-one where it considers that to do so would safeguard or promote his or her welfare. The general duty of a Trust to co-ordinate its activities in respect of children in need with those of other statutory and voluntary agencies finds specific expression in Article 46. Among the agencies which are so required, under Article 27(e) and (f), to lend their co-operation to a Trust is the NIHE.

The legislative intent in Article 21(1)(c) and (3) is clearly to grant a right to homeless young persons (at least to those aged sixteen to eighteen) to claim accommodation from their local Trust, and a corresponding duty is placed jointly on that Trust and the NIHE to make such provision. This may well prove a useful supplement to the provision under the Housing (NI) Order 1988 which restricts applications to those who can prove a 'priority need', e.g. are pregnant, have a child or other dependant or are considered 'to be at risk of sexual or financial exploitation'. The indications (from Char, the national charity for the homeless, and from New Horizon, the oldest such charity in the United Kingdom) are that in England and Wales this provision, designed to assist such children in need, is not being fully implemented. There, as here, this age group is debarred from claiming Income Support. The availability of accommodation to destitute homeless young adolescents unable to claim welfare benefits could be of crucial importance.[22] After the introduction of the 1995 Order such persons will have the right to make their claims against the appropriate Trusts which in turn (if convinced that a young person's welfare is likely to be 'seriously prejudiced') will be obliged to act jointly with the NIHE in meeting them.[23]

Article 27(e) and (f) enables a Trust to request the NIHE to provide accommodation for a homeless family. Although case law[24] in England and Wales has established that the housing authority has no duty under housing legislation, it is clear that such a duty does arise under child-care legislation if the application comes not from a family but from a Trust on behalf of that family. In a case where a Trust's English counterpart was faced with a refusal from the NIHE's English counterpart of its request that accommodation be provided for a family of five children whose parents had rendered them intermittently homeless, the court held that the refusal to consider the request was wrong.[25] The housing authority must consider the request and must comply with it unless compliance would be incompatible with its own obligations and/or it would unduly prejudice the discharge of any of its functions. It was not enough that the housing body had decided that the request did not meet its own criteria.

Article 23 requires a Trust to receive and provide accommodation for children who have been removed or kept away from home under a child assessment order or who have been taken into police protection.

---

22 In Northern Ireland in 1993, 674 homeless persons between the ages of sixteen and eighteen applied to the NIHE for housing.
23 See *R v Northavon DC ex parte Smith* [1993] 2 FLR 897, which seems to continue the rationale of *AG (ex rel Tilley) v Wandsworth London Borough Council,* f/n 19, where it was held that it was not possible to set aside a duty to provide for a child and family purely on the basis that they had been found to be intermittently homeless.
24 See the House of Lords' decision in *R v Oldham Metropolitan Borough Council ex parte Garlick and Related Appeals* [1993] 2 FLR 194, where the court held that a body equivalent to the NIHE had no duty to a homeless dependant child under the legislative counterpart to the Housing (NI) Order 1988.
25 See *R v Wandsworth London Borough Council ex parte Hawthorne* [1995] 2 FLR 238.

(b) The Right

Parents, if they satisfy the above eligibility criteria, are to be provided with relief as of right without any implication that they have been in any way deficient or at fault (evidenced also by the phrase 'for whatever reason') in the execution of their parental duties. An important difference between this and the section 103 provision is that the accommodation must now be the subject of a written and signed agreement between the parties. At no time do the parents lose, nor the Trust acquire, any parental responsibilities. The child is not 'in care' and may be removed by the parents, or by someone with parental responsibility (under Article 22(2)), from Trust accommodation at any time. If the child has reached the age of sixteen, then, under Article 22(5), he or she may not be removed from such accommodation without his or her consent.

(c) Conflict between Parental Right and a Trust's Duty

It is not immediately evident that a Trust has any right to delay yet alone deny a parental request for the immediate return of a child for which it is providing accommodation. However, the requirement in Article 26(1)(a) that any authority (e.g. a Trust) when looking after a child (e.g. by the provision of accommodation) should 'safeguard and promote his welfare' may permit a Trust to resist such a parental request until satisfied that compliance would not be in breach of that duty. Alternatively, under Article 6(5)(b) the Trust, having care but not parental responsibility for the child, would be entitled to 'do what is reasonable in all the circumstances of the case for the purpose of safeguarding or promoting the child's welfare'. If all else fails, however, a Trust could always call upon the police to exercise their powers under Article 65(1)(b) to prevent the removal of an accommodated child in circumstances where there is reasonable cause for a constable to believe that such a removal would be likely to expose the child to significant harm.

(d) The Child

Article 21 also makes some stipulations regarding the position of the child to be accommodated. In particular:

> (4) An authority may provide accommodation for any child within the authority's area (even though a person who has parental responsibility for him is able to provide him with accommodation) if the authority considers that to do so would safeguard or promote the child's welfare.

This provision would seem to grant a Trust maximum discretion to interpret whether, in relation to any particular child, the proposed accommodation would meet the welfare interests of that child. It may have a particular application to private family law circumstances where, for example, either or both parents are so absorbed in mutual acrimony while pursuing divorce proceedings that neither objects to the child's wish to be accommodated elsewhere.

(e) The Child's Wishes

Article 21(6) places a duty on a Trust, insofar as is reasonably practicable and consistent with the child's welfare, to ascertain and give due consideration (having regard to his age and understanding) to the latter's wishes before providing accommodation. If that child is aged sixteen or more and consents to being accommodated (and this is judged to be necessary on welfare grounds), or to being discharged from accommodation, then a Trust is entitled to rely upon that consent regardless of any opposition from a parent or from elsewhere.

The legal situation now has, if anything, firmed since the decision in *Krishnan v Sutton London Borough Council*[26] when the court refused to discharge a child against her wishes to the care of her father.

The position regarding the ascertained wishes of a child aged under sixteen is less certain. Much would depend on the extent to which such a child could be judged to be '*Gillick* competent' (see also Chapters Fifteen and Sixteen). However, given the fact that this provision rests on the consent of all parties, it is unlikely that the wishes of a child under the age of sixteen would be allowed to prevail in the face of parental opposition.

(f) The Costs

Article 24 of the 1995 Order gives a Trust discretionary powers to recover from the principal parties some or all of the costs of the accommodation provided, in accordance with what is reasonable in the light of the means of those parties. Costs incurred in the process of providing services of advice, guidance or counselling are not recoverable. Persons who are in receipt of income support, family credit or disability working allowance are expressly exempted from any liability for costs.

---

26 [1969] 3 All ER 1367.

CHAPTER FOURTEEN

Child Care and Supervision: Significant Harm, the Court, the Trusts and the Orders

Introduction

This chapter focuses, in the main, on the matters provided for under the Children (NI) Order 1995, Part V. Its terms of reference are the principles, the grounds, the parties, the procedures and the orders which permit coercive intervention in parenting matters by a Trust.

There is a well-established pattern of reliance on coercive rather than on consensual intervention to provide 'away from home' care for children in Northern Ireland. This is reflected in the statistics relating to the balance between the coercive measures of fit person orders and parental rights orders and the consensual measure of section 103 admissions. In 1989 the former constituted 76.7 per cent of the total child-care population while the latter comprised 10.5 per cent; the remainder were largely made up of wardship committals. By 1994 the number of children in care under fit person orders or parental rights orders stood at 1,584 and 84 which represents a significant fall from the levels reached in 1990 (1,830 and 168 respectively). Evidence that this balance remains resistant to change is available in the DHSS annual report for 1995:

> While there has been a significant reduction in recent years in the use of Parental Rights Orders and Fit Person Orders, this has been balanced by an increase in Wardship proceedings. The incidence of compulsory interventions has therefore not decreased significantly.[1]

In light of these statistics, this chapter examines the threshold now statutorily set for coercive intervention in a public family law context. It identifies and considers the changes made by the Order to the 'child welfare' remit of the Trusts. It examines, also, the jurisdiction of the courts and the roles of judiciary and guardian ad litem in the management and determination of cases where a Trust alleges a breach of the significant harm threshold. Finally, this chapter outlines the different orders the court may make at the conclusion of child-care proceedings and examines their effects.

---

1 See *Annual Report of the Chief Inspector, Social Services Inspectorate*, NI, DHSS, 1995 64.

Intervention: The Legal Routes into Care

Before the introduction of the 1995 Order a child could be 'in care' on a voluntary or compulsory basis and could have arrived there by one of six different routes. Whether guilty of a criminal offence or of school absenteeism, having been abused or neglected or having simply been temporarily relinquished by a loving but over burdened parent, a child could be committed or admitted to the care of a Trust.

The 1995 Order has tidied-up the rationale, routes and procedures whereby children in Northern Ireland pass from parental to Trust care.

The legal routes into care have been greatly reduced and simplified by the 1995 Order.[2]

The new emphasis in the 1995 Order is on benign intervention by the Trusts to provide the support necessary to maintain vulnerable but viable parenting arrangements (see Chapter Thirteen). The legislative intent is that Trusts should support families so that children can continue to be cared for at home wherever possible.

The 1968 Act, however, has not been repealed; many of its provisions remain in effect. Consequently, the public law relating to children can at times only be ascertained by reading both pieces of legislation in conjunction. In particular, the criminal law provisions of the 1968 Act continue in force and with them continues the law relating to the control of juvenile offenders (see Chapter Seventeen).

The Intervention Threshold

The Principles

The Children (NI) Order 1995 has introduced a new role and weighting for the welfare principle in public family law. This has a direct but different bearing on decision-making by both Trusts and the courts.

1. Welfare and the Role of Trusts

The paramountcy principle is new to child-care legislation in Northern Ireland: it did not form part of the 1968 Act. It is binding on the judiciary, not on the Trusts: there is no statutory requirement on the Trusts under this legislation that they should give any priority to the welfare interests of a child. Indeed, if the Trusts were required in the course of their family support duties to give automatic precedence to the interests of

---

2 Of the six routes available under the 1968 Act only two remain and one new route has been added. No longer are there any voluntary admissions to care (as per section 103), Trust acquisition of parental rights in respect of children in voluntary care (as per section 104), judicial committals to care in matrimonial proceedings (as per the Matrimonial Causes (NI) Order 1978, Article 46, and the Domestic Proceedings (NI) Order 1980, Article 12), adoption proceedings (the Adoption (NI) Order 1987, Article 27), criminal proceedings (the 1968 Act), admissions in relation to school absenteeism (the Education and Library Boards Act (NI) 1972) nor any free access to wardship by a Trust. Intervention by a Trust in the affairs of a family for the purpose of protecting a child rather than supporting parental care now occurs under the powers provided by Part V and Part VI of the 1995 Order.

children, this would be in conflict with the whole partnership ethos. The legislative intent is to leave a Trust free to negotiate the best compromise possible between the conflicting interests of family members which will enable that Trust to safeguard and promote the welfare of any children involved. Only when conciliation has failed are the issues transferred to the court, and it is required to consider changes in the legal status of a child. At this stage the paramountcy principle comes into play (see also Chapter Eleven).

2. Welfare and the Role of the Court

By upgrading and comprehensively applying the principle of the welfare of the child to guide the judicial determination of issues concerning parental responsibilities in most court proceedings, the 1995 Order has radically adjusted the importance to be attached to safeguarding the interests of children. By reinforcing this with the 'welfare checklist', the principle of 'no delay' (Article 3(2)) and the 'no-order' (Article 3(5)) presumption, it enforces the very practical application of this principle. By directing that for most purposes in public family law proceedings the bearing of this principle on the individual circumstances of each child appearing before the court will be assessed by a guardian ad litem, the 1995 Order has ensured that the courts will be fully and independently briefed as to the factors constituting welfare in any particular case.

However, the crucial aspect of the role now played by welfare in public family law is that, strictly speaking, it is legally inoperative until proceedings are commenced. As the Court of Appeal has firmly emphasised,[3] intervention is not permissible unless and until the threshold criteria of 'significant harm' have been met. In many if not in most cases, it will be found that this threshold has not been breached or if it has, that the breach is repairable and on-going Trust intervention is unnecessary. A feature of the 1995 Order is the moral authority which is vested in the presumption favouring family care. Not until the matter comes before the court and breaching of the threshold has been shown to be of such gravity as to displace that presumption will coercive Trust intervention be warranted. In this way the 1995 Order gives effect to the assertion that 'the child is not the child of the state'.[4]

3. Welfare and Partnership between Parent and Trust

The principle governing relationships between Trust and parent in a public family law context is that the interests of children will be best served if the former makes every effort to achieve a partnership with the parents. When this is considered in conjunction with the directive in Article 18(1)(b) of the 1995 Order to 'promote the upbringing of such children by their families', the 'no-order' presumption of Article 3(5) and the absence of any requirement to give priority to the separate interests of a child, the cumulative effect is to place an onus on a Trust to safeguard the welfare interests of a child by maintaining that child in parental care wherever possible. Moreover, even where the 'significant harm' threshold has been breached, a Trust now has a discretion

---

3 See *Nottinghamshire County Council v P (no. 2)* [1993] 2 FLR 134.
4 See *Review of Child Care Law, DoH,* HMSO (1985).

(Article 66(8)), not previously available, to waive its power to instigate care proceedings should it consider that intervention would be contrary to the interests of the child concerned. It is clear that such an exercise of Trust discretion will not be open to judicial challenge.[5] Welfare under the 1995 Order, unlike under the 1968 Act, is seen first and foremost as a matter for the family not the state.

Being 'Looked after' and Parental Responsibility

The concept of partnership has been operationalised through two legal measures: all children in respect of whom a Trust provides away from home care, whether or not under the terms of a court order, are now regarded as being 'looked after' by that Trust, and a parent whose child is being 'looked after' retains parental responsibility for that child.

The effect of the first is, essentially, that a Trust must be guided by the same principles when making arrangements for a child who is the subject of a care order as for one for whom it is merely providing accommodation. This requires a Trust, for example, before taking any decisions in respect of that child to give due consideration to the wishes and feelings of the child, depending on his or her age and understanding and the wishes and feelings of certain others and the child's religious persuasion, racial origin and cultural and linguistic background (Article 26(2)). Insofar as it is practicable and consistent with the child's welfare, a Trust must ensure that the accommodation it provides is near to the child's home and caters also for any other sibling that the Trust might be looking after (Article 27(8)). Also, a duty is placed on a Trust to return any child whom it may be looking after to family care as soon as this is practicable (Article 26(7)).

The effect of the second is to impose upon both parent and Trust a sense of shared responsibility for important decision-making in respect of any child subject to a care order. Parents do not shed responsibility for their children on the making of an order and Trusts do not thereby attain exclusive rights to determine matters affecting the welfare of the children concerned.

Jurisdiction

The Court, Parties, Officials and Procedures

The Children (NI) Order 1995, Parts XV and XVI, together with Schedule 7 and the court rules provide the authority governing matters of court jurisdiction, processes and the roles and responsibilities of those involved.

1. The Court

The jurisdiction and procedure of the court are governed by Part XVI of the 1995 Order. Unlike private proceedings which allow for some flexibility in relation to choice of court, all public proceedings initiated under the 1995 Order must commence at the

---

5 See, for example, *Nottinghamshire County Council v P (no 2)* [1993] 2 FLR 134 CA; *Re S and D (Children: Powers of Court)* [1995] 2 FLR 456 CA.

lowest level in the juvenile court (or 'family proceedings court') from which they may be transferred to a designated county court (i.e. one designated as a 'care centre') and subsequently, if necessary, to the High Court. Where a court is hearing an application for an order under Part V or VI, it is empowered by Article 167 to require the attendance of the child concerned — and that of any parent, or person with parental responsibility, or a person undertaking the care of that child — at such stages of the proceedings as may be specified.

(a) Directions

The court may give, vary or revoke such directions for the conduct of proceedings as the timetable for the hearing or the time for acts to be done, attendance of the child, appointment of a GAL, service of documents, submission of evidence, including experts reports, submission of a welfare report or the transfer of proceedings or consolidation with other proceedings. The court may so act of its own motion or on written request from a party. Notice must be served on the parties who should be given an opportunity to attend or to make written representations.[6]

(b) Legal Aid

Under Article 172 of the 1995 Order (amending the Legal Aid, Advice and Assistance (NI) Order 1981), free legal aid is available to children, parents and others with parental responsibility in respect of applications for care or supervision orders, child assessment orders, emergency protection orders or extensions of same and for children in applications for secure accommodation orders.

2. The Parties

The applicant, respondent, any person with parental responsibilities and the child concerned are automatically the parties in care proceedings instigated under the 1995 Order. Other persons may apply, or the court may direct that they be joined, to become parties to such proceedings. Applications may be made with a minimum of three days' notice. (See Chapter Fifteen 'Evidence: Self-Incriminations' for the position of the court when a party makes a disclosure of criminal conduct.)

(a) Applicants

Under Article 50 of the 1995 Order only a Trust or 'authorised person' may apply for a care order or for a supervision order. For the purposes of these orders, an 'authorised person' is restricted to mean an officer of the NSPCC; neither the RUC nor the ELB may now make application for a care order (see further Chapter Fifteen).

---

6 Directions in magistrates' courts are governed by Rule 15 of the Magistrates' Courts (Children (NI) Order 1995) Rules (NI) 1996; Rule 17 governs attendance at directions appointment and hearing. Directions in the High Court and county courts are governed by Rule 4.15 of the Family Proceedings Rules (NI) 1996; Rule 4.17 governs attendance.

(b) Respondents

The respondents to a care order application are each parent with parental responsibility for the child concerned. Any other parent and certain other persons must be notified and may then elect to become respondents: an unmarried father or person currently caring for the child, for example, must be notified and may then decide to apply to be joined to the proceedings.

(c) Subject

Any child below the age of seventeen (or sixteen if married) may be the subject of proceedings instigated to obtain a care, supervision or interim order. Under Article 60(6) any such proceedings are designated 'specified proceedings' and the child concerned is, therefore, automatically made a party. This will be the case regardless of whether the child does or does not wish to make application for any of these orders.

It has been held[7] that the jurisdiction of the court to hear applications for public family law orders should be determined in accordance with the same rules governing its jurisdiction to do so in respect of private orders. These rules are as stated in the Family Law Act 1986, section 1, viz. that the child's habitual residence is within the jurisdiction or that he or she is physically present within the jurisdiction provided that in the latter case the child was not habitually resident elsewhere when the application was made.

3. The Guardian ad Litem

Article 60 of the 1995 Order states:

> (1) For the purposes of any specified proceedings, the court shall appoint a guardian ad litem for the child concerned unless satisfied that it is not necessary to do so in order to safeguard his interests.

This provision for the appointment of a guardian ad litem (GAL) in all specified (public family law) proceedings, unless the court deems it unnecessary, is one of the most significant changes introduced to child-care law in Northern Ireland by the 1995 Order.

(a) Appointment

Under Article 60(6) of the 1995 Order a GAL must be appointed, regardless of the level of court (unless the court is satisfied that it is unnecessary), in all applications to make, vary, extend or discharge a care or supervision order; in all private family proceedings where the court is considering making a care order; in all proceedings relating to emergency protection orders, child assessment orders and secure accommodation; in all cases concerning a possible change of name, contact, emigration or removal from the jurisdiction; and in all appeal proceedings regarding these matters. The appointment is made from a panel established by regulations under Article 60(7)

---

7 *Re R (Care Orders: Jurisdiction)* [1995] 1 FLR 712.

and may be made by the court of its own motion at any stage in specified proceedings. The procedure for appointment is governed by the Rules.[8]

A GAL has an important but time-limited role in proceedings. He or she should be appointed at the commencement of proceedings but should cease involvement with the child at the close of proceedings[9] or at the close of that part which are designated 'specified proceedings'.[10] There can be no on-going monitoring role for a GAL. The court will not routinely appoint a GAL in all such cases.[11]

(b) Duties

As stated in Article 60(2)(b) the GAL is primarily under 'a duty to safeguard the interests of the child'. This is achieved by conducting an investigation on such interests and compiling a report to the court which the latter, under Article 60(11), 'may take account of'. The GAL is obliged to represent the best interests of the child even if the latter holds contrary views as to what constitutes those best interests. The child concerned may not wish to have such interests represented by a GAL. This has been a source of contention in England and Wales.[12]

The powers and duties of a GAL are further specified in the Rules which require that official to appoint a solicitor (if one has not already been appointed), give such advice to the child as is appropriate having regard to his or her age and understanding, instruct the solicitor, as appropriate, attend all directions appointments and hearings in relation to the proceedings, advise the court on certain matters, notify certain parties, serve and accept service of documents on behalf of the child and carry out such investigations as may be necessary.[13]

For operational aspects of the role of a GAL, see Chapter Nineteen, under 'Representation in Public Proceedings'.

(c) The GAL Panel

Article 60(9) of the Children (NI) Order 1995 together with paragraph 166 of Schedule 9 provide the authority for the setting up of GAL panels. The constitution, administration and procedures of these panels and appointment of panel managers are among the matters which are addressed by the Regulations.[14] Although there is provision to appoint a GAL in private family law proceedings, such an appointment cannot be made from the GAL panel (see the Courts (Children (NI) Order 1995) Rules Magistrates' (NI) 1996, rule 15(2)(d)) and hence there is no public provision for payment.

---

8 Rule 11 of the Magistrates' Courts (Children (NI) Order 1995) Rules (NI) 1996; Rule 4.11 of the Family Proceedings Rules (NI) 1996.
9 As was demonstrated in *Kent County Council v C and Another* [1993] Fam 57.
10 See *Re S (Contact: Grandparents)* [1996] 1 FLR 158.
11 As is illustrated by the decision not to do so in *Re J (A Minor)(Change of Name)* [1993] 1 FLR 699, where it was held that a GAL could do no more than others had already done.
12 See, for example, *Re S (A Minor)(Independent Representation)* [1993] 2 FLR 437 where the Court of Appeal upheld the earlier judicial decision to over-rule the wishes of an eleven-year-old boy who sought to dismiss his GAL in what was a complex case.
13 Rule 12 of the Magistrates' Courts (Children (NI) Order 1995) Rules (NI) 1996; Rule 4.12 of the Family Proceedings Rules (NI) 1996.
14 See the Guardian ad Litem (Panel) Regulations (NI) 1996.

The issue of the independence of GAL panels has been the focus of some debate. In England and Wales the insertion of limited enabling provisions in the Children Act 1975 provided for the appointment of GALs in care and related proceedings. Further legislative changes came into force in May 1984 requiring local authorities to establish and administer country-wide panels of GALs and Reporting Officers (GALROs). The role of the GAL was considerably expanded under the Children Act 1989, but the Panels continued to be funded and administered by the local authorities, so the controversy remained regarding their independence. This issue is considerably more pressing in a small jurisdiction with settled professional staffing arrangements and has already proved to be controversial in an adoption context. The courts in England and Wales have on occasion demonstrated the importance they attach to the principle that the independence of this court officer should not be compromised by the terms of his employment.[15]

In this jurisdiction the issue has been resolved by placing the responsibility for the employment and management of GALs with a newly established free standing GAL agency.

(d) The Northern Ireland Guardian ad Litem Agency (NIGALA)

The DHSS established the NIGALA as a 'special agency' under the Health and Personal Social Services (Special Agencies) (NI) Order 1990 setting it the task of the organisation and management of a regional GAL service. The NIGALA (Establishment and Constitution) Order 1995 makes provisions in relation to the constitution of the Agency and the terms of the office of Agency members. The Guardians ad Litem (Panel) Regulations (NI) 1996 provide the legislative framework for managing the GAL service within this jurisdiction.

4. The Solicitor

Article 60 of the 1995 Order states:

> (3) Where —
>   (a) the child concerned is not represented by a solicitor; and
>   (b) any of the conditions mentioned in paragraph (4) is satisfied, the court may appoint a solicitor to represent him.
> (4) The conditions are that —
>   (a) no guardian ad litem has been appointed for the child;
>   (b) the child has sufficient understanding to instruct a solicitor and wishes to do so;
>   (c) it appears to the court that it would be in the child's best interests for him to be represented by a solicitor.

The appointment of a solicitor is mandatory in proceedings for a secure accommodation order (see further Chapter Nineteen).

---

15 For example, in *Oxfordshire County Council v P* [1995] 1 FLR 552, the court held that the GAL had been wrong to divulge to his employers information concerning child protection matters received while acting in his capacity as GAL. Again, in *R v Cornwall County*

Appointment

The procedure for appointment of a solicitor is governed by the Rules.[16] Usually a solicitor will be appointed by and take instructions from the GAL. However, there will be cases where a child of sufficient understanding will wish to exercise his or her right to appoint and directly instruct a solicitor. There will also be those cases envisaged by the above provisions where the initiative will come from the court. The solicitor is required to represent the child, in furtherance of the latter's best interests, or in accordance with instructions received from either child or GAL. The Rules also provide for the circumstances in which such an appointment may be terminated.

5. The Social Worker

Where the court directs a Trust to conduct inquiries, the resulting written report is to be submitted at least fourteen days in advance of the hearing. Again, the procedure for appointment is governed by the Rules.[17]

6. The Procedures

The Children (NI) Order 1995, Part V, provides the authority for coercive state intervention to determine arrangements for the future care and/or supervision of children. These are procedures for care orders, supervision orders, interim care or supervision orders and educational supervision orders.

The Grounds for Coercive Intervention

Under the Children (NI) Order 1995 a child may be committed to care only under a court order and only where there is evidence of significant harm and either a lack of parental care or of being beyond parental control.

The statutory ground of 'significant harm' as established through evidence adduced by a Trust or other 'authorised person' in conjunction with judicially applied tests of paramountcy, the welfare checklist, the no-order presumption and the no-delay rule now form the threshold for coercive intervention in public family law matters.

7. Significant Harm: Definitions

The concept of significant harm, which now forms the distinguishing characteristic of public family law proceedings, rests on two limbs: that breach of the significant harm threshold has occurred and that this is attributable to either a lack of reasonable parental care or to being beyond parental control. Unless and until this ground can be satisfied there can be no possibility of coercive intervention.

Council [1992] 1 WLR 427, the court quashed a decision made by a Board's counterpart in England which purported to limit the number of hours which a social worker could spend on his GAL duties.

16 Rule 13 of the Magistrates' Courts (Children (NI) Order 1995) Rules (NI) 1996; Rule 4.13 of the Family Proceedings Rules (NI) 1996.
17 Rule 14 of the Magistrates' Courts (Children (NI) Order 1995) Rules (NI) 1996; Rule 4.14 of the Family Proceedings Rules (NI) 1996.

(a) 'Harm'

Article 50 of the 1995 Order states that

> (2) A court may only make a care or supervision order if it is satisfied —
> (a) that the child concerned is suffering, or is likely to suffer, significant harm.

Article 2(2) defines 'harm' as 'ill-treatment or the impairment of health or development' and states that 'ill-treatment' includes 'sexual abuse and forms of abuse which are not physical'. The latter term clearly allows for the inclusion of emotional abuse within the definition of 'harm'.[18] The first requirement of this provision, then, is that 'harm' or the 'likelihood of harm' exists. It is evident that 'ill-treatment', the 'impairment of health' and the impairment of 'development' are each independent and alternative conditions all or any one of which would be sufficient to establish 'harm' or the 'likelihood of harm' and thus satisfy the terms of this requirement. The court considered the meaning of harm in a case[19] where a fifteen-year-old girl had obdurately refused to attend school for three years. The court made a care order holding that harm included social, educational and intellectual development.

(b) 'Significant'

The degree to which such conditions must exist in order to constitute 'significant' harm and thereby satisfy the 'significance' test is problematic (i.e. just how bad does the harm have to be for it to be judged 'significant'?). Clearly, at one extreme, if the harm can be considered very grave as in a recent case[20] where the 'harm' involved the death of an abused child, then there is little difficulty. The uncertainty increases in proportion to the decrease in gravity of harm.

The 1995 Order does not provide any definition for the term 'significant'. The only statutory guidance available is that this be determined by making a comparison with a 'similar' child. This is unsatisfactory although it may be the most realistic test available. In many situations it will be impossible to match the subject child with another yet alone draw any meaningful conclusions about the relative significance of the same harm befalling them. But, as is explained in the Guidance and Regulations:

> The need to use a standard appropriate for the child in question arises because some children have characteristics or handicaps which mean that they cannot be expected to be as healthy or well-developed as others. Equally, if the child needs special care or attention (because, for example, he is unusually difficult to control) then this to be expected for the child. The standard should only be that which it is reasonable to expect for the particular child.[21]

An illustration of the unsatisfactory nature of this test occurred in a case where an application for an FPO was brought in respect of the thirteen-year-old bride of a twenty-

---

18 See *Report of the Inquiry into Child Abuse in Cleveland* (1987) (Cm 412, 4).
19 See *Re O (A Minor)(Care Order: Education: Procedure)* [1992] 2 FLR 7.
20 See *Re D (A Minor)(Care or Supervision Order)* [1993] 2 FLR 43.
21 The Children (NI) Order 1995, Guidance and Regulations, vol. 1 para 9.24.

five-year-old man with a history of promiscuous sexual relationships. As he was receiving treatment for venereal disease, the Trust's counterpart considered that there were good grounds for viewing the girl as being in need of the protection of an FPO. However, the Court of Appeal, overturning the decision by the court at first instance to grant the order, ruled that the court must respect the standards of the parties.[22]

(c) 'Likelihood'

Again, the exact meaning of 'likelihood' has given rise to considerable contention in England. It has been held[23] that the 'likelihood' test would be satisfied by evidence that there was a real risk of future harm. Most recently, the House of Lords consolidated this view in a judgment[24] which, by rejecting the argument that 'likelihood' should be equated with 'probability', has significantly eased the threshold test. The fact that the mere 'likelihood' of a future occurrence of harm could be sufficient to justify coercive intervention provides an important extension to the protective reach of a Trust's statutory powers. It will now no longer be necessary to resort to wardship for authority to remove a new-born baby from an abusing or neglectful mother who has not yet had the opportunity to harm that child. A larger question is whether anticipated harm would extend to cover circumstances of potential damage to a child *en ventre sa mere* from the actions of a substance-abusing mother.

(d) Attributable to Lack of Parental Care or to Being beyond Parental Control

Article 50(2) of the 1995 Order states that the 'harm' or 'likelihood of harm' must be attributable to

(i) the care given to the child, or likely to be given to him if the order were not made, not being what it would be reasonable to expect a parent to give to him; or
(ii) the child's being beyond parental control.

This requirement, therefore, is that the 'harm' or 'likelihood of harm' is attributable to, rather than caused by, either an unreasonable standard of parenting or the child being beyond parental control.

In the former instance, the standard of parental care will be judged by an objective application of the 'reasonableness' test i.e. not what that parent in those circumstances could be expected to provide but what a reasonable parent would provide. However, it has been held[25] that the statutory reference to 'care' (as in Article 50(2)(i) above) referred to the actual parent or carer whose lack of care caused the harm not to that of the hypothetical reasonable parent in that situation.

In the latter case, it is the bare fact that the child is found to be beyond parental control which is all important.[26] This may arise, for example, from drug or alcohol

---

22 See *Mohamed v Knot* [1969] 1 QB 1 (also, see Chapter 1).
23 See *Newham London Borough Council v AG* [1993] 1 FLR 281.
24 See *Re H and Others (Minors)(Sexual Abuse: Standard of Proof)* [1995] 1 FLR 643.
25 See *Re S and R (Minors)(Care Order)* [1993] Fam Law 43.
26 See, for example, *Re O (A Minor)(Care Order: Education: Procedure)* [1992] 2 FLR 7

abuse, sexual promiscuity or anorexia nervosa. Parental fault or default is not at issue; it is the bare fact that there has been a breach of the significant harm threshold, whether by child or parent, which is of concern to the court.

(e) Evidence

The tenses used in this provision have been a source of considerable uncertainty for practitioners in England and Wales. They refer only to present and prospective harm. It has, for example, been held[27] that evidence of significant harm must be sought from the circumstances existing immediately before the proceedings commenced. This would appear to imply that evidence of past harm cannot be relied upon as an indicator of a likely future occurrence. However, the decision in *Re B (A Minor)(Interim Care Order: Criteria)*[28] overturned this view. It was then held that the court was not confined solely to considering the facts existing at the date of the hearing. The court was satisfied that the use of the present tense in the provision indicated a situation over a period of time sufficiently proximate to the date of the inquiry to suggest that it was a present and continuing set of circumstances and not merely past or possible future events.[29]

This point would now seem to have been settled by the decision of the House of Lords in *Re M (A Minor)(Care Order: Threshold Conditions)*[30] which reversed the decision of the Court of Appeal and re-instated that of the court of first instance. The operative time for adducing evidence of significant harm is not the date of hearing. In the words of Lord Mackay,

> the relevant date with respect to which the court must be satisfied (that the child is suffering significant harm) is the date at which the local authority initiated the procedure of protection under the Act.

The spirit behind this ruling and the authority now attached to it became evident in *M v Birmingham City Council*,[31] where the Court of Appeal held that the court was not tied to the facts existing at the time of the hearing but rather the term 'being beyond parental control' should be viewed as describing a state of affairs — in the past, in the future or in the present — according to the context in which it fell to be applied. (For more detailed consideration of the requirements regarding evidential material and standard of proof in the context of child abuse proceedings, see Chapter Fifteen).

---

    where it was considered to be irrelevant to determine whether this established fact was attributable to the fault of child or parent.
27 *Nottinghamshire County Council v S* [1992] 3 WLR 1010.
28 [1993] 1 FLR 815.
29 See, also, *M v Westminster City Council* [1985] FLR 325; *Re D (A Minor)* [1987] 1 FLR 422; and *Northamptonshire County Council v S and Others* [1993] 1 FLR 554, where Ewbank J said: 'In my judgment, the family proceedings court was quite entitled to consider the position when the children were with the mother prior to going into (voluntary) care and was correct in doing so'.
30 [1994] 2 FLR 577 at p. 305.
31 [1994] 2 FLR 141.

Judicial Determination

As referred to above, the 1995 Order imposes specific statutory requirements to govern judicial management of family proceedings cases.

Principles Governing Judicial Determination

The judiciary must apply the paramountcy principle, the 'no-delay' principle, the 'no-order' presumption, the limited litigation principle and, in all public law cases, they must also apply the 'welfare checklist' (see Chapter Eleven, and also see Chapter Fifteen in relation to Part VI proceedings).

1. The Paramountcy Principle

Under Article 3(1) of the 1995 Order when a court is deciding any question with respect to the upbringing of a child then the child's welfare shall be the court's paramount consideration.

Since the introduction of the 1995 Order, the court is now obliged, having satisfied itself that the grounds for the order are met, to apply the 'paramountcy' test in all childcare cases. Paradoxically, the Trusts may now find the court employing this principle to restrain rather than facilitate Trust intervention. In circumstances where, in accordance with the statutory grounds, a Trust intervenes and makes application for a care order the court may still decline to grant the order sought. This may occur, for example, where the court determines that it is of paramount importance not to cause further damage to the psychological bonds between child and parent. The paramountcy principle may thus be used to defeat Trust intentions.

The No-Order Presumption

Under Article 3(5) of the 1995 Order where a court is considering an application for an order it 'shall not make the order or any of the orders unless it considers that doing so would be better for the child than making no order at all'. Again, this places a firm onus on a Trust applicant to not only satisfy the court that the specified statutory grounds can be met but to also convince the court that in the particular circumstances not to grant an order would result in greater harm to the child than to do so; definite evidence has to be produced to rebut the presumption that no order is best. This is not just a reflective exercise, looking back over the child's life and adducing evidence of significant harm. The Trust must also look to the future and present a care plan which shows the court what it hopes to achieve with an order and why this would be better for the child than no order. Otherwise, the no-order approach as neatly summarised in the observation made by Templeman LJ will prevail:[32]

> The best person to bring up a child is the natural parent. It matters not whether the parent is wise or foolish, rich or poor, educated or illiterate, provided that the child's

---

32 *Re KD (A Minor) (Ward: Termination of Access)* [1988] 1 AC 806, 812.

moral and physical health is not in danger. Public authorities cannot improve on nature.

The No-Delay Principle

Under Article 3 of the 1995 Order:

> (2) ... in any proceedings in which any question with respect to the upbringing of a child arises, the court shall have regard to the general principle that any delay in determining the question is likely to prejudice the welfare of the child.

This principle is given teeth by Article 51 which imposes a mandatory duty on a court hearing an application for an order under Part 5 to draw up a timetable 'with a view to disposing of the application without delay'. The importance of this principle was recently emphasised by the Court of Appeal when it overturned the decision of the court at first instance to adjourn care proceedings pending the outcome of a criminal trial.[33] One reason for this statutory requirement was to address the problem of orchestrated delay which by favouring a continuation of the settled care arrangements provided by an applicant, effectively pre-empted judicial discretion and did not necessarily permit a decision which would best promote the long-term interests of the child concerned. Now, once an application is lodged in court, it will in theory be for the court, as advised by the GAL, and not a Trust to determine the pace at which proceedings progress. Adhering to time constraints may well prove problematic for both the Trusts and the courts.

2. The Welfare Checklist

Under Article 3(4) of the 1995 Order when the court is considering whether to make, vary or discharge either a contested Article 8 order or an order under Part V, then it is required to apply the checklist criteria as stated in Article 3, having regard in particular to —

- (a) the ascertainable wishes and feelings of the child concerned (considered in the light of his age and understanding);
- (b) his physical, emotional and educational needs;
- (c) the likely effect on him of any change in his circumstances;
- (d) his age, sex, background and any characteristics of his which the court considers relevant;
- (e) any harm which he has suffered or is at risk of suffering;
- (f) how capable of meeting his needs is each of his parents and any other person in relation to whom the court considers the question to be relevant;
- (g) the range of powers available to the court under this order in the proceedings in question.

While the checklist has a mandatory application only to contested cases in private family law, it must be applied to all public proceedings (though see Chapter Fifteen in

---

33 *Re TB (Care Proceedings: Criminal Trial)* [1995] 2 FLR 80.

relation to Part VI proceedings). Coercive intervention by a Trust under Part V proceedings will not be authorised until the court has applied these criteria to the particular circumstances giving rise to the Trust application and is then satisfied that an order is necessary (for the law relating to judicial application of the welfare checklist, see further Chapter Eleven).

The significance of these requirements was reviewed in the case of *Humberside County Council v B*.[34] The defendant parents successfully appealed against the making of an interim care order on the grounds that although the court at first instance had established a breach of the significant harm threshold it had failed to then consider (in the light of the paramountcy principle, the welfare checklist and its full range of statutory powers) whether the making of that order was the best option open to it. On appeal the court held that the judge at first instance had failed to take into account the risk to the welfare of the child as a consequence of the long-term separation from her parents and had not considered the full range of its powers.

Children in Court

Under Article 168, there is authority to clear the court 'where the evidence of a child is likely to involve matters of an indecent or immoral nature'. The normal rules in respect of hearsay are relaxed in relation to the evidence of children, a principle which has not been greatly affected by the introduction of the Children's Evidence (NI) Order 1995 and the provisions relating to the presentation of evidence by means of video equipment (see further Chapter Eighteen). Article 170 of the Children (NI) Order 1995 prohibits the publication of material likely to identify any child as the subject of proceedings under Part V or VI. Article 172 makes provision for legal aid, advice and assistance.

Public Family Law Orders

1. Care Orders and Supervision Orders

Care orders (COs) and supervision orders (SOs) are available under Article 50 of the 1995 Order if the broad grounds of 'significant harm' and the above tests can be satisfied. A care order subsumes and replaces the variety of different forms of order (FPO, PRO, TSO and section 103 admissions) which previously provided the routes whereby children came into care under the 1968 Act. It is not available in respect of children who have committed offences or are in breach of statutory education requirements. It is available in respect of a child beyond parental control only if 'significant harm' can first be established. A supervision order is now somewhat different from its predecessor under the 1968 Act in that the supervisor is authorised to take steps to give effect to the order including returning to court for a variation of the order. The court has no power to attach conditions to a care order[35] but may attach

---

34 [1993] 1 FLR 257.
35 See, for example, *Re L (Sexual Abuse: Standard of Proof)* [1996] 1 FLR 116 where the Court of Appeal ruled that the judge at first instance had been wrong to issue both a care

directions to a supervision order. Observations recently made by the Court of Appeal in England and Wales regarding the differences between these two orders offer the following guidance for practitioners in this jurisdiction.[36] A care order places a positive duty on a Trust to ensure the welfare of the child concerned and protect him or her from inadequate parenting, which is not inconsistent with the partnership principle as a Trust may place that child with the parents. A supervision order, however, places an obligation on a Trust to help and assist the child but leaves full responsibility with the parents who may choose to ignore both judicial directions and Trust supervision. Because the same threshold requirements apply to both orders, experience in England and Wales indicates that supervision orders are seldom sought.

In *A v Liverpool City Council*[37] the House of Lords ruled that where Parliament has by statute vested certain powers and duties in respect of child welfare in a local authority (or Trust), without reserving for the court a power to review the exercise of those powers and duties, then the court is prevented from interfering in the decisions taken by a local authority (or Trust). Parliament has drawn a clear line dividing executive and judicial exercises of authority. The 1995 Order upholds the spirit of the *Liverpool* ruling by preventing the court from exercising any discretionary power to supervise Trust implementation of the authority granted to the latter by a CO or SO.[38] The legislative intent is that it should be for a Trust and not the court to implement the authority conferred by a CO or SO, subject only to the power reserved to the court by Article 53(1).

1. Initial Hearings: Application for Directions

It will usually be necessary for an application for a care order or supervision order to be preceded by a preliminary court hearing on an application for directions. Such an appointments hearing may, alternatively, be held at any time during the course of proceedings. As is stated in the Guidance and Regulations, directions may then be issued on any of the following matters:

(a) timetable for the proceedings and directions to ensure the timetable is adhered to (this has to be done at some point in the proceedings, and the directions appointment is often the most convenient);
(b) the identity of the parties to the proceedings;
(c) the submission of evidence including experts' reports;
(d) the appointment of a guardian ad litem or solicitor;

---

order and an order (under the provision equivalent to Article 53(4)) authorising a local authority to terminate parental contact so as to save the authority the trouble of applying again for the latter order should it be necessary. For further discussion on the differences between these two orders see, for example, G Brasse, *Supervision or Care Orders?* in Fam Law, vol 27, 1997, P 351–6.

36 See *Re T (A Minor) (Care or Supervision Order)* [1994] 1 FLR 103; also *Re S (J) (A Minor) (Care or Supervision)* [1993] 2 FLR 919.
37 [1982] AC 363.
38 See, for example, *Re B (Minors)(Care: Contact: Local Authority's Plans)* [1993] 1 FLR 543; *Kent County Court v C* [1993] 1 FLR 308; and *Re T (A Minor)(Care Order: Conditions)* [1994] 2 FLR 423.

(e) the date for a subsequent directions appointment, if any, or first hearing;
(f) the attendance of the child concerned;
(g) any other matters considered relevant.

As the Guidance and Regulations go on to note:

> Usually the court will not be able to decide the application for a care order or supervision order at the first application. The applicant should be ready to tell the court at the directions appointment:
>
> (a) whether he or she is applying for an interim order and, if so, any directions under Article 57(6) relating to medical or psychiatric examination or any other kind of assessment (the power to order an examination or assessment relates to the child only);
> (b) what plans the Trust has made for safeguarding and promoting the child's welfare while the interim order is in force and, where an interim care order is sought, what type of placement is envisaged;
> (c) in the case of an interim order, what proposals the Trust has for allowing the child reasonable contact with his parents and others under Article 53.[39]

Under Article 51(1) the court is required, when hearing an application for a Part V order, to draw up a timetable for dealing expeditiously with the proceedings. This management responsibility for controlling the timing and conduct of proceedings is not to be treated lightly.[40]

2. The Grounds

A prerequisite for either a CO or a SO is proof that the child concerned is suffering, or is likely to suffer, significant harm. Under Article 50(2) this must be followed by evidence

> (b) that the harm or likelihood of harm, is attributable to —
>
> (i) the care given to the child, or likely to be given to him if the order were not made, not being what it would be reasonable to expect a parent to give to him; or
> (ii) the child's being beyond parental control.

3. The Applicant

Only a Trust or an 'authorised person', as defined by Article 49(2), is permitted to apply for a CO or a SO; a parent may no longer request a Trust to initiate proceedings on the grounds that a child is beyond his or her control. The onus on a Trust, under Article 66(8), to 'take action to safeguard or promote a child's welfare' will normally require it to apply for a CO where it believes the grounds are satisfied. Before doing so, the advice given in the Guidance and Regulations should be borne in mind:

---

39 Children (NI) Order 1995, Guidance and Regulations, vol. 1, paras 9.38 and 9.39, 6.38.
40 See *Re MD and TD (Minors)(Time Estimates)* [1994] 2 FLR 336.

... the Trust should always seek legal advice on:
(a) whether, in the circumstances of the case and having regard to the Article 3(3) checklist, the court is likely to be satisfied first that the Article 50(2) criteria are satisfied and then that an order should be made under the Article 3(5) test;
(b) the implications of another party to the proceedings opposing the application and applying for an Article 8 order instead;
(c) whether the application falls within criteria of transfer of cases to a higher court and whether representations about this should be made;
(d) whether the court should be asked for an interim care or supervision order, the desired length of the initial interim order and what directions should be sought;
(e) the matters to be provided for in the Trust's advance statement of case, including copies of witness statements that can be made available and a broad outline of the Trust's plans for the child;
(f) notification and other procedural requirements and matters likely to be considered at a directions appointment;
(g) whether the court is likely to consider that in all the circumstances of the case a guardian ad litem does not need to be appointed;
(h) whether use of a residence order linked with a supervision order would be an appropriate alternative to a care order.[41]

However, the onus under Article 66(8) is subject to an accompanying condition that the Trust considers such action to be 'reasonably practicable'. Thus, where a Trust refuses to initiate proceedings, perhaps on the grounds that it lacks the resources to cope with the resulting additional responsibilities, there is now no judicial power available to compel it to do so.[42] This new discretion, enabling a Trust to avoid initiating proceedings to bring before the court a child requiring the protection which can only be authorised by that court, marks a significant change from its previous duty under the 1968 Act to do so. As was stated by Sir Stephen Brown P,

> if a local authority doggedly resists taking the steps which are appropriate to the case of children at risk of significant harm it appears the court is powerless.

Where an authorised person proposes making an application, then if it is reasonably practicable, he or she should first consult the relevant Trust. Applications may also be made in the course of any other family proceedings.

4. The Child

Neither a CO nor a SO may be made with respect to a child who has reached the age of seventeen (or sixteen in the case of a married child). Directions added to a SO but not to a CO may impose certain additional obligations on the child concerned, but as noted in the Guidance and Regulations:

> Requirements as to treatment are wholly the responsibility of the court and have to be specified in the order itself [para 5 of Schedule 3].

---

41 Children (NI) Order 1995, Guidance, vol. 1, para 9.14.
42 Such was the conclusion of the court in *Nottinghamshire County Council v P (no. 2)* [1993] 2 FLR 134, 148.

Requirements as to examinations may be specified by the court in the order or by the supervisor [para 4 of Schedule 3]. Other matters are for the supervisor, provided the supervision order contains the necessary authority.[43]

Where a child has sufficient understanding to make a considered decision, then no direction requiring him or her to undergo a psychiatric or medical examination/treatment may be attached to a SO without the child's consent. That order may impose a broad requirement that the child comply with directions given by the supervisor in respect of living arrangements, reporting arrangements and as to participation or otherwise in activities. This leaves to the supervisor the responsibility of specifying how the judicial directions are to be applied.

5. Care Plan

Before granting a CO or a SO the court is required to scrutinise the Trust's care plan in respect of the child and satisfy itself that the plan is in the child's best interests. The authority for this judicial responsibility lies not in the body of the 1995 Order but in the ancillary regulations.[44] It has been held[45] that the court should only pass responsibility to the Trusts' counterparts by way of COs when all the facts are as fully known as possible and that such facts should be presented to the court by way of a care plan which addressed the headings outlined in the regulations[46] (see further Chapter Sixteen). If the court is not satisfied that the care plan is in the child's best interests, then although it has no power to alter the care plan the advice of Wall J[47] is that the court may refuse to make a CO or SO. There is, therefore, a heavy onus on any Trust applying for a CO to submit sufficient evidence to support its care plan.

Instead of granting a CO application by a Trust the court may, for a limited period, impose its own care plan on the Trust. This is achieved by the court making an interim care order subject to directions designed to provide the information necessary for a valid care plan to be compiled and thereby place the court in a position to decide, when the interim care order has run its course, whether the making of a full CO would be in the child's best interests.[48] This discretionary judicial power to make the order considered by the court rather than the applicant to be most appropriate to the welfare of a child has also been used in England and Wales to give preference to ICOs or indeed EPOs instead of CAOs at the early stages of coercive intervention.

---

43 Children (NI) Order 1995, Guidance, vol. 1, para 9.59.
44 See, Children (NI) Order 1995, Guidance and Regulations, vol. 3 (Family Placements) para 2.62.
45 See *C v Solihull Metropolitan Borough Council* [1993] 1 FLR 290; *Hounslow London Borough Council v A* [1993] 1 FLR 702.
46 See *Manchester City Council v F* [1993] 1 FLR 419.
47 See *Re J (Minors) (Care: Care Plan)* [1994] 1 FLR 253, 258F–G.
48 This was the course of action approved by the Court of Appeal in *Buckingham County Council v M* [1994] 2 FLR 506 when the court rejected a care plan which had as its objective the placing of a child for adoption and instead substituted a phased rehabilitation programme underpinned by an interim care order.

6. Contact Arrangements

Under Article 53 of the 1995 Order,

> (11) Before making a care order with respect to any child the court shall —
> (a) consider the arrangements which the authority has made, or proposes to make, for affording any person contact with a child to whom this Article applies; and
> (b) invite the parties to the proceedings to comment on those arrangements.

Contact arrangements, unlike care plans, have thus been explicitly reserved in the body of the 1995 Order for judicial assessment. This is a significant indicator of the role played by the partnership principle which now governs the joint duties of Trust and parents in the exercise of parental responsibilities to secure the welfare interests of a child. The legislative intent is to require a Trust to declare its hand as regards proposed contact arrangements between child and family of origin before it can be granted a care order (and with it the protection of the *Liverpool* ruling from any further judicial scrutiny). This gives the court an opportunity to satisfy itself as to the *bona fides* of a Trust's rehabilitation care plan and/or satisfy itself that the nature, frequency and duration of the contact arrangements appropriately safeguard the child's welfare interests. The court may then grant a contact order at the same time as it makes the care order. Alternatively, it may grant an interim contact order while making a care order[49] which thereby gives the court an opportunity to review the contact arrangements at a later date. These possibilities are important strategic contributions towards avoiding the adversarial litigation which had become so characteristic of the relationship between parents and Trusts under the 1968 Act.

The fact that a Trust has applied for a SO will not prevent the court from instead issuing a CO. The determining factor will be a combination of the gravity of the prospective harm and the likelihood of it occurring.[50]

7. Effect of a CO

The most immediate consequence of making a care order is that, under Article 180, any wardship order, supervision order, Article 8 order or school attendance order which may be in effect in respect of the child is then discharged (though an emergency protection order will take precedence over the care order). The CO vests parental responsibilities for the child concerned in the Trust not to the exclusion of those responsibilities which remain with the parents but to the exclusion of any further court responsibility. This is in keeping with the principle that under the 1995 Order, unlike the position previously, there shall be a clear line drawn between the authority of the court and that of the Trust. The legislative intent is to place the Trust firmly in the

---

49 See *Cheshire County Council v B* [1992] 2 FCR 572.
50 See *Re D (A Minor)(Care or Supervision Order)* [1993] 2 FLR 423 where the court made such a substitution because it considered that the risk to the children of a current relationship, posed by a father who had previously abused his own children (causing the death of one), was too great to warrant a SO.

driving seat with the certainty of knowing that full responsibility, as detailed in Article 27(5)–(9) and Schedule 2, and accountability for the on-going management of the case rests solely with it. Article 52(5)–(9) details certain restrictions on Trust powers in relation to a child who is the subject of a CO (see further Chapter Sixteen).

8. Effect of a SO

As stated in the Guidance and Regulations:

> A supervision order puts the child under the supervision of a designated Trust.[51]

It also has the immediate effect of terminating any existing SO or care order though it may subsist in conjunction with an Article 8 order (most usually a residence order). Parental responsibility remains unaffected by the order. Under Schedule 3, paragraph 8, of the 1995 Order, a SO shall designate a Trust as supervisor only with the agreement of that Trust and in the event of the child living or being about to live within the Trust's area.

A SO imposes reciprocal legal obligations on three parties: the supervisor (most often a Trust social worker), the child or young person and the 'responsible person'. The latter is defined in Schedule 3, paragraph 1, of the 1995 Order as:

> (a) any person who has parental responsibility for the child and
> (b) any other person with whom the child is living.

The supervisor, the child or anyone with parental responsibility may apply to the court, under Article 58(2), for the SO to be varied or discharged, but the 'responsible person' without parental responsibility can only do so in respect of that part of the order which affects that person. Because an SO offers a less interventionist Trust approach, which is generally to be preferred as being more in keeping with a child's best interests, it rather than a CO should be sought where there is no immediate child protection issue, the child is to remain at home and there is a good prospect of achieving a Trust/parent working partnership. An SO, even if subject to directions and coupled with specific parental agreements, will be perceived by the family as less intrusive than a CO and stands a better chance of enlisting their co-operation.[52]

(a) The Powers and Duties of a Supervisor

The duties of a supervisor are broadly stated in Article 54:

> (1) While a supervision order is in force the supervisor shall —
>   (a) advise, assist and befriend the supervised child;

---

51 Children (NI) Order 1995, Guidance and Regulations, vol. 1, para 9.57.
52 See for example *Re B (Supervision Order: Parental Undertaking)* [1996] 1 FLR 676, *Re S (Care or Supervision Order)* [1996] 1 FLR 753, *Re V (Care or Supervision Order)* [1996] 1 FLR 776, *Re B (Care or Supervision Order)* [1996] 2 FLR 693 and *Re O (Care or Supervision Order)* [1996] 2 FLR 755.

(b) take such steps as are reasonably necessary to give effect to the order; and
(c) where —
  (i) the order is not wholly complied with; or
  (ii) the supervisor considers that the order may no longer be necessary,
    consider whether or not to apply to the court for its variation or discharge.

Under Schedule 3, paragraphs 4 and 5, of the 1995 Order, a SO may direct that the child undergo psychiatric or medical examination and/or treatment, though not if the child, being of sufficient understanding to make an informed decision, refuses to comply. Where such a direction has been attached to the order, then the supervisor has the power, not otherwise available, to require the child to undergo such an examination/treatment. Where a supervisor is faced with obstructive behaviour, as would be the case if he or she were denied access to the child, then the only form of enforcement available would be to return to the court and seek the additional powers of a warrant.[53]

(b) The Obligations of the Child or Young Person

Under Schedule 3 of the 1995 Order:

2. — (1) A supervision order may require the supervised child to comply with any directions given by the supervisor which require him [or her] to do all or any of the following things —
  (a) to live at any place specified in the directions for any period so specified;
  (b) to present himself to any person specified in the directions at any place and on any day so specified;
  (c) to participate in activities specified in the directions on any day so specified.

Also under Schedule 3:

7. — (1) A supervision order may require any supervised child —
  (a) to keep the supervisor informed of any change in his address; and
  (b) to allow the supervisor to visit him at the place where he is living.

(c) The Obligations of a 'Responsible Person'

The obligations of a 'responsible person' are detailed in Schedule 3, paragraph 3, of the 1995 Order and provide that 'with the consent of any responsible person' a SO may include a requirement that such a person will 'take all reasonable steps to ensure that a child complies with' any directions made under paragraph 2(1) above. The co-operation of the parent or other 'responsible person' is necessary if the SO is to be effective. Case law in England has established that, under a SO, a parent may be required to reside at a particular place.[54] A SO may be combined with a RO to facilitate a child's return to family-based care.

---

53 See *Re R and G (Minors)(Interim Care or Supervision Orders)* [1994] 1 FLR 793, *Re B (Supervision Order: Parental Undertaking)* [1996] 1 FLR 676, CA and *Re V (Care or Supervision Order)* [1996] 1 FLR 776 CA.
54 See *Croydon London Borough v A (no. 3)* [1992] 2 FCR 481, [1992] 2 FLR 350.

(d) Duration

A SO lasts for one year, but under Schedule 3, paragraphs 6(1) and (4), it may be extended to a maximum period of three years. A SO may be discharged, under Article 179(3), by a care order or, under Article 58, as a result of an application from the child, supervisor or person with parental responsibility. Otherwise, under Article 179(13), a SO will end on the subject's eighteenth birthday.

II. Interim Order

Under Article 57(1) of the 1995 Order the court is empowered to grant either an interim care order (ICO) or an interim supervision order (ISO) when

    (a) in any proceedings on an application for a care or a supervision order, the proceedings are adjourned; or
    (b) the court gives a direction under Article 56(1).

The court may make an ISO linked to a residence order, instead of making an ICO. It must do so when making a RO in care proceedings, unless satisfied that this is unnecessary. However, it cannot use an ISO to achieve objectives statutorily reserved to an ICO.[55]

1. The Grounds

The court must be satisfied that there are reasonable grounds for believing that the circumstances with respect to the child are as mentioned in Article 50(2). The 'reasonable grounds for believing' test imposes a less onerous burden on an applicant than does the full 'significant harm' test in relation to an application for a CO or SO. However, the grounds for an ICO are still considerably more onerous than those for a child assessment order. In theory, therefore, where a Trust requires time to establish whether the significant harm threshold has been, or is likely to be, breached, then it would be easier and more appropriate for it to seek a CAO rather than an ICO.

The paramountcy principle, welfare checklist and the 'no-order' presumption apply.

2. The Applicant

Only a Trust or an 'authorised person' may apply for either order, though the court may issue such an order in conjunction with a directive to a Trust that the latter undertake an investigation of a child's circumstances. Where in any application for a CO or a SO the court grants a residence order, it will also make an ISO in respect of the child unless satisfied that this is unnecessary.

---

55 See *Re R and G* [1994] 1 FLR 793.

3. The Hearing

Cazalet[56] laid down the following guidelines for courts hearing an application for an ICO or ISO:

> 1. An interim care order is a holding order but the court should nevertheless consider all relevant risks pending the substantive hearing and should ensure perhaps by giving directions that the final hearing takes place at the earliest possible date.
>
> 2. If there is insufficient court time in that court the case should be transferred laterally.
>
> 3. In an interim order hearing the court should only rarely make findings about disputed facts.
>
> 4. Courts should be cautious about changing a child's residence on an interim order.
>
> 5. Where an interim care order would lead to a substantial change in the child's position then the court should permit the hearing of limited oral evidence and for limited cross-examination on that evidence but must ensure that there is not a dress rehearsal of the full hearing.
>
> 6. The court should ensure that it has the written advice of the guardian ad litem but any party opposed to the guardian's recommendations should be given an opportunity to put questions to the guardian.
>
> 7. Justices hearing a case must comply with the mandatory requirements of the Rules.
>
> 8. When granting interim relief, justices should state their findings and reasons concisely and summarise briefly the essential factual issues between the parties. The justices will not however be able to make findings on disputed facts since they will not have heard the evidence in full.

4. The Effect of an ICO

The principal effect of this order is to provide a holding operation, permitting a Trust to carry out its enquiries, gather evidence and prepare reports so as to bring a case before the court in as short a time as possible. Parental responsibility for the child is acquired and held by the Trust (shared also with the parent(s)) for the duration of the order. The court must not pre-judge the substantive issues and should, therefore, restrict itself to maintaining the status quo between the parties by authorising and controlling the minimum level of intervention required in the circumstances for a Trust to prepare its case.[57] A Trust will be entitled to apply for an ICO in circumstances where its need

---

56 See *Hampshire County Council v S* [1993] Fam 158, [1993] 1 FLR 559, [1993] Fam Law 269.
57 See *Re G (Minors)(Interim Care Order)* [1993] 2 FLR 839, 846, where Waite J states that 'Parliament intended the regime of an interim care order to operate as a tightly run procedure closely monitored by the court and affording to all parties an opportunity of frequent review as events unfold during the currency of the order'. Also, see G Brasse, *A Tightly Run Procedure? Interim Care Orders Under Strain* [May 1994] Fam Law.

to carry out the initial investigations necessary to establish whether or not a child is at risk of significant harm is being obstructed by a lack of parental co-operation but neither a CAO nor an EPO are appropriate.[58]

5. Directions

Under Article 57(6) and (7), when granting either order or at any time when either order is in force, the court may add such directions as it considers appropriate regarding any medical, psychiatric or other form of assessment. This is a power it does not have when granting a CO or SO. The ICO may also carry other directions, for example that the child live at home.[59] If the child concerned has sufficient understanding to make an informed decision, he or she may refuse to comply with an assessment requirement and this decision will be valid and legally binding on all parties. Non-compliance without commensurate understanding, however, though invalid in law is likely to produce the same end result in pratice.

There is a view that the court is not entitled to elect to make an ICO instead of a CO simply for the purpose of attaching a direction and achieving a degree of supervision over Trust implementation of care arrangements that it would be prohibited from doing if it made the latter order.[60] As Professor Hayes[61] has succinctly stated,

> ... a care order is still a care order, whether it is an interim or a final order. By drawing a distinction between the two orders the courts are in grave danger of blurring the law and departing from the clear principles relating to the proper exercise of judicial power which were established in *A v Liverpool City Council*.

The alternative view, that the distinction is made by statute to permit in respect of ICOs the exercise of a particular range of judicial discretion not available in respect of COs is steadily gaining ground. This view derives authority from Waite J's definition of the function of an ICO[62] as being

---

58 See *Re B (A Minor)(Interim Care Order: Criteria)* [1993] 1 FLR 815.
59 See *Re G (Minors)(Interim Care Order)* [1993] 2 FLR 839 and also *Re M and C (Minors)(Interim Care Order)* [1995] Fam Law 315. But note also the note of caution sounded by Butler-Sloss LJ in *Re M (Minors)(Sexual Abuse: Evidence)* [1993] 1 FLR 822, when she warned that it was incumbent on the court not to add to the strain on a family, during what is intended to be a short-lived period of intervention, by unnecessarily lengthening proceedings.
60 See *Re J (Minors)(Care: Care Plan)* [1994] 1 FLR 253 per Wall J and *Re T (A Minor)(Care Order: Conditions)* [1994] 2 FLR 423. See also the recent warning given by Butler-Sloss LJ in *Re L (Sexual Abuse: Standard of Proof)* [1996] 1 FLR 116 that an ICO was to be used for its intended purpose and was not to be extended to provide continuing control over the actions of a local authority.
61 'The Proper Role of Courts in Child Care Cases' [1996] Child Fam Law Q 8. See also the CA decision in *Re M (Interim Care Order: Assessment)* [1996] 2 FLR 464 which supports this view.
62 See *Re G*.

... designed to leave the court with the ability to maintain strict control over any steps taken or proposed by a local authority in the exercise of its powers that are by their nature temporary and subject to continuous review.

An important recent judgment by the House of Lords[63] has come down firmly in favour of the latter view. In a unanimous decision the House held that the court does have the power to make an ICO with a direction, under section 38(6) of the 1989 Act (or Article 57(6) of the 1995 Order), that a child and his parents be placed in a residential unit for assessment purposes. The Court of Appeal decision[64] (and the line of cases[65] which it followed) favouring the claim of local authority appellants that it could not be directed to undertake a course of action which lay within the sphere of its discretionary powers but for which it lacked the necessary resources, was overturned. This decision by the House of Lords would seem to provide authority for the following propositions regarding the Trusts' use of ICOs:

- a court is entitled to use the powers of Article 57(6) to require a Trust to arrange such assessment of a child as may be necessary to provide the court with the information it needs to determine the substantive issue of whether or not a care order should be made;
- the financial implications for a Trust of compliance with such a direction must be taken into account by the court when exercising its discretion, but a simple Trust plea of inadequate resources will be insufficient reason for non-compliance;
- a court acting within the scope of its discretionary powers under Article 57(6) will not be in breach of the *Liverpool* ruling;
- an assessment of a child, as permitted under Article 57(6), may be construed as an assessment of parent and child where the quality of their relationship is of crucial legal significance;
- although on issue of an ICO a Trust acquires parental responsibility and thereby has the right to determine a child's place of residence, it cannot use this to avoid compliance with a direction issued under Article 57(6).

Basically, this decision has restored to the courts the use of powers not dissimilar to those previously employed in wardship[66] to require Trusts to undertake short periods of assessment of mother/child relationships (often in the family home) so as to equip the court to make a better informed judgment as to whether rehabilitation, statutory care or non-consensual adoption offered the most appropriate disposal option.

Any reliance on adjournments and a continuation of ICOs as a means of permitting the court to satisfy itself that a care plan is viable will require particular justification.[67]

---

63 See *Re C (Interim Care Order: Residential)* [1997] 1 FLR 1.
64 See *Re C (Interim Care Order: Assessment)* [1996] 2 FLR 708.
65 See, for example, *Re L*, op cit. Also see P. Kidd and P. Storey, 'Interim Assessments and Section 38(6)' in Family Law, vol. 27, pp 185–90.
66 See, for example, *Re W (A Ward)*, unreported, (1988), chap. 6, p 108.
67 See *Re P (Minors)(Interim Order)* [1993] 2 FLR 742; *C v Solihull Metropolitan Borough Council* [1993] 1 FLR 290; *Hounslow London Borough Council v A* [1993] 1 FLR 702; and *Re L (Sexual Abuse: Standard of Proof)* [1996] 1 FLR 116.

6. The Duration

An interim order will have effect for the period stated in the order, unless in the meantime a full order is granted; otherwise an IO will cease eight weeks after the date of issue. An ICO may be renewed, in each instance, for a period not exceeding four weeks.[68] The duration of an ICO is dealt with under Article 57(4) and (5), the convoluted wording of which, while stating that the order will last for a maximum period of eight weeks, places no limit on the number of successive orders that may be obtained.[69] In practice, duration is affected by the court's use of its timetabling powers under Article 51 and by the requirement of Article 57(10) that it 'consider whether any party who was or might have been opposed to the making of an order was in a position to argue their case against the order in full'.

7. Appeal or Discharge

An ICO or an ISO may be challenged by way of appeal[70] or by an application for discharge.

III. Education Supervision Orders

Education supervision orders (ESOs) are the only interventionist orders which are not grounded on 'significant harm' as a basic prerequisite.

1. The Order

Under Article 55 of the 1995 Order the court may, on the application of an education and library board, make an ESO in respect of a child where that child 'is of compulsory school age and is not being educated'. This order does not carry any attached directions from the court; instead it delegates the power to make such directions to the supervisor. These directions may be made at any time while the order is in force. As stated in Schedule 4, paragraph 4:

> (2) Any failure to comply with a direction given by the supervisor under an education supervision order shall be disregarded if it would not have been reasonably practicable to comply with it without failing to comply with a direction given under the other order.

Article 55(5) prohibits the granting of an education supervision order in respect of a child in care. It is assumed that education is an integral aspect of such a child's welfare, which the Trusts are obliged to safeguard and promote.

---

68 See *Re G* f/n 57, p 842, where Waite LJ commented that Parliament's intentions:
> ... would be frustrated if a practice were allowed to grow up under which renewals of interim care orders were sought routinely by local authorities.

69 The difficulties associated with determining the duration of subsequent orders was apparent in *Gateshead MBC v N* [1993] 1 FLR 811. See also *Re B (A Minor)(Interim Care Order: Criteria)* [1993] 1 FLR 815.

70 Rule 28 of the Magistrates' Courts (Children (NI) Order 1995) Rules (NI) 1996; Rule 4.23 of the Family Proceedings Rules (NI) 1996.

2. Circumstances Where an ESO Would Be Appropriate

Where the co-operation of parents is not forthcoming, it is unlikely that an ESO is going to be enforceable; a different approach is indicated. However, as stated in the Guidance and Regulations,[71]

> [a]n education supervision order could help where parents find it difficult to exercise a proper influence over their child and where the child has developed a pattern of poor attendance. It would give the backing of the court to the supervising officer and would complement the efforts of the supervising officer to resolve the child's problems by working with the parents to bring them to accept their statutory education responsibilities.

3. The Role of the Court

The role of the court in dealing with ESO applications arose for consideration in *Essex County Council v B*.[72] This was a case where the application concerned a fourteen-year-old girl who had been a poor attender from the age of five. The magistrates did not appoint a guardian ad litem nor did they make an order — apparently on the basis that an 'enforced change' to full-time education would not produce the desired effect on the girl. The local authority appealed against the 'no-order' decision and the girl appealed against the non-appointment of a GAL.

(a) Welfare Checklist

On appeal it was held that before making an ESO the court must apply the welfare checklist and the no-order presumption.

(b) Guardian ad Litem

The requirement to appoint a GAL is only necessary in 'specified proceedings' and therefore the court was not required to make such an appointment. This case is also authority for the requirement that the court states any findings of fact and gives its reasons when determining an application for an ESO.

(c) Family Proceeding

Application must be made in the first instance to a magistrates' family proceedings court after serving seven days' notice of proceedings on the relevant parties.

Proceedings for an ESO are defined as 'family proceedings' under Article 8(3) and (4) of the 1995 Order. The court must, therefore, apply the paramountcy principle, the welfare checklist, the no-delay principle and the no-order presumption. The fact that they are designated 'family proceedings' also means that the court is free to exercise its discretion and make any Article 8 order instead of an ESO. It may call for welfare reports and for a hearing to be adjourned for preparation of such reports.

---

71 Children (NI) Order 1995, Guidance and Regulations, vol. 1, para 13.12.
72 [1993] 1 FLR 866.

4. The Grounds

The distinctive characteristic of an ESO is that it is confined to school attendance problems:[73]

> (2) A court may only make an education supervision order if it is satisfied that the child concerned is of compulsory school age and is not being properly educated.
>
> (3) For the purposes of this Article, a child is being properly educated only if he is receiving efficient full-time education suitable to his age, ability and aptitude and to any special educational needs he may have.

The corollary is that where the child is the subject of a school attendance order with which there is non-compliance or where the child is simply not a regular school attender, then this ground is automatically satisfied.

In *Re O (A Minor)(Care Order: Education Procedure)*[74] the court considered the possible bearing of the significant harm threshold on a situation of chronic non-attendance. The court found that where a child is not attending school without good reason he or she is either suffering harm due to a lack of adequate parental care or is beyond parental control. In that case it was held that the court at first instance had been right to impose a CO rather than an ESO where the fifteen-year-old child had been truanting for three years and had only attended school for twenty-eight days in the previous year. This is an important ruling which endorses the pre-1989 Act view of Denning MR in *Re S*[75] that '... if a child was not being sent to school or receiving a proper education then he was in need of care'. It demonstrates that, in practice, it will continue to be as difficult under the 1995 Order as it was under the 1968 Act to draw a line between education and general welfare needs.

5. The Applicant

Only an Education and Library Board may make application for an ESO. Before doing so it is required by Article 55(7) to consult with the Trust within whose area the child lives or will live. Because delay can be detrimental to a child's education, the Guidance and Regulations[76] stress that

> [e]ducation and library boards and Trusts should agree time-scales for such consultation and make these public. The outcome should be confirmed in writing, and should indicate whether or not the Trust is involved with the family, if there are any known reasons why an education supervision order would not be considered appropriate and what support the Trust is currently offering or will be offering the child and the family.

---

73 Children (NI) Order 1995, Art. 55.
74 [1992] 2 FLR 7.
75 *(A Minor)* [1978] QB 120.
76 Children (NI) Order 1995, Guidance and Regulations, vol. 1, para 11.13.

Alternatively, if the Trust is already involved with the child, it may request the assistance of the ELB which, under Article 46, it is required to provide, subject to the conditions stated in that provision.

The fact that there is now an order which solely addresses school non-attendance marks a significant change in the legislative approach to non-attending children. Under the 1968 Act, the child with a record of poor school attendance was statutorily defined as vulnerable, the behaviour indicative of welfare needs and the court required to consider a care disposal option. Under the 1995 Order, such a child is viewed as ill-disciplined, the behaviour indicative more of deviancy than of care needs and as such warranting a regulatory form of supervision.

6. Children in Care and ESOs

An ESO cannot be made in respect of a child already subject to a care order. It can be made where a child is merely being accommodated by a Trust. As stated in the Guidance and Regulations[77]

> Trusts have an equal duty to that of parents to discharge their obligations in relation to children in their care i.e. to ensure that the child continues to receive full-time education suitable to his age, ability and aptitude and any special needs he may have.

A Trust is obliged to consult the ELB in respect of any child being accommodated where there are problems in ensuring continued access to education.

7. The Effect of an ESO

As stated in the Guidance and Regulations:[78]

> The intention of education supervision orders is to ensure that a child who is subject to such an order receives efficient full-time education suited to his age, ability, aptitude and any special educational needs, and that sufficient support, advice and guidance are provided to the parents and the child.

One immediate effect of an ESO, under paragraphs 3 and 4 of Schedule 4 of the 1995 Order, is to extinguish any school attendance order, disapply certain provisions of the 1986 and 1989 Orders and remove any requirement relating to school attendance which may have formed a part of a probation order to which the child may at that time be subject. In this way the legislative intent is to purge the order of any connotations of offence and remove school non-attenders from the justice system.

An ESO can, however, co-exist with a supervision order, a probation order or an order made under section 74(1)(c) of the Children and Young Persons Act (NI) 1968 (juvenile offenders).

---

77 Children (NI) Order 1995, Guidance and Regulations, vol. 1, para 13.5.
78 Children (NI) Order 1995, Guidance and Regulations, vol. 1, para 11.3.

An ESO has effect for one year and may then be repeatedly extended though no extension may be for longer than three years. In theory the order could be maintained until the child reached the age of sixteen. It will be terminated on the child's ceasing to be of compulsory schooling age, on the making of a care order or on the successful application for discharge by the child, parent or education and library board.

(a) The Powers and Duties of a Supervisor

Under Schedule 4 of the 1995 Order:

> 2.—(1) Where an education supervision order is in force with respect to a child, it shall be the duty of the supervisor —
>   (a) to advise, assist and befriend, and give directions to—
>   (i) the supervised child; and
>   (ii) his parents, in such a way as will, in the opinion of the supervisor, secure that he is properly educated;
>   (b) where any such directions given to—
>   (i) the supervised child; or
>   (ii) a parent of his, have not been complied with, to consider what further steps to take in the exercise of the supervisor's powers under this Order.

Before giving effect to these duties a supervisor is required, under Schedule 4, paragraph 2, to ascertain as far as is reasonably practicable the wishes and feelings of both child and parents, particularly in relation to the place where the child is to be educated. It is evident that this provision places an onus on the supervisor to be in control in the sense of giving effect to his or her duties in a positive and planned fashion; in the face of non-compliance from child or parent the supervisor is required to do something about it.

(b) The Obligations of the Child or Young Person

Under Schedule 4 of the 1995 Order:

> 6.—(1) An education supervision order may require the child —
>   (a) to keep the supervisor informed of any change in his address; and
>   (b) to allow the supervisor to visit him at the place where he is living.

These basic requirements are reinforced by a warning, under paragraph 8 of Schedule 4, that a failure to inform the supervisor of the child's address or to deny access to the child will be regarded as a criminal offence on the part of child and/or parent.

Under Schedule 4 of the 1995 Order:

> 9.—(1) Where a child with respect to whom an education supervision order is in force persistently fails to comply with any direction given under the order, the education and library board concerned shall notify the appropriate authority.

A referral under this provision will trigger the application of the 'significant harm' threshold thus returning a Trust to the situation as it prevailed under the 1995 Order whereby care orders were often seen as an appropriate disposal option for children presented to the courts with school attendance problems. Now, however, it is for the Trust and not an education and library board to decide whether or not the circumstances are sufficiently grave in their implications for the welfare of the child to warrant an application for a care order.

(c) The Obligations of the Parent

The legal obligation to ensure that a child receives proper education falls firstly on the parents of that child. For the purposes of this legislation, a 'parent' is defined as someone with parental responsibility or a person who has care of the child.

The granting of an ESO has the effect of displacing the parent's rights and duties in respect of a child's education and substituting the authority of a supervisor. The parent then has a duty to comply with any directions given by the supervisor in relation to that child's education. The requirements of paragraph 6(1) in relation to notification of address and access apply equally to the parent. Under Schedule 4, paragraph 8, a persistent failure to co-operate with the supervisor in respect of any of these matters will be a criminal offence unless the directions can be shown to have been unreasonable or that compliance with them would have been incompatible with the directions given under any SO, probation order, or other order under section 74(1)(c) of the 1968 Act to which the child was subject. Parents will also have a good defence if they can show that they took all reasonable steps to induce the child to comply with the supervisor's directions.

It should be noted that in addition, or as an alternative, to applying for an ESO, an ELB may prosecute the child's parents under Article 45 and Schedule 13 of the Education and Libraries (NI) Order 1986 should it consider that this would be a more effective way of proceeding. The court may, however, in the course of such proceedings, direct that the ELB institute ESO proceedings. Should the ELB then choose not to comply with this direction, it must submit a report to the court within eight weeks explaining its reasons for non-compliance.

Private Family Law Orders

Under Article 10 of the 1995 Order:

> (1) In any family proceedings in which a question arises with respect to the welfare of any child, the court may make an Article 8 order with respect to the child if —
>> (b) the court considers that the order should be made even though no such application has been made.

Proceedings initiated for a care order or supervision order under Article 50 are 'family proceedings' for the purposes of the 1995 Order. This means that one possible outcome of such proceedings is that the court will instead decide that an Article 8 order in favour of a private individual affords a more appropriate means of using statutory powers to secure the child's welfare. It may, under Article 11(3), make an Article 8 order in the course of care proceedings, whether or not requested to do so and even if the threshold criteria for a CO or a SO have not been met. It may make an Article 8 order as an interim measure pending the commencement of care proceedings. If, in the latter instance, it should decide to make a residence order, then, under Article 57(3), it must also make an interim supervision order 'unless satisfied that [the child's] welfare will be satisfactorily safeguarded without an interim order being made'. The court's power in respect of Article 8 orders, however, is only exercisable subject to the constraints imposed by Article 9. Also, it is an option which the court will approach with some caution as it precludes the possibility of appointing a GAL with all the added protection for a child that such an appointment entails.[79]

I. Article 8 Orders

The Court and the Trusts

The 1995 Order sets and polices the boundary between private and public family law in relation to the welfare of children. The rule is that parental responsibility should vest exclusively in either the public or in the private domain.

(a) Trust Application for an Article 8 Order

Trusts are prohibited by Article 9(2) from being either an applicant or recipient in respect of residence and contact orders. The legislative intent is that only where the significant harm test has been satisfied and a care order granted will a Trust acquire parental responsibilities. As stated in the Guidance and Regulations:[80]

> Nor can they apply for a prohibited steps or specific issue order as a way of obtaining the care or supervision of a child, nor to obtain an order that the child be accommodated by them, nor can a prohibited steps or specific issue order confer any aspect of parental responsibility upon a Trust (Article 9(5)(b)).

However, where the child concerned is not in care and a Trust can show that the issue affecting that child's welfare is not such as to require an exercise of parental responsibility, then the court may well grant an Article 8 order which falls short of vesting any such responsibility in the Trust. A PSO or a SIO may be granted to a Trust in respect of a child not in care in such circumstances.

---

[79] See *Nottinghamshire County Council v P* [1993] 2 FLR 134. See also *Re S (Contact: Grandparents)* [1996] 1 FLR 158, where the Court of Appeal held that the involvement of a GAL was permissible only for so long as the proceedings were 'specified proceedings'. Once they became Article 8 proceedings, the GAL should have been withdrawn and the Official Solicitor appointed.

[80] Children (NI) Order 1995, Guidance and Regulations, vol. 1, para 5.20.

(b) Private Application for Article 8 Order in Respect of Child in Care of Trust

Under Article 9 of the 1995 Order:

> (1) No court shall make any Article 8 order, other than a residence order, with respect to a child who is in the care of an authority.

A RO is thus the only Article 8 order the court may make in respect of a child who is the subject of a care order. The effect of a RO is to instantly discharge a CO. As stated in the Guidance and Regulations:[81]

> Furthermore, once a care order has been made in respect of a child the court's private law powers should not be used to interfere with the Trust's exercise of its statutory parental responsibilities.

This applies the logic, if not the rule, in *Liverpool* to protect Trusts from possible encroachments upon the sphere of authority granted to them in the form of a care order by Westminster.

Because these orders are mutually exclusive, such an application forces the court to choose between the two and is thus an expedient strategy for attempting to discharge a care order. This was in fact the rationale for the application in *Re A and W (Minors) (Residence Order: Leave to Apply)*[82] in which a foster parent sought leave to appeal a decision of the Trust's English counterpart to prevent her from continuing to foster the four children which that agency had placed with her. The Court of Appeal accepted the applicant's right to pursue a private family law remedy to a matter already subject to a public statutory order, notwithstanding the bearing of the ruling in *Liverpool*. In the particular circumstances of the case, however, it ruled that the applicant had not discharged the heavy onus on her to prove that the agency's actions were not an essential part of a care plan designed to safeguard and promote the welfare of the children in care.

The restriction in Article 9(1) applies only in respect of a child subject to a care order; there is nothing preventing a court from making an Article 8 order where a child is subject to a supervision order or is merely being accommodated by a Trust.

(c) Court Issue of Article 8 Order in Response to Trust Application for CO, SO or IO

When hearing an application to make, vary or discharge any Part V order, the court is required to apply the welfare checklist. This provides an opportunity, in keeping with the underpinning principle of minimal intervention, to consider whether residence orders (ROs) and prohibited steps orders (PSOs), for example, may be used in circumstances where the full imposition of public law is not wholly necessary. Where the court finds that the 'significant harm' threshold either has not been breached or it has but in extenuating circumstances, then instead of granting a care order to the Trust it could make a RO in favour of a third party. Note that the degree of risk is likely to prove all important.[83]

---

81 Children (NI) Order 1995, Guidance and Regulations, vol. 1, para 5.39.
82 [1992] 2 FLR 154, CA.
83 See for example, *Nottinghamshire*, f/n 79, where the Court of Appeal ruled that an application by the Trust's counterpart for a PSO for the purpose of preventing the possible sexual abuse of two girls by their father was misguided; the application should have been for a care order.

However, if there is a realistic alternative to a care order available to the court, then this should be pursued.[84]

This approach has the advantage that the court does not need to be satisfied that there has been a breach of the significant harm threshold. As stated in the Guidance and Regulations:[85]

> It is important for those considering care proceedings to consider the alternative possibilities, and in particular the extent to which the child's needs might be met within the extended family, with an appropriate combination of Article 8 orders and the provision of services by a Trust under Part IV of the Children Order.

When an application for a care order is pending, the court may, of its motion, decide to make an Article 8 order to stabilise the child's circumstances until the care order hearing. Until such time as it makes an order vesting parental responsibility in the Trust, there is judicial discretion to make such Article 8 order or package of orders as it considers necessary and for which the grounds are available.

(d) Court Issue of Article 8 Order in Response to Trust Report under Article 56

In the course of any family proceedings the court may direct a Trust to conduct an investigation and report to the court as to whether or not public proceedings should be commenced in respect of the child or children concerned. If, having conducted its investigation, the Trust reports that it is satisfied that there is no need for public proceedings, then the court may decide to issue an Article 8 order. It should be noted that the appointment of a GAL will be valid only for the period of investigation, unless public proceedings ensue.[86]

II. Residence Order

Where the court considers that on-going coercive intervention is unnecessary to achieve the protection of a child from a future risk of significant harm, it may instead issue a residence order with the consent of the person named in that order. This could be used, for example, to remove the child from the care or from the locality of an abuser to the care and possession of a trusted member of the family. It may be made subject to such conditions as the court considers appropriate or, if necessary, may be coupled with a SO. For example, in a case[87] where a child had sustained an unexplained injury requiring investigation and the consequent lack of evidence made any disruption to the child's care arrangements premature, the court responded to a care order application by issuing instead a RO in favour of the parents and an interim SO. Both were made subject to conditions requiring the parents and the child, respectively, to co-operate with professionals in a programme of assessment over a period of three months. This package of orders, tailored to meet the circumstances of the particular case, avoided reliance on the time-limited CAO or the pre-emptive CO.

---

84 See, for example, *Hounslow London Borough Council v A* [1993] 1 WLR 291.
85 Children (NI) Order 1995, Guidance and Regulations, vol. 1, para 5.53.
86 See *Re S (Contact: Grandparents)* [1996] 1 FLR 158.
87 See *C v Solihull Metropolitan Borough Council* [1993] 1 FLR 227.

A RO can be made in respect of any child already in the care of a Trust, though the latter is neither entitled to apply for such an order nor to have one made in its favour. Under Article 179(1) the effect of making a RO in such circumstances is to discharge the CO. This may provide a useful strategy for a person with parental responsibility who wishes to have a care order discharged. More importantly, it is the only option available to a person without parental responsibility who wishes to achieve the same end (see also Chapter Twelve).

III. Prohibited Steps Order

As stated in the Guidance and Regulations:[88]

> Trusts will, like anyone else, be able to apply for specific issue and prohibited steps orders, provided that they first obtain the court's leave. . . . This will enable them to resolve certain issues which at present can only be resolved by making the child a ward of court, such as whether or not the child should have a particular operation. They may arise where a child who is accommodated voluntarily by the Trust, is felt to be in need of a particular course of treatment urgently and the parents cannot be contacted. If, in all the circumstances of the case, the decision is likely to cause controversy at some future date, the Trust should seek an Article 8 specific issue order.

However, the court may not issue such an order where the objective of a Trust is to prevent an abusing parent from contacting his children. Indeed, in this context the warning given by Sir Stephen Brown[89] should be borne in mind:

> We consider that this court should make it clear that the route chosen by the local authority was wholly inappropriate. In cases where children are found to be at risk of significant harm . . . a clear duty arises on the part of the local authorities to take steps to protect them. In such circumstances a local authority is required to assume responsibility and to intervene in the family arrangements in order to protect the child. A prohibited steps order would not afford the local authority any authority as to how it might deal with the children.

This ruling was subsequently applied in a case where a local authority were denied leave to intervene in private proceedings with an application for a PSO to prevent an abusing father from contacting his children who were being satisfactorily cared for by their mother. The court again held that until the significant harm test could be satisfied, the Trust's counterpart could not intervene in family life. Nor may the court issue such an order where the Trust's objective is to prevent parents from contacting each other.[90]

IV. Contact Order

It will seldom be sufficient to make a contact order instead of a care order in private family law. While the need to define access arrangements between a child and another

---

88 Children (NI) Order 1995, Guidance and Regulations, vol. 1, para 5.20.
89 See *Nottinghamshire*, f/n 79, where the Court of Appeal held that the proper course of action was to seek a CO.
90 See *Croydon London Borough Council v A* (No. 1) [1992] 2 FLR 341.

person may well require court attention after the issue of a CO, it is difficult to conceive of circumstances where dealing with it by way of a contact order could forestall the necessity for a CO (see also Chapters Twelve and Sixteen).

V. Specific Issue Order

There may well be occasions when this order will present a reasonable and sufficient alternative to prolonged coercive intervention as a means of securing a child from possible future harm. Most notably this will be the case in circumstances where that harm is confined to a matter such as access to blood-transfusion treatment.[91] Where a child is not in care, then even if the child is being accommodated, a Trust may with leave of the court apply for either a prohibited steps order or a specific issue order. The latter will direct the named party to do no more than carry out the court's instructions with regard to the identified area of harm. It should be noted, as stated in the Guidance and Regulations[92] that

> ... not only are individuals prevented from applying for prohibited steps or specific issue orders as a means of challenging the decisions of a Trust with respect to a child in its care, but the Trust itself cannot seek guidance from the court on matters concerning the child's upbringing by applying for one of these orders once the child is formally in its care. Instead, the Trust will have to apply for leave to invoke the High Court's inherent jurisdiction under Article 173(2).

It should also be borne in mind that the court has no power to issue a SIO as a means of requiring a Trust to designate a child as being a child in need for the purpose of ensuring appropriate service provision.[93]

VI. Wardship Orders

Under Article 173 of the 1995 Order:

> (1) The court shall not exercise its inherent jurisdiction with respect to children—
>
> (c) so as to make a child who is the subject of a care order a ward of court; or
> (d) for the purpose of conferring on any authority power to determine any question which has arisen, or which may arise, in connection with any aspect of parental responsibility for a child.

Nor may a Trust make application for a wardship order unless it first obtains leave of the court. The legislative intent is clearly to shut down Trust access to the wardship jurisdiction. Having made available a wide range of statutory orders, some of which pointedly incorporate the more characteristic features of wardship, the Trusts are expected to look to those for the powers necessary to discharge their parental responsibilities in respect of a child rather than implicate the courts in on-going case

---

91 See, for example, *Re R (A Minor)(Blood Transfusion)* [1993] 2 FLR 609.
92 Children (NI) Order 1995, Guidance and Regulations, vol. 1, para 5.40.
93 See *Re J (Specific Issue Order: Leave to Apply)* [1995] 1 FLR 669.

management through use of wardship. Care orders and wardship orders are now seen as mutually incompatible and decisions regarding the welfare of children in care are to be taken by the Trusts and not the judiciary.

However, there remain circumstances in which a Trust may be successful in obtaining the leave of the court to commence wardship proceedings. In situations where a Trust requires the court to authorise a limited course of action without otherwise interfering with parental responsibility and no statutory order is appropriate, then recourse to the inherent jurisdiction of the High Court may be possible.[94] There remain circumstances when Trust access to wardship or the inherent jurisdiction will be both necessary and possible (see also Chapter Seven).

VII. Other Orders

There are a small number of what might be termed 'hybrid' orders (in that they belong to neither public nor to private family law) available to the court under the 1995 Order. It may decide to issue one of these instead of the applied for public family law order and/or it may request a Trust report under Article 4(1).

1. Family Assistance Order

Under Article 16 of the 1995 Order, in exceptional circumstances and with the consent of the relevant adult, the court may direct the local Trust 'to make a suitably qualified person available to advise, assist and (where appropriate) befriend any person named in the order'. This may be coupled with a RO and be made for a period not exceeding six months. It should be noted, however, that in circumstances where a court makes a FAO and the relevant Trust decides it has insufficient resources to implement it, the court will then have no alternative other than to discharge the order[95] (see also Chapter Twelve).

2. Order Directing an Investigation of the Child's Circumstances

Under Article 56 of the 1995 Order, the court may decide to respond to an application for a public family law order by directing the local Trust to undertake an investigation of the child's circumstances, rather than for a care or supervision order (where this investigation will have occurred anyway), (see also Chapter Fifteen).

3. Order Appointing a Guardian for the Child

Under Article 159(2) of the 1995 Order, if the court should find that the child has no parent with parental responsibility for him or that the bearer of a residence order in respect of the child has died while the order is still in force, then it may make a guardianship appointment order, even though no application has been made for such an order (see also Chapter Eleven).

---

94 See, for example, *Devon County Council v S and Another* [1995] 2 All ER 243.
95 See *Re C (Family Assistance Order)* [1996] 1 FLR 424.

CHAPTER FIFTEEN

Child Protection: The Law, the Process and the Orders Relating to the Abuse of Children

Introduction

This chapter deals with child abuse and the related responsibilities of the court, the Trusts and others. It therefore focuses on matters governed by the Children (NI) Order 1995, Part VI. However, this area of family law is also shaped and structured by the Guidance and Regulations, volume 6, *Co-operating to Protect Children* and other formal and informal agency procedures. This makes it also necessary to consider the definitions, processes and professional input through which the Trusts and others operationalise the Part VI provisions.

In Northern Ireland, as elsewhere in the United Kingdom, the law and practice relating to child protection has for many years now served to fence off our society's more fundamental need to preserve the life and safety of its children from the main body of its concern for the growth, development and general well-being of children. Child protection constitutes a focus for specialist professional, judicial and agency expertise which is now quite separate from all other rationale for involvement in the lives of children. The Children (NI) Order 1995 challenges the specialists to adjust that focus to accommodate both the principle of partnership with parents and the presumption that care in the family of origin is in every child's best interests. Child protection and family care are not seen as alternatives. Professional concern and agency resources are to be channelled by the concept of 'children in need' to pre-empt or bridge any such gap. No statutory directives require social workers (as opposed to the judiciary) to give priority weighting to the separate welfare interests of a child. Again, this pushes the former to direct their intervention towards maintaining family care rather than towards commencing proceedings requesting the court to substitute care by the state.

This challenge is unlikely to succeed. The machinery of inter-agency collaboration, intra-agency structures, management priorities, staff training and hard won expertise would resist any inducement to fudge the boundaries between child protection and other forms of intervention in the lives of children. Also, the fear of media exposure in the event of another agency failure to provide a child with adequate protection is itself likely to ensure that the child protection system and ethos remains intact.

The DHSS annual report for 1995 notes an overall reduction in the number and rates of children on child protection registers between 1989 and 1993. It also records very significant increases in the number of recorded offences committed against children under seventeen years for 1989 and 1993. While overall figures for cruelty did not increase, serious assaults, wounding and attempted murder increased by 64 per cent child and abduction by 317 per cent, with children aged six to thirteen years being most affected. There was also an increase of 39 per cent in the recorded number of victims of sexual offences between 1989 and 1993, respectively; a 95 per cent increase in the rape of girls aged fourteen to sixteen years and an increase of 72 per cent in the indecent assault of children in all age groups; as well as a decrease of 9 per cent in recorded cases of gross indecency with children.

This data should be viewed in the context of the targets set for the Boards by the DHSS in its *Regional Strategy for Health and Social Well-being 1997–2002* which specifies that by 2002 there should be:

- 20 per cent reduction in the number of children (on CPRs and having suffered significant harm) who are re-abused
- 10 per cent reduction in the number of joint protocol investigations of child abuse
- 10 per cent reduction in the number of children under ten years of age entering care.

This chapter deals with the statutory and administrative procedures which will continue to regulate child protection as a distinct system in this jurisdiction. It considers the definition of child abuse, explains the different types of abuse and the related evidential requirements. It outlines and explains the sequential stages of the child protection process and focuses on the role and responsibilities of the different agencies involved. The orders available, their effects and the arrangements for inter-agency and multi-disciplinary collaboration are outlined. The judicial interpretation of the law, the principles and practice issues arising in England and Wales under the corresponding provisions of the 1989 Act to secure the future care of a child found to be in need of protection are also examined.

Child Abuse

The abuse of a child is a criminal offence. There is probably no form of abuse which gives rise to more social outrage. The Children (NI) Order 1995, Schedule 2, paragraphs 5 and 8 place a specific duty on each Trust to take reasonable steps to prevent a need for it to take child protection proceedings (see further Chapter Fourteen).

The Concept

As has been said,[1]

> ... child abuse is not an absolute concept. Most behaviour has to be seen in context before it can be thought of as maltreatment. With the exception of some sexual abuse, it should also be clear that maltreatment is seldom an event, a single incident that requires action to protect a child.

This approach is evident in the assessment by Jane Gibbons' that[2]

---

1 Dartington Research Centre, *Child Protection: Messages from Research*, HMSO, 1995.
2 Ibid.

as a phenomenon, child maltreatment is more like pornography than whooping cough. It is a socially constructed phenomenon which reflects values and opinions of a particular culture at a particular time.

The construct 'significant harm' now provides the legal benchmark for determining whether child maltreatment has occurred. While there can be no doubt that quite often one incident of maltreatment is, unfortunately, sufficient to constitute significant harm and thus meet the definition of abuse, there is considerably more doubt as to the degree and the types of maltreatment which do so. For example, the systemic abuse of a number of children over an extended period of time has been recognised as a distinct form of abuse, though not very prevalent. Although this jurisdiction has produced examples of systemic abuse,[3] there has been little or no evidence here or across the Irish Sea of so-called satanic or ritualised abuse.[4] In both jurisdictions, the phenomenon of child abuse is represented most often by domestic maltreatment, in the form of a physical or sexual assault, on one child by either a member of that child's family, or a close relative or by a family friend.

Definition in Law

Under Article 62(1)(a) of the 1995 Order a child is abused or at risk of becoming so, when he or she 'is suffering or is likely to suffer significant harm' where 'harm' under Article 2(2) is defined as including both ill-treatment (which 'includes sexual abuse and forms of ill-treatment which are not physical') and the impairment of health ('health' meaning physical or mental health) or development ('development' means physical, intellectual, emotional, social or behavioural development).

The abuse of children takes many different forms. While the primary legal issue is now not the form of abuse but the breaching of the significant harm threshold (see Chapter Fourteen), the categorisation of child abuse has proved necessary because for legal purposes, different forms of abuse require different types of evidential material; whereas for agency purposes, staff skills in detection and treatment together with the need to accurately deploy relevant resources require a similar differentiation.

Administrative Categorisation

The operational distinction made between different forms of child abuse is provided by the definitions given in *Working Together*[5] and replicated in all Health and Social Services Area Child Protection Committee handbooks.

> *Neglect*: Persistent or severe neglect of a child, or the failure to protect a child from exposure to any kind of danger, including cold or starvation, or extreme failure to

---

3 See the *Report of the Committee of Inquiry into Children's Homes and Hostels*, DHSS (NI), HMSO (1986) which examined the Kincora scandal involving a children's home of that name and others; also see the on-going enquiries into abuse perpetrated by members of certain religious orders.
4 See Fontaine J, La, *The Extent and Nature of Organised and Ritual Sexual Abuse: Research Findings*, HMSO, 1994. But also see, for example, *Rochdale Borough Council v A* [1991] 2 FLR 192.
5 *Working Together under the Children Act 1989*, HMSO, 1991.

carry out important aspects of care, resulting in the significant impairment of the child's health or development, including non-organic failure to thrive.
Physical Injury: Actual or likely physical injury to a child, or failure to prevent physical injury (or suffering) to a child including deliberate poisoning, suffocation and Munchausen's syndrome by proxy.
Sexual Abuse: Actual or likely sexual exploitation of a child adolescent. The child may be dependent and/or developmentally immature.
Emotional Abuse: Actual or likely severe adverse effect on the emotional and behavioural development of a child caused by persistent or severe emotional ill-treatment. This category should be used where it is the main or sole form of abuse.

1. Neglect

The liability of a parent, a person with parental responsibility or someone with *loco parentis* standing for any harm which befalls a child as a consequence of his or her failure to afford the child an adequate standard of care or protection is a well-established principle.[6] It has provided grounds for Trust intervention, both consensual and coercive (under section 103 and section 95 of the 1968 Act, respectively, and in wardship), for many years prior to the introduction of the 1995 Order. Traditionally, this liability arose in circumstances where the failure in parenting was associated with low standards of care, maintenance or safety due perhaps to poverty, immaturity or parental incapacity resulting from illness, injury or learning disability.[7] The introduction of the 1995 Order has seen this liability assimilated within the definition of 'harm' in Article 2(2) as meaning 'ill-treatment or the impairment of health or development'.

Fault

Wilfulness is seldom a factor. The distinction between fault and default is not a determinant of Trust or court decision-making in respect of future arrangements for a child found to be neglected. Indeed, it has always been the actual consequences for the child not the intentions of the carer which are of primary concern to Trust and court. The standard of child care required is judged objectively in the sense that the measure applied is that of a hypothetical caring parent, i.e. no allowance can be made for the fact that the actual parent is too young, inexperienced or distressed to cope any better. The standard applied is also subjective in the sense that the level of care expected from such a parent is that actually required to meet the particular needs of the child in question, i.e. the fact that the level of care provided would be adequate for an average child is irrelevant if the child in question requires care of a higher standard due perhaps to a disability.

Although this form of abuse is not mentioned in either the 1995 Order nor in the 1989 Act, it has been the subject of considerable judicial and media attention in recent years as a result of cases arising in the context of medical treatment. Evidence of

---

6 See, for example, *R v Senior* [1899] 1 QB 283 where Russell LJ described neglect as 'the omission of such steps as a reasonable parent would take' (at p. 291). See also *Oakey v Jackson* [1914] 1 KB 216.
7 See, for example, *R v Connor* [1908] 2 KB 26 where a father had deserted, leaving the mother with insufficient money to feed their children. The evidence showed that the children were clean but poorly clad and fed; the father was found guilty of wilful neglect.

parental failure to provide or permit others to provide essential medical treatment for a seriously ill child has repeatedly been found sufficient to ground court intervention (see also Chapters One, Seven, Eighteen and Nineteen).

2. Physical Abuse

Child abuse is most commonly understood to mean the deliberate use by an adult of his or her own personal strength, with or without an implement, to inflict harm on a child. It clearly falls within the definition of 'ill-treatment' given in Article 2(2).

As has been said:[8]

> Physical abuse implies physically harmful action directed against a child; it is usually defined by any inflicted injury such as bruises, burns, head injuries, fractures, abdominal injuries or poisoning.

This is the most frequently recorded form of abuse. The perpetrators are as likely to be parents or other family members as third parties and most often the legal issues are relatively straightforward as evidence in the form of injuries and testimonies from victim and perpetrator are readily available. However, it is the deliberate harm inflicted by a well-intentioned parent or someone acting on his or her behalf for the purposes of disciplining a child that gives rise to most contention.

(a) Chastisement by a Parent

The common-law right[9] of a parent to administer 'moderate and reasonable chastisement' continues to govern the law in this difficult area and to generate debate as to what constitutes 'moderate' or 'reasonable'. It has long been held to be justifiable for a parent to demonstrate disapproval of a child's unacceptable behaviour and to discourage its repetition by physically chastising such a child. However, parental discretion in this area is subject to a legal test of reasonableness.

Paradoxically, it was acceptance of its status as a legal incidence of parenthood that enabled the European Court of Human Rights to rule in favour of parent petitioners who objected to the use of corporal punishment in state schools.[10]

(b) Chastisement by a Third Party

The issue as to who has the right to administer such chastisement has concerned the courts. This arose for consideration in the European Court of Human Rights (ECHR)[11] in a case where a seven-year-old boy had been punished by the headmaster. The chastisement took the form of three strikes on his bottom, through his shorts, with a rubber-soled gym shoe. He alleged breach of Article 3 of the European Convention of Human Rights 1950. The ECHR held that the following factors should be considered

---

8 C Kempe, F Silverman, B Steele, W Droegmueller and H Silver, 'The Battered Child Syndrome', (1962) JAMA, 181.
9 See *R v Hopley* (1860) 2 F&F 202.
10 See *Cambell and Cossans v UK* (1982) 4 EHRR 293.
11 See *Costello–Roberts v United Kingdom* [1994] ELR 1, ECHR. Note, also, Article 37 of the UN Convention on the Rights of the Child, ratified by the United Kingdom in 1991.

in determining whether a breach had occurred: the nature and context of the punishment, the manner and method of its execution, its duration, its physical and mental effects and, in some cases, the sex, age and state of health of the victim. It was decided, by a majority verdict of 5:4, that the punishment had not been so severe as to constitute a breach of Article 3. The court also decided, unanimously, that the punishment had not adversely affected the child's physical or moral integrity to a degree that would have constituted a breach of Article 8 (respect for private and family life) and held that the applicant had an adequate route to a remedy under domestic law.

This headmaster was found to be acting within the scope of his *loco parentis* responsibilities. So, also, was a child-minder[12] who admitted smacking a child in her care but with parental permission.

3. Sexual Abuse

No form of child maltreatment has generated more social outrage and raised more legal difficulties in recent years than sexual abuse. It is recognised in Article 2(2) of the 1995 Order as constituting a specific form of ill-treatment and has been defined as follows.[13]

> Sexual abuse is defined as the involvement of dependent, developmentally immature children and adolescents in sexual activities they do not fully comprehend and to which they are unable to give informed consent or that violate the social taboos of family roles.

This form of abuse, when perpetrated by a family member, is known as incest, and protection has long been afforded under the Punishment of Incest Act 1908, section 1, to any child or young person who is a female member of a household of which a member has committed or attempted to commit such an offence.

(a) Standard of Proof

The normal standard of the balance of probabilities, applicable in all civil proceedings, applies also to cases of child sexual abuse. However, the courts have tended to place a heavy burden on the party alleging such abuse to produce a convincing weight and range of evidential material in support of the allegations. This approach was recommended by the late Higgins J, who, in the first recorded case[14] on child sexual abuse in this jurisdiction, said

> that because of the gravity of the decision, which the Court has to make, the Court should require a very high degree of probability, which is appropriate to what is at stake. For the purposes of this case, I shall accept that as the correct standard of proof having regard to the consequences which may follow, if the Board's case is proved.

In England and Wales, the Court of Appeal has recently lent more weight to this approach in a judgment which endorsed the views of the judge at first instance who

---

12 See *London Borough of Sutton v Davies* (No 2)[1995] 1 All ER 65; also see Chapter Five.
13 M Schechter and L Roberge, 'Sexual Exploitation' in *Child Abuse and Neglect*, eds. R Helfer and C Kempe, Balinger, 1976, 127–42.
14 See *In Re PB (A Minor)* unreported (1986).

had in turn relied on the well-worn assertion of Ungoed-Thomas J[15] that 'the more serious the allegation the more cogent is the evidence required to overcome the unlikelihood of what is alleged'. This was a case which rested on the single issue of whether the elder of four sisters had been sexually abused by her step-father who had been acquitted of rape on that issue; subsequently, the court had to consider an application for care orders in respect of the other three sisters on the grounds that they were 'likely to suffer significant harm' (as per Article 50(2)) if the orders were not made. The president of the family division then stated[16] that the standard was

> that evidence of primary fact relating to past events had to be established on the balance of probabilities proportionate to the gravity of the allegations concerned.

Any remaining doubt on the matter was laid to rest by the final ruling on this case by the House of Lords in what has now become the leading case[17] on the standard of evidence applicable in cases of alleged sexual abuse. Having considered possible different interpretations of the requisite standard and reviewed related case law, the House concluded that the correct rule was to apply the simple balance of probabilities test.

Additionally, Sheldon J has suggested[18] that a distinction may be usefully made between the standard of proof required to establish the fact of such abuse and that required to establish the identity of the perpetrator. Particularly where parental sexual abuse is alleged, he suggests that the long-term consequences for the child, the perpetrator and the family as a whole are so serious as to justify a higher standard of proof for the second stage than the first.

It has also been noted[19] that the ultimate decision as to the accuracy of the statements of children is a matter for the court and not for the experts (the latter may express a view on the credibility of the child in relation to the allegations, they may not express a view about the truth of those allegations) so that expert evidence of opinion on that issue is inadmissible.

(b) Burden of Proof

The ruling in *Re H and Others* also serves to underline the basic obligation of applicants in such cases to discharge the burden of proof lying on them to show that the child concerned is likely to suffer significant harm.

(c) Evidence

In the absence of an admission of guilt, allegations of child sexual abuse present the court with greater difficulties than other forms of abuse. In the words of Browne-Wilkinson LJ:[20]

---

15   See *Re Dellow's WT* [1964] 1 WLR 451.
16   See *Re H and Others (Minors)(Sexual Abuse: Standard of Proof)* [1995] 1 FLR 643, 650.
17   Ibid.
18   See, for example, *Re G (no. 2) (A Minor)* [1988] 1 FLR 314.
19   See Johnson J in *Re B (Child Sexual Abuse: Standard of Proof)* [1995] 1 FLR 904, 912A–C. Also see *Re S and B (Minors) (Child Abuse: Evidence)* [1990] 2 FLR 489.
20   [1996] 1 All ER 4.

Child abuse, particularly sexual abuse, is notoriously difficult to prove in a court of law. The relevant facts are extremely sensitive and emotive. They are often known only to the child and to the alleged abuser.

Reliance solely on the testimony of an alleged victim is particularly fraught with legal difficulties. Corroboration must be sought in the form not only of medical evidence but also in verifiable psycho-social disturbance (see further Chapter Nineteen).

(d) Proof of Past Abuse as Evidence of 'Likely to Suffer Significant Harm'

A central issue in *Re H and R* was whether, even if the abuse had occurred in respect of one child, that would be sufficient evidence to ground a finding of risk of future abuse to that child's siblings. As Browne-Wilkinson LJ[21] stated:

> If legal proof of actual abuse is a prerequisite to a finding that a child is at risk of abuse, the courts will be powerless to intervene to protect children in relation to whom there are the gravest suspicions of actual abuse but the necessary evidence legally to prove such abuse is lacking.

The House of Lords acknowledged that in relation to the initial allegation of abuse the court had not been satisfied that 'the child concerned is suffering, or is likely to suffer, significant harm' (as per section 31(2)(a) of the 1989 Act or Article 50(2)(a) of the 1995 Order). However, the House held that the issue of whether the girl's siblings were exposed to 'harm, or the likelihood of harm . . . attributable to (i) the care given to the child, or likely to be given to him if the order were not made, not being what it would be reasonable to expect a parent to give to him' (as per section 31(2)(b) of the 1989 Act or Article 50(2)(b) of the 1995 Order) was not dependent upon the initial finding. The two parts of this provision may stand separately: 'the likelihood of future harm does not depend on proof that disputed allegations are true' (per Lord Lloyd of Berwick). In principle, it was possible for the court to find that a risk of future abuse existed to a child's siblings despite there being insufficient evidence to confirm past abuse in respect of the child concerned.

Further, the evidence which was adduced in the course of the unsuccessful proceedings under the first part of this provision could, nonetheless, be relied upon in subsequent proceedings under the second part. As noted by Lord Lloyd of Berwick[22]:

> Evidence which is insufficient to establish the truth of an allegation to a required standard of proof nevertheless remains evidence in the case. It need not be disregarded.

However, the problem facing the House was that no facts had been established in the first set of proceedings which could form the basis of evidence to satisfy the grounds

---

21 Ibid.
22 Ibid at 10. Cases relied upon in support of this assertion were: *H v H and C (Kent CC Intervening)(Child Abuse: Evidence), K v K (Haringey London BC intervening)(Child Abuse: Evidence)* [1989] 3 All ER 740, 750, [1990] Fam 86, 101; *Re W (Minors)(Wardship: Evidence)* [1990] 1 FLR 203.

of the second set. Proof of relevant facts is required for the success of any proceedings. A child cannot be removed from parental care on the grounds either that he or she is suffering significant harm or that he or she is likely to do so unless the court is presented with facts not suspicion. The House dismissed the appeal.

(e) Severity of Sentence

AG's Reference[23] concerned a case referred to the Court of Appeal by the Attorney General under section 36 of the Criminal Justice Act 1988. The issue was whether the sentence of five years handed down by the Belfast Crown Court was a sufficiently severe punishment for a twenty-seven-year-old man convicted on one count of rape and six counts of gross indecency against a six-year-old girl, the daughter of a couple with whom he had been close friends for ten years. In a judgment which raised the sentence to eight years, Hutton LCJ[24] said:

> The threat of sexual abuse to children in modern society has become so grave and the duty resting on the courts to deter those who may be tempted to harm little children sexually has become so important that severe sentences must be passed on those who commit rape against little children even if before the offence they had good records and good reputations.

The Court of Appeal has also considered[25] a father's petition for leave to appeal from a sentence of nine years imposed following a conviction on two counts of incest with his daughter, one occurring while she was below the age of fourteen. Granting leave and confirming the sentence, Hutton LCJ and Kelly LJ also endorsed a sentencing policy provided by Lane LJ in England. This policy calibrates sentences — factors such as the age of the child, the frequency and duration of the abuse, whether additional perversion was practised and the level of coercion, physical brutality or indeed affection employed by the perpetrator.

4. Emotional Abuse

Emotional abuse is clearly intended for inclusion within the 'forms of ill-treatment which are not physical' for the purposes of Article 2(2) of the 1995 Order. Like neglect, emotional abuse may be more a sin of omission than commission. Deprivation of a sense of warmth in a relationship with a parent can in itself engender serious psychological problems for a child. Deliberate emotional cruelty (e.g. parental taunting in respect of a child's disability) or inappropriate emotional demands (e.g. that an adolescent should assume a relationship of confidante/therapist with a sole parent) may amount to abuse. Whether resulting from deprivation or deliberation, emotional abuse like all other forms of child abuse[26] is a consequence of the misuse by an adult

---

23 Unreported (1989) CA.
24 Ibid at 251.
25 See *R v Charters* [1990] 6 BNIL 70.
26 See, for example, *Re M and R (Child Abuse: Evidence)* [1996] 2 FLR 195, CA where the Court of Appeal upheld the finding of emotional abuse by the court at first instance and the consequent making of interim care orders.

of the authority they bear as such in their relationship with a child. Once the level of abuse breaches the threshold of significant harm, it satisfies the grounds for coercive intervention by a Trust or 'authorised person'.

Child Protection

I. The Agencies Involved

Arrangements for the protection of children are not the sole responsibility of any one agency. The Trusts are of necessity the lead agency as they are statutorily assigned the duty of determining whether a case goes to court and for implementing any related orders issued by the court. They give effect to their pre-court duties, however, by co-ordinating the involvement of other agencies. The operational roles and responsibilities of all involved in this child protection network are governed more by administrative rules and regulations than by statute law.

1. The Trusts

The Children (NI) Order 1995 places the following duties on the Trusts in respect of child protection: to investigate (Article 66); to take such steps as may be reasonable to prevent a need for child protection proceedings (Schedule 2, para 5 and 8) to make or cause to be made such inquiries as may be necessary to determine whether action should be taken to safeguard or promote a child's welfare (Article 65(1)(b)) and to seek court orders for the assessment, urgent removal or care of a child (Articles 62, 63 and 50, respectively). The Trusts give effect to these duties through structures which predate the introduction of the 1995 Order but continue to facilitate efficient management of their child protection remit.

(a) The Area Child Protection Committees (ACPC)

Each Health and Social Services Board has its own area child protection committee (ACPC) which is responsible for establishing the policies and strategies, formulating the standards of practice and monitoring professional effectiveness in respect of child protection within its area. The ACPC negotiates the inter-agency working arrangements which prevail in relation to the detection of abuse and the management of subsequent inter-disciplinary involvement.

(b) The Child Protection Panels (CPP)

Each Trust within each Board has its own child protection panel (CPC) which acts as a conduit for relaying data affecting policy and practice between the ACPC and the managers of local child protection teams. Primarily, though, this body implements the ACPC child protection policies and procedures, and conducts case reviews.

(c) Case Management Reviews

Each Trust has its own core review team, consisting of representatives locally drawn from the relevant professions, which meets as necessary to conduct a review of any case where a child has suffered significant harm and the circumstances are considered to have implications for agency practice. This body will serve advance notice on its Board and DHSS of an intention to hold such a review and, if requested, will extend membership rights to their representatives.

2. The National Society for the Prevention of Cruelty to Children

An 'authorised person' for the purposes of the child protection powers outlined in Part V is, as defined under Article 49(2) of the 1995 Order, the National Society for the Prevention of Cruelty to Children (NSPCC) and any of its officials. This voluntary organisation continues, as under the 1968 Act, to be legislatively recognised as the sole non-statutory agency entitled to conduct enquiries and commence court proceedings in relation to child protection matters.

3. The Royal Ulster Constabulary

Child abuse is a crime and the statutory authority governing police investigations into actual or suspected criminal offences is provided by the Police and Criminal Evidence (NI) Order 1989.

In 1994 the Royal Ulster Constabulary (RUC) established CARE (Child Abuse and Rape Enquiry) units as the basis for pursuing its enquiries into child protection matters. Each of the nine RUC divisions now has its own CARE unit.

The Joint Protocol Arrangements

The *Regional Protocol for the Joint Investigation by Social Workers and Police Officers of Alleged and Suspected Child Abuse*, or the so-called 'joint protocol' arrangements, established between the Boards and the RUC to give effect to their complementary child protection responsibilities under the 1968 Act, continue to provide the framework for managing the involvement of police officers and social workers (and such other health or social services staff as may be appropriate) in each case of suspected child abuse. However, in practice the separation of a social worker's primary concern to secure protection and appropriate treatment for a child victim from that of the police to conduct an investigation, gather evidential material and pursue a criminal prosecution has proved problematic.

4. The Medical Profession

Health care practitioners can often play a crucial role in cases of actual or suspected child abuse. While their role in offering treatment to an abused child following the conclusion of court proceedings is usually legally non-contentious, the involvement of health practitioners in cases of alleged abuse prior to proceedings has at times given rise to controversy and, in particular, the role of Forensic Medical Officers and paediatricians is now governed by agency procedures. Most legal difficulties stem from the necessity to obtain parental consent for the medical examination of a child and for most intrusive types of treatment.

5. The Teaching Profession

Schools necessarily play a vital role in identifying child abuse. Designated teaching staff are now offered special training in child protection, are appointed to liaise with their local Trust child protection team on operational matters and are required to participate in formal inter-agency procedures for ensuring effective practice arrangements. Under such procedures, teachers are required to attend child protection case conferences where a child known to them is the subject of inquiries.

II. The Trusts

The child protection process is that period, from detection of actual or suspected abuse to a Trust decision to initiate or dispense with court proceedings, in which a child must be safeguarded, inquiries conducted and professional involvement co-ordinated. The management of agency responsibilities during this period is governed by procedures set out in the area child protection committee handbooks. These in turn have been drawn up to comply with the guidelines set out in *Co-operating to Protect Children*.[27] The guidelines structure the child protection process into a series of sequential stages: initial investigations, case conference, registration and decision to initiate either statutory proceedings or take other forms of action.

This agency-constructed process for the management of child abuse inquiries does not draw its authority from the substantive provisions of the 1995 Order: neither the child protection case conference nor the child protection register are mentioned there and the process itself remains materially unaffected by legislative change. However, it has for some time been endorsed and utilised by all relevant agencies and professionals as the appropriate vehicle for carrying cases of suspected abuse from point of detection to point of judicial determination. It is now formally addressed in the Children (NI) Order 1995, Guidance and Regulations, volume 6: *Co-operating to Protect Children.*

Initial Investigations: The Statutory Authority

Investigations may be initiated either by request of the court under Article 4, by directive of the court under Article 56, by referral procedures provided for in the schedules, from the RUC under Article 66(1)(a) or by Trust initiative under Article 66(1)(b) of the 1995 Order. The latter will be used with the greatest frequency as disclosure by child is the most common trigger for intervention.[28] Article 66 inquiries may follow on from police-initiated intervention to remove and accommodate a child under Article 65.

Authority to Conduct a Child Welfare Inquiry

(a) Under Article 4

  (i) A court considering any question with respect to a child under this Order may ask an authority to arrange for a suitably qualified person to report to the court

---

27 DHSS, 1989, a document which was based on its English predecessor *Working Together,* 1988.
28 This power of the court to direct a Trust to carry out investigations is also available when convicting of a 'Schedule 1' offence under section 96 of the 1968 Act.

on such matters relating to the welfare of that child as are required to be dealt with in the report.

This is a sweeping discretionary power available to the judiciary as and when they feel the need to avail of it. Unlike investigations conducted under Articles 56 or 66, the authority to request Trust intervention under Article 4 is not tied to the 'significant harm' threshold.

(b) Under Article 56

(1) Where, in any family proceedings in which a question arises with respect to the welfare of any child, it appears to the court that it may be appropriate for a care or supervision order to be made with respect to him, the court may direct the appropriate authority to undertake an investigation of the child's circumstances.

Article 56(2) and (3) requires that a Trust, when undertaking such an investigation, report to the court as to whether it proposes to apply for a CO or SO and, if not, its reasons for so deciding; whether, instead, it has provided or proposes to provide services or assistance for the child and/or the family and, if so, the nature of any such services or assistance; or whether it has taken or proposes to take any other form of action with respect to the child and, if so, the nature of that action. Article 56(4) requires the Trust to make its report to the court within eight weeks from being so directed unless the court otherwise directs.

Such action, taken under the corresponding provision of the 1989 Act, determined the subsequent course of events in a case[29] which illustrates the usefulness of consolidated family proceedings. Separation proceedings, interrupted by an application for a residence order brought jointly by one party (the father) and an aunt, were further compounded when a child of the parties to the initial action alleged sexual abuse by the father. The court's direction that an assessment be undertaken was thwarted by the father's refusal to co-operate. Faced with this obstruction and believing that grounds existed to satisfy the significant harm test the court granted the Trust's counterpart an interim care order permitting the removal of the child to a place where the required investigation could proceed. This court-initiated investigation by a Trust replaces the previous discretionary judicial power under matrimonial and other legislation to simply commit a child directly into care.

(c) Under Schedule 4, paragraph 7

(2) On discharging an education supervision order, the court may direct the authority within whose area the child lives, or will live, to investigate the circumstances of the child.

Judicial discretion will give rise to the referral of a small number of such cases every year.

---

29   See *Re B (A Minor)(Interim Care Order: Criteria)* [1993] 1 FLR 815.

(d) Under Schedule 4, paragraph 9

>(1) Where a child with respect to whom an education supervision order [ESO] is in force persistently fails to comply with any direction given under the order, the education and library board concerned shall notify the appropriate authority.
>
>(2) Where an authority has been notified under sub-paragraph (1) it shall investigate the circumstances of the child.

Persistent non-compliance with the requirements of an ESO will give rise to an assumption that the child and his or her circumstances require investigation from a welfare perspective; which in turn may on occasion lead into a child protection enquiry.

(e) Under Article 66

>(1) Where an authority —
> (a) is informed that a child lives, or is found, in the authority's area
>   (i) is the subject of an emergency protection order; or
>   (ii) is in police protection;
> (b) has reasonable cause to suspect that a child who lives, or is found, in the authority's area is suffering, or is likely to suffer, significant harm,
>
>the authority shall make, or cause to be made, such enquiries as it considers necessary to enable it to decide whether it should take any action to safeguard or promote the child's welfare.

A Trust-initiated investigation will occur in respect of a child who is already the subject of an emergency protection order or, having been taken into police protection under Article 65, is then the subject of a referral to the relevant Trust.

Most Trust investigations are generated by this provision. The latter part of it places a much firmer onus on a Trust to conduct inquiries than existed under the 1968 Act. It is now required to make such enquiries as will enable it to rule out the need to take protective measures. Also, as stated in the Guidance and Regulations:[30]

>An application for an emergency protection order or a child assessment order should always be preceded by some kind of Trust investigation where the Trust is the applicant. Indeed the applicant is not likely to be able to satisfy the court of either set of grounds without being able to point to findings of an investigation, however limited this might be in some circumstances and especially in sudden emergencies. Action under Article 66 (the Trust's duty to investigate) should be seen as the usual first step when a question of child protection arises . . .

Article 66 requires that:

>(3) The inquiries shall, in particular, be directed towards establishing —
> (a) whether the authority should make any application to the court, or exercise any of the authority's other powers under this Order, with respect to the child; and

---

30 Children (NI) Order 1995, Guidance and Regulations, vol. 1, para 8.6.

(b) whether, in the case of a child —
  (i) with respect to whom an emergency protection order has been made; and
  (ii) who is not in accommodation provided by or on behalf of the authority, it would be in the child's best interests (while the emergency protection order remains in force) for him to be in such accommodation.

Any Trust pursuing inquiries under this provision is empowered by Article 65(4) to 'take such steps as are reasonably practicable' to obtain access to the child concerned, or allow access to be obtained by someone authorised by the Trust, unless it is satisfied that it already has sufficient information about the child; refusal of access provides grounds, under Article 65(6), for an EPO. As stressed in the Guidance and Regulations,[31] this provision:

> imposes a positive duty on Trusts making enquiries to see the child and to take legal action if access is denied.

If it should become apparent, during the course of inquiries, that 'there are matters connected with the child's education which should be investigated' then Article 66(5) requires the Trust to consult with the relevant Education and Library Board. The importance of inter-agency co-operation which is addressed by Article 46 is also apparent in Article 66(9) which places a specific duty on certain named bodies (and such others, under Article 66(10) and (11), as the Trust considers appropriate) to provide assistance to any Trust pursuing inquiries under this provision if called upon to do so. However, as noted in the Guidance and Regulations:[32]

> ... this provision does not oblige any agency to assist a Trust where doing so would be unreasonable in all the circumstances of the case. What constitutes 'unreasonable' will depend on local circumstances ...

If, having completed its investigation, the Trust concludes that no further action is required, it must consider whether it would be appropriate for it to review the case at a later date; if so, then it is required under Article 66(7) to set a date for such a review.

The link between a Trust's investigative/coercive intervention duties and its powers under Part IV (specifically, the link between Articles 66 and 18 in which the circumstances described and the services are the same) may not be readily made.[33] Alternatively, Article 18 enquiries are seen by some professionals as a 'passport to services'.[34]

---

31 Children (NI) Order 1995, Guidance and Regulations, vol. 1, para 8.10.
32 Children (NI) Order 1995, Guidance and Regulations, vol. 1, para 8.14.
33 See Gibbons et al, *Operating the Child Protection System: A Study of Child Protection Practices in English Local Authorities*, HMSO, 1995, where a study of CPRs revealed that in more than fifty per cent of the cases, though a finding had been made of grave concern, no services were provided.
34 See Dingwall and 'diagnostic inflation'.

Initial Investigations: Professional Inquiries

Many referrals are filtered out following internal agency inquiries.[35] A case is most likely to be dropped if the allegation concerns neglect, the physical abuse is judged to be not very serious, the perpetrator is not a member of the household, the source of referral is anonymous or non-professional or there has been no previous contact with social services.

1. Referral

There is no specific legal requirement for the mandatory reporting of actual or suspected incidents of child abuse. However, failure to disclose to the proper authorities knowledge of criminal conduct is itself an offence which may give rise to prosecution. Members of the general public are encouraged to report any suspicions they may have (to the Trust, NSPCC or the police) and information given will be treated as confidential.[36] Once a referral has been received, then under Article 66(9), certain specified agencies have a duty to assist a Trust in its inquiries 'by providing relevant information and advice'.

2. Home Visit

An investigation, including a home visit, is carried out. At this stage the senior social worker usually plays a critical role. Again the same factors tend to determine the outcome: about two-thirds of the referrals are filtered out and do not reach the case conference stage. Some agencies employ standardised Investigation Report Forms including a formal Risk Assessment Summary to be signed by the investigating social worker, countersigned by the senior social worker or relevant manager with reasons stated for any non-service disposal.

3. Interviewing the Child

At this stage the child must be seen by the investigating officer from the Trust and, if the child is of sufficient age and understanding, should be interviewed in relation to the presenting issues. The professional problems which arise at this stage concerning the roles of police officer, doctor and social worker, the compatibility of forensic and therapeutic modes of intervention and consent for conducting intrusive investigations/ examinations have been the subject of inter-agency procedural guidance and judicial comment. Butler-Sloss LJ, for example, offered guidance in the *Cleveland Report* on interviewing children[37] and has more recently observed:[38]

> Generally, it is desirable that interviews with young children be conducted as soon as possible after the allegations are first raised, should be few in number and should have investigation as their primary purpose.

---

35 See Gibbons et al, who estimate that about one quarter are filtered out.
36 See *D v NSPCC* [1978] AC 171; [1977] 1 All ER 589.
37 See *Report of the Inquiry into Child Abuse in Cleveland*, HMSO (Cmnd 412, 198).
38 See *Re M (Minors)(Sexual Abuse: Evidence)* [1993] 1 FLR 822. See also Chapter Fifteen.

Child Protection Case Conference

Following the report of the inquiry into the death of Maria Colwell, the DHSS advised[39] the setting up of Area Review Committees (now Area Child Protection Committees, or ACPCs) to oversee local policy and training arrangements, to ensure that case conferences were held following every suspected case and to set up a 'good record of information' (the 'child protection register') which was 'essential to good communication between the many disciplines involved'.

1. Functions

The remit of such a case conference is to address the specific issue of whether the name of a particular child should be placed on, retained on or removed from the register. It does not make judgments about parental culpability.[40] The official guidelines[41] state that before a child's name can be placed on a CPR,

> the conference must decide that there is, or is a likelihood of, significant harm leading to the need for a child protection plan. One of the following requirements needs to be satisfied:
> (i) there must be one or more identifiable incidents which can be described as having adversely affected the child. . . . Professional judgment is that further incidents are likely; or
> (ii) significant harm is expected on the basis of professional judgement of findings of the investigation in this individual case or on research evidence.

Research shows that only about a quarter of referrals lead to child protection case conferences.[42] The placing or retaining of the name of a child on a register requires current evidence of abuse which meets the criteria set out in one of the categories mentioned above (at 15.2.3). The decision to place the name of a child on the 'child protection register' is taken at a multi-disciplinary case conference after evidence has been heard from all professionals who have been involved with the child. These case conferences are governed by the ACPCs.[43]

---

39 DHSS, 1974.
40 The *Working Together* paper (f/n 5) suggests that 'it is good practice to invite parents solicitors to child protection case conference'; no guidance is offered as to the circumstances in which this would be appropriate. However, in *The Challenge of Partnership: Practice Guide* (HMSO, 1994), the Social Services Inspectorate emphasises the importance of proper consultation, involvement, participation and partnership with children and their parents if good quality, acceptable decision-making is to be practised for family support and child protection.
41 See *Working Together*, f/n 5, para 6.39.
42 See Gibbons et al.
43 These were established as a result of guidance provided by the DoH in *Working Together* (HMSO, 1991), which drew from *Protecting Children* (HMSO, 1988).

2. Professional Involvement

It has been estimated[44] that, on average, 7.4 professionals (excluding the chair) attend such case conferences with (apart from social services staff) police officers and nurses being most often represented and doctors least often. Non-professionals, such as child-minders, may also be invited to attend.

3. Involvement of Parent and Child

The parents or guardian of the child concerned should be invited to attend the case conference and be given an opportunity to explain the basis of any cause for concern. The reason for registration must be explained to them. Indeed, it has been held[45] to be a breach of natural justice to deny an alleged abuser the opportunity to attend a case conference and to be heard by it. However, recent research has shown that in practice parental involvement is variable:[46] twenty-one per cent of parents were found to have attended the whole case conference; forty per cent attended part; eight per cent attended the end; nineteen per cent did not attend at all and thirteen per cent were not invited.

It has been held[47] that although the parent had not been invited to the conference, the mother nevertheless knew the reasons for professional concern and had been given opportunities to address these concerns. Despite her protests of unfair procedure and stigmatisation, the court ruled that the child's name was properly entered on the register.

4. Decision-Making

On average, six out of every seven children who enter the child protection system are filtered out without their names being placed on the register. Factors determining registration seemed to be certainty that abuse or neglect had occurred, its seriousness, the characteristics of the parents indicating a future risk to the child and 'chronic concern on the part of community agencies'.

Child Protection Register (CPR)

As stated in the Guidance and Regulations:[48]

> The purpose of the register is to provide a record of all children in the area for whom there are unresolved child protection issues and who are currently the subject of an inter-agency protection plan and to ensure that the plans are formally reviewed at least every six months. The register will provide a central point of enquiry for professional staff who are worried about a child and to provide useful information for the individual child protection agencies and for the ACPC.

---

44 See C Hallett and E Birchall, *Co-ordination and Child Protection,* HMSO, 1992.
45 See *R v Norfolk County Council, ex parte M* [1989] 2 All ER 359. Also see *R v Harrow ex parte D* [1989] 3 All ER 12, CA and *R v Devon County Council ex parte L* [1991] 2 FLR 541.
46 See J Thoburn, A Lewis and D Shemmings *Paternalism or Partnership? Family Involvement in the Child Protection Process,* HMSO, 1995.
47 See *R v Harrow London Borough, ex parte D* [1990] Fam 133.
48 Children (NI) Order, Guidance and Regulations, vol. 6, para 8.2.

Thus the main function of a CPR is to provide a central record of those children defined by a panel of inter-agency professionals as currently in need of an inter-agency protection plan. When a child's name is entered on a Trust's Child Protection Register under one of the above categories, the entry is further designated as either 'potential', 'suspected' or 'confirmed'. Notification of the fact that such an entry has been made will be given to the parents or carer, the relevant school and, where practicable, to the child concerned.

The operational use of CPRs has been the subject of studies which show that: a CPR is not consulted in most cases where there is professional concern for a child,[49] different criteria are employed in different regions,[50] and they sometimes serve different purposes that those for which they were intended.[51] CPRs are nonetheless seen by professionals as an essential tool in the child protection process. In addition to their primary function, they also serve to protect professionals, foster inter-agency co-operation and perhaps act as a passport to service provision for families in need.

In Northern Ireland the annually recorded numbers of children on Trust CPRs provide evidence that fewer may now be at risk. In 1990 a total of 1,556 children were so registered, in 1991 there were 1,502, in 1992 this had fallen to 1,444 and by 1993 only 1,345 children were registered as being 'at risk'.[52]

1. Effect of Registration

Research findings indicate that placing a child's name on the register provides little assurance that thereafter effective professional intervention will ensure either adequate protection for the child concerned or appropriate support services for the family. One study[53] revealed that on average: thirty-one per cent of cases originally placed on the register and nineteen per cent of those not so placed experienced further harm in the six-month period from original conference; fifty-seven per cent of the former remained safely placed at home compared with seventy-three per cent of those not registered. Being assessed as 'in need of protection' rather than as 'in need' probably accounted for the fact that a high proportion received no services at all as a result of their referral. In the words of the researchers:

> Too many families struggling with child rearing problems who came to the attention of social services departments were prematurely defined as potential child protection cases, rather than as families containing children in need.

Most registered children and their families receive monitoring and limited practical help rather than specific services aimed at compensating for the effects of maltreatment.

---

49 See reports: BASW, 1978; ADSS, 1981, 1987; DHSS, 1990.
50 See Tilley and Burke, (1988); Cann, (1989).
51 For example, procuring resources for families in need; see Corby & Mills, (1986); Jones et al, (1986).
52 See *Annual Report of the Chief Inspector*, DHSS (SSI), 1995.
53 See J Gibbons, S Conroy and C Bell, *Operating the Child Protection System*, London: HMSO, 1995. See also, Gough et al, (1987); Corby, (1987).

2. Child Protection Review

Every registered child should be formally reviewed six months after registration and a decision then taken as to whether or not the current circumstances continue to justify retention of his or her name on the register.

Conclusion of Child Protection Process

The Options Available

Under the 1995 Order, unlike the 1968 Act, the legislative intent is to provide a Trust with a broad range of options at the conclusion of its protective procedures.

(a) Decision That Suspicions Are Unfounded

If satisfied that the initial suspicions were totally unfounded, then clearly, no further action will be taken. A decision to that effect will be recorded and the parents advised accordingly.

(b) Decision That Child Is a 'Child in Need'

Where an investigating Trust determines that a child is vulnerable but the significant harm threshold has not been breached, then it should consider whether the circumstances are such as to require it to treat the child as coming within the definition of 'in need'. If so, then this will give rise to a duty under Article 18 to provide an appropriate 'range and level of personal social services'.

(c) Decision That Private Proceedings for Acquiring Parental Responsibility Are Appropriate

Again, where a Trust concludes that a child is vulnerable, the significant harm threshold has not been breached but that no one person has parental responsibility for the child, then in keeping with the 'family care is best' principle, the Trust may support a private proceedings application from a suitable member of the family for an Article 8 order (e.g. a residence order). The Trust itself has no authority to apply for an Article 8 order.

(d) Decision That Sufficient Evidence Exists to Warrant Further Inquiries

A Trust may decide that there is cause for concern and more time is needed for a thorough investigation. Under the 1995 Order it will then consider whether an application for an interim care order (see further Chapter Fourteen) or for a child assessment order will best enable it to complete its inquiries. Although both orders are public family law measures, they each allow a Trust to hold a fairly neutral position in relation to the child and family and permit the status quo care arrangements to continue while inquiries are being pursued.

(e) Decision Not to Initiate Proceedings

Under the 1995 Order, unlike the position under the 1968 Act, a Trust has discretion to decide whether to commence proceedings in respect of a child which it has found to be in need of protection. While Article 66(8) places an onus on an investigating Trust 'to take action to safeguard or promote the child's welfare', this duty is conditional upon it being 'within the power' and 'reasonably practicable' for the Trust to do so. A Trust will, therefore, be justified in concluding that although the significant harm test is satisfied it will not commence proceedings as it would not, for example, be in a position to allocate the staff or resources necessary to implement any order granted (see further Chapter Fourteen). Where it decides not to initiate any court proceedings, a Trust must nevertheless consider whether it should review the case at a later date. In the event of it determining that such a review would be appropriate, then under Article 66(7), it must fix a date for that review.

The fact that a child's circumstances do not warrant the initiation of proceedings under Part VI of the 1995 Order should not distract a Trust from a further examination of those circumstances so as to establish whether it should be providing support and assistance under Part IV. Care proceedings may be inappropriate but an offer of accommodation, or an arrangement for placement with extended family or for respite care could prevent the necessity for such proceedings from arising later.

(f) Decision That Public Proceedings for Acquiring Parental Responsibility Are Appropriate

Where there is clear evidence of significant harm and it is 'within the power' and is 'reasonably practicable' for it to do so, then the Trust is required to initiate the appropriate proceedings. This it may do by ensuring that appropriate care arrangements are made for the children concerned away from the family home. The Trust may achieve the latter either on a consensual basis by 'looking after' such children within the meaning of Article 27, on a coercive basis by applying directly for a care order or supervision order (see Chapter Fourteen) or it may need to intervene coercively and immediately using the powers of Part VI.

III. The Principles, the Trusts' Investigatory Practices and the Orders

The 1995 Order draws a clear line between the remit of court and Trust in relation to the protection of children.

Part VI Proceedings

(a) The Principles

Proceedings commenced under the Children (NI) Order, Part VI, are excluded from the definition of 'family proceedings' given in Article 8(4). This means that, when hearing Part VI proceedings, the court is unable to make any Article 8 order, either on its own motion or in response to an application. It can only make or refuse to make the order applied for with the exception that it may make an EPO instead of a CAO.

(b) Paramountcy Principle and the Checklist

When considering an application for an order under Part VI, the court must have regard to the paramountcy principle but it is not required to apply the 'welfare checklist'. Child protection is statutorily set aside to facilitate urgent professional intervention and prompt judicial determination as to whether or not emergency powers should be used to secure a child's immediate protection. The time taken to rigorously examine an application under each heading of the checklist would cause undue delay and risk defeating the purpose of the protective provisions. However, the actions of the court will be governed by the 'no-delay' principle, by the 'no-order' presumption and the requirement to draw up a timetable to expedite the proceedings.[54]

2. Significant Harm

In England and Wales, the judicial approach to proceedings commenced under the 1989 Act, Part V (equivalent to proceedings under the 1995 Order, Part VI) has been to relax the rule in respect of significant harm. The sense of urgency which characterises these proceedings allowed the Court of Appeal[55] to rule that such applications should not be delayed by an unduly legalistic analysis of whether the presented evidence fully satisfied the significant harm test. The application of the test must, nonetheless, be considered. This represented a deviation from the normal judicial approach that a condition precedent to the commencing of proceedings for coercive intervention is proof that the 'significant harm' threshold has been, or is at imminent risk of being, breached. It has been re-visited by the House of Lords in a judgment[56] which overturns the approach in *Newham* and has now fully restored significant harm as a condition precedent in applications for an EPO, a CAO or an order for the police to exercise their powers of protection.

3. Evidence: Self-incrimination

Part VI proceedings (and those commenced under the provisions of Part V) are governed by the principle stated in Article 171 that no person may refuse to give evidence on the ground that to do so 'might incriminate him or his spouse of an offence'. Also, under Article 171:

> (2) A statement or admission made in such proceedings shall not be admissible in evidence against the person making it or his spouse in proceedings for an offence other then perjury.

This provision exactly replicates section 98(2) of the Children Act 1989 which in England has recently attracted considerable judicial attention. The case[57] in question

---

54 See J Plotnikoff and R Woolfson, *The Pace of Child Abuse Prosecutions*, DoH (1995) which reveals that instead of child abuse cases receiving priority treatment within the court system, they are in fact taking longer to reach the disposal stage then other cases. Other important findings from this research include: child abuse cases were not identified systematically when they entered the system; joint medical examinations in child sexual abuse cases were in the minority; there was little correlation between the strength of the medical evidence and the likelihood of a conviction; social workers were not involved in a quarter of child interviews conducted by officers in child protection units; and decisions to issue a notice of transfer were taken sparingly, only in mainstream abuse cases and too late.
55 See Sir Stephen Brown P in *Newham London Borough v AG* [1992] 2 FCR 119, 120.
56 See *Re H and R (Child Sexual Abuse: Standard of Proof)* [1995] 1 FLR 643.
57 See *Re EC (Disclosure of Material)* [1996] 2 FLR 725, as reported in *Family Law*, March 1997, vol. 27, p 160.

concerned care proceedings during the course of which the court at first instance heard an admission of guilt by a father in relation to criminal conduct resulting in the death of a child. On advice from the court the Trust's counterpart wrote to the police informing them of the admission. The police replied with an application for disclosure of certain documents including statements made by the parents, medical reports, evidence from doctors and excerpts from the transcript of evidence and from the judgment where these related to the death. The court granted leave for disclosure to be made in respect of the medical evidence, but not as regards the parents' statements nor the transcript or judgment excerpts. The Court of Appeal overturned the decision ruling that the above provision does not prevent admissions made in care proceedings from being used in the course of police inquiries. It is a matter for judicial discretion whether such admissions should be disclosed, but when carrying out the balancing act necessary to determine how to exercise its discretion the court should consider the following factors:

(a) the welfare and interests of the child concerned in the care proceedings (if the child is likely to be adversely affected by the order in any serious way, that will be a very important factor);
(b) the welfare and interests of other children generally;
(c) the maintenance of confidentiality in children's cases;
(d) the importance of encouraging frankness in children's cases;
(e) the public interest in the administration of justice (barriers should not be erected between one branch of the judicature and another);
(f) the public interest in the prosecution of serious crime and the punishment of offenders (there is a strong public interest in making available material to the police which is relevant to a criminal trial; in many cases this is likely to be a very important factor);
(g) the gravity of the offence and the relevance of the evidence to it (if the evidence has little or no bearing on the investigation or trial this will militate against a disclosure order);
(h) the desirability of co-operation between various agencies concerned with children's welfare;
(i) where section 98(2) applies, the terms of the section itself — namely that the witness is not excused from answering incriminating questions and that any statement of admission will not be admissible against him in criminal proceedings — fairness to the person who has incriminated himself and any others affected by the incriminating statement and any danger of oppression will also be relevant considerations;
(j) any other material disclosure which has already taken place.

Part VI Proceedings: A Trust's Investigatory Practices

The point at which, in an investigation of alleged child abuse, priority should be given to forensic rather than to therapeutic functions has been open to contention. The Trust practice, at the conclusion of a case conference where evidence of probable child abuse has been uncovered, of then giving priority to facilitating police investigations into the conduct of an alleged offender instead of continuing to hold responsibility for pursuing its own enquiries while also assessing and treating the needs of an alleged victim was criticised by the late Higgins J:[58]

> I have reservations about the wisdom of starting police investigations immediately. In my opinion the commencement of police investigation at that early stage must have rendered more difficult the investigation and assessment by the Social Services in that, not only those suspected of abusing the child, but also their relatives, were liable to react much more defensively to enquiries by social workers once the involvement of the police was known.

The authority governing investigatory procedures is intended to make the route into care less peremptory and less accessible at the unilateral discretion of the court or Trust. Since the introduction of the 1989 Act, the courts in England and Wales have had the opportunity to consider some problems which have arisen in regard to this investigatory phase of coercive intervention[59] (see also Chapter Fifteen).

The Orders Available

The proceedings available under the 1995 Order, Part VI, are applications for a child assessment order, an emergency protection order, a recovery order and a police protection order. Part VI also makes provision for the setting up and running of children's refuges.

1. Child Assessment Order (CAO)

A child assessment order is available under Article 62 of the 1995 Order and may be utilised in conjunction with private but not public law orders (though it may co-exist with an education supervision order). Its function is to authorise the means whereby a Trust can establish whether the subject is suffering or is likely to suffer significant harm. By issuing a CAO the court can permit an applicant to bring a child to a named assessor and ensure that such assessment as the court specifies is conducted by that assessor. It is intended to be used with discretion, not in circumstances where more interventionist powers are required (e.g. an EPO), nor where less may be sufficient (e.g. counselling). The balance should be determined within the context of a child protection case conference. As stated in the Guidance and Regulations:[60]

> The child assessment order, established by Article 62, deals with the single issue of enabling an assessment of the child to be made where significant harm is suspected but the child is not thought to be at immediate risk, the applicant considers that an assessment is required and the parents or other persons responsible for the child have refused to co-operate.

---

58 See *Re PB (A Minor)* unreported (1986).
59 For example, in *Re A and Others (Minors) (Child Abuse: Guidelines)* [1992] 1 FLR 439, Holings J offered definitive guidance on the conduct of such interviews.
60 Children (NI) Order 1995, Guidance and Regulations, vol. 1, para 15.1.

In England and Wales, however, experience indicates that little use is being made of CAOs; instead interim care orders, with assessment conditions, are preferred to achieve the same end result.[61]

(a) The Grounds

Under Article 62(1), the court must be satisfied in relation to three matters, that —

> (a) the applicant has reasonable cause to suspect that the child is suffering, or is likely to suffer, significant harm;
> (b) an assessment of the state of the child's health or development, or of the way in which he has been treated is required to enable the applicant to determine whether or not the child is suffering, or is likely to suffer, significant harm; and
> (c) it is unlikely that such an assessment will be made, or be satisfactory, in the absence of an order under this Article.

For obvious reasons, the grounds for a CAO are more readily satisfied than those for a CO.

(b) The Applicant

Under Article 62(1) only a Trust or an 'authorised person' (as defined by Article 49(2)) is permitted to apply for a CAO. An application should only be made when efforts to achieve an assessment by parents and Trust working together on a partnership basis have failed. Parents should always be warned in advance that a persistent refusal to co-operate on their part will place the Trust in the position of having to apply for a CAO.

(c) Notice Is Served

The fact that a CAO is not intended for use in emergency situations is illustrated by the requirement that seven days' notice be given of an intention to make application. An applicant must take such steps as are reasonably practicable to ensure that such notice is served on the child's parents, any other person with parental responsibility or who is caring for the child, any person with a contact order or who is allowed contact by virtue of an order under Article 53 and the child.

(d) Appointment of a Guardian ad Litem

Once proceedings have been commenced the court must, under Article 60(6)(g), take the necessary steps to appoint a GAL for the child concerned, unless it is satisfied that such an appointment is unnecessary; subsequently the court or GAL may then appoint a solicitor.

(e) The Alternative

The court is required to apply the paramountcy principle but is not required to apply the welfare checklist. It will need to be satisfied that inquiries made by the applicant were thorough and that all reasonable efforts were made to induce the relevant parties

---

61 See Dickens, *Assessment and the Control of Social Work, An Analysis of Reasons for the Non-Use of the Child Assessment Order* 88 19 JSWFL.

to co-operate voluntarily. Under Article 62(4) the court is not permitted to make the order if it is satisfied that there are grounds for making an EPO and that the latter order should instead be made. This point is also emphasised in the Guidance and Regulations:[62]

> It is less interventionist than the emergency protection order, interim care order and interim supervision order and should not be used where the circumstances of the case suggest that one of these orders would be more appropriate.

Under Article 62(3) the court may treat an application for a CAO as one for an EPO.

(f) The Child's Consent

The court may make the order, but if the child is of sufficient understanding to make an informed decision, he or she is then entitled to refuse to undergo the assessment. As stated in the Guidance and Regulations:[63]

> Providing the child with further advice may result in the child withdrawing his opposition, but all professionals should take particular care to avoid coercing the child into agreement even where there is a belief that the refusal to comply is itself the product of coercion by a parent, relative or friend.

(g) Right of Appeal

There is a right of appeal against the making, or the refusal to make, a CAO. Under Article 62(12) persons specified in the Rules and entitled to notice may apply for a variation or discharge.

(h) The Effect

Under Article 62 the principal effects of this order are twofold.

> (6) Where a child assessment order is in force with respect to a child it shall be the duty of any person who is in a position to produce the child—
> (a) to produce him to such person as may be named in the order; and
> (b) to comply with such directions relating to the assessment order as the court thinks fit to specify in the order.
>
> (7) A child assessment order authorises any person carrying out the assessment, or any part of the assessment, to do so in accordance with the terms of the order.

This order is a court directive to the applicant. It specifies the assessment date and the assessment period (a maximum of seven days) and authorises the person responsible to conduct the assessment. There is no provision for the assessment period to be extended. Under Article 179(15) no application may be made for another order in respect of the same child within a period of six months from the termination of the last unless the court gives leave to do so. The court may attach directions to the order

---

62 Children (NI) Order 1995, Guidance and Regulations, vol. 1, para 15.2.
63 Children (NI) Order 1995, Guidance and Regulations, vol. 1, 15.13.

relating to the assessment and under paragraph 10 to 'the contact he must be allowed to have with other persons while away from home'.

(i) The Limitations of a CAO

The CAO, like an EPO, is a tightly defined grant of authority to an applicant, intended to license coercive intervention in family affairs for a specific purpose and for a restricted time period. A CAO does not give the applicant any powers for use in emergency situations, nor does it vest in him or her any degree of parental responsibility. As stated in the Guidance and Regulations:[64]

> A CAO will usually be most appropriate where the harm to the child is long-term and cumulative rather than sudden and severe.

Article 62 stresses the limitations of the authority conferred by this order. The court is prohibited from granting a CAO in situations where an EPO would be more appropriate (paragraph 4); the child, if of sufficient understanding to make an informed decision, may refuse to submit to the assessment (paragraphs 7 and 8) and the child may only be kept away from home for the period or periods specified in the order (paragraph 9).[65] The necessity for the child to be away from home will only arise if the court is convinced that this is necessary for the purposes of the assessment (and not, for example, to ensure the child's protection), can be limited to a period or periods less than the statutory maximum and can otherwise be accomplished within such directions as the court may decide to attach to the order, including directions regarding contact arrangements with family and others.

A failure to produce the child in compliance with this order should be regarded with grave concern. Non-compliance must suggest the appropriateness of resorting instead to an emergency protection order under Article 63(1)(b).

2. Emergency Protection Order (EPO)

An emergency protection order is available under Article 63 of the 1995 Order. The court is specifically required to make an EPO, in the context of proceedings for a CAO, where it considers that the grounds for the former exist. It is significant that the court has been given the power to question a Trust's grounds for optimism, which may lie behind a Trust application for a CAO, and the capacity to substitute of its own motion an order giving absolute priority to the protection of the child concerned.

As the name suggests, an EPO is intended to provide court authorisation for urgent protection to be given to a child by ensuring his or her immediate removal to, or retention in, a secure place. The child should be named in the order. The tightly defined powers of an EPO reflect the professional and public disquiet aroused by the Cleveland

---

64 Children (NI) Order 1995, Guidance and Regulations, vol. 1, para 15.7.
65 It may be queried whether both the CAO and the EPO are in accord with Article 51(d) of the European Convention on Human Rights; detention is not for the purposes of educational supervision nor is it for the purposes of bringing the child before the competent legal authority.

affair and the guidance offered in the subsequent *Cleveland Report.* Unlike its predecessor, the place of safety order, an EPO is of much shorter duration, focuses attention on the child rather than the place (so if, having located the child, the bearer of an EPO should discover that he or she is no longer at risk, then the child should not be removed), and allows for continued contact between child and family. An EPO is not to be used as an expedient means of commencing care proceedings. However, as emphasised in the Guidance and Regulations:

> ... decisive action to protect the child is essential once it appears that the circumstances fall within one of the grounds in Article 63(1).[66]

(a) The Grounds

There are two sets of grounds. The first, under Article 63(1)(a), requires evidence that there is a risk of 'significant harm' to a child if

> (i) he is not removed to accommodation provided by or on behalf of the applicant; or
> (ii) he does not remain in the place in which he is then being accommodated.

This rests solely on the test of prospective harm. Evidence of past or present harm is insufficient but may be relevant to indicate the likelihood of a future occurrence; there is no requirement relating to fault for, or causation of, such harm.

The second, under Article 63(1)(b) and (c), is relevant only to applications from either a Trust or from an authorised person where inquiries are being pursued in relation to actual or suspected significant harm and

> those inquiries are being frustrated by access to the child being unreasonably refused to a person authorised to seek access and the applicant has reasonable cause to believe that access to the child is required as a matter of urgency.

An application may be made by an authorised person where that person has reasonable cause for a belief that a child is presently suffering, or is likely to suffer, significant harm.

There must be a dimension of urgency in the circumstances necessitating an EPO as opposed to a CAO. During the hearing the court is free to take into account all relevant evidence regardless of the application of any statutory provision or rule of law.

(b) Aspects of the Grounds: Unreasonable Refusal of Access

Where, under Article 63(1)(b), a Trust (or authorised person) is making application on the grounds that access in respect of a child is being unreasonably refused, then the court will need to be convinced that the significant harm test can be satisfied, the refusal of access is unreasonable and the circumstances indicate that access to the child is required as a matter of urgency.

Where access to a child, or information regarding his or her whereabouts, is being denied, then Article 66(6) places a strict duty on a Trust or other 'authorised person'

---

66 Children (NI) Order 1995, Guidance and Regulations, vol. 1, para 14.5.

to apply for an EPO, CAO, CO or SO unless satisfied that the child's welfare may be otherwise safeguarded.[67] This legal presumption, that in such circumstances the Trust must seek a court order, will only be rebutted by definite evidence that it is unnecessary.

(c) Aspects of the Grounds: The Significant Harm Test

As noted in the Guidance and Regulations:[68]

> There is a clear distinction to be made in relation to the significant harm test in Article 63(1)(a) as against subsections (b) and (c).... In the former it is the court that must have reasonable cause to believe; in the latter it is the applicant who must have reasonable cause to suspect.

This difference in effect places a heavier onus on private applicants than on Trust applicants to convince the court that evidence exists to satisfy the significant harm test.

Where the likelihood of significant harm is attributable to the presence of an alleged abuser, then the Trust should explore the possibility of effecting the removal of that person as an alternative to EPO procedures. This may be achieved through either public or private law measures. Under the former, a Trust could advise and assist the voluntary departure of the alleged abuser through reliance on resources available in the provisions of the 1995 Order, Schedule 2, paragraph 6. Under the latter, a Trust could suggest that a non-abusing parent or guardian apply for an ouster injunction or exclusion order.

(d) Aspects of the Grounds: The Limitations

Even if the grounds are satisfied, the court need not make an EPO. The court may conclude, after applying the paramountcy principle and the no-order presumption but not the welfare checklist, that the child's interests would be best served by not granting the order sought.

(e) The Applicant

The first set of grounds permit an application for an EPO from any person under Article 63(1)(a). Should an application be made by a private individual, then Court Rules require that person to also notify the local Trust which will trigger the latter's investigatory duties under Article 66. The second set of grounds is restricted to applications from a Trust or from an 'authorised person' and represents a legislative response to the case of Kimberley Carlile and others.[69] An 'authorised person' (as defined in Article 49(2) will be an officer of the NSPCC.

---

67 Ensuring prompt access to a child suspected of being abused was a primary legislative objective following the report in respect of Kimberley Carlile and such others as *A Child in Trust: Report on the Death of Jasmine Beckford*, London Borough of Brent, 1988; *Whose Child: Report on the Death of Tyra Henry*, London Borough of Greenwich, 1987.
68 Children (NI) Order 1995, Guidance and Regulations, vol. 1, para 14.19.
69 *A Child in Mind: Protection of Children in a Responsible Society*, Report of the Commission of Inquiry into the Circumstances surrounding the death of Kimberley Carlile, 1987.

(f) The Application

An application may be made *ex parte* or on notice and may be made orally. The application should name the child or should otherwise provide a close description. There is provision for a single justice to make an order. The applicant is required, by the Court Rules, to serve a copy of the application and the order within forty-eight hours on the parties to the proceedings, any person who is not a party but has care of the child and the relevant Trust, where the latter is not the applicant. The court must make arrangements for the appointment of a GAL, unless it considers that such an appointment is unnecessary, and subsequently the GAL or the court may appoint a solicitor.

(g) Judicial Directions

Under Article 63(6)–(9) the court may, when issuing an EPO or at any time when the order is in force, add certain directions. These specifically enable the court to deal with issues of contact between the child and his or her family or any other person and the need for a medical or psychiatric examination or assessment of the child. Under Article 62(7) the child may, if of sufficient understanding to make an informed decision, refuse to undergo such an examination or assessment. Under paragraph 8 the court reserves the right to attach conditions to any arrangements regarding contact and to the commencement or not of any examination or assessment.

The court also has the power to add directions relating to the enforcement of an EPO; any directions in the order may be varied at any time.

(h) Transfer of Responsibilities under an EPO

Under the regulations made pursuant to Article 71(3), a Trust is permitted to take over an EPO made in favour of a private person and with it the entailed powers and responsibilities in respect of the child where:[70]

(a) an emergency protection order has been made with respect to a child;
(b) the applicant for the order was not the authority within whose area the child is ordinarily resident; and
(c) that authority is of the opinion that it would be in the child's best interests for the applicant's responsibilities under the order to be transferred to it,

The legislative intent is to facilitate any individual who, in an emergency, seeks to secure immediate protection for a child but to spare that person from having to subsequently bear the responsibility of complying with any judicial directions which may be attached to the resulting EPO.

In forming its opinion under Regulation 2(c) the Trust is required to consult with the person and to consider the following factors:[71]

---

70 The Emergency Protection Orders (Transfer of Responsibilities) Regulations (NI) 1996, Regulation 2.
71 The Emergency Protection Orders (Transfer of Responsibilities) Regulations (NI) 1996, Regulation 3.

(a) the ascertainable wishes and feelings of the child having regard to his age and understanding;
(b) the child's physical, emotional and educational needs for the duration of the emergency protection order;
(c) the likely effect on him of any change in his circumstances which may be caused by a transfer of responsibilities under the order;
(d) his age, sex and family background;
(e) the circumstances which gave rise to the application for the emergency protection order;
(f) any directions of the court and other orders made in respect of the child;
(g) the relationship (if any) of the applicant for the emergency protection order to the child; and
(h) any plans which the applicant may have in respect of the child.

Having concluded that such a transfer is desirable, the Trust is required under Regulation 3 to serve notice to that effect on the person concerned, the court that made the order and the parties on whom the person initially served notice. The date and time of the transfer must be entered on the transfer notice and, under Regulation 4, will be treated as the date and time at which the Trust acquired responsibilities under the order. If, however, the transfer notice was served later, then the date and time of receipt will be taken as the point at which the Trust assumed its responsibilities. A certified refuge, at which the child subject to an EPO is residing, is exempted from the effect of the regulations.[72]

(j) The Effect of the Order

Under Article 63(4) of the 1995 Order the three immediate effects of an EPO are that it:

(a) operates as a direction to any person who is in a position to do so to comply with any request to produce the child to the applicant;
(b) authorises —
  (i) the removal of the child at any time to accommodation provided by or on behalf of the applicant and his being kept there; or
  (ii) the prevention of the removal from any hospital, or other place, in which he was being accommodated immediately before the making of the order; and
(c) gives the applicant parental responsibility for the child.

The power of removal to, or retention in, a safe place is the main authority conferred on the applicant and one which may be exercised at any stage in the duration of the order.

However, the act of removal is only authorised if, at that point in time, it is necessary to do so in order to 'safeguard' the child; should it become apparent to the applicant at time of implementing the EPO that the child is no longer in danger, then the removal ceases to be authorised.

---

[72] The Emergency Protection Orders (Transfer of Responsibilities) Regulations (NI) 1996, Regulation 5.

Article 64(12) permits an EPO to be served and executed on a Sunday, notwithstanding the Sunday Observance Act (Ireland) 1695, section 7. Under Article 67(1), where it is apparent that information regarding the child's whereabouts is not available to the applicant but is available to another person, then the court may include in the order a requirement that the latter person disclose to the applicant, if so requested, any such information. Additional directions may be included under paragraph 3 of this Article to 'authorise the applicant to enter premises specified by the order and search for the child with respect to whom the order is made' and under Article 67(4) to do so in respect of any other child at risk on the same premises. Under paragraph 9 a direction authorising the issue of a warrant permits a constable to accompany the applicant and to use such reasonable force as may be necessary to ensure entry to premises or access to the child concerned, where this has been or may be denied to the applicant. Under paragraph 11 a constable, in executing the warrant, may 'be accompanied by a medical practitioner, registered nurse or registered health visitor if he so chooses'. The order may authorise the removal of the child and his or her retention in a place specified by the applicant; it may prevent the unauthorised removal of the child from a specified place. Any person obstructing the implementation of an EPO will be guilty of a criminal offence.

(k) Limitations of an EPO

The power vested in the holder of an EPO to exercise parental responsibility is hedged around with restrictions. Indeed, an important principle behind this order, as is clear from Article 63(5)(b), is that it should permit the minimum degree of interference with parental authority necessary to achieve security for the child; discretionary action is limited to the minimum necessary to 'safeguard the welfare of the child'. It would, therefore, be inappropriate to seek to make any decisions which would have a long-term effect on the child's life. Similarly, paragraphs 10 and 11 place an onus on the bearer of an order to arrange for the child to return home to the care of the person from whom he or she was removed, or returned to a parent, a person with parental responsibility or someone judged (by the bearer of the order and the court) to be appropriate, just as soon as this is reasonably practicable.

Article 63(13) provides that, unless the court issues contrary directions, reasonable contact shall be permitted between the child and

  (a) his parents;
  (b) any person who is not a parent of his but who has parental responsibility for him;
  (c) any person with whom he was living immediately before the making of the order;
  (d) any person in whose favour a contact order is in force with respect to him;
  (e) any person who is allowed to have contact with the child by virtue of an order under Article 53; and
  (f) any person acting on behalf of any of those persons.

This provision is fully in line with the general statement of principle governing the obligation of the Trusts to promote and maintain contact between a child and family as expressed in Article 29. The provisions of Article 30 also apply. These enable a

Trust to make payments in respect of any 'travelling, subsistence or other expenses' incurred by child or parent (and/or other specified persons) in the course of visits undertaken for the purpose of maintaining such contact.

There is a requirement to establish and take into account the views of the subject of an EPO. Moreover, the provision in paragraph 13 is framed more as a right of the child rather than of the parent or other persons.

(l) Duration

Article 64 of the 1995 Order states that:

> (1) An emergency protection order shall have effect for such period, not exceeding eight days, as may be specified in the order.

At the expiry of that period Article 64(4) and (5) permits the court to grant an extension but 'only if it has reasonable cause to believe that the child concerned is likely to suffer significant harm if the order is not extended'. There is no means whereby a Trust can challenge a court refusal to grant an extension. Only one extension is possible and only for a further period not exceeding seven days; this should be sufficient for an applicant to judge whether or not an application under Article 57 for an interim care order is necessary. The total possible period of retention is thus fifteen days under an EPO as opposed to fifteen weeks under a PSO.

(m) The Right of Appeal

Article 64(9) of the 1995 Order prevents the making of an appeal application.[73] However, while such a right does not technically exist, there is nothing to prevent an interested party (i.e. the child, the parent/s, the person/s with direct care responsibility for the child immediately prior to removal or the person/s with parental responsibility) from challenging the making of the order at the hearing. Any of those parties may apply, under Article 64(7), for the order to be discharged, though, under Article 64(8), not if they had notice of the initial application for the order and attended the hearing. Article 64(8) also prevents an application for discharge from being heard within seventy-two hours of the order being made, though the application may be lodged in court within that period.

3. Recovery Order

The recovery order is available under Article 69 of the 1995 Order and applies to a child, defined in Article 68, as being in care, the subject of an EPO or in police protection. Any person who knowingly and without lawful authority or reasonable excuse removes such a child will be guilty of an offence.

---

73 In *Essex County Council v F* [1993] 1 FLR 847 it was held that the equivalent provision under the 1989 Act did not permit an appeal against either the making of or the refusal to make an EPO. Also see *Re P (Emergency Protection Order)* [1996] 1 FLR 482.

(a) The Grounds

A recovery order may be made

> (1) Where it appears to the court that there is reason to believe that a child to whom this Article applies —
> - (a) has been unlawfully taken away or is being unlawfully kept away from the responsible person;
> - (b) has run away or is staying away from the responsible person; or
> - (c) is missing.

(b) The Applicant

As stated in the Guidance and Regulations:[74]

> ... the court's powers to make a recovery order are restricted to those children who are in care, are the subject of an emergency protection order or are in police protection (Articles 68(2) and 69).

Therefore the only person eligible to make application for a recovery order is any person who has parental responsibility for the child by virtue of a care order or emergency protection order or, where the child is in police protection, the designated police officer.

(c) The Application

The application is made by submitting the appropriate form to the court; this must name the person with parental responsibility and the child. The hearing may be *ex parte* or on one day's notice.

(d) The Effect

Under Article 69(3) a recovery order directs any person in a position to do so to produce the child on request to an authorised person, authorises the removal of a child by an authorised person, requires the disclosure of information as to the child's whereabouts from those with information to a constable or officer of the court and on request, authorises a constable to enter and search specified premises for the child, using reasonable force if necessary.

(e) The Authorised Person

As stated in the Guidance and Regulations:[75]

> An 'authorised person' in this context means any person specified by the court or a constable. It can also mean anyone specifically authorised for the purpose after the recovery order is made, by a person who has parental responsibility for the child by virtue of a care order or an emergency protection order. A Trust may therefore arrange for someone else to remove the child on its behalf once the order has been made.

---

74 Children (NI) Order 1995, Guidance and Regulations, vol. 1, para 17.3.
75 Children (NI) Order 1995, Guidance and Regulations, vol. 1, para 17.6.

Such an authorised person should always produce proof of his or her authority to act as such.

(f) The Child

It should be noted that a child will always be justified in leaving an abusing or threatening environment.

4. Police Protection Order

Under Article 65:

> (1) Where a constable has reasonable cause to believe that a child would otherwise be likely to suffer significant harm, he may —
> (a) remove the child to suitable accommodation and keep him there; or
> (b) take such steps as are reasonable to ensure that the child's removal from any hospital, or other place, in which he is then being accommodated is prevented.

This is a new power which may be used in circumstances where either the police are the first to discover that a child is suffering or is likely to suffer significant harm or the urgency is such that immediate intervention is required. As there are no powers to search, it may only be used where the police have already located the child. However, in situations of extreme urgency, Article 19(1)(c) of the Police and Criminal Evidence (NI) Order 1989 gives the police powers to enter and search, without a warrant, while Article 27(3)(e) of that Order provides a power of arrest without warrant where necessary to protect a child. It may be augmented by a warrant to enter and search a premises.

(a) The Effect of Police Protection

The Article 65 power of police protection enables a police constable to remove a child to, or retain a child in, a secure place such as a hospital (Article 65(1) and (5)). Under Article 65(8) the child may be retained in police protection for no longer than seventy-two hours. If the police consider that the period should be extended, then they may contact the local Trust with a view to that agency applying for either an EPO or an ICO or alternatively they may apply for and obtain an EPO on behalf of the Trust. The power should be called upon, as stated in the Guidance and Regulations:[76]

> If the developing circumstances make the case so urgent that there is not time to apply for an emergency protection order, the police should be asked to use their powers under Article 65 of the Children Order to take the child into police protection. These can only be exercised, however, where access is not an obstacle and the police can in effect 'find' the child since there are no powers of search attached to Article 65. In dire emergencies and for the purposes of saving life and limb, the police have reserve powers under the Police and Criminal Evidence (NI) Order 1989 to enter and search premises without a warrant.

---

76 Children (NI) Order 1995, Guidance and Regulations, vol. 1, para 15.20.

Having taken the child into police protection, a constable may (under Article 65(5)(e)) remove him or her to accommodation provided for such children under Article 23.[77] Although the police do not thereby acquire parental responsibility, they must nonetheless do all that is reasonable to safeguard and promote the child's welfare while he or she remains in their care.

(b) The Designated Officer

As soon as is reasonably practicable, the constable who removed the child must ensure that the case is enquired into by a designated police officer who in turn is required, under Article 65(5)(a) and (b), to inform the relevant Trust/s of the steps taken and the reasons for taking them. He is also required, under Article 65(5)(c), to inform the child (if he or she appears capable of understanding), the child's parents, any person who is not the parent but has parental responsibility and any other person with whom the child was then living of the steps taken and those which may be taken. He must take such steps as are reasonably practicable to ascertain the wishes and feelings of the child.

(c) Inter-Agency Liaison

As is stated in the Guidance and Regulations:[78]

> Trusts will find it necessary to monitor and review at regular intervals their channels of communication with the police so that effective inter-agency working is achieved. Trusts will need to build on existing practice and guidelines developed under the aegis of the Area Child Protection Committee and the principles set out in volume 6: *Co-operating to Protect Children*. This should ensure that no child taken into police protection need be accommodated in a police station. It should also ensure that police action to safeguard a child is not prompted because of a belief that the evidence is not sufficient for an application for an emergency protection order.

Refuges

Under Article 70 the Trusts may provide or arrange for others to provide, refuges for children at risk of harm (such harm need not be 'significant'). Once a child's safety is secured by means of an EPO, for example, the Trust may then give effect to its duty to provide reception and accommodation facilities by means of provision within a designated refuge for children at risk. The possibility of persons providing shelter for children being open to prosecution is avoided by the introduction of a system of certification.

---

[77] Article 23:

(2) Every authority shall receive, and provide accommodation for, children in police protection whom the authority is requested to receive under Article 65(5)(e).

[78] Children (NI) Order 1995, Guidance and Regulations, vol. 1, paragraph 16.7.

CHAPTER SIXTEEN

Children Being 'Looked After' by a Trust: In Care and in Accommodation

Introduction

The law relating to children being 'looked after' by Trusts, is largely governed by Part V of the Children (NI) Order 1995 and is the subject of this chapter. The care arrangement actually made by a Trust may be consensual or coercive, of short- or long-term duration, be restricted to one location, entail a succession of similar settings or lead into a mix and match of different types of placement. In Northern Ireland, as elsewhere in the United Kingdom, the changes in emphasis in the 1980s from prevention to protection, care to control, residential to foster placement and from being looked after by strangers to upbringing by family have contributed to the current uncertainty surrounding the definition of 'care'.

The marked swing away from placements in children's homes towards family-based care, if necessary with approved foster-parents, has been due to a fundamental change in child-care philosophy. There is now a general recognition that the maintenance of significant relationships can be crucial to the healthy psychological development of children. This is apparent in the growing number of judicial rulings which aim to protect or restore contact between children in care and the parents, relatives, friends and schools which form every child's network of attachments. It is also a philosophy now underpinned by legislative directive. This chapter sets out the law and the professional issues affecting children being looked after by the Trusts, whether in care or being accommodated, under the powers of the Children (NI) Order 1995.

Historically, the Children and Young Persons (NI) Act 1968 provided the legal basis for the transfer of responsibility for some 20,000 children from parental to state care (see Appendices). A notable trend in such transfers was the gradual reversal of the grounds on which they took place. In the early years of that legislation, intervention in family affairs by social work practitioners was with parental consent to facilitate the admission of children to the short-term residential care service offered by the Health and Social Services Boards. (In 1970 of the total child-care population 1,176 were voluntary admissions and 542 were committals.) Towards the close of that legislative era its provisions, supplemented by recourse to wardship (see Chapter Seven), were being used by legal and social work practitioners mainly to ensure the committal of children to the long-term foster care service provided by the Boards (i.e. in 1989, 76.7 per cent of the child-care population consisted of committals and only 10.5 per cent were voluntary admissions).

The child-care population steadily increased during those years from 1,717, or a rate of 3.33 per 1,000 in 1970 to 2,783, or a rate of 6.0 in 1989, but has declined more recently. As stated in the DHSS annual report for 1995:[1]

> ... between 1989 and 1993 there was an overall reduction of 4.5% in the number of children in care ... across the four Boards there was an overall reduction from 76.7% to 63.8% in the number of subjects of either a Fit Person Order or a Parental Rights Order ... the change in the use of Section 103 was relatively small ... there were marked increases in the use of Wardship ... all Boards increased their percentage of children in foster care ... there has been an overall downward trend in the use of residential care.

Being 'Looked After' by a Trust

Children are 'looked after' by a Trust when they are in accommodation provided by it or by other bodies as a consequence of its coercive or consensual intervention. This provision puts in place one of the Order's strategic bridgeheads which serve to bind together the relevant public and private sectors of family law. In the former instance the authority of a care order compels a family to accept a placement provided by or on behalf of a Trust for their child. In the second the voluntary consent of all parties makes the Trust offer of accommodation acceptable to all. In both sets of circumstances the Trust has a duty to make accommodation available, and in both it is now obliged to apply the same uniform standards of care.

Definition of Being 'Looked After'

Article 25 of the 1995 Order states:

> (1) In this Order any reference to a child who is looked after by an authority is a reference to a child who is —
>
> (a) in the care of the authority; or
> (b) provided with accommodation by the authority.
>
> (2) In paragraph (1)(b) 'accommodation' means accommodation which is provided for a continuous period of more than twenty-four hours.
>
> (3) Paragraph (1) is subject to Article 2(6).

From the cross-reference to Article 2(6) it is apparent that the range of children who may come within the definition of being 'looked after' by a Trust is in fact broader than might be inferred from the simple distinction between those in care and those accommodated.

Article 2 states:

---

1 *Annual Report of the Chief Inspector*, Social Services Inspectorate, Northern Ireland, 1995, DHSS.

(6) References in this Order to accommodation provided by or on behalf of an authority are references to accommodation so provided in the exercise of its personal social services functions including such functions exercisable on behalf of the Department by virtue of Article 17(1) of the Health and Personal Social Services (Northern Ireland) Order 1972.

'Looked After'

1. Provided with Accommodation

The status of a child in need who is being accommodated by or on behalf of a Trust remains wholly unqualified. The legal standing of Trust, parent and child relative to each other remains the same before and after the provision of accommodation.

(a) The Voluntary Agreement

In keeping with the spirit of partnership between parents and Trust which underlies the provision of accommodation for children in need, there is no statutory requirement that the acceptance of this support service be conditional upon the signing of a written agreement between the parties. However, because the statutory body does not acquire any degree of parental responsibility in respect of a child for whom it provides this service, it has been necessary to deal with the resulting areas of uncertainty in the Guidance and Regulations.[2]

The new statutory duty to seek out and take into account the wishes and feelings of a child (and indeed those of any parent or other relevant person) in relation to any decision affecting his or her welfare has placed an onerous responsibility on the Trusts but aptly demonstrates the legislative intent to ensure that children are treated as more than 'objects of concern' (see Chapter Fifteen).

(b) Terms and Conditions

In order to avoid the perennial problems which have long been associated with the dilemma of having responsibility but no authority in respect of a child entrusted to its care by parental agreement, a Trust needs to reach an early, clear and explicit understanding with the parent in relation to certain aspects of the care arrangement. The place, carers and duration of the arrangements are the most obvious matters upon which there needs to be agreement. Decisions also need to be reached about schooling, plans for the holiday periods and visiting arrangements. Most importantly, however, is the issue in relation to medical treatment. Over recent years there have been many instances where difficulties have arisen because a Trust, or its English counterpart, has been unable to acquire the parental consent necessary to authorise treatment for a child in voluntary care. Faced with parental unavailability or refusal to co-operate and being itself devoid of the authority necessary to sanction treatment, the agency has often been forced to make hurried wardship applications in order to secure judicial authority for urgently required medical intervention (see further Chapter Seven). It is envisaged

---

[2] *Arrangements for Placement of Children (General) Regulations* 1996.

that, in future, a written agreement between parents and Trust will provide for such matters as Trust permission to authorise medical treatment in respect of a child being 'looked after' in voluntary accommodation.

2. In the Care of the Authority

Under Article 50(1) of the 1995 Order (see also Chapter Fourteen), following an application by a Trust or an 'authorised person', the court may make a care order:

> (a) placing the child with respect to whom the application is made in the care of a designated authority.

(a) Powers and Duties of the Trust

Under Article 52 of the 1995 Order:

> (1) Where a care order is made with respect to a child the authority designated by the order shall receive him into its care and keep him in its care while the order is in force.

The most immediate effect of the order is thus to direct the designated Trust to take physical possession of the named child. Further:

> (3) Where a care order is in force with respect to a child, the authority designated by the order shall —
> (a) have parental responsibility for the child; and
> (b) have the power (subject to paragraphs (4) and (9) to determine the extent to which a parent or guardian of the child may meet his parental responsibility for the child.

Paragraph (b) is particularly important. As stated in the Guidance and Regulations:[3]

> Subject to the specific restrictions in Article 52, a Trust has all the rights, duties, powers, responsibilities and authority to act as parent of the child in care and to discharge all its responsibilities to the child positively and effectively. These include having to decide how to best care for the child in accordance with Article 52. It may not transfer any part of its parental responsibility to someone else, but can arrange for some or all of it to be met on its behalf by others (e.g. a foster parent or a voluntary organisation).

A Trust has the power to specify exactly how parents are to exercise many of the responsibilities they retain in respect of their child. This may include determining such matters as accommodation, direct care responsibilities, contact with named persons, school attendance or attendance, for example, at an assessment centre (subject to prior consultation with the child). The principle may be that Trust and parent should work

---

3 Children (NI) Order 1995, Guidance, vol. 1, para 9.50.

in partnership to further the best interests of a child subject to a care order but the legislative intent is to make it clear that it should be the Trust and not the parent who has the final say.

(b) Legal Standing of the Parent

The legal position of the parent of a child subject to a care order is apparent not so much from Article 52 of the 1995 Order but from Article 5:

> (4) More than one person may have parental responsibility for the same child at the same time.
>
> (5) A person who has parental responsibility for a child at any time shall not cease to have that responsibility solely because some other person subsequently acquires parental responsibility for the child.
>
> (7) The fact that a person has parental responsibility for a child shall not entitle him to act in any way which would be incompatible with any order made with respect to the child under this Order.

As is clear from paragraphs (4) and (5), the fact that a Trust has acquired parental responsibilities by virtue of the issue of a care order does not mean that the parent concerned has been simultaneously divested of them. This is reinforced in Article 52:

> (5) Nothing in paragraph (3)(b) shall prevent a parent or guardian of the child who has care of him from doing what is reasonable in all the circumstances of the case for the purpose of safeguarding or promoting his welfare.

Among the powers which are retained by the parent of a child subject to a care order are those enumerated under Article 52(6): the right to determine religious upbringing and the right to give or refuse consent to a freeing order for adoption, an adoption order and to the appointment of a guardian. The Guidance and Regulations[4] lay some emphasis on the obligation of a Trust to respect parental choice regarding a child's religious upbringing:

> It must not cause the child to be brought up in any religious persuasion other than that in which he would have been brought up had the order not been made . . . requires the Trust not to bring about any change by its own action or inaction.

In this context it should be noted that the late Higgins J[5] expressed his reservations as to the Trusts' record of diligence in this regard:

> Speaking generally, it has been my experience that the Board in placing children in short-term foster care, which frequently turns out to last for much longer than intended, is not as sensitive to the need to match the religious belief of the child's parent or parents to that of the foster parents as I think it should.

4　Children (NI) Order 1995, Guidance and Regulations, vol. 1, para 9.51. See also in this jurisdiction, *Re McC, T and B*, unreported (1982), as discussed in Chapter Seven.
5　See *Re T (A Minor)*, unreported (1993).

Under Article 52(7) any attempt to remove a child from the United Kingdom or to change his or her surname is prohibited.[6] Also the written consent of any parent who has parental responsibility is required before a child's name may be changed. Other powers not enumerated under the 1995 Order by implication remain with the parent including those aspects of parental responsibility which have not been addressed by the Trust under Article 52(3)(b). However, although retaining parental responsibility in respect of a child in care, a parent nevertheless loses his or her entitlement to child benefit.

(c) Legal Standing of the Child

Greater and more explicit recognition is given to the rights of a child in care under the 1995 Order than under the 1968 Act. These include such rights as to have their welfare safeguarded and promoted, to have their wishes and feelings sought and taken into account in decisions affecting their welfare, to retain contact with parents, relatives and others and to be placed with or in close proximity to their family of origin. A child in care who has sufficient understanding also has the right to apply for an Article 8 order and the right to representation when doing so.

Placements for a Child Being Looked After by a Trust

There are three principal alternatives considered by a Trust when deciding how best to give effect to its responsibilities towards a child or young person entrusted to it by parent or court. These are residential placements in a children's home, family placements with approved foster-parents and family placements with parent/s or a relative. Under the terms of a care order, the right to select the type considered most appropriate to the needs of a particular child vests in a Trust. Where a child is being accommodated by consent of parent or child then choice of placement type will be determined on a consensual basis. In addition, there have always been a small number of children for whom placement in a training school (now 'justice' rather than 'care' placements; see further Chapter Seventeen) or with foster-parents 'with a view to adoption' (see Chapter Six) has been the most appropriate care arrangement.

Residential Care Placements

Residential care has traditionally been the Trusts' placement of choice, provision of which has been shared with the voluntary sector.[8] In Northern Ireland, however, the use of this option has decreased during the past two decades as it has throughout the rest of the United Kingdom. For example, in 1979 some 1,889, or 57.9 per cent, of the total care population were in residential care whereas by 1988 only 705, or 26.9 per

---

6 This accords with Article 7 of the UN Convention on the Rights of the Child which states that a child shall, from birth, have the right to assume a name. Article 8 obliges State Parties to respect the right of children to preserve their identity including their names.
7 See *McLavery v Secretary of State for Social Security (Child Benefit: Child in Care)* [1996] 2 FLR No 6.
8 See *The Role of the Voluntary Homes in the Child Care Service*, HMSO, 1996.

cent, were in such placements; by 1992 there were only 457 children in residential care in this jurisdiction.[9] In a recent policy review[10] a further reduction of 15 per cent of placement is recommended during this period.

The reasons for this decline are attributable not only to the influence of a policy change which favoured family-based rather than institution-based care for children but also to the impact of a number of cases where children were found to have been abused by the staff into whose care they had been entrusted. Following a number of enquiries into abuse in residential settings in the United Kingdom, there were recommendations[11] that foster care offered a greater likelihood of safety for children. In this jurisdiction much the same conclusions had been drawn by the report of the Hughes Inquiry[12] following the scandal associated with the Kincora Boy's Hostel. That report included recommendations in relation to issues of staffing in homes, the need for clear procedures, inspections, contact with residents, treatment plans for children, consultation with children and the rights of children to make complaints. A more recent report[13] adopts a rights approach to the establishment of standards against which children's residential services should be monitored and inspected and suggests that any guidelines to standards and practice in substitute care should be constructed from the child's perspective.

Residential Care under the 1995 Order

Under Article 26 of the 1995 Order, a Trust may provide residential care for any child it is looking after (i.e. whether by court order or by consent of parent and/or child) by maintaining him or her in either a community home (paragraph 2(b)), a voluntary home (paragraph 2(c)), a registered children's home (paragraph 2(d)), a home or institution provided by a government department or a prescribed public body or by making other arrangements (paragraph 2(e)). These forms of residential care provision, with the exception of Trust-run children's homes (exempted by Article 149 of the 1995 Order from inspection requirements), are all equally subject to the requirements of the 1995 Order, the Children's Homes Regulations 1996 and to the Guidance and Regulations issued by the DHSS (NI). However, the 1995 Order in keeping with its progenitor the 1989 Act is flawed in that its provisions relating to the registration and inspection of children's homes apply only to those who cater for four or more children. It has been estimated that the number of care situations in England and Wales which thereby escape the rigorous supervision required by the either the Children's Homes Regulations or the foster-care regulations, could be as high as three thousand.

---

9 See *Residential Child Care*, Social Services Inspectorate, 1989.
10 See *DHSS Child Care Strategy 1992–7*.
11 See *Warner Report* (1992), para 3.36.
12 See *Report of the Committee of Inquiry into Children's Homes and Hostels*, HMSO, 1986.
13 *Quality Living: Standards for Services — Children Who Live Away from Home*, DHSS/Barnardos, 1992. Also see G Horgan and R Sinclair *Caring for Children: A Study of Residential Care in Northern Ireland*, DHSS (1995).

Family Placements

I. Foster Care

The decline in residential care provision has been mirrored by a corresponding increase in the use of foster care. In the United Kingdom the increase was from 48 per cent of the total 'in care population' in 1970 to 54 per cent in 1987. In Northern Ireland the increase was from 37.8 per cent in 1979 to 71 per cent in 1988, resulting in a total of 1,621 children in foster care in 1992. In this jurisdiction the pace of change has been fuelled by a DHSS policy[14] which set a target of 75 per cent placements in foster care (excluding children home-on-trial) to be achieved by each Trust by 1997; a target exceeded by most Trusts. This trend is now showing signs of at least slowing down according to the findings of recent research studies.[15] These draw attention to the fact that foster care can also give rise to abuse situations. One researcher claims that simplistic notions about transferring children in residential care to the presumed safety of foster care seem not only misplaced but positively dangerous.[16]

1. Foster-Parents

Under Article 27(2) of the 1995 Order, a Trust which is looking after a child may provide accommodation for him or her by placing the child with a family, a relative of the child or any other suitable person on such terms as to payment by the Trust and otherwise as the Trust may determine. Where a child is so placed then that person will be deemed to be a Trust foster-parent unless he or she is a parent of the child, has parental responsibility or was a person in whose favour a residence order had been made, prior to the issue of the care order, in respect of the child. Under Schedule 5 of the 1995 Order:

> . . . a person fosters a child if —
> (a) he is an authority foster parent in relation to the child;
> (b) he is a foster parent with whom the child has been by a voluntary organisation; or
> (c) he fosters the child privately.

Article 28 of the 1995 Order provides the authority for regulations which govern the approval of foster-parents and the working arrangements between them and a Trust. As stated in the Guidance and Regulations:[17]

> Each responsible authority will have its organisational and procedural arrangements, including management and staffing structures, for the recruitment, assessment, approval, preparation, training and support for foster parents. These arrangements make up what may be described informally as a fostering service.

---

14 See *Regional Strategy for Health and Personal Social Services* 1992–97 DHSS.
15 See Pringle (1993); and D Berridge and H Cleaver, *Foster Home Breakdown*, Oxford: Blackwell (1987); and D Berridge, *Foster and Residential Care Reassessed: A Research Perspective*, Children and Society, vol. 8 (1994).
16 See Pringle (1993), p. 247.
17 The Children (NI) Order 1995, Guidance and Regulations, vol. 3, para 4.5.

2. Arrangements for Fostering Children in Care

As stated in the Guidance and Regulations:[18]

> The intention of the Children Order is that both the immediate and long-term needs of the child should be considered and provided for in the Trust's planning for the child. In undertaking that planning for a child in care the Trust is required to give the same attention to the wishes of the child, parents, and others as it must when providing accommodation under voluntary arrangements. The Trust should also take into account and consider the child's religious persuasion, racial origin and cultural and linguistic background. Children with a physical and/or sensory disability or a learning disability will require particular consideration and the accommodation provided for them should not be unsuitable to the needs of the child (Article 27(9)).

The relationships between a Trust, a foster-parent and a child (where the latter is being looked after by a Trust and is placed with that foster-parent) are governed by two sets of regulations. One deals with the child and the other with the placement. These relationships may also be affected by statutory rights accruing to foster-parents by virtue of the duration of their care relationship with a child.

(a) Arrangements for Placement of Children (General) Regulations (NI) 1996

The arrangements for Placement of Children (General) Regulations (NI) 1996 stipulate certain matters which a Trust is required to address with the parents of any child being placed with Trust foster-parents. An agreement or care plan must be drawn up between Trust and parents which includes statements as to the type of accommodation to be provided, the name and address of the foster-parents, details regarding any services to be provided for the child. the anticipated division of responsibility among parent, foster-parent, Trust and any other relevant party for the duration of the placement, the arrangements for the day-to-day management of the child's needs, including the identification of decision-making opportunities, such as case reviews, which will allow or require parental participation and perhaps also that of the child. Looking After Children (LAC) forms have been specially drawn up to facilitate a Trust in dealing with these specific matters.

The agreement will also set out the agreed contact arrangements between child and parents and between child and such relevant others as siblings, grandparents, other relatives or any person bearing parental responsibility in respect of the child. The consent or otherwise of all parties must be recorded and provision made for arrangements to be reviewed and adjusted as necessary. The agreement must make a statement regarding the estimated duration of the placement, the conditions under which it could be terminated and the preparations which will then be made to facilitate the child's return to pre-committal care arrangements or to alternative accommodation if that should be appropriate.

---

18 The Children (NI) Order 1995, Guidance and Regulations, vol. 1, para 2.4.

(b) Foster Placement (Children) Regulations 1996

The Foster Placement (Children) Regulations 1996 stipulate the matters which a Trust is required to address with the foster-parents in respect of any child-care placement to be made with them. An agreement drawn up between Trust and foster-parents should include statements about training, support, payment and procedures for review of the service provided by the foster-parents. It should give an account of the relevant care arrangements made by the Trust with the parents of any child to be placed in the foster home. It must also address the respective responsibilities of Trust, parent and foster-parent including details regarding respective liabilities for any difficulties which may occur. It should also provide information as to the Trust's complaints procedure.

A foster-parent will owe certain specific duties to the employing Trust and these will be listed in the agreement. Foster-parents, for example, have to undertake not to administer corporal punishment to any child placed with them, to respect the confidentiality of certain information and to notify the Trust in particular circumstances such as when a child becomes ill. They will also have to agree to contact arrangements between the child and such others as the Trust considers appropriate, to supervisory visits from Trust social workers and to the programme of case reviews.

3. Rights of Foster-Parents

Under Article 26(2) and (3) of the 1995 Order, foster-parents have a general right to have their wishes and feelings ascertained and given due consideration by a Trust in relation to the 'making of any decision with respect to a child it is looking after'. They also have the right to attend any case reviews held by a Trust in respect of a child placed with them.

Apart from the rights of 'tenure' which a foster-parent may acquire under the provisions in the Adoption (NI) Order 1987 (see Chapter Six), their legal standing may also be reinforced under similar provisions in the 1995 Order. Under Article 10(5)(b) 'any person with whom the child has lived for a period of at least three years' may apply for a residence or contact order. Under Article 10(5)(c)(ii) an application may be made by a person 'in any case where the child is in the care of a Trust, has the consent of that Trust'. Applications from foster-parents are, however, subject to the restrictions of Article 9:

> (3) A person who is, or was at any time within the last six months, an authority foster parent of a child may not apply for leave to apply for an Article 8 order with respect to the child unless —
>
> (a) he has the consent of the authority;
> (b) he is a relative of the child; or
> (c) the child has lived with him for at least three years preceding the application.

In effect, a Trust foster-parent may make application after one year with Trust consent or after three years without such consent. In the absence of Trust consent for a foster-parent application, the child concerned could, under Article 10(8), make the application without being subject to any time constraints but only with leave of the court if the latter 'is satisfied that he has sufficient understanding to make the proposed application'.

As noted in the Guidance and Regulations:[19]

> Trust foster parents fall into four categories:
> (a) those with whom the child had lived for a total of at least three years during the previous five, who may apply as of right for a residence or contact order;
> (b) those who have the consent of the people whose rights will be affected by the order, who may apply as of right for a residence or contact order;
> (c) relatives of the child, who will need leave to make any application if they do not fall within the first two rules, but do not need the additional consent of the Trust; and
> (d) everyone else, who will need both the consent of the Trust and the leave of the court to make an application for any sort of Article 8 order; this restriction is to prevent application by foster parents at a stage when the Trust is still trying to assess what is best for the child in the long term and also so that parents will not be deterred from asking for their child to be accommodated with a Trust foster parent if the need arises.

Under the Children (NI) Order 1995, Schedule 1, paragraph 2, the court may make an order for financial relief against the parents and for the benefit of 'any person in whose favour a residence order is in effect with respect to a child'. Under paragraph 17:

> (1) Where a child lives, or is to live, with a person as the result of a residence order, a Trust may make contributions to that person towards the cost of the accommodation and maintenance of the child.

II. In Care at Home

There has always been a limited practice of placing some children subject to care orders at home, usually on a 'home on trial' or 'on leave' basis. Initially those placed at home tended to be subject to matrimonial care orders or wardship and the placement decision to let them stay was the result of changes in the household which removed the source of risk. More recently this practice has grown to become, in some instances, the planned placement of choice for the duration of a care order.

1. Advantages of Home Placements

In Northern Ireland, of the 1,573 children subject to a care order in 1964 only forty (3 per cent) were at home whereas by 1980 this had risen to 481 out of 2,444 and in 1989 reached 750 out of 2,783. There have been two major studies in England and Wales on this practice[20] and two in Northern Ireland.[21]

---

19 The Children (NI) Order 1995, Guidance and Regulations, vol. 1, para 5.35.
20 *Captive Clients – Social Work with Families of Children Home on Trial*, Thorburn, 1980; and *Trials and Tribulations: Returning Children from Care to Their Families*, Farmer/Parker, 1989.
21 G Kelly, *Patterns of Care — Child Care Careers and the Decisions that Shape Them*, Dept. of Social Studies, QUB (1990). J Pinkerton, *In Care at Home*, Avebury (1994).

The studies completed in this jurisdiction followed from the work done in England. Firstly, in a longitudinal study which recorded the care careers of eighty-three children over some eighteen months, Kelly[22] revealed large numbers of children in care, often following a PSO, who were shortly afterwards returned home. This gave rise to the supposition that the reason for care proceedings was to strengthen home-based intervention rather than to displace family care. Secondly, Pinkerton[23] showed that many of the children and young people 'home in care' came from households known to social services for considerable periods of time prior to their change in legal status and were returned to those same households after a relatively short episode of substitute care. This finding, that whatever the care plan and wherever the placement, the majority of children taken into Trust care reverted to their families of origin as soon they were able, called into question the point of substitute care arrangements and did much to legitimate the policy of placing children in care where possible with their families.

2. In Care at Home under the 1995 Order

Under Article 27(2)(a) the Trust has the right to place at home any child it is looking after, a right subject to the Placement of Children with Parents Regulations drawn up by the DHSS under paragraph (5). Not only does the Trust have a right to make such a placement but, under paragraph (7), it has a duty to do so as its first preference 'unless that would not be reasonably practicable or consistent with his welfare'. However, where the child is subject to a care order, then special safeguards will have to put in place to ensure the safety of the child.[24] These Regulations address only the situation of children in care under a care order and placed with a parent, other person with parental responsibility or a person in whose favour a residence order has been made. If a child is aged sixteen or over, then their placement is governed only by Regulations 4, 5, 10 and 11.

As stated in the Guidance and Regulations:[25]

> The Placement of Children with Parents etc. Regulations reflect the philosophy of the Children Order that children in need can be assisted most effectively if the Trust works in partnership with the child's parents and that for most children the best place for him to be brought up is in his own family.

There is a heavy onus on a Trust to satisfy itself that if a child should be so placed that a care order is also necessary.

Trust Duties in Relation to Children Being Looked After by the Trust

Principles

The principles stated in two Conventions have exercised a direct influence on the development of the law relating to children in the United Kingdom: the European

---

22 See Kelly above.
23 See Pinkerton, f 21 above.
24 See *A Child in Trust — The Report of the Panel of Inquiry into the Circumstances Surrounding the Death of Jasmine Beckford,* London: Blom-Cooper, 1985.
25 Children (NI) Order 1995, Guidance and Regulations, vol. 3, para 7.1.

Convention for the Protection of Human Rights and Fundamental Freedoms[26] and the UN Convention on the Rights of the Child. Article 6 of the former, dealing with parental rights of access, was found to have been breached in *O v UK, B v UK, H v UK, R v UK, W v UK*.[27]

In the UN Convention, under Article 3.3,

> the State Parties shall ensure that the institutions, services and facilities responsible for the care or protection of children shall adhere to the standards established by competent authorities, particularly in the areas of safety, health, the number and suitability of their staff as well as competent supervision.

Article 25 of the UN Convention requires States to recognise the right of a child placed in care for care, protection or treatment of his or her physical or mental health, to periodic review of the treatment provided to the child and all other circumstances relevant to the placement.

1. Welfare of the Child

The more general duty of a Trust in relation to a child in care is as stated in Article 26 of the 1995 Order:

> (1) Every authority looking after a child shall —
> (a) safeguard and promote his welfare.

The directive that every Trust should 'safeguard' is an unambiguous reminder that this most basic obligation, to keep a child safe, is one which the Trusts have on occasion failed to honour: it is not to be left as an unstated assumption that a Trust will positively plan and provide for a child's safety. Evidence of past failures are well documented in such reports as 'An Abuse of Trust', DHSS (SSI) (1993) and *Report of the Committee of Inquiry into Children's Homes and Hostels*, HMSO (1986). Again, the directive to 'promote' welfare makes explicit the legislative intent that every Trust should be proactive after the issue of a care order in ensuring that a child benefits and continues to benefit from the experience of being in care. It is not acceptable for a child 'to drift in care'.

The general thrust of the principles is that Trust intervention in family life should be kept to a minimum and that a child's welfare interests are usually best served by parental care. This is evident in Article 27(7) which requires a Trust to work towards rehabilitation of the child with the family of origin by placing that child in the care of parents or relatives 'unless that would not be reasonably practicable or consistent with his welfare'. When providing accommodation for a child, and subject to the same condition, paragraph (8) requires a Trust to do so close to the child's home and to arrange for any siblings in care to be accommodated together.

---

26 Cmnd 8969 (1953).
27 See (1987) 10 EHRR 29.

2. Wishes of the Child

The requirement that a child or young person be consulted before any decisions are taken affecting his or her interests is a significant step forward for the legal position of children in Northern Ireland. This requirement is stated initially in Article 3(3)(a) of the 1995 Order and is subsequently repeated at various points. Article 26, for example, states:

> (2) Before making any decision with respect to a child whom it is looking after, or proposing to look after, an authority shall, so far as is reasonably practicable, ascertain the wishes and feelings of —
> (a) the child . . . regarding the matter to be decided.
> (3) In making any such decision an authority shall give due consideration —
> (a) having regard to his age and understanding, to such wishes and feelings of the child as the authority has been able to ascertain . . .

This principle is binding not only on the Trust in respect of the subject of a care order but also on such others as voluntary organisations, staff of children's homes, foster-parents, medical practitioners and education authorities. It derives from the decision in *Gillick*, has been shaped by the European and UN Conventions and has the broad effect of separating the legal interests of child and parent so as to give some legal standing to those of the former in relation to third parties (see also Chapter Fifteen).

Care Plans

A Trust is required to produce a care plan in respect of any child who is on the child protection register, is being 'looked after' or is the subject of either a judicial inquiry or of court proceedings. Guidance on the formulation of such plans has been offered by the Department of Health.[28]

1. The Requirements

Regulation 3 of the Arrangements for Placement of Children (General) Regulations (NI)1996 governs the making of a care plan. Whether the placement is being provided on a voluntary or compulsory basis, an agreement or care plan must be drawn up in respect of the child concerned. Planning should begin prior to placement however, as stated in the Guidance and Regulations:[29]

> In an emergency or immediate placement, it may not be possible to draw up a long term plan prior to placement. However, a provisional outline plan should always exist. The firm plan should then be drawn up as soon as possible after the child has been looked after or accommodated and in any case not later than 14 days after the placement started.

---

28 See DoH, *Protecting Children*, HMSO, 1988.
29 The Children (NI) Order 1995, Guidance and Regulations, vol. 3, para 2.16.

The plan must be in writing and be drawn up after consultations among Trust, parents and child (where possible) and such other individuals and agencies as may be playing an important part in the child's life. After placement, the plan should be scrutinised and if necessary adjusted at the first review which must occur within four weeks of the Trust's commencing to look after the child.

Regulation 4 governs the considerations on making a care plan and the contents of arrangements refers further to Schedule 4 of the Regulations.

The Looking After Children (LAC) forms establish a format for a care plan and refers further to Schedule 1–4 of the Regulations.

2. Purpose

The purpose of a care plan is to outline the way in which a Trust intends to give effect to its responsibility under Articles 18(1), 26(1), 76 and 92 to safeguard and promote the welfare of the child concerned, thereby giving focus to the work and avoiding drift. As stated in the Guidance and Regulations:[30]

> This will be achieved in broad terms by:
> - assessing the child's needs;
> - determining objectives to be met to safeguard and promote the child's welfare;
> - consulting with parents, the child and others whom the responsible authority consider are relevant;
> - appraising the options available to meet those objectives;
> - making decisions in full consultation with the child, his parents and other agencies and individuals with a legitimate interest;
> - designating individuals to undertake specific tasks; and
> - setting a time scale in which tasks must be achieved or reassessed.

3. Matters to Be Addressed

A care plan must provide for the carrying out of parental responsibilities in respect of the child. These responsibilities are the same under the 1995 Order as they were under the 1968 Act. Their distribution between Trust and parent is dependent upon whether the child is accommodated on a voluntary basis or is in care under a court order. They are now to be found in the Order, listed in Regulation 4 and as specified in Schedules 1–3 of the Regulations (General). These matters are addressed under the headings of welfare, health, consent to medical examination or treatment, education, religion, culture and race.

Contact with a Child in Care

Under Article 53:

> (1) Where a child is in the care of an authority, the authority shall (subject to the provisions of this Article) allow the child reasonable contact with —

---

30 The Children (NI) Order 1995, Guidance and Regulations, vol. 3, para 2.18.

(a) his parents;
(b) any guardian of his;
(c) where there was a residence order in force with respect to the child immediately before the care order was made, the person in whose favour the residence order was made; and
(d) where, immediately before the care order was made, a person had care of the child by virtue of an order made in the exercise of the High Court's inherent jurisdiction with respect to children, that person.

This provision replicates section 34 of the 1989 Act which was drawn up against the background of the decisions taken by the European Court of Human Rights in four cases.[31]

The parental right of access to a child in care was recognised by Article 8 of the European Convention and enforced against the United Kingdom in *R v United Kingdom*[32] where it was held that a parental right of access exists independently of considerations of the child's welfare. However, this right had proved to be unenforceable in Northern Ireland. The importance attached to the Strasbourg rulings by the United Kingdom courts is evident in the judgments of Lords Templeman and Oliver in *Re KD (A Minor)(Access: Principles)*.[33]

The legislative intent is that contact arrangements will have been determined between Trust and parent and be subjected to judicial scrutiny prior to the issue of the care order (see Chapter Twelve). If, despite such opportunities to pre-empt later conflict, a dispute should arise among Trust, parent and/or child, then the above Article 53(1) will come into play.

1. Contact Arrangements in Respect of a Child Being Looked After by a Trust

As stated in the Guidance and Regulations:[34]

> In the case of children looked after by a Trust, Article 27(8)(a) specifically requires the Trust to place a child near his home, so far as practicable, subject to his welfare being safeguarded.

Child Being Accommodated

As stated in the Guidance and Regulations:[35]

> ... limitations, controls and postponements of contact should be agreed by all those concerned.

Child in Care

Article 53(1) creates a presumption that placement arrangements will provide for 'reasonable contact' between parents and a child in care, i.e. there is now an onus on

---

31 See *O, B, W and R v UK* ECHR Series A, No. 120–121 (1987) and Series A, No. 136 – A and C–E (1988).
32 [1988] 2 FLR 445.
33 [1988] 2 FLR 139.
34 Children (NI) Order 1995, Guidance and Regulations, vol. 3, para 8.17.
35 Children (NI) Order 1995, Guidance and Regulations, vol. 3, para 8.33.

a Trust to achieve this of its own volition rather than doing so in response to a challenge from parent or child, a presumption which does not extend to facilitating contact with members of the extended family.[36] As stated in the Guidance and Regulations:[37]

> Parents should be involved in the assessment and planning prior to placement wherever possible.

Also, under Articles 26(2), 76(2) and 92(2) of the Children Order:

> Consideration of contact is an essential element in the planning process. So far as is reasonably practicable, the views of the child, the parents and the child's carers must be ascertained before a decision about contact arrangements is made.

The value and purpose of contact should be clearly understood and agreed so far as possible by all concerned. There should be a clear understanding from the outset about all the arrangements and what is expected of the parents, the responsible authority and the child's carers in connection with the arrangements.[38]

The presumption of reasonable contact is strengthened by Article 29(1) which, in respect of a child being looked after by a Trust, requires the latter to 'endeavour to promote contact between the child and his parents' and other parties. Further, as noted in the Guidance and Regulations:[39]

> In some cases it may be appropriate to identify relatives, who may include a parent, with whom contact has lapsed and to follow up the prospects of re-establishing contact.

The emphasis, however, should be on preserving the child's existing close and positive relationships rather than deliberately cultivating new relationships among members of the extended family.

2. Child in Care: Decision-Making by the Trust

Once a care order is made it is for the Trust and not the court to determine the contact arrangements unless any of the parties concerned bring an application for a contact order before the court. Generally, as stated in the Guidance and Regulations:[40]

> ... all decisions about contact should be explained to parents and discussed with them. The Trust should also confirm in writing to the parents all decisions and agreements about contact arrangements and any changes to the arrangements and the outcome of all formal and informal reviews of contact. Where limitations or control on contact have been imposed, these should be clearly stated. Similarly any postponement of contact should be confirmed in writing together with the reasons.

---

36 This is apparent from the decision in *Re A (A Minor)(Contact Application: Grandparent) The Times*, March 6, 1995 CA.
37 Children (NI) Order 1995, Guidance and Regulations, vol. 3, para 8.11.
38 Children (NI) Order 1995, Guidance and Regulations, vol. 3, para 8.15.
39 Children (NI) Order 1995, Guidance and Regulations, vol. 3, para 8.16.
40 Children (NI) Order 1995, Guidance and Regulations, vol. 3, para 8.33.

When a Trust wishes to refuse contact, then it is only entitled to do so where, under paragraph (6) of this Article:

> (a) the authority is satisfied that it is necessary to do so in order to safeguard or promote the child's welfare; and
> (b) the refusal—
> > (i) is decided upon as a matter of urgency; and
> > (ii) does not last for more than seven days.

Any such Trust refusal of contact, departure from the terms of an order made under Article 53 and notification of variation or supervision of contact arrangements must be made after serving notice on those concerned in accordance with Regulation 2 of the Contact with Children Regulations (NI) 1996. The matters to be addressed in the notification are detailed in the Schedule to the Regulations and include the decision taken, the date of the decision, reasons for taking it, its duration and the rights of the parties affected. A Trust should always be aware that it may not be in a child's best interests to be induced to persist in contact arrangements which produce stress and unhappiness. Also, as stated in the Guidance and Regulations:[41]

> A child in care has a right to make an application to the court to authorise the Trust to refuse to allow contact between the child and a named person (Article 53(4)). It may be that the Trust will decide that it is in the child's best interests to initiate such proceedings if the child so wishes.

Where disagreements about contact arrangements persist between the parties and the Trust, the dissatisfied party should be advised to seek independent legal advice.

The right to take decisions governing contact arrangements between children in care and their families is an area of child-care practice in Northern Ireland which has been radically changed by the 1995 Order. The absence of any equivalent to the Child Care Act 1980 had left such decisions totally to the discretion of Trust social workers, a discretion very frequently exercised to terminate contact in preparation for adoption placements. Where controversy arises the law now places the authority to take contact decisions in the hands of the court.

3. Applications for a Contact Order

An Order under Article 53

Where a child is the subject of a care order, then an application for judicial determination of a dispute concerning contact arrangements may be made by the Trust, the child, any of the parties listed in paragraph (1) above or any other person with leave of the court. Under Article 53(5), the court may of its own volition when making a CO also make a contact order. Should a Trust, for example, wish to extend the period of suspended contact from the seven days permitted under Article 53(6)(b)(ii) or to permanently terminate all contact, then it must seek authority from the court. Although

---

41 Children (NI) Order 1995, Guidance and Regulations, vol. 3, para 8.25.

not mentioned in this provision, it is most probable that an unmarried father, grandparents, siblings or other relatives would have little difficulty in obtaining leave to make application. The court may then 'make such order as it considers appropriate'. Application may also be made by the Trust or the child under Article 53(4) asking the court to 'make an order authorising the Trust to refuse to allow contact' between the child and any of the parties listed in paragraph (1) above. A number of applications made by children seeking termination of contact have been heard by the courts in England and Wales.

An Order under Article 8

Where a child is being accommodated by a Trust, then a dispute concerning access may be judicially resolved following an application for an Article 8 contact order by child, parent or other person.

4. Child in Care: Decision-Making by the Court

Under Article 53:

> (4) On an application made by the authority or the child, the court may make an order authorising the authority to refuse to allow contact between the child and any person who is mentioned in sub-paragraphs (a) to (d) of paragraph (1) and named in the order.

If the application is made under paragraph (2) or (3), 'the court may make such order as it considers appropriate with respect to the contact which is to be allowed between the child and any named person'. However, in considering any such application, the court is entitled to review a Trust's management of contact arrangements and test their reasonableness against the presumption imposed upon the Trust by Article 53(1).[42] Recently, in rejecting an application to terminate parental access to a child in care so as to facilitate the placement of that child for adoption, the President of the Family Division said:[43]

> The emphasis is heavily placed on the presumption of continuing parental contact ... since the court has a duty to consider contact between the child and the parents, it may require the local authority to justify its long-term plan where their plan excludes contact between the parents and the child.

By refusing to authorise a termination of contact, the court may effectively demolish a care plan. While it is clear that the court is entitled to respond in this way when the

---

42 This was confirmed by the decision of the Court of Appeal in *Re B (Minors)(Care: Contact: Local Authority's Plans)* [1993] 1 FLR 543 which considered the bearing of the equivalent provision in the 1989 Act on the Trusts' counterparts and the decision in *Re P (Minors)(Contact with Children in Care)* [1993] 2 FLR 156 which held that long-term care plans which excluded contact could be reviewed by the court.
43 See in *Re E (A Minor)(Care Order: Contact)* [1994] 1 FLR 146, 151D, 153F which followed the decision in *Re B* above. See also *Re L (Sexual Abuse: Standard of Proof)* [1996] 1 FLR 116.

matter is brought before it or arises in the context of proceedings, it is less clear whether it has the power to itself initiate such a review. It has been suggested[44] that the court may respond to such an application in respect of a child in care by making a contact order subject to a condition that the matter be reviewed by the court some months later. It is unlikely that such a blatant attempt to impose on-going judicial review of how a Trust implements the statutory authority conferred on it by a CO (as opposed to the quite different type and extent of authority conferred by an ICO) would be sustainable.

Where the application is made by a child in care, it will be governed by the paramountcy principle. The House of Lords has considered the relative weighting to be allocated to welfare interests where the applicant and the party in respect of whom a contact order was being sought were both children and both in care.[45] It ruled that the paramountcy principle attached to the interests of the subject of the application.

The protection hitherto enjoyed by the Trusts, as a result of the *Liverpool* ruling and in the absence of any equivalent to the Child Care Act 1980, to determine access arrangements in respect of children in care would seem to have been swept away by Article 53(1). However, in a recent case[46] the court considered an appeal against the making of a contact order by the family proceedings court. The assumed power of the court at first instance derived from the wording of section 34(2) of the 1989 Act, replicated as follows in Article 53 of the 1995 Order:

> (2) On an application made by the authority or the court, the court may make such order as it considers appropriate with respect to the contact which is to be allowed between the child and any named person.

On appeal it was argued that the use of the words 'which is to be allowed' disclosed a presumption that it fell to the appropriate statutory authority (the Trusts under the 1995 Order) to determine the existence and extent of any contact between a child in care and a named person. In view of the authority's statutory duty to promote contact between a child in care and his or her family of origin, it was unnecessary for the court at first instance to add an order to the same effect. The appeal was allowed.

Under Article 53(7), where the issue is the nature rather than the fact or otherwise of contact, the court has a discretion to 'impose such conditions as the court considers appropriate'. In effect this gives it the power to define all aspects of the contact. Where no application has been made but the court is either making a care order or is involved in proceedings concerning a child in care, then the court may nonetheless make an order under this Article if it considers this to be necessary (see also Chapter Twelve).

5. Effect of an Order

Regulation 3 permits a Trust to depart from the terms of any order made under Article 53 in circumstances where the agreement of the parties and child is available

---

44 See G Brasse *After the Care Order — Into Forbidden Territory*, (1995) Fam Law 75.
45 See *Birmingham City Council v H* (no. 3) [1994] 1 All ER 12. Also see *Re W (Application for Leave)* where the court ruled that an application made by a fifteen-year-old, the subject of a care order, did not require prior leave of the court.
46 See *Re F (Contact: Child in Care)* [1995] 1 FLR 510.

and seven days' advance notice is served. Once an order is made under Article 53, the Trust will need to review its care plan for the child.

Because the court has the power under paragraph (9) to 'vary or discharge any order made under this Article', the fact that it has previously decided a contact issue will not be a bar to subsequent applications on the same issue.

6. Conflict of Interests Where All Parties Are Children

A problem not addressed by the Children Act 1989, but posing a recurring dilemma for the courts in England and Wales and likely to do so in this jurisdiction under the equivalent provisions of the 1995 Order, has been how to respond to the interests of children where these are in conflict in the same proceedings. This has most often occurred in circumstances where the children are either siblings or where one is the underaged mother of the other.

An example of the former was in *Re T and E (Proceedings: Conflict of Interests)*[47] where the court was faced with three applications. The first was an application from the father of one of two half-sisters, both of whom were in the same short-term foster placement, to revoke a care order in respect of his daughter. The other two were applications for freeing orders from the local authority in respect of both girls, one being contested. Given that the close relationship between the two girls was an important component in the legal interests of both, the court acknowledged that the success of any application would jeopardise the welfare of the remaining child. The legal interests of each child required that contact with the other be maintained. The question therefore arose as to how the court should distinguish between the competing sets of interests and what part the paramountcy principle should play in determining the applications. It was held that, where in such cases the interests of children are in conflict, the court must balance the potential benefit to one against the potential detriment to the other before deciding on any particular course of action.

An example of the latter was *Birmingham City Council v H (No 2)*[48] where the mother, a minor, applied for contact with her child. The Court of Appeal held that in making its decision the Court must balance the welfare of the two children. However, on appeal the House of Lords considered that the paramountcy principle applied to the child who was the subject of the proceedings, in this case the child with whom contact was sought, and that the Court's decision must reflect a weighting which favoured that child (see also Chapter Fifteen).

Disciplining a Child

Following a number of well-publicised scandals in relation to the discipline procedures used against children in care, most notably the use of 'pin-down',[49] there is now a greater awareness of what is and what is not an acceptable use of discipline. While

---

47 [1995] 1 FLR 581.
48 [1993] 1 FLR 883.
49 See *The Pindown Experience and the Protection of Children*, the Report of the Staffordshire Child Care Inquiry (1990).

parents may have a right to discipline their children, it is not readily apparent what degree of force, if any, can be used by designated care staff in relation to a child being looked after by a Trust. This matter is addressed in Regulation 8(2).

1. Unacceptable Discipline

In the words of Hoggett:[50]

> The following sanctions are not allowed: any form of corporal punishment, deprivation of food, or drink, or sleep, restriction of visiting or other outside contacts (unless necessary in order to protect or promote the child's welfare), requiring the child to wear distinctive or inappropriate clothes (apart from school and other uniforms), fines, using or withholding medication or medical or dental treatment, and intimate physical examination.
>
> Exceptions are made for action authorised by a doctor or dentist which is necessary to prevent injury to anyone or serious damage to property, and for directions given by the Secretary of State.

However, it has long been accepted that in law those with parental responsibility have the right of 'reasonable chastisement'.[51]

2. Permissible Restraint

The restraining of children in residential care has recently been addressed in a training pack, commissioned by the Department of Health and introduced to staff in this jurisdiction by SSI (NI), entitled *Taking Care, Taking Control*. That material is now incorporated within the Guidance and Regulations.[52]

Physical restraint is allowed to prevent 'detained or remanded' children from escaping or where immediate action is needed to prevent injury to the person or serious damage to property. Talking to a child who is misbehaving or threatening to leave may be reinforced by standing in his or her way, placing a hand on his or her arm or holding a highly distressed child, if these are intended to be persuasive rather than coercive. However, any intervention should be tailored to the particular child and the incident which gave rise to it.

Recent case law[53] in England has confirmed that a child-minder is justified in administering a light smack to a child in his or her care with or without parental permission (see also Chapter Thirteen).

Review Procedures and Parental Participation

Under Article 45 of the 1995 Order:

---

50 See Hoggett, *Parents and Children*, 1993, p 149.
51 See *R v Hopley* (1860) 2 FLR 202.
52 See Children (NI) Order 1995, Guidance and Regulations, vol 4, *Residential Care*, 'Good Order and Discipline', pp 28–44.
53 See *London Borough of Sutton v Davies* [1994] 1 FLR 737.

(1) The Department may make regulations requiring the case of each child who is being looked after by an authority to be reviewed in accordance with the provisions of the regulations.

The Review of Children's Cases Regulations was made pursuant to this provision and was applied to all children and young persons being looked after by a Trust whether or not they are the subject of statutory orders and whether they are looked after by a Trust or accommodated by a voluntary organisation or in a registered children's home. As stated in the Guidance and Regulations:[54]

> The purpose of the review is to ensure that the child's welfare is safeguarded and promoted in the most effective way throughout the period he is looked after or accommodated. Progress in safeguarding and providing for the child's welfare should be examined and monitored at every review and the plan for the child amended as necessary to reflect any significant change.

This provision accords with Article 25 of the United Nations Convention on the Rights of the Child which recognises the right of a child in care to a periodic review of the circumstances relevant to being placed in care.

1. Review Requirements

Regulation 2 places a specific statutory duty on the responsible authority to review the case of a child looked after or accommodated in accordance with the Regulations.

Regulation 3 requires a first review to be conducted on every case within two to four weeks of a child's accommodation by or committal to the care of a Trust, a second within three months of the first and thereafter at intervals of not more than six months. These are minimum standards; reviews should take place more frequently if the circumstances of a case require it.

The Looking After Children (LAC) forms provide the recommended format for recording review material. As stated in the Guidance and Regulations:[55]

> A review system should provide for —
> - the full participation of both children and parents in the decision-making process;
> - a structured, co-ordinated approach to the planning of child care work in individual cases and;
> - a monitoring system for checking the operation of the review process.

Before conducting any review the Trust must seek the views of the child, the parents, any person other than a parent who has parental responsibility and such other persons as the Trust considers relevant. The review should provide, as far as is practicable, for the attendance and participation of such persons, all of whom should be advised of the outcome.

Schedule 2 to the Regulations provides a checklist of matters, mainly relating to the care plan, to be considered at every review. This list is neither comprehensive nor

---

54 Children (NI) Order 1995, Guidance and Regulations, vol. 3, para 3.1.
55 Children (NI) Order 1995, Guidance and Regulations, vol. 3, para 3.8.

exclusive but merely the minimum that should be addressed. Certain matters must be examined at each review: whether any care order in effect should be discharged or any change to the child's status be sought, whether contact arrangements between the child and family should be altered, the views of the child, carer, parent and any independent visitor, whether any special arrangements should be made to meet the child's, the immediate and long-term arrangements for looking after the child and whether the child's needs indicate permanency planning or re-unification with the family.

2. Reviews, Representations and the Rights of the Child

A Trust is required to explain to the child, insofar as is reasonably practicable, any steps that he or she may take under the 1995 Order. In particular the Trust must advise the child of the right under Article 10 to apply with leave for an Article 8 order or, if in care, the right under Article 58(1)(b) to apply for a discharge of the care order. The child must also be advised of the procedure established pursuant to Article 45(3) for him or her to make representations (including a complaint) to the Trust.

3. Representations and Participation of Parents and Child

Under Article 45(3) the right of participation by child and parent, in the child-care decision-making, review and complaint procedures of a Trust is introduced for the first time. This right to participate or to make representations extends to any person bearing parental responsibility in respect of the child, any Trust foster-parent and to any other person whom the Trust should consider to be relevant to securing or promoting the child's welfare. The right applies to any matter relating to the exercise of a Trust's functions arising under Part IV of the 1995 Order and is given effect by Regulation 7(2) which requires the involvement of the child (subject to age and understanding) and parents, unless there is good reason not to. Both would normally attend the entire review. The child may benefit from being accompanied by someone who could provide friendly support. Separate times for attendance of child and parent may be necessary.

Articles 26(2), 76 and 92 state that before taking any decision the review should obtain and take account of the wishes and feelings of the child, parents, person with parental responsibility and any other person considered relevant. 'Other person' may include a current carer, an independent visitor, a GP, an appropriate Trust and ELB, the relevant teacher and any other involved professional.

Regulation 8 requires each responsible authority to put in place arrangements for implementing the decisions taken. Under Article 46, the ELB, NIHE and others have a duty to comply with a request from a Trust for assistance with the exercise of its functions under Part IV; unless to do so would be incompatible with that body's own statutory or other duties and obligations or would unduly prejudice the discharge of any of its functions. Under Article 47 the Trust has a duty to consult with an ELB before accommodating a child in an establishment which provides education.

Regulation 9 requires responsible authorities to put in place a system for monitoring the operation of the review system.

Secure Accommodation

Any child already being looked after by a Trust, whether on a voluntary basis or as the consequence of a care order and regardless of the type of accommodation being provided (foster home, psychiatric hospital, hostel, children's home etc.), is eligible for a judicially sanctioned removal to or retention in secure accommodation, provided the legal requirements are satisfied.

Authority to Provide Secure Accommodation

The authority to provide secure accommodation is to be found in Article 44 of the 1995 Order and in the Children (Secure Accommodation) Regulations (NI) 1996. The Regulations govern restrictions on the liberty of children being looked after by Trusts, protecting them from unnecessary and inappropriate placement in secure accommodation.

Definition of Secure Accommodation

Under Article 44(1) of the 1995 Order 'secure accommodation' means accommodation provided for the purpose of restricting liberty. Whether or not a particular place or practice meets the terms of this definition is ultimately a matter for the court to determine. Any practice which prevents a child from leaving a room of its own volition, however, could amount to a restriction of liberty. It has been held[56] that a behaviour modification unit in a hospital, where the programme entailed a restriction on person liberty, was a form of secure accommodation.

Criteria for Use of Secure Accommodation

Under Article 44(2) a child who is being looked after by a Trust may not be placed and, if placed, may not be kept, in secure accommodation unless it appears

(a) that —
  (i) he has a history of absconding and is likely to abscond from any other description of accommodation; and
  (ii) if he absconds, he is likely to suffer significant harm; or
(b) that if he is kept in any other description of accommodation he is likely to injure himself or other persons.

Intended as a 'last resort', there are thus only two types of situation justifying secure accommodation.

When Secure Accommodation May Not Be Used

Secure accommodation is never justified as a punishment nor by the lack of an alternative.

---

56 See *R v Northampton Juvenile Court, ex parte London Borough of Hammersmith and Fulham* [1985] FLR 193.

Under the Children (Secure Accommodation) Regulations (NI) 1996 the DHSS has excluded certain categories of children and young persons from eligibility for placement in secure accommodation. No child in a voluntary or privately run children's home may be so placed; neither may any child already detained under the Mental Health (NI) Order 1986; nor may any child under the age of thirteen years be detained without the prior approval of the DHSS; nor may a child convicted of a grave offence whose detention is subject to the discretion of the Home Office; and no young person aged between sixteen and twenty-one years who is being provided with accommodation by a Trust in order to safeguard or promote that person's welfare or who is the subject of a CAO and is being kept away from home pursuant to that order may be so detained.

Retention in Secure Accommodation

Under Article 44(3) provision is made for regulations to specify a maximum period during which a child may be retained in secure accommodation without recourse to the court. Under Regulation 11(1) a child in care may only be so retained for a maximum period of seventy-two hours in any period of twenty-eight days, unless a further period has been sanctioned by the court.[57]

Role of the Court

Where a child is to be detained in secure accommodation for a period exceeding seventy-two hours, then authority to do so must be sought from a family proceedings court (or county court or High Court where a secure order is made in the course of civil proceedings being heard in either court).

As stated in the Guidance and Regulations:[58]

> It is the role of the court to safeguard the child's welfare from inappropriate or unnecessary use of secure accommodation, by satisfying itself that those making the application have demonstrated that the statutory criteria in Article 44(2) have been met (Article 44(4)). If the court determines that the criteria are satisfied, the court shall make an order authorising the child to be kept in secure accommodation and specifying the maximum period the child may be so kept (Article 44(5)). This, however, is subject to the power of the court to make an interim order under Article 44(6).

The court must be satisfied that the order will positively contribute to the child's welfare and must not make an order unless it considers that doing so would be better for the child than making no order at all.

The Rules require copies of written reports to be made available before the hearing to the applicant, parent/guardian, the solicitor for the child, the GAL and the child. In the latter instance the court may direct otherwise.[59]

---

57 See Children (Secure Accommodation) Regulations (NI), 1996; see also Regulation 11(3) for exceptional arrangements at weekends and public holidays.
58 Children (NI) Order 1995, Guidance and Regulations, vol. 1, para 18.7.
59 The Magistrates' Courts (Children (NI) Order 1995) Rules (NI) 1996, Rule 26.

1. Family Proceedings

In *Oxfordshire County Council v R*[60] the court advised that secure accommodation proceedings were family proceedings for some purposes of the 1989 Act and, therefore, hearsay evidence was admissible and the welfare principle and the 'no-order' presumption applied. Under Article 60, they are also 'specified proceedings' and therefore the court must appoint a guardian ad litem unless satisfied that it is not necessary to do so in the interests of the child. From the judicial comments made in this case it is clear that when considering an application for secure accommodation, magistrates should use the statutory criteria set out in Article 44 as a checklist.

2. Welfare Principle

In *Re M (Secure Accommodation Order)*[61] the court ruled that the paramountcy principle must not be brought to bear on any judicial consideration of whether or not a secure accommodation order should be made.

3. The Order

Before making the order the court must, under Article 44(7) ensure that legal representation is provided for the child 'unless, having been informed of his right to apply for legal aid and having had the opportunity to do so, he refused or failed to apply'. The availability of legal aid for secure accommodation proceedings is provided for under Article 172 (amending the Legal Aid, Advice and Assistance (NI) Order 1981, Article 5).

Under Regulation 12, the order may authorise the retention of a child for a period not exceeding three months. Under Regulation 13, on subsequent applications, a Trust may seek six-month extensions.

Once the criteria cease to be met, the child should be removed. Under Article 22 a person with parental responsibility has the right to remove a child retained in secure accommodation.

4. Appeals

Under Article 166 of the 1995 Order arrangements are provided for appeal procedures in relation to the making or otherwise of secure accommodation orders.

Trust Responsibilities for Children in Secure Accommodation

In addition to its normal responsibilities in respect of children whom it is looking after, a Trust has other duties which are specific to children in secure accommodation. In particular it must establish a review panel of at least three members, one of whom at least must not be employed by the Trust, which shall conduct a review of every child in secure accommodation within one month of a child's admission and at intervals of

---

60 [1992] 1 FLR 648.
61 [1995] FLR 418.

not less than three months thereafter. The panel should address not only the matters relating to the child's welfare as detailed in Article 45 but must also satisfy itself that the criteria for retention in secure accommodation is still being met. When making its deliberations the panel is required to ascertain and take into account the wishes and feelings of the child and those of any person bearing parental responsibility or having had care responsibility in respect of him or her. All involved must be advised of the outcome of the review and proper records must be maintained.

Discharge from Care

The discharge procedure for a child or young person 'being looked after by a Trust' will vary according to whether he or she is merely being accommodated or is in the care of the Trust. In the first instance, Article 22(2) permits any person with parental responsibility for a child to remove that child at any time from accommodation provided by a Trust. In the second instance, there are a number of alternative formal procedures for effecting discharge.

Discharge from a Care Order

A child or young person may be discharged from a care order by a successful application for discharge, by a successful application for a residence order, by the court on application substituting a supervision order, by adoption or by the young person reaching the age of eighteen.

1. Application for Discharge from a Care Order

Under Article 58 of the 1995 Order:

>   (1) A care order may be discharged by the court on the application of —
>   (a) any person who has parental responsibility for the child;
>   (b) the child himself; or
>   (c) the authority designated by the order.

This extension of a right to apply for the discharge of a care order, from being the exclusive prerogative of a Trust to the others listed above, is a significant step in the implementation of the partnership principle which runs through the Children (NI) Order 1995. In a recent decision[62] Thorpe J made it clear that the right of the subject of an order to make an application for the discharge of that order is not conditional upon first obtaining leave of the court. The primary issue is — does the child have sufficient understanding to make application? — an issue which will fall to be decided in the first instance by the solicitor chosen to take instructions from the child. Ultimately the issue will be determined by the court.

---

62   See *Re A (Care: Discharge Application by Child)* [1995] 1 FLR 599.

2. The Making of a Residence Order

Under Article 179:

> (1) The making of a residence order with respect to a child who is the subject of a care order discharges the care order.

The authority of the court to make such an order arises under Article 9(1). This power under paragraph (2) may be exercised in favour of a Trust foster-parent if that person is a relative of the child, with Trust consent or after three years of undertaking direct care responsibility. The child may make such an application stating in whose favour the residence order should be made out, i.e. with whom he or she proposes to reside following the discharge of the care order. As stated in the Guidance and Regulations[63]

> A care order is automatically discharged by the making of a residence order (Article 179(1)). This route extends opportunities to bring a care order to an end to the following persons not having parental responsibility: Trust foster parents (if they satisfy the conditions in Article 9(3)), an unmarried father (Article 10(4)(a)), any person with whom the child has lived for at least three years (Article 10(5)(b)), any person who has the consent of a Trust to apply for a residence order (Article 10(5)(c)(ii)) and any person who succeeds in an application for leave to bring an application (Article 10(9)).

3. The Making of a Supervision Order

Under Schedule 3:

> 9. The making of a supervision order with respect to any child brings to an end any earlier care or supervision order which —
> (a) was made with respect to that child; and
> (b) would otherwise continue in force.

4. Substitution of a Supervision Order

Under Article 58:

> (4) Where a care order is in force with respect to a child the court may, on the application of any person entitled to apply for the order to be discharged, substitute a supervision order for the care order.

The authority for the court to make such an order in response to an application from a Trust or an authorised person arises under Article 50(6)(7a). The court is not obliged to seek evidence that the significant harm threshold has been breached as, presumably, it is entitled to rely on the existence of the care order as proof that this is the case.

---

63 Children (NI) Order 1995, Guidance and Regulations, vol. 1, para 9.74.

5. Adoption

The making of an adoption order or a freeing order extinguishes any subsisting order made under the 1995 Order.[64]

6. Attaining Eighteenth Birthday

Under Article 179, if not discharged by the court, then:

> (12) Any care order, other than an interim care order, shall continue in force until the child reaches the age of 18, unless it is brought to an end earlier.

After Care

A particular weakness of the Children and Young Persons Act (NI) 1968 was its failure to place any specific duties on the Health and Social Services Boards in relation to the on-going needs of children and young persons after they had been discharged from care. The 1995 Order addresses this omission.

I. A Young Person's Eligibility for Services

1. Age

The young person must be aged at least sixteen but be less than twenty-one when requesting after-care services.

2. Been Looked After

It is not necessary for the young person to have been the subject of a care order only that he or she has been either 'looked after by an authority', been accommodated (by or on behalf of a voluntary organisation) or been in a children's home or, for a consecutive period of at least three months been in an ELB facility, a residential care home, a nursing home or in any prescribed accommodation or has been privately fostered. In either case, this must have occurred (or, more likely, continued) after reaching the age of sixteen.

3. Be in Need

Under Article 35(5) the conditions to be met are that:

(a) it appears to the authority that the person concerned is in need of advice and being befriended;
(b) where that person was not being looked after by the authority, the authority is satisfied that the person by whom he was being looked after does not have the necessary facilities for advising or befriending him.

---

64 The Adoption (NI) Order 1987, Articles 12(3) and 17(3) as amended by the Children (NI) Order 1995, Schedule 9, paras 140(1) and 143(2).

II. A Trust's Duty to Provide Services

1. Duty to Prepare

Under Article 35 of the 1995 Order:

> (1) Where a child is being looked after by an authority, the authority shall advise, assist and befriend him with a view to promoting his welfare when he ceases to be looked after by the authority.

This is the first time such a specific duty has been placed on the Trusts. The duty is to prepare the young person, while he or she is still in care (or while still being looked after by the Trust), to cope with the responsibilities of independent living when he or she leaves.

2. Duty to Continue to Support

A Trust's aftercare duty arises when notice is served on it that there is in its area a person qualifying for advice and assistance who meets the conditions of paragraph (5) above and who has asked for help which, under this Article, it is able to give. Under Article 37(3) where this duty has arisen but the young person has moved or is moving to another area, then the Trust is required to notify the Trust for that area. A similar obligation falls on anyone providing accommodation in respect of a young person who, having reached the age of sixteen, ceases to be so accommodated. The Trust for the area in which the young person is to reside must be notified accordingly.

3. Nature of Support

The aftercare duty to provide assistance may under Article 36(1) 'be in kind or, in exceptional circumstances, in cash' and under paragraph (2) may take the form of:

> (a) contributing to expenses incurred by him in living near the place where he is or will be —
>   (i) employed or seeking employment; or
>   (ii) receiving education or training; or
> (b) making a grant to enable him to meet expenses connected with his education or training.

Financial assistance may be in the form of a grant or a loan, but the young person does not have to first satisfy statutory welfare benefits criteria before becoming eligible for a Trust grant and cannot be required to make loan repayments while he or she is in receipt of income support or family credit. Under the 1995 Order, Schedule 2, paragraph 2, the Trusts have a duty to publish information about aftercare services.

CHAPTER SEVENTEEN

Children, Young Persons and Juvenile Justice

Introduction

In Northern Ireland, the division between the care and justice systems has been far from watertight. The history of the problematic relationship between the two,[1] associated with the use made of their permeable boundaries,[2] coupled with the fact that this situation will not end with the implementation of the 1995 Order[3] provides the justification for including a criminal law chapter in a civil law book.

The gap between the two is set to widen following the introduction of the Children (NI) Order 1995 which makes a clear and firm distinction between care and criminal proceedings. Those for whom state intervention is indicated for care reasons will now be the subject of proceedings governed by the 1995 Order. All other children and young persons, the perpetrators rather than the victims of criminal offences, will be the subject of proceedings governed by other legislation. This gap and the firming up of the justice response to offending juveniles will eventually be consolidated by the Criminal Justice (NI) Order 1996.

The juvenile population in Northern Ireland, in decline for the past decade or so, has been increasing since 1993. The number of juvenile offenders, however, has steadily decreased: in 1980 some 2,225 juveniles were prosecuted compared with 1,373 in 1990, 1,133 in 1993 and only 1,031 in 1994.[4] There were 879 disposals by the juvenile courts in 1994 of which 219 were custodial, 304 were supervision in the community and 241 were conditional discharges.

This decrease in prosecutions is partially a measure of the success of what is termed the 'diversion policy' which has its origins in a recommendation made in the *Black*

---

1 See, for example, Ministry of Home Affairs (NI), *Juvenile Offenders and Those in Need of Care and Protection*, Belfast: the Ministry, 1963; B Caul and S Herron, *A Service for People*, Belfast: The Universities Press, 1992.
2 The trend whereby young persons who are committed by the courts because of their needs to the care disposal of an FPO but nevertheless end up in the control setting of a training school has hardened. On 2 December 1993, the training school population consisted of 267 committals and 143 young people on remand. The basis for committal were: care orders, 56 per cent; offenders, 29 per cent; and education, 15 per cent.
3 Until legislation is introduced to establish youth courts, repeal the residual provisions of the Children and Young Persons Act (NI) 1968 and re-designate training schools exclusively for offenders, there will continue to be areas of overlap.
4 See *Annual Reports of the Chief Constable of the RUC*, HMSO.

Report[5] that there should be an increase in the use of police cautioning and in non-custodial sentences so as to divert offending juveniles away from possible prosecution. In short, the main trends show a decreasing proportion of juvenile offenders being taken to court of whom far fewer now receive a custodial sentence than occurred ten years ago.

The juvenile justice system in Northern Ireland, as governed primarily by the 1968 Act, is the subject of this chapter. It considers the implications arising from certain provisions of the 1995 Order and those which may be predicted to arise as a consequence of anticipated changes to existing criminal justice legislation.

The Jurisdiction, Parties and Bodies of the Juvenile Justice System

Jurisdiction

In Northern Ireland the jurisdiction of the juvenile justice system relates to those children and young persons who are aged between ten and sixteen, resident within (or alleged to have committed an offence within) the province, against whom the DPP or the RUC have brought charges of involvement in summary or indictable offences or in respect of whom a Health and Social Services Board ('Trust') or other authorised person has commenced proceedings alleging lack of parental control.

1. The Legislation

In Northern Ireland the law relating to the criminal activities of children and young persons is currently governed primarily by the Children and Young Persons Act (NI) 1968[6] and the Probation Act (NI) 1950.[7] Other legislation such as the Emergency Provisions Act (1973 (as renewed), the Criminal Justice (NI) Order 1980 and the Treatment of Offenders (NI) Order 1989 also exercises a considerable influence.

2. The Court

Under the Children Act 1908, section III:

> A court of summary jurisdiction when hearing charges against children or young persons, or when hearing applications for orders or licences relating to a child or young person at which the attendance of a child or young person is required, shall, unless the child or young person is charged jointly with any other person not being a child or young person, sit either in a different building or room from that in which the ordinary sittings of the court are held, or on different days or at different times from those at which the ordinary sittings are held, and a court of summary jurisdiction so sitting is in this Act referred to as a Juvenile Court.

---

5 The Black Committee, *Report of the Children and Young Persons Review Group*, Belfast: HMSO, 1979, para 6.2.
6 The juvenile justice provisions of the 1968 Act basically re-enact those of the 1950 Act with amendments and with the incorporation of some of the major provisions of the 1963 Act.
7 Replacing the 1907 Act.

This section was subsequently amended[8] to allow two persons to sit with the resident magistrate in each petty sessions district. Currently, the Children and Young Persons Act (NI) 1968 provides the governing statutory authority for juvenile courts in this jurisdiction. A juvenile court generally sits in the same building as the adult court but at different times so as to minimise opportunities for contact between adult and juvenile offenders.

The juvenile court is presided over by a resident magistrate who has at least six years' experience as a qualified solicitor or barrister and two members of a lay panel, one of whom must be a woman. The lay members usually have no legal qualifications but some training and are selected by the clerk of petty sessions from panels appointed by the Lord Chancellor for each county court division. The magistrate who is the chairman of the court may sit alone and has a casting vote if one member is absent. When fully constituted, the court reaches a decision on the basis of the unanimous or majority opinion of its members. In doing so it is required, by section 48 of the 1968 Act, to 'have regard to the welfare of the child' and to ensure that proper provision is made for his or her education and training.

The juvenile court has jurisdiction to hear and determine summary offences, and under section 79 of the 1968 Act, it also has authority to deal summarily with indictable offences (except murder) if it is considered expedient to do so by the court and with the agreement of parents and subject. The court may then make such order as would have been available to it if the case had been tried on indictment. However, the vast bulk of juvenile offences concern burglary and theft, including car theft.[9]

The 1968 Act, unlike the equivalent legislation in England and Wales (the 'welfare'-oriented 1969 Act), retained important decision-making powers under the control of the court. Thus a training school order made by a court did not allow for social work discretion to send a child 'home on trial'. Nor were there any provisions which explicitly addressed the responsibility to assist juveniles not to engage in criminal activities. This legislative omission has to some extent been remedied in the 1995 Order.

Parties

The following are the essential participants in any criminal proceedings brought in the juvenile court: the DPP (or in some less serious cases, the RUC), the juvenile who has been charged and the parents (unless excused by the court).

1. The Director of Public Prosecutions (DPP)

The office of the DPP was established by the Prosecution of Offences (NI) Order 1972, as amended. This official is appointed by the Attorney-General and may also be removed by him or her on the grounds of incompetence or misconduct. The Director is assisted by staff based in the main office at the Royal Courts of Justice and in each of the seven county court divisions.

---

8 By the Children (Juvenile Courts) Act (NI) 1942 in response to the recommendations of the Lynn committee.
9 See NIO Statistics Office, 1992.

The responsibility of the DPP is to bring prosecutions in respect of all major criminal offences and certain minor ones. He or she determines whether to bring a prosecution on the basis of evidence gathered by the RUC in the course of conducting their investigations and then passed in a file to the DPP.

The role of the DPP in relation to juvenile offenders is to bring prosecutions in respect of any indictable offences and such less serious criminal offences as considered necessary.

2. The Juvenile

Any child or young person between the ages of ten and sixteen (inclusive) suspected to be in need of care, protection and control or suspected of being an offender may be brought before the juvenile court. The age of criminal responsibility is fixed, by section 69 of the 1968 Act, at ten years. It is the child, rather than his or her parents, who is regarded in law as a party to proceedings in the juvenile court. These proceedings are a legacy from an era dominated by the criminal law when a child was required to appear as a party so that he or she could be named as a defendant in a prosecution which alleged the criminality or delinquency of that child.

In Northern Ireland as in England and Wales the definition of juvenile, for the purposes of criminal proceedings, continues to be determined in accordance with traditional common-law rules; the commission of a crime requires that the *actus reus* be accompanied by the appropriate *mens rea*. The *doli incapax* presumption sets the age of criminal responsibility at ten years, below which a child cannot be held to have the requisite *mens rea* to commit an offence and must be dealt with under the care rather than the criminal jurisdiction of the juvenile court. A child between the ages of ten and fourteen is presumed to be incapable of committing a crime but this presumption may be rebutted by evidence[10] which demonstrates that he or she knew the activity was wrong. The younger the child the stronger the presumption.[11] In respect of a young person aged between fourteen and sixteen, a reverse presumption applies, i.e. from the age of fourteen a person is presumed to have intended the consequences of his or her actions. Thereafter, young persons are held to have full capacity and are as criminally liable for their actions as any adult.

The law on this matter was recently well scrutinised by the courts in *C v DPP*[12] which concerned a twelve-year-old boy charged with the offence of tampering with a motor vehicle. In the magistrates' court he was convicted, it being held that on the evidence the presumption of *doli incapax* was rebutted. He appealed to the divisional court by way of case stated on the issue of whether there was any or sufficient evidence that at the time he knew his act to be seriously wrong. The appeal was denied, it being held that the *doli incapax* presumption was out-dated and could no longer be regarded as a part of the law of England. However, on appeal to the House of Lords, the *doli incapax* presumption[13] was re-affirmed: it may only be rebutted by showing clear,

---

10   As in *JM (A Minor) v Runeckles* (1984) 79 Cr App Rep 255.
11   See *X v X* [1958] Crim LR 805.
12   [1994] QBD 3 All GR 191.
13   See *C v Director of Public Prosecutions* [1995] 1 FLR 933 HL.

positive evidence — not consisting merely in the evidence of the acts amounting to the offence itself — that the child knew the act was seriously wrong.

3. The Parents

The law relating to juvenile offenders gives some recognition to both the rights and duties of parents. In the first instance, where juveniles are arrested or detained for questioning, then their parents must be notified as soon as is reasonably practicable and should be present when their children are being interviewed. In the event of charges being laid and the juveniles being brought before the court, parents may be required to attend throughout the hearing and must attend in the case of a child under sixteen. Should the court reach a finding of guilt and decide to impose a fine, then in acknowledgement of parental responsibility to exercise proper supervision and control, it will require payment to be made by the parent rather than the juvenile, unless the court is satisfied that there is a good reason for not penalising the parent.

The Bodies

The following are the bodies most prominently concerned with the implementation of the juvenile justice system in Northern Ireland: the NIO; the Probation Board; the Trusts; and the RUC.

1. The Northern Ireland Office (NIO)

The NIO was established by the Northern Ireland Constitution Act 1973 and is the arm of government with responsibility for overseeing the functions of the juvenile justice system in Northern Ireland. This Office is led by the Secretary of State with assistance from his four ministers. All aspects of policy, reform and administration of the juvenile justice system come within the remit of the NIO.

2. The Probation Board

The probation service in Northern Ireland is administered by the Probation Board which was established by the Probation Board (NI) Order 1982. The service then ceased to be an integral part of the NIO, though remaining funded by it, and became a relatively independent public body. It is managed by a Board whose members hold office for three-year terms (maximum of two terms) on appointment by the Secretary of State.

The remit of the Probation Board in relation to juvenile offenders includes responsibility for supervising those who have been made the subject of probation orders, developing intermediate treatment schemes to assist in the prevention of offences, the rehabilitation of offenders and the reduction of recidivism. The Board works closely with such voluntary bodies as Extern and the Northern Ireland Association for the Care and Resettlement of Offenders (NIACRO) and contributes to the funding of their activities.

3. The Health and Social Services Boards ('Trusts')

The integrated health and social services administrative bodies were established by the Health and Personal Social Services (NI) Order 1972 and subsequently re-organised by the Health and Social Services (NI) Order 1991 together with the Health and Personal Social Services (NI) Order 1994.[14] The brief of the Trusts in relation to juvenile offenders includes ensuring the provision of services which contribute to the prevention of offences, securing the welfare interests of offenders and, where appropriate, providing secure accommodation.

4. The RUC

Established, or re-constituted, in 1922 the RUC is now organised on the basis of three regions, sub-divided into a total of twelve divisions. Its primary responsibilities are the protection of the community, prevention of crime and the detection and prosecution of offenders. In common with other UK police forces, the RUC retains some discretion in relation to the prosecution of less serious offences.

In relation to juvenile offenders, the role of the RUC includes bringing prosecutions for most minor criminal offences. Among the strategies it has developed to give effect to its discretionary power in respect of minor offences is the Juvenile Liaison Scheme. This was initiated in 1975, as an extension of the practice of cautioning, to allow for the on-going police supervision of juvenile offenders.

Juveniles, Offences and Social Policy

The Background to the Present Juvenile Justice System in Northern Ireland

The approach to juvenile offenders has differed in Northern Ireland from that developed elsewhere in the United Kingdom. This may be seen in the trends relating to the output of the juvenile justice system, judicial interpretation of disposal provisions under the 1968 Act and in the proposals put forward in recent discussion papers.

Juveniles and Offences — The Broad Statistical Trends

The rate of juveniles offending is recorded as being consistently lower in this jurisdiction than in England and Wales. However, this may be partially attributable to the impact of civil disturbance on this jurisdiction.[15] It is probably fair to say that decreased detection by the RUC has been associated with an under-reporting of juvenile offences in certain communities. A comparison between the jurisdictions of England and Wales and Northern Ireland, as regards the number of juvenile offenders found guilty of indictable offences per thousand of the population, for the period 1964–1980 reveals:

(i) a fairly constant level of recorded indictable offences in Northern Ireland, though evidence of some increase between 1979 and 1980;

---

14 The four HSSBs (Eastern, Western, Northern and Southern) which had been established to develop, provide and deliver services to vulnerable social groups have now become the purchasers of services provided to such groups by independent Community Trusts (prior to the 1994 Order, the latter were the constituent units of management of each Board).

15 For example, the overall detection rate for offences known to the RUC fell from an estimated 58.3 per cent in 1968 to 21.9 per cent in 1977.

(ii) a substantially lower rate of juvenile offending in Northern Ireland than in England and Wales.[16]

A recent report[17] shows that '. . . the number of juveniles convicted by the courts has fallen markedly over the past ten years, from 1,717 in 1982 to 804 in 1991'. However it must be remembered that, though the rate of offending is lower in this than in the neighbouring jurisdiction, the incorporation of scheduled offences within the total of juvenile crimes in Northern Ireland means that here a greater proportion of the population of offending juveniles has committed serious offences than elsewhere in the United Kingdom.

Justice and Care

The Children and Young Persons Act (NI) 1968 gave an equivocal response to the debate as to whether juvenile offences are most appropriately dealt with under child care or justice legislation. In England and Wales this was resolved in legislation favouring a 'care' approach to juvenile offenders. In Northern Ireland, however, the 1968 Act permitted a 'twin-track' approach whereby the juvenile court processed those children in need of care, protection and control differently from those who had committed offences. This clear distinction between the court's 'care' and 'offence' procedures was compromised by the potential exercise of judicial discretion at the point of case disposal. Under section 95 of the 1968 Act, the court could make the custodial option of a training school order available in respect of a juvenile found to be in need of care, protection and control. Conversely, the same provision gave it the power to make the 'care' option of a fit-person order available in respect of a juvenile found to have committed an offence. In recent years, judicial use of this cross-over provision has been characterised by the decreased issue of FPOs in favour of offenders and a very considerable increase in the proportion of the training school population who had appeared before the court on care rather than offence grounds (see Appendices). To some degree this has been attributable to a Trust (or Board) practice of seeking to retain 'difficult' children in the care system (albeit it in the care regime of a training school) rather than have them criminalised by pressing formal charges for criminal damage, assault or other misconduct occurring while they were the subject of care orders.

The Jurisdiction of the Courts

Some of the uncertainties inherent in this twin-track approach were evident in the case of *McGrillen v Cullen*.[18] This case concerned a claim for damages brought by a plaintiff who had earlier appeared before a magistrates' court on a charge of poor school attendance under Schedule 9, paragraph 5 of the Education and Library (NI) Order

---

16 See B Caul, J Pinkerton and F Powell *The Juvenile Justice System in NI*, Polytechnic Series, Jordanstown (1983).
17 See NIO, *Crime in the Community*, HMSO (1993) a discussion paper on criminal justice in Northern Ireland.
18 [1991] NILR 53.

1972. On the charge being upheld, she was made the subject of a TSO under section 95 of the Children and Young Persons Act 1968 and then sent to a training school where she remained for five days. At that time the plaintiff had not been represented and when an application for bail was lodged on her behalf it was refused by the magistrate on the ground that as it was a civil matter bail was not appropriate. On application being made to the county court, however, bail was granted and the TSO was reversed. The plaintiff subsequently brought proceedings against the magistrate.

The plaintiff's case rested on the assertion that she should not have been sent to the training school without first being offered legal assistance under Article 15 of the Treatment of Offenders (NI) Order 1976 and bail. The plaintiff claimed damages on the grounds that in so deciding the magistrate had been acting outside his jurisdiction or in excess of his jurisdiction.

The court relied on the ruling in *Re McC v Mullan*[19] where the House of Lords established that if a magistrates' court fails to comply with Article 15(1) of the Treatment of Offenders (NI) Order 1976 before passing sentence, it is acting without jurisdiction or in excess of jurisdiction and its members are liable in a civil action for damages. Such a magistrates' court is acting without jurisdiction if the condition precedent to its passing sentence, the offer of legal aid, has not been fulfilled.

The court found that the jurisdiction to make a TSO stems from Schedule 9 of the 1972 Order. Under paragraph 4 the parent may be found guilty of an offence and is liable on 'summary conviction' to specified penalties if the child fails to attend school regularly. Under paragraph 7 the court may make any order under section 95 of the 1968 Act. It was found that while the mother had been prosecuted and convicted the plaintiff had been dealt with under the civil law.

It was held that as the action in respect of the plaintiff had not led to a conviction, then Article 15 of the 1976 Order did not apply. Thus in failing to offer legal aid the defendant had not been acting without jurisdiction or in excess of jurisdiction. It was also held, however, that he had been wrong to consider that he did not have jurisdiction to grant bail.

Discussion Papers

The consultation paper, *Proposed Changes to Some Aspects of the Law Relating to Children in Northern Ireland,*[20] anticipated that a separate order dealing with juvenile justice matters would

> ... consolidate and amend the provisions of the Children and Young Persons Act (NI) 1968 which relate to offences against children and young persons and those which relate to juvenile offenders. The consolidation would incorporate the amendments made by the Treatment of Offenders (NI) Order 1989 while amendments would be required to reflect the revised role of training schools following the separation of care and criminal cases.

---

19 [1984] 3 All ER 908.
20 Compiled by the Office of Law Reform and the DHSS, HMSO, para 1.9. 1989.

This proposal, which endorsed a similar recommendation made in the *Black Report*,[21] received support from SACHR:[22]

> The Commission believes it to be important that child care cases should, as is mooted in the Consultation Paper, be separated from juvenile offenders cases.

Following its review of criminal justice policy conducted during 1991 and 1992, the NIO issued the *Criminal Justice Policy Proposals* (1994) paper. This contained a number of proposals relating to the options available to the juvenile court as well as to the remit of the court itself. Among these were that the court should determine the length of a training school order from a range of fixed period options on a continuum from one week to two years. It also suggested the abolition of a committal to a remand home and the introduction of new arrangements for post discharge supervision by training school staff (viz. fixed period supervision for periods of three to six months). In addition it proposed that seventeen-year-olds should be amenable to the jurisdiction of the juvenile court, which could make training school orders and assessment orders in respect of them. Parents and guardians of convicted juvenile offenders would be made liable for any fines imposed.

Subsequently, the Criminal Justice Directorate of the NIO issued its paper *Juvenile Justice: The Way Forward* (1996). Among the recommendations it makes, in respect of offenders, are the abolition of fit-person orders and supervision orders; the retention of conditional discharges, fines, compensation orders, probation orders, community service orders (for sixteen- and seventeen-year-olds) and attendance centre orders; the provision of sufficient non-custodial/diversionary facilities across Northern Ireland; the re-naming of the juvenile court as 'the youth court'; and the extension of its jurisdiction to include those aged seventeen; a restricted use of custodial sentences in relation to those aged seventeen or younger; and the re-naming of training schools as 'juvenile offenders centres'.

Juvenile Offences

I. Prevention

The statutory onus placed on bodies such as the Trusts and the Probation Board to provide services which would assist the prevention of juvenile crime has not been onerous. Much preventative work has been undertaken by voluntary bodies. However, there is every indication that future legislation will give effect to the proposals in the *Black Report*[23] that the statutory authorities should be required to invest more in preventative and diversionary service provision.

1. By Statutory Bodies under the Children and Young Persons Act (NI) 1968

Under the 1968 Act, section 163:

---

21 See f/n 5, para 4.5.
22 See introduction to: Submission by SACHR.
23 See f/n 5, para 3.31.

> ... where, in consequence of any investigation arising out of the alleged commission of an offence, a member of the RUC is of the opinion that a child or young person may be in need of advice, guidance or assistance for any reason and is not to be brought before a court, it shall be his duty to notify the welfare authority.

This is a discretionary power, resting as it does on an opinion. It enables a police constable to interpret a juvenile's behaviour as indicating a need for assistance and allowing the juvenile to be diverted from the justice to the care system. The duty of the Trust receiving a referral under section 163, or in any other way, is as stated in section 164:

> ... the welfare authority shall make available such advice, guidance and assistance as may promote the welfare of children by diminishing the need to receive them into or keep them in care under this Act or to bring children before a court.

2. By Statutory Bodies under the Children (NI) Order 1995

Under Schedule 2(8) of the Children (NI) Order 1995:

> Every Board shall take reasonable steps designed —
>   (a) to reduce the need to bring —
>   (ii) criminal proceedings against such children
>   (b) to encourage children within the Board's area not to commit criminal offences; and
>   (c) to avoid the need for children within the Board's area to be placed in secure accommodation.

This specific statement requires the Trust to be proactive in its duty to prevent children and young persons from entering the justice system. As such it complements and gives focus to the general duty placed on the Trusts by Article 18 to provide personal social services to children 'in need'. However, there is no indication of any overall strategy nor of precisely what services they might deploy in giving effect to these duties.

Article 21 does link a preventative duty to specific objectives and services:

> (3) Every authority shall provide accommodation for any child in need within the authority's area who has reached the age of sixteen and whose welfare the authority considers is likely to be seriously prejudiced if the authority does not provide him with accommodation.

By requiring the Trusts to provide accommodation for such young persons 'in need', this provision should assist those at risk of being drawn into the juvenile justice system.

3. By Voluntary Bodies

In Northern Ireland the voluntary agencies have played a significant role in the prevention of juvenile offending. Agencies such as Save the Children Fund, Extern and NIACRO have done much to supplement preventative statutory provision.[24]

---

24 See, for example, the *Turas* project, which is a scheme established in 1991 and run jointly by the Probation Board and the West Belfast Parent/Youth Support Group. It aims to provide

II. Committal Proceedings

The committal process whereby a juvenile is brought before the juvenile court to answer charges of an alleged offence is governed by the Children and Young Persons Act (NI) 1968 and the Magistrates' Court (Children and Young Persons) Rules (NI) 1969. There are several different stages in the process from the time charges are made to the actual court appearance.

1. Charges Are Brought

Care proceedings are initiated under section 94 of the 1968 Act by a constable or authorised person who, after consultation with the appropriate Trust, may bring before the juvenile court any child or young person who is thought to be out of parental control. The Trust, under the same provision, must do so unless it thinks it undesirable with regard to the child's interests or that proceedings are about to be brought by someone else. Justice proceedings may be initiated by a constable preferring charges against any juvenile suspected of committing or of being involved in the committing of a summary or indictable offence. In justice proceedings it is not necessary for the constable to consult the appropriate Trust before charges are laid; section 53(2) of the 1968 Act does require notification to certain parties after charges are laid.

(a) Arrest

Where a juvenile who is arrested without a warrant is not released within twenty-four hours, he or she must be brought before a magistrates' court within forty-eight hours of arrest (juveniles held under the emergency legislation may be held for up to seventy-two hours; section 14 of the Prevention of Terrorism (Temporary Provisions) Act 1984 allows for seven days' detention). While being detained section 45 of the Northern Ireland (Emergency Provisions) Act 1973 allows for the deferral of access to a solicitor in certain circumstances.

The position of the arrested juvenile is governed by Part IV (arrest) and Part V (detention) of the Police and Criminal Evidence (NI) Order 1989. Under Article 38(9) a duty is placed on the custody officer to keep a custody record, detain in police custody a person not in a fit state to be otherwise dealt with, take steps to ascertain the identity of a person responsible for the welfare of an arrested juvenile and inform that person of the arrest, if practicable. Article 58 states that a person responsible for the welfare of a child must be informed of the arrest, the reason for it and the place of detention.

A juvenile may be brought to court by way of a summons or by police recognisances.

(i) By Summons

Where a juvenile is summoned to appear as a defendant to answer a criminal charge, the parent or parents will also be required to attend through inclusion on the same

---

alternatives for hard-core joyriders who live in high risk areas of West Belfast. Again, the *Time Out* project was established in 1993 and is run jointly by the WHSSB and Extern. It provides a voluntary time-out residential service for juveniles who are at risk of removal from home by the statutory authorities.

summons or by separate summons. The parent is a co-defendant with the juvenile in criminal cases.

(ii) By Police Recognisances

Where a juvenile is arrested with or without a warrant and cannot be brought forthwith before a magistrates' court, then the officer in charge of the police station may inquire into the case and release the juvenile to appear before the magistrates' court or a juvenile court.

(b) Separation from Adult Offenders

Where any juvenile is detained in a police station either after arrest, while being conveyed to or from any criminal court or while waiting before or after attendance at any criminal court, he or she should be kept apart from adult offenders. This does not apply in circumstances where the adult and juvenile are jointly charged in respect of the same offence or where the adult is a relative of the juvenile. In the case of a female juvenile, arrangements should be made, as soon as is practicable, for her to be placed under the care of an appropriate female adult, usually a woman police constable.

(c) Bail

Where a person under the age of seventeen is arrested for an offence and cannot be brought before a magistrates' court immediately, the officer in charge at the police station may release that person on bail unless: (1) he is charged with murder or other grave offence; (2) he ought in his own interest to be removed from association with a criminal or prostitute; or (3) his release would defeat the interests of justice.

(d) Remand

If, instead of bail, he is remanded in custody, then he must be detained in a remand home unless it is impracticable to do so, he is so unruly that he cannot be safely detained there or his state of health makes it inadvisable. In such circumstances he or she may then be remanded in a hospital (with the consent of the court or of a Justice of the Peace) or in prison. The option of bail or remand may also occur during the course of proceedings under the court's general power of adjournment.

2. Commencement of Proceedings

There are certain basic requirements for commencing proceedings against a juvenile.

(a) Notice Is Served

Where a juvenile is to be brought before the court on a charge of having committed an offence or of being out of parental control, then the complainant, or other person responsible for bringing the juvenile to court, must serve notice (as soon as is practicable) of their intention to do so on the local probation officer and the local Trust. The notice should include details regarding the court at which the hearing is to be held and the date, time and nature of the charges or grounds on which the proceedings are based.

(b) Social Enquiry Report

Following receipt of this notification the Trust is required to make investigations and submit to the court a Social Enquiry Report which addresses such matters as home circumstances, school record, physical and mental health, character and the availability and suitability of such disposal options as training school. A Social Enquiry Report from a Trust will not be necessary where the offence is of a trivial nature or where a probation officer has agreed to provide it.

3. Court Attendance

Children or young persons charged with offences are usually required to attend their local juvenile court. However, in some circumstances their attendance is required in a magistrates' court, other than a juvenile court. Once before the court, their right to silence is governed by the Criminal Evidence (NI) Order 1988. Article 3 permits the court or jury to draw inferences from the exercise of this right. Article 4 emphasises the obligation of an accused person (i.e. over fourteen years of age) to give evidence and explains that a refusal to do so will serve to corroborate other evidence against that person. Where the police believe that a substance, mark or article provides evidence against the accused, then Article 5 requires them to state this belief and to request an explanation.

(a) Juvenile Court

The juvenile court hearing is held *in camera*. The court must explain the substance of the charges or application in simple language appropriate to the juvenile's age and understanding. Where a juvenile appears before the court, a parent or guardian should also be in attendance; while social workers or training school staff may be asked to attend, they cannot be required to do so. Any newspaper or broadcast reports in respect of proceedings in a juvenile court must not disclose the name, address or school of the juvenile nor include any particulars likely to lead to the identification of that person or of any other juvenile involved in the proceedings.

The social enquiry report must be considered by the court before a decision is reached. If one has not been submitted, then the court will be adjourned pending its availability. Alternatively, if it has been submitted and the juvenile or parent/guardian wishes to produce evidence relating to its contents, then again the court should adjourn for this purpose and if necessary require the attendance of the person who compiled the report at the next hearing. The juvenile may be remanded in custody or on bail depending on the circumstances.

If the court needs more time before making a decision, then it may make an interim order committing the juvenile to a place of safety for five weeks. It may direct that a juvenile attend for a comprehensive assessment at a Day Assessment Centre to provide information to assist appropriate sentencing.

If a finding of guilt is made or if the juvenile is found to be in need of care, protection and control, the court must inform the parent or guardian of the manner in which it proposes to deal with the juvenile and must allow representations from such a person.

(b) Magistrates' Court

If jointly charged with an adult, a juvenile may be tried at a magistrates' court other than a juvenile court and, if convicted, will then be remitted to the juvenile court for a determination of the case. Only in the following circumstances may a charge against a juvenile be heard by a magistrates' court which is not a juvenile court:

(a) the juvenile is jointly charged with a person aged seventeen or over;
(b) the juvenile is charged with an offence arising out of circumstances which are the same or are connected with the offence with which an adult is charged;
(c) the juvenile is charged with an offence and an adult is also charged with aiding, abetting, causing, counselling, procuring, allowing or permitting that offence;
(d) an adult is charged with an offence and the juvenile is charged (at the same time) with aiding, abetting, causing, counselling, procuring, allowing or permitting that offence;
(e) it appears to an adult court, in the course of proceedings, that the accused is a juvenile and the court thinks fit to proceed with the hearing and determination.

Adult courts may or may not proceed with the hearing of charges against juveniles in the circumstances mentioned above. If, having chosen to proceed, the adult court makes a finding of guilt, it must then remit the juvenile to the appropriate juvenile court. A juvenile so remitted under section 64 A(2) has no right of appeal against the order of remission. This remission, after the finding of guilt, can be effected by means of an order for custody, bail (by recognisance) or by summons.

A Crown court may also, having found a juvenile guilty of an offence, remit the case to the juvenile court for determination. A certificate to this effect should be sent to the Clerk of Petty Sessions by the Chief Clerk. The same certification procedure should be followed where the juvenile is remitted from one magistrates' court to a juvenile court in another district.

Terrorist-Type Offences by Juveniles

Committal Proceedings

The twenty-five years of civil unrest in Northern Ireland have brought an added dimension to the definition of juvenile offences. A considerable number of children and young persons have been implicated in terrorist-type activities. Such offenders have been brought before the courts on proceedings initiated under either the 1968 Act or the Northern Ireland (Emergency Provisions) Act 1973 (as renewed).

1. Brought under the Children and Young Persons Act (NI) 1968

Under section 73 of the 1968 Act —

> (1) Sentence of death shall not be pronounced on or recorded against a person convicted of an offence if it appears to the court that at the time when the offence was committed he was under the age of eighteen, nor shall any such person be sentenced to imprisonment for life under Section 9(2) of the Criminal Justice Act

(NI) 1966, but in lieu thereof the court shall sentence him to be detained during the pleasure of the Governor (now Minister of State), and if so sentenced, he shall be liable to be detained in such a place and under such conditions as the minister may direct.

Between 1972 and 1975 the rate of convictions under this provision, expressed as a proportion of the total population, was approximately twenty-two times the rate of convictions confirmed under the equivalent legislation in England:[25]

> (2) Where a child or young person is convicted on indictment of any offence punishable in the case of an adult with imprisonment for fourteen years or more, not being an offence the sentence for which is fixed by law, and the court is of opinion that none of the other methods in which the case may be legally dealt with is suitable, the court may sentence the offender to be detained for such period as may be specified in the sentence; and where such a sentence has been passed, the child or young person shall, during that period, notwithstanding anything in the other provisions of this Act, be liable to be detained in such place and under such conditions as the Minister may direct.

During the same period, the rate of convictions under this provision for young persons under sixteen expressed as a proportion of the total population was approximately thirteen times that achieved under equivalent legislation in England.[26]

2. Brought under the Northern Ireland (Emergency Provisions) Act 1973

The Northern Ireland (Emergency Provisions) Act 1973, as periodically renewed, has enabled the DPP to designate certain offences, deemed to have terrorist connotations, as 'scheduled offences'. These offences are listed in Schedule 4 of the Act and are normally dealt with according to the special trial procedures in the 'Diplock courts' (non-jury). To date, offences which have been so designated are murder and attempted murder, malicious wounding, grievous bodily harm, possession of firearms and/or ammunition, causing an explosion or possessing explosives, membership of a proscribed organisation, armed robbery and hijack. The Probation Board has a practice of not preparing reports on a pre-trial basis for defendants charged with scheduled offences, unless the defendant is already subject to statutory supervision. The level of juvenile involvement in scheduled offences reached a peak in 1975 and 1976 but by 1979 had fallen to less than four per cent of all scheduled offences.[27]

Juvenile Offenders — The Disposal Options

Under the Children and Young Persons Act 1968 and the Probation Act (NI) 1950, a wide range of disposal options is available in respect of juvenile offenders; most of these are community orders, very few are custodial. The following is a statement of the law relating to these disposal options.

---

25 See Northern Ireland Court Service: Statistics and Research Branch, Annual Statistical Reports and annual *Commentary on Northern Ireland Crime Statistics.*
26 Ibid.
27 Ibid.

I. Non-Judicial Disposal Option

The *Black Report* recommended that juveniles should be diverted from prosecution by the increased use of police cautioning and the use of other community-based options. This diversion policy still rests largely on the non-judicial disposal option of a juvenile caution, administered by a juvenile liaison officer under the JLO scheme, as instituted by the RUC in 1975. In the overall context of rolling back the powers of state intervention in family life, a philosophy which prevailed in the 1980s, this scheme may be seen as representing in the criminal law relating to children, a role equivalent to that played by the 'no-order' presumption in the civil law.

1. Juvenile Caution

Under section 53 of the 1968 Act the RUC is required to serve notice on the local Trust of any intention to formally caution a juvenile who has admitted an offence. The administering of a caution is performed with parental consent as an alternative to prosecution. In *R v Chief Constable of Kent and Another ex parte L*[28] the Divisional Court ruled that a decision by the Crown Prosecution Service to prosecute a juvenile, against the advice of the JLO who considered a caution to be sufficient, was within the powers of the CPS. A juvenile caution leaves the recipient with a criminal record.

More juveniles are dealt with by way of police caution than by prosecution; though the overall trend is now decreasing.[29] According to the *Chief Constable's Report*, only 8.6 per cent of those cautioned are subsequently referred for other offences.[30] The *Criminal Justice Policy Proposals*[31] promote the use of cautioning, especially the use of juvenile liaison panels, and also suggest that proposals be developed for the caution to be accompanied by a requirement to undertake, in appropriate cases, treatment or other restorative measures.

2. Other Diversion Options

In Northern Ireland there has never been a clear strategy on how best to implement a diversion policy. There are many diverse projects, mostly centred on Belfast, which have been established with the objective of keeping juveniles out of the justice system. They operate at different levels or tiers, offer flexible individual programmes, rapid response and simple referral procedures. Many, such as *Turas*, are projects run jointly by statutory and voluntary agencies.

---

28 [1991] Crim LKR 841.
29 According to the Juvenile Liaison Scheme (NI) reports, official cautions rose from forty-eight per cent of total prosecutions in 1982 to seventy-four per cent of the total in 1992. In 1991, 2,233 juveniles were cautioned (which represented sixty-eight per cent of the total of juveniles cautioned or found guilty of offences in that year) compared with 2,042 in 1993 and 1,831 in 1994. Indeed the numbers of prosecuted juveniles fell by more than fifty per cent between 1984 and 1993 due mainly to the use of cautioning. This is the most commonly used and, arguably, the most successful of the diversion policy options.
30 See f/n 4, (1993), p. 64.
31 31 January 1994.

II. Judicial Disposal Options

1. Non-Treatment Orders

There is a tariff of disposal options from which the court may draw following a successful prosecution. At this stage, or at any other point in the proceedings, the court must avoid terms appropriate to adults, such as 'conviction' and 'sentence'. If found guilty, then after four years that finding shall — with certain exceptions — be deemed not to have been made and no criminal record will exist. The court is not empowered to impose a period of imprisonment on a 'child', however a young person (aged between fourteen and seventeen inclusive) may be imprisoned for an offence or in default of payment of a fine, costs, damages or compensation if the court certifies that the subject is both so unruly and/or so depraved a character that no other method of dealing with him or her is appropriate. Neither may it impose a sentence of death or of life imprisonment under section 9(2) of the Criminal Justice Act (NI) 1966 on any person who at the time of the offence was under the age of eighteen; instead, the court may sentence him or her to be detained at the pleasure of the Secretary of State.

The forthcoming legislation will change the name of the juvenile court to the 'youth court'. It will also bring seventeen-year-olds — who presently inhabit a kind of limbo between juvenile and adult status — within its ambit and within the discretionary power of the court to order parents or guardians to attend court and pay financial penalties.

(a) Discharge

The court may decide that the offence was sufficiently trivial and the offender suitably apologetic to permit it to discharge the offender either absolutely or on condition that he or she commit no further offences for a specified period not exceeding three years. In 1993, thirty-five per cent of all juveniles sentenced in Northern Ireland received a conditional or absolute discharge.

(b) Bind Over and Deferred Sentence

A person involved or suspected of being involved in an affray or incident of public disorder may be dealt with by a magistrate exercising the traditional common-law power to 'bind over' under a direction not to disturb the peace for a specified period. This may be coupled with a decision to defer any sentencing until the end of that period when the person's behaviour will then determine disposal. This option requires the subject's consent.

(c) Fines and Compensation

From a sliding scale of financial penalties the court may impose a fine suited to the gravity of the offence and to the means of an offender. The fines are set by section 72 of the 1968 Act, as amended by the Criminal Penalties (Increase) Order (NI) 1984, at a maximum of £100 in respect of a child and at £400 for a young person. A fine may be levied against the juvenile's parents or guardian or, if he or she is the subject of a care order, against the Trust. Alternatively, where the young person is employed, the fine is for a considerable amount and there are doubts as to the subject's willingness to co-operate, the court may make an 'attachment of earnings' order. This directs that a certain amount be deducted at source from the young person's earnings. Instead of or in addition to a fine, the court may order that the victim be paid compensation for any loss or personal injury suffered as a consequence of the offender's criminal conduct. The maximum amount which an offender may be ordered to pay in compensation is set at £400. Again, this may be levied against the juvenile or the parents. In certain types of offences (e.g. involving drugs), the court has also the power to order the seizure and sale of property associated with the crime to ensure that an offender does not accrue any long-term benefit.

The forthcoming legislation will require the court to take due account of the means of parents or guardians in assessing the level of any fine ordered to be paid by them.

(d) Parental Recognisances

The court may decide that the preferable way of dealing with a young person's problematic behaviour is to require the subject and his or her parents to form a more mutually constructive and co-operative relationship. This is achieved by an order discharging the child into parental care, with parental consent, on the understanding that if the child re-offends, then the parent will forfeit a specified sum of money to the court. By holding the parents responsible for the subject's actions for a specified period of up to three years, the court seeks to, literally, bring home to the child the consequences of his or her actions.

2. Community Orders

In certain circumstances the court may make a community order instead of a custodial order. The different types of community orders are community service, supervision, fit-person, probation and attendance centre orders. Before the court makes such an order it must be satisfied that three requirements can be met. Firstly, the gravity of the offence must have been such that the court would be justified in making a custodial order. Secondly, the particular order must be suited to the offender. Finally, the restrictions which the community order would impose on the liberty of the offender must be commensurate with the seriousness of the offence. In 1993, twenty-five per cent of all juveniles sentenced in Northern Ireland received a community sentence.[32]

(a) Community Service Order

The requirements of a community service order are governed by Article 8 of the Treatment of Offenders (NI) Order 1976 as amended by the Criminal Justice (NI) Order 1980 and then by the Treatment of Offenders (NI) Order 1989. This order can only be made with the consent of the offender. The period specified in the order must be at least forty but not more than one hundred and twenty hours and should be completed within twelve months. The juvenile must be at least sixteen years of age and the offence one which would, in the case of an adult, be punishable by imprisonment but is not fixed by law. Any breach of the order's requirements may result in court proceedings and the imposition of a fine not exceeding £400 or the order may

---

32 See f/n 25.

be revoked and the subject sentenced afresh for the original offence. The subject has a right to apply to have the order revoked and the right to appeal against the conviction.

(b) Supervision Order

Under section 95 of the Children and Young Persons Act (NI) 1968 the court has the power to direct that an offender, aged between ten and seventeen (inclusive), be placed under the supervision of a Trust social worker or a probation officer for a fixed period of not longer than three years. The younger the child the stronger the presumption that the supervisor should be a Trust social worker rather than a probation officer.

Both supervisor and subject can apply for a supervision order to be varied or discharged. In the event of an order made under section 95 (as opposed to one under section 74) being breached, the supervisor may bring fresh court proceedings to seek a fit-person order.

(c) Fit Person Order

Section 74 of the 1968 Act gives the court authority to make an FPO in respect of a juvenile offender. The child or young person must be more than ten years of age and less than eighteen. It can only be imposed if the offence is one which would attract a term of imprisonment in the case of an adult, the child is in need of care or control which he or she would otherwise be unlikely to receive and a serious curtailment of the child's liberty is called for.

(d) Probation Order

The law governing the requirements of a probation order is as stated in the Probation Act (NI) 1950. This details the grounds for and the duration of a probation order and the various powers of the court in relation to breaches of that order. It also provides for a mental health treatment condition to be attached to an order.

Any person, from the age of ten (unlike England and Wales where the equivalent age is sixteen), found guilty of an offence (except an offence carrying a mandatory life sentence and most driving offences) can be placed on probation. This order directs that an offender be placed, with his or her consent (or, if less than fourteen years of age, with the consent of a parent or guardian), under the supervision of a probation officer for a fixed period of not less than six months and not more than three years. The Treatment of Offenders (NI) Order 1989 added the 'fourth condition' to probation orders, i.e. the subject could be required either to attend a day centre or participate in a specified programme of activities up to a maximum of sixty days.

The court must be satisfied that the issuance of a probation order offers a reasonable prospect of effecting the successful rehabilitation of the offender.

(e) Attendance Centre Orders

The attendance centre order requires a juvenile to attend a designated venue at a time and day fixed by the court or determined by the Probation Board. At present there are two such centres, one in Belfast and another in Lisburn. It is intended, when resources permit, to provide additional attendance centre facilities, particularly in those parts of the province where their absence now makes it difficult for the courts to impose a non-custodial sentence.

3. Custodial Orders

These orders all require the subject to be detained in a residential facility. In 1993, only 19 per cent of all juveniles sentenced in Northern Ireland received a custodial sentence.[33]

(a) Training School Order

Under section 95, section 108(a) or section 143(6)(b) of the 1968 Act, a juvenile court can make a training school order on care grounds. Such an order is more usually made in respect of a juvenile found to be, in the terms of section 95(1)(b), 'beyond the control of his parent or guardian'. This will be the case even if the standard of control offered by the parent is inadequate. In this jurisdiction, for example, the case of *Irwin v Brown and Others*[34] concerned a youth brought before the juvenile court under paragraph 5(2) to Schedule 8 of the 1968 Act. It was then held that the court may make any order under section 95 of that Act which would be available to it if the matter had come before it under section 94. A TSO was made.

Proceedings in such cases may be instigated by a Trust, the RUC, an ELB or an interested person, following the serving of notice on the local Trust under section 53.

Under Article 27 of the 1995 Order the Trusts may place a child in any care setting; this will permit a continuation of the present practice whereby the recalcitrant subjects of a care order may be placed in the care section of a training school, the latter now being designated as children's homes. Under Schedule 8 paragraph 30(3) of the 1995 Order, after implementation, any person the subject of a TSO and so placed in the care sector is deemed to have become instead the subject of a care order, remaining in the training school and, under Article 45, being reviewed as if the 'child is looked after by a Trust'.

The order is a semi-determinate sentence which previously provided for a maximum period of three years' detention until the Treatment of Offenders (NI) Order 1989 reduced this to two years. It must cease on the juvenile's eighteenth birthday.

(b) Long-Term Detention

There are two different forms of long-term detention: fixed term and indeterminate.

(i) Fixed-Term Detention

Fixed-term detention is applicable in the case of a child or young person convicted on indictment either: under section 73(2) of the Children and Young Persons Act (NI) 1968 of an offence which in the case of an adult would be punishable by a sentence of fourteen years or more; or, under section 10(1) of the Northern Ireland (Emergency

---

[33] See f/n 25. For a recent study of serious offending among male juvenile offenders sentenced to secure and open forms of residential custody in training schools, see Curran, Kilpatrick, Young and Wilson *Longitudinal Aspects of Reconviction: Secure and Open Intervention with Juvenile Offenders in Northern Ireland* (1995) 34(2) Howard J Crim Just.

[34] [1993] 6 NIJB 18.

Provisions Act) 1978, of a scheduled offence which in the case of an adult would be punishable by a sentence of five years or more. The court must be satisfied that no other disposal option is appropriate. As there is a minimum age limit of fourteen in respect of juvenile appearances in the crown court, fixed-term detention cannot be applied to those aged between ten and fourteen. A child within the latter age bracket can only be committed into Trust care, regardless of the seriousness of the offence.

(ii) Indeterminate Detention

Indeterminate detention is restricted to those juveniles who have been found guilty of murder. If the juvenile is below the age of eighteen when the murder was committed, then under section 73(i) of the 1968 Act, he or she is sentenced to be detained 'at the Secretary of State's pleasure'. Under section 73(4) of the 1968 Act or section 1(3) of the 1978 Act, he or she may be released on licence at any time following consultation with the Lord Chief Justice and the trial judge (if available). Under section 73(5) of the 1968 Act, the Secretary of State has the power to attach such conditions as he thinks fit to the licence including supervision by a probation officer. The licence may be revoked at any time.

Arguably indeterminate sentences do not conform with Article 37 of the UN Convention on the Rights of the Child. Also, as has become apparent from the attention given by the Court of Appeal and the House of Lords to the sentences imposed in the Jamie Bulger case, the exercise of a Secretary of State's discretionary powers may be at least controversial.

(c) Treatment Orders

Under the Mental Health (NI) Order 1986 the court has the power to make a hospital order or a guardianship order in respect of a juvenile charged with an offence which, if he or she did not require treatment, would, if found guilty, merit a term of imprisonment. The juvenile must be suffering from mental illness or psychopathic disorder or have a significant or severe mental impairment. Evidence to this effect will be required from two medical practitioners, one of whom must be a psychiatrist. Eligibility for a guardianship order requires the juvenile to be not less than sixteen years of age, and for a hospital order the condition must be 'treatable'. Each order lasts for an initial period of six months and may subsequently be renewed for twelve-month periods indefinitely; subject to confirmation by the Mental Health Review Tribunal.

Remand

At any time the proceedings in a juvenile court or the proceedings concerning a juvenile but held in a different court may be adjourned. The purpose of an adjournment is usually to enable the court to obtain further information. On such occasions the court may remand the juvenile either in custody or on bail.

When so remanded, the court may at any time order the juvenile to appear before it.

Purpose of the Remand

Following a finding that the juvenile is guilty of an offence, the court is required to then consider and to take into account the information submitted in the form of a 'social enquiry report' and in the form of a statement regarding any record of previous convictions. Usually, the latter will be made by the DPP or the RUC, and the former will have been prepared by the officer from the relevant Trust or Probation Board, in accordance with the notification procedure, and lodged in court. Where either has not occurred or the court requires additional information (perhaps in relation to the juvenile's physical or mental health), then it may order an adjournment and remand the juvenile pending receipt of the necessary information.

Remanded in Custody

A juvenile may be committed to the custodial care of a remand home either on final disposal of a case (under sections 74 and 75 of the 1968 Act) or pending determination of a final disposal. The court may order a child or young person to be held on remand for a maximum period of one month in certain circumstances. If found guilty of a scheduled offence, a young person may also be sentenced to a period, not exceeding six months, in a remand home.[35]

In Northern Ireland each of the five training schools is registered as a remand home and has a capacity to accommodate juveniles on remand. Under section 132 of the 1968 Act, all remand homes must be registered and inspected; regard must be had to the religious persuasion of the young person being held on remand. Under section 133 any child or young person being detained in a remand home or being conveyed to or from such a place 'shall be deemed to be in legal custody'.

The decision as to which training school a juvenile should be sent is one made by or on behalf of the Secretary of State not the court. The period for which a juvenile or adult can be held on remand before a court determination of guilt should not exceed eight days. However, if both prosecutor and defendant agree, then this period may be extended to fourteen days from the day following the date of the order. The exclusion of the day on which the order was made is due to the statutory guidance that: 'Where in an enactment a period of time is expressed to begin on, or to be reckoned from, a particular day, that day shall not be included in the period'. The forthcoming legislation will abolish the sentence of committal to a remand home.

Instead of being remanded in custody to a designated remand home, a juvenile may, in certain circumstances, be held in prison. This will be the case where a court certifies that a young person (i.e. aged between 14 and 17 inclusive) is either so unruly a character that he cannot be safely committed to a remand home or that he is so depraved a character that he is not a fit person to be detained in a remand home. Again, even if remanded to a remand home, a young person may prove to be so unruly or depraved that he or she ends up in a Young Offenders' Centre (defined as a prison for the purposes of the Prison Act).

---

35 See the Northern Ireland (Emergency Provisions) Act 1978, section 10(2) and Schedule 4.

Remanded on Bail

Where a juvenile is remanded on bail for either an eight-day or fourteen-day period, this may be extended without limitation subject to the consent of both defendant and prosecution. In relation to juveniles who have attained the age of fourteen and are charged with 'scheduled offences', the court's power to grant bail is restricted. In such circumstances, only where an offence is being tried summarily or where the DPP submits a certificate stating that in his or her opinion an offence is suitable to be tried summarily will the court be able to grant bail.

Extended Remand

Where the purpose is to obtain the information necessary to make a determination, then the court may remand on bail only for a maximum period of twenty-eight days or until the next sitting of the court, whichever is the longer. In such circumstances, whether remanded on bail or in custody, the period of remand may be extended in the absence of the juvenile by any court of summary jurisdiction or by a resident magistrate acting for the same petty sessions district. However, at least once every five weeks the juvenile must be brought before a court of summary jurisdiction or before a resident magistrate sitting out of petty sessions.

Release and Remission

Under section 132(4)(a) of the 1968 Act a child or young person being held in a remand home may be temporarily released or may, on grounds of industry or good conduct, be granted remission.[36]

Treatment of Offenders

The majority of offenders are the subject of 'diversion policy' options. They are diverted away from the juvenile justice system. Those found guilty of serious or repeated offences will, following determination, be retained within the system by an order which will require that they undertake treatment in either a community or custodial setting. The following is a statement of the outcome of treatment disposal options made in respect of juvenile offenders in Northern Ireland.

I. Community Treatment Options

The wide range of community disposal options allows the treatment of juvenile offenders to be individually tailored to a greater extent than elsewhere in the United Kingdom.

1. Community Service

The child or young person is required to undertake a specified number of hours of unpaid work on a named vocational project which is run for the benefit of the community (e.g. a youth club). For the duration of the order the subject must report

---

36 See the 1968 Act as amended by section 9(5) of the Northern Ireland (Emergency Provisions) Act 1978.

to the relevant officer in the Probation Board (usually the Community Service Officer), notify that person of any change of address and perform such work at such times as may be directed by the officer within the hours specified in the order.

2. Attendance Centres

The main attendance centre is located in Belfast, although there is now another in Lisburn. They cater for juveniles of both sexes aged ten to sixteen. The objective of attendance is to restrict the liberty of juveniles without interfering with their school or work and without removing them from home.

3. Supervision

The primary duties of a supervisor are to advise, assist and befriend the subject of the order who in turn has a duty to inform the supervisor of any change of address, keep in touch at all times and allow home visits. The court may attach a condition to the order requiring the subject to live with a named person, with that person's consent, or requiring participation in a specified intermediate treatment programme or perhaps not to participate in certain activities or not to frequent certain premises. Usually, much of the finer detail of therapeutic intervention is left to the discretion of the supervisor.

4. Fit Person

The child or young person placed in the care of a 'fit person' is in effect being given the benefit of a care disposal instead of a justice disposal option. This is very seldom utilised.

5. Probation

In the words of the Probation Board 'the purpose of the Probation Order is to provide the probationer with a structured and positive opportunity to desist from committing offences'. The duty of the probation officer is to advise, assist and befriend the probationer and ensure that the requirements of the order are carried out.

The order states that the subject must be of good behaviour and must lead an industrious life. The subject must agree to co-operate with a probation officer, notify him or her of any change of address and remain in contact with that officer at all times. If so required, the subject must permit the officer to make home visits. The court has the power to attach conditions to a probation order concerning, for example, the place of residence or attendance at a clinic for treatment. Failure to comply with any of the requirements of the order may be regarded as a breach of probation and result in court proceedings at which a fine may be imposed or the order may be revoked and the subject sentenced afresh for the original offence. Both the subject and the probation officer have the right to initiate proceedings to discharge or vary the order and the subject is entitled to legal representation.

II. Custodial Treatment Options

The use of custodial treatment options is proportionately greater here than elsewhere in the United Kingdom and the framework of custodial facilities is somewhat different.

The training schools (all of which are designated as remand homes) provide accommodation for juveniles aged between ten and sixteen at the time of their committal by the courts. As a result in Northern Ireland there is less need for detention in the young offenders' centre or for imprisonment.

The Home Secretary in a recent 'Green Paper'[37] has indicated that while the range of community disposals in England and Wales will remain as they are, the custodial options may well be strengthened. This initiative is likely to transfer to Northern Ireland in due course and will add to the concern expressed by the UN Committee on the Rights of the Child in their 1995 report[38] which called for a review of the criminal justice system as it relates to juveniles in Northern Ireland (particularly in the context of the principles stated in Articles 37 and 40 of the UN Convention).

1. Training School

Under the Children and Young Persons Act (NI) 1968, section 137, a training school is an approved facility providing residential care

> ... for the reception and training of children and young persons who are considered by the courts to be in need of a period of residential treatment away from their home environment.

Training schools are residential institutions which provide education and training for juveniles sent to them by the courts; they also provide facilities for juveniles remanded into custody. They were initiated as the primary disposal option available to the juvenile courts by the Children and Young Persons Act (NI) 1950 and continue to be governed primarily by the Statutory Rules and Orders of Northern Ireland No 32 (Training School Rules). Their classification, administration and management is subject to section 139 of the 1968 Act.

Four training schools were initially established; the one each for Catholic boys (St Patrick's) and girls (St Joseph's) being matched by similar provision for Protestants (Rathgael and Whiteabbey, respectively). Rathgael (now accommodating both girls and boys) and St Patrick's operate open residential systems, each on a dual campus with separately accommodated juvenile offenders and children and young persons detained on care orders.[39] Two other facilities have since been added: Whitefield House, an inter-agency day unit with a mixed population (by gender and religion), and Lisnevin, a unit offering secure accommodation for the more difficult and disruptive offenders on referral from the two male training schools.

Training schools provide secure accommodation for offenders aged from ten to seventeen years who have been found guilty of an imprisonable offence, to be chronic non-school attenders or to be in need of care, protection and control. They have also been commonly used for the subjects of care orders who cannot be contained within the Trusts'

---

37 See *Strengthening Punishment in the Community* (1995).
38 See f/n 17, Chap. 17.
39 St Joseph's is now also an open facility for girls, while the Whiteabbey school has since closed.

range of community provision and for those convicted of a scheduled offence.[40] The total training school population has changed considerably in recent years.[41]

The juvenile may be released by the training school after six months on licence or before on permission of the Secretary of State. After release the juvenile is subject to supervision in the community by the staff of the training school for a period of three years or until he or she reaches the age of twenty-one, whichever is the shorter.

The *Criminal Justice Policy Proposals*[42] recommended retention of the training school order. Forthcoming legislation will permit the court to determine the length of sentence for a range of fixed periods from one week to two years. It will also introduce new arrangements for supervision after release from training school — supervision being by school staff for a set period of between three months and six months (depending on the length of the order). As in England and Wales, seventeen-year-olds will be brought within the remit of the juvenile court which will be re-named the 'youth court'. This legislation will also increase the community element in supervision after release from training school by confining the direct involvement of school staff to a set period of between three and six months (depending on the length of the order), any subsequent care or support being provided in the offender's community. It will ensure the appointment of fully independent visitors to training schools by obliging the Secretary of State to satisfy himself or herself that the training school board of management has made such appointments.

2. Detention in Secure Accommodation

Lisnevin is a highly secure unit consisting of a remand unit with a maximum capacity for twenty-five boys and a fifteen-bed special unit which takes referrals of juveniles with particularly problematic behaviour from the other units.

3. Detention in a Young Offenders' Centre (YOC)

Hydebank Wood (YOC), a secure unit, was established in June 1979 and provides both for the detention of young males who have been convicted of offences and for those who have not. Its management is governed by rules and regulations contained in the Prison and Young Offender Centre Rules (NI) 1994. Article 7 of the Treatment of

---

40 For example, in autumn 1996 approximately fifty per cent of the justice population consisted of persons initially referred to training schools for care or protection reasons. Also, nine out of thirty-eight schedule offenders were sent to training schools in 1980.
41 In 1993, for example, only 116 training school orders were made, which is the lowest number in recent years and about half the level reached in the mid-1980s. By autumn 1996 the justice population — both sentenced and remand — in the training schools stood at approximately one hundred. The composition of the population has also changed. In 1988, 1990 and 1991 the care committals out-numbered offenders. This trend peaked during 1991 when care committals reached fifty-three per cent of the total for that year while offenders constituted thirty-one per cent. This phenomenon is directly linked to a sustained increase in the number of male committals on care grounds, from nineteen per cent of total intake in 1982 to forty-six per cent in 1991.
42 See f/n 31.

Offenders (NI) Order 1989 restricts admissions to young persons aged not less than sixteen years. However, under section 72(3) of the 1968 Act, it also receives fourteen- to seventeen-year-old convicted offenders, disposed of under Article 74, in respect of whom 'certificates of unruliness' have been issued because they are deemed to be unmanageable, too depraved or to have committed grave offences. Detention in a YOC is permissible in the following circumstances:

(a) if he or she is aged fifteen or more, has absconded from training school and with the consent of the Secretary of State is brought before a juvenile court;[43]
(b) he or she has been guilty of serious misconduct at the school and the school managers, with the Secretary of State's consent, bring him or her before the court;[44]
(c) he or she is so seriously unruly or subversive that his or her removal is necessary to maintain school discipline. He or she may then be removed to a YOC for a period of five weeks pending an enquiry as to the best means of disposal.[45]

When the subject of a TSO is sentenced to a YOC, then the TSO ceases to operate[46] and will not normally revive on discharge from the YOC.[47] It will, however, revive in the following sets of circumstances:

(a) where someone sentenced to a period of detention in the YOC is released on appeal;
(b) where someone sentenced to a period of detention in the YOC is granted bail pending appeal; and
(c) where someone sentenced to a period of detention in the YOC is serving that sentence for fine default.

The Secretary of State may direct the transfer of a young person from a YOC to a prison, for the remainder of the sentence, if a visiting committee reports that he or she is 'incorrigible' or a 'bad influence' on other inmates.[48]

Of the 371 committals in 1992, ninety-eight per cent were male and only two per cent were female. Between 1982 and 1992 the unit's average population declined by thirty-nine per cent,[49] including those on a suspended term.

---

43 See 1968 Act, section 140(ii)(b).
44 See 1968 Act, Schedule 5, para 11(1)(b).
45 See the 1968 Act, Schedule 5, para 10(i); this being a purely administrative provision.
46 See the Criminal Justice (NI) Order 1986, Article 5.
47 See the Criminal Justice (NI) Order 1986, Article 5(b).
48 See the Treatment of Offenders Act (NI) 1968, section 7(1)(b).
49 Digest of Information on the Northern Ireland Justice System.

CHAPTER EIGHTEEN

The Views and Legal Interests of the Child

Introduction

Rights for children is a concept which traditionally has never rested comfortably with lawyers. This is curious as the law has never had any difficulty in holding that children have responsibilities for which they can and should be held accountable before a court. In Great Britain, children were sentenced to penal servitude, hard labour and whipping until these were abolished by the Criminal Justice Act 1948 (sections 1(1), 1(2) and 2 respectively). In Northern Ireland there are currently children in our prisons.[1] Being a child has never been a legal impediment to enlistment in the armed forces at times of national emergency, to acquiring a driving licence nor to securing employment. Many children are currently in employment, yet children are not permitted to enrol on the electoral register, to marry without parental permission nor to purchase cigarettes. It would seem that the courts have considerably less difficulty in accommodating the legal capacity of children as bearers of duties than of rights. Why should this be?

Some of the problems associated with the legal standing of children are to do with definition. This is apparent at either end of childhood: the concept of 'welfare' in relation to babies and to adolescents can obscure the legal interests of those involved and confuse the ownership of such interests. The younger the child, the more difficult it is to be certain that his or her welfare can be defined separately from that of the caring parent or guardian. The older the child, the more certain it is that they should be. Indeed, for adolescents, the law is such a minefield of different age thresholds for different levels of responsibility that it is becoming increasingly difficult to be sure that the eighteenth birthday marks any legally significant passage from minor to adult status. When does the status of dependency give way to personal responsibility?

The Children (NI) Order 1995 introduced the requirement to ascertain the wishes and feelings of the child as the first item on a 'welfare checklist'[2] to be judicially

---

1 For example, a fifteen-year-old girl, the subject of a care order, was committed to the Young Offenders' Centre in Maghaberry Prison in 1995 as this was the only form of secure accommodation then available for adolescent females.
2 See Article 3 —
    (3) In the circumstances referred to in paragraph (4), a court shall have regard in particular to —
        (a) the ascertainable wishes and feelings of the child concerned (considered in the light of his age and understanding).

applied in all public and some private proceedings instigated under this legislation. It also makes some decisions by judiciary and Trusts conditional upon their acceptance by the child concerned and requires the Trusts to involve a child in other areas of decision-making.

This chapter considers the resulting implications for the legal standing of children. It examines when and to what effect the views of a child may contribute to a decision taken by the judiciary, Trust or others in relation to that child's legal interests. It assesses the inter-relationship among a child's views, welfare and legal interests. It leaves to Chapter Nineteen, however, the supplementary questions as to the means by which a child's views are to be ascertained and represented.

The Views of the Child — The Law, the Parties and the Principle

I. Law

1. Pressure for Change

The Children (NI) Order 1995, in particular Article 3(3)(a), is now the primary source of legal authority for the principle that a child's views should be ascertained and taken into account when decisions are to be taken on matters concerning that child's welfare. This important, comprehensive and very recent legislative recognition of the changed *locus standi* of a child in family proceedings has been brought about by a gradual convergence of pressures emanating from international sources, from across the Irish Sea and from local judicial practice.

(a) International Pressure

There is considerable evidence to suggest that legislative recognition of the importance of a child's views on matters concerning his or her welfare was in response to pressure from outside the United Kingdom (see also Chapter Eleven).[3] In particular, the United Nations Convention on the Rights of the Child which was adopted by the UN General Assembly in November 1989 and ratified by the United Kingdom in December 1991 has influenced the shaping of some of the more formative principles governing the 1995 Order.[4] It may be that the assimilation (though not the formulation and develop-

---

3 For example, in 1984 the Parliamentary Assembly made a recommendation to the ministers of the Council of Europe on the subject of 'parental responsibilities' and incorporated advice in relation to the views of children. It then argued that when decisions are to be taken affecting the legal interests of children, the latter 'should be consulted if their degree of maturity with regard to the decision so permits'.

4 Article 5 of the Convention, for example, recognises the inherent mutuality between the rights of parents and the welfare of their children in its declaration:

> States Parties shall respect the responsibilities, rights and duties of parents . . . to provide, in a manner consistent with the evolving capacities of the child, appropriate direction and guidance in the exercise by the child of the rights recognised in the present Convention.

See also Article 12 which deals with the right of a child to freely express his or her opinion, and have that opinion taken into account, in any matter or procedure affecting him or her.

ment) of the paramountcy principle within the Children Act 1989 and subsequently within the Children (NI) Order 1995 owes at least as much to Strasbourg initiative as to indigenous case law.[5]

(b) Judicial Initiative in England and Wales

The ruling in *Gillick* was a landmark decision for recognition of the separate legal interests of children[6] (see also Chapters Two, Seven and Eleven). Arguably, however, it may with hindsight be seen as forming a watershed in United Kingdom jurisprudence in the area of children's rights: subsequent case law reveals, if anything, a steady constriction of the *Gillick* principle. The judicial approach to the views of children and the weighting accorded to such views have remained essentially paternalistic (see also Chapter Two).

2. The New Statutory Duty

For the first time there is a legal requirement that, in certain circumstances, when matters concerning the welfare of a child are being decided the views of that child will be sought and taken into account. Not until after problems have arisen, however, and decisions then need to be taken in the circumstances allowed for under the 1995 Order does this requirement come into play. There is no general principle that a child has a right to participate in decisions affecting his or her welfare.

(a) The Duty of the Courts

Under Article 3 of the 1995 Order:

> (3) In the circumstances mentioned in paragraph (4), a court shall have regard in particular to —
>
>> (a) the ascertainable wishes and feelings of the child concerned (considered in the light of his age and understanding).

(i) The Circumstances

These are contested proceedings to make, vary or discharge an Article 8 order and proceedings to make, vary or discharge an order under Part V. The mandatory application of this duty to 'have regard' etc. in all public but only in contested private family law proceedings reflects the legislation's underpinning philosophy of minimal judicial intervention in consensual family law matters, but comprehensive and consistent judicial scrutiny of public law matters, where the welfare interests of children are involved. The breadth of application of this principle is apparent also from the Children's Evidence (NI) Order 1995, Article 3 provides:

---

5 This is not to detract from the example set by the Court of Chancery which, in the course of exercising its jurisdiction for the benefit of a child, developed the practice of ascertaining and giving due consideration to the views of the child concerned. See, for example, *R v Smith* (1734) 2 Strange 982.
6 *Gillick v West Norfolk and Wisbech Area Health Authority* [1986] 1 AC 112 HL.

(3) A child's evidence shall be received unless it appears to the court that the child is incapable of giving intelligible testimony.

(See also Chapter Sixteen.)

(ii) Shall Have Regard

The requirement that the court 'shall have regard' for the wishes and feelings of the child gives statutory effect to the trenchant observation made by Butler-Sloss LJ:[7]

> The child is a person and not an object of concern . . . . Children are entitled to a proper explanation appropriate to their age . . . . The views and wishes of the child, particularly as to what is to happen to him/her, should be taken into consideration by the professionals involved . . . and should be placed before whichever court deals with the case.

However, this requirement stops well short of importing any suggestion that a child's consent should be sought. Indeed, the court may over-rule a *Gillick* competent minor[8] and the parents or any professional.

(iii) Ascertainable Wishes and Feelings

There are some very basic reasons why the court should establish the wishes and feelings of the child. Firstly, the court needs to confirm that children understand the issues which have a bearing on their future welfare. Secondly, it is an appropriate means for the court to demonstrate its respect for any views the child might have on matters which concern him or her. Primarily, however, the spirit of the paramountcy principle requires that the child, the subject of the proceedings and intended beneficiary of the principle, be directly engaged by the court. In acknowledgement of the importance of the occasion to the child, the probable confusing and intimidating effect of courtroom procedure and in order to pave the way for the child to express their views, it is critical that judicial skills be deployed to facilitate the constructive involvement of the child in the proceedings.

This composite duty heads the checklist of factors to be considered by the court when giving effect to the paramountcy principle, but it remains only one of seven such factors, all of which require judicial consideration and none of which will necessarily weigh more than any other in the circumstances of a particular case. The judicial checklist is not a definitive slide rule to be uniformly applied to all cases.

The clear implication of this provision is that while the judiciary are to be guided by it in their application of the paramountcy principle, their discretion is not to be fettered in the interpretation and relative weighting they give to the different factors which will constitute the welfare of the child in each case. The views and the legal interests of the child are not synonymous, and while the first may inform judicial appreciation of the latter, they may also be biased, wrong and obscure the legal issues (see also Chapter One).

---

7 See *Report of the Inquiry into Child Abuse in Cleveland 1987*, Cmnd 412 (1988) p. 245.
8 See *Re R* [1991] 4 All ER 177.

(b) The Duty of the Trusts

There is no requirement that the Trusts apply the paramountcy principle to resolve issues affecting the welfare of a child. The duty placed on the Trusts is therefore limited in application to certain circumstances, unlike the comprehensive nature of the judicial duty.

II. Parties

1. The Child

Prior to the decision in *Gillick* a valid consent for a third party to undertake a course of action affecting the welfare interests of a child could only be obtained from a parent, guardian or court but not from the child. Since the introduction of the Children Act 1989 the courts, when taking into account the views of an older child to determine a welfare-related issue, can be seen looking as much to the *Gillick* decision and consent considerations as to the new statutory directive and considerations of wishes and feelings. In Northern Ireland the similar practice of the High Court indicates that in the years following the introduction of the Children (NI) Order 1995, the judicial leaning towards the *Gillick* decision as the preferred reference point in such cases is likely to continue.

(a) The Age and Understanding of the Child

The legal standing of a child in any decision-making process affecting his or her interests will depend on his or her age and understanding of the issues involved. This has long been the governing principle in Northern Ireland where, as MacDermott J[9] has stated:

> The older a child gets the greater the weight which can be given to its wishes.... These girls are twelve and ten and quite mature ... of an age to express a meaningful opinion and I bear it in mind.

However, since the decision in *Gillick* this approach has hardened into a 'competence' test. As Lord Scarman[10] then explained:

> [A] minor's capacity to make his or her decision depends upon the minor having sufficient understanding and intelligence to make the decision and is not to be determined by reference to any judicially fixed age limit.

The *prima facie* presumption that a child below the age of sixteen is non-competent, in the above sense, may be rebutted by evidence based on age and understanding; a child over that age will be presumed to have the necessary competence. The law now requires that the views and feelings of a child in either group be sought in relation to a decision materially affecting his or her interests but, where a child is aged sixteen or is deemed to be '*Gillick* competent', then the law goes further and requires that his or her consent be sought in relation to the matter at issue.

---

9 See *In Re CB and AJB (Minors)*, unreported (1983).
10 F/n 5 at 252 G.

The effect of *Gillick* in the post-Children Act 1989 era is apparent in recent case law. For example, the court has indicated that it would respect the wishes of a fourteen-year-old regarding his education but also commented that had he been eleven, it would not have hesitated to 'pack him off to boarding school'.[11] The critical factor in this and many similar cases is the age and understanding of the child concerned. As Sir Thomas Bingham MR[12] has observed:

> Children have different levels of understanding at the same age. And understanding is not absolute. It has to be assessed relative to the issues in the case.

(b) The Views of the Child

The child's 'wishes' and 'feelings' are not to be seen as the sole indicators of his or her appreciation of the matters at issue, nor are these necessarily to be accorded the same weighting in each case. The subjects on which a child refuses to communicate or refers to obliquely may be of greater importance. An assessment of a child's wishes and feelings is a very difficult task and can only be sensibly achieved if conducted in the context of factors such as particular attributes and/or needs, personality and character development, attachments and each child's understanding of where he or she fits into the family dynamics. How the views of children, in relation to matters concerning them, are to be ascertained has been as controversial here as in England and Wales.

In the courts and in the course of agency proceedings in relation to child-care matters, the task of ascertaining a child's wishes and feelings has usually been left to Trust social workers. The latter, unlike their counterparts across the Irish Sea, have had responsibility for furnishing the courts with social history reports in all matrimonial proceedings involving children and in all child-care proceedings. This report, whether produced for agency or for court proceedings, would note the views of the child and offer an opinion on their significance. In agency proceedings, recent good practice developments would allow for a child to participate to some extent in, for example, reviews of care arrangements.

In court proceedings, other intermediaries such as the guardian ad litem in adoption proceedings, the Official Solicitor and/or expert witnesses such as psychologists and child psychiatrists might also be available to assist the court to ascertain a child's wishes and feelings. It should be noted, however, that the court has held[13] that evidence, in the form of such views and wishes, could only be withheld from a party to proceedings (the mother) in the most exceptional circumstances, disclosure to all parties being the normal rule (see also Chapter Sixteen). The High Court judiciary, particularly in wardship/ adoption cases, have an established practice of supplementing the information made available through intermediaries by making their own direct enquiries of a child wherever practicable, either in open court or in the judge's chambers.

A variation of this practice was recently the subject of judicial comment. In *Re W (A Minor) (Contact)*[14] the children were aged ten and twelve and expressed a wish to

---

11 See *Re P (A Minor)(Education)* [1992] 1 FLR 316 CA.
12 See in *Re Section (A Minor)(Independent Representation)* [1993] 2 FLR 444H.
13 See *Re M (Minors)(Disclosure of Evidence)* [1994] 1 FLR 6.
14 [1994] 2 FLR 441.

see the judge to explain why they wanted to live with their father. Butler-Sloss[15] in the course of her judgment stated that:

> If children of 10 and 12 express the view that they wish to see the judge, that is in line with Section 1(3)(a) of the 1989 Act [Article 3(3)(a) of the 1995 Order].... If children have views which they wish the court to hear that is entirely in accordance with Parliament's requirement for the first time that courts should ascertain the wishes and understanding of children who are of an age and maturity to give them.

(c) The Consent of the Child

Where the child is aged at least sixteen or though younger is deemed to be of an age and understanding to give an informed consent, then parents, the court and other third parties will be legally obliged to do more than ascertain and have regard to his or her views. If the child satisfies the 'competence test', then that child may assert his or her views by instigating proceedings, instructing a solicitor and/or by participating as a full party in proceedings. Such a child may also give or withhold consent in relation to the proposals of such others as parents and Trust. There are circumstances in which others may have to defer to the views of a child; some of these circumstances are stated in or arise from the Children (NI) Order 1995.

2. The Parents

Where consent is needed to authorise a course of action in a matter affecting the welfare of a child, then traditionally, the consent sought will have been that of the child's parent. This usually occurs when the proposals of a third party, such as those of a medical practitioner to conduct an intimate physical examination or to administer anaesthetic, could lead to a possible charge of trespass to the person of the child unless properly authorised. The question of the circumstances in which a child may give such a full and independent consent and the extent to which this may prevail against the wishes of others have greatly exercised the judiciary in recent years.

(a) Parental Consent Displaced by Child's Wishes and Feelings

As was stated in the *Gillick* case:[16]

> An underlying principle of the law ... is that parental right yields to the child's right to make his own decisions when he reaches a sufficient understanding and intelligence to be capable of making up his own mind on the matter requiring decision.

This clear statement of principle has proved quite complicated to apply in practice. That 'the parental right yields' infers that it continues in existence, presumably until the child ceases to be a minor. But to what effect? It can at least be stated with some certainty that where a child is aged sixteen or satisfies the competence test, then the courts will be extremely reluctant to impose a parental decision against the wishes of

---

15 Ibid.
16 F/n 5 at 251 B.

that child. Further, where parental consent is unavailable, for whatever reason, then a third party would be entitled to rely on the authorisation of such a child. However, it is when a third party is faced with a clear contradiction between the wishes of parent and such a child that legal certainties become hardest to find. A more recent decision[17] provides authority for the limited proposition that where a child, aged sixteen or *Gillick* competent, has given a valid consent, then this cannot be subsequently overridden by the parent.

(b) Parental Consent Concurrent with Child's Wishes and Feelings

In keeping with the spirit of the Children Act 1989, particularly the approach which has substituted for the previous exclusivity of parental rights, a new concept of shared parental responsibility, the courts in England and Wales have recently been interpreting consent in relation to welfare decisions as a power which may be vested jointly in a number of office-holders. The significance of this being that either parent or a competent child could unilaterally exercise their joint authority to give a valid consent. It would thus be open to a third party to choose the office-holder from whom they would seek authorisation; a refusal by one would not debar the other from granting authorisation.[18]

3. Other Third Parties

Consent for a course of action relating to the welfare interests of a child can only be given by a parent, the court, someone or body with parental responsibility or by the child concerned if he or she is of an age and understanding to do so. Among the third parties who would be recognised as having capacity to give consent are any Trust vested with a care order, a putative father (if he has legally acquired parental responsibility), a guardian or any person in whose favour the court has made a residence order. Relatives without parental responsibility are unable to give a valid consent.

The Principle

The legislative intent is that when, in certain circumstances, decisions are taken by the state on matters affecting the welfare of a child, those taking such decisions should only do so after having fully assessed the legal interests of the child concerned. The views of the child on the presenting issue are not determinative and may not even be very relevant; they are merely an ingredient in the totality of factors which constitute an overall assessment of the child's legal interests.

The statutory duty placed on the courts is to apply the paramountcy principle in certain specified proceedings when determining matters affecting the welfare interests of a child. In so doing the court is required, among other things, to seek the views but not the consent of the child concerned. There are many issues on which the court will

---

17 See *Re W (A Minor)(Medical Treatment: Court's Jurisdiction)* [1992] 3 WLR 785, [1992] 4 All ER 627.
18 This approach can be seen in *Re R (A Minor)(Wardship: Medical Treatment)* [1992] 1 FLR 190 where Donaldson LJ held that a parent retained the right to consent to treatment on behalf of a child, even though the child was of age and understanding and had refused her consent.

seek the views of a child of sufficient age and understanding. There are also some few issues where consent rather than views will be sought.

Public Family Law

I. Ascertain the Wishes and Feelings of the Child

The Children (NI) Order 1995 gives more prominence to the views of the child in public family law proceedings than in private proceedings. Whereas the application of Article 3(1) is selective in relation to the latter, it is universal to all public proceedings.

1. The Duties of the Court

(a) To Ascertain Wishes and Feelings

How the child's wishes and feeling are to be ascertained will to some extent vary in accordance with the age and assertiveness of the child concerned. Where a guardian ad litem (GAL) is appointed, which will be in virtually all public law cases, that person will ascertain and present such wishes and feelings to the court. In a minority of cases the child will be the applicant and proceedings will in effect be driven by his or her views. In many the child's views will be represented by a solicitor engaged by the GAL and/or be the subject of assessment by expert witnesses (see further Chapter Nineteen). Whether elicited by intermediaries, sought by judicial interview or directly expressed at the insistence of the child, the 1995 Order now requires the latter's wishes and feelings to be ascertained by the court.

However, in some cases it may not be in a particular child's best interests to be subjected to enquiries regarding his or her wishes and feelings. This is most likely to occur in public family proceedings where, for example, a child has been seriously traumatised and clearly indicates that he or she does not wish to participate in any enquiries or court proceedings. Then compliance with the paramountcy principle will entail not exposing the child to the risk of further stress or even abuse by attempting to ascertain his or her wishes and feelings.

(b) To Have Regard for Wishes and Feelings

The requirement to have regard for the child's wishes and feelings clearly leaves to judicial discretion the crucial issue of how much weight is to be attached, in any particular instance, to the views of a child when determining a matter affecting his or her welfare. The fact that such a consideration will seldom be the deciding factor was apparent in a recent ruling of the Court of Appeal in England.[19] In considering the equivalent provision of the 1989 Act, it was held that the court should always elicit and respect the views of a child which it may not be able to act upon but which may tip the balance in a difficult case.

19　See *Re P (A Minor)(Education)* [1992] 1 FLR 316 CA.

2. The Duties of a Trust

Once a Trust incurs responsibilities in respect of a child, it will now, thereby, incur an obligation to ascertain the wishes and feelings of that child. This may arise by implication in the context of service provision for children with special needs. It may arise by explicit statutory directive in relation to children being either accommodated or being 'looked after' by a Trust. It may also arise from the considerable body of regulations which detail a Trust's implementation of its various statutory duties towards children, including those being adopted.

(a) In Relation to Children Being Accommodated by a Trust

Under Article 21:

> (6) Before providing accommodation under this Article, an authority shall, so far as is practicable and consistent with the child's welfare—
>
> > (a) ascertain the child's wishes regarding the provision of accommodation; and
> > (b) give due consideration (having regard to his age and understanding) to such wishes of the child as the authority has been able to ascertain.

The form of words relied upon in this and the following provisions to delineate the duty of the Trust differs slightly from that used above in respect of the equivalent judicial duty. It may be that the change from 'have regard' to 'give due consideration' and the occasional absence of a Trust's duty to do so in relation to 'feelings' is intended to imply a subtle distinction in the extent and weighting to be attached to the views of a child by Trust and judiciary.

The regulations governing the agreements made between a Trust and parents, in respect of arrangements for a child being accommodated, provide for the views of the child concerned to be ascertained. The requirement is that every Trust shall record the arrangements it makes for ascertaining the views of the child in relation to the matters dealt with in the accommodation agreement.

(b) In Relation to Children Being 'Looked After' by a Trust

Under Article 26:

> (2) Before making any decision with respect to a child whom it is looking after, or proposing to look after, an authority shall, so far as is reasonably practicable, ascertain the wishes and feelings of —
>
> > (a) the child and
>
> (3) In making any such decision an authority shall give due consideration—
>
> > (a) having regard to his age and understanding, to such wishes and feelings of the child as the authority has been able to ascertain.

When so considering a child's views, in the context of such decision-making, a Trust is further directed to consider also the child's religious persuasion, racial origin and cultural and linguistic background.

By imposing the requirement that a Trust consult, where practicable, with a child before making decisions affecting that child and before making arrangements regarding his or her future home, this provision very sensibly ensures that the child is at least briefed and at best given a chance to participate in the choices to be made as to the manner in which he or she is looked after by the Trust.

(c) In Relation to the Reviews of Children Being 'Looked After' by a Trust
Under Article 45:

> (1) The Department may make regulations requiring the case of each child who is being looked after by an authority to be reviewed in accordance with the provisions of the regulations.
> (2) The regulations may, in particular, make provision . . .
>> (d) requiring the authority, before conducting any review, to seek the views of
>>> (i) the child.

The regulations emanating from this provision provide comprehensively for the responsibility of Trusts to ascertain and take into account the wishes and feelings of children across the full range of settings in which they may be accommodated, including those of children in secure accommodation.

Bringing the views of the child concerned before the case review panel has been a part of the Trusts' good practice arrangements in relation to children in care for many years. How this is achieved so as to ensure that the child is therapeutically engaged, his or her legal interests effectively and assertively represented, while welfare interests are not compromised, remains a principal challenge for the practice of a Trust as much as for the court.

(d) In Relation to Receiving Representations, Including Complaints, from Children
The duty of a Trust to establish a complaints procedure in relation to children whom it is 'looking after' is addressed in regulations which give effect to Article 28:

> (2) Regulations under Article 27(2)(f) may, in particular, make provision as to . . .
>> (b) the opportunities such persons are to have to make representations in relation to the arrangements proposed.

The regulations governing a similar duty in respect of children for whom a Trust provides 'advice and assistance' derive from the authority of Article 27:

> (1) Every authority shall establish a procedure for considering any representations (including any complaint) made to the authority by a person qualifying for advice and assistance about the discharge of the authority's functions under this Part in relation to him.

3. The Duties of Others

(a) Of a Voluntary Organisation

Under Article 76:

> (1) Where a child is accommodated by or on behalf of a voluntary organisation, the organisation shall . . .
>> (c) advise, assist and befriend him with a view to promoting his welfare when he ceases to be so accommodated.
>
> (2) Before making any decision with respect to any such child the organisation shall, so far as is reasonably practicable, ascertain the wishes and feelings of
>> (a) the child regarding the matter to be decided.
>
> (3) In making any such decision the organisation shall give due consideration
>> (a) having regard to the child's age and understanding, to such wishes and feelings of his as the organisation has been able to ascertain.

This provision extends a particular standard of good practice to voluntary organisations.

(b) Of a Person Carrying on a Private Children's Home

Under Article 92(1)(c), (2)(a) and (3)(a) of the 1995 Order, the stated duties of any persons carrying on a private children's home replicate those outlined in the corresponding provisions of Article 76 above. The inclusion of private children's homes within the scope of this mandatory duty thereby ensures its uniform legal application across both the statutory and voluntary sectors of child care.

(c) Of Other Persons and Bodies

Under Article 65(1) a constable has the power to remove and provide accommodation for a child in an emergency. The exercise of this power is subject to a requirement in paragraph (5) of the same Article that as soon as is reasonably practicable after the child has been taken into police protection, the designated officer shall

>> (d) take such steps as are reasonably practicable to discover the wishes and feelings of the child.

However, under Article 65(10), the issue of whether the child is then to have contact with parents or any other stated persons is a matter to be determined by the designated officer in light of his or her assessment of the child's best interests; there is no requirement that he or she seek the views of the child on this matter.

Under Schedule 4, paragraph 2, the duties of a supervisor in respect of a child who is the subject of an education supervision order include the power to give such directions to the child as may be necessary to ensure that he or she is properly educated. This power is subject to the instruction in sub-paragraph (2) that the supervisor

> . . . shall, so far as is reasonably practicable, ascertain the wishes and feelings of
>> (a) the child.

Sub-paragraph (3) adds the further instruction that

... when settling the terms of any such directions, the supervisor shall give due consideration
  (a) having regard to the child's age and understanding, to such wishes and feelings of his as the supervisor has been able to ascertain.

These instructions do not lie solely in relation to the child; they are exactly replicated in respect of the child's parents. Not only are the views of the child thus accorded no greater weight than those of the parents but there is no suggestion in this provision that the supervisor should comply with the views of either party.

II. The Duty to Defer to the Views of the Child

There is no such thing as a sweeping statutory duty directing that a child's views, as opposed to his or her legal interests, must prevail over all other considerations in the determining of issues affecting the welfare of that child. The essential point of the paramountcy principle, after all, is a recognition that the responsibility for decision-making is to be placed not in the hands of a child but in the hands of certain authorised others. Additionally, the party primarily bound by the outcome of any decision to which the principle applies is the child concerned.

However, there are now some areas of decision-making governed by the 1995 Order where such authority has been extended to enforce the views of a child that in effect responsibility for a decision rests with that child. There are also other areas where, because decisions turn on the consent rather than the views of a *Gillick* competent child, the outcome will be the same.

1. The Duties of the Court

(a) Non-Consensual Medical Treatment of a Child in Care

The circumstances in which the wishes and feelings of an older child may, in public family proceedings, be permitted to override a refusal of parental consent produce an area of law which seems set to experience an exponential increase in litigation. The issues arise most commonly and most urgently in relation to medical treatment where consent of parent or child is an essential pre-condition for doctors to commence treatment except in an emergency. Such cases most usually appear before the courts in private family proceedings (see Chapters Two and Seven) where the criteria to be applied and the appropriate forum for hearing them have greatly exercised the judiciary in recent years. In public family proceedings where the child is in care, it is evident[20] that the appropriate forum is the inherent jurisdiction of the High Court.

(i) No Consent Available

Occasionally, circumstances arise in which the person whose consent is required to authorise treatment lacks the capacity to do so, usually due to mental illness. In this jurisdiction this was the situation in a recent case[21] where a Trust (hospital Trust) sought

---

20 See *Re R (A Minor)(Blood Transfusion)* [1993] 2 FLR 757.
21 See *Re TC (A Minor)* [1994] 4 BNIL.

permission to disconnect a life support system which was sustaining the life of a two-year old severely brain damaged child. The High Court, exercising its inherent jurisdiction, provided the necessary authority (see also Chapter Seven).

(ii) Parental Consent Unavailable

Where the child is a mature minor and parental consent is, for whatever reason unavailable, then there is authority under the ruling in *Gillick* for the courts to endorse the consent of the child.

(iii) Child's Consent Withheld

The Trusts are frequently faced with problems in relation to older adolescents in care who make reasoned decisions which are not in keeping with their welfare interests. The question then arises as to what authority a Trust might have to override the decision of a *Gillick* competent minor. In *Re W (A Minor)(Medical Treatment: Court's Jurisdiction)*[22] the court considered an application made by a Trust's English counterpart in respect of a sixteen-year-old anorexic girl in care for permission to arrange medical treatment and for this to be provided without her consent if necessary. The Court of Appeal unanimously gave its consent holding: that it had authority to do so under the court's unlimited inherent *parens patriae* jurisdiction; the authority of those holding 'parental responsibility' for a child would be insufficient to override the decision of a *'Gillick* competent' child; its authority when exercising this jurisdiction exceeded that which came within the definition of 'parental responsibility'; and that the High Court's inherent jurisdiction may apply regardless of whether the child in question was a ward.

(iv) Child's Consent Opposed by Parent

In this jurisdiction the courts have a long-established practice of ascertaining the views of the child when determining matters affecting the child's welfare. Where the views of a mature minor in care are being unreasonably opposed by a parent, the court will not hesitate to give precedence to the views of the child if the evidence shows that to do so would be compatible with welfare interests. In this jurisdiction, for example, Shiel J considered[23] a Trust wardship application in respect of a proposed abortion for a fourteen-year-old girl who was thirteen weeks' pregnant, the subject of an FPO and resident in a children's home. The application was contested by the child's mother. Having received evidence that the minor was '*Gillick* competent', that she was steadfast in her desire for a termination and threatened suicide if her wishes were obstructed and following evidence from Trust staff, doctors and a psychiatrist as to the minor's mental health, the court granted the application.

This approach is very much in keeping with the decision in *Re O (A Minor)(Medical Treatment)*[24] which provides authority for the view that the inherent jurisdiction is the most appropriate forum to authorise a blood transfusion for a child against the wishes of the child's parents who, in the latter case, were Jehovah Witnesses.

---

22 [1992] 3 WLR 785 [1992] 4 All ER 627.
23 See In *the matter of K (A Minor)*, unreported (1993).
24 [1993] 2 FLR 149.

(b) Specific Provisions of the Children (NI) Order 1995

The fact that the court is bound by the paramountcy principle in its determination of most proceedings arising under the 1995 Order does not of itself give rise to any presumption that other factors must give way to the views of a child. Indeed, quite the opposite is the case: such views acquire their legal status in relation to the presenting issues only after the most careful judicial assessment. However, in the following circumstances the courts have little or no option when faced with a resolute child.

(i) In Relation to Authorising Trust Arrangements for a Child in Care to Live Abroad

Under Article 33(1) the authority of the court is necessary to approve any arrangements which a Trust has made, or assisted in making, for a child to live abroad. Rule 2(2) of the Magistrates' Court Rules makes provision for a GAL to be appointed to advise the court on the implications then arising for the welfare of the child. The court, in certain circumstances, is prohibited from giving such approval unless satisfied that, among other considerations:

> (c) the child has consented to living in that country and that the child does have sufficient understanding to give or withhold consent.

This provision is noteworthy as it provides a very rare instance of legislative insistence that a right held by an adult or body and affecting the upbringing of a child is only exercisable subject to the consent of that child.

(ii) In Relation to Child Assessment Orders

Article 62 of the 1995 Order empowers the court, on the application of a Trust or authorised person, to make a child assessment order if satisfied that the requirements stated in that provision have been met. However, under paragraph (8) 'if the child is of sufficient understanding to make an informed decision he may refuse to submit to a medical or psychiatric examination or other assessment'. This effectively gives the child a power of veto over an entire court order.

(iii) In Relation to Assessment Conditions Attached to Other Court Orders

Under Article 63(1) of the 1995 Order the court may make an emergency protection order which can be subject to a direction made under (6)(b) requiring a medical, psychiatric or other form of assessment for the child. However, paragraph (7) of the same Article states that the child concerned may 'if he is of sufficient understanding to make an informed decision, refuse to submit to the examination or other assessment'. The child is thus given a power of veto, restricted to an ancillary aspect of the order.

Under Schedule 3, paragraph 4, the power of a court to attach a direction to a supervision order made under Article 54(1) requiring the child to attend for psychiatric or medical examination is subject to the provision that:

> (4) No court shall include a requirement under this paragraph in a supervision order unless it is satisfied —
>> (a) where the child has sufficient understanding to make an informed decision, that he consents to its inclusion.

The power of a court to make or vary a supervision order on advice provided by a medical practitioner appointed for the purposes of Part II of the Mental Health (NI) Order 1986 to direct the treatment of a child is also subject to exactly the same condition.

(iv) In Relation to Applications for the Discharge and Variation of Certain Orders

Under Article 58(1) and (2) the court may discharge a care order or a supervision order, respectively, on the application of the child concerned. Under Article 64(7)(a) the court may do the same where the child's application is in respect of an emergency protection order. Similarly, under Schedule 4, paragraph 7, the court may do so where the child's application is in relation to an education supervision order. Again, under Schedule 8, paragraph 10(3), the court may discharge 'any existing order which is in force with respect to a child' on application by the child concerned. These provisions require the court to treat an application from a child in the same way it would if the application had been made by a Trust, parent or a person with parental responsibility: if the applicant satisfies the conditions, then the court must defer and discharge the order.

2. The Duties of a Trust

Under the 1995 Order it is, generally speaking, for the courts not the Trusts to decide on the rights of the parties involved in matters where the welfare interests of children are at stake. However, in the following circumstances, under the 1995 Order and other legislation, a Trust may find that its obligation to defer to the views of a child is such that in effect it is recognising and conceding a right held by that child.

(a) In Relation to the Provision of Accommodation

Article 22(5) removes both a Trust's right not to provide accommodation and the right of any person with parental responsibility to remove a child from Trust accommodation (rights as defined in Articles 21 and 22) 'where a child who has reached the age of sixteen agrees to being provided with accommodation under Article 21'. Effectively, this provision would seem to place a duty on the Trusts to provide accommodation to such a child or allow him or her to remain in Trust accommodation if so requested by that child.

The independent legal status of such a child is further recognised by Article 39(3)(b) under which a Trust is authorised to recover from that child (when aged sixteen or more) contributions towards the maintenance costs incurred in looking after him or her.

(b) In Relation to the Appointment of Visitors for a Child Being 'Looked After' by a Trust and Not Being Visited

The duty of a Trust under Article 31(1) of the 1995 Order to appoint a visitor in such circumstances or to continue that appointment may, under paragraphs (5) and (6), respectively, be overridden by the views of the child if:

(a) the child objects . . . and
(b) the authority is satisfied that the child has sufficient understanding to make an informed decision.

This, again, is a situation where it would seem that a Trust has no option but to accept and implement the views of the child.

(c) In Relation to the Right of a Child in Care to Seek Advice and Assistance

The duty or power of a Trust under Article 35 in relation to 'a person qualifying for advice and assistance' is extended by Schedule 8, paragraph 17, to include 'a person within the area of the Trust in question who is under twenty-one and who was, at any time after reaching the age of 16 but while still a child a person falling within paragraph 11(1), 15(1) or 31(1)'. This means that in some circumstances a Trust would be unable to deny the claim of a child to advice and assistance.

(d) In Relation to the Right of a Child to Seek Information

Arguably, a *Gillick* competent minor is eligible to apply for access to personal information held on an agency's file. The relevant Trust, medical practitioner or other statutorily specified agency will have a duty to disclose the requested information subject to the provisions of the Data Protection Act 1984, the Access to Personal Files and Medical Reports (NI) Order 1991 and the Access to Health Records (NI) Order 1993.

Private Family Law

I. The Duty to Ascertain the Wishes and Feelings of the Child

The requirement that the child's wishes and feelings are to be ascertained has a restricted application to private family proceedings. It falls as a statutory duty on the judiciary only in respect of contested proceedings and its bearing on Trust procedures is virtually limited to forming an item in the court reports of social workers and GALs in adoption and in some wardship and matrimonial proceedings.

The Duties of the Court

(a) In Relation to Uncontested Proceedings Affecting Welfare

In uncontested private family law proceedings the welfare 'checklist' has no application and therefore there is no statutory requirement that the wishes and feelings of the child concerned be ascertained. This non-interventionist stance is well illustrated by the two provisions in the 1995 Order relating to the intention to change a child's surname. Article 13(1)(a) states that:

> (1) Where a residence order is in force with respect to a child, no person shall—
>> (a) cause the child to be known by a new surname except with written consent of every person with parental responsibility or leave of the court.

Under Article 52(7)(a) 'no person shall cause the child to be known by a new surname' — except in the same circumstances. In neither instance is there a requirement to seek the child's views. Indeed, where the child's views are brought before the court,[25] they may be discounted. This was precisely what occurred in *Re B (Change of Surname)*[26] when the unequivocal wishes of three children (aged twelve, fourteen and sixteen),

---
25 See *W v A (Child: Surname)* [1981] 1 All ER 100.
26 [1996] 1 FLR 791.

supported by mother and social worker, proved insufficient to convince the court that a change of surname to that of their step-father would be justified. This is an approach which contrasts with that advocated in Articles 2 and 8 of the UN Convention on the Rights of the Child.

(b) In Relation to Contested Proceedings Affecting Welfare

In adoption, wardship and matrimonial proceedings where an application is being contested, the judiciary have a well-established practice of seeking the views of the children concerned. Information on their views will also be made available to the court in the form of reports from Trust social workers in respect of all such proceedings, augmented by reports from GALs in adoption applications, and in all cases by occasional evidence from expert witnesses.

In adoption proceedings the statutory requirement in Article 9 of the Adoption (NI) Order 1987 to '. . . ascertain the wishes and feelings of the child . . . having regard to his age and understanding' is binding on both court and Trust in relation to any decision. The significance attached to this requirement was apparent in *In Re B (Minor) (Adoption: Parental Agreement)*[27] where the court's decision to dispense with the need for parental agreement was significantly influenced by the wishes of the eleven-year-old subject.

In matrimonial proceedings the checklist considerations as stated in Article 3(3) of the 1995 Order now apply to any disputes concerning the parties' proposed care arrangements for their children. Such is the significance attached to the requirement to seek the views of the children concerned that it has been held[28] that a failure to do so ought to be a ground of appeal.

The case law of the wardship jurisdiction reveals a consistent judicial concern to establish a direct relationship with the children who come before the court. In recent years this has been accompanied by a judicial willingness to solicit and give more weight to their opinions.

II. The Duty to Defer to the Views of the Child

The fact that in private family proceedings the duty upon others in relation to the views of a child is at its weakest is balanced by the powerful right of a child in such proceedings to assert his or her views at the expense of others. After all, the decision in *Gillick* resulted from private family proceedings and remains the leading case and reference point for a developing body of jurisprudence on the autonomous legal interests of children and the weighting of such interests relative to those of parents and others. It is private family proceedings which have since witnessed the emergence of such child 'rights' as to sue for damage caused while a foetus, to 'divorce' parents, to have access to parents and to have access to information on pre-adoption family background. This is in keeping with the general philosophy underpinning the 1995 Order that state intrusion in family matters should be minimised while the capacity of family members to assert their autonomous legal interests should be facilitated.

---

27   [1990] 2 FLR 383.
28   See *M v M (Minor: Custody Appeal)* [1987] 1 WLR 404.

However, it is possible that the decision in *Re B*[29] indicates a firming-up of the judicial approach towards children's 'rights': where a child's wishes are in conflict with rights traditionally regarded as hallmarks of parental status (the right to determine religious upbringing, surname etc.), they may not prevail.

The Duties of the Court

(a) In Relation to Leave to Apply for Article 8 Orders

Under Article 10 of the 1995 Order:

> (8) Where the person applying for leave to make an application for an Article 8 order is the child concerned, the court may only grant leave if it is satisfied that he has sufficient understanding to make the proposed application for the Article 8 order.

This would seem to imply that where the condition is satisfied the court is then virtually required to grant the leave sought.

(b) In Relation to Contact Arrangements

Ever since the decision in *M v M (Child: Access)*[30] the courts will defer to the views of a child, where these are judged to be compatible with his or her welfare interests, when faced with a conflict between such views and those of a parent in respect of contact arrangements.

(c) In Relation to Applications for the Termination of Guardianship Appointments

Under Article 163(1) the court may, at any time, order the termination of an appointment of a guardian made under Articles 159 or 160:

> (b) on the application of the child concerned, with leave of the court.

Again, the court is required to treat the application on its merits and will be obliged to accede to the child's wishes if satisfied that to do so would be in keeping with his or her welfare interests.

(d) In Relation to Assessments

In private law cases the assessment of a *Gillick* competent child is dependent upon the prior consent of that child. However, his or her right to refuse might depend upon mental competence.[31] This may also be overridden by the court if the latter should be of the opinion that an examination is in his or her best interests.[32]

---

29 See f/n 26.
30 [1973] 2 All ER 81.
31 See *R v Waltham Forest London Borough ex parte G* [1989] 2 FLR 138.
32 See *Re W (A Minor) (Consent to Medical Treatment)* [1993] 1 FLR 1.

CHAPTER NINETEEN

Representing the Views and Legal Interests of the Child

Introduction

Audi alteram partem — the right of a person directly affected by the outcome to put their case to the court — is a right of natural justice which has long been denied to children. Instead, a person below the age of eighteen has been construed as *sui juris*,[1] their legal interests subsumed within those of a parent or guardian. The latter would therefore be the party named in family proceedings to represent the interests of a child. Where it was considered appropriate by the court (most usually in wardship proceedings) the Official Solicitor might be invited to 'speak for the child'. Occasionally, such a duty might have been statutorily assigned to a guardian ad litem (for example, in adoption proceedings) or to a Trust social worker (in matrimonial proceedings). Neither court nor legislation required a child's wishes or independent legal interests to be brought before a judge. The duty of official intermediaries was to provide factual information and advice as to what, in the presenting circumstances, they considered to be a child's best interests. Their views were often at variance with the wishes of the child concerned.

In this jurisdiction it was the *Black Report*[2] which drew attention to the need for separate representation for a child. The Black Committee considered 'it essential that a child should be adequately represented in legal proceedings'. The committee advised that this should be provided 'in any case where there could be a conflict between the interests of a child and that of his parent or guardian'. It 'examined closely the arguments for the appointment of child advocates, in addition to, or instead of, guardians ad litem . . . that the child should be represented in legal proceedings by either a lawyer or a social worker . . . the merits of setting up a separate Office of Child Advocate, or an extension of the duties of the Official Solicitor in juvenile proceedings'. The committee concluded by recommending 'that a guardian ad litem be appointed by the court in every case where there is any doubt as to whether the interests of the child are being adequately protected, and a child should have the right to separate legal representation'.[3]

---

1 Beneath the law.
2 The Black Committee, *Report of the Children and Young Persons Review Group*, Belfast: HMSO, 1979.
3 Ibid at paras 4.6 and 4.7.

This chapter examines the extent to which the Children (NI) Order 1995 finally fulfils the promise of the *Black Report*. The previous chapter having considered when, where and to what effect a child's views may now be taken into account in decisions affecting his or her welfare, this one deals with how and by whom such views are to be represented. It identifies the range of professionals to whom a child may look for representation and the circumstances in which it would be both possible and appropriate for a child to rely on self-representation.

The Law, Jurisdiction of the Courts and the Child as a Party

The Children (NI) Order 1995 now provides the means whereby a child's own views may form part of the decision-making process in court and agency proceedings where public or private matters concerning his or her welfare are being determined. Moreover, by making the appointment of a child as a party possible in some proceedings and mandatory in others, this legislation has provided a mechanism for giving effective weighting to those views and has thereby made what may prove to be its single most important change to the law relating to the interests of children.

The Law

1. Civil Proceedings Excluding Family Proceedings Commenced under the Children (NI) Order 1995

Capacity to engage in civil litigation has always been governed by a competency test. Certain 'categories' of persons were deemed to be inherently non-competent and thus lacking the legal capacity necessary to initiate proceedings, to be a full party to proceedings initiated by others or to give evidence as competent witnesses. Children constituted such a class of non-competent persons. In common with all other such classes, therefore, the rule has been that children must be represented by an adult when their interests need to be spoken for in civil proceedings. Where a child's participation was as applicant or plaintiff, then his or her interests would be represented by a 'next friend'. Where that participation was as defendant or respondent, then representation would be by a guardian ad litem. Except to the extent to which this rule has now been amended by the 1995 Order and the Family Proceedings Rules, it continues to govern representation of children in civil proceedings.

(a) A Next Friend

(i) Who May So Act

Any person within the jurisdiction[4] with capacity[5] who is neither the defendant[6] nor a friend of the defendant[7] nor in anyway connected with the defendant, nor otherwise

---

4 See *Jones v Lloyd* (1874) LR 18 Eq 265.
5 See *Re Duke of Somerset, Thynne v St Maur* (1877) 34 Ch D 465.
6 See *Lewis v Nobbs* (1878) 8 Ch D 591, 593.
7 See *Re Burgess, Burgess v Bottomley* (1883) 25 Ch D 243 CA.

having any interest in the proceedings adverse to the minor's interests,[8] may act as the 'next friend' of an infant plaintiff or applicant.[9]

Preference is given to a parent, though a guardian, testamentary guardian or the Official Solicitor may so act. A person acting in the capacity of a 'next friend' should be a person of substance and a relative or someone with tangible connections with the family. If actively providing assistance during the course of proceedings, such a person is sometimes referred to as a '*McKenzie* man'.[10]

Otherwise a 'next friend' can only actively intervene in proceedings by instructing a solicitor.

(ii) Duties of a Next Friend

A next friend is an officer of the court appointed to safeguard the interests of the minor[11] with responsibility for the conduct of proceedings but without being a party[12] nor being entitled to appear in person.

(iii) Removal/Replacement of a Next Friend

Where a parent, acting as a 'next friend', is doing so improperly or in such a way as to damage the interests of the child,[13] then the court may remove that parent and appoint instead a more suitable 'next friend' or a GAL. For example, a 'next friend' will be removed if he improperly refuses to continue the proceedings.[14] However, if the actions of a 'next friend' cannot be construed as detrimental to the interests of a minor, as where parents refused to accept a class settlement for children affected by the drug thalidomide,[15] then the court will not order his or her removal. An application for such a removal may be made, with leave, by the child concerned where he or she wishes to conduct the remaining stages of the proceedings by means of self-representation.

(b) A Guardian ad Litem (GAL)

The appointment of a GAL has in the past been associated with adoption proceedings and is now also associated with care proceedings commenced under the 1995 Order. However, this official status has a long history, and appointments have never been confined to such matters. The person appointed must have no interest in the proceedings which could be adverse to those of the minor.[16] Preference will be given to a person of substance who is not already a party and who is a relative of the child or a friend of the family. A minor may engage a GAL to defend his or her interests in any family

---

8   See *Jacob v Lucas* (1839) 1 Beav 436.
9   See *Whittaker v Marlar* (1786) 1 Cox EEq Cas 285 at 286; *Harrison v Harrison* (1842) 5 Beav 130.
10 See *McKenzie v McKenzie* [1971] P 33, [1970] 3 All ER 1034, CA where the plaintiff was accompanied by a learned 'friend' who assisted in presenting the case by taking notes and giving advice.
11 See *Morgan v Thorne* (1841) 7 M&W 400.
12 See *Sinclair v Sinclair* (1845) 13 M&W 640.
13 See *Gee v Gee* (1863) 12 WR 187.
14 See *Ward v Ward* (1863) 3 Mer 706.
15 See *Re Taylor's Application* [1972] 2 QB 369, [1972] 2 All ER 873 CA.
16 See *Smith v Palmer* (1840) 3 Beav 10.

proceedings (except where the court rules provide otherwise) and that appointment need not be made by the court. In such an instance, the GAL is not appointed from the GAL panel. The Official Solicitor may be appointed to act in this capacity but only with his or her prior agreement. A GAL can only act through a solicitor.

2. Family Proceedings Commenced under the Children (NI) Order 1995

The *audi alteram partem* principle, which found authoritative recognition in Article 12 of the UN Convention,[17] has now been incorporated into the civil law of this jurisdiction. The statutory authority for the appointment of professional representation on behalf of a child in family proceedings is now governed by the Children (NI) Order 1995, which disapplies the 'next friend' rule. Article 60 provides for the representation of a child by the appointment of a guardian ad litem and a solicitor in public law proceedings, while the Family Proceedings Rules makes provision for a solicitor to do so in private proceedings. Unlike the situation which prevailed under the 1968 Act, a solicitor will no longer take instruction on matters concerning the welfare of a child from that child's parents acting in their capacity as 'next friend'. The SACHR has acknowledged the significance of this legislative change by recording its support for the provisions in the 1995 Order which promote the child's own views and reflect the Article 12 principle.

Jurisdiction

Family proceedings, the only proceedings in which a child may hold full party status, must be commenced in the magistrates' courts (subject to the guidance given below by the President of the Family Division) but thereafter may be transferred to and concluded in any court. Civil proceedings, other than family proceedings, will be commenced in the court designated as being appropriate to the level of the action.

1. The High Court

The interests of a child may be represented in civil proceedings, other than family proceedings, in the High Court only through the offices of an adult acting on the child's

---

17   Article 12:

   1. States Parties shall assure to the child who is capable of forming his or her own views the right to express those views freely in all matters affecting the child, the views of the child being given due weight in accordance with the age and maturity of the child.
   2. For this purpose, the child shall in particular be provided the opportunity to be heard in any judicial and administrative proceedings affecting the child, either directly, or through a representative or an appropriate body, in a manner consistent with the procedural rules of national law.

   In their recent audit of the implementation of the Convention in the UK, the UN Committee on the Rights of Children recommended that 'greater priority be given to incorporating the general principles of the Convention especially the provisions of . . . Article 12 concerning the child's right to make their views known and have those views given due weight, in legislative and administrative measures and in policies undertaken to implement the rights of the Child'. (CRC/C/15Add.34 Feb 1995)

behalf. If acting as a plaintiff or applicant in proceedings, that adult representative will be serving as a 'next friend'. If acting as defendant or respondent, the adult will be serving as a guardian ad litem. Any financial benefit to the child resulting from the proceedings must be paid into the court and may only be paid out as directed by the court.

The interests of a child in proceedings conducted under the amendments introduced by the Family Proceedings Rules may be represented by a solicitor instructed by that child. In *Re AD (A Minor)*[18] Sir Stephen Brown, the President of the Family Division, advised that any application by a child to initiate proceedings under the 1989 Act should be made in the High Court or, if made elsewhere, should be promptly transferred to the High Court.[19]

2. The County Court

The county court is and will continue to be the court of first recourse in divorce proceedings and will therefore be the court where most judicial decisions affecting the welfare interests of children are made. The Family Proceedings Rules now permit children to prosecute or defend any family proceedings (other than 'specified' proceedings) by retaining a solicitor rather than, as in all other civil proceedings, having to do so by way of a 'next friend' or GAL. If the child has not already retained a solicitor, then he or she will have to either convince a solicitor of his or her ability to give instructions or obtain leave of the court. Any monies recovered for the benefit of a child as a result of proceedings must be paid into court and will only be paid out as directed by the court.

3. The Magistrates' Court

The only form of civil proceedings heard in a magistrates' court to which a child may be made a party are family proceedings commenced under the Children (NI) Order 1995. In 'specified' proceedings this is automatic and mandatory; otherwise it is permissible only in circumstances where the child is the applicant and with leave of the court.

4. The Duty of the Court

The court has a duty under Article 60 of the 1995 Order to appoint a GAL to represent a child in specified family proceedings. Where, in such proceedings, a solicitor has not been retained to represent a child and the court considers such an appointment to be necessary, then, subject to the conditions specified in Article 60, it may make the appointment. Invariably, when a GAL is appointed it then falls to that GAL to appoint the solicitor (under the Rules).

The Child

The United Nations Convention on the Rights of the Child has, in recent years, provided an inescapable reference point for Westminster legislators drafting provisions relating

---

18 [1993] Fam Law 43.
19 See *Practice Direction, Children Act 1989 — Applications by Children* [1993] 1 FLR 668.

to the treatment of a child in court. For example, Article 5 gives recognition to the evolving capacities of the child,[20] while Article 8 acknowledges a child's right to an identity. The issue of the Draft Convention on Children's Rights by the Council of Europe in November 1994 serves to indicate the likely future importance of influence from this quarter.

1. Child as a Party

In any public law proceedings, the child concerned (in addition to the Trust, parents, any other person with parental responsibility and such other persons as may be granted leave by the court to be joined) will by right automatically have full party status. In private law proceedings a child will not have party status by right but may, with leave of the court, acquire it.

2. Child's Right to Representation

Full party status, in public law proceedings, brings with it a right to attend court, to be represented in court by a panel GAL and to appeal from the decision of the court (Article 166). It also entitles the court to compel the attendance of a child where necessary. In private law proceedings, even where a child acquires party status, representation by a panel GAL is not possible; the child is dependent upon the court inviting the Official Solicitor to act on the child's behalf.

Representation, properly understood, can only be provided by a solicitor acting on and abiding by instructions from their client whether or not in agreement with them. A child with 'sufficient understanding' is entitled to retain and instruct a solicitor to act as his or her representative in any family proceedings, with leave of the court in some circumstances. Where a child is not of 'sufficient understanding' or chooses not to instruct a solicitor, then the court will require that a GAL or Trust social worker be appointed as a 'court officer' to advise it on matters relating to the child's best interests.

The child will rarely control the representation being provided for him or her, though in private proceedings he or she is more likely to do so. Allowing or expecting a child to exercise such control, or even to attend the proceedings, may, in some circumstances, amount to 'secondary abuse' of that child; in public proceedings, there is a discretion available to the court, under Article 167(1) of the 1995 Order, to waive the necessity for a child's attendance, even where the child is a party.

3. The 'Sufficient Understanding' Test

The leave of the court for a child to apply for an Article 8 order, the retaining of a solicitor by a child and the right of a child to participate in proceedings without a next friend

---

20 Article 5:

> States Parties shall respect the responsibilities, rights and duties of parents or, where applicable, the members of the extended family or community as provided for by local custom, legal guardians or other persons legally responsible for the child, to provide, in a manner consistent with the evolving capacities of the child, appropriate direction and guidance in the exercise by the child of the rights recognised in the present Convention.

or GAL are each dependent upon the statutory requirement (Article 10(8), Article 60(4)(b) and Rule 12(3),[21] respectively) that the child concerned first satisfies the 'sufficient understanding' test. There have, in recent years, been a number of important judicial decisions which offer some measures for determining when a child's understanding may be construed as 'sufficient'.

(a) Age and Maturity of Child
In considering whether a child is competent to instruct a solicitor, much will depend on the age and maturity of the child concerned.[22]

(b) Understanding Relative to the Issues
A crucial point was made by Sir Thomas Bingham in *Re S and B (Minors)(Child Abuse: Evidence)*[23] when he observed that understanding 'has to be assessed relative to the issues in the case'. This is an approach he later returned to in a case[24] where the Court of Appeal considered whether an eleven-year-old boy should be granted leave to apply for the removal of the Official Solicitor appointed to represent his interests in a bitter dispute between parents who each sought a residence order in respect of him. In ruling that leave should not be granted, Bingham MR reasoned that the child did not have the maturity to sufficiently understand the complex emotional context of the dispute and thus would be unable to undertake the role of a party in the proceedings. Two years later Johnson J took the view that the child had attained sufficient maturity to instruct his own legal representative and, dismissing the Official Solicitor, gave the child permission to leave the jurisdiction and live with his father.[25] Again, in *Re K, W, and H (Minors)(Medical Treatment)*[26] the Court of Appeal was unconvinced that children had the capacity to give independent instructions.

(c) Understanding and Emotional Disturbance
The fact that a child is emotionally disturbed will necessarily affect that child's capacity to instruct a solicitor.[27] The judgment as to whether the emotional disturbance is affecting rationality to the extent that a capacity to issue valid instructions is impaired is one for a doctor to make.

---

21 The Magistrates' Courts (Children (NI) Order 1995) Rules (NI) 1996.
22 In *Re T (A Minor)(Wardship: Representation)*, The Times, May 10, 1993, the court upheld the right of a thirteen-year-old girl to instruct a solicitor. In *Re S (A Minor) (Independent Representation)* [1993] 2 FLR 437 the court denied the same right to an eleven-year-old boy (see also Chapter Fifteen).
23 [1990] 2 FLR 489, 444 H.
24 See f/n 22, *Re S (A Minor)*.
25 Note that the judge's view, as expressed in *Re C (A Minor)(Leave to seek Section 8 Orders)* [1994] 1 FLR 26, to the effect that the issue of self-representation by a child should be governed by the paramountcy principle, has not been followed by subsequent cases.
26 [1993] 1 FLR 854.
27 This was the view of the court in *Re H (A Minor)(Care Proceedings: Child's Wishes)* [1993] 1 FLR 440 where Thorpe J ruled that a child must be rational as well as having 'sufficient understanding'.

4. The Effect of a Judgment Made against a Child

The effect of a judgment made against a child will be exactly the same as one made against an adult.[28] However, if that judgment was made in the mistaken belief that the plaintiff was an adult, then it may be set aside.[29] Again, it will also be set aside in the event of the plaintiff having signed the judgment without having first applied for a GAL to be appointed.[30]

An injunction may be granted against a minor[31] but not an order for specific performance.[32] However, as the Court of Appeal ruled in *Re Section (A Minor)*[33] an injunction can only be enforced by committal to prison, by sequestration of property or by fine. No power exists to commit a minor under the age of seventeen to prison; it would be unrealistic to order sequestration of property; and a minor would be unable to pay a fine. Injunctions against minors are therefore unenforceable and inappropriate.

5. Costs Awarded against a Child

The court may order costs to be paid by an infant defendant.[34] This is most likely in situations where the child has been found guilty of fraud or has been cited as a respondent or co-respondent in divorce proceedings.

Representation

1. The Evidence of Children

The evidence of children is governed mainly by the Children's Evidence (NI) Order 1995, Articles 168–171 of the Children (NI) Order 1995, the Criminal Justice (Evidence, Etc.)(NI) Order 1988 and the Rules.

1. Evidence Given by Children

The principle of the welfare of the child has, in recent years, been brought to bear on the manner in which the court treats children appearing before it as witnesses, particularly where such a child is giving evidence as the victim of alleged abuse.

(a) Evidence on Oath

The 'competency test' has traditionally had a particular relevance to the standing of evidence given by children. In order to impress upon a witness the solemnity of his or her duty to be truthful, the general rule has always been that the court will require that person to swear an oath before giving testimony. Persons presumed non-competent, such as young children and the mentally impaired, were considered incapable of

---

28   See *Henry v Archibald* (1871) 5 IR Eq 559.
29   See *Furnival v Brooke* (1883) 49 LT 134.
30   See *Leaver v Torres* (1899) 43 Sol Jo 778; *Stanga v Stanga* [1954] 2 All ER 16.
31   See *Lempriere v Lange* (1879) 12 Ch D 675.
32   See *Lumley v Ravenscroft* [1895] 1 QB 683 CA.
33   [1991] FCR 811.
34   See *Woolf v Woolf* [1899] 1 Ch 343; but also see *Elsey v Cox* (1858) 26 Beav 95.

swearing a valid oath and thus could not bear witness in a court of law. The legal presumption has been that children aged fourteen years or more are competent to give evidence on oath while those of a younger age are not. Evidence to be given by a child under the age of fourteen would be considered as hearsay and thus be normally inadmissible. However, the courts have long recognised that some children under the age of fourteen have the maturity and understanding to provide credible evidence but not to fully comprehend the significance of an oath. Rather than nullify the evidence of such children under the hearsay rule, the legislature has instead introduced measures to provide for the admissibility of the unsworn evidence of children. These legislative exceptions to the hearsay rule only apply in relation to a child under the age of fourteen who is judged not competent to swear an oath.[35]

(b) Unsworn Evidence

(i) Criminal Proceedings

Article 3 of the Children's Evidence (NI) Order 1995 removes section 57 of the Children and Young Persons Act (NI) 1968 and amends section 58 by inserting section 58A:

> (1) A child's evidence in criminal proceedings shall be unsworn.
>
> (2) A deposition of a child's unsworn evidence may be taken for the purposes of criminal proceedings as if that evidence had been given on oath.
>
> (3) A child's evidence shall be received unless it appears to the court that the child is incapable of giving intelligible testimony.

(ii) Civil Proceedings

Under Article 169 of the 1995 Order, in civil proceedings, where the court is of the opinion that the child does not understand the nature of an oath, then the court may dispense with the necessity to administer it and instead:

> (4) The child's evidence may be heard by the court if, in its opinion —
> (a) he understands that it is his duty to speak the truth; and
> (b) he has sufficient understanding to justify his evidence being heard.

These provisions bring civil proceedings into line with criminal proceedings.

(iii) Children's Evidence and the Hearsay Rule

Under Article 169(5)–(8) of the Children (NI) Order 1995 the Lord Chancellor is given authority to make orders to provide for 'the admissibility of evidence which would otherwise be inadmissible under any rule of hearsay'. The Children (Admissibility of Hearsay Evidence) Order (NI) 1996 has been enacted in pursuance of that provision. This legislation disapplies the hearsay rule in relation to any evidence given in connection with the upbringing, maintenance or welfare of a child in civil proceedings heard in the High Court, county court or in family proceedings heard in the magistrates' courts.

---

35 See *R v Hayes* [1977] 1 WLR 234.

In *R(J) v Oxfordshire County Council*[36] the court considered the effect of equivalent legislation and held that it permitted hearsay evidence to be admitted in all proceedings instituted under the Children Act 1989 including proceedings for secure accommodation and child assessment orders. In this jurisdiction the hearsay rule was the subject of judicial consideration in *Northern Health and Social Services Board v YB (A Minor)*,[37] heard in the wardship jurisdiction (see Chapter Seven).

(d) The Weighting of Hearsay Evidence

Judicial discretion is the sole determinant of the weighting given to the hearsay evidence of a child. Where the evidence is considered too remote, the court may decide to completely ignore it.[38]

Article 13 of the Police and Criminal Evidence (NI) Order 1988 abolished the requirement of corroboration for the unsworn evidence of children. The common-law rule requiring the judge to warn a jury about the dangers of finding a defendant guilty on the basis of the uncorroborated evidence of a child has thus been removed except where the offence alleged is one of sexual abuse. The unsworn evidence of a child will now be sufficient to secure a conviction or to corroborate the unsworn evidence of another child.

(e) Children's Evidence: The Use of Video Technology

In this jurisdiction, the appropriateness of video technology in child sexual abuse cases arose for consideration in a preliminary hearing prior to the substantive hearing of *In Re PB (A Minor)*[39] before the late Higgins J. The case concerned a four-year-old girl who had been made a ward of court by the NHSSB which then requested that care and control be given to that body and not to the respondent, the child's mother. The contention of the NHSSB was that the child had been sexually abused by an adult male or males in the child's family and that the child would be in physical and moral danger if permitted to reside with the respondent. The child had been interviewed by a doctor and the interview had been video recorded. The NHSSB intended to rely at the substantive hearing on the evidence of the doctor and on the video recording to prove what the child had said and done during the interview. The respondent objected to such evidence being given by the doctor and to the video recording being shown on the ground that it offended against the hearsay rule and therefore was not admissible. At the preliminary hearing, Higgins J[40] ruled that although evidence by the doctor of what the child said during the interview offended against the hearsay rule, the court had discretion to admit such evidence because: (i) in wardship proceedings the first and paramount purpose is the welfare of the child; (ii) it was almost the only evidence available for the purpose of proving the alleged sexual abuse. He held that the court

---

36 [1992] 3 All ER 660.
37 Unreported (1986).
38 See *Re W (Minors)(Wardship: Evidence)* [1990] 1 FLR 203; *R v B County Council ex parte P* [1991] 1 FLR 470.
39 Unreported (1986).
40 Ibid.

should hear the doctor's evidence and that, since it was as much in the respondent's interests as the NHSSB's, the court should see and hear the video recording.

This was followed by *R v Brown*[41] where the appellant had been convicted on a charge of rape against a fifteen-year-old girl. The evidence of the injured party had been presented to the court by way of a 'live' TV link, pursuant to Article 81(1)(b)(i) of the Police and Criminal Evidence (NI) Order 1989, on the grounds that the witness would not otherwise give evidence through fear. The appellant averred that the evidence adduced in support of the injured party had been hearsay. The court held that the evidence in question was not hearsay (see also Rule 44B of the Crown Court (Amendment No 2) Rules (NI) 1989).

The Pigot Committee,[42] in addition to recommending the abolition of the exception to the corroboration rule relating to sexual abuse cases, also advocated the use of closed-circuit television technology as a means of reducing stress for children giving evidence in abuse cases. The latter recommendation finally found statutory endorsement in this jurisdiction with the introduction of the Children's Evidence (NI) Order 1995. Article 5 of that Order inserted Article 81A, 'Video recordings of testimony from child witnesses', after Article 81 in the Police and Criminal Evidence (NI) Order 1988. The further insertion of Article 81B prohibits the cross-examination of a child victim or witness in an abuse case in most circumstances.

Most recently, in England the decision of the Court of Appeal in *Re N (Child Abuse: Evidence)*[43] serves as a reminder that evidence from a videotaped interview will have to comply with certain quality standards if the court is to accept that it meets the standard of proof required in sexual abuse cases. The Court of Appeal ruled that the judge at first instance should have reminded himself that the video recording was a form of hearsay evidence and treated the videotape as unreliable evidence because the child was in the presence of a parent and exposed to leading questions. It further ruled that the GAL had strayed beyond his area of expertise when giving evidence.

2. The Evidence of Others in Relation to Children and the Self-Incrimination Rule

Under Article 171 of the 1995 Order:

> (1) In any proceedings in which a court is hearing an application for an order under Part V or VI, no person shall be excused from
>
> > (a) giving evidence on any matter; or
> > (b) answering any question put to him in the course of his giving evidence, on the ground that doing so might incriminate him or his spouse of an offence.

This provision disapplies the privilege against self-incrimination from emergency proceedings and also from proceedings concerning care and supervision orders. In return for giving evidence which would otherwise have been incriminating, the person

---

41   [1991] NI 290.
42   See *Report of the Advisory Group on Video Evidence,* Home Office, 1989.
43   [1996] 2 FLR 2.

concerned shall be excused by the court from the consequences of any admission or incriminating statement made, except where the offence disclosed is one of perjury. This exemption may be of considerable significance in care proceedings grounded on allegations of child abuse.[44]

3. Evidence Given by Expert Witnesses Following Examination of Children

As stated in the Rules:[45]

> (1) No person may, without leave of the court, cause the child to be medically or psychiatrically examined, or otherwise assessed, for the purpose of the preparation of expert evidence for use in the proceedings.

Any application for leave under paragraph (1) must be served, unless the court directs otherwise, on all parties and on the GAL. Where such leave has not been obtained, then any evidence gained from an examination or assessment is inadmissible without permission of the court. The problems which arise in relation to the evidence of children resulting from disclosures made to professionals have been apparent in a number of cases.

II. *The Role of the Professionals*

There is no tradition in this jurisdiction of professionals initiating actions on behalf of children's 'rights'. There has never been any equivalent to the Children's Legal Centre which has long been established elsewhere in the United Kingdom. No advocacy services exist for children, and the lobbying from some voluntary bodies for the creation of a Children's Commissioner has, so far, had little effect[46] (though, as of autumn 1996, it seemed probable that funding for a commissioner would be made available). The absence of a collective and strategic professional initiative to assert and develop the 'rights' of children should not, however, deflect from an acknowledgement of the more pervasive role played by professional representatives on behalf of children's interests in this region of the United Kingdom. The professional contribution to judicial decisions affecting the welfare of children in private family law proceedings has for many years been provided more comprehensively in Northern Ireland than on the other side of the Irish Sea.

---

44 See *Rochdale Borough Council v A and Others* [1991] 2 FLR 192; *Re A and Others (Minors)(Child Abuse: Guidelines)* [1992] 1 FLR 439; and *Cleveland CC v F* [1995] 2 All ER 236. Also, see Spencer and Flin, *The Evidence of Children*, 2nd ed, London: Blackstone, 1993.
45 Rule 19 of the Magistrates' Courts (Children (NI) Order 1995) Rules (NI) 1996; Rule 4.19 of the Family Proceedings Rules (NI) 1996.
46 The Children's Rights Development Unit (CRDO) was established in the United Kingdom in 1992 to promote implementation of the UN Convention on the Rights of the Child; an office was maintained in Belfast. The CRDU ceased to function in 1995 but its work is continued through the Office to Establish a Children's Rights Commissioner which has a representative in Northern Ireland. However, NIACRO have for some years maintained an independent representation scheme for children detained in secure accommodation. This is dependent upon the goodwill of the training school management; the volunteers have no statutory right of access.

1. The Official Solicitor

The appointment and duties of the Official Solicitor are governed by section 75(2) of the Judicature (NI) Act 1978.

(a) Appointment of the Official Solicitor

Traditionally, the appointment of the Official Solicitor has been associated with wardship, adoption and occasional child-care proceedings where he or she would undertake the role of guardian ad litem or, subsequently, be assigned responsibility to act as guardian of the child's estate. In Northern Ireland this involvement in such proceedings has been usual in cases involving a clear conflict of interests between the child and another party, an international dimension or some complex legal issue such as arises from time to time in the legal/medical field. The significance of this involvement is apparent from the fact that in autumn 1996 the Official Solicitor had a caseload of 337 including 145 wards of court. Henceforth this role will be considerably restricted in public proceedings both because of the virtual disappearance of wardship in that context and because of displacement by the GAL of responsibilities which previously fell to the Official Solicitor. However, as the GAL panel will not be available to the court in private proceedings, the Official Solicitor may on occasion be invited to fill the gap, and he or she will also continue to have a role in wardship as this continues to be a growth area in private family law. When, in exceptional circumstances, the Official Solicitor is appointed to act in proceedings instigated under the 1995 Order or in wardship and heard in the High Court, then he or she will act as both solicitor and as GAL.

(b) Duties of the Official Solicitor

The Official Solicitor has been described as

> ... much more than a mere guardian ad litem. He is at once *amicus curiae*, independent solicitor acting for the children, investigator, advisor and sometimes supervisor.[47]

He or she has a duty to communicate a child's wishes to the court but is not obliged to follow 'instructions' if these do not coincide with what he or she believes to be in the child's best interests. This role is, therefore, a hybrid one.[48] On the one hand he or she is obliged to 'give the child a voice in proceedings' by representing the child's views, defending his or her legal interests, instructing specialist consultants, or negotiating with overseas officials and generally acting as a solicitor to the client: the child. On the other hand, as an officer of the court the primary duty is directed towards discovering and then representing to the court what he or she conceives to be the child's

---

47 See *Re G* [1982] 1 WLR 438.
48 See *Re T (Child: Representation)* [1993] 3 WLR 602 where Waite LJ said of the Official Solicitor: 'He owes a loyalty which has by its very nature to be divided: to the child whose views he must fully and fairly represent; and to the court, which it is his duty to assist in achieving the overriding or paramount objective of promoting the child's best interests.'

best interests, which may conflict with the child's wishes.[49] He or she may consent to be appointed as GAL to defend the interests of a minor with a disability. A solicitor may ask the court to invite the Official Solicitor to act, or in adoption proceedings involving an alleged illegal placement, he or she may be appointed by the High Court[50] and he or she may be dismissed by the appointment of a solicitor.[51] The ultimate decision is for the court, which may override the child's wishes.[52]

2. The Guardian ad Litem

The GAL, as a court official, is appointed in specified proceedings, usually child-care cases but also, most notably, in adoption proceedings (see respectively Chapters Fourteen and Six). His or her primary responsibilities include a duty to communicate a child's wishes to the court, to advise the court as to what he or she considers are in the child's best interests, to carry out an independent investigation, examine all options available to the courts and to appoint a solicitor to represent the child as a client. He or she also has the duty to advise the court on the appropriate form for the proceedings and the appropriate timing of proceedings or any part of them. Where there is conflict between the views of the child and those of the GAL, the latter may present his or her separate views personally or through a solicitor and thereby continue to assist the court. The child may, however, choose to dismiss the GAL and prosecute or defend the remainder of the proceedings by directly instructing the solicitor.[53] For operational aspects of the role of a GAL, see further below.

3. The Solicitor

Under the 1995 Order, the court of its own motion may appoint a solicitor to represent a child in any private proceedings or in any public proceedings where a GAL has not been appointed, the child is of sufficient understanding and if such an appointment is in the child's best interests. A solicitor may be retained by and take instructions from a child whenever, in 'specified proceedings', the child has 'sufficient understanding' or in private proceedings has such understanding and chooses to make that appointment. A solicitor will take instructions from the GAL only when the child is not sufficiently mature to directly instruct or the mature child's views do not conflict with the views of the GAL. A preliminary interview will be necessary to establish 'sufficient understanding' on the basis of whether the child fully comprehends the nature of the proceedings and appreciates the likely long- and short-term consequences of the proceedings.[54] Where a child instructs a solicitor (which may occur either in specified

---

49   See *L v L (Children: Separate Representation)* [1994] 1 FLR 890, 893.
50   See *Practice Direction* [1986] 2 All ER 832.
51   See *Re H (A Minor)(Role of Official Solicitor)* [1993] 2 FLR 552.
52   See *Re CT (A Minor)(Wardship: Representation)* [1993] 2 FLR 278.
53   As in *Re H* in f/n 51.
54   In this context the guidance of the Official Solicitor to his staff on the procedure to be followed is helpful:
    The advice runs along these lines. Whatever the age of the child, if at any time the child asks about having his own solicitor the case worker is instructed always to explain

proceedings when the wishes of a mature child conflict with those of the GAL or in private proceedings where no GAL involvement is necessary), then such instructions must be followed even if they conflict with the solicitor's views.[55] However, as in any other case, the solicitor must remember his or her duty to the Legal Aid Board in respect of unreasonable instructions.

As the true representative of the child and advocate of the latter's wishes, the solicitor must ensure that proceedings are at the child's pace and must give the child space and permission to express his or her views. The responsibility to equip the child with sufficient information to make an informed decision falls on the solicitor. As with any other client, the solicitor is under a general duty of disclosure to a child in respect of documentary evidence held by the solicitor in preparation for the case; but discretion is called for in the manner in which this is done.[56]

4. Expert Witnesses

The role of an expert witness is to provide the court with specialist information and, where appropriate, with a considered opinion on matters which lie within the witness's area of specialist expertise. It has been said that expert witnesses should only express opinions genuinely held and which are not biased towards one party or the other.[57] Considerable judicial dissatisfation has been expressed regardng the use of expert witnesses in proceedings instigated under the 1989 Act.[58]

---

what may be done — unless the child clearly has no idea what he is talking about! At the first interview if the child is obviously competent (typically a sensible sixteen-year-old) the case worker explains that if the child takes a different view from the Official Solicitor he has the right to ask the court to let him have another solicitor. In all other cases, the case worker waits to see whether the child raises the question, but throughout the interview the case worker must be forming his own assessment of the child's competence in the light of the issues. At the end of the interview, if the child has not asked about a solicitor, provided the case worker thinks that the child has an understanding of the issues and may have the capacity to take a full part in the proceedings, the case worker will offer a brief explanation of the child's right to ask the court to allow him to have his own solicitor . . . . The next step, once the assessment of the child's capacity has been made, is to ascertain the child's perception of priorities, and following that the weight to be given to the views of the child (See P Harris, the Official Solicitor, *Representing Children*, vol. 8, no 2, 1995.)

55 The Family Proceedings Rules (NI) 1996, Rule 4.13(1)(a). See *Re M (Minors) (Care Proceedings: Child's Wishes)* [1994] 1 FLR 749.
56 See M I'Anson, *Guide to Good Practice*, SFLA, PO Box 302, Orpington BR6 8QX, DX 86853 Locksbottom.
57 See *Re R (A Minor) (Expert's Evidence)(Note)* [1991] 1 FLR 291 per Cazalet J.
58 See Dame Margaret Booth, *Avoiding Delay in Children Act Cases*, (1996) a report to the Lord Chancellor which recorded that: eighty per cent of courts thought that more expert reports were requested than were actually of use; issues should be more clearly defined before an expert was instructed and one party should take responsibility for providing the papers to experts; instructing an expert should be discussed at an early directions hearing, having first clearly established the issues upon which expert evidence was needed; clear, prompt, precise instruction should be sent to an expert whose availability had been previously checked; and the lawyers concerned need to co-ordinate on issuing instructions without delay (as reported in *Family Law*, October 1995, vol. 26, p. 644).

The contribution of an expert witness is confined to illuminating the court's understanding of complex factors and cannot be permitted to usurp the court's responsibility to determine the weighting to be given to such factors when deciding the matters at issue.[59] Psychiatric evidence, for example, is admissible to determine the child's propensity to fantasise or invent, to assess his or her current psychiatric state and to establish the credibility of a child's account of his or her previous history.

(a) Confidentiality of Documents

As stated in the Rules:[60]

> ... no document, other than a record of an order, held by the court and relating to relevant proceedings shall be disclosed, other than to —
> (a) a party,
> (b) the legal representative of a party,
> (c) the guardian ad litem,
> (d) the Legal Aid Department, or
> (e) a welfare officer
>
> without leave of the court.

In effect this rule provides a presumption of disclosure of documents among the above listed. Moreover, in the words of Wall J:[61]

> ... the current practice of the courts in children's cases is to require disclosure of all medical reports and to invite experts to confer pre-trial.

(b) Disclosure of Evidence

The court has the power to direct that evidence be withheld from a party to proceedings brought under the Children (NI) Order 1995.[62] This power should only be exercised in exceptional circumstances.[63] As Butler-Sloss stated in *Re M (Minors)(Disclosure of Evidence)*[64] when considering whether to order non-disclosure:

> The test was not one of significant harm, but of whether disclosure would be so detrimental to the welfare of the children as to outweigh the normal requirement of a fair trial that all evidence must be disclosed.[65]

In *Oxfordshire County Council v M*[66] the Court of Appeal ruled that the court has the power to override legal professional privilege and order disclosure of an otherwise

---

59 See *Re M and R (Child Abuse: Evidence)* [1996] 2 FLR 195, CA.
60 Rule 23 of the Magistrates' Courts (Children (NI) Order 1995) Rules (NI) 1996; Rule 4.24 of the Family Proceedings Rules (NI) 1996.
61 See *Re AB (Child Abuse: Expert Witnesses)* [1995] 1 FLR 191.
62 See *Re B (A Minor) (Disclosure of Evidence)* [1993] 1 FLR 191.
63 See *Re G (Minors) (Welfare Report: Disclosure)* [1993] 2 FLR 293; also see *Re C (A Minor: Irregularity of Practice)* [1991] 2 FLR 438.
64 [1994] 1 FLR 6.
65 See also *Official Solicitor v K* [1965] AC 201.
66 [1994] 1 FLR 175.

privileged expert's report. The parents were thereby prevented from withholding an unfavourable report from a psychiatrist in respect of whom they had obtained leave to disclose the papers in the case. Wall J[67] recently gave the following guidance in relation to the disclosure of evidence provided by an expert witness:

> It is essential that medical experts are fully instructed, and that the context in which the expert's opinion is sought and the specific questions to be addressed are set out in the letter of instruction. Careful thought should be given to the selection of the papers to be sent to the expert, which should be disclosed to the other parties and included in the court bundle.

He went on to advise that expert witnesses should feel free to request further information or documentation and should be prepared for the sharing of all their clinical information with other experts and with the court.

The significance of this advice lies in the extent of the material to which the disclosure duty applies: including all notes, records, photographs, correspondence, x-rays and related material from previous medical histories held by other medical staff. This continues the approach he outlined earlier[68] when he endorsed the view of Thorpe J in *Essex County Council v R*[69] that there is a positive duty of disclosure. It is clear that the judiciary are no longer to be neutral umpires as counsel field their expert witnesses but are resolved to play a positive part in the business of protecting children in the course of court proceedings.

Most recently, the House of Lords in *Re L (Police Investigation: Privilege)*[70] has taken this approach a step further by ruling that the right of a party to proceedings not to produce documents is an incident of adversarial proceedings which can have no place in the inquisitorial proceedings of the Children's Act 1989. The report of an expert witness adverse to the interests of the party who held it was ordered to be disclosed to the police.

Representation in Private Proceedings

Whilst full party status is now automatic for minors in all specified public law proceedings commenced under the Children (NI) Order 1995 and their representation is then also required, the same applies to only a minority of the Order's private proceedings. Indeed, with the removal of mandatory social work reports in uncontested matrimonial cases, the number of private proceedings where the court will be required to have the benefit of impartial information on the best interests of the child is now

---

67 See *Re M (Minors)(Care Proceedings: Child's Wishes)* [1994] 1 FLR 749.
68 See *In Re DH (A Minor)(Child Abuse)* [1994] 1 FLR 679.
69 [1993] 2 FLR 826. Also see *Oxfordshire County Council v P* [1995] 1 FLR 552 where it was said:
> In all cases where the welfare of children is the court's paramount consideration, there is a duty on all parties to make full and frank disclosure of all matters material to welfare.
70 [1996] 1 FLR 731.

significantly lower than before the introduction of the 1995 Order. The reason for this is unambiguous. Decisions regarding the future care arrangements of children following a breakdown in parenting arrangements occurring in a private family law context are presumed to lie within the authority of the family choosing to dis-assemble its collective legal interests. This presumption is rebutted by contested proceedings which, self-evidently, demonstrate evidence of disagreement that could prove prejudicial to the future welfare interests of their children. The opposite presumption arises where the breakdown occurs in a public family law context. In both areas of law the common denominator triggering state involvement is that evidence exists to substantiate grounds of unreasonableness or parental fault/default respectively (see also Chapters Two and Twelve). Representation, and the entailed costs, will be provided only where breakdowns in parenting arrangements involving such grounds explicitly disclose a presumption that decisions affecting the future care arrangements of children need to be subject to judicial scrutiny.

Self-Representation by a Minor — Instructing a Solicitor

A child may instruct a solicitor to represent his or her legal interests in proceedings instigated by that child or by others. If the child has applied for an order under the 1995 Order, then he or she will have full party status and an entitlement to representation in court (usually on legal aid). If the child is not the applicant or plaintiff, then he or she will not automatically be a party to proceedings but, with leave of the court, may be made a party and a GAL may be appointed by the court to act on the child's behalf. However, any application for leave for separate representation in private law proceedings must now be made in the High Court; an application may be made *ex parte*.[71] A minor who wishes to prosecute or defend a family proceedings action will no longer have to do so by through the offices of a 'next friend'.

Under the Family Proceedings Rules (NI) (Rule 6.3(1)), the child concerned in any private law proceedings may commence, conduct or defend an action where either of the following two sets of circumstances exist:

>   where he has obtained
>   - (a) the leave of the court for that purpose; or
>   - (b) where a solicitor
>   - (i) considers that the minor is able, having regard to his understanding, to give instructions in relation to the proceedings; and
>   - (ii) has accepted instructions from the minor to act for him in the proceedings and, where the proceedings have so begun, is so acting.

The court does not have the power to appoint a solicitor to act for a child in private proceedings; though it may invite the Official Solicitor to do so.

---

71 See *Re Section (A Minor)(Independent Representation)* [1993] Fam 263 and [1993] 2 FCR 1 where it was clearly stated that a judge has discretion, in the interests of justice, to hear any party and that it would further such interests if applications were made on notice to all other parties.

Self-Representation

(a) The Legal Aid Test

The child seeking to directly instruct a solicitor in private family law proceedings has to undergo a number of preliminary tests. He or she must first acquire the necessary information on his or her rights in this respect and must then locate a solicitor willing and able to lend appropriate assistance. There is a further test in the sense that the Legal Aid Board must be satisfied (subject to the child's means) as to the merit of the child's application.

(b) Leave to Apply for Article 8 Orders: Application of the 'Sufficient Understanding' Test

Under Article 10(2)(b) of the 1995 Order a child is entitled to seek leave to apply for any Article 8 order. Applications under the equivalent provision in the 1989 Act gave rise to a number of well-reported cases of children seeking to 'divorce' their parents and led to a cautionary note being sounded by the President of the Family Division[72] that applications from children for orders under this provision are not expected to occur frequently. Leave will, however, be granted subject to the court being satisfied that the child meets the 'sufficient understanding' criteria.

Indeed, even if emotionally disturbed, an otherwise mature minor could still have sufficient understanding to instruct a solicitor.[73]

(c) The Participation Test

Where the court accepts that a child, having passed the above tests, could participate in proceedings, it has not always accepted that the child should participate. There has been some judicial concern that exposing a child to the experience of giving evidence, being cross-examined and hearing the evidence of other parties might in itself be placing him or her at risk of suffering significant harm. Booth J has indicated in *Re H*[74] that once the court has satisfied itself as to the 'could' issue, then it is not open to it to consider the 'should' issue; where a child has a right which he or she is capable of exercising, then the court must not place further obstacles in the child's way.

(d) The 'Welfare' Test

Finally, though the child may instruct a solicitor to represent his or her wishes and the latter may, through skilful advocacy and rigorous pursuit of the case, give full professional effect to those wishes, nonetheless the court will apply the Article 3(1) test that 'the child's welfare shall be the court's paramount consideration' to determine two further matters. First, on the issue of the extent to which the child should participate in proceedings, the court will consider the risk of 'significant harm' befalling the child

---

72 See *Re AD (A Minor)(Child's Wishes)* [1993] Fam Law 405. Also see Houghton, *Children Divorcing their Parents* (1994) JSWFL 185.
73 See *Re H (A Minor)(Care Proceedings: Child's Wishes)* [1993] 1 FLR 440.
74 [1993] 2 FLR 552.

as a consequence of being exposed to damaging evidence or stressful procedures. Unless convinced that the child's right as a party to fully participate in the proceedings is not outweighed by the risk of harm, the court will refuse or restrict such participation. Second, before giving judgment the court must be satisfied that, all other things being equal, the welfare interests of the child (not the child's wishes, wants, desires or needs as defined by him or her) will be best advanced by it. The older the child, however, the greater the probability that the court, influenced by the *Gillick* ruling, will be disinclined to impose a ruling which is at variance with his or her wishes.

Representation by a Guardian ad Litem

The role of a GAL in proceedings commenced under the Children (NI) Order 1995 will in practice be almost entirely confined to public law matters. The involvement of this official in adoption proceedings continues as before the 1995 Order (see Chapter Six).

Representation by a Trust Social Worker

Article 4 provides a broad judicial discretion for the appointment of a Trust social worker to report to the court on the welfare of a child in any public or private family proceedings. Only in those private proceedings where the interests of a child are among the matters being disputed does the 1995 Order (supplementing the requirement in the adoption statute and substituting for that in matrimonial legislation) specifically provide for such an appointment. The social worker then acts as the court's officer rather than as the child's representative.

1. Proceedings under the Children (NI) Order 1995

If the subject of proceedings, then the child may be made a party and may have his or her views represented by a social worker in a report requested by the court. In the course of proceedings a child may represent his or her own interests, for example, by seeking a self-referral into care or refusing a medical or psychiatric examination.

2. Matrimonial Proceedings

The mandatory requirement that in this jurisdiction, unlike in England and Wales, a report from a Trust social worker should be submitted to the court in respect of all divorce proceedings where children were involved[75] was ended by the 1995 Order. Ironically, this means that one major effect of the 1995 Order has been to remove the safety net of professional scrutiny, previously provided by Trust social workers in respect of child welfare considerations, from most judicial decisions affecting the future of children. Such reports continue, however, to be required in contested matrimonial proceedings which involve children.

The submission made to the court by the Trust social worker in report form and perhaps also in person, is not required to represent the child's views or legal interests

---

75 Matrimonial Causes (NI) Order 1978, Article 43(1)(b)(ii), required 'a report . . . on the children and the suitability of any arrangements which have been made, or are proposed, by either party to be made, for their welfare'.

on the matters at issue. The Trust social worker functions as a court officer to investigate family circumstances and provide the court with background factual information on the family, its individual members, its history and present difficulties; he or she co-ordinates the provision of information from other disciplines and agencies and assesses the proposed future care arrangements for the children. Arguably, then, even in those remaining cases which require a professional to speak on behalf of a child, that contribution falls far short of representation.

3. Adoption, Wardship and Other Private Proceedings

Again, the role of the Trust social worker is to act as a court officer and provide the court with information in relation to the child and to his or her family circumstances rather than to act as the child's representative. An example of the role of this official in a private proceedings conducted in the wardship jurisdiction of Northern Ireland was provided in *In re TC (A Minor)*[76] (see Chapter Seven). In adoption proceedings the role of the Trust social worker was considered by Hutton J in *In re EB and Others*[77] (see Chapter Six).

Representation in Public Proceedings

In public family law proceedings instigated under the 1995 Order, to authorise coercive state intervention in the affairs of a family for the purpose of safeguarding the welfare of a child, there is now an effective package of measures available to ensure representation for the welfare interests of such a child. These measures include a requirement that the child be automatically granted full party status and free legal aid, that a guardian ad litem be appointed to represent the child's best interests and provision be made for the appointment of a solicitor to represent the child's views. Representation in wardship cases is of little significance because wardship no longer has any significant bearing on public law, except for narrowly defined areas such as child abduction (see Chapter Ten), though it will be of growing significance in criminal law cases (see Chapter Seventeen).

Appointment of Representatives

In public law cases, under the 1995 Order, the views of the child will normally be represented by both a GAL and a lawyer. Under Article 60 their appointments are required in the following circumstances:

> (1) For the purpose of any specified proceedings, the court shall appoint a guardian ad litem for the child concerned unless satisfied that it is not necessary to do so in order to safeguard his interests.
>
> . . .
>
> (3) Where
>
> > (a) the child concerned is not represented by a solicitor; and

---

76 Unreported (1994).
77 [1985] 5 NIJB 2.

(b) any of the conditions mentioned in paragraph (4) is satisfied, the court may appoint a solicitor to represent him.

(4) The conditions are that
- (a) no guardian ad litem has been appointed for the child;
- (b) the child has sufficient understanding to instruct a solicitor and wishes to do so;
- (c) it appears to the court that it would be in the child's best interests for him to be represented by a solicitor.

1. Specified Proceedings

'Specified proceedings' are those listed in Article 60(6) of the Children (NI) Order 1995 and consist, basically, of any proceedings instigated under that legislation which sanction coercive state intervention in a family for the purpose of safeguarding a child's welfare. In such proceedings a child is automatically a party and therefore a GAL must be appointed by the court 'unless it is satisfied that it is not necessary to do so in the child's interests'. However, if he or she has sufficient understanding to give instructions, then a solicitor may be retained by the child. The courts in England and Wales have determined that the appointment of a GAL is, therefore, not mandatory for all 'specified proceedings'. In *Re J (A Minor)(Change of Name)*,[78] for example, where proceedings were undertaken in respect of a twelve-year-old girl in long-term care who wished to change her name to that of her foster parents, the court held that the appointment of a GAL would not result in any more being done for the child than had already been done by others.

2. Legal Aid, Advice and Assistance

Under Article 172(3) of the 1995 Order legal aid must be made available to the child concerned in any application for a care or supervision order, a child assessment order, an emergency protection order or for an extension or discharge of an emergency protection order.

Representation by a GAL

The GAL appointment should be made as soon as possible after the commencement of an action but may be made at any stage during the course of proceedings. It is then the responsibility of that court officer to appoint a solicitor to act as the child's representative. Where both a solicitor and a GAL are appointed, then the former must take instruction from the GAL unless the child is directly instructing the solicitor. The appointment made by the GAL must be based upon the needs of an individual child and the particularities of the case.

---

78   See [1993] 1 FLR 699.

1. Duties of a GAL

A GAL is appointed by the court with the general duty to 'safeguard the interests of the child' as stated in Article 60(2)(b). The role of this court officer has been described[79] as being 'proactive' in relation to the conduct and time-tabling of proceedings and the disposal options available. The more particular duties attached to this role are outlined in the Rules[80] and include advising the court in relation to:

(a) whether the child is of sufficient understanding for any purpose including the child's refusal to submit to a medical or psychiatric examination or other assessment that the court has the power to require, direct or order;
(b) the wishes of the child in respect of any matter relevant to the proceedings, including his attendance at court;
(c) the appropriate forum for the proceedings;
(d) the appropriate timing of the proceedings or any part of them;
(e) the options available to it in respect of the child and the suitability of each such option including what order should be made in determining the application;
(f) any other matter concerning which the court seeks his advice or concerning which he considers that the court should be informed.

In pursuance of the above, the GAL must carry out such investigations as may be necessary (including examining and taking copies of Trust case files) and submit to the court a full report on all matters relating to the welfare interests of the child not later than seven before the hearing. As is apparent from these duties, the role of the GAL is to act as a court officer rather than as a representative of the child. There is a difficult professional balance to be struck here between a fact-finding investigatory role designed to furnish the court with background information on the general circumstances of the family and an advocacy role on behalf of what in each case are the particular welfare interests of the child concerned.

2. Disclosure of Information to a GAL

The GAL is empowered by Article 61 to have access to records and may seek expert advice. He or she may examine and take copies of any records held by a Trust which are relevant to the welfare of the child concerned, including adoption records; but should never purport to offer confidentiality to a child in respect of any disclosure made by the latter.[81]

A GAL may seek out expert advice, co-ordinate the pooling of information from experts and analyse the issues for the court.[82]

---

79 See *The Children (NI) Order 1995, Guidance and Regulations Vol. 7, Guardians ad Litem and Other Court Related Issues* (1996).
80 Rule 12 of the Magistrates' Courts (Children (NI) Order 1995) Rules (NI) 1996; Rule 4.12(5) of the Family Proceedings Rules (NI) 1996.
81 See *Re T (A Minor) (Guardian ad Litem)* [1994] 1 FLR 632 CA.
82 See *Re C (Expert Evidence: Disclosure: Practice)* [1995] 1 FLR 204.

3. Disclosure of Information by a GAL

The significance of the GAL's appointment as a court officer was illustrated in *Oxfordshire County Council v P*,[83] when the court held that the GAL had been wrong to disclose to the police information obtained from a parent concerning child protection matters. The GAL was accountable to the court, which should have been appraised and whose permission should have been sought, prior to the divulging of *sub judice* matters to a third party. The GAL report is a confidential court document. Leave of the court is required before disclosure of the report, or any part of it, can be made to anyone other than those listed in the Rules.[83a]

Once proceedings are over any further disclosure of information in a GAL's report, for example to the staff of a family centre,[84] is a matter for the court.

4. The Advisory Role of a GAL

The advisory role of a GAL may arise in the context of a Trust giving effect to its general duty under Article 26:

> (2) Before making any decision with respect to a child whom it is looking after, or proposing to look after, an authority shall, so far as is reasonably practicable, ascertain the wishes and feelings of . . .
>
>> (d) any other persons whose wishes and feelings the authority considers to be relevant, regarding the matter to be decided.

The court has held that this provision placed a duty on a Trust's counterpart to consult with a GAL, where one had already been appointed, before making a decision materially affecting a child's welfare.[85]

5. Removal/Replacement of a GAL

Where a GAL acts improperly or in a manner prejudicial to the interests of the minor or where there is other good reason for his or her removal, then the court may direct that he or she be replaced.[86] Any attempt by a GAL to conclude proceedings in a manner detrimental to the interests of the child will be invalid: the office must be used for the child's benefit. If the child chooses to discharge the GAL[87] then the court will apply the 'sufficient understanding' test to establish — not whether the child is acting

---

83   See [1995] 1 FLR 552.
83a Rule 4.24(1) of the Family Proceedings Rules (NI) 1996; Rule 23(1) of the Magistrates' Courts (Children (NI) Order 1995) Rules (NI) 1996.
84   See *Re C (Guardian ad Litem: Disclosure of Report)* [1996] 1 FLR 61. But see also *Re G (Social Worker: Disclosure)* [1996] 1 FLR 276. Also 'Guardians ad litem and Disclosure' by Prof. N. Lowe in Family Law, vol. 26, pp 618–20 where he suggests that oral admissions made to a GAL can be disclosed to a social worker without court leave and may then be reported to the police in a child protection case conference.
85   See *R v North Yorkshire CC ex parte M* [1989] 1 All ER143.
86   See *Re Duke of Somerset, Thynne v St Maur* (1887) 34 Ch D 465.
87   See *Re Section (A Minor)(Independent Representation)* [1993] 2 FLR 437.

in his or her best interests — but whether the decision itself is valid. In public law cases, unlike private proceedings, where the child succeeds in removing the GAL and proposes to prosecute or defend the remaining proceedings by directly instructing a solicitor, then the court will have to arrange for separate representation to be provided for the GAL.[88]

6. Appointment of the Official Solicitor as GAL

Article 60(8) of the Children (NI) Order 1995 retains the power of the Lord Chancellor, under section 75(2) of the Judicature (NI) Act 1978, 'to confer or impose duties on the Official Solicitor'. The corresponding provision in the 1989 Act (s 41(8)) gave rise to a direction requiring the appointment of the Official Solicitor where, in any specified proceedings, a child does not have a GAL and the court considers that there are 'exceptional circumstances which make it desirable in the interests of the child'.[89] The direction will only apply when a case is in the High Court and contains an element of complexity, for example, an extra-jurisdictional dimension, concerns a number of children or in such other circumstances as the court should consider the appointment to be appropriate.

Representation by a Solicitor

While the GAL will speak for that which he or she construes to be in the best interests of the child, it is the solicitor to whom the child must look for his or her views to be represented and rights asserted in court. In certain circumstances the court is prohibited from making orders under the 1995 Order unless the child is legally represented. This, for example, is the case in relation to orders for secure accommodation. Under Article 44:

> (7) No court shall exercise the powers conferred by this Article in respect of a child who is not legally represented in that court unless, having been informed of his right to apply for legal aid and having had the opportunity to do so, he refused or failed to apply.

1. Appointed by a GAL

A solicitor will normally be both appointed by the GAL and take instructions from that court officer; should the further appointment of counsel be necessary, this will be made by the solicitor.

2. Appointed by or Instruction Undertaken by the Child

Where the child has sufficient understanding to give instructions and wishes to do so, then the solicitor will be obliged to respect the child's wishes and act independently of the GAL. It has been held that the level of understanding required of a child to

---

88 The Family Proceedings Rules (NI) 1996, Rule 4.12(4) and (5).
89 See the *Lord Chancellor's Directions: Duties and Functions of the Official Solicitor under the Children Act 1989* [1991] 2 FLR 471.

instruct a solicitor is less than that required to make an informed decision to refuse medical treatment or psychiatric assessment.[90] However, before granting leave for a child to directly instruct a solicitor, the court will require to be convinced that the child has sufficient understanding.[91]

3. Conflict between the Views of GAL and Child

In *Re M (Minors)(Care Proceedings: Child's Wishes)*[92] the court considered the procedure which should be followed where the child has sufficient understanding to instruct a solicitor and wishes to do so because the child's views were in conflict with those of the GAL. In giving judgment Wall J[93] offered the following guidance:

> It was important for the court to make an informed decision about the child's representation at an early stage. Guardians must therefore be alert to the possibility that the child may be seeking to instruct the solicitor direct or that there may be a conflict between the guardian's recommendations and the views of the child. In such cases, the guardian must take an early opportunity to discuss the difficulties with the solicitor instructed on behalf of the child, and either take out a summons for directions for the point to be resolved or, where such a summons is already fixed, bring the matter to the attention of the court and other parties at that appointment.

Where a solicitor, being aware of a conflict of views, is of the opinion that the child has sufficient understanding to give instructions then this will seldom be challenged by the court. As Wall J observed in the above case 'the courts in public law cases are content to rely on the good sense and expertise of local solicitors who . . . are developing a keen sense of a child's competence or otherwise to give instructions'.[94]

4. Appointed by the Court

Under Article 60(3) of the 1995 Order the court may appoint a solicitor if one has not already been appointed, subject to the conditions specified in Article 60(4).

This power of appointment is one which the court does not have in private proceedings.

Representation in Proceedings Initiated by the Child

Under Article 58(1)(b) of the 1995 Order the applicant in proceedings for discharge of a care or supervision order may be the child concerned. In England and Wales the corresponding provision[95] has given rise to controversy in relation to the right of the child to make application without first obtaining leave of the court. In *Re A (Care:*

---

90 See *Re H (A Minor)(Care Proceedings: Child's Wishes)* [1993] 1 FLR 440.
91 See *Re Section (A Minor)(Independent Representation)* [1993] 2 FLR 437 and *Re K, W and H (Minors)(Medical Treatment)* [1993] 1 FLR 854, where the court remained unconvinced.
92 [1994] 1 FLR 749.
93 Ibid.
94 Ibid.
95 The Children Act 1989, section 39(1)(b).

Discharge Application by Child)[96] the High Court considered the question, which had arisen in the county court, as to whether a fourteen-year-old boy could apply as of right for the discharge of the care order relating to him and also the further question as to the extent to which he should be allowed to participate in the discharge hearing.

1. Leave to Apply

The court held, in *Re A*, that the provision did not suggest a requirement that the applicant first obtain leave to apply. It would fall to the county court judge, when the applicant appeared before the court, to then determine whether or not the child was of sufficient understanding to make representations under the Rules. In making this decision the judge would take into account the fact that the child had already been accepted by a solicitor as a client with sufficient understanding to give direct instructions. This is an important ruling, marking a significant point of difference between the *locus standi* of a child applicant in public and private family proceedings commenced under this legislation. Unlike the situation in respect of applications for Article 8 orders, a child of 'sufficient understanding' to instruct a solicitor will not require prior leave of the court to commence proceedings to discharge a care order. Given that the distinction between private and public family law in this legislation seems to rest, to a considerable extent, on a pervasive legislative intent to facilitate autonomous decision-making by family members in the former while requiring this to be subjected to prior authorisation from court or Trust in the latter, there is now arguably a logical inconsistency in the legal standing accorded to a child applicant in each area.

2. Participation in Proceedings

The court in *Re A* also held that the right of children who are parties to public proceedings instigated under this legislation to participate must be balanced against the risk that in doing so they may be exposed to harm; the decision as to whether the child should participate was one for the court to make as soon as practicable after the commencement of an action. This is in keeping with the view expressed by Waite J in *Re C*[97] that 'the presence of children should not be encouraged to develop into settled practice'. However, this is at variance with the approach followed by the judiciary in private proceedings but readily facilitated by the discretionary judicial power available under Article 167(1) of the 1995 Order to waive the necessity for a child's attendance.

Representation in Relation to Service Provision by the Trusts

For the first time in this jurisdiction, a right and a procedure has been provided under the 1995 Order for those affected by the provision or lack of provision of services governed by child-care legislation to make representations (including complaints) about such services.

---

96 [1995] 1 FLR 599.
97 [1993] 1 FLR 832.

1. Complaints Procedure

Under Article 37 of the 1995 Order:

> (1) Every authority shall establish a procedure for considering any representations (including any complaint) made to the authority by a person qualifying for advice and assistance about the discharge of the authority's functions under this Part in relation to him.

This provision requires that complaints procedures be set up, publicised and operationalised by all Trusts in respect of the services they provide. This duty is extended, by Article 37(4) and Schedule 2 paragraph 2(1), to all voluntary organisations and children's homes.

2. Complainant

A person is deemed to be 'qualifying for advice and assistance' under the terms of this provision if he or she is under twenty-one and if at any time after reaching the age of sixteen had been looked after by a Trust or accommodated in any of the settings specified under Article 35(2). Those entitled under Article 45 to make a complaint or representations to a Trust include children, parents and any person with parental responsibility, any Trust foster-parent and any other person whom the Trust considers has good reason to be interested in a child's welfare.

3. Complaint

The services in respect of which representations may be made include accommodation and those provided or needed but not provided by any Trust, voluntary organisation or registered children's home. Under Article 45(2)(g) a Trust is required to inform any child, so far as is reasonably practicable, of the steps he or she may take under the 1995 Order to seek redress for any perceived grievance and in particular:

> (3) Every authority shall establish a procedure for considering any representations (including any complaints) made to it by
>> (a) any child who is being looked after by the authority or who is not being looked after but is in need about the discharge of any of the authority's functions under this Part in relation to the child.

Such representations may, for example, be in relation to a Trust's failure to meet its obligation under Article 45(2)(d)(i) to seek the views of a child being looked after by it before conducting any review in respect of him or her. They may relate to a perceived Trust failure in relation to specific powers and duties to provide services for families under Schedule 2 of the 1995 Order, e.g. undertaking an assessment of a child with 'special needs' under Schedule 2(4). The representations are made in the first instance in writing or in person to the appropriate Trust where they are considered by Trust officials and an independent person.

4. Response

A response must be made within twenty-eight days and must be accompanied by guidance as to the procedure to be followed in the event of continued dissatisfaction. The complainant then has the right to request that the matter at issue be referred to a Representations Panel for further consideration.

5. The Representations Panel

The representations panel is constituted to provide a formal hearing for any person who has registered his or her dissatisfaction with the Trust's response to initial enquiries. The panel must include an independent person and must meet to consider the matter at issue within twenty-eight days of notification. It must receive any written or oral submission made by the complainant, the Trust or by the independent person involved in the initial enquiry (if different from the panel representative). The Legal Aid Board may provide financial assistance to enable a child to be legally represented at such a panel. When the panel has reached a conclusion, this must be recorded, together with the reasons for it, within twenty-four hours of the meeting. All parties and any other person judged to have a *bona fide* interest must then be notified by the panel of the conclusion reached. The Trust, assisted by the independent appointee, must then consider what action if any it should take in relation to the child or children, the subject of the enquiries, in the light of the conclusions reached by the representation panel. Finally, a complainant seeking further redress may consider an application to the court for a judicial review.

PART THREE

Property and Finance

Introduction

This Part sets out the law relating to the ownership of property and to a lesser extent of finances, prior to, during and after the life of a family unit. Of the three parts which constitute this book on family law in Northern Ireland, the law is least satisfactory and most difficult to state with certainty in this part.

Family law is no longer structured iconoclastically around matters of status. It is now mostly to do with everyday disputes regarding property and children. The latter area has been recently and comprehensively updated by the introduction of new legislation and the repeal or amendment of statutes, some of which were relics from the Victorian era. Property law, however, has yet to receive equivalent legislative attention. Such new legislation as has been introduced is patchy, issue specific and largely addresses financial matters (e.g. child support and pensions). The judiciary have been left to rely on case-law precedents as the means of introducing, where possible, modernising legal reforms. Whereas, in other areas of family law (most notably in relation to children), this case law would have originated in the courts of England and Wales, in the area of property disputes the reliance may be upon precedents forged in the Irish courts. The Partition Acts of 1868 and 1876, long since repealed in England and Wales, continue in effect in this jurisdiction and, to that extent, property law in Northern Ireland can at times more readily find common ground with existing Irish law than with modern developments across the Irish sea. The Northern Ireland practitioner may find that he or she turns almost as frequently to Irish texts as to English for reference purposes when dealing with a third party creditor seeking to realise an ownership share in matrimonial property.

Consequently, this area continues to display the more traditional characteristics of private family law. The effects of the distinction between marital and non-marital relationships, for example, are very evident. It is also a primary growth area for litigation as many couples who form serial relationships may have avoided the ties of marriage and/or children but not those of property and finance. As the litigation largely occurs at times of family breakdown, this Part is mostly concerned with disputes between parents and between parents and third parties.

This Part is presented in three sections. The first section (containing Chapters Twenty and Twenty-one) deals with the disputed ownership of property and finance in the context of intact family units. By beginning with an explanation of some core concepts, principles and case law, the initial chapter lays the foundation for this Part. In particular those differences in the rights of family members resulting from differences in marital status and the relevance of equity and the doctrine of trusts are closely examined. Third-party rights are also outlined.

The second section (containing Chapters Twenty-two to Twenty-four) deals with the disputed ownership of property and finance in the context of family breakdown.

The provision made for the support of children is dealt with separately in Chapter Twenty-two which explains the workings of the child support scheme. In recognition of the particular significance of judicial separation for a society where religious principles often preclude recourse to divorce, attention is given to the statutory provisions governing maintenance payments. The main focus, however, is on ancillary relief as judicially determined in divorce proceedings.

The third and final section (containing Chapters Twenty-five and Twenty-six) closes the book with an examination of the consequences of death, particularly of a parent, for property ownership in a family. The differences between testate and intestate deaths and the implications arising for the rights of the parties concerned are outlined. The characteristics of a valid will are identified. Again, the legal relevance of a distinction between marital and non-marital families is considered as are the rights of third-party claimants.

CHAPTER TWENTY

Property, Finance and the Marital Family

Introduction

This chapter deals with the rights of spouses and their children in relation to property and finance. It examines how the ownership of property is acquired, the different forms this may take and the basis on which disputes are resolved. In particular it considers the respective rights of the spouses *vis-à-vis* each other and *vis-à-vis* third parties in respect of the matrimonial home and family property. These matters are considered in the context of a legally intact marriage.

Most difficulties between spouses concerning the ownership of property occur at or after marriage breakdown. During marriage the difficulties are more likely to lie between spouses and third parties. The emphasis in this chapter is, therefore, on first parties acquiring the ownership of property and on their subsequent disputes with third parties regarding that ownership. The law relating to maintenance is dealt with in Chapter Twenty-three and in relation to the distribution of marital property and finance on divorce and on death is to be found in Chapters Twenty-four and Twenty-five respectively.

Matrimonial Property

I. The Development of the Law Relating to Rights of Ownership

Property may be either 'real' (e.g. land or house) or 'personal' (e.g. jewellery, paintings or shares). When the ownership of marital property is disputed in the courts, this is most likely to concern real property as the value of personal property often does not warrant the costs of litigation.

In this jurisdiction the law governing the property rights of spouses is to be found in the general body of property law, in a series of modifying statutory provisions which have sought to take account of the spousal relationship, in the principles of equity and in a number of key judgments which extend to this jurisdiction precedents forged in the courts of England and Wales. A blend of statutory provisions and equitable principles have shaped the law in this jurisdiction.

Marital Status

In the law relating to property disputes between spouses, the marital status of the parties when the dispute comes before the court determines the degree of judicial discretion available. Where the marriage is subsisting, then the normal law of property applies and there is virtually no discretion; the court is restricted to merely declaring the parties' respective rights. Where the marriage is ending or has already ended, then there are extensive discretionary powers available to re-distribute property; the court may create rather than merely declare property rights. In the former instance the law is governed mainly by the Married Woman's Property Act 1882. In the latter it is governed by the Matrimonial Causes (NI) Order 1978, the Law Reform (Husband and Wife) Act (NI) 1964, the Domestic Proceedings (NI) Order 1980 and the Family Law (Miscellaneous Provisions)(NI) Order 1984 (see further Chapter Twenty-four).

Legislation

In this jurisdiction the legislative provisions which address the respective rights of spouses to property during rather than at the end of a marriage are the Married Woman's Property Act 1882, section 17, as amended by the Family Law (Miscellaneous Provisions) (NI) Order 1984, Articles 4–13 and 20 together with the Law Reform (Husband and Wife) Act (NI) 1964. Provisions addressing the rights of spouses *vis-à-vis* third parties continue to be found mainly in the Partition Acts of 1868 and 1876, except where the claims of a third party arise in the context of bankruptcy when the Insolvency (NI) Order 1989 provides the primary legislative framework.

(a) The Married Woman's Property Act 1882

Until the introduction of the Married Woman's Property Act 1882 a wife's property would, on marriage, vest in her husband. The draconian effect of the law on the property rights of a wife was, to some extent, balanced by the common-law duty of a husband to provide his wife with the necessities of life. In practice, by allowing her to live with him in their home he was held to have fulfilled his duty.[1] This common-law reciprocation — a wife's duty to provide consortium and the husband's duty to provide a right of occupation — persisted to the extent that a wife without legal or equitable title would forfeit her right to occupy the matrimonial home if she defaulted on her marital obligations.[2] If she left him, she abandoned also not only any claim to his property but all entitlement to that property which she had brought with her into the marriage. During their marriage any property rights continued to vest solely in the husband. Only on death would certain limited rights to the property owned by the husband then vest in his widow.

The 1882 Act gave a wife the right to have and to hold a legal interest in property. She could retain ownership of property on marriage, could thereafter acquire it and could hold her rights quite separately from those of her husband. She was thus statutorily enabled to exercise her rights as if she were a *femme sole*[3] and able to sue

---

1 See *McGowan v McGowan* [1948] 2 All ER 1032, 1035.
2 See *Chilton v Chilton* [1952] 1 All ER 1322.
3 This expression refers to a construct in the law of equity which, by the end of the sixteenth century, had established that if property was settled by trust on a single woman 'for her separate use' then she would continue to hold her rights, exclusive of her husband, for the duration of her marriage and had complete discretion to dispose of it by will.

others, including her husband, to protect her property. This Act, paradoxically, is often used by men. Proceedings are usually instigated in the county courts, depending on the rateable value of the property.

For many years the courts interpreted section 17 as permitting the exercise of judicial discretion to re-distribute matrimonial property between the spouses in whatever proportions seemed appropriate, regardless of rights being vested exclusively in one party. This practice was ended by the decisions of the House of Lords in *Pettitt* and *Gissing* (see p. 475–6).

(b) The Law Reform (Husband and Wife) Act (NI) 1964

The Law Reform (Husband and Wife) Act (NI) 1964 was introduced primarily to remove the common-law rule[4] that ownership of any property acquired by a wife, using savings made from the housekeeping expenses provided by her husband, vested in the husband exclusively. Instead, it provided that ownership of such property would vest in them both jointly.

(c) The Family Law (Miscellaneous Provisions) (NI) Order 1984

Article 4 of the Family Law (Miscellaneous Provisions) (NI) Order 1984 confers on a spouse without legal title a 'right of occupation' which will bind third parties and will be protected by the court as a matrimonial charge. This should be registered. A matrimonial charge which has not been registered is void only as against the purchaser of an estate.[5]

(d) The Partition Acts of 1868 and 1876

The statutory right to apply to the court for an order compelling the sale of property owned by joint tenants was first made available under the Act for Joint Tenants 1542. This right was consolidated and enlarged under the Partition Acts which now provide the authority, where joint tenants are unable to reach agreements, for the court to order partition or sale in lieu of partition and thereby enable the parties to realise their separate interests in the property. An order compelling sale may be made under sections 3, 4 or 5 of the 1868 Act.

(e) The Insolvency (NI) Order 1989

The Insolvency (NI) Order 1989 provides a creditor with a statutory right to apply to the court for an order transferring the ownership of a bankrupt spouse's assets in satisfaction of debts incurred by the latter. The provisions govern the rights of spouses *vis-à-vis* third party creditors in the context of bankruptcy.

---

4 See, for example, *Blackwell v Blackwell* [1943] 2 All ER 579 CA.
5 See, for example, *The Matter of Folio 3540 Co Tyrone* [1991] NI 273 where Murray LJ held that the making of an order charging land under the Judgments Enforcement (NI) Order 1981 was not a transaction for valuable consideration.

Equity

(a) The Doctrine of Trusts

The 1882 Act did nothing to clarify the rights which a 'non-owning spouse' might have to an interest in the matrimonial home or in the savings from or property bought with normal housekeeping expenses. It was left to equity to provide a remedy.

(i) Ownership Rights in Equity: The Doctrine of Trusts

The doctrine of resulting, implied, or constructive trusts developed from judicial initiatives which gave recognition to an interest acquired by one spouse in property wholly owned by the other. It was judged inequitable that because a property, such as the matrimonial home, was registered solely in the name of one spouse this should operate as a bar preventing any acknowledgement of an interest to which the other may be entitled. This might arise, for example, on the basis of that other having paid a part of the purchase price. Where a non-owning spouse (now mostly a cohabitee), can show no contractual evidence to support a claim in statutory proceedings for a share in property, the court will allow that party to rely instead on evidence adduced through the doctrine of trusts. This doctrine has little relevance to the parties of a failed marriage, as ancillary proceedings will almost always settle ownership without regard to beneficial interest (see Chapter Twenty-four). It is of considerable importance to property disputes between spouses and between spouses and third parties. It is of great relevance to failed non-marital relationships where property disputes will normally have to be judicially resolved outside the statutory framework (see Chapter Twenty-one).

As has been explained by Lord Diplock:[6]

> A resulting, implied or constructive trust . . . is created by a transaction between the trustee and the *cestui que trust* in connection with the acquisition by the trustee of a legal estate in land, whenever the trustee has so conducted himself that it would be inequitable to allow him to deny the *cestui que trust* a beneficial interest in the land acquired. And he will be held so to have conducted himself if by his words or conduct he has induced the *cestui que trust* to act to his own detriment in the reasonable belief that by so acting he was acquiring a beneficial interest in the land.

(ii) Resulting Trust

A resulting trust arises where one party is vested wholly with the legal rights to property, there is evidence of a common intention that the other party should hold a beneficial interest in it, that other party has clearly acted to his or her detriment by making a direct contribution to the purchase price and that action is directly attributable to the common intention. The trust results from and is in proportion to the direct financial contribution made by that other party towards the cost of the property.

(iii) Implied Trust

The court will imply the existence of a trust where there is evidence of an oral agreement to the effect that it was the parties' common intention to share the beneficial

---

6   See *Gissing v Gissing* [1971] AC 886; [1970] 2 All ER 780, HL.

interest in the property and that the party in whom the legal estate was not to be vested would make a contribution in some way towards the purchase price. This has now, in effect, become subsumed within the concept of a constructive trust.

(iv) Constructive Trust

Unlike a resulting trust, a constructive trust does not rest on the applicant's direct financial contribution. Again, however, there must be evidence of a common intention and evidence that the party with no legal rights acted to his or her detriment based on that common intention. The courts will require such intention to be verified by evidence of express conversations accompanied usually by indirect financial contributions; it will not be sufficient to claim that it can be inferred from the behaviour of the parties. Where common intention and referable detrimental action can be demonstrated, then the court will hold that the parties have in effect constructed a trust giving the party without legal rights a beneficial interest in the property (see further *Rosset* at p. 476).

The constructive trust would seem to best represent the equitable intent to ascribe a beneficial right of ownership to a spouse or partner in circumstances where this is required in the interests of justice but is not attainable through the provisions of statute. Basing a claim on a constructive trust can prove more advantageous than struggling to meet the evidential requirements necessary to substantiate the existence of a resulting trust. For example, in a recent case[7] the court found that it defied common sense to ascribe a beneficial interest to a wife on the basis of her financial contributions when the marital couple had lived together for many years in their family home and had never any cause to consider their respective ownership rights to that property. Accordingly, rather than endorse the resulting trust approach of the court at first instance (which, on that basis, awarded the wife a 6.4 per cent share) Waite J instead held that a constructive trust could be inferred, resting on an implied agreement that the couple would hold their beneficial interests in the property in equal shares.

It is in such cases, as in *Rosset*,[8] where the reason for determining the extent of the beneficial interest accruing to a spouse without legal ownership rights is so that third party claims to the property may be established, that the relevance of the doctrine of trusts plays a crucial part in deciding the future of a family home.

The court is unable to recognise an equitable right of ownership where the contribution is in the nature of maintenance rather than significant improvement or where there is no evidence of the required intention; but this will have a considerable bearing on an eventual financial settlement.[9]

(b) The Presumption of Advancement

Again, like constructive trusts, this equitable doctrine can also be readily distinguished from the doctrine of resulting trusts. As explained in the literature[10]:

---

7 See *Midland Bank v Cooke and Another* [1995] 2 RLR 915.
8 See *Lloyds Bank v Rosset and Another* [1990] 2 FLR 155 HL.
9 As in *Britannia Building Society v Johnston and Others* [1994] 10 BNIL 75.
10 *Snell's Principles of Equity*, 29th ed.

Presumption of advancement
As the doctrine of resulting trusts is based upon the unexpressed but presumed intention of the true purchaser, it will not arise where the relationship existing between the true and the normal purchaser is such as to raise a presumption that a gift was intended. This presumption of advancement, as it is called, applies to all cases in which the person providing the purchase-money is under, or expects to be under, an equitable obligation to support, or make provision for, the person to whom the property is conveyed, i.e. where the former is the husband or father of, or stands in *loco parentis* to, the latter.

Accordingly, if a man buys property and has it conveyed to his wife (or intended wife), *prima facie* this is a gift to her.[11]

Rebutting the Presumption
Evidence of Intention
Both the presumption of a resulting trust and the presumption of advancement can be rebutted by evidence of the actual intention of the purchaser. Indeed, in the case of an asset purchased for the joint use of husband and wife, the presumption of advancement is readily rebutted. The clearest evidence is an express declaration of trust on the face of the conveyance of the legal estate, but even where this is absent the court puts itself in the position of a jury, and considers all the circumstances of the case, so as to arrive at the purchaser's real intention; it is only where there is no evidence to contradict it that the presumption of a resulting trust, or of advancement, as the case may be, will prevail.[12]

Improper Purposes
The presumptions are not rebuttable by evidence of an improper purpose. Thus where a husband puts property into his wife's name, he cannot be heard to say that he did so to defeat his creditors, or to evade government restrictions on taxes. The rules of equity cannot be used to aid iniquity, and the presumption will apply unless a proper ground for rebutting them is both pleaded and proved.[13]

While most frequently considered in the context of marital relationships, the application of this doctrine is by no means restricted to spouses. For example, a recent case[14] concerned a father who had sought to avoid the claims of creditors by transferring shares in the family business to his son for no consideration. The father resolved his difficulties with the creditors and sought the return of his shares; the son refused to comply. The court at first instance held that the presumption of advancement applied as it was the father's presumed intention to vest ownership of the shares in the son. However, the Court of Appeal, while conceding that the presumption applied, held that his action was governed by the intention to avoid his creditors and this remained unfulfilled as he had changed his mind in that regard. Accordingly, the presumption

---

11 Ibid at 179.
12 Ibid at 180.
13 Ibid at 181.
14 See *Tribe v Tribe* [1995] 2 FLR 968.

of advancement was rebutted, the son did not receive a gift and ownership of the shares remained with the father.[15]

It may be fair to comment that in the context of current sensitivity to discriminatory practices, this doctrine can no longer be accorded the same judicial weight as formerly, at least not as it has been applied to spouses.

(c) Proprietary Estoppel

As explained by Balcombe LJ,[16] the essential elements of this doctrine are:

(a) That an applicant must act to his detriment in reliance on promises made by the defendant; although there must be a sufficient link between the promises relied on and the conduct which consists of the detriment.
(b) The promises need not be the sole inducement, so long as they are an inducement.
(c) Once it has been established that the promises were made and there has been sufficient conduct by the applicant then the burden of proof shifts to the defendant to prove that the applicant did not rely on the promises.

The proofs required are of a lesser order than is necessary to support a claim that a constructive trust has arisen. Also the court has discretion to make such award as it considers equitable. For these reasons claims are increasingly being made in proprietary estoppel in preference to constructive trusts.

(d) Precedents

A small number of frequently quoted cases are so fundamental to an understanding of the modern law of equity on property disputes between family members and between them and third parties that they are best briefly outlined at the outset of this part and chapter.

(i) Pettitt v Pettitt

The case of *Pettitt v Pettitt*[17] concerned the proceeds of the sale of a couple's matrimonial home. The house had been bought by the wife (with money from the sale of another house wholly owned by her) and registered solely in her name. The husband had done some work on the house of a DIY nature. Their relationship broke down, they divorced, she sold the house and he then commenced proceedings under section 17 of the Married Woman's Property Act 1882 claiming a small share of the proceeds on the basis of his work having enhanced the value of the property. The House of Lords considered the wife's appeal from the decision of the court of first instance, as upheld by the Court of Appeal, that the husband had an entitlement amounting to one-third of the estimated value of his work.

Giving judgment on behalf of the House, Lord Morris[18] stated that:

---

15 See also *Tinsley v Milligan* [1993] 2 FLR 968 Chapter 21.
16 See *Wayling v Jones* [1995] 2 FLR 1029, 1031 H.
17 [1969] 2 All ER 385 HL.
18 Ibid.

> ... all the indications are that section 17 was purely a procedural section ... the procedure was devised as a means of resolving a dispute or question as to title rather than as a means of giving some title not previously existing.

It was held that the court could not vary the existing proprietary rights of the parties. The court had no discretionary power unless it was established that each party had a substantial beneficial interest in which case its discretionary power was restricted to the option of holding that both parties had an equal entitlement. The rights of the parties could be affected by evidence that an agreement of an express, implied or imputed nature existed between them, by estoppel, fraud or mistake. In this case the only evidence was of possible imputed agreement arising from the husband's work on the property. However, as a matter of fact this had been too insubstantial to confer a beneficial interest.

(ii) Gissing v Gissing

Again, the case of *Gissing v Gissing*[19] concerned an application brought by a former spouse under section 17 of the 1882 Act claiming a beneficial interest in what had been the matrimonial home, bought in the name of the other and in respect of which the applicant had made no contribution to the purchase price. This time the applicant was the former wife and her claim rested on the assertion that she had worked throughout their married life, had secured employment for her husband with her employer and had used some of her savings to pay for furnishings and for the laying of a lawn. Mortgage payments were made exclusively by the husband who had also provided his wife with a housekeeping allowance, though she bought all clothing for herself and their son. The House of Lords upheld the decision of the court at first instance, overturning that of the Court of Appeal, to rule that the wife had not acquired any beneficial interest.

The decision was based on a finding that there was no evidence of a common intention, expressed or inferred, that the wife should acquire any such interest. It was not possible to impute to parties an intention which they did not have, nor for the court to substitute for that lack an intention which it believed reasonable spouses in that position would have had if they stopped to consider the position. The House also took the opportunity to adjust its earlier ruling in *Pettitt* on the matter of the court's ambit of discretion. This time it ruled that the maxim 'equality is equity' should not prevent the awarding of shares in unequal proportions if this was required in the interests of justice, nor should it be prevented by any difficulty in arriving at a fair apportioning.

(iii) Lloyds Bank v Rosset and Another

Lloyds Bank v Rosset and Another[20] concerned a farmhouse in Switzerland purchased by Mr Rosset (the first respondent) in his name as a family home for himself and his wife (the second respondent). There had been no agreement that the wife should have a beneficial interest in the property, nor did she make any contribution towards the

---

19 [1970] 2 All ER 780 HL.
20 [1991] 1 AC 107, 130; [1990] 1 All ER 111, 117 HL.

purchase price although she did assist in renovation work. Immediately before the purchase, and unknown to his wife, Mr Rosset entered into a loan arrangement with a bank (the appellant) using the farmhouse as security. Within two years of the purchase the marriage had broken down, Mr Rosset had moved out and the bank had commenced proceedings for possession of the farmhouse due to non-repayment of the loan. The bank's claim was not contested by Mr Rosset but it was by his estranged wife who alleged that she had been entitled to a beneficial interest in the property under a constructive trust since the date of its acquisition.

In giving judgment for the House of Lords, Lord Bridge of Harwich stated:[21]

> The first and fundamental question which must always be resolved is whether, independently of an inference to be drawn from the conduct of the parties in the course of sharing the house as their home and managing their joint affairs, there has at any time prior to acquisition, or exceptionally at some later date, been any agreement, arrangement or understanding reached between them that the property is to be shared beneficially. . . . Once a finding to this effect is made it will only be necessary for the partner asserting a claim to a beneficial interest against the partner entitled to the legal estate to show that he or she has acted to his or her detriment or significantly altered his or her position in reliance on the agreement in order to give rise to a constructive trust or proprietary estoppel.

However, as his Lordship then went on to point out,[22]

> . . . where there is no evidence to support a finding of an agreement or arrangement to share . . . and where the court must rely entirely on the conduct of the parties both as the basis from which to infer a common intention to share the property beneficially and as the conduct relied on to give rise to a constructive trust . . . contributions to the purchase price . . . will readily justify the inference necessary to the creation of a constructive trust. But, as I read the authorities, it is at least extremely doubtful whether anything less will do.

It was held that the wife had no entitlement to a beneficial interest in the property.

II. Engagement

The act of engagement does not confer any new legal status on the couple concerned: neither the relationship between the parties nor the relationship between them and third parties are legally altered. However, for some purposes, the law recognises that arrangements entered into by an engaged couple cannot be treated as if they had been made by two wholly independent individuals; indeed there are circumstances in which they are now required to be treated as though made by a married couple.

1. Property of Engaged Couples

The Family Law (Miscellaneous Provisions) (NI) Order 1984, Article 15(1), abolished the common-law right to seek damages for 'breach of promise to marry'. Articles

---

21 Ibid.
22 Ibid.

15–17 of the 1984 Order now place engaged couples in much the same position as married couples in relation to any property in which either or both parties have a beneficial interest. This gave statutory effect to judicial practice in cases such as *Toner v Toner*.[23] There the purchase of a house, the initial assurance policy and extensive refurbishment of that house all took place before and in contemplation of the parties' marriage. During the subsequent dispute as to ownership of the matrimonial home, counsel for both parties proceeded on the basis that the principles to be applied were the same as if the house had been acquired after the marriage.[24]

Case law[25] would indicate that the agreement to marry may be expressed or implied and, provided it is enforceable, may ground an action even if contrary to public policy.

In this jurisdiction the case of *Ridgeway v Murray*[26] illustrates the common approach taken by the courts to property disputes between couples whether married or engaged. The plaintiff who had lived all her life in Plymouth met the defendant, a long-distance lorry driver, in 1975 and shortly afterwards accepted his marriage proposal. It was an informal engagement, he bought her a ring and they agreed to be married on her next birthday. When that date arrived he, in fact, was delivering goods in Holland. However, the engagement was never broken off nor was it ever at risk of being broken off.

In 1978 the defendant bought a house in Northern Ireland. He then invited the plaintiff to his parent's house in Scotland where he would make the necessary arrangements for their marriage before they took up residence in the newly acquired house. He never made the arrangements. Instead they moved directly to Northern Ireland where they lived together as man and wife, she doing much decorating and home maintenance, and in due course she became pregnant. During a discussion about marriage, the plaintiff mentioned that she was worried about the security of her position and (according to her account) the defendant then offered to add her name to the title deeds of the house. This he did not do. Eventually their relationship broke down and she petitioned the court claiming a beneficial interest in the house.

The court found that the house had been acquired for the purpose of being the matrimonial home and 'that to say the plaintiff, as the prospective wife, has no interest therein would be to do her a grievous wrong in all the circumstances'.[27] It was held that, given the work the plaintiff had done to the house, the defendant would be regarded as holding the legal estate on trust in the proportions of 4/5th for him and 1/5th for her. The plaintiff was granted an injunction preventing the defendant from interfering with or otherwise obstructing the plaintiff's enjoyment and occupation of the premises.

A person suffering loss as a consequence of a broken engagement is also placed in the same position as a spouse following marital breakdown for the purposes of pursuing a claim to property under section 17 of the Married Woman's Property Act 1882. Section 2(2) of that Act requires proceedings to be commenced within three years of the engagement ending.

---

23 [1972] NILR 1.
24 See *Ulrich v Ulrich* [1968] 1 WLR 180 and also *Cooke v Head* [19072] 2 All ER 38.
25 See *Shaw v Fitzgerald* [1992] 1 FLR 357.
26 [1981] 7 NIJB.
27 Ibid.

(a) Gifts between Fiancées

Gifts between fiancées are now governed by statute rather than by common law. In keeping with the general principle that the rights of parties in private family law proceedings should not be subject to a condition that the applicant is without fault in relation to the subject of the proceedings, there is now no bar to the defaulter claiming a return of gifts. As stated in Article 17 of the 1984 Order: a person 'shall not be precluded from recovering the gift on termination of the agreement by reason of the fact that he (or she) was responsible for the termination'. However, not all gifts are recoverable. The test to be applied is — was it given to the other and accepted with the intention that it be utilised on or during marriage? Thus incidental gifts made during the engagement (e.g. birthday presents etc.) will not be recoverable, while a contribution to a deposit made to secure the prospective matrimonial home will be. No expenses may be recovered by either party, or by their relatives, in respect of preparations made for the wedding. In this context, it might be noted that wedding gifts are not jointly owned by the couple. Where a friend or relative of one of the parties provides a gift that item is in law a gift not to the couple but to the party with whom the giver had a particular relationship.[28]

(b) Engagement Ring

Under Article 17(7) of the 1984 Order, the engagement ring is specifically designated an absolute gift unless there is evidence to show that it was given on condition that it be returned in the event of the marriage not taking place.

2. Pre-Nuptial Agreements

A formal agreement between an engaged couple to take effect on marriage or, more likely, in the event of the marriage breaking down will be actionable under the same principles provided for in the 1984 Order. These are usually drawn-up to apportion rights to property and/or finance, and any resulting proceedings will be determined in accordance with normal principles of contract law. Should the matter subsequently arise in the context of divorce proceedings etc., then any stipulated rights of the parties will be subject to the discretionary right of the court, under Article 26(1)(c) of the 1978 Order, to 'vary for the benefit of the parties to the marriage and of the children of the family or either or any of them any ante-nuptial or post-nuptial settlement.'

III. First-Party Contests; Ownership Rights under Statute and in Equity

The introduction of the 1882 Act gave a wife a statutory right to bring proceedings to establish or defend a claim to an ownership interest in matrimonial property. This right has been significantly extended by judicial development of the equitable doctrine of trusts.

Proceedings to Establish Ownership

Proceedings to establish ownership are governed by the Married Woman's Property Act 1882 as extended by equity. Section 17 of the 1882 Act enables the court to

---

28 See *Samson v Samson* [1982] 1 WLR 252, [1982] 1 All ER 780. But see also *Midland Bank v Cooke and Another* [1995] 2 FLR 915 and the findings of the Court of Appeal as discussed below at p. 492.

consider any question 'as to the title to or possession of property' which may arise in a dispute between husband and wife.

The Parties

Those who may apply under section 17 of the 1882 Act are a husband or wife, a former husband or wife (if application is made within three years of divorce or annulment) and either fiancée (again if application is made within three years of their engagement being terminated).

The Orders

Under section 17 of the 1882 Act, the court may make 'such orders with respect to the property in dispute as it thinks fit'. Since the decisions in *Pettitt* and *Gissing*, this power is understood as being to declare rather than create the respective rights of spouses in relation to property such as the matrimonial home. In disputes between spouses, other than in divorce or nullity suits, this provision continues to provide the means whereby the court determines ownership of the matrimonial home.

The Property

(a) Income

Where a fund is explicitly set up for a joint purpose agreed by the spouses and each spouse makes some contribution to it, then few legal difficulties arise. This will be the case when a joint bank account is set up for the purpose of meeting the day-to-day 'running expenses' of both working spouses, to which both transfer some or all of their earnings. The fact that their contributions are unequal is beside the point: in law and in equity the couple will have established joint ownership of that fund.

However, problems arise where either the purpose of the fund is mutually agreed but the financial contribution to it is made wholly or mostly by one spouse or the couple never actually explicitly agreed on the purpose of the fund though both thereafter contributed to it. In the first instance, case law[29] demonstrates that an intent to set up a 'common purse' is the determining factor; ownership is then joint. Conversely, in the second instance, in the absence of such an intent, ownership will follow the money; there is a presumption that the fund belongs to the person who created it.[30] This presumption may be rebutted by evidence of an implied intent to establish a 'common purse'[31] which will be the case where, for example, a wife can show that the 'presumption of advancement' operated in her favour.[32]

---

29 See *Jones v Maynard* [1951] Ch 572, [1951] 1 All ER 802 where, though the bank account was in the husband's name and he was the main contributor, he had authorised his wife to draw from it and thereafter both had treated it as being a joint account. Held: it was a joint account, where the wife was entitled to half the money in the account when it was closed; she was also entitled to half the value of all investments made by the husband from money which he had withdrawn from that account since giving her authorisation.
30 See *Heseltine v Heseltine* [1971] 1 All ER 952.
31 See *Re Figgis* [1969] 1 Ch 123, [1968] 1 All ER 999.
32 See *Transfer of Money between Spouses* (Law Com Working Paper no. 90, p 574).

(b) Housekeeping Funds

Problems may also arise where one spouse provides the sole financial contribution and the other acquires a fund of savings made as a result of good housekeeping or acquires property bought with the proceeds of such savings. The common-law rule was that any such savings, or property derived therefrom, belonged exclusively to the provider, who was assumed to be the husband. In this jurisdiction,[33] the Law Reform (Husband and Wife) Act (NI) 1964, section 3, removed that inequity and instead required ownership to vest in both equally. This rule only applies in circumstances where the provider is the husband, not where the roles are reversed.

(c) Matrimonial Home; Statute Law

A married couple can establish their equal rights to the matrimonial home in accordance with the normal laws governing contract and conveyancing. By deed, creation of a trust or by conveyance a married couple may, in common with any other group of persons, complete the necessary legal formalities to expressly create joint ownership in a specific property. It is of no consequence whether one of the parties was wholly responsible for purchasing the property. Once so established and both names have been registered on the title deeds of the property, the ownership is verifiable in law and equity, is binding on all parties and provides absolute proof of ownership in any subsequent dealings with third parties. Breach of the terms of such an express agreement will provide a spouse with grounds for commencing proceedings.

(d) Matrimonial Home; Equity

Where the matrimonial home has been purchased by the husband and ownership registered exclusively to him, the legislators and the courts have nonetheless sought to recognise rights which his wife may acquire to a share in the ownership of that home. Legislative reforms to that effect introduced in England and Wales have largely,[34] but not wholly, been eventually transferred to this jurisdiction.

The courts will imply to one spouse an intention to permit the other to acquire an equitable right to a share in ownership where there is evidence to support the existence of a trust. Two crucial elements must be present: a common intention and the suffering of a detriment attributable to that intention. If the plaintiff can establish both, then the court will go on to consider which type of trust has been created, a resulting trust or a constructive trust, and apportion the respective beneficial interests.

(i) Common Intention

There must be evidence of an intention on the part of both spouses that the beneficial ownership in the property was to be shared. Where, for example, correspondence can

---

33 Following the Married Woman's Property Act 1964.
34 The relevant legislation in this jurisdiction being: the Married Woman's Property Act 1882, section 17, as amended by the Matrimonial Causes (NI) Order 1978, Article 55; the Law Reform (Husband and Wife) Act (NI) 1964, section 3; the Domestic Proceedings (NI) Order 1980, Articles 18, 19 and 21, and; the Family Law (Miscellaneous Provisions)(NI) Order 1984, Articles 4–13 and 20.

be produced in which the sole registered owner states that this was his intention, then he will be held to have been holding his legal title subject to a constructive trust in favour of his spouse.[35] Where the parties have not committed their common intention to writing, the courts may nonetheless accept other evidence which shows that the behaviour of both parties is only explicable on the basis that they were acting in accordance with such an intention. However, conduct giving rise to the inference of an agreement, arrangement or even of an understanding between spouses that they would share the beneficial ownership in a property is now subject to more sceptical judicial scrutiny than formerly. Since the decision in *Rosset* (see above) the courts will be slow to infer common intention in the absence of reinforcing evidence of direct contributions (resulting trusts) or conversations (constructive trusts).

(ii) Suffering a Detriment

There must be evidence that the common intention was relied upon by the claimant and as a consequence she suffered a detriment. The fact, for example, that a wife produced evidence of a common intention that she and her husband should share everything was insufficient to establish her claim to a beneficial ownership in their home, in the absence of any additional evidence that she had relied on this intention and in doing so had suffered a specific detriment.[36]

The Ownership of Property

I. First-Party Contests; Resulting Trusts Based on Direct Contributions

A spouse basing a claim on the grounds of a resulting trust will prove the existence of a common intention and the suffering of a referable detriment by providing evidence of having made direct contributions to the purchase price of the property. If established, the trust will result in an ownership entitlement reflecting the proportion of the contribution to the purchase price.

Direct Contributions

In situations where there is no evidence of an arrangement or agreement between the spouses, then, in the words of Lord Bridge of Harwich,[37]

> ... the court must rely entirely on the conduct of the parties both as the basis from which to infer a common intention to share the property beneficially and as the conduct relied on to give rise to a constructive trust. In this situation direct contributions to the purchase price by the partner who is not the legal owner, whether initially or by payment of mortgage instalments, will readily justify the inference necessary to the creation of a constructive trust. But, as I read the authorities, it is at least doubtful whether anything else will do.

---

35 See *Re Densham* [1975] 1 WLR 1519, [1975] 3 All ER 726.
36 See *Midland Bank v Dobson* [1986] 1 FLR 171.
37 See *Lloyds Bank v Rosset* [1990] 2 WLR 867.

The claimant must prove that he or she has made a reasonable contribution to the purchase price. This will be readily confirmed where that contribution takes the form of a regular and substantial proportion of mortgage repayments or a proportion of the deposit[38] paid to secure the house; even if this has been paid by the groom's father in the form of a pre-wedding present,[39] post-wedding gift,[40] or loan[41] to both parties. So, also, where the contribution of a spouse took the form of substantial home improvements[42] or a substantial role in the other's business[43] and was accompanied by evidence of the necessary common intent, then such a spouse would have an equitable claim to a share in ownership.

Direct Contributions: Insufficient

A claim asserting the existence of a resulting trust may be rebutted by evidence that the financial sum in question was not intended as a direct financial contribution to the purchase price. The necessary common intention, as evidenced by a direct contribution, will be shown to be absent by evidence that in fact the sum given by the claimant had been a gift, loan[44] or payment of rent.[45] The claim may also be defeated by evidence that the sum was insufficient to constitute a real 'contribution'.

In this jurisdiction the decision of the court in *Toner v Toner*[46] serves as a cautionary warning that occasional payments will not suffice to establish the necessary intention. This case also illustrates the common approach taken to property disputes whether ownership was acquired during engagement or during marriage. The wife's summons under section 17 of the 1882 Act concerned the marital home which had been purchased by the husband, in his name, prior to and in contemplation of the marriage. Part of the purchase price consisted of a cash payment made by the husband, part was in the form of a loan advanced by the wife's mother to cover the deposit and the balance was made up by a building society mortgage linked to a life assurance policy in his name. The house was extensively re-decorated and furnished prior to the marriage: much of the materials and labour involved was provided by the wife's father. Most of the cost of the furniture was borne by the wife's mother. During their marriage, the wife remained in part-time employment and used her wages to meet their daily living expenses. The husband was in full-time employment and paid for all other outgoings, made all repayments in respect of the mortgage debt and paid all instalments on his life assurance policy. The house was purchased in 1967, the parties married in 1968, separated in 1970 and the house was sold in 1971. The wife's summons, claiming a beneficial interest in the proceeds from the sale of the former matrimonial home and its contents, was heard by Gibson LJ in 1972.

---

38 As in *Re Roger's Question* [1948] 1 All ER 328.
39 As in *Midland Bank v Cooke and Another* [1995] 2 FLR 915.
40 As in *McHardy and Sons (A Firm) v Warren and Another* [1994] 2 FLR 338.
41 As in *Halifax Building Society v Brown* [1996] 1 FLR 103.
42 As in *Smith v Baker* [1970] 1 WLR 1160.
43 As in *Nixon v Nixon* [1969] 1 WLR 1676.
44 As in *Re Sharpe* [1980] 1 WLR 219.
45 As in *Savage v Dunningham* [1973] 3 WLR 471.
46 [1972] NILR 1.

The court found that the substantive issue of the wife's claim in respect of the house rested on her assertion that by making a direct contribution to the initial purchase price (attributing the loan from her mother as a gift to her) and by making regular payments towards household expenses she had thereby acquired a beneficial interest in the property. The first leg of her claim was found to be substantiated by evidence of bank withdrawals made by the mother, attributed as a gift to the wife not to the couple. As regards the second leg, the court held that it was bound by the judgment in *McFarlane v McFarlane*[47] subject to the rule in *Pettitt v Pettitt*[48] that the court cannot impute to the parties an agreement they never made. In this case Gibson LJ[49] took the view that

> ... the mere payment of household expenses such as the cost of food by one spouse is not sufficient to constitute a contribution towards the purchase of the home — quite regardless of whether it must be pursuant to an arrangement — unless it can be shown that the payments were referable to the purchase of the house in the sense that they freed the husband's personal money and enabled him to use it to meet the current building society instalments or the premiums on the life assurance policies.

He concluded there was no evidence that had the wife not paid for the food the husband would have been unable to continue the payments in respect of the house. The wife's contributions were therefore disregarded.

II. First-Party Contests; Constructive Trusts Based on Evidence of Conversations and Referable Detriment

Where there is no evidence of a direct and substantial contribution to the purchase price, then a spouse will usually frame a claim in equity on the grounds of a constructive trust. That claim will rest on proof of indirect contributions and evidence of conversations which show the existence of a common intention to share beneficial ownership. Evidence of an agreement, arrangement or understanding and of a referable detriment will enable the court to construct a trust giving the claimant an ownership entitlement fixed at judicial discretion.

Conversations

There must be clear evidence of conversations in which both parties expressed a common intention to share the beneficial interest in the property, even though the legal ownership was vested solely in the name of one of the parties. The court will require 'evidence of express discussions between the partners, however imperfectly remembered and however imprecise their terms may have been'.[50]

---

47 [1972] NI 59.
48 [1970] AC 777, 816; [1969] 2 All ER 385, 408 HL.
49 See f/n 46.
50 Per Lord Bridge of Harwich in *Rosset*, f/n 17.

Referable Detriment

There must be evidence that the claimant acted on the proven common intention with the result that he or she suffered a detriment. This will take the form of evidence of having made an indirect contribution such as the investment of time, skill and work in the management of the property.

Combination of Indirect Contributions and Agreement as to Purpose

It is essential to prove that where indirect contributions have been made, this was done in pursuance of the common intention of both parties that the non-legal owner would thereby acquire a beneficial interest in the property. The leading case on the importance of indirect financial contributions being tied to this common intention is *Gissing*.[51]

In this jurisdiction, the leading case and reference point for much subsequent decision-making in this area has long been *McFarlane v McFarlane*.[52] This case was heard in the first instance by Brown J in the county court, then by Gibson LJ in the High Court and on appeal by MacDermott J and Lowry LCJ for the Court of Appeal. Its significance is such that it must be considered in some detail.

The contesting parties were a husband and wife and the property at issue comprised two dwelling houses. The parties were married in 1946, four children were born of the marriage, they separated in 1968 and by the time the property dispute came to court the wife had commenced divorce proceedings.

At the time of the marriage the husband had his own car dismantling business and had opened and thereafter maintained a personal bank account in respect of that business, the wife was a teacher and for some years continued in that career, becoming a principal. During the course of the marriage the husband commenced a second business in insurance broking and again opened and maintained a personal bank account to deal with related business matters; the wife at first provided assistance with this business in conjunction with her teaching duties but eventually ceased the latter and worked full time in the business. At all times she also provided for the needs of their children and maintained the family home. The properties in question were bought in the same year. One house was paid for out of his first account, the other out of both accounts. Both were bought in the husband's name and each was bought to be the matrimonial home. The second was in fact used in that capacity until the couple separated in 1968. The wife brought proceedings against her husband claiming that she had a beneficial interest in the ownership of both properties by virtue of the indirect contributions she had made to their purchase price.

At the initial hearing, Brown J relied largely on *Pettit v Pettit* and *Gissing* and held that the wife's claim failed and should be dismissed. At the second hearing, Gibson LJ held that the cases relied upon did not preclude the wife's claim and found that she was entitled to a beneficial interest in each of the properties, a 2/5ths share in the total.

---

51 See f/n 19.
52 F/n 47.

MacDermott LJ[53] considered the bearing of *Pettit* and *Gissing* on the issues in the present case. It was his view that, before the decision in *Pettit*, section 17 of the 1882 Act was interpreted as conferring a wide discretionary power,

> ... which enabled the Courts to dispense a kind of palm-tree justice in property disputes between spouses or former spouses, unshackled by the rules of law which had previously obtained in this particular field. This development was to some extent formalised by the emergence of what may be called the 'family assets' doctrine as described by Denning LJ in *Gissing*:
>
>> 'It comes to this: where a couple, by their joint efforts, get a house and furniture, intending it to be a continuing provision for them for their joint lives, it is the *prima facie* inference from their conduct that the house and furniture is a 'family asset' in which each is entitled to an equal share. It matters not in whose name it stands, or who pays for what, or who goes out to work and who stays at home. If they both contribute to it by their joint efforts the *prima facie* inference is that it belongs to them both equally at any rate when each member makes a financial contribution which is substantial.'

MacDermott LJ noted that the net effect of the decisions in *Pettit* and *Gissing* was to put an end to the 'family assets' doctrine and to impose a restricted interpretation on section 17 which was held to be only a procedural provision not empowering the court to alter the existing rights of the parties. It was his view that the present law could be summarised in two propositions. Firstly, that in the absence of proof to the contrary, a spouse who has acquired the legal title to property purchased with the aid of a substantial monetary contribution from the other spouse will hold the property subject to a beneficial interest therein belonging to the other spouse. Secondly, in certain circumstances the first proposition can also apply in favour of the spouse without the legal title where that spouse has contributed to the purchase, not directly by finding a part of the price, but indirectly and in a manner which has added to the resources out of which the property has been acquired as, for example, by work done or services rendered or by relieving the other spouse of some, at any rate, of his or her financial contributions.

Applying these propositions to the case in hand, MacDermott LJ[54] considered that the central issue was

> ... whether the contributions mentioned in the second proposition (i.e. indirect contributions) have to be the subject of some agreement or arrangement between the spouses before they can be held to found a claim to a beneficial interest in the property acquired with their aid; or whether, as in the case of direct monetary contributions to the price of what was acquired, a resulting trust in favour of the contributor will follow as a matter of course in the absence of rebutting evidence?

He concluded[55] that

---

53 See f/n 46.
54 See f/n 46.
55 Ibid.

> ... there is a relevant distinction between the two kinds of contribution and the indirect contribution, if it is to earn a beneficial interest in the property acquired, must be the subject of agreement or arrangement between the spouses ... includes any understanding between the spouses which shows a mutual intention that the indirect contributions of one or the other will go to create a beneficial proprietary interest in the contributor.

That being the case, he was unable to agree with Gibson LJ's finding that the wife's substantial but indirect contribution over the years, to the funds out of which the properties in dispute were bought, was sufficient for her to establish a beneficial interest. He was[56]

> ... unable to discover anything to support the existence of any agreement or arrangement or understanding between the parties ... nothing sufficient to establish even the most informal of understandings from which the necessary intention regarding the wife's indirect contributions could be inferred.

The wife was held to be a volunteer (a 'volunteer' is someone who has provided no consideration, i.e. has not evidenced their contractual intent by giving something to balance a transaction) and therefore the doctrines of equity had nothing to give her (it is a rule of equity that 'Equity will not assist a volunteer').

Indirect Contributions and the Presumption of Advancement

In this jurisdiction the High Court had an opportunity to consider a claim based on indirect contributions from a wife in *Watters v Watters*,[57] which was heard on appeal from a county court. This was a case where a separated wife with four dependant children had applied under section 17 of the Married Woman's Property Act 1882 for a declaration that she had an equitable interest in a dwelling house, the matrimonial home. The facts may be briefly stated as follows. The couple married in 1963 and opened a joint account with a building society in 1965. The husband entered into a contract to purchase the matrimonial home in 1967 for £2,800 and paid a deposit of £700 of which £600 came from the joint account and £100 was provided by the husband; the balance was to be met by a mortgage arrangement with the building society which required monthly repayments of £15.00. In 1975 the husband converted a personal bank account into a joint account into which his employers paid his wages and from which he and his wife made withdrawals to meet daily household running costs. Throughout the marriage the husband was in virtually continuous employment while the wife was not employed at any time. Marital difficulties arose in 1977 which led to a magistrates' court finding the husband guilty of cruelty, making a maintenance order in favour of the wife and as a consequence the wife and children found alternative accommodation. Since the separation, the husband had consistently met all mortgage repayments.

The wife claimed that the first lodgement in the joint account with the building society had been made by her with money received from an aunt, that the opening of

---

56 Ibid.
57 [1979] 3 NIJB.

that account had been discussed and agreed upon between her husband and herself with the common objective of buying a house and that throughout their marriage her mother had given her cash presents amounting to £10–12 per month which had been used to make up mortgage repayments. The court at first instance found that the wife had received some money from her mother and some of that had been used for repayments.

The High Court ruled that[58]

> [t]he money for the initial investment in the joint account and many subsequent payments were provided by the husband out of his own money, but the presumption of advancement applied and, accordingly, the wife jointly with the husband became entitled beneficially to the money in the account. There is clear authority for the proposition that the presumption of advancement can apply to a joint husband and wife account (see *Re Figgis* [1969] 1 Ch 123).

Finding that the husband had failed to rebut the presumption of advancement, the court held that on the opening of the joint account the wife then acquired a joint beneficial interest of 6/28ths (the £600 deposit as a proportion of the purchase price of £2,800), even though the legal title to the house was put solely in the husband's name (see *McFarlane* above for the legal effect of a direct contribution by a wife to the purchase price). The court found no evidence of the wife having made any specific direct contributions to the cost of the house such as would entitle her to an increased beneficial interest. However, in view of the modest payments made by her mother which may have indirectly contributed to the cost of the house, the court fixed the wife's whole, severed and equitable interest at 1/8th.

The Matrimonial Home

First-Party Contests; Rights of Occupation

The Family Law (Miscellaneous Provisions) (NI) Order 1984, Articles 3–13, transferred to this jurisdiction the provisions set out in the Matrimonial Homes Act 1983 protecting the right of a non-owning spouse to occupy the marital home, the principles to be applied and the orders available for that purpose. This following deals with the law relating to those matters (for the application of the law in the context of domestic violence, as governed largely by the 1980 Order, see Chapter Eight).

1. Rights

Under the 1984 Order:

> 4.—(1) Where one spouse is entitled to occupy a dwelling house by virtue of any statutory provision giving him or her the right to remain in occupation, and the other is not so entitled then, subject to this Part, the spouse not so entitled shall have the following rights (in this Part referred to as 'rights of occupation').

---

58 Ibid.

(a) if in occupation, a right not to be evicted or excluded from the dwelling house or any part thereof by the other spouse except with leave of the court given by an order under this Article;
(b) if not in occupation, a right with the leave of the court so given to enter into and occupy the dwelling house.

Under Article 4(11) these rights continue for as long as the marriage subsists. The rights are registerable, in accordance with the Land Registration Rules (NI) 1994 and the Matrimonial Charges Regulations (NI) 1989, as a charge against the matrimonial home in the Land Registry or Registry of Deeds.

(a) The Matrimonial Home

The Order only applies to a matrimonial home. Where the couple have more than one dwelling the applicant spouse must choose which one is to be the named matrimonial home. The protection is not available in respect of a dwelling house which is otherwise used. It may apply to an entire building despite the fact that only a part of it was ever in use as the matrimonial home (e.g. a hotel in which the owners had their own quarters). As stated in Article 13(1) of the 1984 Order, the protection is available in respect of a dwelling house held by the two spouses either jointly or as tenants-in-common which, at any time, served as the matrimonial home.

(b) 'In Occupation'

The right to occupy is dependent upon the continuation of both the marriage and the legal rights of the other spouse. The Order applies regardless of whether the occupation is in respect of a home legally owned wholly by one spouse, is owned subject to a mortgage, is jointly owned by both or where both share the joint tenancy of a public or privately owned dwelling.

2. Principles

The 1984 Order requires the court to apply four criteria when considering an application for an order: the conduct of the spouses in relation to each other and otherwise, their respective needs and financial resources, the needs of any children and all the circumstances of the case. The Court of Appeal[59] has held that the reference to 'all the circumstances of the case' indicates a legislative intent to allow the court to take into consideration not only the interests of the spouses and any children but also the interests of third parties.

The Rule in Richards v Richards

The introduction of the 1984 Order also had the effect of transferring to this jurisdiction the decision of the House of Lords in *Richards v Richards*.[60] This is a significant ruling, the facts of which can be briefly stated.

---

59 See *Kaur v Gill* [1988] Fam 110, [1988] 2 All ER 288.
60 [1984] AC 174, [1983] 2 All ER 807 HL.

The case concerned a married couple who lived in the marital home with their two children. It was an unhappy marriage during which the wife, on several occasions, left the husband to live briefly with other men. She eventually petitioned, unsuccessfully, for divorce on the grounds of her husband's behaviour; the court held that her allegations were 'flimsy in the extreme'. They continued to live in the marital home but in separate bedrooms until she finally left, taking the children, to live in an overcrowded house. She then sought an exclusion order to oust the husband from the home. This was granted by the court and upheld by the Court of Appeal, despite the judge at first instance finding that she had no reasonable ground for refusing to return, because her present accommodation was unsuitable for the children. The husband appealed to the House of Lords.

The House upheld the appeal on the grounds that the wife had never made out a case for the exclusion of her husband. It ruled that the law governing the occupation of the matrimonial home was now to be found exclusively in the 1983 Act (or 1984 Order) and therefore the power to issue an ouster order was only exercisable subject to the above four criteria being satisfied. Moreover, it ruled that each of the criteria must be given an equal weighting, where the weighting given to any one depended on the facts of the case and the inapplicability of the paramountcy principle.

However, in giving judgment in *Richards*, Hailsham LJ recognised[61] that there may be some circumstances in which the welfare interests of children will have to be made paramount. This acknowledgment of possible exceptions to the rule in *Richards* has been steadily reinforced by other decisions[62] in recent years.

3. Orders

The 1984 Order provides that rights of occupation may be claimed by the non-owning spouse applying to the court for an order:

(a) declaring, enforcing, restricting or terminating those rights, or
(b) prohibiting, suspending, or restricting the exercise by either spouse of the right to occupy the dwelling-house, or
(c) requiring either spouse to permit the exercise by the other of the right to occupy the dwelling-house.

These are very sweeping judicial powers. Effectively, a spouse is thereby given a right to apply for an 'ouster' order to debar the other from their home and/or a 're-entry' order permitting the former to resume living there. Once acquired the order should be registered, even if the acquiring spouse is not actually in occupation. It then takes effect as an equitable charge binding not only on the other spouse but also on third parties. A spouse with registered rights may continue mortgage payments which the building society is required to accept.

---

61   Ibid at 204.
62   See, for example, *Gibson v Austin* [1992] 2 FLR 437, where it was held that in proceedings for an injunction to restrain a respondent from molesting a child living with the applicant it would be appropriate to apply the paramountcy principle.

The Matrimonial Home and Beneficial Interests

Contests between First and Third Parties

Disputes between a spouse or spouses and third parties regarding the ownership of matrimonial homes are the cause of much litigation. If the legal title to the property is clearly vested in both parties, then the application of the law is quite straightforward. However, if legal ownership is vested in one spouse but the other claims a beneficial interest, then the rights of a third party are not as readily determined.

Beneficial Interests and Third Parties

(a) The Principles

Where a third party is put on formal notice of a non-owning spouse's established beneficial interest in the property (i.e. when this is registered as a notice, caution or charge), then, whether or not they knew of it, the third party will be bound by such interest and any title acquired will be subject to it. Where the interest of a non-owning spouse in occupation[63] is not registered but could have been readily discovered if the third party had made reasonable enquiries, then the court will hold that the latter had constructive notice of it and the same consequences will ensue. Where such a non-owning spouse has an unregistered beneficial interest but has no notice of a legal right given by the owning spouse to a third party, then the latter's right will defer to the beneficial interest.[64]

(i) The Rule in *Rosset*

Where a non-owning spouse has made no direct contribution towards the purchase price of the matrimonial home and is unable to provide evidence of any agreement, arrangement or understanding that the property is to be shared beneficially, then that spouse will not have acquired a beneficial interest and the rights of a third party will prevail against him or her whether or not those rights were acquired with the latter's knowledge. *Rosset*[65] remains the leading case illustrating this proposition in circumstances where the claimant did not have notice of third-party rights.

(ii) The Decision in *Cooke*

Where a non-owning spouse is able to establish some beneficial interest, the court may then go on to take into account all dealings between the parties relating to the property when apportioning beneficial interests between first parties and determining the priority of a third-party claim.

This rule is a consequence of the recent Court of Appeal judgment in *Midland Bank v Cooke and Another*[66] which concerned a matrimonial home registered and mortgaged

---

63 See *Abbey National Building Society v Cann* [1990] 1 All ER 1085 for authority that the claimant spouse with a beneficial interest must be in occupation of the matrimonial home at the time when the third party acquired their legal rights.
64 See *William and Glyn's Bank v Boland* [1980] 2 All ER 408 HL.
65 See f/n 20.
66 [1995] 2 FLR 915.

in the husband's name. At time of purchase he had contributed £1,000 and her parents £1,100 to the purchase price (amounting to approximately one-quarter of the total). After their marriage in 1971 both parties remained in employment. The wife did a considerable amount of work on the property, paid contractors bills and met the cost of much household expenditure. The husband made all mortgage repayments, though it was not established that his capacity to do so was due in part to his wife bearing the burden of other costs. In 1978 the bank made a loan, secured on the house, to further the interests of the husband's business. In 1979 the wife signed a waiver form, postponing any interest she may have in the property in favour of the bank's charge. A second loan and charge were then secured. The bank brought proceedings claiming repayment of the loans or possession of the matrimonial home. The judge at first instance held that the waiver had been obtained as a result of the husband's undue influence (itself a significant finding and one which was not appealed) and that the wife was entitled by resulting trust to a proportion amounting to 6.7 per cent of the total beneficial interest of the property (this representing a half share in her parents' contribution to the purchase price).

On appeal the court held that the wife was entitled to a fifty per cent share in the beneficial interest. It was found that where the parents of one spouse make a contribution to the purchase price of a matrimonial home, as a wedding present, the correct inference is that this is a gift in equal shares to the marital couple which operates to vest a beneficial interest, proportionate to the total purchase price, in them both. The court re-affirmed the ruling in *Rosset* but added that once an entitlement to some beneficial interest has been established then, in the words of Waite LJ,[67]

> ... the duty of the judge is to undertake a survey of the whole course of dealing between the parties relevant to their ownership and occupation of the property and their sharing of its burdens and advantages. That scrutiny will not confine itself to the limited range of acts of direct contribution of the sort that are needed to found a beneficial interest in the first place. It will take into consideration all conduct which throws light on the question what shares were intended.

Further, the court held that the claims of a non-owning party should not be foreclosed by the absence of an agreement between the couple as to ownership of the property. The fact that ownership had never been discussed was not conclusive.

This decision seems to have the effect of confining the rule in *Rosset* to the preliminary issue of whether or not an entitlement to beneficial interest can be established, ameliorating the harshness of the ruling in *Gissing* and giving permission for contributions based on parental and housekeeping services to be taken into account when quantifying the amount of beneficial interest accruing to a non-owning spouse in occupation.

(b) The Practice

The precedent value of the cases outlined below must now be read subject to the ruling in *Cooke*.

---

67 Ibid.

(i) A Spouse with Notice of a Third Party's Rights Will Only Prevail against Those Rights Where She Can Establish a Beneficial Interest

In this jurisdiction the case of *Britannia Building Society v Johnston and Others*[68] provides a good illustration of circumstances where the claimant did have notice of a third party's rights. This was a case where the first defendant was the registered owner of a farm inherited from his father on the latter's death in 1982. He lived on the farm with his wife, the second defendant, since their marriage in 1967. Throughout the marriage the second defendant kept the house, helped with the livestock on the farm and bore primary care responsibility for the upbringing of their children. Indeed, for some years, both prior to and since the death of the first defendant's father, the farm was effectively worked by the joint efforts of the first and second defendants.

In 1990 the first defendant obtained a loan of £45,000 repayable over thirteen years. This was secured by a charge on the farm in favour of the plaintiff. The charge was registered in the Land Registry in 1992. The second defendant was not included in the loan arrangement and no attempt was made to have her sign a deed of postponement. No instalments of principal or interest were ever paid and the plaintiff applied to the court for an order for possession. The first defendant entered an appearance but took no part in the proceedings and it was accepted on behalf of the third, fourth and fifth defendants (their children) that no defence to the claim for possession could be put forward on their behalf. The second defendant, however, claimed that a constructive trust had arisen in her favour, entitling her to share in the lands and giving her an overriding right which should prevail against the plaintiff's claim. It was further argued that the facts gave rise to a proprietary estoppel in favour of the second defendant.

It was held,[69] granting the order for possession, that:

1. Circumstances which are capable of giving rise to a constructive trust in cases of this nature are (a) an agreement, arrangement or undertaking reached between the spouses that the property is to be shared beneficially, or (b) conduct on the part of the claimant, amounting to a direct contribution to the purchase price of the property, which gives rise to the inference of such a common intention to share the beneficial interest in the property [see *Rosset*[70]].
2. There is insufficient evidence given by the second defendant to hold that anything approaching a definite agreement, arrangement or understanding was ever reached between her and her husband. Moreover, the necessary element of acting to her detriment was wholly lacking. The highest at which her case could be put is that she continued to work on the farm following discussions about her entitlement to a share in the lands. However, she was doing this work since her marriage as part of her daily life, long before her husband succeeded his father as owner, and the evidence does not support a conclusion that she undertook any more or increased her efforts for the benefit of the farm on the strength of such discussions.

---

68 [1994] 10 BNIL 75.
69 Ibid.
70 See f/n 20.

3. It was laid down in this jurisdiction in *McFarlane v McFarlane*[71] that an indirect contribution will not suffice to establish a constructive trust in favour of a claimant. When one adds to this fact that no payments were ever made on foot of the mortgage debt, it could not be readily said that she has made contributions of a type which are capable of giving rise to a constructive trust in her favour of an equitable trust in the lands.
4. To establish a proprietary estoppel the second defendant would have to show expenditure of money on the lands or at least an equivalent action to her detriment, allied to representation or encouragement on the part of the owner of the lands, sufficient to make it inequitable for the owner to insist on his strict legal rights. The actions of the first defendant were insufficient to constitute the necessary element of encouragement, nor did the second defendant change her position to her detriment in any way sufficient to give rise to an estoppel. The plaintiff was granted an order for possession of the lands.

(ii) The Beneficial Interest of a Spouse with Notice of a Third Party's Rights Will Not Prevail against Those Rights Where the Beneficial Interest Is Relatively Insignificant

The proposition that the beneficial interest of a spouse with notice will not prevail against the rights of a third party when that interest is relatively insignificant is illustrated by the facts of *Northern Bank v McNeill*.[72] In this case the plaintiff brought proceedings by way of mortgagee's summons with the aim of realising securities held by the bank against overdraft liabilities of the defendants, the latter being a husband and his wife and the securities being the matrimonial home. This was a complicated suit which also concerned the ownership of two failed businesses with which the first defendant (the husband) but not the second (the wife) was involved with others. The husband had an arrangement with the plaintiff whereby business debts were secured by way of a charge registered in favour of the plaintiff against the matrimonial home of which the husband was the sole owner. In March 1982 the husband lodged a planning application to build fifty-two houses on land attached to the matrimonial home. The plaintiff agreed to assist him with this scheme by lending him and his wife £15,000 together with an assurance that consideration would be given to a further loan of £35,000 within the next year. In return the plaintiff sought and obtained the agreement of the wife that she would make herself jointly liable with her husband for his existing indebtedness and for the future liabilities of them both. This arrangement was secured by a second charge against the matrimonial home. A year later the plaintiff called in the joint debt.

Among the issues facing the court was whether the wife had an equitable interest in one-half (or some other fraction) of the matrimonial home. Also, the question was raised as to whether the second charge on the matrimonial home should be set aside as regards the wife's interest on the grounds (i) that it was an unconscionable bargain, or (ii) undue influence, or (iii) misrepresentation.

---

71   See f/n 47.
72   [1988] 7 BNIL 79.

In relation to the first issue, the court held that where a wife claims an equitable interest in the matrimonial home against her husband's mortgagee (the husband being the sole registered owner of the fee simple in the home), the onus is on the wife to establish that interest. Furthermore, in accordance with the rule in *McFarlane*, if the wife relies on indirect contributions by herself to the purchase price she must also prove an agreement between herself and her husband or at least an arrangement and understanding (not necessarily contractual in status) with her husband that she was to have such an interest. The court considered that evidence regarding the wife's direct and indirect contributions to the purchase price of the home was unsatisfactory. Applying equitable principles, the court judged the sum of her direct and indirect contributions amounted to 1/6th of the total purchase price. The court also found that there was an understanding or agreement between the husband and wife that her contributions should go towards the purchase of the home. It was held that she was therefore entitled to a corresponding beneficial interest in the home.

In relation to the second issue, the court held that the wife's claim failed on each of three counts.

Accordingly, the court upheld the order for possession of the matrimonial home.

(iii) The Beneficial Interest of a Spouse without Notice of a Third Party's Rights Will Prevail against Those Rights

The proposition that the beneficial interests of a spouse will prevail against the rights of a third party of whom that spouse has no interest is usefully illustrated by the case of *Allied Irish Banks Ltd v McWilliams and Another*.[73] The case concerned two summonses. In the first the plaintiff was the bank and the husband and wife were the defendants, the property at issue was the matrimonial home and the proceedings were commenced under section 46 of the Judgments (Enforcement) Act (NI) 1969 in respect of a charge registered in 1980 by the bank against the property. In the second the plaintiff was the wife, the husband the defendant and the proceedings were brought under section 17 of the Married Women's Property Act 1882 whereby the wife sought a declaration that she was entitled to an absolute interest in the matrimonial home subject only to a building society mortgage and certain other charges imposed on the property under the 1969 Act.

The facts may be briefly stated. In 1962 the couple were married and three children were born of the marriage (aged eleven, fifteen and eighteen at the time of proceedings). In 1975 the husband and wife acquired the property, subject to a mortgage, as joint owners. The marriage was unhappy and unsuccessful. The husband lived apart from his family for long periods, became unemployed shortly after the marriage, was never thereafter in secure employment, never provided any kind of regular income and gambled. The wife decided, shortly after the birth of the first child, that she would have to be the sole breadwinner for the family and secured employment as a teacher which she thereafter maintained, becoming a department head. The wife first learned of a charge against the property in 1981 when the bank sought leave to sell the house.

---

73 [1982] NILR 156.

The wife claimed that despite both assignment and mortgage being in the joint names of herself and her husband, she was the sole owner in equity and the bank's charge, being subsequent to her equitable interest, could not prevail against it. The wife's claim rested on two alternative arguments. Firstly, it was contended that before the acquisition of the property no agreement was made between the husband and wife as to the beneficial ownership of it when acquired, and since in the event the wife paid the whole of the deposit and the whole of the repayments to date to the building society out of her own money, she was in equity entitled to the ownership under the principle of resulting trusts (as applied in *Pettit*). Secondly and alternatively, it was argued that if a pre-acquisition agreement was made between the husband and wife as to the beneficial ownership, the agreement was that she should have the sole beneficial ownership of the property.

The court found that the house was acquired at the wife's initiative; the husband's name had been added as an owner only because of the wife's conviction that her name alone would be insufficient to secure a loan. There was no agreement between husband and wife before the property was acquired as to what was to happen to the beneficial ownership in it afterwards. After acquisition the husband made sporadic payments into the wife's bank account but there was no agreement or arrangement between them that those payments were to go towards the repayment of the mortgage debt or for any other specific purpose. The bank account could not be regarded as a joint one in which the husband as well as the wife had an interest.

On the facts thus established, the court was of the view that as the parties had made no express agreement regarding the equitable ownership before joint acquisition of the property, it must therefore rest in the spouse who paid the purchase price (see *Pettitt*[74] per Lord Upjohn).

The court held that, as between the husband and wife, the latter was entitled to the whole equitable interest in the property and the husband was to be regarded as trustee of his interest in it for her. The prior equitable interests of the wife had priority over the subsequent legal charge of the bank, unless it could be shown that the bank acquired its charge *bona fide* for value and without actual or constructive notice of the wife's equitable interest. The onus of proof lay on the bank; no proof was offered.

(iv) The Beneficial Interest of a Spouse without Notice of a Third Party's Rights Will Only Prevail Where the Interest Is Substantial

In *Northern Bank Ltd v Beattie*[75] the applicant bank sought (i) possession of the 'mortgaged premises' (the matrimonial home), (ii) alternatively, determination of the wife's beneficial interest in the premises and (iii) sale in lieu of partition.

The relevant facts were as follows. The couple married in 1959 and had five children none of whom continued to be dependent on their parents. The premises in dispute was purchased by the husband in 1974 for £5,500, a deposit of £360 being paid by

---

74 See f/n 17 at 813–14B.
75 [1982] NIJB 18. See also Wallace, *Mortgagees and Possession*, NILQ, vol. 37 (1986) No. 4 (p. 352 et seq) and Wallace, *Mortgagees and Charges*, Annual Review of Property Law (1995) (p. 35 et seq). Also, further at end of chapter.

him. At the same time he secured, solely in his name, a mortgage with the NIHE. In 1974 he obtained a second mortgage, by sub-demise of the house, with the Northern Bank. His wife knew nothing of this mortgage. In 1980 the couple separated. In 1981 the husband's financial difficulties led to the bank issuing a summons. One year later the husband ceased repayments to the NIHE which then also issued a summons. If the house was sold and both mortgages paid off there would be no remaining monies.

The issues before the court were as follows. Could the wife establish a one-half (or other share) equitable interest in the premises on the trust basis as outlined in *McFarlane*? If so, would the equitable interest have priority over the legal estate vested in the bank under the bank's mortgage? Again, if the wife could establish such a prior equitable interest, would the bank be entitled to an order for sale of the premises under the Partition Acts?

The court heard evidence from the wife, judged to be somewhat flimsy, of her long periods of employment during the marriage when, she claimed, her wages went into the housekeeping and home maintenance expenses. In the light of this evidence the judge stated:[76]

> It is well established that the first question to be asked in this type of case is whether the spouses agreed that the wife was to acquire a beneficial interest in the matrimonial home. If they did, then the court will do its best to ascertain what precisely the agreement was and will give effect to it. However, if no agreement is proved but it is shown that the wife has *directly* contributed a substantial sum of money towards the purchase of the home then normally, in the absence of contrary intentions, the court will apply the resulting trust principle and hold that the wife acquired a share in the home proportionate to her contribution to the cost of it. Where, however, as in the present case, the wife claims an interest on the basis of *indirect* contributions then different considerations apply. In *McFarlane*[77] Lord MacDermott described that basis in the following words:
>
> > '... not directly, by finding a part of the price, but indirectly and in a manner which has added to the resources out of which the property has been acquired as, for example, by work done or services rendered or by relieving the other spouse of some, at any rate, of his or her financial obligations.
> >
> > '... Indirect contribution, if it is to earn a beneficial interest in the property acquired, must be the subject of agreement or arrangement between the spouses ... includes any understanding between the spouses which shows a mutual intention that the indirect contributions of one or the other will go to create a beneficial proprietary interest...
> >
> > 'But circumstances may arise, even in the best regulated marriages, where the spouses agree in thinking it provident and right that some form of wealth to be produced by the indirect contributions of one or other of them should enure and be held for the benefit of the contributor.

---

76 Ibid.
77 See f/n 47 at 67.

> ... a court of equity ... is entitled to say that the holder of the fund or property in question was bound as a matter of fair dealing to hold the same or some share thereof on behalf of the contributor. At this point the indirect contribution has become, by virtue of the arrangement or undertaking between the spouses, as much the basis of a resulting trust as a direct contribution in money to the cost of acquiring a particular property'.

As Lord Lowry,[78] in the same case, said:

> 'Thus a tacit, or even express, agreement that the wife in the present case should use her salary as she did is not an agreement or an arrangement that by doing so she was to acquire an interest in the property. Or, as Mr Murray put it, indirect contributions which are unrelated to the acquisition of the property cannot found an equitable interest in it'.

Lord Lowry, referring to *Gissing*, added:

> 'The House of Lords has further made it plain that imputed intention is not enough; the intention must be a real one and not a legal fiction introduced for the purpose of achieving a result thought by the court to be just but not intended by the parties. A real intention may be either express or to be implied from the conduct of the parties.'

The court found that there never was an express agreement; the wife made no direct contributions either to the payment of the deposit or to the payment of any of the instalments of the mortgage debt which had been paid; there was much exaggeration and some serious inaccuracies in the wife's evidence; the wife's earnings were undoubtedly applied to discharge household bills, which otherwise the husband would have had to meet, and that this enabled him to make mortgage payments. Accordingly, returning to the questions it had initially set, the court held (i) that the wife had acquired a beneficial interest which could be set at one-quarter for her and at three-quarters for the husband, (ii) that priority should be given to the wife's interest due to the bank's failure to make any inquiry of a person in occupation at the time the mortgage was made and (iii) that the bank had a right to sell the property under the Partition Acts.

The Matrimonial Home and Legal Interests

Contests between First Parties and with Third Parties

In this jurisdiction the claims of a creditor against the property of a debtor are generally made under the Partition Acts of 1868 and 1876 rather than, as in England and Wales, under the Law of Property Act 1925. The law relating to the rights of spouses when one is declared bankrupt is largely governed by the Insolvency (NI) Order 1989, Article 302 (dealing with claims between spouses) and Article 309(2)(a) (dealing with the rights of the spouse of a bankrupt in relation to third-party claims in respect of the matrimonial home).

---

78 Ibid. at 76.

Bankruptcy

(a) The Principles

A bankrupt spouse without any dependant children is exposed to the full rigour of the Insolvency (NI) Order 1989. A creditor's claims will lie against all assets (excepting trade tools) including the matrimonial home. Such a claim cannot lie against assets owned by the spouse of the bankrupt, including any legal title or established beneficial interest in their home. Bankrupts and/or their spouses are afforded some protection under the 1989 Order where dependant children are involved but their rights of occupation may be dispensed with by the judiciary. Protection may also be available, to a degree, under the provisions of the Children (NI) Order 1995. A spouse of the bankrupt with dependent children, who has no legal title to the matrimonial home but has a beneficial interest, could look to equity rather than statute for protection. An equitable trust, arising from the beneficial interest, may afford some protection for that spouse for the duration of the children's dependency. This was demonstrated in *Re Holliday*[79] where one reason given by the court for deferring the sale of a bankrupt's home was to avoid hardship to his wife and disruption to their children's education.

The 1989 Order now provides a creditor with statutory rights which, in most circumstances, will prevail against the equitable interests of the spouse of a bankrupt. This is so despite the fact that, in keeping with the recommendations of the *Cork Report*,[80] it directs the court to give specific consideration to the needs of the bankrupt's spouse and children. Before making an order in relation to the matrimonial home, there is a judicial duty under Article 309(5) to apply the following criteria:

(a) the interests of the bankrupt's creditors;
(b) the conduct of the spouse or former spouse, far as contributing to the bankruptcy;
(c) the needs and financial resources of the spouse or former spouse;
(d) the needs of the children; and
(e) all the circumstances of the case other than the needs of the bankrupt.

However, the courts have elected to adopt a conservative approach to this duty.

(b) The Law and the Rights of Spouses vis-à-vis Each Other

Under the Law Reform (Miscellaneous Provisions) Act (NI) 1937, section 9, for the purposes of the legal effects of bankruptcy, a married and an unmarried woman are to be treated in the same way.

(c) The Law and the Rights of a Spouse vis-à-vis Third Parties

In theory, statute law now affords some limited recognition to the rights of a blameless spouse and protection for his or her dependant children in the face of a claim for possession of the matrimonial home from the bankrupt spouse's trustees. The dilemma facing the court when considering the conflicting claims of a bankrupt's spouse and

---

79 [1981] Ch 405; [1980] 3 All ER 385 CA.
80 The *Cork Committee on Insolvency* (Cmnd 8558) (1982).

children on the one hand and the trustee for the bankrupt's creditors on the other was summarised by Goff LJ in the words 'whose voice in equity in all the circumstances ought to prevail'.[81] In practice, judicial restraint in applying the protective provisions of the Insolvency (NI) Order 1989 has had the result that, most usually, the best an innocent spouse and mother can hope for is to have the sale briefly deferred. One year after the creditor has obtained on order vesting the property of a bankrupt in the creditor:

> ... the court shall assume, unless the circumstances are exceptional, that the interests of the bankrupt's creditors outweigh all other considerations.

In effect there is now a rebuttable presumption that a creditor's claim to matrimonial property, including the family home, will prevail against all other considerations. Case law has confirmed the need for circumstances to be truly exceptional if a creditor's claim is to be deferred.

(i) Transactions to Deprive Creditors

A primary reason for introducing the 1989 Order was to protect the interests of creditors. A practice had developed whereby a spouse with full legal title who was threatened with insolvency would enter into a 'transaction of convenience' with the other, transfer some legal right to the matrimonial property for nominal consideration, and so hope to forestall the claims of a creditor. This has been addressed by a provision which allows a trustee to apply to the court, in circumstances where such a transaction 'for undervalue' has been made within five years preceding the bankruptcy, and authorises the court to remove the effect of that transaction and to then make such order as it thinks fit.

(ii) Creditor and Spouse without Legal Ownership

The 1989 Order provides that the trustee in bankruptcy may make application in the bankruptcy court for sale or partition of matrimonial property and the court will then apply the above criteria and make such order as it considers to be fair and reasonable. A spouse without legal ownership will effectively have twelve months in which to make out a case that her circumstances are exceptional if the creditor's claim is to be defeated. As stated, exceptional hardship will be hard to prove. For example, the fact that wives and their dependent children would suffer hardship if two matrimonial homes were sold by the trustees on failure of a business owned by two brothers who also had exclusive legal title to the houses has been held not to meet this test.[82]

(iii) Creditor and Spouses with Joint Ownership

The case of *Official Assignee for Bankruptcy for Northern Ireland and Assignee of the Property of Helen Beattie v Beattie and Another*[83] concerned the effect of a wife's bankruptcy on ownership of the matrimonial home, which was valued at £30,000. The husband sought to prevent the Official Assignee from disposing of the home.

---

81 See f/n 79.
82 See *Re Citro (A Bankrupt) and Another* [1991] 1 FLR 71; [1990] 3 All ER 95 2 CA.
83 [1992] 12 NIJB 11.

An application was brought under the Partition Acts 1868 and 1876 by the Official Assignee of the estate of Helen Beattie (the second defendant) who was adjudged a bankrupt on July 6, 1987. The plaintiff sought a determination of the interests of Helen Beattie and the interests of her husband (the first defendant) in the matrimonial home and either a partition of the premises, which were held by the defendants as tenants-in-common in equal shares, or a sale and equal distribution of the proceeds between the plaintiff and the first defendant.

In the Registry of Deeds each defendant was registered as a tenant-in-common owner of land held in fee simple, each with an entitlement to an undivided half share in that land. The entry in the Registry also showed, in the margin against ownership of premises (the matrimonial home), the wording:

Registered 16th May 1977
Consideration: — Natural love and affection.

The first defendant claimed the entire beneficial interest. He asserted that he purchased the land in his sole name, provided the purchase price (£1,000), had a dwelling-house constructed on the land and that the second defendant made no financial contribution whatsoever towards the repayment of the mortgage. He further asserted that the above entry had been made only because he feared that his medical condition would prevent him from obtaining a mortgage solely in his name. For that reason alone (i.e. to satisfy the risk criteria of the building society and thereby secure a mortgage), he had extended a right of tenant-in-common to his wife.

It was accepted that prior to the second defendant's bankruptcy the legal estate in the premises was indisputably vested in equal shares in both defendants as tenants-in-common. The issues requiring determination by the court were whether the beneficial interest in the premises was apportioned equally, whether the apportioning was affected by the fact that the first defendant made all mortgage repayments and whether that defendant should now be given credit for the repayments made.

The court gave full consideration to the presumption of advancement and to the doctrine of resulting trusts. It was found that the first defendant was[84]

> attempting to use the rules of equity to prove that the deed of transfer to his wife was not effected for the natural love and affection which is stated in the deed of transfer. He is estopped from denying that the gift to his wife was made for natural love and affection. He is moving the goal posts. 'He who comes into equity must come with clean hands'. The presumption of advancement applies unless a proper ground for rebutting this is both pleaded and proved.

The court ruled that the premises were held by both defendants immediately prior to the bankruptcy as tenants-in-common in equal shares in both law and equity. It therefore upheld the building society charge of £21,848.47 on the property.

---

84   Ibid.

(iv) Creditor and Divorced Spouses with Joint Ownership: Dependent Children

The facts of *Re Gorman*[85] are sufficiently apposite to warrant their being set out in this context, even though they concern the circumstances of a legally dissolved family unit. This case illustrates the court's concern to extend some protection to the family home of a divorced mother and children (and the limitations on its capacity to do so), even in the face of the rightful claims of a third party.

Initially, the family home had been transferred to the spouses in equal shares and there was an unsigned declaration of interests. At the time of transfer, the largest contribution to the purchase price had been made by the woman as a result of a gift from her father. No property adjustment order was made during the course of subsequent divorce proceedings. The mother and children remained in residence and she continued the mortgage repayments and paid for improvements to the property. The father, who lived elsewhere, became bankrupt three years after the divorce. As his only asset was his share in the former family home, the trustee in bankruptcy applied for this to be sold and claimed one-half of the proceeds of such sale. The decision of the judge at first instance to refuse to order the sale was reversed on appeal. That the largest contribution to the purchase price had been made by the mother was irrelevant when the transfer document clearly declared that the couple were to hold the property in equal shares. The creditors were entitled to claim the father's one-half share in the property. This share would be subject to equitable accounting to allow for her mortgage repayments and improvement costs and his loss of occupancy rights. However, the order was deferred for six months to permit the mother to sue her solicitor for failing to take the steps necessary to protect her position during the divorce proceedings.

Mortgages and Charges

Proceedings by Third Parties

Bankruptcy proceedings are not the only means by which creditors may seek to realise their interests in marital property. But, where such an interest extends to less than one moiety in the value of the property, a creditor may need to proceed with great care if he or she is to succeed against a debtor spouse. Much will depend on whether the creditor has standing as mortgagee or chargee.

1. Mortgages and a Creditor's Right of Enforcement

A mortgagee is vested with rights in the property subject to the mortgage.[86] To establish those rights the mortgagee may bring proceedings under section 4 of the Partition Act 1868 requesting the court to direct the partition (or sale in lieu) of the property. If granted, the order may be enforced by powers provided under Article 52 of the Judgments Enforcement (NI) Order 1981 which specifically recognise a mortgagee's right of sale. The recent case of *Northern Bank Ltd v Adams*,[87] heard before Master

---

85 [1990] 2 FLR 284.
86 See *Northern Banking Company v Devlin* [1924] IR 90.
87 Unreported (1996).

Ellison, provides authority for the view that a creditor must have an interest in the property which extends to one moiety or more in the property if the court is to have jurisdiction to deal with an application under section 4. This was a case concerning a couple (with two children aged sixteen and nineteen at the time of hearing) registered as joint owners in fee simple of a house bought for £30,000 in or about 1988 and valued at £80–90,000 when the matter was before the court. This matrimonial home was subject to two mortgages: a joint mortgage with the National Building Society, on which a debt of £10,000 was outstanding; and a mortgage solely in the name of the husband (the first defendant) with the Northern Bank (the plaintiff) on which a debt of approximately £9,000 was outstanding. The wife (the second defendant) had no knowledge of the second mortgage. The husband, who had left the home, did not contest the proceedings. Having ruled that the court could not proceed under section 4, Master Ellison found that he did have both jurisdiction under section 3 of the 1868 Act and a discretion to make an order for sale in lieu of partition. He endorsed the view of Professor Wallace that:

> If the mortgage affects less than a moiety of the property the position will be governed by section 3 of the 1868 Act and will presumably depend on the court's view of whether or not a sale 'would be more beneficial for the parties than a division of the property'. Since physical partition would seem to be equally impracticable in such a case the likelihood of a request for sale being successful must be considerable.[88]

In guiding the exercise of his discretion Master Ellison applied the criteria listed in Article 209(5) of the Insolvency (NI) Order 1989. He determined that the interests of the creditors should prevail over those of an innocent spouse without notice, but that the criteria indicated the presence of sufficiently 'exceptional circumstances' to justify an eighteen-month postponement of sale.

2. Charges and a Creditor's Right of Enforcement

A chargee has no rights in property, merely certain rights over property. As has been said:

> A charge is the appropriation of real or personal property for the discharge of a debt or other obligation, without giving the creditor either a general or special property in, or possession of, the subject of the security.[89]

In *Tubman v Johnston*,[90] for example, a judgment creditor with a registered charge against the property of a debtor and his wife, sought an order under Article 52 of the Judgments Enforcement (NI) Order 1981 for possession of the property with a view to sale. Murray J (as he then was) affirmed the view of the Master that a creditor armed only with a registered charge does not have an interest or 'estate' in the property and is therefore unable to call upon the power of sale available under Article 52. A chargee, wishing to realise the value of his loan through sale of the property charged, must

---

88 See *Mortgages and Possession*, NILQ (1986), vol. 37, no. 4 at p. 354.
89 See Fisher and Lightwood *Law of Mortgage* (10th ed., p. 4).
90 [1981] NI 53.

proceed by way of application under section 4 of the Partition Act 1868. Where, as in *Tubman*, the chargee's interest in the value of the property extends to one moiety or more in the value of the property charged, then that chargee will have *locus standi* to proceed under section 4 and 'the Court shall, unless it sees good reason to the contrary, direct a sale of the property accordingly'. Where, as in *Northern Bank Ltd v Haggerty*,[91] that interest is less than one moiety, then the chargee will not have *locus standi* under section 4 of the 1868 Act and, as they cannot proceed under Article 46 of the 1981 Order then, in the words of Campbell J in *Haggerty*, 'the 1981 Order has left the holder of an order charging land, in these circumstances, without a satisfactory method of realising his security'.

---

91 Unreported (1995).

CHAPTER TWENTY-ONE

Property, Finance and the Non-Marital Family

Introduction

Marital status continues to allow sufficient difference in the treatment of couples appearing before the court in connection with a dispute regarding family property and finance to justify dealing with such matters in a separate, if brief, chapter. A dispute between persons in a non-marital relationship may involve cohabitees of the same or different gender. It may entail persons in any combination of relationships and generations within the nuclear and/or extended family. The matters in dispute which attract a rather different legal response in a non-marital rather than a marital context include rights in relation to the ownership of property, occupation of the family home and rights in bankruptcy. This chapter deals with such matters as disputed between persons in cohabiting and, almost exclusively, heterosexual relationships.

Statute Law, Unmarried Persons and Property

The law relating to the ownership of (and succession to) family property continues, in the main, to be largely predicated on marriage. A cohabiting couple has little of the statutory and few of the equitable protections available to a marital couple. Thus:[1]

> ... disputes between cohabitants or former cohabitants over the ownership, occupation or use of property must be resolved, generally speaking, by applying the ordinary legal rules applicable to strangers.

Statutory Rights

Essentially, the statutory law relating to the property of cohabitees falls outside the boundaries of family law. Any statutory rights of the parties must be sought in the general law of property. Where dependent children are involved, however, the provisions of the Children (NI) Order 1995 may apply.

1. During Cohabiting Relationship

The power to redistribute family assets, available to the court in relation to applications made under section 17 of the Married Woman's Property Act 1882, does not apply to cohabiting couples.

---

1 See *Bromley's Family Law*, 8th ed, 583.

2. On Breakdown of Cohabiting Relationship

The property adjustment powers available to the court on breakdown of a marital relationship are not available to it on breakdown of a non-marital relationship. In particular neither the Law Reform (Husband and Wife) Act (NI) 1964 nor the principle in *Richards v Richards*[2] have any application.

Where a couple appear before the court as registered joint tenants of their family home then, in this jurisdiction, the Partition Acts provide statutory authority for the recognition and realisation of their separate legal interests. The law on such matters was confirmed in a recent case[3] which concerned an unmarried couple with no children who had bought a site, built a bungalow and set up home together in 1983. Both parties had made fairly equal contributions to the site purchase price. The cost of the bungalow was largely funded by a first joint mortgage, with the balance made up by the man (the plaintiff) who in due course secured a second mortgage. Eventually the relationship broke down in considerable acrimony and in 1992 a point was reached where the plaintiff found himself locked out.

In that year, and repeatedly thereafter, he sought to have the property sold and the proceeds divided equally between himself and his former partner. However, his co-habitee (the defendant), for reasons which were never explained, refused to co-operate, undertook sole responsibility for meeting the mortgage repayments and resided elsewhere. When the matter came before the court at first instance the plaintiff's application was granted, whereupon the defendant 'driven by an overwhelming sense of grievance' lodged an appeal.

In the High Court, Girvan J made a preliminary finding that both parties were entitled to a joint tenancy and to equal beneficial interests in the property. The learned judge then embarked upon a lengthy review of the law to determine whether the court had jurisdiction to make the order sought. He began by examining the common law prior to the Act for Joint Tenants 1542; he then considered the effect of that Henry VIII statute; he studied the authorities prior to the Partition Act 1868, including some case law; he assessed the significance and effect of the Partition Acts of 1868 and 1876; and he concluded with an analysis of sections 3 and 4 of the 1868 Act. His review led Girvan J to the conclusion that the court had retained jurisdiction to make the order sought and the appeal was rejected. He also took the opportunity to endorse the opinion of his colleague Murray J:

> My reading of the law is that if the owner or mortgagee demands a sale this is strictly an alternative remedy to a physical partition and if physical partition is not practicable then sale is the only possible order. I draw attention to the words 'sale ... instead of a division of the property' in section 4, indeed they also appear in section 3, and I record that I asked counsel for authority for the proposition that sale can be refused for good reason in a case where physical partition is not practicable. No such authority was produced to me and I certainly have not been able to find any myself. Indeed, the cases point against any such proposition being good law.[4]

---

2 [1984] 1 AC 174.
3 See *Glass v McManus*, unreported (1996).
4 See *Northern Bank Limited v Beattie* [1982] 18 NIJB.

Equity, Cohabitees and the Family Home

Rights of Ownership

In the absence of an express legally binding agreement or dependent children, any rights which may arise from a party's status as a non-owning cohabitee will be determined in accordance with the law governing trusts. The principles applied by the courts to ascertain whether or not the conduct of the parties gave rise to a trust are essentially the same regardless of the parties marital status. The governing precedents are provided mainly by the rulings in *Rosset* and in *Midland Bank*[5] (therefore, see also, Chapter Twenty).

Beneficial Interest Not Applicable

It is not always necessary to apply the doctrines of resulting, implied or constructive trust in order to determine the interest, if any, of an unmarried cohabitee in respect of a house where he or she lives with the legal owner. Where the parties have themselves explicitly agreed on the matter, the role of the court is confined to declaring their respective rights as established in the agreement. There is then no need for the court to seek to discover intentions and construe trust relationships.

This can be illustrated by the circumstances of two cases. In *Goodman v Gallant*[6] an unmarried couple purchased a house the conveyance for which was registered solely in the man's name. They agreed between them, however, that she was to be entitled to a half share in the beneficial ownership. Their relationship then broke down, he left and another man moved in to cohabit. The registered owner was 'bought out' by the others, his freehold interest was transferred and the new couple became beneficial joint tenants on trust for sale. That cohabiting relationship then broke down, she served notice to terminate the joint tenancy and he issued a summons to determine their respective beneficial interests. She claimed an entitlement to a three-quarter share of the beneficial interest on the basis that she started with a half share and then acquired a further half of the registered owner's interest. The court held that the plaintiff and respondent held equal shares as joint tenants in accordance with the express declaration of their intentions made at the time they acquired the registered owner's share.

In the more straightforward case of *Turton v Turton*[7] the deed of conveyance in respect of the home purchased by an unmarried couple (she having made no contribution towards the purchase price) stated that they held the property as beneficial joint tenants. On the breakdown of their relationship she sought a court declaration as to her share of the beneficial interest. The court held that their interests were as declared in the deed of conveyance.

In both cases the courts in effect ruled that a party having made an express agreement was barred from later relying on the doctrine of trusts.

---

5 See *Lloyds Bank v Rosset and Another* [1990] 2 FLR 155 HL; *Midland Bank and Another v Cooke* [1995] 2 FLR 915.
6 [1986] 1 All ER 311.
7 [1987] 2 All ER 641.

Acquiring a Beneficial Interest — The Principle

The difficulties facing an unmarried woman who seeks to establish a beneficial interest in property owned by her cohabitee have been outlined by Waite J:[8]

> ... in general, their financial rights have to be worked according to their strict entitlement in equity, a process which is anything but forward looking and involves, on the contrary, a painfully detailed retrospect.
>
> The template for that analysis has recently been restated by the House of Lords and the Court of Appeal in *Lloyds Bank v Rosset*[9] and *Grant v Edwards*.[10] The court first has to ask itself whether there have, at any time prior to acquisition of disputed property, or exceptionally at some later date, been discussions between the parties leading to any agreement, arrangement or understanding between them that the property is to be shared beneficially. Any further investigation carried out by the court will vary in depth, according to whether the answer to that initial enquiry is 'yes' or 'no'. If there have been discussions of that kind and the answer is therefore 'yes', the court then proceeds to examine the subsequent course of dealings between the parties for evidence of conduct detrimental to the party without legal title referable to a reliance upon the arrangement in question. If there have not been discussions and the answer to that initial enquiry is therefore 'no', the investigation of subsequent events has to take the form of an inferential analysis, involving a scrutiny of all events potentially capable of throwing evidential light on the question, whether in the absence of express discussion, a presumed intention can be spelt out of the parties' past course of dealing.

In essence such an application must pass through two stages. First, to establish a beneficial interest, common intention must be proven by evidence of either an express agreement or direct/indirect contributions, and then, it must be proven that the applicant suffered a detriment as a consequence of relying on that common intention. Secondly, the court will go on to fix the proportion of the applicant's beneficial interest in accordance with either the terms of any express agreement made by the parties, their respective contributions to the purchase price (in the case of a resulting trust) or all the circumstances (in the case of a constructive trust).

Acquiring and Apportioning Beneficial Interests — The Practice

There must be evidence of an intention, shared equally by both parties, accompanied by evidence that one party acted in reliance upon that intention and as a consequence suffered a detriment (see *Rosset* above and, generally, Chapter Twenty).

(a) Evidence of Express Common Intention and Referable Detriment

Cooke v Head,[11] which has long been a leading case, relates to the acquisition of a beneficial interest by one cohabitee in property bought, mortgaged and registered by

---

8 See *Hammond v Mitchell* [1991] 1 WLR 1127.
9 See f/n 3.
10 [1986] Ch 638, [1986] 2 All ER 426.
11 [1972] 2 All ER 38.

the other. The Court of Appeal then held that the parties had acquired the property with the intention of using it as their family home and that the subsequent actions of the non-owning party, her physical labour in sharing the building work and her contribution towards mortgage repayments, had given rise to a constructive trust. In the circumstances the court awarded her one-third of the proceeds resulting from the sale of the house. The facts and outcome of this case were mirrored more recently in *Drake v Whipp*[12] where, at first instance, the plaintiff's claim had been wrongly argued on the basis of a resulting trust.

Again, in *Eves v Eves*[13] a couple, who had lived together for some years and had two children, purchased a house with his money and in his name. At the time of purchase he stated that it was to be their family home and claimed that his reason for not putting the house into their joint names was that she was not yet twenty-one. In the ensuing period of three years, before their relationship broke down, she acted on this common understanding and did considerable manual work to restore what was a very dilapidated house. He left, married someone else and eventually caused her and the two children to leave the house. She then sought a court declaration that she had acquired a beneficial interest in the ownership of the property by virtue of the expressed common intention and her consequent investment of time and labour. The court found that the link between the promises relied upon and the conduct constituting the detriment was sufficiently proximate and accordingly held that his assurances had given rise to a constructive trust entitling her to a one-quarter interest in the property.[14]

Finally, *Hammond v Mitchell*[15] concerned a cohabitee relationship formed between a second-hand car dealer (married but separated from his wife) and a 'bunny girl'; they had two children. On the relationship breaking down, she applied to the court for a share in both the bungalow which had been their family home and a house in Spain. As evidence of the existence of a common intent that she should acquire a beneficial interest in the bungalow she submitted that, although he had registered it solely in his name (for tax purposes, as he had explained at the time) he had also declared that on their marriage she would own half the property. Subsequently, she had allowed him to use the house as security for his risky business ventures. If these ventures had failed, they would have had to forfeit the house but in fact they succeeded to the point where he was able to purchase a second house in Spain, again with his own money and solely in his name, though she had made some contribution to the running expenses. Waite J, giving judgment, stated:[16]

> ... the law requires me in determining the beneficial title to apply the principles enunciated in *Lloyds Bank plc v Rosset* and *Grant v Edwards*. It will involve asking this question first: is there any, and if so which, property which has been the subject of some agreement, arrangement or understanding reached between the parties on the basis of express discussion to the effect that such property is to be shared

---

12 [1996] 1 FLR 826.
13 [1975] 3 All ER 768.
14 See also *Wayling v Jones* [1995] 2 FLR 1029.
15 [1991] 1 WLR 1127.
16 Ibid.

beneficially; and (if there is) has Miss M shown herself to have acted to her detriment or significantly altered her position in reliance on the agreement so as to give rise to a constructive trust or proprietary estoppel?

The court held that she had no beneficial interest in the house in Spain but was entitled to a half share in the bungalow in respect of which there was evidence that a constructive trust had been established.

(b) Evidence of Implied Common Intention

In *Grant v Edwards*,[17] evidence of common intention was found to be implied in the explanation given by a man for not putting his cohabitee's name on the title deeds. The house was purchased in his name and registered in the names of his brother and himself in order, as he explained at the time to the plaintiff, not to compromise her divorce proceedings. When a fire subsequently badly damaged the house, they shared the insurance payments between them equally. They both worked and although he met all mortgage repayments he would not have been able to do so without her financial contributions to the household expenses. After their relationship broke down, her claim for a share in the beneficial ownership was rejected by the court at first instance. In the Court of Appeal, Nourse LJ[18] stated the plaintiff's legal position as follows:

> In a case such as the present, where there has been no written declaration of agreement, nor any direct provision by the plaintiff of part of the purchase price so as to give rise to a resulting trust in her favour, she must establish a common intention between her and the defendant, acted on by her, that she should have a beneficial interest in the property. If she can do that, equity will not allow the defendant to deny that interest and will construct a trust to give effect to it.

The court found that the defendant's initial explanation and their sharing of the insurance money provided evidence of common intention while her financial contributions constituted action to her detriment which was referable to that intention. It was held that she was entitled to a half share in the beneficial ownership.

However, evidence of implied common intention must demonstrate both real 'intention', not something more ephemeral, and that it was 'common' to both parties, not merely assumed by one to be so. This was illustrated in the case of *Springette v Defoe*,[19] where the court emphasised the need for both strands to be proven. In that case, despite the fact that when the parties bought their council house it was transferred into their joint names and thereafter they contributed equally to the mortgage payments, it was found that neither had ever addressed the issue of their respective beneficial interests. An uncommunicated belief of equal ownership was held to be an insufficient basis for sustaining a claim in law. The court ruled that in the absence of a verifiable common intention the parties held the property on a resulting trust with ownership divided in proportion to their respective contributions towards the purchase price.

---

17 [1986] 2 All ER 426 at p. 433.
18 Ibid.
19 [1992] 2 FLR 437, [1992] Fam Law 489.

(c) Evidence indicating Contractual Licence

The court may hold that a contractual licence has come into being where there is evidence of an intention to create a legally binding relationship and evidence that the plaintiff provided consideration in pursuance of that intention. For example, in *Tanner v Tanner*[20] the mistress in a non-cohabiting relationship appealed against the making of an order for possession of the house bought by her lover for her to live in and in which she and their twin daughters had lived for some years. The Court of Appeal heard that neither plaintiff nor defendant had ever declared any intention of marriage, he had purchased the house in his name and she had made no contribution to the purchase price nor to its maintenance. It was held that although there was insufficient evidence to sustain an explicit contract there was enough to infer the existence of an implied contractual licence entitling her to accommodation for herself and children while the latter were of school age or until their circumstances changed. Breach of this licence would entitle her to damages.

(d) Evidence Indicating Proprietary Estoppel

Evidence of proprietary estoppel requires a plaintiff to show that he or she had a right in relation to property owned by another, that the latter knew of and encouraged that belief and that in acting upon that belief the plaintiff suffered a detriment. In such circumstances the owner will be 'estopped' from relying solely on his or her legal rights to deny the interests of the plaintiff in the matter. For example, in *Coombes v Smith*[21] the plaintiff relied on such a belief but failed to provide sufficient evidence to substantiate her claim. This was a case concerning two married persons, an unhappily married woman (the plaintiff) who left her husband and marital home and a married man who provided a house for that woman but remained living with his own wife and family. The plaintiff became pregnant by that man, gave up her job and moved into a house which he had bought in his name with the intention that it would be their family home. In fact he never did live there although he took responsibility for meeting all mortgage payments and for financially supporting mother and child. In time that house was sold, was replaced by another and the same arrangements continued. Again the house was solely in his name though he gave verbal assurances that he would look after her and ensure that she would always have a roof over her head. She decorated the house and maintained the garden. Ten years later he formed a relationship with another woman and offered the plaintiff £10,000 to vacate the premises. She lodged a claim for maintenance against him. He offered to allow her to remain in the house until their child reached seventeen. She responded with an application for an order that the house be conveyed to her or for a declaration of her entitlement to occupy the house for life based on proprietary estoppel and contractual licence. The claim based on contractual licence failed due to a lack of evidence that, at the time of the initial arrangements, the necessary elements of a contract ever existed: initially, their mutual intention was only that they should live together; there was no evidence of a formal

---

20   [1975] 3 All ER 776.
21   [1987] 1 FLR 352.

agreement that she was entitled to be accommodated by him for the rest of her life; nor had she provided any consideration, she merely chose a preferable place to live. The claim based on proprietary estoppel fared no better. There was no evidence that she believed she had any right of occupation of that particular premises other than at his discretion; in any event, there was no evidence of her having suffered any detriment as a direct consequence of reliance on such a belief (the court considered that she had given up her job simply because she was pregnant). The evidence was that she believed that he had given an undertaking to provide a roof over her head, but this was of general application; and there was no evidence that they had ever discussed what they would do if their relationship broke down. The court held that her application would be dismissed but imposed a requirement that he honour his undertaking to permit mother and child to remain in occupation until the latter reached the age of seventeen.

(e) Evidence of Indirect Contributions

A plaintiff who claims a beneficial interest in property owned by another, in respect of which the plaintiff has made no contribution to the purchase price, may succeed where there is evidence of a common intention that he or she should acquire such an interest. This intention may be evidenced by express agreement or otherwise may be inferred from evidence that the plaintiff made, and was allowed to make, a significant indirect contribution to costs.

Such a contention was made, for example, in *Thomas v Fuller-Brown*[22] where the male cohabitee had not contributed to the purchase price of the house in which he lived with the registered owner. However, following the breakdown of their relationship, he claimed a right to a beneficial interest in the property on the basis that he had acquired an improvement grant on the property, designed and built a two-storey extension, completed extensive interior construction and decorating work and landscaped the grounds. While accepting that his work had greatly improved the value of the property, the court nonetheless held that this in itself could confer no right to a beneficial interest in it.

For many unmarried mothers the possibility of basing a claim on their indirect contributions offers the only opportunity to establish a beneficial interest.

In *Burns v Burns*[23] the court considered the case of a cohabitee who had lived with her partner for nineteen years, changed her name to his, reared their two children and had decorated and maintained the home which he had purchased in his name. On the break up of their relationship she claimed to have acquired a beneficial interest because of her work in the home, her contributions to the housekeeping expenses and because she had bought some furnishings and fittings. The court dismissed her claim and this decision was upheld by the Court of Appeal which ruled that to succeed the plaintiff would have had to establish her legal interest in the home by proof of a common intention to create a trust. There was no evidence to show that this was intended. In particular, she had made no contribution to the purchase price of the house and no substantial contribution towards running costs. This decision stands as a reminder of

---

22 [1988] 1 FLR 237.
23 [1984] 1 All ER 244.

how the interests of an unmarried mother in the home where she reared her family can be left wholly unprotected. It also points up the uncertainties inherent in basing claims on constructive trusts.[24]

More recently the position of such a mother would seem to have been improved by the decision in *Midland Bank v Cooke and Another*.[25] Where she can show evidence of common intention (perhaps by having made some contribution towards the purchase price, however slight, even if made by her parents by way of gift or loan), then despite her never having discussed the question of ownership, the court may now take into account such indirect contributions as housekeeping and child rearing when quantifying her proportion of the total beneficial interest in the family home. She must still, however, clear the initial hurdle of 'common intention'.

Equity, Cohabitees and Ownership of Property Other Than the Family Home

Again, because statute law makes no specific provision for property adjustment in disputes between cohabitees, an unmarried plaintiff without legal title must base a claim for ownership rights on the doctrine of trusts.

Business

In *Tinsley v Milligan*[26] the House of Lords considered the division of beneficial interests between a cohabiting female couple in respect of a bed-and-breakfast business. The couple had shared their finances to buy the property, had expressly acknowledged that it was to be jointly owned and had thereafter pooled their resources to cover running costs. However, in order to facilitate Milligan's defrauding of the DHSS (she claimed various social security means-tested payments on the basis of having no property rights), title to the property was in Tinsley's sole name as were all related bank and building society accounts. When their relationship broke down Tinsley moved out, serving notice on Milligan to quit and bringing an action for possession. Milligan countered with a claim that she was entitled to a half share in the property.

The court had little difficulty in resolving the substantive issue of ownership rights. On the basis of the couple's joint contributions to the purchase price, express common intention of joint ownership and sustained shared investment in the running of the business, the court held that a resulting trust had arisen giving each party rights to the beneficial interest in proportion to their respective contributions to the purchase price. The question which exercised the House of Lords, as it had the Court of Appeal, was whether Milligan was barred on the grounds of public policy from claiming her entitlement: did her fraudulent activity trigger the rule that 'those who come to equity must come with clean hands' and debar her from deriving benefit from the proceedings? The court found that the illegal activity was beside the point. It had no immediate

---

24   See also *Layton v Martin and Others* [1986] 2 FLR 227.
25   [1995] 2 FLR 915.
26   [1993] 2 FLR 968.

bearing on the ownership issue and the court did not need to take it into account. The doctrine of advancement (which would have had the effect of raising a presumption that Milligan had intended to make a gift of her share of the business to Tinsley) did not apply.

Bought with Savings from Housekeeping

In *Paul v Constance*[27] the court differentiated between the *locus standi* of married and unmarried couples for the purposes of establishing ownership of property bought by one partner with savings 'derived from' an allowance made by the other partner in respect of 'expenses of the home or for similar purposes'. It was held that the presumption of 'common intent', which would allow the court to regard both partners in a marital relationship as joint owners of the property, does not extend to cohabitees. A cohabitee in a similar situation must prove the nature of both partners' intentions before the court can settle any such ownership dispute.

Presumption of Advancement

Much the same rationale lies behind the well-established rule that the presumption of advancement does not apply (unless the couple are engaged) in the context of a non-marital relationship. Because the presumption is a corollary of the husband's common-law duty to maintain his wife, it has no bearing on cohabitees.

The Law, Unmarried Parents and the Family Home

Ownership and Occupation

To a limited extent both statute and equity address the special position of an unmarried parent with a dependent child or children in relation to the family home.

1. Equity and Ownership

In disputes between unmarried parents regarding ownership of the family home, occurring in the context of a breakdown of their relationship, the courts attach over-riding importance to safeguarding the interests of the parent who retains care responsibility for the children. For example, in *Re Evers' Trust*[28] the couple, who had lived together for some years with children of their relationship and of his previous marriage, bought a house with a combination of both their finances and registered it in their joint names. Three years later their relationship broke down and he left, leaving her and all the children in the house. He then commenced proceedings to have the house sold immediately so that he could realise his share of the proceeds. The court upheld his right to order the sale of the property but directed the sale to be postponed until the youngest child attained the age of sixteen on the ground that at time of

---

27 [1977] 1 All ER 195.
28 [1980] 1 WLR 1327.

purchase the common intention of the parties had been to acquire a home not merely for themselves but also for their children. In effect a constructive trust had arisen which afforded protection to the children's right to a home during their minority.

In *Richards v Richards*[29] Lord Hailsham recognised (p 204) that there may be some cases where the needs of the children are such as to require them to be given paramountcy. It has been suggested[30] that such a case would be where the upbringing of a child is directly raised as an issue in a contest between parents for exclusive ownership/ occupation rights in respect of the family home.

2. Statute and Occupation Rights

(a) The Domestic Proceedings (NI) Order 1980

Under Article 18 of the 1980 Order, as extended by Article 20 of the Family Law (Matrimonial Provisions)(NI) Order 1984:

> (10) This Article applies to a cohabiting couple, that is to say a man and a woman who are or have been living with each other in the same household as if they were husband and wife, in the same manner as it applies to the parties to a marriage.
>
> (11) In determining whether for the purposes of paragraph (10) a man and a woman are a cohabiting couple the court shall have regard to all the circumstances of the case, including
>
> > (a) the time for which it appears they have been living together; and
> > (b) whether there are any children of the relationship.

In the leading case of *Davis v Johnson*,[31] the cohabitees were registered as joint tenants and lived together as man and wife. On two occasions Davis inflicted 'horrifying' violence on Johnson causing her eventually to flee with their child to a refuge. Her successful application for an exclusion order, under the provision equivalent to Article 18 of the Domestic Proceedings (NI) Order 1980[32] was rescinded, restored by the Court of Appeal and then appealed to the House of Lords. The grounds for the appeal were that the relevant provision could not exclude a person who had proprietary rights in a dwelling from entering it. The court held that while the provision could not affect property rights, it could affect the enjoyment of such rights. In the words of Scarman LJ:[33]

> Section 1 of the Act [*Article 18 of the Order, sic*] is concerned to protect not property but human life and limb. But, while the section is not intended to confer, and does not confer upon, an unmarried woman property rights in the home, it does enable the county court to suspend or restrict her family partner's property right to possession

---

29 F/n 2 at 204.
30 See *Gibson v Austin* [1992] 2 FLR 437.
31 [1978] 2 WLR 553.
32 The equivalent provisions in the law for England and Wales are to be found in the Domestic Violence and Matrimonial Proceedings Act 1976, section 1.
33 See f/n 29.

and to preserve her right of occupancy ... for as long as may be thought necessary by the court to secure the protection of herself and the children.

However, subsequent case law has narrowed the application of this principle. The Court of Appeal has ruled[34] that setting aside the enjoyment of property rights is a draconian measure and it must be demonstrated that it is just and reasonable to do so. In that case, an unmarried man had been excluded by ouster order from the flat, which he held on a joint tenancy basis with a cohabitee and their child, and successfully appealed on the ground that though they quarrelled he had never resorted to violence. The court found that although it was not necessary to ground an ouster order on violence, or the threat of violence, it was necessary to address separately the issues of which party had the greatest need for the accommodation and whether the conduct of the defendant warranted such a draconian order. The first issue was addressed in the four matters as stated in the grounds of Article 20 of the Family Law (Miscellaneous Provisions) (NI) Order 1984,[35] viz. the conduct of the parties, their needs and resources, the needs of the children and other considerations. The court at first instance had correctly considered this but it had failed to address the second issue.

(b) The Children (NI) Order 1995

The contentious interface between the traditional bulwarks provided for private rights by the law of property and the modern intrusiveness of an extensive public interest in the welfare of children has recently been the subject of judicial attention in England with results which will be felt also in this jurisdiction. The case of *Pearson v Franklin*[36] concerned an unmarried couple, with two children, who were joint tenants of a house. The relationship eventually broke down, without violence, and the mother with the children left to live with her parents. Some six months later she applied for a specific issue order to enable her to live in the former family home and to exclude the father, who had remained in residence. The father then applied for a contact order. In giving judgment the judge at first instance granted the father's application but dismissed that of the mother stating that he had no jurisdiction, under the 1989 Act, to grant her an order for that purpose. On appeal it was held that the sought-for specific issue order, which would have brought into play the paramountcy principle, was merely an ouster order in disguise and Parliament could not have intended the functions of ouster orders to be introduced in this way. However, the Court of Appeal then drew attention to an alternative remedy available to the applicant, i.e. she could instead have brought an application for a transfer of the tenancy for the benefit of the children.

Under Article 15 of the Children Order (NI) 1995 such an order may be made by the court employing the powers available to it in Schedule 1, paragraph 2, 2(e)(i). The court must then consider all the matters set out in Schedule 1, paragraph 5; it may not simply apply the paramountcy principle. In fact, in England, this course of action was pursued

---

34 See *Wiseman v Simpson* [1988] 1 All ER 245.
35 Under section 1(3) of the Matrimonial Homes Act 1983.
36 [1994] 1 WLR 186; [1994] 2 All ER 137.

by an applicant under provisions equivalent to those in Schedule 1, paragraph 1(1)(d) of the 1989 Act.[37] Indeed, the powers under Schedule 1 have become an important means for ensuring provision of accommodation for the children of cohabitee parents whose relationship has broken down.

In exercising its powers the court may not make a property adjustment order capable of conferring a benefit on the child concerned after he or she has attained maturity. The order may only direct that property be transferred and held on trust for the child's benefit and to revert to the original owner when the child attains independence. An order to that effect was in fact made in *A v A (A Minor)(Financial Provision)*[38] where the court ruled that during this period the mother should have the right to occupy the property to the exclusion of the father and without having to pay any rent.

3. Statute, Bankruptcy and Ownership/Occupation Rights

The Insolvency (NI) Order 1989

Cohabitees have no rights under the 1989 Order. The provisions governing the right of a bankrupt or his or her spouse with dependant children to the continued occupation of the family home apply regardless of the bankrupt's marital status (see further Chapter Twenty). The rights of ownership or occupation, if any, of a bankrupt but childless cohabitee fall to be determined in accordance with the general case-law principles as established before the introduction of this legislation.

Finances

There is no assumption of a common ownership of finances.

Income and Savings

Money, in the form of income or savings, is owned separately by each cohabitee. The general law of property allows a joint ownership arrangement to be established between cohabitees, as it does between any combination of married persons or 'strangers'. Savings will only be owned jointly where the parties have clearly agreed to hold their monies on that basis.

Financial Provision for a Non-Marital Child under the 1995 Order

In addition to directing the transfer or settlement of property, the court also has the power under Schedule 1 to make a lump sum order for the benefit of a non-marital child during his or her minority. For example, in *H v P (Illegitimate Child: Capital Provision)*[39] the court directed an unmarried father to settle a sum of £30,000 for the benefit of the mother and child for so long as she provided a home for the child during his minority or until he ceased full-time education. The sum was to enable the mother

---

37 See *K v K (Minors: Property Transfer)* [1992] 1 WLR 530.
38 [1994] 1 FLR 657.
39 [1993] Fam Law 515.

to purchase suitable accommodation. Again, in *A v A (A Minor: Financial Provision)*[40] the court used its powers under Schedule 1 to order the unmarried father to pay his daughter's school fees and extras and to make annual payments of £20,000 for her maintenance.

In deciding whether or not to exercise its powers under Schedule 1 the court is not permitted to apply the paramountcy principle but instead must have regard to the guidelines stated in the Schedule.

Tax and Social Security Assessments

The court has held[41] that the reference to 'wife' in section 8(1)(a) of the Income and Corporation Taxes Act 1970 does not include a 'common law wife'; the definition of 'wife' is to be restricted to its statutory meaning within the Marriage Acts.

Compensation

A cohabitee's right to compensation as a consequence of the injury or death of a partner is governed by the Criminal Injuries (NI) Order 1988, Article 5(2), and the Fatal Accidents legislation.

---

40 [1994] 1 FLR 657.
41 See *Rignal (HM Inspector of Taxes) v Andrews* [1990] 8 BNIL 73.

CHAPTER TWENTY-TWO

Family Breakdown: The Child Support Scheme

Introduction

This chapter deals with the law represented in particular by the provisions of the Child Support (NI) Orders 1991 and 1995 as it relates to maintenance issues arising in respect of children following family breakdown. It provides a separate but supplementary focus to earlier chapters dealing with other aspects of family breakdown and is itself supplemented by the following chapter on the court's residual jurisdiction in respect of maintenance.

The law permits the parties to a marriage to extinguish their legal relationship and obligations to each other through proceedings for divorce, nullity and judicial separation. It does not, however, permit them to extinguish their legal relationship or obligations in respect of any children of that marriage. Divorce dissolves the spousal but not the parental relationship.

The Child Support Legislation

The Child Support (NI) Order 1991, the principal statute, became law on April 5, 1993. The subsequent introduction of the Child Support (NI) Order 1991 (Consequential Amendments) Order (NI) 1994 amends Article 85 of the Magistrates' Courts (NI) Order 1981 so as to provide that an order issued by a court of summary jurisdiction for periodical payments to be made through a collecting officer will not have effect at any time when the DHSS is arranging for the collection of periodical payments under Article 30 of the 1991 Order.

The Child Support (NI) Order 1995 amends the principal statute to improve provision for the assessment, collection and enforcement of maintenance payments. A number of technical amendments are introduced to permit greater flexibility in certain circumstances.

I. Purpose

The purpose of this legislation, as stated in the explanatory note accompanying the 1991 Order, is to

> ... make provision for Northern Ireland with regard to the assessment, collection and enforcement of periodical maintenance payments payable by certain parents with respect to children of theirs who are not in their care.

This broadly means that in any application following family breakdown, where there are financial arrangements to be made for the future maintenance of children, then referral for assessment will now most usually be made from the court to the child support agency. This will apply in the context of divorce (see Chapter Nine) and separation (see Chapter Eight) proceedings instigated under either the Matrimonial Causes (NI) Order 1978 or the Domestic Proceedings (NI) Order 1980 for divorce, nullity or judicial separation. It will also apply if the issue of such financial arrangements should arise in the context of proceedings instigated under the Children (NI) Order 1995 (Part 11) or even, though this will become increasingly unusual, in wardship. However, excluded from this transfer of responsibility from court to child support agency are the judicial powers to order periodical or lump sum payments and/or property settlements for the benefit of children in the course of matrimonial proceedings (see Chapters Twenty-Three and Twenty-Four).

II. The Principles

Like the Child Support Act 1991, which it virtually replicates, the origins of the Child Support (NI) Order 1991 are traceable to the White Paper *Children Come First*.[1] This document paved the way for both pieces of legislation by criticising the former judicial process for determining maintenance as being 'unnecessarily fragmented, uncertain in its results, slow and ineffective . . . based largely on discretion' and leading to 'uncertainty and inconsistent decisions'.

However, the resulting legislation does not blend seamlessly with the provisions of the Children (NI) Order 1995. There are some areas of significant difference.

The Main Principles

(a) That an Absent Parent, Not the State, Has a Duty to Provide Maintenance for a Child

Article 5 of the Child Support (NI) Order 1991 states the principle, later emphasised in the corresponding provision of the Children (NI) Order 1995, that the law now firmly recognises a presumption placing responsibility for ensuring the welfare interests of a child, including maintenance, on the parents of that child. The definition of 'parent' in Article 2 makes it clear that this responsibility falls 'on the mother and father of the child and, in the case of an illegitimate child, includes the father'. Article 7(4) gives teeth to the principle articulated in Article 5(2) that it is the responsibility of an absent parent to make 'periodical payments in respect to the child' by placing a specific duty on an applicant for maintenance assessment. This duty is to provide the information necessary to locate an absent parent, determine the maintenance payable and permit the recovery of the amount due from that parent. The clear legislative intent behind this provision is to ensure that an absent parent, in practice almost always a deserting father, will be pursued and held accountable for a share of the cost of maintaining any natural children he has left behind.

---

1 Cmnd 1264 (1990).

This principle was perhaps the primary driving force behind the child support legislation. The legislators were faced with a situation where parenting arrangements were becoming increasingly fluid, with many thousands of absent parents forming new family units which absorbed maintenance costs due to the former unit and leaving this to be retrieved by many sole-caring parents from the DHSS. The displacement of costs from absent parent to State was also compounded by the judicial practice of facilitating clean-break settlements. This is a practice whereby one parent would agree to waive any future claim to periodic maintenance payments in lieu of the other making a once-off lump sum or property transfer. Ironically, a major criticism of the effect of the child support legislation has been the inequity that may now result from the child support agency's policy of ignoring such settlements and computing maintenance liability as though the financial or property transfer had never taken place. The retrospective effect of this legislation has, in some cases, undoubtedly produced unanticipated and unjust results.

(b) That a Caring Parent Should Not Be Consigned Indefinitely to a Poverty Trap as a Consequence of Her Abandonment

Large numbers of abandoned sole-caring parents were being left with the possibility of pursuing a claim for maintenance only against the State. This in effect debarred them from seeking or continuing in paid employment. The fact that they should be punished in this way was inequitable, a strain on the quality of care available for their children and generated a widespread and effective public outcry.

However, although the Child Support (NI) Order 1991 increased the certainty and regularity of maintenance payments, it did so only to the level normally payable through state benefits: many families were no better off, they had only the security of subsistence level payments. The 1995 Order introduced the child maintenance bonus enabling some caring parents to acquire the means whereby they could seek training and hope to eventually secure employment. Not until 1997, when this provision came into effect, did such parents benefit.

(c) That the Making of Maintenance Assessments Should Be an Administrative Rather Than a Judicial Matter

Article 41 of the 1991 Order provides that the jurisdiction to award maintenance for children, previously vested in the courts, should in future be assumed by the child support agency. The rationale for this principle was grounded mainly on considerations of procedural cost coupled with the uncertainty and ineffectiveness of the judicial process.

Burdened by the ever-increasing weight of administrative duties which accompanied the hearings for divorce and separation, judicial time in Northern Ireland as elsewhere in the United Kingdom was being inappropriately tied up with non-adjudicative business. One major reason for this legislative initiative was to free up the judicial process and increase judicial availability for other business.

The unpredictability of outcome in judicial determination of maintenance issues was a factor which concerned the authors of the *Children Come First* paper. Judicial discretion, exercised to achieve an equitable resolution according to the different circumstances of each case, resulted in a great disparity in decision-making. Applying a standardised formula for assessing maintenance liability to all cases would, it was felt, bring more overall consistency and fairness to the settling of maintenance issues.

(d) That the Enforcement of Maintenance Obligations Is More Effectively Managed by the Child Support Agency Than by the Courts

Given the number of cases coming before the courts, both for initial determination and thereafter for a variation of the maintenance order, the frequent changes of address of the parties involved and the proportion who were in receipt of welfare benefits, it was proving impossible for the judiciary to respond sufficiently promptly to the problems associated with non-payment of maintenance. A great many single parents were left in the position of receiving irregular amounts of payment at irregular intervals, or none at all. Expediency dictated the transfer of responsibility for enforcing payments to an agency which, being constituted under the umbrella of the DHSS, already possessed the data base and the obligation to monitor financial matters in relation to a high proportion of the parties appearing before the courts.

III. The Main Differences in Principle between the Child Support (NI) Orders 1991 and 1995 and the Children (NI) Order 1995

1. Public and Private Family Law

The effect of Article 41 of the 1991 Order is to transfer responsibility for making maintenance assessments from the judiciary to child support officers, in most circumstances. Most obviously, the thrust of the child support legislation differs from that of the Children Order by moving an important volume of family law litigation from the private into the public sector. When seen in conjunction with the very considerable body of rules and regulations which will eventually accompany the 1991 Order, it raises the question as to whether the declared legislative intent to 'roll back the state' in child care has been sustained in child maintenance.

2. The Paramountcy Principle

Under Article 6 of the 1991 Order the Child Support Agency, or child support officer, is only required to 'have regard to the welfare of any child likely to be affected by its or his decision'. This is in marked contrast to the role of the paramountcy principle as stated in Article 3 of the Children Order. Again the effect achieved seems paradoxical when set against the legislative intent behind the Children Order to bring a new synthesis and coherence of principle to the law relating to children.

3. A 'Natural' Child

Article 3 of the 1991 Order, which defines a 'child' for the purposes of this legislation, makes no reference to one who may be treated as a 'child of the family'. This gives rise to a significant difference in principle in that while 'child' is defined inclusively in the Children Order to embrace anyone treated as a 'child of the family', in the child support legislation this term is in effect defined exclusively as restricted to mean a 'natural' child or one to whom a parent is biologically related.

The Child Support Scheme

In marked contrast to established practice in relation to other UK social legislation, the Child Support (NI) Order 1991 was introduced simultaneously with its counterpart the Child Support Act 1991. Thereafter, the phasing in of both sets of provisions has been co-ordinated and managed in tandem.

On April 5, 1993 the child support scheme was launched with immediate application to all new cases (i.e. cases in which judicial orders for maintenance had not yet been made). Until April 1996 those, together with all cases where the applicant is in receipt of welfare benefits, fall to be determined under the scheme. Thereafter the assessment of all cases where the applicant is not on welfare benefits and a variation is required in respect of an existing court order, together with responsibility for the collection and enforcement duties in relation to maintenance payments including those arising on foot of certain court orders, will be conducted under the scheme.

Administrative and Judicial Jurisdictions

The transition period, from the introduction of the child support legislation in April 1993 until its full implementation, has been characterised by considerable jurisdictional uncertainty. As the transfer of responsibilities from court to administrative body is gradually phased in, underpinned by the staged release of related rules and regulations, so practitioners are being hard pressed to keep up with the re-direction of procedures from one jurisdiction to the other.

1. Administrative Jurisdiction

For the most part the effect of the child support legislation will be to remove responsibility for dealing with maintenance in respect of natural and adopted children, habitually resident in Northern Ireland, from the courts and place it with the child support agency. This is the broad effect of Article 7 of the 1991 Order as applied to post-April 1993 cases and ensures that all but a minority of cases will eventually be the responsibility of that Agency. However, the jurisdiction of many pre-April 1993 cases continues to lie with the court. During the transition phase certain applicants will be entitled to be heard by the court. Later the court will retain a residual jurisdiction in respect of some matters and exclusive jurisdiction in relation to certain categories of applicants and children.

2. Judicial Jurisdiction

A minority of cases will be excluded, some temporarily and others permanently, from determination by the child support agency.

(a) Phasing-in Cases

Where the parties consent to maintenance arrangements for their children, have concluded a written agreement to that effect and are not in receipt of welfare benefits, then under Article 10(5) it is acknowledged that the court's jurisdiction should not be ousted by the Agency. Article 11(2) then goes on to state that nothing in the 1991 Order shall prevent any person from entering into a maintenance agreement. The following provisions of that article, however, make it clear that after the phasing-in period any party to such an agreement, or indeed any other person, may apply to the Agency for a maintenance assessment in respect of the children who are the subjects of the agreement. In such circumstances it will then fall to the Agency, not the court, to vary the terms of the agreement (i.e. the jurisdiction of the court will have been ousted).

There is uncertainty as to the status of so-called clean-break settlements.[2] It would seem likely, however, that where such a court-sanctioned settlement later comes before the Agency, probably as a consequence of the person with care becoming dependent upon welfare benefits, then the Agency will have power to set aside the terms of the settlement, make a fresh assessment and direct payment of maintenance.

(b) Exceptions

Certain types of matters are excluded from the scope of the child support legislation. For example, because the scheme is solely concerned with income not capital, it will not apply to any issues relating to capital provision for a child. Therefore, the courts rather than the Agency will have jurisdiction in disputes relating to lump-sum payments or property adjustments to be made in favour of children in the course of matrimonial proceedings. Recourse may then be had to the Children (NI) Order 1995.

Cases concerning certain categories of children have been exempted from Agency jurisdiction. One such category results from the wording used to define 'child' in Article 3(1)(b). This would seem to indicate that if a child is under the age of nineteen and receiving full-time advanced education (perhaps at a university), then the court and not the Agency will have jurisdiction. Another arises where a child is habitually resident outside the United Kingdom. Article 41 provides powers for the Agency to cancel any maintenance assessment made in respect of a child who has ceased to be habitually resident within the United Kingdom. Finally, step-children and other 'children of the family' have been deliberately excluded from the definition of 'child' and therefore must be presumed to fall outside the application of the child support scheme. Again, by implication, the court rather than the Agency will have jurisdiction to deal with maintenance issues in respect of such children.

(c) Residual Jurisdiction

The courts will continue to have a limited jurisdiction to deal with cases concerning certain categories of children. Under Article 10(8) of the 1991 Order, for example, a

---

2 See *Minton v Minton* [1079] AC 593 where Scarman LJ described the purpose of such settlements as being to enable the parties 'to put the past behind them and to begin a new life which is not overshadowed by the relationship which has just broken down'.

court will have jurisdiction to make a maintenance order in respect of a disabled child (as defined in section 9) and in respect of whom a disability allowance is or is not being paid, provided the order is in relation to expenses attributable to the disability. Children who are married, those with high-income parents or where school fees are involved will also come within the jurisdiction of the court rather than the Agency for the purposes of determining maintenance issues (see also Chapter Twenty-Three).

(d) Appeals

Finally, the courts retain their customary appellate jurisdiction. This was exercised, for example, in *Department of Health and Social Security v Lowry*[3] which concerned a case stated by a Social Security Commissioner following his ruling regarding the decision taken by the Appeal Tribunal that a plaintiff was not eligible for a payment in respect of ten years of child benefit arrears. The Commissioner stated a case on a point of law, the court ruled that he had been wrong in his interpretation and referred the matter back to an Adjudications Officer for re-assessment.

A right of appeal will lie from a decision of the Child Support Commissioner to the Court of Appeal. In addition, the usual rights of access to the Ombudsman or to the process of judicial review may be available to an aggrieved person.

(e) The EEC

In this context it is also relevant to note the background influence of Strasbourg. For example, in *Adjudication Officer v Una McMenamin*[4] the Court of Appeal, acting under Article 177 of the EEC Treaty, referred to the Court of Justice of the European Committee for a preliminary ruling on the application of EEC regulations.

The Administrative Framework

The child support legislation provides for the setting up of a whole new administrative framework operating under the umbrella of the DHSS. The statutory provisions will also be augmented by a substantial body of regulations detailing matters of implementation and enforcement. This new framework rests on a Child Support Agency, with a head office in Belfast (branch offices in Omagh, Antrim, Foyle and Newry), serviced by teams of Child Support Officers accountable to a Chief Child Support Officer.

1. The Child Support Officers

Article 15(1) of the 1991 Order makes provision for the appointment of child support officers. Their role is to make assessments, arrange for collections, enforce payments and facilitate appeals in respect of child maintenance. Under Article 20 the assessment of a child support officer, or the refusal of an officer to accept an application for assessment, may be reviewed on application by the applicant to the Department which will then appoint another officer to conduct the review. Article 21 permits officers to instigate their own reviews when satisfied that an assessment is defective by reason of:

---

3 [1993] 10 NIJB 42.
4 [1993] 11 NIJB 29.

(a) having been made in ignorance of a material fact;
(b) having been based on a mistake as to a material fact; or
(c) being wrong in law.

2. The Chief Child Support Officer

Article 15(3) of the 1991 Order provides for the appointment of the chief child support officer. His or her duties are, as detailed in Article 15(4), to

(a) advise child support officers on the discharge of their functions in relation to making, reviewing or cancelling maintenance assessments;
(b) keep under review the operation of the provision made by or under this Order with respect to making, reviewing or cancelling maintenance assessments; and provide annual reports to the Department on such matters.

3. The Child Support Appeals Tribunals

Article 23(1) of the 1991 Order provides for the setting up of child support appeals tribunals to hear appeals instigated under Article 22 (subject to any order made under Article 42). Schedule 3 of this Order details matters relating to the presidency, chairmanship, membership, administration and expenses of such tribunals.

4. The Child Support Commissioners

Article 25(1) of the 1991 Order permits an appeal on a point of law, with leave of the chairman of the appeal tribunal, from either an aggrieved applicant or from a child support officer to a child support commissioner. If satisfied that the decision of the tribunal was wrong in law, the commissioner may set it aside and then, under Article 25(3), he may

(a) if he can do so without making fresh or further findings of fact, give the decision which he considers should have been given by the child support appeal tribunal;
(b) if he considers it expedient, make such findings and give such decision as he considers appropriate in the light of those findings; or
(c) refer the case, with directions for its determination, to a child support officer or, if he considers it appropriate, to a child support appeal tribunal.

Schedule 4 of the 1991 Order provides for the making of regulations to govern proceedings heard before a commissioner and details matters relating to the setting up of a tribunal of commissioners in certain circumstances, the finality of a commissioner's decisions and the pensions or payments which may be payable.

In this jurisdiction, the appeal procedure was illustrated in *Northern Ireland Child Support Commissioners Unreported Decision CSC6/94*.[5] This case concerned a maintenance payment made on August 26, 1993. The respondent, the absent parent, requested a review of the assessment on August 31, 1993. On October 8, the Child

---

5 [1994] 6 BNIL 56.

Support Officer (CSO) reviewed the decision of August 26th and made a fresh assessment. The respondent appealed the CSO's decision on the basis that the fresh assessment was incorrect. At the Child Support Appeal Tribunal (CSAT) hearing, evidence was given of a change in the respondent's circumstances since August 26th. The tribunal considered the change in the respondent's circumstances and took it into account in arriving at its decision. The CSO appealed to the Child Support Commissioner (CSC).

In upholding the appeal the CSC held as follows.

1. The right of appeal in this case arose under Article 22 of the 1991 Order which is an appeal against an Article 20 or 'second tier' review. There is no direct right of appeal to a CSAT against other types of review such as an Article 18 'periodical review' or an Article 19 'change of circumstances review'. As the change of circumstance had not been considered by the CSO as part of a 'second tier' review, the tribunal had no jurisdiction in relation to it.

2. Unlike the Social Security Appeal Tribunal and the Disability Appeal Tribunal, which have the power to consider matters arising on appeal (see section 34 of the Social Security Administration (NI) Act 1992), the CSAT has no inherent power to consider matters which are not otherwise the subject of the appeal. Accordingly, the tribunal exceeded its jurisdiction by considering the change of circumstances.

The Parties to Whom the Child Support Scheme Applies

The child support legislation has equal application to marital and non-marital families. The parties are the parent with care, the absent parent and a qualifying child. While the latter, being the actual or potential subject of a maintenance payment, is the main focus of concern, the Agency is also required to take into account the likely impact of its assessment on the welfare of any other children for whom the absent parent has responsibility.

I. Persons Eligible to Make Application under the Child Support Scheme

Article 7(1) of the 1991 Order confers eligibility to make application for an assessment of maintenance under the child support scheme. Only two classes of applicant are permitted — 'either the person with care or the absent parent'— subject to the Article 41 requirement that such a person is habitually resident in the United Kingdom. However, the political thrust behind this legislation, contrary to that generating most change in modern family law, is that private discretion should not be the main determinant of access to its procedures. Provision is therefore made for some applications to be compulsory. Also, while the parties may make a private arrangement to agree on maintenance payments, either may nonetheless later apply for an assessment to be carried out under the scheme. Any subsisting contractual agreement which purports to prevent such action will be considered void.

1. Voluntary Application from a 'Person with Care'

A 'person with care' is defined under Article 4(3) of the 1991 Order as someone with whom the child has his or her home and who provides day-to-day care for that child.

If such a person is not in receipt of welfare benefits, then he or she is free to elect whether or not to make an application. An application for assessment may be made by both parents acting together (the levying of a fee in respect of each application has been deferred for two years). Alternatively, on submission of a written agreement specifying the terms on which both parties undertake to support their children, the court may make an order endorsing that agreement.

2. Voluntary Application from an Absent Parent

Article 4(2) of the 1991 Order defines an absent parent as one who does not live in the same household with the child, the latter having his or her home with a person who provides day-to-day care. Both these requirements must be satisfied for the definition to be met. Such a person may make application on the same basis as a person with care, and indeed they will usually make it jointly.

3. Mandatory Application from a Parent Who Is a Person with Care

While neither of the above parties have to make an application under the child support scheme, any parent being a person with care who is in receipt of welfare benefits may well be compelled to do so. Article 9(1) states that 'where income support, family credit of any other benefit of a prescribed kind is claimed by or in respect of, or paid to or in respect of' such a parent, then that parent may be required by the Agency to initiate proceedings under the scheme. Only if the Agency has reasonable grounds for believing that such action would cause the parent or any child living with that parent a risk of suffering harm or undue distress is that body permitted to waive the parental obligation to make an application for assessment.

A person with care who refuses to authorise an application for assessment or fails to provide the Agency with the information necessary to locate the 'absent parent' will be penalised by a reduction in benefits unless he or she can show good reason for being unco-operative. The recent case of *Northern Ireland Child Support Commissioner's Unreported Decision No CSC 8/94*[6] demonstrates the importance attached to this requirement, the relative significance accorded to the principle of the welfare of the child and graphically illustrates the procedural process. The Commissioner was then considering an appeal made by a Child Support Officer against the decision of the Child Support Appeal Tribunal which had allowed the appeal of a mother against the decision of that Officer to reduce her benefit entitlement on the grounds that she was refusing to disclose the identity of the father of one of her two children. The mother's failure to disclose, on the form and during subsequent interviews with the Officer, was purportedly on the ground that she did not know the identity of the father. This defence was rejected on the evidence by the tribunal but it then allowed her appeal on the grounds that the reduction in benefits would impair the welfare interests of her children. The Commissioner held that the Appeal Tribunal had misdirected itself by not focusing on whether the mother had reasonable cause for non-disclosure. There was no evidence to show that she or her children would be placed at any particular risk by complying

---

6 [1995] 3 BNIL 57.

with the disclosure requirement. The Commissioner further held that, while a reduction in benefits may have adverse effects on the welfare of the children, this was not in itself a sufficient ground for appeal against the decision of the Officer.

4. Deferred Application for Maintenance Assessment

Article 7(10) of the 1991 Order, as inserted by Article 12 of the 1995 Order, prevents the making of an application for a maintenance assessment in circumstances where the parties are bound by a written maintenance agreement made before April 1993 or by a maintenance order or where benefit is currently being paid in respect of a child. The effect of Article 7(10) is extended to similarly restrict the power of the court under Articles 10 and 11 of the 1991 Order in respect of maintenance for children.

II. Persons Liable to Pay Maintenance under the Child Support Scheme

1. A 'Parent'

The main principle underpinning this legislation is that both parents have an equal responsibility to maintain their child throughout childhood. In practice this is applied by tracing and assessing the absent parent and ensuring that his or her contribution redresses the financial burden carried by the parent with care. A parent, for the purposes of the 1991 Order, is a person who has either adopted the child in question, is so by virtue of an order under section 50 of the Human Fertilisation and Embryology Act 1990 or is the biological mother or father of that child.

2. Blood Tests

Under Article 27(1) of the 1991 Order, a person who denies parentage in respect of a specific child cannot be subjected to a maintenance assessment except in specified circumstances. Instead, under Article 28(1A), as amended by Article 15 of the 1995 Order, the agency or the person with care may apply to a court for a declaration 'as to whether or not the alleged parent is one of the child's parents'. Then the matter may be resolved by recourse to blood tests under the Blood Tests (Evidence of Paternity) (Amendment) Regulations (NI) 1990. Failure to provide a sample for such testing is not an offence but, in the absence of just cause under Articles 8–13 of the Family Law Reform (NI) Order 1977, the court is entitled to draw its own conclusions. In determining whether or not to direct a blood test, the court will do so unless satisfied that this would be contrary to the best interests of the child concerned.[7]

The resulting declaration is one which will have effect only for the purposes of the child support legislation. Under Article 27A of the 1991 Order, as inserted by Article 14 of the 1995 Order, costs are made recoverable against a person not excluded as a parent by the results of such tests.

---

7   See *S v S* [1972] AC 24, 3 All ER 107. Also, see *Re E (A Minor)(Child Support: Blood Test)* [1994] 2 FLR 548.

3. An Absent Parent

First, an absent parent is one who meets the twin requirements of Article 4(2) and satisfies the Article 41 condition. Second, it is clear from the statutory definition that to be an absent parent such a person must first be a natural parent in respect of the child in question. Only the child's biological mother or father, whether married or not, can meet this definition; though this will in fact include adoptive parents it will not extend to step-parents. Both of a child's parents may be absent parents for the purposes of the 1991 Order.

Article 5(2) clearly states the absent parent's responsibility to 'maintain any qualifying child of his by making periodical payments of maintenance with respect to the child of such amount, and at such intervals, as may be determined in accordance with the provisions of this Order'. Article 5(3) places a firm duty on that parent 'to make those payments' following a maintenance assessment made under the Order. This on-going responsibility will not be ousted by the existence of an earlier clean-break settlement nor by the terms of an agreed and subsisting maintenance order.

III. Children for Whom Persons Are Liable to Pay Maintenance under the Child Support Scheme

A child for whom persons are liable to pay maintenance is referred to, for the purposes of the child support legislation, as a 'qualifying child' and is defined under Article 4(1) as someone in relation to whom one or both parents may be construed as 'absent parents'.

1. Natural Child

This exclusionary provision deliberately attaches an on-going liability for maintenance to a person in respect of any child to whom he or she is a 'biological' or adoptive parent. The legislative intent, being to ensure that parental responsibility will be firmly fixed in relation to every child, will follow a biological or adoptive parent into any subsequent familial situation and take precedence over any assumed responsibility for other children in that situation. While liability in respect of the maintenance of a natural child will automatically be determined in accordance with the child support scheme, liability for step-children or other children of the family will require referral to the court.

2. Age of Child

The age of the child has generated considerable controversy. The political decision to exclude from the definition of 'child', for the purposes of this legislation, any person aged between sixteen and eighteen years who is not in education/training, at a time of economic recession, was certain to generate widespread dissatisfaction. As it is, to meet the definition of 'child' for the purposes of this Order, a person is required by Article 3 to be either:

(a) aged less than sixteen years; or
(b) aged less than nineteen years and be receiving full-time education (which is not advanced education) at a recognised educational establishment or elsewhere if the education is recognised by the Department; or
(c) aged less than eighteen years and prescribed conditions are met in respect of him.

3. Marital Status of Child

A person will not meet the definition of 'child' for the purposes of this Order if he or she either:

(a) is or has been married or
(b) has celebrated a marriage which is void or
(c) has celebrated a marriage in respect of which a decree of nullity has been granted.

4. Habitual Residence of Child

Article 41 of the 1991 Order prevents a child support officer from making an assessment in respect of any child who is habitually resident outside the United Kingdom.

5. Welfare of Child

Under Article 9(2) a child support officer has discretion to waive the requirement to co-operate if he or she is of the opinion that to proceed would risk causing the parent 'harm or undue distress'. This could well be the case in situations, for example, where the child concerned has been conceived by means of rape or incest. Such stress on a parent would necessarily impact also on the welfare of the child. Although this provision is framed to protect the position of the parent with care, the latter can authorise the officer to ignore the risk and pursue the absent parent.[8] The latter has no right of challenge under this provision.[9]

Procedures

The application of the child support scheme is governed not only by the terms of the Child Support Orders but also by a considerable body of regulations. The assessment of maintenance payable by an absent parent in respect of a qualifying child is in fact a complex process. It is conducted in strict accordance with a mathematical formula which, being based on income support rates, therefore necessitates carrying out periodic adjustments to that assessment. The maintenance assessment is arrived at by a consideration of both the child's requirements and the parent/s' income.

I. The Assessment of Maintenance

Article 13(1) of the 1991 Order empowers a child support officer to make maintenance assessments in respect of a person with care, an absent parent and a qualifying child. The Child Support (Maintenance Assessment Procedure) Regulations 1992 provide the procedural framework necessary to guide the officer in carrying out such assessment duties. For the purposes of gathering information in relation to an absent parent's income, an officer is empowered to require persons such as parents and employers and

---

8 See, for example, *R v Secretary of State for Social Security ex parte Biggin* [1995] 1 FLR 851.
9 See *R v Secretary of State for Social Security ex parte Lloyd* [1995] 1 FLR 856.

bodies such as the Inland Revenue to make a full disclosure of details relating to income. The Child Support (Information, Evidence and Disclosure) Regulations (NI) 1992 detail the type of information which is to be sought.

If difficulties arise in a particular case, then, under Article 17, the agency is empowered to appoint a person to act as an inspector who may enter upon such premises and carry out such examinations of persons, premises and documents as may be appropriate. It is a criminal offence to knowingly obstruct or delay an inspector, and penalties may be applied for failure to co-operate.

II. The Review of Maintenance Assessments

Under Articles 18 and 19 of the 1991 Order the agency is obliged to review its original assessment within a prescribed period and thereafter to conduct reviews at periodic intervals and/or as required by any significant change of circumstances. Under Article 21(1) the child support officer may also initiate a review if and when he or she has reason to believe that the original assessment is defective by reason of:

(a) having been made in ignorance of a material fact;
(b) having been based on a mistake as to a material fact or;
(c) being wrong in law.

Under Article 20(7) any such review may be itself reviewed, on application, by a child support officer who was not previously involved. The provisions relating to reviews were amended by the Child Support (NI) Order 1995 to broaden the powers of a reviewing officer.

III. Appeals

Under Article 22 of the 1991 Order a person aggrieved by a decision of a child support officer is permitted to appeal to a child support appeals tribunal in circumstances where either the application for a review was not accepted by an officer or when dissatisfied with the result of such a review. Appeals must be brought within twenty-eight days of notification of the decision in question, though this period may be extended with leave from the chairman of an appeals tribunal. Article 10 of the Child Support (NI) Order 1995 amends this provision to allow for appeals to lapse in circumstances where a review is conducted while the appeal is pending and the outcome is judged, by the child support officer concerned, to have produced much the same result as would be the case if the appeal succeeded.

IV. The Collection of Maintenance Payments

Article 29 of the 1991 Order enables assessed maintenance to be collected and payments to be then made directly to the person caring for the child or through the agency or through such other intermediary as the latter may determine. For administrative purposes a distinction is made between two different types of maintenance: that which is assessed under Article 9 ('benefit cases'), where the applicant is in receipt of income support, family credit or any other prescribed benefit; and where an application has been made under Article 7(2). The Child Support (Collection and Enforcement) Regulations (NI) 1992 detail the arrangements which may be made for the collection of assessed maintenance.

V. *The Enforcement of Maintenance Payments*

Articles 29–37 of the 1991 Order, together with the considerable body of ancillary regulations, provide a wide range of methods for the enforcement of maintenance payments. These include arrangements for collection by way of direct debit or standing order. Provision is also made for enforcement by means of employing the old common-law device of levying distress whereby a debtor's goods may be forcefully removed and, if necessary, sold and the proceeds used to clear his or her debt.

1. Deduction of Earnings

Article 31 provides a power to direct, where necessary, the deduction of maintenance payments at source from the liable parent's earnings. This is done by issuing a 'deduction from earnings order'; a court order is unnecessary. Before doing so, considerable weight should be given to the welfare principle as stated in Article 6 of the 1991 Order.[10] The employer is required to make the deductions and inform the employee accordingly. It is an offence to refuse to comply with a deduction from earnings order and in such circumstances an application may be made under Article 33 to a court of summary jurisdiction for a 'liability order'. This directs a person who has failed to make one or more maintenance payments to do so, together with any interest which may have accrued, or face the enforced sale of such goods as may be necessary to meet the payments due. Application under Article 37, for committal to prison, is the ultimate means of enforcement available.

2. Jurisdiction of the Court

The High Court does not have jurisdiction to support the statutory powers of the Agency. Matters which are reserved to the Agency cannot also be the subject of duplicatory High Court proceedings; the Agency must look to its own comprehensive code of collection and enforcement powers. This is apparent from a recent Court of Appeal decision[11] which upheld the refusal of the High Court to grant a *Mareva* injunction in favour of the Department of Social Security (on behalf of the Child Support Agency) to restrain an absent parent who owed substantial arrears from disposing of the proceeds from sale of the matrimonial home.

The divisional court has no jurisdiction to hear an appeal against a refusal to remit arrears. This may only be done by case stated on the grounds of error of law or excess of jurisdiction.[12]

---

10 See, for example, *ex parte Biggin,* f/n 8.
11 See *Department of Social Security v Butler* [1996] 1 FLR 1.
12 See *Berry v Berry* [1987] 1 FLR 105 and *E v C (Maintenance)* [1996] 1 FLR 472.

VI. Arrears

Article 38 of the 1991 Order allows the Agency to recover, or seek to recover, arrears (or an 'additional sum' under the 1995 Order) amounting to one or more payments which an absent parent has failed to make. Interest will be levied at current rates. Article 38(6) provides that any sums recovered should be paid into the Consolidated Fund. There are no time limits in law or in practice restricting the period for which arrears are recoverable; however, the 1995 Order makes provision for Regulations which may give the Agency some discretion to fix a period or waive liability. It has been a criticism of Agency practice that, due to the calculation of the 'effective date' from which liability to pay child support commences, very frequently in new cases the absent parent has unknowingly accrued arrears before notification of assessment.

Applying the Assessment Formula

The child support scheme provides for the administration of a means-tested benefit. Assessments are therefore conducted in a standardised fashion. Part 1 of Schedule 1 of the 1991 Order outlines the complex mathematical formula which is to govern all assessments. The formula is calculated by reference to the child's maintenance requirement and the assessable income of both parents.

I. The Child's Maintenance Requirement

The child's maintenance requirement, in fact, is worked out on the basis of the maintenance requirement for the family unit as a whole rather than the particular requirements of the individual child. It is computed by, firstly, aggregating the Income Support allowances payable in respect of each child of the family, to any member of the family aged twenty-five or more, and to the caring parent. Secondly, the aggregated Child Benefit payable in respect of all children is then deducted from that first amount. However, this computation fails to take into account the housing costs for any such family unit.

II. The Parent/s' Income

The assessable income of both parents provides the basis for computing liability for maintenance. In general terms this is arrived at by deducting a reasonable allowance for living costs from each parent's actual net income. Liability is then calculated with reference to both a 'floor' and a 'ceiling' for maintenance payments. The former is acknowledged by a 'protected level of income' which prevents a liable parent from being forced on to Income Support. The latter is given recognition in a statutory formula for fixing a maximum payment level beyond which maintenance needs have no reasonable claim.

In practice what happens is that a calculation is made of each parent's total income from all sources (excluding most-means tested benefits, tax, personal insurance contributions and half any pension contributions less 'exempt income'). This 'assessable income' is then subject to a fifty per cent 'reduction rate' to allow for a notional equally shared financial responsibility for child maintenance, until such time as the child's maintenance requirement level is reached.

III. Departure Directions

Articles 28A–28I of the Child Support (NI) Order 1991, as inserted by Article 3 of the 1995 Order, provide lengthy directions to deal with departures from the usual rules for determining assessments.

1. Fresh Assessments

Article 28A permits the person with care or the absent parent to apply for a 'departure direction' requesting a fresh assessment in which specified factors will be either taken into account or be excluded. Under Article 28A, such an application must state whether it is based on:

(a) the effect of the current assessment; or
(b) a material change in the circumstances of the case since the current assessment was made.

An application may be made even though a normal review has been applied for or is underway. Pending the outcome of an application by an absent parent, the Agency may impose a regular payments condition.

2. Principles to Be Applied

In determining the application the Agency is required under Article 28E(2) to be guided by the general principles that:

(a) parents should be responsible for maintaining their children whenever they can afford to do so;
(b) where a parent has more than one child, his obligation to maintain any one of them should be no less of an obligation than his obligation to maintain any other of them.

The Agency is also required to have regard to the financial circumstances of both the absent parent and the person with care, together with the welfare interests of any child likely to be affected by the direction it may give. In any event, the Agency is prevented from giving a direction unless satisfied that it would be just and equitable in all the circumstances of the case to do so.

3. Special Expenses

Paragraph 3 of Schedule 4B of the 1991 Order, as inserted by Schedule 2 of the 1995 Order, increases the Agency's flexibility in conducting reviews of assessments. It does so by instancing circumstances (a non-exhaustive list) giving rise to special expenses 'which were not, and could not have been, taken into account in determining the current assessment'. These include expenses attributable to travel, illness or to some types of debt.

4. Property or Capital Transfers

Schedule 2, paragraph 3 of the 1995 Order makes provision for property transfers to be taken into account, in some circumstances, for the purpose of reducing maintenance payments. This is a significant amendment which will give child support officers a future opportunity to avoid some of the inequitable consequences of past assessments which, under the 1991 Order, were based solely on finances and ignored clean break house transfers.

Schedule 4B, paragraph 4 overcomes the blind spot in the 1991 Order, to similar effect, regarding lump sum payments.

Financial Provision for Children

The Children (NI) Order 1995

A new statutory code governing financial provision for children has been put into place by Article 15 and Schedule 1 of the Children Order.

The New Arrangements

The relevant provisions previously dispersed among the Guardianship of Infants Act 1886, the Children and Young Persons Act (NI) 1968 and the Family Law Reform (NI) Order 1987 are now to be found in a consolidated and amended form in the 1995 Order. As noted in the Regulations:[13]

> All applications concerning financial relief for a child only, and not for an adult as well, will now have to be made under the Children Order and qualify as 'family proceedings' as defined in Article 8(3), so that the court is also able to make any Article 8 order in those proceedings. The courts will still have power, however, to make orders for financial provision for children in matrimonial proceedings under the Matrimonial Causes (NI) Order 1978 and the Domestic Proceedings (NI) Order 1980. Applications under the Schedule may be made by a parent or guardian or by any person in whose favour a residence order is in force with respect to the child.

The equivalent provisions under the 1989 Act have proved particularly useful in circumstances where the liquidity problems of a liable parent are such that he has no regular income but he does have considerable capital assets. Recently, in such a case[14] in England, the High Court made an order under Schedule 1 settling a lump sum for the child where the liable father had previously been assessed by a child support officer as having a nil contribution to make towards the support of that child on the basis of his lack of income, despite the fact that his house was valued at £2.6 million and his three cars at £190,000. Schedule 1, paragraph 2(2)(c) of the 1995 Order provides the courts of this jurisdiction with authority to make a similar order.

---

13 Sch. 1, para 2(1), Reg. 2.65.
14 See *Phillips v Peace* [1996] 2 FLR 230.

CHAPTER TWENTY-THREE

Separation: Maintenance

Introduction

Spouses, unlike cohabitees, have a duty to provide mutual support (see Chapters Two and Three). Issues in relation to this duty will most usually be brought before the court following family breakdown in the context of proceedings for a judicial separation or for alleged breach of a separation by agreement. This chapter deals with the relevant law as applied in the context of separation. Elsewhere in the United Kingdom marriage breakdown would mean an almost exclusive focus on divorce proceedings. In Northern Ireland, however, religious beliefs quite often dictate recourse to measures which fall short of, or serve as lengthy preliminaries to, the final legal dissolution of a marriage. Attention is also given to maintenance agreements. The concern of this chapter is thus with the legal means whereby the court and spouses regulate the financial aspects of a dead marriage. For the law in respect of such matters in the context of a continuing marital or cohabiting relationship, see Chapters Twenty and Twenty-One; on divorce see Chapter Twenty-Four; and for those matters which fall within the remit of the Child Support (NI) Orders of 1991 and 1995, see Chapter Twenty-Two.

Jurisdiction

The marital duty to provide maintenance for a spouse and children is now largely enforced through the Child Support (NI) Orders 1991 and 1995. The court, however, continues to hold jurisdiction to make maintenance orders in certain circumstances.

Legislation

A claim for maintenance by one spouse against the other will be determined by the court under either Article 29 of the Matrimonial Causes (NI) Order 1978 or Article 4 of the Domestic Proceedings (NI) Order 1980 (as amended by the Matrimonial and Family Proceedings (NI) Order 1989, subject to the Child Support (NI) Order 1991). The relevant procedure is set out in Part III of the Family Proceedings Rules (NI) 1996. The provisions of the Family Law (NI) Order 1993, particularly Articles 6–11, on the methods by which payment on foot of maintenance orders can be made (including maintenance orders registered in or confirmed by courts of summary jurisdiction or registered in the High Court) should also be noted.

Courts

Under the Domestic Proceedings (NI) Order 1980 the magistrates' courts have jurisdiction to make financial provision orders of unsecured periodical payments and lump sum payments under £1,000.00 (also, personal protection orders and exclusion orders; see Chapter Eight).

Under the Matrimonial Causes (NI) Order 1978, the High Court and the county court have jurisdiction to make financial provision orders including those for secured periodical payments and for lump sums exceeding £1,000.00. They are most likely to do so in the context of divorce proceedings (see Chapter Twenty-Four).

Parties

Under the Domestic Proceedings (NI) Order 1980, Article 3:

> Either party to a marriage may apply to the court for an order under Article 4.

The Rules permit a party, proceeding under Article 3(c) or (d) and wishing to make application under Article 4 for financial provision, not to furnish particulars of the adultery or behaviour in the summons.[1] Should the respondent request such details, then they are to be provided by the applicant's solicitor. The criteria governing the eligibility and liability of the parties is the same as in divorce proceedings (see further Chapter Twenty-Four).

Maintenance by Private Agreement

Instead of resorting to legal proceedings, spouses often choose to amicably draw up their own private agreement which, usually in addition to other matters, will set out the agreed arrangements in respect of maintenance. The law relating to such maintenance agreements is governed by Articles 36–38 of the Matrimonial Causes (NI) Order 1978.

Maintenance Agreement

1. Definition

Under Article 36:

> (2) ... 'maintenance agreement' means any agreement in writing made, whether before or after the commencement of this Article, between the parties to a marriage, being —
> (a) an agreement containing financial arrangements, whether made during the continuance or after the dissolution or annulment of the marriage; or
> (b) a separation agreement which contains no financial arrangements in a case where no other agreement in writing between the same parties contains such arrangements.

In this context, 'financial arrangements' means:

---

1 See the Magistrates' Courts (Domestic Proceedings) Rules (NI) 1966, Rule 3(2).

> ... provisions governing the rights and liabilities towards one another when living separately of the parties to a marriage (including a marriage which has been dissolved or annulled) in respect of the making or securing of payments or the disposition or use of any property, including such rights and liabilities with respect to the maintenance or education of any child, whether or not a child of the family.

The first requirement of this definition is that the agreement be in writing though not necessarily in a formal contract. It may, for example, be included in a personal letter.[2] The reference to 'disposition or use of property' has been held to be sufficiently wide to include agreements in respect of the ownership or occupation of the matrimonial home.[3]

2. Validity

As with any other contractual document, a maintenance agreement must meet the usual evidential requirements in respect of contractual intent, consideration and of full and free consent (see also, Chapter Eight).

3. The Courts

The courts look favourably on agreements reached privately between the parties concerned. However, the law is a matter for the courts and the terms of any such agreement must therefore remain subject to possible review and alteration.

(a) Court's Power to Review

Under Article 36:

> (1) If a maintenance agreement includes a provision purporting to restrict any right to apply to a court for an order containing financial arrangements, then—
> (a) that provision shall be void, but
> (b) any other financial arrangements contained in the agreement shall not thereby be rendered void or unenforceable and shall, unless they are void or unenforceable for any other reason (and subject to Articles 37 and 38), be binding on the parties to the agreement.

The intention of the separating spouses may well be to draw up a once and for all settlement to finalise their mutually agreed financial arrangements, but this is rendered impossible by the above provision. Any attempt to construct a private and final agreement will not succeed. A spouse cannot prevent the possibility of the agreement being subject to court review, on application by either party; there is a public interest[4] to be safeguarded. This, in effect, provides a spouse (usually the wife) with an insurance policy: while insisting that the other party acknowledges a 'floor' to their financial arrangements, a spouse may also decide to raise the 'ceiling' by seeking a more

---

2 See *MH v MH* [1981] FLR 429.
3 See *D v D* (1974)118 SJ 715; also see *Sutton v Sutton* [1984] 1 All ER 168.
4 See *Hyman v Hyman* [1929] AC 601 HL, and *Sutton* at f/n 3.

favourable settlement from the court. However, as in *Edgar v Edgar*[5] where the court held that there was no good reason to go behind a *bona fide* agreement, this may not succeed. Any attempt to forestall such a strategy by including a barring clause to that effect in the agreement will be void under the above Article; the agreement itself, however, will remain valid.

(b) Endorsement by the Court

Under Article 8 of the 1980 Order (as amended by Article 13 of the 1989 Order) the court may transform the legal standing of a maintenance agreement by incorporating it into a consent order. The effect is that the agreement no longer rests on the consent of the parties[6] but on the authority of the court; any alteration or termination is not at the discretion of the former but may be achieved only by court order (as was the case in *Crozier v Crozier*,[7] see Chapter Twenty-Four). The Rules permit an application made under Article 8 to be made orally, before a Justice of the Peace or clerk of petty sessions, specifying the type of payment though evidence of consent must be provided in writing and witnessed.[8]

Under Article 9 of the 1980 Order the same process may occur in circumstances where the couple have been living apart for three continuous months, neither having deserted the other and one of whom has been making periodical payments for the benefit of the other or a child of the family. Again, the Rules permit an application under this Article to be made orally.[9]

(c) Endorsement by the Court: A 'Consent Order'

Under Article 35A[10] of the 1978 Order, in response to an application for financial relief from a party to a maintenance agreement, the court may grant a 'consent order' in the terms as stated in the agreement. Such orders are subject to several restrictions. Firstly, they may be made only in relation to financial provision, property adjustment and the sale of property. Moreover, once made, they are naturally only binding in respect of the agreed terms; there is nothing to stop the parties litigating on matters not covered by the consent order. Secondly, they can only be made if the parties make a full and frank disclosure of the 'prescribed information' as specified in Rule 2.72 of the Family Proceedings Rules (NI) 1996. As has been said:[11]

> It has long been established that when parties seek the assistance of the courts in resolving their financial differences they, the parties, are under an obligation to disclose all their resources, to be full, frank and clear in their disclosures. If either party fails to do so the court may either refuse to adjudicate upon the matter as

---

5 [1980] 3 All ER 887.
6 See *De Lasala v De Lasala* [1980] AC 546, 550.
7 [1993] 10 BNIL 34.
8 See the Magistrates' Courts (Domestic Proceedings) Rules (NI) 1966, Rule.
9 See the Magistrates' Courts (Domestic Proceedings) Rules (NI) 1966, Rule 5.
10 Inserted by the Matrimonial and Family Proceedings (NI) Order 1989, Article 10.
11 See *J v J* [1955] 2 All ER 617.

presented or proceed, drawing such inferences as can be properly drawn against the party in default.

The House of Lords more recently ruled that where a party wilfully fails to make disclosure of a significant fact, then a consent order must be set aside.[12] It is imperative that the terms of consent orders be defined with precision[13] as the lump sum and property adjustment components of consent orders cannot be subsequently varied. In addition to material non-disclosure, a consent order may also be set aside on the usual grounds that it was obtained by fraud or mistake or has subsequently been affected by a *Barder*-type new event.[14] Thirdly, they may not be made unless the court has considered all the circumstances of the case, applied the Article 27 guidelines and the 'clean break' test of Article 27A.[15]

If granted, however, the outcome for the parties is that a consent order will operate to give them all the secure finality of a clean break settlement. It will cease to have effect if the parties resume living together.

(d) Alteration by the Court During the Lifetime of the Parties

Under Article 37(2) the court has authority to vary, revoke or insert new provisions in an agreement if satisfied either

(a) that by reason of a change in the circumstances in the light of which any financial arrangements contained in the agreement were made or, as the case may be, financial arrangements were omitted from it (including a change unforeseen by the parties when making the agreement), the agreement should be altered so as to make different, or, as the case may be, so as to contain, financial arrangements, or

(b) that the agreement does not contain proper financial arrangements with respect to any child of the family.

The court is always concerned to uphold an agreement freely reached between the parties. However, as stated above, the court may intervene on application by one of the parties, to review and vary the terms of an agreement where either as a result of a change in circumstances the applicant has been unduly disadvantaged or proper provision has not been made for a child of the family. Rule 3.4 of the Family Proceedings (NI) Order 1996 makes provision for such an application and details the matters to be addressed in the supporting affidavit.

The court will need to be satisfied that the maintenance agreement is still subsisting and that both parties to it are either domiciled or resident within the jurisdiction.

---

12 See *Livesey (formerly Jenkins) v Jenkins* [1985] AC 424, [1985] 1 All ER 106, [1985] FLR 813 where the applicant failed to disclose the fact of her engagement which immediately preceded her consent order application.
13 See *Dinch v Dinch* [1987] 1 All ER 818, [1987] 2 FLR 162, where the comments were obiter.
14 See *Barder v Barder (Caluori Intervening)* [1987] 2 FLR 480.
15 Both guidelines and test having been inserted into the 1978 Order by the Matrimonial and Family Proceedings (NI) Order 1989, Article 6.

In the first instance, the disadvantaged applicant will have to show that when the agreement was drawn up the change in circumstances which subsequently occurred could not then have been reasonably foreseen.[16] If the court should conclude that while the applicant did not foresee the change in circumstances, a reasonable person in the same position would have done so, then the claim will fail and the applicant will be bound by the terms of the agreement. The applicant will also be required to prove that the disadvantage resulting from the change in circumstances flows from the terms of the agreement not from any other source. The courts have been particularly alert to the possibility of an agreement being prejudiced by a party's wilful or reckless conduct.[17] Where assets have been needlessly squandered by one party the courts have taken the view that to disregard such conduct would be inequitable to the other.[18] This approach was demonstrated in a recent case[19] where a husband made a separation agreement concerning the family farm which he had bought with financial assistance from his wife and subsequently mismanaged. It was agreed that the farm would be sold and the wife would receive a substantial amount 'in full and final settlement' from the sale which would be deferred for a period. During the interim the husband became bankrupt and was evicted from the farm. The trustees paid out almost the full agreed amount to the wife but a considerable debt remained outstanding. The husband, who was then living with his parents and subsisting on income support, sought a lump sum order against his wife for funds sufficient to buy himself a house, establish a new business and pay off some creditors. The court held that the financial disparity between the spouses was now so great as to justify it making some financial adjustment in the husband's favour. However, his conduct in allowing the bankruptcy situation to come about had been so obstinate, selfish and unrealistic that it amounted to conduct which it would be inequitable to disregard. Accordingly, the agreement would be adjusted but only to allow the husband reasonable provision for basic accommodation.

In this jurisdiction the case of *M v M*[20] (see Chapter Twenty-Four) provides a good example of how the existence of a formal legal agreement concerning the matrimonial home, reached prior to the grant of a decree absolute, need pose no impediment to a subsequent application for a property adjustment order in respect of the same property. This is particularly so in situations where a petitioner has relied on either of the separation facts and the respondent wishes to ensure that adequate financial provision will be made available before the decree absolute is granted. Because in such cases there can be no suggestion of fault on the part of the respondent, the court will always respond positively to a request from the latter for assurance of adequate provision even if this is made during the course of proceedings.

The High Court or county court has the power to alter the agreement by revoking or varying any of the financial arrangements or by inserting fresh arrangements for the

---

16 See *Gorman v Gorman* [1964] 3 All ER 739 CA.
17 See, for example, *Ratcliffe v Ratcliffe* [1962] 3 All ER 933 CA where the court held that the agreement should stand as it was the applicant's conduct in abandoning his career and assuming a less well paid position that rendered him unable to meet the terms.
18 See, for example, *Martin v Martin* [1976] Fam 335; [1976] 3 All ER 625.
19 See *Beach v Beach* [1995] 2 FLR 160.
20 [1983] 7 BNIL 1.

benefit of a disadvantaged party or a child of the family. Such a court may not, however, make alterations which have the effect of placing a party in a position which is more advantageous than if he or she had instituted divorce proceedings.[21] The powers of a magistrates' court are more limited.

(e) Alteration by the Court after Death of One of the Parties

Under Article 38(2) the High Court or county court has authority to alter a maintenance agreement on the application of either a surviving party to that agreement or the personal representatives of the deceased. The latter must have died within the jurisdiction, provision must have been made for continuing payments and, under Article 38(3), the application has to be brought within six months of the date on which representation in regard to the estate of the deceased is first taken out unless permission for a later application is obtained from the High Court or county court. Rule 3.5 of the Family Proceedings (NI) Order 1996 makes provision for such an application and details the matters to be addressed in the supporting affidavit. The powers of the court are the same as when applications are brought during the lifetime of the parties, and under Article 38(4), any alteration made by the court takes effect as if made immediately before the death by agreement between the parties and for valuable consideration.

Maintenance

I. The Matrimonial Causes (NI) Order 1978

Rule 3.1 of the Family Proceedings (NI) Order 1996 deals with an application made by a spouse under Article 29 of the 1978 Order for failure to maintain the applicant or any child of the family.

Application for maintenance may be made by summons to the High Court or to a county court. Rule 3.1 of the 1996 Order details the matters which must be addressed in a supporting affidavit.

1. The Grounds

Under the 1978 Order:

> 29. Either party to a marriage may apply to the court for an order under this Article on the ground that the other party to the marriage ('the respondent')
>
> (a) has failed to provide reasonable maintenance for the applicant; or
> (b) has failed to provide, or to make a proper contribution towards; reasonable maintenance for any child of the family.

A 'child of the family', for the purposes of this provision, means a child of both parties to the marriage and any other child, not being a child who has been boarded-out with those parties by a Trust or voluntary organisation, who has been treated by the parties as a child of the family (as defined in Article 2 of the Children (NI) Order 1995.

---

21 See *Pace v Doe* [1977] Fam 18, [1977] 1 All ER 176.

The ground is now 'has failed to provide' which replaces the long-standing 'wilful neglect to provide'.[22] This ground, as adjusted, gives statutory effect to the common-law duty of one spouse to maintain the other and carries with it the corollary defence that if the other is in default then the duty lapses.[23] The fact that the law governing the defence to a charge of failure to maintain continues to be exercised in accordance with common law principles was demonstrated in *Megarry v Megarry*,[24] which remains the leading case in this jurisdiction.

This case concerned a wife with two teenage children who, having complained to no avail about the choice of matrimonial home (it belonged to the company formed and owned by the husband and his parents) for the full sixteen years of her marriage, eventually left with the children following a row during which her husband had used very rejecting language. Thereafter he refused to provide any maintenance for her, on the grounds of her desertion, though he did support the children and pay their school fees. She refused to return and instead brought proceedings for periodical payments alleging 'wilful neglect to pay maintenance' under section 4 of the 1951 Act. Kelly J held that the words 'wilful neglect' no longer added an extra burden of proof to be satisfied by the applicant (removed by the Summary Jurisdiction (Separation and Maintenance) Act (NI) 1945). The essential question, as put by Kelly J, is as determining in its relevance today as it was then and earlier under the common law:[25]

> [H]as the husband been excused from his duty to provide reasonable maintenance by reason of some grave fault on the part of his wife?

The learned judge formed the view that as the husband had become more successful in his business and more pre-occupied with it, he had neglected his marriage to the point where he wanted rid of it. As his words had been intended to drive his wife from the home and to keep her away, he was therefore guilty of constructive desertion. The order sought was granted.

2. The Orders

Under Rule 3.3 of the Family Proceedings (NI) Order 1996:

> (3) On the hearing of the application the judge may make such order as he thinks just or may refer the application (except any application under Article 8 of the Order of 1995), or any application for an order under Article 29(5) of the Order of 1978 to the Master for him to investigate the means of the parties to the marriage.

The Master, on undertaking such an investigation, will report the results to the judge. The High Court has authority to make the same orders regarding periodical payments and lump sums as the magistrates' courts except that it is not subject to the latter's financial ceiling when making awards and it may make them on a 'secured' basis so that they continue after the death of the respondent.

---

22 See Married Women (Maintenance in Case of Desertion) Act 1886 and the Law Reform (Matrimonial Provisions) Act (NI) 1951, section 4.
23 See, for example, *Northrop v Northrop* [1968] P 74. See also, Rule 3.2(1) of the 1996 Order.
24 [1978] 7 NIJB.
25 Ibid.

II. The Domestic Proceedings (NI) Order 1980

Most applications for maintenance during marriage are made to the magistrates' courts under Articles 3–9 of the 1980 Order, as amended by the 1989 Order. Article 30 of the 1980 Order prevents an application under Article 4 from being heard if proceedings are already underway in the divorce court.

Either or both parties may also have a right to claim maintenance from the State as a consequence of an entitlement to contributory or non-contributory benefits from the Department of Social Security.

1. The Grounds

Under the 1980 Order:

> 3. Either party to a marriage may apply to the court for an order under Article 4 on the ground that the other party to the marriage ('the respondent')—
> - (a) has failed to provide reasonable maintenance for the applicant; or
> - (b) has failed to provide, or to make a proper contribution towards; reasonable maintenance for any child of the family; or
> - (c) has, since the date of the marriage, committed adultery; or
> - (d) has behaved in such a way that the applicant cannot reasonably be expected to live with the respondent; or
> - (e) has deserted the applicant.

A 'child of the family' has the same meaning as in Article 29 of the 1978 Order. An application must be brought within one year of the behaviour which provides the ground relied upon.

2. The Orders

Orders for financial provision may be made under Article 4, Article 8, Article 9 or Article 13(2). The magistrates' court cannot make orders for secured periodical payments nor can it make property adjustment orders.

(a) Article 4

Where an applicant satisfies any of the grounds listed in Article 3 above, then the court may make one or more of the following orders, under Article 4:

(a) an order that the respondent shall make to the applicant such periodical payments, and for such term as may be specified in the order;
(b) an order that the respondent shall pay to the applicant such lump sum as may be so specified;
(c) an order that the respondent shall make to the applicant for the benefit of a child of the family to whom the application relates, or to such a child, such periodical payments, and for such term, as may be so specified;
(d) an order that the respondent shall pay to the applicant for the benefit of a child of the family to whom the application relates, or to such a child, such lump sum as may be so specified.

The court thus has authority to issue orders for a lump sum and/or periodical payments and for such period as the court sees fit. Lump sums are restricted to amounts not exceeding £1,000, may be paid in instalments and the amount payable in each instalment may, under Article 24, be varied. The court also has the power, under Article 20, to make an interim maintenance order.

Article 5 of the 1980 Order (as substituted by Article 12 of the 1989 Order) specifies a number of considerations which the court is required to take into account before making an order under Article 4. In all material respects these are identical to the matters which the court is required to consider in the context of proceedings for financial provision under the 1978 Order (see further Chapter Twenty-Four).

(b) Article 8 (as Amended by Article 13 of the 1989 Order)

Where the spouses have drawn up a private maintenance agreement, then either may apply to the court for an order, under Article 8, for financial provision on the ground that the other is in breach of that agreement. If satisfied that the respondent has agreed to make provision, has breached that agreement and that it would not be contrary to the interests of justice, then the court may exercise its powers by granting an order for the making of lump-sum payments and/or periodical payments to the applicant. Such payment/s are payable by the respondent to the applicant for the latter's benefit and/or for the benefit of any child of the family and are subject to review under the Child Support (NI) Order 1991.

(c) Article 9

Where the parties have been living apart by mutual agreement for a continuous period exceeding three months, neither being in desertion, and one has been providing maintenance to the other or in respect of a child of the family, then that other is entitled to apply to the court for a maintenance order pursuant to Article 9.

(d) Article 13(2)

Where the court has made an order under Article 10(2) in respect of a child of the family and in favour of the respondent, then Article 13(2) enables it to it make an order directing financial provision to be paid for the benefit of that child. The order may require the applicant to make such provision by lump sum and/or by periodical payments.

3. Appeal

An appeal may lie to the county court against the decision of a magistrates' court. Under Article 31, it is enforceable until such time as the appeal is heard.

4. Enforcement

When made, Article 27 then provides that the orders may thereafter be enforced while the parties are living together but that periodical payments in favour of a spouse will lapse where the parties continue living together for a continuous period of more than six months. Enforcement is, as usual, by way of application to the Enforcement of Judgments Office. Where there are outstanding arrears, then an arrears summons may be issued requiring the respondent to account to the court for his non-payments. The courts, unlike the Child Support Agency, have discretion to enforce rather than a discretion to remit arrears.[26] The court appearance may, if necessary, be followed by a committal to prison under Articles 36 and 39 of the 1980 Order. Case law in England and Wales demonstrates that before making a committal order, a magistrate must clearly record that consideration has been given to the ability of the liable relative to pay the arrears and to the most appropriate means by which this may be achieved.[27]

III. Child Support/Care Legislation

Although the jurisdiction of the court to make maintenance orders has been severely curtailed by the Child Support (NI) Orders 1991 and 1995, it will continue for some years to carry responsibility for those orders already made, until these are eventually taken over by the Child Support Agency. In addition it will hold responsibility for maintenance in certain circumstances excluded from the remit of that agency. The jurisdiction of the court has also been affected by the Children (NI) Order 1995.

1. Maintenance Payments

(a) Child Support (NI) Orders 1991 and 1995 to or on Behalf of Children, Reserved to the Court

The court retains some jurisdiction to make maintenance orders despite the broad sweep of the child support legislation both because certain types of cases have been specifically excluded from the remit of the child support scheme and because others have not been included. It also retains jurisdiction in respect of those cases in which it has already made maintenance orders. But, where maintenance orders are already in force and a maintenance assessment is carried out under the child support scheme, then the order will cease to have effect to the extent that it conflicts with the assessment.

(b) Relating to Disabled Children, Adolescent Education or High Parental Income

Article 3(1) of the 1991 Order excludes persons between the ages of sixteen and eighteen who are not in full-time education from the definition of 'child', but their circumstances may bring them within the jurisdiction of the court for the purposes of maintenance orders. Article 10 outlines the protected jurisdiction of the court in relation to maintenance payments in respect of certain children. Article 10(6)(c) allows the court to make maintenance orders for payments additional to those fixed by the Child Support Agency where the court is satisfied that this is appropriate. Article 10(7) permits the court to make a maintenance order solely for the purpose of requiring a person to meet the costs of school fees. Article 10(8) prevents the child support scheme from

---

26 See *B v B (Periodical Payment: Transitional Provisions)* [1995] Fam Law 223 and *B v C (Enforcement: Arrears)* [1995] Fam Law 243.
27 See *SN v ST (Maintenance Order: Enforcement)* [1995] 1 FLR 868.

usurping the jurisdiction of the court to make maintenance orders in respect of disabled children (as defined by sections 9); whether or not they are in receipt of disability benefits.

Article 10(10) continues the court's authority to 'make a maintenance order in relation to a child if the order is made against a person with care of the child'.

2. Separation — Maintenance Agreements and the Children (NI) Order 1995

The law looks as favourably on maintenance agreements made privately by separating parents in respect of provision for their children as it does where that provision is made for the benefit of the parties. The validity of any such agreement will be determined in accordance with the same tests. Again there are some circumstances where the court may intervene, on application by a parent, to alter an agreement. A parent wishing to challenge an agreed arrangement made with the other parent, during the lifetime of the latter, regarding provision for their child will now have to make application to the court under the Children (NI) Order 1995, Schedule 1.

(a) Maintenance Agreement for a Child

(i) Jurisdiction of the Courts

Under Schedule 1, paragraph 12(2), where an agreement is subsisting and each of the parties to it is resident or domiciled within the jurisdiction, then either parent may apply to the court for an order to alter that agreement. Application may be made to the High Court, a county court or to a magistrates' court. In the latter case, paragraph 6 of this Schedule prohibits an application in respect of property; a magistrates' court is restricted by sub-paragraphs (a) and (b) to making, increasing, reducing or terminating periodical payments.

(ii) Definition

Under Schedule 1, paragraph 12:

> (1) . . . 'maintenance agreement' means any agreement made in writing with respect to a child (including an agreement made before the commencement of this paragraph) which
>
> > (a) is or was made between the father and mother of the child; and
> > (b) contains provision with respect to the making or securing of payments, or the disposition or use of any property, for the maintenance or education of the child.

It makes no difference whether or not the parents were married to each other but they must be the actual mother and father of the child in question (i.e. a step-parent or any other form of parental status will not suffice). The agreement must be in writing.

(b) Alteration by the Court During the Parties' Lifetime

Under Schedule 1, paragraph 12, where the agreement still subsists and the parties are both domiciled or resident in Northern Ireland, then:

(3) If the court to which the application is made is satisfied either
   (a) that, by reason of a change in the circumstances in the light of which any financial arrangements contained in the agreement were made (including a change unforeseen by the parties when making the agreement), the agreement should be altered so as to make different financial arrangements; or
   (b) that the agreement does not contain proper financial arrangements with respect to the child, then that court may by order make such alterations in the agreement by varying or revoking any financial arrangements contained in it as may appear to the court to be just having regard to all the circumstances.

This provision has a retrospective application enabling the court to use its wide discretionary powers of adjustment in respect of agreements made before as well as after implementation of the 1995 Order.

(c) Alteration by the Court after the Death of One of the Parties

Under Schedule 1, paragraph 13:

(1) Where a maintenance agreement provides for the continuation, after the death of one of the parties, of payments for the maintenance of a child and that party dies domiciled in Northern Ireland, the surviving party or the personal representatives of the deceased party may apply to the High Court or a county court for an order under paragraph 12.

Such an application should be made within six months of the day in which representation in regard to the deceased is first taken out: after that period an application may only be made with leave of either designated court.

CHAPTER TWENTY-FOUR

Divorce: Ancillary Relief

Introduction

This chapter deals with the law relating to the finance and property of spouses in the context of proceedings for the termination of marriage. Ancillary relief at the time of, or following, the commencement of proceedings for divorce, nullity or judicial separation is its sole concern. The law in relation to settlements of finance and property made in other contexts must, therefore, be sought elsewhere: during the continuation of a marital or cohabiting relationship (see Chapters Twenty and Twenty-One); during a separation (see Chapter Twenty-Three); and for those matters which fall within the remit of the Child Support (NI) Orders of 1991 and 1995 (see Chapter Twenty-Two).

Jurisdiction

The Child Support (NI) Orders have removed much responsibility for settling financial arrangements on family breakdown from the judicial process. The Children (NI) Order 1995 has transferred much judicial responsibility for settling the future care arrangements of dependent children from matrimonial to child-care proceedings. However, in the context of proceedings for divorce, nullity or judicial separation, the courts do continue to hold a considerable jurisdiction to grant ancillary relief. This is now exercised to a limited extent by way of orders for the adjustment of finances but extensively as regards property adjustment orders for the benefit of the respondent and any dependent children.

Legislation

Ancillary relief is governed by Articles 23–31 of the Matrimonial Causes (NI) Order 1978, as amended by Articles 5–11 of the Matrimonial and Family Proceedings (NI) Order 1984 and subject to the provisions of the 1991 Order. Articles 25 and 26 of the 1978 Order provide specific authority for judicial orders to regulate matters of finance and property, respectively. The relevant procedure is as set out in Rules 2.55–2.73 of the Family Proceedings Rules (NI) 1996.

The aim of the Married Woman's Property Act 1882 was to protect the property rights of women by enabling a wife to take back, at the end of a marriage, the property she had brought with her into it. The 1882 Act, however, did not take account of any contribution made to marital property by the wife during the course of the marriage. The aim of the Matrimonial Causes (NI) Order 1978 was to place a wife not in the position she was when she entered the marriage but the position she would have been in had the marriage continued.

Courts

Proceedings under the 1978 Order may be commenced either in the High Court or in a county court; both have jurisdiction to make orders for the financial provision of any child of the family. Their authority to do so, by making lump sum payments or property adjustment orders, remains undiminished by the introduction of the 1991 Order.

In implementing the provisions of the 1978 Order, the courts have further developed the law. It is now judicially recognised that if, following marriage breakdown, two separate homes have to be established, then one party cannot continue to enjoy the same standard of living as he or she would have enjoyed had the marriage subsisted. Consequently, the courts strive to provide a fair distribution of assets which, while taking account of the matters listed in Article 27 (as amended), aims to provide a home with a degree of financial stability for the custodial parent.

The Lord Chancellor's Ancillary Relief Advisory Group has for some years now been designing a new procedure for expediting ancillary relief cases through the court system. A pilot scheme was implemented in the autumn of 1996 in England and Wales, involving (among other innovations) new forms to provide for the uniform and full disclosure of parties' assets. It is anticipated that when the results of that scheme have been thoroughly assessed, new procedures will be introduced for the more effective and economical processing of ancillary relief cases.

Applicants

Under Rule 2.56 of the 1996 Rules any of the following may apply for ancillary relief in respect of an eligible child:

(a) a parent or guardian of any child of the family;
(b) any person in whose favour a residence order has been made with respect to a child of the family, and any applicant for such an order;
(c) any other person who is entitled to apply for a residence order with respect to a child;
(d) an authority, where an order has been made under Article 50(1)(a) of the 1995 Order placing a child in its care;
(e) the Official Solicitor if appointed the guardian ad litem of a child of the family under Rule 6.6; and
(f) a child of the family who has been given leave to intervene in the cause for the purpose of applying for ancillary relief.

1. Eligible Child

Under Article 2 of the Matrimonial Causes (NI) Order 1978 an eligible child is:

(a) a child of both parties; and
(b) any other child, not being a child who has been boarded-out with those parties by or on behalf of the Department of Health and Social Services or a voluntary organisation, who has been treated by both parties as a child of their family.

This definition encompasses any illegitimate children of one or both parties and any step-children or any child privately fostered with them. It stands in marked contrast to the definition of 'child' in the Child Support (NI) Order 1991 where only a biological or adoptive relationship will suffice. An unborn child however, does not come within this definition. For example, *in A v A (Family: Unborn Child)*,[1] it was held that a husband could not be held liable for the maintenance of a child conceived before but born after his marriage to the mother, even though he had known that he could not be the father and had given every assurance of his intention to treat the child as his own.

Article 31(1) of the 1978 Order states that to be eligible for a financial provision order or an order for a transfer of property under Article 26(1)(a) a child must not have attained the age of eighteen. In the case of a periodical payments order or secured periodical payments order in favour of a child, they may be paid only until the child's first birthday past the upper limit of the compulsory school age (as set by Article 36 of the Education and Libraries (NI) Order 1986), though this may be extended at the court's discretion but not beyond the child's eighteenth birthday.

Article 31(3) of the 1978 Order provides an exception to the upper age limit of eighteen years by allowing payments to continue in respect of an older child who is, or would be if proper arrangements were made, 'receiving instruction at an educational establishment or undergoing training for a trade, profession or vocation'. This applies whether or not the child is also, or will also be, in gainful employment.

Article 31(3)(b) of the 1978 Order provides that where there are special circumstances the court has discretion to waive the age and/or the education/training conditions and make an order for periodical payments or secured payments in favour of a 'child' older than eighteen.

In England this provision provided the grounds for an order in *Downing v Downing (Downing Intervening)*.[2] It was then held that a 'child' over the age of eighteen was entitled to intervene in matrimonial proceedings to claim financial provision for his educational/training costs despite the fact that his parents' divorce decree had been finalised many years previously.

The eligibility of children for financial or property provision in their own right on the divorce or separation of their parents has been considerably reduced by the 1991 Order. The thrust behind this legislation is that children are best supported by directing provision towards the caring parent.

2. Eligible Spouse

Under the Matrimonial Causes (NI) Order 1978, Article 29:

> Either party to a marriage may apply to the court for an order under this Article on the ground that the other party to the marriage ('the respondent')
>
> (a) has failed to provide reasonable maintenance for the applicant; or
> (b) has failed to provide, or to make a proper contribution towards; reasonable maintenance for any child of the family.

---

1 [1974] Fam 6; [1974] 1 All ER 755.
2 [1976] Fam 288.

The fact that the parties have drawn up a maintenance agreement does not prevent either of them applying to the court under this provision (for consent orders, see Chapter Twenty-Three).

3. Liable Spouse/Parent

A parent need not be the biological mother or father of a child to be found liable in divorce proceedings to contribute a share of their assets for the benefit of that child. The legislative preference for 'child of the family' is, in this context, deliberately intended to bring in step-parents and other informal carers to the circle of those who in law may be held to bear parental responsibility. This indicates legislative recognition of the realities of modern family life. Given the increase in the number of parents who have serial marital or non-marital relationships and those who acquire parentage by artificial means, there are now an ever-increasing number of children in respect of whom primary parental responsibility is difficult to ascertain. Conversely, very many children now each have several persons to whom they may legally look for a degree of parental acknowledgement.

The law has determined that a significant test of parental liability is whether a person has chosen to treat a child as one of the family. This formulation will confer liability on someone who while not having a formal legal relationship with a child (e.g. a lodger, grandparent, step-parent or even a neighbour) does currently undertake direct care responsibility. Others who do not bear such responsibility but are so related to the child (e.g. a natural father or mother or an adopter) may be pursued under other legislation (specifically under the 1991 Order).

In deciding whether to exercise its power under Articles 25 or 26 of the 1978 Order against one of the parties to the marriage in favour of a child of the family who is not the child of that party, the court is required by Article 27(3), as amended by Article 6(4) of the Matrimonial and Family Proceedings (NI) Order 1984, to have regard:

(a) to whether that party had assumed any responsibility for the child's maintenance and, if so, to the extent to which, and the basis upon which, that party assumed such responsibility and to the length of time for which that party discharged such responsibility;
(b) to whether in assuming and discharging such responsibility that party did so knowing that the child was not his or her own;
(c) to the liability of any other person to maintain the child.

Court Orders Pending Hearing for Ancillary Relief

The court will use its powers of injunction to restrain a party from activity which threatens to frustrate the full exercise of its powers to grant ancillary relief. It may make orders under Article 39(2) of the 1978 Order to restrain a party from having dealings with any finance or property likely to be the subject of ancillary relief proceedings or to set aside any transactions made where there is evidence of an intention to frustrate the scope of such proceedings. Application may be made under this provision for an injunction by way of either a *Mareva* injunction where there are equitable interests to be protected or an *Anton Pillar* injunction where there is a suspicion that full disclosure of assets will be avoided (but only if the applicant can show a very strong case and establish a real possibility that documents or materials would be destroyed resulting in a denial of justice to the applicant). Application may also be made for a writ of *ne exeat regno* where there is a possibility that a party may attempt to flee the jurisdiction, with matrimonial assets, prior to ancillary relief proceedings.

Ancillary Relief

1. Definition

Under Rule 1.3 of the Family Proceedings Rules (NI) 1996, 'ancillary relief' means

- (a) an avoidance of disposition order,
- (b) a financial provision order,
- (c) an order for maintenance pending suit,
- (d) a property adjustment order, or
- (e) a variation order.

The orders made will be for lump-sum or periodical payments and/or for the transfer, sale or other disposition of specified property.

2. Enforcement

The court will enforce orders for lump-sum payments by issuing an order for sale of specified property, a writ of execution, garnishee proceedings, a charging order or a judgment summons. Orders for periodical payments will be enforced by any of the above and/or also by an attachment of earnings order or by registration in a magistrates' court. Maintenance enforcement in the High Court and divorce county courts is provided for under Article 96A of the Family Law (NI) Order 1993.

Ancillary Relief

I. Maintenance Pending Suit

'Maintenance pending suit' is the term used to describe the interim maintenance arrangements made for a spouse until substantive proceedings can be concluded.

The Order

Under Article 24 of the 1978 Order:

> On a petition for divorce, nullity of marriage or judicial separation, the court may make an order for maintenance pending suit, that is to say, an order requiring either party to the marriage to make to the other such periodical payments for his or her maintenance and for such term, being a term beginning not earlier than the date of the presentation of the petition and ending with the date of the determination of the suit, as the court thinks reasonable.

The court is not required to take into account the matters referred to in Article 27 when determining an application for maintenance pending suit. Its view of what constitutes 'reasonable' maintenance will depend on the parties' circumstances.[3] The court may make an order (a 'corresponding order') for periodical payments to provide for payments to be made at the same rate as those provided for by order of maintenance pending suit.[4]

II. Financial Provision

When an issue of financial provision for children arises in the course of matrimonial proceedings, the judiciary must first consider whether their jurisdiction in relation to that issue has been ousted by the Child Support Orders of 1991 and 1995. However, because that legislation is concerned with income payments rather than capital assets, issues relating to the latter will always fall for judicial determination.

1. Orders Available

Under Article 25 of the 1978 Order:

> (1) On granting a decree of divorce, a decree of nullity of marriage or a decree of judicial separation or at any time thereafter (whether, in the case of a decree of divorce or of nullity of marriage, before or after the decree is made absolute), the court may make any one or more of the following orders, that is to say
>
> (a) an order that either party to the marriage shall make to the other such periodical payments, for such term, as may be specified in the order;
> (b) an order that either party to the marriage shall secure to the other to the satisfaction of the court such periodical payments, for such term, as may be so specified;
> (c) an order that either party to the marriage shall pay to the other such lump sum or sums as may be so specified;
> (d) an order that a party to the marriage shall make to such person as may be specified in the order for the benefit of a child of the family, or to such a child, such periodical payments, for such term, as may be so specified;
> (e) an order that a party to the marriage shall secure to such person as may be so specified for the benefit of such a child, or to such a child, to the satisfaction of the court, such periodical payments, for such term, as may be so specified;
> (f) an order that a party to the marriage shall pay to such person as may be so specified for the benefit of such a child, or to such a child, such lump sum as may be so specified subject, however, in the case of an order under subparagraph (d), (e) or (f), to the restrictions imposed by Article 31(1) and (3) on the making of financial provision orders in favour of children who have attained the age of eighteen.

---

3 See, for example, *Re T (Divorce: Interim Maintenance: Discovery)* [1990] 1 FLR 1 where this was fixed at £25,000 per annum because of the husband's relative wealth.
4 The Family Proceedings Rules (NI) 1996, Rule 2.70.

(2) The court may also, subject to those restrictions, make any one or more of the orders mentioned in paragraph (1)(d), (e) and

(f)(a) in any proceedings for divorce, nullity of marriage or judicial separation, before granting a decree; and
(b) where any such proceedings are dismissed after the beginning of the trial, either forthwith or within a reasonable period after the dismissal.

An order for financial provision will direct that funds be made available either by way of periodical payments or by a lump-sum payment. These are made payable to the spouses and to or on behalf of their children.

2. Periodical Payments

Periodical payment orders require payment of funds to a spouse and/or to or for the benefit of a child of the family on a regular basis such as weekly, monthly or quarterly. They can be made on a secured or unsecured basis. If there is reason to doubt the good intentions of a respondent, then he or she will be required to lodge security in the court which will be forfeited if there is a default on payments. On the death of the respondent, unsecured periodical payments will cease but secured payments can be set against the estate and continue until death or re-marriage of the recipient spouse.

3. Lump-Sum Payments

Lump-sum payment orders again require payment of funds to a spouse and/or to or for the benefit of a child of the family. They are 'once and for all' payments which are often made in the context of clean break settlements and may be for substantial amounts.[5] Under Article 25(7) of the 1978 Order (inserted by Article 5 of the 1989 Order), where the court directs that payment of a lump sum be deferred or be paid in instalments, it shall state the period and rate for additional interest charges.

Computation of lump sums is achieved through a *Duxbury* calculation[6] which uses a computer programme to aggregate disposable income (taking into account variables such as life expectancy, tax and inflation) to calculate the amount sufficient to produce an annual income to sustain the recipient for life.

Lump-Sum Payments to or on Behalf of a Child

Under Article 25(4) of the 1978 Order lump sums are not 'once and for all' payments as the power of the court to make an order is exercisable 'from time to time'. In the past the divorce courts have been unenthusiastic about making orders for capital as opposed to income payments. As Booth J has pointed out,[7] lump-sum orders in favour of children, particularly where their parents were of modest means, have been comparatively rare. Lump-sum payments, as an alternative rather than as a supplement

---

5 See, for example, *Gojkovic v Gojkovic* [1990] 2 All ER 84 where the lump sum was £1.3 million.
6 See *Duxbury v Duxbury* [1987] 1 FLR 7.
7 See *Kiely v Kiely* [1988] 1 FLR 248 CA.

to orders for maintenance, did not appeal as the most appropriate means of meeting a child's long-term welfare needs. Such an order cannot be made to take effect when the subject attains the age of majority.

Following the introduction of the child support legislation and the Children (NI) Order 1995, the courts have retained authority to make lump-sum payments for children (see also Chapter Twenty-Two), confirm terms of a written agreement between the parties for periodical payments where the terms are equivalent to those which would have been incorporated in a maintenance order, revoke an existing maintenance order, supplement the authority of the maintenance assessment made under child support legislation, order financial provision for some children over the age of eighteen and order anyone other than a natural parent to provide for a 'child of the family'. However, there can be little doubt that the observation made by MacDermott LJ is likely to hold true for the future:[8]

> In this jurisdiction there have been comparatively few cases in which a judge has been called upon to readjust the financial position of the parties to a marriage which has already been dissolved.

4. Pensions

On July 1, 1996, the Pensions (NI) Order 1995 came into effect. This enables the courts to include pension benefits in its calculations of the parties' total wealth. The following pension benefits are earmarked by Article 166 for inclusion in the court's calculations: death benefit lump sums pre-retirement, lump sums at retirement, death benefits post-retirement and pensions in payment. A system based on cash equivalent value transfers is used to quantify and then allocate pension benefits on divorce. In addition, the pension splitting provision introduced in England and Wales by the Family Law Act 1996 will, when implemented in this jurisdiction, enable the court to divide pension entitlements at the time of divorce.[9]

5. Variation and Discharge

Under Article 33 of the 1978 Order the court has a power to vary or discharge the orders made for ancillary relief on the grounds of a change of circumstances. Usually this is applied to periodical payments. It can also be applied to lump sums where these are being paid in instalments, to maintenance pending suit and to the sale of property. It has no application to normal 'once-off' lump sums nor to property adjustment orders.

Under Article 33(7), when exercising its powers to vary or discharge orders, the court must consider all the circumstances of the case 'including any change in any of the matters to which the court was required to have regard when making the order to which the application relates'. It must, therefore, apply the clean break test and give first consideration to the welfare of any children involved.

---

8 In *M v M* [1983] 7 BNIL 1.
9 See the government's green paper *The Treatment of Pension — Splitting on Divorce* (Cmnd 3345), 1996. Also, see *K v K (Financial Relief: Widow's Pension)* [1997] 1 FLR 35 for an illustration of the unsatisfactory nature of the present law.

Recently, under the equivalent provisions of the Matrimonial Causes Act 1973, Bracewell J in *Benson v Benson (Deceased)*[10] considered a spouse's claim, brought out of time, that the death of the other party six months after the consent order amounted to such a change. She found against the applicant, ruling that the substantial delay which occurred before proceedings were brought compromised his claim.

III. Property Adjustment and Sale

Applications for the redistribution of property in divorce proceedings were formerly brought before the court on proceedings commenced under section 17 of the 1882 Act. This is no longer necessary.

1. Orders in Relation to Adjustment of Property

Under Article 26 of the 1978 Order:

> (1) On granting a decree of divorce, a decree of nullity of marriage or a decree of judicial separation or at any time thereafter (whether, in the case of a decree of divorce or of nullity of marriage, before or after the decree is made absolute), the court may make any one or more of the following orders, that is to say
>> (a) an order that a party to the marriage shall transfer to the other party, to any child of the family or to such person as may be specified in the order for the benefit of such a child such property as may be so specified, being property to which the first-mentioned party is entitled, either in possession or reversion;
>> (b) an order that a settlement of such property as may be so specified, being property to which a party to the marriage is so entitled, be made to the satisfaction of the court for the benefit of the other party to the marriage and of the children of the family or of any of them;
>> (c) an order varying for the benefit of the parties to the marriage and of the children of the family or any of them any ante-nuptial or post-nuptial settlement (including such a settlement made by will or codicil) made on the parties to the marriage;
>> (d) an order extinguishing or reducing the interest of either of the parties to the marriage under any such settlement; subject, however, in the case of an order under sub-paragraph (a) to the restrictions imposed by Article 31(1) and (3) on the making of orders for a transfer of property in favour of children who have attained the age of eighteen.
>
> (2) The court may make an order under paragraph (1)(c) notwithstanding that there are no children of the family.

For the purposes of this provision, 'property' is broadly defined. It includes purchases made before marriage and rights to prospective pensions and inheritances. Since the introduction of Article 27A of the Matrimonial Causes (NI) Order 1978 (as inserted by Article 6 of the Matrimonial and Family Proceedings (NI) Order 1989), the court

---

10   [1996] 1 FLR 692.

in divorce proceedings has had wide powers, in addition to ordering a sale, in respect of property belonging to either or both of the spouses. The court may direct that it be transferred, settled or that a variation be made in the terms of a settlement. Before exercising such powers, however, the court is required to apply the guidelines of Article 27 of the 1978 Order (as amended by the 1989 Order), give first consideration to the child's welfare and consider also the possibility of effecting a clean break under Article 27A.

(a) Transfer of Property

Under Article 26(1)(a) of the 1978 Order the court may direct one spouse to transfer his or her ownership of a specified property to the other and/or to or for the benefit of a child of the family. Usually the property is the matrimonial home and it is transferred to the parent who is to undertake direct care responsibility for the children. It may be transferred wholly and irrevocably or subject to a charge. The transfer might be ordered in exchange for a lump sum or for an agreement to waive or accept reduced periodical payments.

Under the Matrimonial and Family Proceedings (NI) Order 1989, Article 41 and Schedule 1, the court may order the transfer of tenancies. Rule 3.9 of the Family Proceedings Rules (NI) 1996 allows this power to be exercised by the master.

A transfer can be directed so as to achieve a clean break. In *Hanlon v Hanlon*,[11] for example, the Court of Appeal ordered the husband's share in the matrimonial home to be transferred to the wife in return for which she would forgo any entitlement to periodical payments in respect of their two daughters. In *Crozier v Crozier*[12] the applicant was seeking leave to appeal out of time against a consent order made with his wife in ancillary proceedings following their divorce in 1989. The consent order provided that the husband would transfer his half share in the former matrimonial home to his former wife in full and final settlement of all her financial claims against him. The order also provided a nominal financial contribution towards the maintenance of the one child of the family who was then aged five and lived with the wife. The latter was in receipt of income support. The husband had received documents from the Child Support Agency and it was expected that his liability for his son's maintenance would increase to about £29 per week. The applicant sought to vary the consent order to recover his half share in the former matrimonial home. His earnings were £9,390 gross per annum and he now lived with another woman who earned about £4,800 per annum and the two-year-old child of their union. The former wife was living with a man whom she intended to marry. The former matrimonial home had been sold. The applicant was seeking to recover his share of the proceeds of that sale so as to meet his son's maintenance requirements as estimated by the Child Support Agency. The court held that while the parties could obtain a 'clean break' as between themselves, they could not do so in respect of their child.[13] There was a well-established legislative history,

---

11 [1978] 1 WLR 592.
12 [1993] 10 BNIL.
13 See *Preston v Preston* [1982] Fam 17; [1982] 1 All ER 41 CA.

evidenced most recently by the child support legislation, whereby the State could claim a contribution from the liable relative for the State support of a child living with a single parent of limited means. The State was, therefore, never bound by the agreement entered into by the parties and they would be unable to achieve a clean financial break in respect of their son. The legal liability to maintain him remained with them both. As there were no grounds for setting aside the consent order, leave was refused to appeal out of time.

(b) Settlement of Property — Mesher and Martin Orders

Under Article 26(1)(b) of the 1978 Order the court can direct one spouse to settle property for the benefit of the other and/or any child of the family. Under Article 26(4) it may register a charge against the family home rendering it unsellable by either parent until such time as the children have grown up. Sometimes referred to as a *Mesher* order the origins of this type of arrangement lie in the case of *Mesher v Mesher*[14] where both divorcing spouses intended to re-marry, the matrimonial home was in their joint names and there was a dependent child of the marriage. The Court of Appeal ruled that it was more appropriate that the wife and child should retain the family home 'rather than she should have a large sum of available capital' but it would also be inequitable to permanently deprive the husband of a rightful share in the proceeds of an eventual sale. The compromise determined by the court, setting a precedent for very many subsequent cases, was to order that the family home be held on trust for both parents and not be sold until the child reached the age of eighteen. This was also the preferred judicial action in *Allan v Allan*[15] where the court ordered that the marital home was not to be disposed of until the children had completed their education. The main disadvantage of *Mesher* orders is their lack of flexibility. They are property adjustment orders and cannot therefore be subsequently varied.[16]

Martin orders[17] are somewhat similar in that the court seeks to protect the matrimonial home in the short term from the threat of sale. The difference lies in the fact that the court seeks retention of the home for the benefit not of children but for one of the parties. The order made gives one party, usually the wife, a right of occupation until her death, remarriage or cohabitation. It also determines the division of the proceeds of sale after the expiry of that life interest.

(c) Variation of a Trust Settlement

Under Article 26(1)(c) and (d) of the 1987 Order the court can vary a settlement by which property is being held on trust for certain beneficiaries with life interests. This is very seldom directed.[18]

---

14 [1980] 1 All ER 126.
15 [1974] 1 WLR 1171.
16 See (Law Com *Family Law: The Ground for Divorce* no 192) (1990) which recommends new statutory powers to vary such orders in exceptional circumstances.
17 See *Martin v Martin* [1978] Fam 12; [1977] 3 All ER 762.
18 But see *E v E (Financial Provision)* [1990] 2 FLR 233 where the court ordered the transfer of £1.25 million from a settlement to the wife and children.

2. Orders in Relation to Sale of Property

Under Article 26 of the 1978 Order:

> (4) Where the court makes an order under any provision of paragraph (1) it may give such consequential directions as it thinks fit for giving effect to the order (including directions requiring the making of any payments or the disposal of any property).

This provision incorporates the power to order a sale in ancillary relief proceedings. It is now used, in preference to the Partition Acts 1868 and 1876 (see also *Beattie*[19] in Chapter Twenty), when the court considers that only by sale of the property and division of the proceeds will an equitable distribution between the parties be ensured.

Matters to Which the Court Must Have Regard

When exercising its authority under Articles 25 and 26 of the 1978 Order in relation to a child of the family, the court has wide discretionary powers. In exercising these powers it is required by Article 27 to have regard to certain matters.

I. Welfare

Under Article 27 of the Matrimonial Causes Order (NI) 1978, as amended by Article 6 of the Matrimonial and Family Proceedings (NI) Order 1989:

> (1) It shall be the duty of the court in deciding whether to exercise its powers under Article 25 or 26 and, if so, in what manner, to have regard to all the circumstances of the case, first consideration being given to the welfare while a minor of any child of the family who has not attained the age of eighteen.

This definition of 'child' removes from the court's consideration any individual aged eighteen or more and who may be dependent for reasons of involvement in higher or further education, vocational training, disability or illness. The provision clearly does not permit the child's welfare to be the paramount concern of the court. The weighting given to the welfare factor was considered by the Court of Appeal in *Sutter v Sutter and Jones*[20] where the identical provision in the Matrimonial Causes Act 1973 came under scrutiny. The court then held that the judge at first instance had been wrong to order a husband to meet his wife's mortgage repayments on their house of which she was to have ownership so as to best provide for the children. This was to place undue importance on welfare relative to the burden imposed on the husband. It was considered that the wife's cohabitee should bear some of the costs. The principle of the welfare of the child is not the factor of paramount significance in this context.

---

19 *Northern Bank Ltd v Beattie* [1982] NIJB 18.
20 [1987] 2 FLR 232.

II. Other Considerations

Under Article 27(2) of the 1978 Order, as amended by Article 6(3) of the 1989 Order, the court is required to have regard to all the circumstances of the case. The following matters are specifically required to be considered, though there is no legislative guidance as to the weighting each is to be accorded.

1. Parties' Present and Future Resources

Under Article 27(2) the court is required to have regard to

> (a) the income, earning capacity, property and other financial resources which each of the parties to the marriage has or is likely to have in the foreseeable future, including in the case of earning capacity any increase in that capacity which it would in the opinion of the court be reasonable to expect a party to the marriage to take steps to acquire.

All actual or potential finances or property of both parties must be taken into account. The courts have adopted a very broad interpretation of 'financial resources' encompassing possible inheritance rights,[21] damages for personal injury[22] and assets outside the jurisdiction[23] and the income of a new spouse or cohabitee.[24]

In the UK, however, unlike the US, the courts have been guided by the principle that intervention in private family finances should be restricted to satisfying a public interest in ensuring that the requirements of a spouse are, in all the circumstances of the case, reasonably met. This principle comes into play where the parties have very considerable assets and provides the basis for what has become known as 'the millionaire's defence'.[25] In such circumstances, when exercising their discretion under Article 27, the judiciary will stop well short of a comprehensive re-organisation of family finances. Instead the judicial test to be applied is — What, having regard to all Article 27 criteria, does the spouse reasonably require?[26]

2. Parties' Future Needs

Under Article 27(2) the court is required to have regard to

> (b) the financial needs, obligations and responsibilities which each of the parties to the marriage has or is likely to have in the foreseeable future.

---

21 See, for example, *Michael v Michael* [1986] 2 FLR 389.
22 See, for example, *Wagstaff v Wagstaff* [1992] 1 FLR 333.
23 See, for example, *Browne v Browne* [1989] 1 FLR 291. See also *H v H (Financial Provision: Conduct)* [1994] 2 FLR 801.
24 See, for example, *Macey v Macey* (1981) 3 FLR 7.
25 See further *Van G v Van G (Financial Provision: Millionaire's Defence)* [1995] 1 FLR 328.
26 A test most recently and graphically demonstrated by the Court of Appeal in *Dart v Dart* [1996] 2 FLR 286 which concluded with an order requiring the husband to pay his wife £9 million plus costs from assets estimated at approx. £400 million.

All actual or potential needs of both parties must also be taken into account. Where one party has care responsibility for children, even if these are not children of the marriage[27] this will be a particularly important factor. Where the other party requires accommodation for his or her visiting children, then this too may be taken into account.[28] Where a party has formed a second family, the court must make proper allowances for the new obligations thereby acquired.[29] This provision requires future funding to be estimated relative to needs rather than to available assets.[30]

3. Parties' Accustomed Standard of Living

Under Article 27(2) the court is required to have regard to

> (c) the standard of living enjoyed by the family before the breakdown of the marriage.

Again, this provision has been interpreted so as to require the court to look to future needs rather than available resources. Where resources permit, it will seek to place a party in a financial position sufficient to maintain his or her marital lifestyle but will resist any additional broad claim to a proportion of the other party's assets. The court has indicated that 'need' might not be the determining criteria in circumstances where the parties had enjoyed a good lifestyle, the divorce was recent and the ex-husband had since acquired more assets.[31] This approach was consolidated in *F v F (Duxbury Calculation: Rate of Return)*[32] where the parties had been married for twenty-three years, the plaintiff had always been a housewife, the husband was a successful businessman and they had no dependent children. The court considered it more appropriate to address reasonable need than to attempt an equal distribution of available assets. After methodically applying the statutory criteria (equivalent to Article 27(2)), the court awarded the wife one-third of her husband's total assets of £3,400,000.

Where resources do not permit the retention of a marital standard of living, the court will merely seek to place the parties in comparable financial positions.

4. Parties' Ages

Under Article 27(2) the court is required to have regard to

> (d) the age of each party to the marriage and the duration of the marriage.

The courts differentiate between the prospective financial needs of young and older couples. The younger the party and the briefer the marriage, the greater will be the court's expectation that he or she can attain financial independence and should be encouraged to do so.[33]

---

27 See, for example, *Fisher v Fisher* [1989] 1 FLR 423.
28 See, for example, *Calderbank v Calderbank* [1975] 3 All ER 333.
29 See, for example, *Stockford v Stockford* (1982) 3 FLR 58.
30 See, for example, *Leadbetter v Leadbetter* [1985] FLR 789.
31 See *Cornick v Cornick* [1995] 2 FLR.
32 [1996] 1 FLR 833.
33 See, for example, *Attar v Attar* (No 2) [1985] FLR 653.

5. Parties' Disabilities

Under Article 27(2) the court is required to have regard to

> (e) any physical or mental disability of either of the parties to the marriage.

Clearly, the fact that one party suffers from a serious physical or mental disability and the other does not is a matter which affects his or her relative capacity to achieve future financial independence. The court will take this into account.[34] However, the fact that a party is disabled could work to his or her disadvantage when the court comes to determine appropriate financial provision. Where, for example, it was pleaded that the wife had a life-threatening illness, the court interpreted this as justification for viewing her needs as being correspondingly reduced.[35]

6. Parties' Past and Future Contributions

Under Article 27(2) the court is required to have regard to

> (f) the contributions which each of the parties has made or is likely in the foreseeable future to make to the welfare of the family, including any contribution by looking after the home or caring for the family.

This provision gives statutory effect to the equitable rule that a party without legal title to the family home may acquire a beneficial interest in it by virtue of his or her indirect contributions. The fact that it applies solely in the context of a marital relationship demonstrates an important difference between spouses and cohabitees on family breakdown. Where spouses are concerned, in the words of Denning LJ:[36]

> If the court considers that the home has been acquired and maintained by the joint efforts of both, then, when the marriage breaks down, it should be regarded as the joint property of both of them, no matter in whose name it stands.

This provision has the potential to lift a party's entitlement beyond the resources/needs calculation and establish a claim to a proportion of available assets.[37]

7. Parties' Conduct

Under Article 27(2) the court is required to have regard to

> (g) the conduct of each of the parties, if that conduct is such that it would in the opinion of the court be inequitable to disregard it;

This provision is in keeping with the broad legislative intent to minimise the significance of fault in the modern law of divorce. An intent which has been mirrored in the

---

34 See, for example, *B v B* (1982) 3 FLR 299 where the fact that the wife suffered from multiple sclerosis was reflected in a higher award.
35 See *M v M (Property Adjustment: Impaired Life Expectancy)* [1993] 2 FLR 723.
36 See *Watchel v Watchel* [1973] 1 All ER 829.
37 See, for example, *O'Donnell v O'Donnell* [1975] 2 All ER 993.

judicial effort to bury the so-called principle of the 'unimpeachable parent'. Its effect is to rule out of the equation any suggestion of fault based on the conduct of a party, when consideration is being given to adjusting the parties' property and finances, unless that conduct is exceptional. The courts have taken the view that conduct will be relevant when it is 'exceptional and gross'[38] as when it involves wounding a spouse,[39] squandering the family's assets[40] or adultery with relatives by marriage.[41]

8. Parties' Loss of Future Benefits

Under Article 27(2) in the case of proceedings for divorce or nullity of marriage, the court is required to have regard to

> (h) ... the value to each of the parties to the marriage of any benefit (for example, a pension) which by reason of the dissolution or annulment of the marriage, that party will lose the chance of acquiring.

This provision entitled the court to take into consideration the effect that divorce would have on a spouse's entitlement to future benefits such as would derive from pensions, insurance policies and inheritance. A petitioner or respondent required to make full disclosure of all property and income is also required under Rule 2.73 of the Family Proceedings Rules (NI) 1996 to give similar particulars in relation to any pension scheme to which he or she may belong. A lump-sum award could then be made to compensate a disadvantaged party.

However, the rule that any entitlement to a future benefit would terminate on divorce has been amended by the Pensions (NI) Order 1995. This applies to petitions lodged after July 1, 1996 and provides for the 'earmarking' of pensions for the benefit of an ex-spouse.

III. Further Considerations in respect of a Child

Under Article 27(3) the court is further required, in relation to a child of the family, to have particular regard to the following:

(a) the financial needs of the child;
(b) the income, earning capacity (if any), property and other financial resources of the child;
(c) any physical or mental disability of the child;
(d) the manner in which he was being and in which the parties to the marriage expected him to be educated or trained; and
(e) some considerations mentioned earlier in relation to the parties to the marriage (income, financial needs, standard of living and the physical or mental disability of either of the parties).

---

38 See Denning LJ in f/n 36.
39 As in *Jones v Jones* [1975] 2 All ER 12. Also see, *A v A (Financial Provision: Conduct)* [1995] 1 FLR 345 where again the conduct was physical violence.
40 As in *Martin v Martin* [1976] 3 All ER 625.
41 As in *Bailey v Tolliday* [1983] 4 FLR 542 and *Dixon v Dixon* (1974) Fam Law 58.

The general approach of the courts to this provision has been expressed by Scarman LJ[42] as one of pursuing a 'public interest that spouses, to the extent that their means permit, should provide for themselves and their children'. The courts have relied on this provision to direct a party to make an increased payment where a child had a disability,[43] was in boarding school[44] and is dependent but is not related.[45]

IV. Consideration of Transactions Made with a View to Avoid Liability

Under Article 39 of the 1978 Order the court can set aside dispositions made by a party with the intention to avoid a claim for financial relief. This will apply to any such disposition of funds or property made within three years of the application for relief.

The 'Clean Break'

The legislative intent behind the clean break principle is that on marriage breakdown the spouses should be encouraged to make arrangements regarding their property and finances which enable them to finalise entitlements, put the past behind them and avoid further litigation. It gives statutory effect to the recommendation of the Law Commission that the courts should take into account the capacity of both spouses to earn a living and become financially independent.[46] It was formulated to address, in particular, the circumstances of childless couples who were either divorcing after short marriages during which both parties were employed or after long marriages during which considerable assets had been accumulated.

The clean break principle applies only to the legal relationship between the spouses. The principle of parental responsibility ensures the continuation of the legal relationship between parent and child.

I. The Duty

The Matrimonial Causes (NI) Order 1978, as amended by Article 6 of the Matrimonial and Family Proceedings (NI) Order 1989, imposes a duty on the court to consider, when making an order for the sale of property or for the adjustment of an entitlement to finance or property, whether instead a clean break would be more appropriate. The relevant provision is Article 27A of the 1978 Order (inserted by the 1989 Order) and, as it exactly duplicates section 25A of the Matrimonial Causes Act 1973, the related case law developed in the courts of England and Wales is equally applicable to this jurisdiction.

The test to be satisfied is whether it be more 'just and reasonable' for the court to terminate all financial obligations? Article 27A sets out three different situations in which this duty is to be applied.

---

42   See *Minton v Minton* [1979] AC 593; [1979] 1 All ER 79.
43   As in *Smith v Smith* [1991] 2 All ER 306.
44   As in *O'Donnell v O'Donnell* [1975] 2 All ER 993.
45   As in *Day v Day* [1988] 1 FLR 278.
46   See *The Financial Consequences of Divorce* (Law Com no. 112) (1982).

II. At or Shortly after Grant of Decree

Under Article 27:

> A. — (1) Where on or after the grant of a decree of divorce or nullity of marriage the court decides to exercise its powers under Article 25(1)(a), (b) or (c) or 26 in favour of a party to the marriage, it shall be the duty of the court to consider whether it would be appropriate so to exercise those powers that the financial obligations of each party towards the other will be terminated as soon after the grant of the decree as the court considers just and reasonable.

This imposes a duty on the court to consider making a clean break settlement 'soon after the grant of the decree' rather than orders for the adjustment of property and long-term maintenance. The court may achieve a clean break by an order for transfer of property in lieu of periodical payments.[47]

Clean break orders are most often appropriate where both parties are young and employed or with strong employment prospects,[48] the marriage has been brief,[49] they are wealthy[50] or where they are poor and the finances involved are largely from public funds[51] and where there are no dependent children involved.

A clean break order, made on the basis of a fraudulent misrepresentation of one party's financial circumstances, may be subsequently set aside by the court on application of the other party, even if many years have elapsed since the making of that order.[52]

Delayed Applications for Ancillary Relief

There is no time limit for making such applications. Once a petition for ancillary relief has been lodged in court, which is usually automatically incorporated in the divorce petition, the actual application can follow at any time thereafter. The fact that a delayed application for a lump-sum payment has the capacity to overturn the clean break philosophy and revive proceedings presumed by court and respondent to be finalised was considered in the case of *Twiname v Twiname*[53] where the time lapse between grant of decree absolute and application for ancillary relief was fifteen years. The Court of Appeal held that the words 'or at any time thereafter' in section 23(1) of the Matrimonial Causes Act 1973 (Article 25(1) of the 1978 Order) allowed a party who had not yet claimed ancillary relief the opportunity to re-think a settled clean break approach.

---

47 As in *Hanlon v Hanlon,* f/n 11.
48 As in f/n 33.
49 Ibid, where it lasted six months.
50 As in *Gojkovic v Gojkovic* [1991] 3 WLR 621.
51 As in *Ashley v Blackman* [1988] 2 FLR 278.
52 See *T v T (Consent Order: Procedure to Set Aside)* [1996] 2 FLR 640 where the court ruled that the misrepresentation was such that it had prevented the proper exercise of the court's powers 6-and-a-half years earlier when the clean break order was made. A re-hearing was ordered.
53 [1992] 1 FLR 29.

III. Fixed-Term Periodical Payments

Under Article 27:

> A.—(2) Where the court decides in such a case to make a periodical payments or secured periodical payments order in favour of a party to the marriage, the court shall in particular consider whether it would be appropriate to require those payments to be made or secured only for such term as would in the opinion of the court be sufficient to enable the party in whose favour the order is made to adjust without undue hardship to the termination of his or her financial dependence on the other party.

The court can make a deferred clean break by granting a short-term order and fixing a date at which periodical payments must cease. Factors indicating the appropriateness of such an order are: children likely to be soon independent,[54] probability of shortly attaining financial independence[55] or an acrimonious relationship.[56] The court is less likely to make such an order where the parties are older[57] or young children are involved.[58] The duty on the court is merely to consider whether a clean break is appropriate; it is not obliged to impose such an order.[59]

IV. Dismissal of Applications for Periodical Payments

Under Article 27:

> A.—(3) Where on or after grant of a decree of divorce or nullity of marriage an application is made by a party to the marriage for a periodical payments or secured periodical payments order in his or her favour, then, if the court considers that no continuing obligation should be imposed on either party to make or secure periodical payments in favour of the other, the court may dismiss the application with a direction that the applicant shall not be entitled to make any further application in relation to that marriage for an order under Article 25(1)(a) or (b).

The court can impose a clean break by dismissing an application for periodical payments, by refusing to renew an order made for a fixed term or in any proceedings

---

54 As in *CB v CB* [1988] Fam Law 471 where they were aged eighteen and thirteen.
55 As in *Hedges v Hedges* [1991] 1 FLR 196 where, after four and a half years of marriage, there were no children, both parties were employed and the wife was aged thirty-seven.
56 As in *Evans v Evans* [1990] 2 All ER 147 where a short-term order was held to be sufficient, until the children went to boarding school and the wife resumed secretarial employment, after which the order would cease so as to avoid further mutual acrimony.
57 As in *Morris v Morris* [1985] FLR 1176 where it was held that the fifty-six-year-old wife would suffer undue hardship if payments were to cease.
58 As in *Sutter v Sutter and Jones* [1987] 2 All ER 336 where the children were aged fourteen and eight.
59 See *Barratt v Barratt* [1988] 2 FLR 516 CA where, although the parties had lived apart for eight years and the youngest child was aged sixteen, the Court of Appeal held that the judge at first instance had been wrong to consider that this provision required him to impose a clean break deferred for four years; factors such as the wife's lack of employment experience and pension rights indicated that she would suffer undue hardship if such an order was made.

brought to vary an order. This can be reinforced by adding a direction denying leave to make any further application.

V. *Inappropriate*

A clean break order is not always appropriate. This is most likely to be the case where the court needs to ensure on-going financial security for young children. Other factors have also influenced the court against making such orders.

1. Inappropriate due to Dependent Children

The court has refused to make a clean break order where a young wife, divorced after six weeks, with no previous employment experience had responsibility for the upbringing of her two teenage daughters from a previous relationship.[60]

2. Inappropriate due to Presence of Cohabitee

The principle is now well established that in circumstances where a wife or ex-wife cohabits in the matrimonial home, the cohabitant has a responsibility to make a financial contribution, which in turn must reduce the level of periodical payments that a husband should be expected to make. It also, however, introduces sufficient uncertainty into the situation to prevent the court from making a clean break order.

The governing precedent is the case of *Sutter*[61] where the ex-husband, who had since re-married, appealed against a maintenance order in favour of his wife who lived with their two children (aged fourteen and eight) and a cohabitee in the former matrimonial home. He claimed that the judge at first instance should not have regarded the welfare of the children as the overriding consideration, should have taken into account the wife's conduct in cohabiting and should have imposed a clean break. The appeal was allowed on the restricted ground that the court was required to take into account all the circumstances of the case which included the presence of the cohabitee and his obligation to contribute towards household expenses. Accordingly, the maintenance order was reduced to a nominal sum. A clean break, however, was not imposed because it was not possible to predict at what stage during the children's dependency the wife, who had no employment record and no intention of marrying her cohabitee, would achieve financial independence. Keeping the proceedings open, by making only a nominal maintenance award (a 'backstop' order), allows the possibility of a future review at the initiative of either party.

That decision was followed in, for example, *Atkinson v Atkinson*[62] where there were no children involved but the facts were otherwise substantially the same. Again, intriguingly, in *Atkinson v Atkinson*,[63] where the cohabitee was a prosperous businessman, the court held that weight must be given to his capacity to make a reasonable contri-

---

60 See *Day v Day*, f/n 45.
61 See f/n 58.
62 [1987] 3 All ER 849.
63 [1995] 2 FLR 356.

bution in return for the benefits of a home and therefore it was appropriate to reduce the amount of periodical payments. As the ex-husband was not prepared to make a lump-sum payment, the court ruled that it should not impose a clean break.

3. Inappropriate due to Need to Protect Public Funds

The decision in *Barnes v Barnes*[64] is authority for the broad rule that the court will refrain from action which achieves no more than the displacing of a spouse's maintenance obligations onto the State. In that case the divorced husband, who had re-married, sought to avoid paying any maintenance to his ex-wife, while accepting his obligation to do so in respect of their children. The court at first instance duly made an order requiring him to pay 5p per annum to his first wife. On appeal the court increased the payments to £2.00 per week, despite the fact that the recipient would be no better off as her state benefits would be deducted by that amount. The court took the view that in the interests of justice the husband should be required to meet his maintenance obligations rather than be allowed to stand aside and permit this to fall wholly on the State.

The Practice in Northern Ireland

1. Clean Break Upheld by the Court

In this jurisdiction the court had an opportunity to consider the clean break principle in *J McC v A McC*.[65] The facts may be briefly stated. The twenty-three-year-old marriage was dissolved in 1981; the only 'child' of the marriage was then aged twenty-three and living apart from her parents. The wife was aged forty-five and earning £654 per month. Since 1962 she had suffered from rheumatoid arthritis and wished to continue living in what had been their home as it was on a level site and had been made suitable for her needs. The husband was aged forty-eight and earned £840 per month. Each was self-supporting and no sum was being paid by the husband to the wife as maintenance or under an order for periodical payments. Both parties were very attached to their former matrimonial home which was jointly owned and valued at £47,500, subject to a mortgage of £3,000. Both parties sought a property adjustment order in respect of the home.

The master ordered that the husband should transfer his interest in the home to the wife; the latter was to be responsible for mortgage repayments and was to pay the husband the sum of £10,000 within three months of the transfer. The husband lodged an appeal on the grounds that the master had failed to take into account his equitable entitlement resulting from the work he had done to the home: he had helped to draw up the initial plans for the dwelling, ordered the materials and assisted in its construction.

On appeal, before MacDermott J, the court held as follows[66]:

> (1) Article 27 of the Matrimonial Causes (NI) Order 1978 requires the court to resolve disputes over property by applying the criteria set out in the Article rather

---

64 [1972] 3 All ER 872.
65 [1982] 14 NIJB.
66 Ibid.

than starting from some pre-conceived arithmetical baseline. The parties interests in the property were also to be taken into account because the end result to be achieved was to place the parties in the financial position they would each have been had the marriage not broken down, so far as that was practical.

(2) The judicial aim must be to meet the justice of the particular case. The criteria set out in Article 27 must be followed and decisions reached in other cases must be viewed with caution as every case depends upon its own particular and peculiar facts.

(3) The single most relevant factor in this case is the wife's ill health which makes relevant item (e) in Article 27(1) and the wife should be allowed to remain in the matrimonial home.

(4) This was a case for the application of the so-called 'clean break' principle. Having regard to the factors set out in Article 27 the proper compensating figure for the husband was less than 50 per cent of the value of the home.

(5) The husband was to transfer his interest in the home to the wife; the wife was to be responsible for the mortgage repayments and was to pay the husband £15,000 within three months of the transfer.

2. Clean Break Over-Ruled by the Court

M v M[67] was a case resulting from an application under Article 27(1) of the Matrimonial Causes (NI) Order 1978, heard before Hutton J (as he was then), concerning a couple who had married in 1968 and by the time of the proceedings had three children aged eighteen, sixteen and thirteen. Throughout the marriage the husband had been employed as a policeman while the wife had never been in employment. The matrimonial home was bought in 1972, valued at £20,000 and was subject to a £5,000 mortgage.

In 1975 the husband left the matrimonial home to live in a rented flat with a Miss R, whom he planned to marry. He continued to pay the mortgage instalments, rates, full costs and a housekeeping allowance of £140 per month to his wife. These expenses amounted to £335 per month.

In 1981 the husband contacted solicitors with a view to commencing divorce proceedings. An agreement was negotiated with the wife's solicitors to the effect that she would accept a transfer to her of the matrimonial home (the husband undertaking to discharge the mortgage) in full settlement of her claims and those of her children.

In 1982 divorce proceedings were commenced by the husband on the basis of five years' separation. Shortly afterwards he and Miss R contracted to buy a house costing £19,750, the monthly mortgage repayments being £214. The wife then applied for a property adjustment order and for financial provision, despite their 1981 agreement.

The husband's net monthly earnings in 1981/2 were £925 and had increased subsequently. Those of Miss R were £400 approximately. The wife had a part-time job and earned £120 per month. Her only other income was child allowance and her monthly outgoings were £328. By an order made in 1983, the master directed the husband to transfer his interest in the matrimonial home to the wife (the husband to

---

[67] [1983] 7 BNIL 1.

be responsible for the discharge of the £5,000 mortgage) and to pay £230 less tax to the wife until the decree absolute. Thereafter, periodical payments at the same monthly rate were to be made (one-third of their joint incomes) and £52 per month to the youngest child. The husband appealed.

Held, dismissing the appeal and varying the order:[68]

1. Agreement by the wife to accept the house in full settlement of her claims did not prevent her seeking orders for financial provision and property adjustment. The agreement was not a reasonable one, particularly as it made no provision for the youngest child, therefore it would not be just for the wife to be bound by it, even though it had been made with legal advice (*Edgar v Edgar*[69] distinguished on the facts).
2. Although the husband had contracted to buy another house after the agreement had been reached, the court was not satisfied that he had altered his position solely in reliance on the agreement. It was probable that he would have bought a house following his divorce even if he had thought that his wife would obtain a maintenance award.
3. Having regard to the duration of the marriage, the age of the wife, the dependency of the youngest child and the financial needs and obligations of the parties the wife should receive a monthly sum of £230 (approximately £160 net) which represented 1/3rd of the joint incomes. The husband should have a deferred charge of 1/3rd of the proceeds of sale of the house when the wife remarries, or ceases to permanently reside in the house or dies, whichever event happens first.

---

[68] Ibid.
[69] [1980] 3 All ER 887.

CHAPTER TWENTY-FIVE

Testate Succession

Introduction

This chapter considers the law relating to the making of wills, the role and powers of a testator and testacy in general. Particular attention is given to judicial determination of testacy disputes.

There is now little difference between such law as it applies in this jurisdiction and in England and Wales, though it remains very different from that pertaining in Scotland.

Wills

The last will and testament is the means whereby an adult makes gifts of property and finance, taking effect on death, to whomsoever that adult may choose. This is dependent upon the Probate Office being satisfied that the will has been validly executed.

I. Statute Law

The law relating to the construction of a valid will is now governed by the Wills and Administration Proceedings (NI) Order 1994 which came into effect on January 1, 1995 (except for Articles 32–35). This, in the main, repeals and replaces the Wills Act 1837 and consolidates provisions previously found in such legislation as the Wills (Amendment) Act 1852, the Wills (Amendment) Act 1954 and the Administration of Estates Act (NI) 1955. The 1994 Order has relaxed the legal formalities relating to the construction and valid execution of wills and in doing so effectively brings the law in Northern Ireland into line with that in England and Wales since the introduction there of the Administration of Justice Act 1982.

1. The 1994 Order

(a) Prospective Application

The 1837 Act will continue to govern the law relating to testacy in many cases where death has occurred prior to the commencement date of the 1994 Order. The latter, broadly speaking, only applies to cases where the testator's death occurs after that date, i.e. it is generally not retrospective.

(b) Matters Exempted

The 1837 Act has not been totally repealed. The Northern Ireland Act 1974[1] precludes the repeal of those provisions of the 1837 Act (as extended by the Wills (Soldiers and

---

1 Under which matters relating to the 'armed forces' are 'exceptional matters' and as such are exempted from being dealt with by Orders in Council.

Sailors) Act 1918) dealing with the making of wills by serving members of the army, navy and airforce. Thus, section 11 of the 1837 Act continues in effect, permitting servicemen to make 'privileged' wills, i.e. wills which are exempted from normal legal formalities. This, for example, allows a serviceman who is a minor to be a testator, a will to be oral and a written will to be exempt from the requirements regarding signature and witnessing.[2] In this jurisdiction, the case of *Re Hamilton*[3] demonstrates that though a serviceman may make a verbal will, be unaware that he is doing so and be exempt from the usual formalities, it must nevertheless be clear that he acted with testamentary intent in that he intended to make a disposition to take effect on his death.

(c) Other Changes

If issue of a child of the testator who has predeceased the testator can save a gift from lapsing, then he or she will automatically take the saved gift (Article 22). In contrast, under section 33 of the 1837 Act the saved gift goes with the estate of the dead child — which obviously might not be to the issue who saved it.

The rules as to what contingency gifts carry the intermediate income (thus enabling the statutory power of maintenance under section 32 of the Trustee Act (NI) 1958) will change to come into line with section 175 of the Law of Property Act 1925. The present position will change for gifts of residuary realty, specific realty and specific personalty, which will all carry intermediate income.

II. The Contents

A testator is entitled to make arrangements for the disposal of all property owned at the time of his or her death. The disposal of immovable property owned overseas is subject to the law of the country in which the property is owned. The testator, by executing a will, makes a devise of land and a legacy or bequest of personal property to named beneficiaries.

1. Matters Exempted from Disposal by Will

(a) Pensions

As a rule pensions cannot be the subject of a will.

(b) The Corpse

Under common law a corpse belongs to no one.[4] However, in normal circumstances, the executors named in a will (administrators or other persons in cases of intestacy) have a right and duty to custody and possession of a testator's body until, and solely for the purpose of, burial. In abnormal circumstances the coroner has the right, under section 11 of the Coroners Act (NI) 1959, to immediate possession of the body where death results from violence, misadventure or unfair means; negligence, misconduct or

---

2 See *Re Coventry* [1979] 2 WLR 853, [1979] 3 All ER 815; *Re Jones* [1981] 1 All ER 1.
3 [1982] NI 197.
4 See, for example, *Williams v Williams* [1880] 20 Ch D 659.

malpractice on the part of others; any cause other than an illness or disease requiring attention and treatment from a medical practitioner in the twenty-eight-day period preceding death; or in otherwise suspicious circumstances. Once the post-mortem is completed the coroner has a duty to release the body to the executors or appropriate others.

A testator may, under the Human Tissue Act (NI) 1962, make arrangements to donate organs or other parts of his or her body for the purposes of medical research or for the benefit of others. Any such arrangement may be made in a will or in a properly attested written or verbal declaration. Because a testator has no legal rights in his or her corpse, such donations are unenforceable. Moreover, the next-of-kin has no right to the body, or to any part of it, other than for the limited purpose of burial. This was emphasised in the recent case of *Dobson v North Tyneside Health Authority*[5] where the Court of Appeal ruled that the next-of-kin had no right of possession in the deceased's brain after it had been removed for the purposes of an autopsy.

III. The Formalities

The legal requirements of a will made prior to January 1, 1995 are governed by section 9 of the 1837 Act; after that date Article 5 of the 1994 Order provides the relevant statutory authority. Neither statute makes any prescriptive requirements regarding the format of a will.

1. In Writing

A verbal declaration or audio-visual recording is insufficient. A will must be in writing. Any alteration to an extant will (substitution, addition, or subtraction) must be freshly attested.

2. Intentions Clearly Stated

The intentions of the testator should be evident on the face of the will. Beneficiaries should be clearly identified and the nature and quantity of related bequests specified. In this jurisdiction the case of *Hull v Mullan and Others*[6] illustrates the importance of minimising ambiguity. In his will the testator had stated:

> In the event of my eldest [sic] son Roger dying without issue ... then in such case ... I direct that my Trustees shall hold all my said property upon trust for my said son William Joseph and his issue.

However, under the Wills Act 1837, section 29:

> 'Die without issue' shall be construed to mean want or failure of issue in the lifetime or at the time of death.

Roger had three sons and one grandchild. The question that arose for the court to consider was in what circumstances would Roger and his issue inherit the deceased's

---

5 [1997] 1 FLR 598.
6 [1985] NIJB 4.

estate? Did the testator envisage a possibility that Roger might have issue but that he, she or they would predecease him (in which case, William and his issue would only inherit if, when Roger died, all four of his descendants were already dead)? Alternatively, did he envisage a possibility that Roger might never have any issue (William and his issue then inheriting on Roger's death). The court held that there was nothing in the will to suggest that in order for Roger to inherit he must have issue which would survive him. Thus there were no circumstances in which William and his issue would inherit.[7]

3. Signed

The testator must make or acknowledge his or her signature; the signature may be made by way of a mark. Under Article 5(b) of the 1994 Order the signature may be placed anywhere on a will made after the date of commencement provided that 'it appears from the will or is shown that the testator intended by his signature to give effect to the will'. Under section 1 of the Wills (Amendment) Act 1852 the requirement in respect of wills made earlier is that the signature be 'at or after, or following, or under or beside or opposite to the end of the will'. In the latter case, any disposition appearing after the signature will be void.

Both the 1837 and 1994 statutes make provision for a testator who is unable to write or make a mark, most usually as a result of serious illness. A valid signature may be made by a person acting under the direction and in the presence of a testator. There must be evidence that the person so acting was wholly controlled by the intention of the testator. In this jurisdiction the case of *Fulton v Kee*[8] provides authority for the view that this will be negated by evidence of a testator's passivity at the time of the agent's actions.

The test of a valid signature is evidence that it was intended to serve that function. The use, therefore, of a thumbprint or cross, initials, inconsistency in reference to forenames, an abbreviated surname or the incorporation of a nickname will not in itself constitute an invalid signature.

4. Witnessed

A will must be witnessed by at least two persons. Both witnesses must be present when the testator makes, or acknowledges, his or her signature. Each witness must attest the will and authenticate the signature of the testator though this need not be done in the presence of the other. As the function of the witnesses is merely to attest the signature of the testator, it is unnecessary that they first read or have any knowledge of the contents of the will. There is no statutorily prescribed form of words to be used by a witness when attesting a will.

It is not possible to be a witness and a beneficiary of a will. Under both section 15 of the 1837 Act and Article 8 of the 1994 Order any gift made to a witness or to the spouse of a witness is treated as void and lapses into the residual estate, or if the gift is residuary, then a partial intestacy arises. However, under Article 8(3), a gift made

---

7   See also *Ulster Bank v McCullough and Others* [1985] 11 NIJB 1 where the court was faced with an issue of construction.
8   [1961] NI 1.

in such circumstances will be valid if the attestation in question is unnecessary to the proper execution of the will. This provision removes the possibility of such gifts failing even though such an attestation was superfluous.[9] It is possible for a witness to be a minor but he or she must be *Gillick* competent (see further Part One).

A witness, unlike a testator, cannot direct another person to act on his or her behalf. In this jurisdiction the case of *Re Bullock*[10] demonstrates that where a witness purports to so act (by stamping the latter's signature onto the will), then the will has been invalidly executed.

Unlike the situation under the 1837 Act, a witness now has the option, under Article 5(d)(ii) of the 1994 Order, of either signing a will after the signature of the testator or of acknowledging a signature made earlier. This change overturns the harsh decision made in *Re Colling*,[11] where one witness had been briefly absent during the period when the enfeebled testator completed his signature,[12] and its effect was recently demonstrated in the not dissimilar case of *Couser v Couser*.[13]

In this jurisdiction, the judgment of Carswell J in *Grieve v Grieve*[14] offers a graphic reminder of the importance of attestation. As he then said:

> The purported will was the most remarkable document which I have seen propounded as a testamentary instrument in all my experience. It was written on an ordinary cheque form from the deceased's Northern Bank cheque book. It bore what was apparently the signature of the deceased on the part of the document where a cheque would normally be signed . . . the signatures of (the two witnesses) appeared immediately below that of the deceased. The date inserted at the top was 9.8.1984, then the words were written above in two segments. 'The will of James Grieve, Claudy, Londonderry' was written on the right hand portion, and on the left hand portion were the words 'I bequeath all my worldly goods to my nephew, (Michael B Grieve, Executors to be John Brown, Patrick Grieve', and then the words appear 'Witnessed by', followed by the signatures of (the two witnesses).

The two 'witnesses' stated in their evidence that, after delivering hay to the testator's farm they had been requested by him to append their signatures to the said document which, as he informed them, was his 'testament'. This they did without first reading the document to which the testator then added his signature. Carswell J had heard enough to rule the will invalid.

5. Dated

It is not a formal requirement that a will be dated, but because of the possibility of successive wills, this should be done.

---

9 As was the case in *Re Bravda* [1968] 2 All ER 217 where two of four witnesses were beneficiaries.
10 [1968] NI 96.
11 [1972] 3 All ER 729.
12 See, for example, *Moore v King* (1842) per Sir Herbert Jenner Fust at p 253 and the decision of the House of Lords in *Hindmarsh v Charleton* (1861) 8 HLC 160.
13 [1996] 2 FLR 46.
14 [1993] 6 NIJB 34.

IV. Alterations

Article 11 of the 1994 Order, replicating the provisions of the 1837 Act, provides the relevant statutory authority and continues the precedent value of previous case law in relation to the legal alteration of wills. It remains the case that any such alteration must itself be executed in compliance with the formalities required for the making of a valid will. There is a requirement, therefore, that the signature of the testator as attested by the witnesses, should appear in respect of each alteration. Where a will bears incorrectly executed alterations it will be read devoid of any reference to them.

Alternatively, the terms of a will may be altered by appending a codicil. Again this must be executed in accordance with the usual formalities.

As a 'will speaks from death' a testator is free to make such alterations to it and to dispose of property (subject to Article 12 of the 1979 Order) as he or she wishes right up to the moment of death.

V. Revocations

Under Article 14 of the 1994 Order a will may be revoked by the testator during his or her lifetime. The different ways in which this may be achieved have attracted the attention of the Law Commission.[15]

1. By Destruction

Article 14(1)(d) repeats the provision under the 1837 Act permitting a will to be destroyed by 'burning, tearing or otherwise destroying'. For a will to be revoked in this way the act must be executed either by the testator or by someone acting in the presence of and under the direction of the testator. The act must be accompanied by an intention to revoke. The act will not constitute a revocation if the testator is not physically present,[16] if it does not conform to the statutory definition of destruction or if it is destroyed by mistake. A lost will is not a revoked will.

2. By Making a New Will

A new will revokes one made earlier only if it carries a declaration to that effect. Revocation is most commonly achieved in this way. Where a deceased has left two or more wills, none containing a clause or specific codicil revoking earlier versions, then any inconsistencies will be construed in favour of the one made last. Where a new but invalid will is made, followed by the destruction of an earlier version, then evidence may be admitted to show that the act of destruction did not constitute a revocation as the intention to revoke was dependant upon a belief in the validity of the new will. In such circumstances the doctrine of dependant relative revocation permits revival of the earlier will, by admitting a copy to probate or admitting evidence as to its contents.

---

15 See *The Making and Revocation of Wills* Cmnd 7902 (HMSO) (1980).
16 See *Re Gilliland* [1937] NI 156.

3. By Marriage

Under Article 12(1)(3) of the 1994 Order a will is automatically revoked by the marriage of a testator. Whereas under the 1837 Act a will was wholly revoked unless it could be shown to have been made in contemplation of that marriage, under the 1994 Order it will only be partially revoked to the extent that in such circumstances the specific marriage-related gifts will stand.

The Testator

The broad rule that gifts are made at the total discretion of the testator is subject to statutory conditions affecting the capacity of the testator and the priority rights of certain claimants.

I. The Legal Requirements

A testator is a person who makes a will. There are certain legal requirements to be satisfied before a person can be held to have had the capacity to act as a testator.

1. An Adult

A child cannot normally make a will. The testator must be aged eighteen or over, except in the circumstances governed by section 11 of the 1837 Act. However, under Article 4 of the 1994 Order the law now permits married minors (or minors who have been married) to make a valid will.

2. Being 'of Sound Mind'

To be of sound mind a testator must understand the nature and effect of individual bequests. The validity of a will is conditional upon the testator having been so either at the time of its execution or when it was being drawn up provided, in the latter instance, that at the time of execution he or she at least realised the significance of the document then being signed and witnessed.

Where the testator is known to have suffered from mental illness, it will then depend on the individual's circumstances whether or not he or she was of unsound mind at the operative time. A mentally ill person may make a valid will during a lucid intermission in their illness. Where the illness is of such severity that the person has been made the subject of an order under the Mental Health (NI) Order 1986, then special provision is made under Article 99(1)(e) of that Order for a will to be drawn up on behalf of the patient subject to advice from the Master for Care and Protection.[17] The formalities in respect of such wills are governed by Article 100(1)(a) and (b) of the 1986 Order.

---

17 See *Re S (Gifts by Mental Patients)* [1997] 1 FLR 96 for an example of how this procedure (under the equivalent provisions of the Mental Health Act 1983) can be utilised to allow *inter vivos* dispositions to be made.

3. Testamentary Intent

The court will be concerned to give effect to a testator's intentions. The presumption of due execution, which has long found expression in the maxim *omnia presumuntur rite esse acta*, has now been reinforced by Article 29(1) of the 1994 Order which permits the court to order limited rectification of a will to insert as well as to delete words. This enables the court to bring the wording of the will into accord with the testator's intentions where the court is satisfied that the will as expressed fails to carry out those intentions either as a consequence of 'clerical error' or of failure to understand the testator's instructions.

Where ambiguity arises, established judicial practice has been to construe legal interpretation in accordance with testator's intent and extrinsic evidence may be admitted to clarify the exact nature of the deceased's intentions. As Kelly J ruled in *Murphy v Murphy*,[18] if inadvertence or misunderstanding should threaten to frustrate the clear intention of a testator, then the Probate Court will admit so much of two or more documents to probate so as to ensure that the testator's intention is achieved.

More recently, in this jurisdiction, the Court of Appeal had cause to consider how best it might give effect to a testator's intent where this had been jeopardised by a solicitor's incompetence. The case of *Hutchinson v McSorley*[19] concerned a testator in his late sixties who had lived with his daughter on her husband's farm. She had looked after him for several years until his death. The court was required to ascertain the intentions of the deceased who had made two wills in the space of three days: one was hand-written, the other purported to be a typed version of the first, prepared by the same solicitor but witnessed by a husband of a beneficiary. The court had little difficulty in ruling that the second will had been nullified under section 15 of the 1837 Act by the involvement of the husband. The issue for the court, given the presence of the second document, was whether the first could stand as a duly executed will, properly acknowledged by the testator, such as would satisfy the requirements of section 9 of the 1837 Act. The court held that 'it was abundantly plain that the testator intended his daughter to take his whole estate'. It determined that it should not allow other considerations to subvert an intent, clearly expressed in two documents before the court, which the testator had sought to present in a properly executed will. The hand-written will was declared valid.

II. Effect of Marriage

Under the 1994 Order, as previously under section 18 of the Wills Act, a will is revoked by the marriage of the testator unless made in contemplation of that marriage. So, where a married testator has died leaving provision for next-of-kin, then that provision will be displaced by the prior claims of the surviving spouse and those of such children as there may be of their marriage. Under Article 12 of the 1994 Order, individual gifts in a will, made in the expectation of surviving a particular marriage, will not be revoked by that marriage.

---

18   [1980] 3 NIJB.
19   [1993] 6 NIJB 49.

III. Effect of Divorce

A will is not revoked by the divorce or judicial separation of the testator.[20] However, under Article 13 of the 1994 Order, where a divorced testator has died, then any provision made in favour of the ex-spouse will pass as if that former spouse had died on the date of the divorce. Further, any appointment of that ex-spouse as executor or trustee will lapse, and in the absence of a contrary intention, any appointment by the deceased of the ex-spouse as guardian will be deemed to have been revoked at the date of the divorce.

In *Re Sinclair*,[21] the testator left his entire estate to his wife but in the event of her predeceasing him, it was to go to a charity. At the time of his death she was still alive but they were divorced. It was held that the gift to her lapsed on the divorce and as she had not predeceased him the gift to the charity could not take effect, so the entire will was void. The rules of intestacy were held to apply.

Rights of a Former Spouse

Where a testator has made no provision or inadequate provision in his will for a former spouse, the latter may have a right to claim against the estate. Under Article 4 of the Provision for Family and Dependants (NI) (Order)1979 such a spouse, who has not remarried, may make a claim unless barred by court order under Article 11 of the Matrimonial and Family Proceedings (NI) Order 1989.

IV. Effect of Murder

A sane person who causes the death of a testator by murder or manslaughter is barred on the grounds of public policy from being a beneficiary under any will previously executed by the deceased. This rule is subject to the Forfeiture (NI) Order 1982 which permits some discretion to be exercised in circumstances where murder was not the cause of death. To date, two unreported cases have been brought under this Order: in one, the court varied the effect of the Order; in the other, the case was withdrawn as it was outside the three-month time limit which, it would appear, there is no discretion to extend.

V. Effect of Mutual Testation

The practice whereby two persons, usually spouses, execute mutual wills in favour of a common intended beneficiary can give rise to difficulties.[22]

---

20 See *The Effect of Divorce on Wills* (Law Com no. 217) (1993) which followed the publication of a Consultation Paper in 1992.
21 [1985] 1 All ER 1066.
22 See, for example, *Re Dale, Proctor v Dale* [1994] Ch 31. Also see *Re Goodchild (Deceased) and Another* [1996] 1 FLR 591 where the decision of the court at first instance was subsequently upheld by the Court of Appeal. In the absence of evidence of a clear agreement between testators to be bound not to change their intentions after the death of the first testator, wills made simultaneously and in similar terms will not be regarded in law as mutual wills. The survivor will be entitled to dispose of the entire estate at his or her discretion.

1. The Legal Requirements

Mutual wills contain reciprocal clauses to the same effect such as 'I leave all my worldly goods to my spouse, but should he/she predecease me, then to our children'. However, the mere fact that wills contain such clauses is not enough. If they are to be regarded as mutual, it must be proven that there was a clear agreement between the parties that they intended to be mutually bound. In the words of Carnwath J, 'There must be evidence of a precise agreement'.[23] This may be most satisfactorily achieved by the inclusion of an additional clause which expressly declares that neither party will alter or revoke the agreed dispositions without the consent of the other.[24]

In the absence of an explicit agreement the court will consider all the circumstances of the case to establish whether any evidence exists which, on the balance of probabilities, demonstrates a mutuality of testator intent.

A claimant who fails to satisfy the court that a mutual will exists may have to settle for making a claim under Article 2(1) of the Inheritance (Provision for Family and Dependants) Order 1979 (see Chapter Twenty-Six).

2. The Effect

Once the existence of a mutually binding agreement is established, then the designated property is regarded in law as being held on trust for the intended beneficiary. A surviving testator, who re-marries and acquires a new family, remains bound by the terms of that will and cannot otherwise dispose of the designated property. Wills which carry a degree of mutuality are, however, exposed to the risk of uncertainty in circumstances where the testators die in an accident. It may then become crucial to establish the order of death.

VI. Effect of Avoidance Dispositions

Under Article 12 of the Inheritance (Provision for Family and Dependants) (NI) (Order) 1979 any disposal of property made by a testator with the intention and effect of avoiding meeting a statutory right to provide for family and dependants can be set aside by the court if it was made for inadequate consideration and within six years of the testator's death.

The Administration of Wills

To be a valid legal instrument for the distribution of the property of a deceased, a will must first be 'proven'. This process involves certain key officials.

I. Executors

An executor is a person appointed by a testator in a will to act after the latter's death as his or her personal representative by ensuring the proper execution of directions given in a will.

---

23 Ibid in *Re Goodchild*, citing as his authority *Dufour v Pereira* (1769) 1 Dick 420. See also L Ross *Mutual Wills — an exceptional case?* in Child and Family Law Quarterly, vol. 8, no. 3, P 253–260 (1996).
24 As in *Re Hagger, Freeman v Ascot* [1930] 2 Ch 190.

1. Appointment

The appointment of an executor is made at the discretion of the testator. An appointment is most often made in the will by means of a specific direction naming the appointee and takes effect on death of the testator. An intention to make such an appointment may also be inferred from the wording used. As the appointment is subject to the usual rules regarding capacity, a minor or person suffering from a mental disability cannot act as an executor. Moreover, the appointee may choose not to accept the appointment by lodging a written declaration to that effect in the Probate Office. The lack of an executor does not affect the validity of a will. In Northern Ireland there is no limit on the number of executors who may be appointed; at least two would be customary.

2. Role and Responsibilities

From the date of a testator's death his or her estate vests in the named executor. The latter is required not only to administer the bequests in accordance with testator's wishes but also to take overall responsibility for the management of the testator's fiduciary affairs including accounting for all assets, liabilities and taxes. While it is usual to charge an executor with responsibility for the testator's entire estate, it is also possible to allocate separate areas of responsibility to a number of different executors. An executor of a will may also be one of its beneficiaries.

II. Probate Office

Authority to administer the estate of a deceased must be sought from the Probate Office which is under the management of the Master for Probate and Matrimonial Proceedings.

1. Application

Under the Administration of Estates Act (NI) 1955 an executor is obliged to expedite the administration of a deceased's estate 'as soon as is reasonably practicable'. An application for a grant of probate is made to the Probate Office most usually by the solicitor acting on behalf of the deceased's family, but it may be made by an executor or other personal representative acting directly. This must be accompanied by the original will (i.e. not a photo-copy), death certificate, oaths sworn by such executors or administrators as may have been appointed, such affidavits if any as may be required and the fee. The application will not be accepted until the Probate Office receives notification that any tax due under the Inheritance Tax Act 1984 has been paid; this is payable six months after the end of the month in which death occurred.

2. Grant of Probate

On application from an executor, or alternatively from a *bona fide* personal representative, the Probate Office will issue a grant of probate. This cannot be issued within seven days of the death. The Administration of Estates Act 1971 provides that where the deceased was domiciled in Northern Ireland but the estate is partially or wholly located elsewhere in the United Kingdom, then the grant taken out in this jurisdiction will also have effect throughout the United Kingdom.

3. Revocation of a Grant of Probate

Under Article 11 of the Administration of Estates (NI) Order 1979 the court may revoke a grant of probate. This is most likely to occur in circumstances where a later will is discovered. It may also be necessary where the grant issued contains serious mistakes or was issued on the basis of wrong or false information.

Contested Wills

The discretionary right of a testator to dispose of property as he or she thinks fit is only exercisable subject to prior satisfaction of the statutory rights of certain persons and bodies.

I. Statutory Rights

The right of an applicant to challenge dispositions made by a testator is provided by the Inheritance (Provision for Family and Dependants) (NI) Order 1979. Its provisions largely replicate those of the Inheritance (Provision for Family and Dependants) Act 1975.

1. Application

Under Article 2 of the 1979 Order, applications may be made only in respect of persons who die after 1980 and who, at the time of death, are domiciled in this jurisdiction. As proceedings are expensive, there may be no point in making application where the estate is small.[25]

2. Grounds for Application

The 1979 Order governs claims against the estate of a deceased by those with an entitlement for whom no provision was made in a valid will, the provision was in an invalid or ineffective will or where no will was made. Both the High Court and the county court have jurisdiction to hear proceedings instigated under the 1979 Order.

3. Applicants

Under Article 3(1) of the 1979 Order the following are recognised as eligible to make application:

1. the wife or husband of the deceased;
2. a former wife or husband of the deceased who has not remarried;
3. a child of the deceased;
4. any person (not being a child of the deceased) who, in the case of any marriage to which the deceased was at any time a party, was treated by the deceased as a child of the family in relation to that marriage;

---

25 See, for example, *Jelly v Iliffe* [1981] 2 WLR 801.

5. any person (not being a person included in the foregoing paragraphs of this subsection) who immediately before the death of the deceased was being maintained, either wholly or partly, by the deceased.

4. Probate

A condition precedent to implementation of the statute's provisions is that a grant of probate has been made or letters of administration have been issued.[26]

5. Time as a Bar

Applications must be made within six months of the issue of the grant of representation. However, with leave of the court, good reason having been shown (which, in this jurisdiction, will need to be very good as the courts are reluctant to grant extensions), an application may be made at a later date.[27]

6. Cohabitee

In the near future statutory protection will also be extended to an unmarried cohabitee of at least two years' standing.

II. Judicial Determination

1. General Principles

Notwithstanding the 1979 Order the principle governing judicial determination continues to be as stated by Oliver J:[28]

> ... an Englishman still remains at liberty at his death to dispose of his own property in whatever way he pleases. [An able-bodied applicant (other than a spouse) must establish] some sort of moral claim ... to be maintained by the deceased or at the expense of his estate beyond the mere fact of blood relationship, some reason why it can be said that, in the circumstances, it is unreasonable that no or no greater provision was in fact made.

The powers exercisable by the courts under the 1979 Order are essentially discretionary in nature. The process by which the court decides whether or not to exercise its discretion is fairly straightforward.

(a) The Two-Stage Test

The 1979 Order imposes a two-stage test for all claimants: has the deceased failed, by will or intestacy, to make 'reasonable financial provision for the claimant'? If so, should the court exercise its discretion to order such provision to be made from the deceased's estate?

---

26 See, for example, *Re McBroom Deceased* [1992] 2 FLR 49.
27 See, for example, *Re Salmon* [1986] 3 All ER 532; *Re Dennis* [1981] 2 All ER 140; and *Re Freeman* [1984] 3 All ER 906.
28 In *Re Coventry, deceased* [1980] Ch 461, 474, 475.

(b) Matters to Be Taken into Account

Under Article 5(1) of the 1979 Order the court is required to consider the following factors when determining an Article 3(1) application.

(i) The Means of the Applicant

The court seeks to establish the current and projected financial circumstances of the claimant relative to his or her commitments and responsibility for any dependants.

(ii) The Applicant's Circumstances Relative to Others

The court will compare the applicant's financial circumstances with those of other applicants or beneficiaries who stand to benefit from the estate.

(iii) The Deceased's Obligations towards the Applicant

Again, the court will be concerned to establish how the deceased's obligations towards the applicant compare with those towards any other person who stands to benefit from the estate.

(iv) The Size and Nature of the Estate

In particular the court will wish to consider any link between the substantive content of the estate and the applicant.

(v) Any Special Needs of the Applicant

Should the applicant have particular needs, such as a physical or mental disability, the court will weigh this in the balance with the needs of other applicants and beneficiaries.

(vi) Any Other Matter, Including Conduct

The conduct, whether by deceased or applicant and whether good or bad, will be taken into account by the court. Any statements made by the deceased, indicating his or her intentions toward the applicant, will similarly be of interest to the court.

2. Spouses

Under the terms of the 1979 Act, there are three respects in which spouses are regarded more favourably than other applicants. First, a spouse is not required to produce evidence of dependency in order to establish a right to claim against the deceased's estate. Second, unlike other Article 3(1) applicants, the test to be applied in respect of spouses is not whether the deceased failed to make reasonable financial provision for his or her maintenance but whether such provision was 'reasonable in all the circumstances of the case for a husband or wife to receive, whether or not that provision is required for his or her maintenance'. Third, in addition to the Article 5(1) factors, when considering an application from a spouse or former spouse the court must also take into account under Article 5(2):

(i) the age of the applicant and the duration of the marriage;
(ii) the contribution made by the applicant to the welfare of the family of the deceased, including any contribution made by looking after the home or caring for the family;
(iii) in the case of an application by a spouse (unless there was a decree of judicial separation in force at the date of death and the separation was continuing) the provision which the applicant might reasonably have expected to receive if, on the day the deceased died, the marriage had been terminated by divorce instead.

The court tends to give particular weight to the latter factor. Paradoxically, however, there may be an inverse correlation between that weighting and the duration of the marriage: the longer the marriage the less the factor, relative to others, may influence judicial determination of the amount to be awarded. This can be seen in the different emphasis placed on the factor in two recent cases, one concerning a marriage of six years and the other of sixty-four years duration.

The case of *Weir and Others v Davey and Others: Watts v Weir and Others*[29] concerned a constable in the RUC who in 1988 in his late thirties committed suicide. An application was subsequently lodged for financial provision to be made from his estate for his estranged wife. The grounds for her application were that in the disposition of his estate, effected by will in 1983, he had failed to make reasonable provision for her.

The court heard that the couple had married in 1972 and a daughter had been born in 1977. In 1978 marital difficulties caused a separation and the wife was awarded a maintenance order on evidence of her husband's persistent cruelty; an order was also issued in favour of the daughter. The marital home was sold and the proceeds were lodged in a joint account with a building society. The wife, fearing that the husband might squander the money, withdrew approximately one-quarter of the total and lodged it in a separate account under her sister's name. In 1979 the couple were briefly reconciled during which period they bought a house, using the money from the sister's account but registering the house in his name. In 1981 the wife and daughter left, ultimately setting up home in NIHE rented accommodation. At the end of that year maintenance orders for mother and child were awarded against the husband. A year later the wife issued a summons under the Married Woman's Property Act 1882 to protect her interest in the house and caused a *lis pendens* to be registered against the property.

In 1982 the husband met Mrs M, a divorcee with three children. They set up home together and for several years he was their sole source of support. During this period he suffered an accident while on duty which resulted in his medical discharge from the RUC in 1987. Enduring ill effects of the accident led him to institute proceedings for damages against the police authority. This action came to court in 1992 having been brought by his executors; the estranged wife and daughter were parties.

The deceased had made a will in 1983 which contained no provision for his wife but left 'whatever dwelling house I may own at the date of my death together with all contents and any motor car which I may own at the date of my death to my friend

---

[29] [1993] 2 NIJB 46.

Mrs M (the cohabitee) absolutely'. He left the residue and remainder of his estate upon trust to hold for his daughter until she attained the age of twenty-one. The net value of the estate amounted to £78,000 together with a TSB Life Bond of £16,535.

The legal principles for the making of orders under Articles 4 and 5[30] establish that when determining the widow's application for relief, the court should apply the two-stage test. Firstly, under Article 2(1)(a) of the 1979 Order, it must be determined whether in the disposition of his estate effected by his will the deceased failed to make reasonable provision for his wife and if so, what financial provision should be made having regard to the matters set out in Article 5. In determining what reasonable provision should be made, the court should also have regard to what reasonable provision she would have received on divorce. As Waite J said in *Re Moody*:[31]

> Nevertheless, in cases where the applicant is a surviving spouse, the logical starting point . . . would be an appraisal of the claimant's notional entitlement under the amended sections 25 and 25A of the Matrimonial Causes Act 1973, assuming there has been a decree of divorce at the date of death.

The court found as follows:

1. The wife, the sole applicant under Article 3(1)(a) was left nothing in the will. As the deceased did not make reasonable provision for her the court would do so under Article 4(1)(6) i.e. ' . . . an order for the payment of . . . a lump sum of such amount as may be so specified'.
2. The court took into account the wife's circumstances. She was aged forty-four, an experienced typist with rented accommodation who had her own car. The court was unimpressed by her professed wish to buy a house holding that, on the evidence, she was content and comfortable living in rented accommodation. The court noted that as the deceased had made provision for his daughter it was unlikely that her needs would, in future, significantly impact upon the mother's resources.

Also, under Article 5, the court was obliged to take into account any financial needs and resources which Mrs M, a beneficiary under the will, had or was likely to have and the obligations and responsibilities which the deceased had towards her.

The court awarded the wife £38,000 and costs.

The case of *Re A McGuigan v B and E McGuigan*[32] concerned a testator, aged ninety-three at the time of his death in 1994, who had been a man of 'active and frequently changing testamentary intentions'. He had made many wills including nine between 1965 and 1989. In his final will he had made no provision for any of his three non-dependent children. To his wife (the plaintiff) he bequeathed the matrimonial home and attached farm for her life and thereafter this was to pass to his grandson Eugene, son of Brian (a defendant) to whom he also left the remainder of the estate.

---

30 See *Re Moody Deceased, Moody v Stevenson* [1992] 2 All ER 524; *Re Banning Deceased, Banning v Salmon and Others* [1984] 3 All ER 1 and *Re Patton, McIlveen and Another v Patton* [1986] NI 45.
31 Ibid at 534B.
32 Unreported (1996).

The total value of the estate was estimated at £95,000. The widow, aged eighty-one, after almost sixty-five years of marriage, during which she had always played a full and active role in running the farm, was dissatisfied with the terms of the will and applied under Article 4 of the 1979 Order for reasonable provision to be made for her from the deceased's estate.

Kerr LJ methodically applied the checklist of statutory requirements: the two stage test; the six different matters to be taken into account under Article 5(1); and then he finally considered the three Article 5(2) factors. The dilemma presented by the latter provision was that:

> On one view, the age of the applicant may be regarded as a factor weighing against making substantial capital provision for her. As against this, however, the view may be taken that throughout her long marriage she contributed significantly to the success of the farming enterprise and made it possible for the deceased to preserve his ownership of the lands which now form the bulk of his estate.

While acknowledging that 'the length of the applicant's marriage to the deceased and the daily contribution which she made must not be lost sight of' Kerr LJ stressed that 'the need for capital provision for the applicant is obviously not as great as would be the case of a young widow'. He found that the deceased had failed to make reasonable provision for the applicant and that her current financial requirements and the contribution she had made to the family and farms had been insufficiently recognised. In his assessment of reasonable provision Kerr LJ bore in mind three other matters: the testator's freedom, even if qualified, to dispose of his estate as he should think fit; the likely effect of an increase in provision from the deceased's estate on the applicant's entitlement to income support; and the substantial depletion of the estate due to the costs incurred by the litigants. He held that the applicant should have a life interest in all the deceased's lands and buildings including the matrimonial home, with the remainder to the grandson Eugene absolutely. He ordered that a further £5,000 should be settled on the applicant from the estate.

In the case of a former spouse, however, there is a heavy burden on such an applicant to rebut the presumption that adequate provision was made at the time of the divorce.

3. Children

In addition to the Article 5(1) factors, when considering an application in respect of a child of the deceased or one treated as a child of the family in relation to that marriage, the court must also take into account:

> (i) the manner in which the applicant was being, or in which he might be expected to be, educated or trained.

Where the child is one who has been treated as a child of the family in relation to that marriage, then the court is further required to consider:

> (ii) whether the deceased has assumed any responsibility for the applicant's maintenance and, if so, the extent to which the deceased assumed that responsibility and the length of time for which the deceased discharged it;

(iii) whether, in discharging that responsibility, the deceased knew that it was not his own child;
(iv) the liability of any person to maintain the applicant.

(a) Dependant Child

Parental responsibility follows the child. It is terminated by neither the divorce nor the death of a parent. Part of that responsibility is in the form of a statutory duty requiring a testator to make 'reasonable financial provision' for the future needs of any child of the testator's marriage, any non-marital child or any child adopted, treated as a child of the family or *en ventre sa mere* at time of the testator's death. Any such child, who remains both a dependant minor and is inadequately provided for, will have little difficulty in pursuing a claim for provision to be made from the testator's estate.

It should be noted that a non-marital child of the deceased has the same right as a marital child to claim against the latter's estate, where the death occurred after December 31, 1977.[33]

(b) Non-Dependant Child

Most applications are made by 'children' who have attained the age of majority. The 1979 Order removed all age limits in respect of such applicants. However, the applicant's status of dependency is crucial to the reciprocal duty resting on a testator parent to make 'reasonable financial provision'. Only where it can be shown that the inadequate provision was made by a testator parent whose death occurred during the applicant's minority, or if it occurred after the applicant had attained the age of majority, but without having attained financial independence, and was unreasonable in all the circumstances of the case, will the court order appropriate provision to be made out of the deceased's estate.

In the recent case of *Goodchild*,[34] once the court had ruled that the applicant son had failed to establish the existence of mutual wills, it then went on to find that, nonetheless, his claim could be grounded on the testator's moral obligation under the 1975 Act to make reasonable provision. The court made an order giving effect to a verbal maternal promise that the son would inherit certain property, thereby undoing the father's disposition in favour of his second wife, on the grounds that it was unreasonable of the father to disinherit his son.

In this jurisdiction the case of *Re Creeney, Creeney v Smith*[35] illustrates the judicial approach to non-dependant child applicants. The plaintiff was the son of the deceased who had died in 1982. He had worked for many years for low pay in the deceased's shoe shop in the expectation that he would succeed to the business. In 1968 the deceased retired from the business leaving it to be managed by the plaintiff. The busi-

---

33 See, for example, *Re Patton* [1986] NI 45.
34 See f/n 22. Also, see *Re Abram (Deceased)* [1996] 2 FLR 379 where the court held that the applicant must show both: an unreasonable failure to make provision which required proof of special circumstance and evidenced, for example, by the testator's breach of a moral obligation; and a maintenance requirement from the estate.
35 [1984] NI 397.

ness, however, failed to prosper. In 1972, following a quarrel with the deceased about the disposal of the proceeds of the house which the plaintiff had expected to come to him, the plaintiff abandoned the business and went to live in England. In his will the deceased left all his property to his daughter, the defendant. The plaintiff brought proceedings under the Inheritance (Provision for Family and Dependants) (NI) Order 1979 seeking reasonable provision from the deceased's estate. Article 2(2) of the 1979 Order defines reasonable provision in cases where the applicant is a person other than the spouse of the deceased as 'such financial provision as it would be reasonable in all the circumstances of the case for the applicant to receive for his maintenance'.

The court held that the disposition of the deceased's estate effected by the will did not make reasonable financial provision for the plaintiff and that a lump sum, representing one-third of the value of the net estate, should be paid to him.

4. Cohabitees

A cohabitee may succeed to the estate of a deceased person who died testate in the same way as anyone else. A testator may make specific provision in a will for whomsoever he or she chooses.

(a) Grounds

The right of a cohabitee (any friend, relative or partner who lives in domestic circumstances with the testator) to provision from a testator's estate will rest on two grounds. First, the applicant must demonstrate that he or she was dependant upon the testator at the time of the latter's death. Second, it must be shown that the testator made unreasonable provision for the needs of that dependant. Any such right will have to be pursued in accordance with established equitable principles (see further Chapter Twenty).

In *Jelley v Iliffe*,[36] for example, the Court of Appeal considered the application of a male cohabitee who sought provision from the estate of a deceased female testator with whom he had lived for many years but from whom he received nothing in her will. The court ruled that as the facts showed that the deceased contributed more than the plaintiff to the continuance of their relationship, then there was sufficient evidence of probable dependency to permit the matter to go to trial.

The case of *Wayling v Jones*[37] illustrates the modern judicial approach to an applicant seeking to assert such a right. The Court of Appeal considered the claim of a beneficiary in proprietary estoppel that the deceased had failed to honour a promise on which the beneficiary had relied to bequeath him the ownership of a hotel. This was a case where a cohabiting male couple had bought and sold a succession of business premises in each of which they then lived and worked. The age difference between the plaintiff and the deceased was thirty-five years: the former bore the brunt of the responsibility for running the businesses which the deceased purchased; the latter, in return, made promises that the plaintiff would inherit the relevant business

---

36 [1981] 2 All ER 29.
37 [1995] 2 FLR 1030.

and, therefore, paid the plaintiff only pocket-money in addition to providing for his living expenses. The deceased had made a will, giving effect to this express declaration of intent, in which he left the then current business to the plaintiff. However, that business was sold, another bought and, despite the deceased's assurances that he would alter his will to honour his promise, he died without having done so. The only provision made for the plaintiff was the gift of a car and some furniture of little value.

The court at first instance dismissed the plaintiff's claim against the estate of the deceased holding that although there was evidence of such a promise and evidence that the plaintiff had acted to his detriment, there was insufficient proof of a causal link. The court was not satisfied that, in the event of the promise being withdrawn, the plaintiff would have left; it was at least possible that he would have remained and incurred the detriment anyway. The Court of Appeal reversed this decision holding that the foregoing of any wages by the plaintiff in return for his work implied the existence of a link (he did not have to prove reliance in proprietary estoppel) between the promise of the deceased and the conduct of the plaintiff which was detrimental to the latter. Once that link was established, showing that there was an inducement for the plaintiff's subsequent conduct (it was of no consequence that there may have been other inducements), then the burden of proof shifted to the defendant to show that the plaintiff had not relied on that promise to his detriment. The defendant had failed to discharge this burden. The Court of Appeal was also satisfied that evidence existed to show that the plaintiff would not have remained with the deceased had the latter withdrawn his promise. The plaintiff was awarded the net proceeds of the sale of the hotel plus interest.[38]

(b) Orders

Under Article 4(1) of the 1979 Order the court has the power to make any one or more of the following orders:

    (i) interim order (if the applicant needs immediate assistance),
    (ii) periodical payments,
    (iii) lump-sum payments,
    (iv) order for transfer or settlement of property,
    (v) order for acquisition of property,
    (vi) order varying an ante-or post-nuptial settlement.

These are similar to the orders available to the court when considering applications for ancillary relief in the context of proceedings for divorce, nullity or judicial separation under the Matrimonial Causes (NI) Order 1978.

---

38 See also *Tinsley v Milligan* [1992] 2 All ER 391 CA.

CHAPTER TWENTY-SIX

Intestate Succession

Introduction

The law of intestate succession makes a distinction between the administration of an estate in accordance with rules which determine the equal and rightful shares of an intestate's family and next-of-kin and the determination of claims against such an estate made by those who were dependent upon the deceased at the time of death. The first set of circumstances is governed by the Administration of Estates Act (NI) 1955 where determination is by the mandatory application of rules set out in that statute. The second is governed by the Inheritance (Provision for Family and Dependants) (NI) Order 1979 where determination is at judicial discretion. This chapter examines and outlines the differences between the two.

Intestacy

Succession to the estate of a deceased, where that person has died either without having made a will or having made a will which proves to be invalid or ineffective, is determined wholly or partially in accordance with the law of intestacy.

I. Definitions

A number of terms are either exclusive to the law of intestacy or have a particular meaning in that context.

1. Whole and Partial Intestacy

Where the entire assets of a deceased remain undisposed of by a will, either because a will was not executed or was executed but failed completely, then the deceased has died wholly intestate and all of his or her estate falls to be disposed of in accordance with the rules of intestacy. Where a will is executed but fails to dispose of a testator's entire assets, then the deceased has died partially intestate and that remainder is treated as being subject to the rules of intestacy.

2. Beneficiaries

Those entitled to succeed to an intestate's estate are usually the next-of-kin within a certain class, e.g. all first cousins. Identifying and tracing the full membership of that class can often be a much more complicated process than contacting the beneficiaries named in a will. For that reason, and in order to allow administrators to settle the distribution of an estate within a reasonable period, section 28 of the Trustee Act (NI)

1958 makes provision for notice to be publicly served in respect of any missing possible beneficiaries requiring them to lodge details of their claims within two months. At the expiration of that period the administrators are free to distribute the estate among known and qualifying next-of-kin.

3. Administrators

Administrators are the persons entitled under the 1955 Act to take out letters of administration in respect of an intestate's estate; application is made to the Probate Office. The appropriate administrator in a particular case is the person who, as next-of-kin, stands in the closest degree of blood relationship to the deceased; more than one may therefore be equally entitled. Once the inheritance tax, if any, has been paid and letters of administration have been taken out, the estate vests in the administrator who then becomes the personal representative of the deceased. As such his principal duty is to administer the estate in accordance with the rules stated in the 1955 Act and outlined below.

4. Hotchpot

The hotchpot is a device instituted to guard against the possibility of a child of an intestate receiving a double benefit and thereby ensures that issue take on a *per stirpes* basis. Section 18 of the Administration of Estates Act (NI) 1955 provides that when it comes to dividing out the assets among the issue of an intestate, any benefit already received by one should 'be brought into hotchpot'. The aggregated 'pot' is then distributed in equal shares. The Law Commission has recommended the abolition of hotchpot[1] on the ground that it is discriminatory as it applies only to issue. In this jurisdiction the hotchpot rule does not apply to partial intestacies.

II. *Statute Law*

The Administration of Estates Act (NI) 1955 provides the statutory framework for distribution among those with a right to a share in the estate of an intestate. Others, without such a specific right or those who are dissatisfied with their share under the 1955 Act may bring a claim under the Inheritance (Provision for Family and Dependants) (NI) Order 1979. Each piece of legislation governs a quite separate legal process: the former is of greater importance both because it deals with the firmly established rights of the parties and attracts a much larger volume of litigation whilst the second is purely discretionary.

It should be noted that the draft Succession (NI) Order 1996 (in effect in early 1997), will in some respects bring the law into line with England and Wales by introducing provisions equivalent to those contained in the Law Reform (Succession) Act 1995 (in effect since January 1996). In particular the 1996 Order will: abolish hotchpot, give cohabitees automatic *locus standi* under the 1979 Order and introduce a survivorship clause requiring a claimant to survive a deceased spouse by twenty-eight days.

---

1 See *Distribution on Intestacy* (Law Com no 187, para 47) (1989). For a recent and thorough study, see S Grattan, *Succession Law in Northern Ireland*, Belfast: SLS (1996).

The Marital Family

Marital status is a significant determinant of succession rights in respect of an intestate's estate. A spouse is treated more favourably in law than a cohabitee. Where the deceased died intestate then, in most cases, unless the estate is substantial, a surviving spouse will inherit everything. Where the estate is solvent, then regardless of its size and whether or not there are children, the surviving spouse will always have an exclusive statutory entitlement to all personal chattels (as defined in section 45 of the 1955 Act). Where the estate is large, the surviving spouse will have a statutory right to a majority share in all other assets.

The legislative intent, informing the Administration of Estates Act (NI) 1955, is that the deceased's family should be placed, insofar as is practicable, in a position approximate to that which they would have been in had the deceased died testate.

I. *Definitions*

1. Spouse of the Intestate

The rights of the spouse of an intestate are dependent, in the first instance, upon actual marital status at the time of the intestate's death. The marriage must have been, at that time, valid and subsisting.

(a) A 'Spouse'

For the purposes of intestacy a spouse is the person legally married to the intestate at the time of the latter's death. This definition includes a party to a voidable marriage where a decree of annulment has not been issued but excludes a party to a void marriage and a cohabitee.

(b) A Separated Spouse

Under the Matrimonial Causes (NI) Order 1978, Article 20:

> (2) If while a decree of separation is in force and the separation is continuing either of the parties to the marriage dies intestate as respects all or any part of his or her real or personal property, the property as respects which he or she died intestate shall devolve as if the other party to the marriage had then been dead.

Thus a separated spouse is only disentitled if a decree of judicial separation is in force. A spouse who is otherwise merely living apart from the intestate, even if so doing for many years prior to and at the time of death, does not come within this definition.

(c) A Divorced Spouse

The succession rights of a former spouse terminate on the grant of a decree absolute. A person in respect of whom only a decree *nisi* has been issued is not a divorced spouse and is therefore in a position to succeed as the surviving spouse.[2]

---

2 See, for example, *Re Seaford* [1968] 1 All ER 482.

2. Child of the Intestate

For the purposes of the 1955 Act, a child of the intestate is any child born in and of the marriage, one who has been adopted by the intestate,[3] or is a non-marital child or was conceived but not born before the death of the intestate.[4] A child 'treated as one of the family' does not come within this definition, though such a child does do so for the purposes of the 1979 Order.

II. Entitlement of Surviving Spouse

1. Personal Chattels

Under section 45(1) of the Administration of Estates Act (NI) 1955 the 'personal chattels' to which the surviving spouse has an exclusive entitlement are defined as:

> ... carriages, horses, stable furniture and effects, motor cars and accessories, garden effects, domestic animals, plate, plated articles, linen, china, glass, books, pictures, prints, furniture, jewellery, articles of household or personal use or ornament, musical and scientific instruments and apparatus, wines, liquors and consumable stores, but does not include any chattels used at the death of the intestate for business or professional purposes nor money or security for money.

There is no upper or lower limit to the value of any such items, only a requirement that they be used for personal and not business purposes. So, for example, collections of unmounted diamonds,[5] clocks and watches[6] a sixty-foot yacht[7] and racehorses kept for recreational use have all been classified as personal chattels. The entitlement of the surviving spouse is subject to the estate being solvent; on insolvency, the personal chattels will be sold by the administrators to defray debts.

2. The Matrimonial Home

In normal circumstances, where the matrimonial home is owned exclusively by an intestate, or jointly with a spouse, then on the former's death the latter will have a priority right to claim full ownership. However, unlike their counterparts in England and Wales, surviving spouses in this jurisdiction are not entitled to opt for ownership of all or part of a matrimonial home instead of taking all or part of their designated financial share of the estate. There are circumstances in which a spouse will have to forego a claim to the matrimonial home and settle for an entitlement to a lump sum.

3. The Residual Estate

A surviving spouse is entitled to a statutorily fixed share of an intestate's estate. This size of the share is dependant upon whether or not the intestate is also survived by

---

3   See Article 40 of the Adoption (NI) Order 1987.
4   See section 13 of the 1955 Act.
5   See *Re Whitby* [1944] 1 All ER 299.
6   See *Re Crispin's Will Trusts* [1974] 3 All ER 772 CA.
7   See *Re Chaplin* [1950] 2 All ER 155.

issue and, if so, by the number of same. The rules governing the fixing of such shares are as stated below. In practice, their application may be upset by proceedings instigated by a claimant under the 1979 Order.

(a) Spouse with Children

Under the Administration of Estates Act (NI) 1955, the following rules apply on intestacy.

    1. Where the estate, exclusive of personal chattels, is worth £125,000 or less, the spouse succeeds to the entire estate.

    2. Where the estate, exclusive of personal chattels, is worth more than £125,000 and there is one child, the spouse succeeds to the first £125,000 and to half the remainder; the child succeeds to the balance of the estate.

    3. Where the estate, exclusive of personal chattels, is worth more than £125,000 and there is more than one child, the spouse succeeds to the first £125,000 and to one third of the remainder; the children succeed in equal shares to the balance of the estate.

The share of any child of the intestate who has predeceased him or her passes *per stirpes* to the issue, if any, of that child. Neither the parents nor any siblings of the intestate have any claim to any part of the estate.

(b) Spouse without Children

Under the Administration of Estates Act (NI) 1955, the following rules apply on intestacy.

    1. Where the estate, exclusive of personal chattels, is worth £200,000 or less, the spouse succeeds to the entire estate.

    2. Where one or both parents of the deceased are still living, the spouse succeeds to the first £200,000 plus half the balance, the remainder is shared equally between the parents or devolves wholly to one surviving parent.

    3. Where there are no surviving parents of the deceased, but there are brothers and sisters of the deceased, the spouse succeeds to the first £200,000 and half the balance, the remainder is shared equally between the brothers and sisters.

    4. Where there are no surviving parents or no brothers or sisters of the deceased, then the spouse succeeds to the entire estate.

Again, the share of any child of the intestate who has predeceased him or her passes to the issue, if any, of that child.

III. No Surviving Spouse

Under the Administration of Estates Act (NI)1955, the following rules apply on intestacy.

1. If there are children, they succeed *per stirpes*, to the entire estate.
2. If there are no children, but one or both parents of the deceased are still alive, the surviving parent succeeds to the entire estate or both succeed in equal shares to the entire estate.
3. If there are no children and no surviving parents of the deceased, but there are brothers and sisters of the deceased, then they succeed in equal shares to the entire estate.
4. In the absence of the above, if there are surviving grandparents then they succeed in equal shares to the whole estate.
5. In the absence of the above, if there are surviving uncles and aunts of the deceased then they succeed in equal shares to the whole estate.
6. In the absence of the above, then rights of succession are determined by proximity of blood relationship to the intestate of any surviving next-of-kin.
7. In the absence of the above then, under section 16 of the 1955 Act, the Crown succeeds to the entire estate.

Basically, in the absence of any spouse or children of the intestate (or issue of any children), then the estate devolves in accordance with the rules governing next-of-kin. Those who stand in the closest degree of blood relationship to the intestate at the time of death will have the strongest claim. Under section 14 of the 1955 Act, relatives of the half-blood take equally with those of full-blood. Where there is more than one person of the same degree of kinship, then they take in equal shares. Only siblings, uncles and aunts may be represented by issue in the event of their predeceasing the testator.

The Non-Marital Family

The Administration of Estates Act (NI) 1955 governs the rules for succession on intestacy. These rules make provision for the surviving members of an intestate's marital family. They give no recognition to a non-marital family unit.

Succession

1. Cohabitee

A cohabitee has no statutory rights of succession nor does he or she enjoy the same right as a spouse to occupy the matrimonial home in the event of the death or bankruptcy of a partner.

If the deceased died intestate, then the surviving partner is placed at a considerable disadvantage in comparison with a surviving spouse. The relative injustice of the cohabitee's position was of concern to the Law Commission which recommended changes to the statutory provisions to ensure greater protection (though not parity with spouses) for their interests.[8] These recommendations have not been implemented.

Any claim on the estate of an intestate by a surviving cohabitee will fall to be decided under the Inheritance (Provision for Family and Dependants)(NI) Order 1979.

---

8 See f/n 1.

The provisions of the Family Law Reform (NI) Order 1977 (as amended by the Children (NI) Order 1995, Schedule 8, paragraph 33)[9] should also be noted.

Rights of a Cohabitee

Under the 1979 Order, a cohabitee and/or an illegitimate child will be entitled to claim for reasonable provision for maintenance to be made from the estate of a deceased. However, while such a child has an unconditional right of application, a cohabitee will have to show that the deceased had been treating the applicant as a dependant for at least two years and was continuing to do so immediately prior to death.

(i) The Public Sector Family Home

The law governing a cohabitee's rights of succession on the death of a partner who is a public housing tenant is to be found in the Housing (NI) Order 1983, Article 24(3) and the Housing (NI) Order 1986, Schedule 1.

The term 'secure tenancy' was introduced to the law of this jurisdiction by Article 25 of the 1983 Order. A cohabitee will not qualify as a successor to such a tenancy unless he or she occupied the premises as the principal or only home at the time of the tenant's death (see further Chapters Twenty-Three and Twenty-Four).

(ii) Tenancies

A cohabitee's tenancy rights are largely governed by the Rent (NI) Order 1978, Article 4 and Schedule 1. In most cases the surviving cohabitee will enjoy the same right to succeed to the tenancy as would a surviving spouse. Succession for both is conditional upon proof of living together as husband and wife. Cohabitees will be held to have provided such proof where their relationships displayed features of settled permanence characteristic of marriage.[10] This will not be the case where the relationship is casual, purely platonic[11] or homosexual.[12] There will be occasions when a cohabitee may have difficulty in proving that, at the time of death, the couple's domestic arrangements demonstrate such a settled sustained relationship.

2. Non-Marital Child

A non-marital child now has the same statutory right as a marital child to apply under the intestacy rules for provision to be made from an intestate parent's estate. This results from the removal by the Family Law Reform (NI) Order 1977 of the previous statutory distinction made between the inheritance rights of legitimate and illegitimate children in relation to the estate of their parents, extended under Articles 155–7 and Schedule 6 of the Children (NI) Order 1995 to include the estates of other family members. Application may be made under the Administration of Estates Act (NI) 1955.

---

9 The amendments repeal Article 3 (rights on intestacy) and Article 4 (presumption in dispositions of property) from the date of the coming into effect of the 1995 Order.
10 See *Dyson Holdings v Fox* [1976] QB 503; [1975] 3 All ER 1030 CA and *Watson v Lucas* [1980] 1 WLR 1493.
11 See *Carega Properties v Sharratt* [1979] 2 All ER 1084.
12 See *Harrogate Borough Council v Simpson* [1986] 2 FLR 91 CA.

Judicial Determination of Claims Brought against an Intestate's Estate

Proceedings asserting a claim to a share in an intestate's estate may be brought by any dependant of an intestate regardless of the latter's marital status. This allows claims from the family or next-of-kin of a married intestate, the cohabitee or child of an unmarried intestate or indeed anyone else. In all cases the proceedings must be commenced under the Inheritance (Provision for Family and Dependants) (NI) Order 1979. This provides a safety net for specified applicants.

Statutory Proceedings

Applications may be brought in the High Court or county court under the 1979 Order by persons dissatisfied with their designated statutory entitlement under the 1955 Act. Applications must be brought under the 1979 Order by those, such as cohabitees, who are debarred from doing so under the 1955 Act. In both cases the right of an applicant is restricted to making an application. The court, as explained by Carnwath J,[13] then applies a double test. The first is

> ... to determine the reasonableness of the provision actually made (if any) and secondly to determine the extent to which the court should exercise its powers.

Any remedy is totally at the discretion of the court.

1. Legislative Purpose

To claim against the estate of an intestate, applicants must bring their case within the terms of reference of the 1979 Order. This legislation replicates the provisions of the Inheritance (Provision for Family and Dependants) Act 1975 which has been described by Stephenson LJ[14] as an Act

> ... to remedy, wherever reasonably possible, the injustice of one, who has been put by a deceased person in a position of dependency upon him, being deprived of any financial support, either by accident or by design of the deceased, after his death.

The judicial finding that pre-1975 cases no longer have any precedent value must, therefore, have equal application in this jurisdiction to pre-1979 cases.[15]

2. Applicants

Eligibility to apply for provision to be made from the estate of an intestate, as from the estate of a testator, is defined by Article 3(1) of the 1979 Order. The following are recognised as eligible to make application:

---

13 See *Re Goodchild (Deceased) and Another* [1996] 1 FLR 591.
14 See *Jelley v Iliffe* [1981] 2 All ER 29, 36.
15 See *Moody v Stevenson* [1992] 2 All ER 481.

1. the wife or husband of the deceased;
2. a former wife or husband of the deceased who has not remarried;
3. a child of the deceased;
4. any person (not being a child of the deceased) who, in the case of any marriage to which the deceased was at any time a party, was treated by the deceased as a child of the family in relation to that marriage;
5. any person (not being a person included in the foregoing paragraphs of this subsection) who immediately before the death of the deceased was being maintained, either wholly or partly, by the deceased.

In the context of non-marital relationships, most applicants are drawn from the last category.

3. Grounds

A claim is based on an assertion that the intestate failed to make reasonable provision for the applicant. Any such claim requires evidence that a state of dependency existed between the applicant and the deceased immediately prior to the death; that, in fact, the deceased had accepted responsibility for maintaining the claimant and was doing so at that time.

4. Time Limits

An application must be made within six months of letters of administration being taken out. Later applications may be accepted with leave of the court if good reason is shown.[16]

5. Orders

Under the 1979 Order the court has the power to make the same orders in relation to proceedings instituted in the context of intestacy as it does in the context of testacy. Under Article 4(1) it may make any one or more of the following orders:

    (i) interim order (if the applicant needs immediate assistance),
    (ii) periodical payments,
    (iii) lump-sum payments,
    (iv) order for transfer or settlement of property,
    (v) order for acquisition of property,
    (vi) order varying an ante-or post-nuptial settlement.

Claims Made against the Estate of a Married Intestate

1. Spouse

The discretionary powers of the court, as it strives to do justice to the conflicting claims of an intestate's family, were demonstrated in *Re Coventry Deceased*.[17] In that case

---

16 See *Re Dennis* [1981] 2 All ER 140 where leave was refused for lack of a good reason for the delayed application.
17 [1980] Ch 461; [1979] 3 All ER 815 CA.

the claimant was a son who was in employment and who had lived with the deceased for the nineteen years preceding death. His mother, the spouse of the deceased who subsisted on state benefits, had left the family home during this period because of their attitudes towards her. The Court of Appeal held that the deceased had no special obligation towards the son (who was clearly financially independent) and awarded the estate to the spouse.

2. Child

The age of such a child claimant is not a factor,[18] and it is sufficient that the deceased had treated the claimant as a child of the family.[19] In this jurisdiction the case of *Campbell v Campbell*[20] provides a good example of judicial discretion when applying the law on intestacy to favour a non-dependant child in a marital family context. The relevant facts were that the deceased had eleven children, one of whom had predeceased her. As she had died a widow and intestate, the normal rules would lead to a straight division of the estate, or its net value, into eleven equal shares.

The estate consisted of the family farm (and other assets) which had been run by the father until his death in 1963 and since then by the mother, with the help of son A who had spent virtually his whole life working on the farm, until her death in 1981. Her grandson W, son of A's deceased sister, had been brought up on the farm and had also always worked there. Applications were brought by A (aged fifty-three) and W (aged twenty-eight) under Article 4(1) and 5(1) of the Inheritance (Provision for Family and Dependants)(NI) Order 1979 and were heard by Murray J.

The court heard that the effect of applying the law of intestacy would be to put A out on the street with no job and perhaps £6,500 and to leave W with nothing. It also heard of the circumstances of a Mrs S, a sister of A, who was a widow with an unemployed son living with her and who subsisted on payments from Supplementary Benefits. It found that both plaintiffs were entitled to apply for orders as, under Article 2(1), the intestacy law did not make 'reasonable financial provision' within the meaning of Article 3:

> (1) . . . such financial provision as it would be reasonable in all the circumstances of the case for the applicant to receive for his maintenance.

The court held that A was to occupy the dwelling house on the farm, rent free for life and was to be awarded a larger share of the deceased's net estate; W was to have a share of the net assets (but smaller than that apportioned between A's siblings); and Mrs S was to receive a larger share than that allocated to the siblings.

---

18 Ibid, where the 'child' was aged forty-eight.
19 See, for example, *Re Leach (Deceased)* [1985] 2 All ER 754 CA where a step-daughter, in her fifties, succeeded despite opposing claims from next-of-kin.
20 [1982] NIBJ 18.

Claims Made against the Estate of an Unmarried Intestate

1. Cohabitee

Any claimant will have a case if he or she can demonstrate that the state of dependency upon the deceased existed at the time of the latter's death; that deceased had accepted responsibility for maintaining the claimant; and that the deceased had failed to make reasonable provision for the claimant. A surviving sibling or other relative, for example, would be as entitled as a mistress to make such a claim.

The significance of marital status in the context of intestacy is well illustrated by *Harrington v Gill*,[21] in which the deceased and the claimant lived together in the former's house following the death of their respective spouses. The deceased had paid all outgoings while the claimant paid for all clothes and household extras but did not pay for her board and lodging. On his death intestate, the claimant who was aged seventy-four subsisted on her pension while the entire estate went to the deceased's daughter who lived in financially secure circumstances. The claimant's appeal for reasonable provision was ultimately determined by the Court of Appeal which ruled that all necessary conditions to establish a claim were satisfied and that she was entitled to such provision as a reasonable man in the deceased's position would make. She was granted a lump sum and a life interest in the house.

Where there is evidence that the deceased repudiated responsibility for maintaining the claimant, then the latter's claim under the 1979 Order must fail.[22]

2. Child

A child of any age, whether legitimate, illegitimate, adopted or conceived before the death of an intestate parent, has a right to claim against the estate where reasonable provision was not made for him or her. The court, however, has a power rather than a duty to make provision and may not make an order in circumstances where it considers that a reasonable person in the deceased's position may have chosen not to do so.[23]

---

21 [1982] 4 FLR 265.
22 As in *Kourkey v Lusher* (1983) 4 FLR 65 where the deceased had ended his relationship with his mistress nine days before his death.
23 See, for example, f/ns 16 and 17 supra where in both cases the court took the view that the claimants should be encouraged to fend for themselves.

APPENDIX 1

The Eight Principles of the Honourable Justice MacDermott

1. The first and paramount consideration for the Court is the welfare of the child. This rule has its roots in the practice of the Court of Chancery. Decision and legislation has only served to strengthen and develop it. As Lindly LJ said in *In re McGrath*: 'The dominant matter for the consideration of the Court is the welfare of the child. But the welfare of a child is not measured by money only, nor by physical comfort only. The word welfare must be taken in its widest sense. The moral and religious welfare of the child must be considered as well as its physical well-being. Nor can the ties of affection be disregarded.' (*Re B. (an infant)*, per MacDermott J, [1946] NI 1).

2. In considering the welfare of a child the court 'must not only address itself to the child's present comfort and happiness but must also endeavour to look forward and try to consider what is ultimately best in the interest of the child.' (*Re B.*, per Black J, [1946] at p. 4)

3. In considering this type of case in Northern Ireland, regard must be had to the provisions of s. 5 of the Guardianship of Infants Act 1886 as to whether the father or the mother be the applicant to the court. This section prescribes three matters for the consideration of the court: 'the welfare of the infant, the conduct of the parties, and the wishes as well of the mother as of the father'. But as Viscount Cave said in *Ward v Laverty*, [1925] AC 101 at p. 108: 'It is the welfare of the children which, according to rules which are now well accepted, forms the paramount consideration in these cases.'

4. 'In having regard to the conduct of the parents under s. 5 of the Act of 1886 the Court should consider the spouses as of equal status and ignore the inequality of their rights at common law.' (*Re B.*, [1946] NI 1 per MacDermott J, at p. 8)

5. If the welfare of the child is equally assured irrespective of which parent obtains custody, there exists, in Northern Ireland at least, a sufficient residue of the father's common law right to custody to tip the balance in his favour. See *Re R.A.W. and M.W. (infants)*, [1949] NI 1: 'In practice however I would doubt if today a full analysis of the ingredients which make up the concept of welfare will often achieve such a finely balanced conclusion and in this case I have reached my decision without having to involve this principle.

604

6. In England, the most relevant statutory provisions is s. 1 of the Guardianship of Infants Act 1925. It prescribes not three matters but one for the consideration of the court in this type of case: 'The Court shall regard the welfare of the infant as the first and paramount consideration'. In the 'Spanish boy' case, [1970] AC 668, Lord MacDermott defined that phrase at p. 710 in these words:

> Reading these words in their ordinary significance, and relating them to the various classes of proceedings which the section has already mentioned, it seems to me that they must mean more than that the child's welfare is to be treated as the top item in a list of items relevant to the matters in question. I think they connote a process whereby, when all the relevant facts, relationships, claims, wishes of parents, risks, choices, and other circumstances are taken into account and weighed, the course to be followed will be that which is most in the interests of the child's welfare as that term has now to be understood. That is the first consideration because it is of first importance and the paramount consideration because it rules upon or determines the course to be followed.

To my mind the courts in Northern Ireland faced with the consideration of the welfare of a child embark on a similar process and despite the differences in legislative background, guidance and assistance can be found in the English decisions.

7. There is no rule of law that a mother is entitled to the custody of young children; see *Re B.*, [1962] 1 All ER 872 at p. 873. As a factor in the overall concept of welfare, the presence of a mother must receive considerable weight, but at the same time no mother is entitled to seek to take advantage of that foreseeable judicial view by acting arbitrarily and without due regard to the wishes of her husband.

8. Not only are the husband and wife mutually entitled to each other's society but children of the marriage are entitled to the joint care and affection of both parents. A parent who sees fit to leave the matrimonial home must justify his or her action if a claim to care and control of a child is to succeed; this is a heavy onus and the Court will require to be satisfied that sufficiently grave and weighty reasons exist to justify such actions. Such generalisations must of course be applied cautiously the outcome of each case turns on its own peculiar facts. It is obvious that to destroy a marriage which has hitherto been successful and happy is a much more irresponsible act than to leave a matrimonial home where, though the parents had both been living under the same roof, the real heart of the marriage had long since died and actual separation was inevitable sooner or later. In recent years, the question of the effect of parental fault, in the sense which I have described above, has been considered many times and I would refer to *Re F.*, [1969] 2 Ch. 238 (Megarry J); *Re L.*, [1962] 1 WLR 886 (The English Court of Appeal) and *Re P.D.J.M.* and *R.J.M.* (1974) No. 196, a decision of Lord MacDermott in our Chancery Division.

These judgments satisfy me of the following:

(a) Parental conduct is relevant not simply because it is one of the matters which s. 5 of the Act of 1886 requires to be considered, but because such conduct may

indicate whether or not a parent is a person who is capable of bringing up a child properly and in a satisfactory home environment.
(b) Even if a parent's conduct is blameworthy, he or she may be preferred to the innocent parent if the Court is satisfied that the future welfare of the child will best be secured by that course being taken.
(c) If the welfare of the child will be equally satisfactorily secured no matter which parent it is with, justice entitles the innocent parent to preference.

APPENDIX 2

The Changing Context of Private Family Law Since 1967

YEAR	MARRIAGES No.	MARRIAGES Rate per 1,000	DIVORCES Number	ILLEGITIMATE BIRTHS No.	ILLEGITIMATE BIRTHS Rate per 1,000 live births	ABORTIONS Number	ADOPTIONS Number	ADOPTIONS No. of family adoptions	RELEVANT LEGISLATION
1967	10,924	7.3	174	1,205	3.6		424		Adoption (NI) Act 1967
1968	11,240	7.5	263	1,245	3.8		456		
1969	11,587	7.7	240	1,210	3.7		514		Age of Majority Act (NI) 1969
1970	12,297	8.1	309	1,214	3.8	199	554		
1971	12,152	7.92	339	1,207	3.8	648	393		
1972	11,905	7.7	355	1,263	4.2	775	426		
1973	11,212	7.2	393	1,195	4.1	1,007	407		
1974	10,783	7.0	382	1,296	4.8	1,092	332	115	
1975	10,867	7.1	437	1,338	5.1	1,115	369	150	
1976	9,914	6.4	574	1,330	5.0	1,142	388	167	
1977	9,696	6.4	569	1,383	5.4	1,244	309	155	Family Law Reform (NI) Order 1977
1978	10,304	6.7	599	1,523	5.8	1,311	313	153	Matrimonial Causes (NI) Order 1978
1979	10,214	6.7	601	1,668	5.9	1,425	292	132	
1980	9,923	6.4	896	1,751	6.1	1,565	326	167	Domestic Proceedings (NI) Order 1980
1981	9,636	6.2	1,355	1,902	7.0	1,441	309	155	
1982	9,913	6.32	1,383	2,112	7.8	1,510	242	128	
1983	9,990	6.4	1,657	2,383	8.7	1,460	294	144	
1984	10,361	6.7	1,552	2,802	10.1	1,530	253	125	
1985	10,343	6.6	1,669	3,195	11.6	1,637	255	140	
1986	10,225	6.5	1,539	3,580	12.7	1,724	264	134	
1987	10,363	6.6	1,514	3,976	14.3	17.46	285	167	Adoption (NI) Order 1987
1988	9,960	6.3	1,550	4,464	16.1	1,815	270		
1989	10,019	6.3	1,818	4,412	16.9	1,816			
1990	9,588	6.0	1,897	4,972	18.8	1,855	144		
1991	9,221	5.8	2,310	5,306	20.2	1,775	222		
1992	9,392	5.8	2,280	5,603	21.9	1,794	236	89*	
1993	9,045	5.5	2,213	5,459	21.9	1,629	192	84*	Family Law (NI) Order 1993*
1994	8,683	5.3	2,303	5,353	22.0	1,678	192	63*	
1995	8,576	5.2	2,302	5,503	23.1	1,548	163	66*	Children (NI) Order 1995*

* High Court only.

APPENDIX 3

The Changing Context of Public Family Law Since 1967

YEAR	IN CARE No.	IN CARE Rate per 1,000	CARE ROUTE Vol Admis.	CARE ROUTE FPO	CARE ROUTE PRO	WARDSHIP ORDERS No.	WARDSHIP ORDERS Board/Trust	ADMISSIONS/DISCHARGES Admit	ADMISSIONS/DISCHARGES FPO	ADMISSIONS/DISCHARGES Discharge	DISPERSAL Boarded Out	DISPERSAL At Home etc.	RELEVANT LEGISLATION
1967	1,484												Children and Young Persons Act (NI) 1968
1968	1,521								701				
1969	1,644								700				Age of Majority Act (NI) 1969
1970	1,717	3.33	1,176	542	192			1,290	95	1,049	719	122	
1971	1,770	3.44	1,270	500	178			1,158	57	1,059	763	117	
1972	1,734	3.37	1,184	550	192			1,131	81	1,080	801	187	
1973	1,782	3.33	1,259	513	177			1,028	68	1,065	757	181	
1974	1,735	3.24	1,273	462	133			1,122	99	783	795	133	
1975	1,788	3.45			160			990	177	913	752	148	
1976	1,810	3.45						1,089	193	937	811	218	
1977	1,936	3.72	792	809	211			1,099	218	892	829	282	
1978	2,021	3.93			250	56		1,016	286	818	831	295	
1979	2,127	4.1			255	80		982	288	879	864	413	
1980	2,444	4.8	781	1,346	255	77		1,016	360	920	863	481	
1981	2,584	5.12	762	1,548	287	55	46	1,143	306	945	1,076	607	Legal Aid Advice and Assistance (NI) Order 1981
1982	2,559	5.07	591	1,675	303	99		1,070	298	928	1,125	619	Probation Board (NI) Order 1982
1983	2,547	5.17	625	1,751	318	106		894	325	961	1,162	621	
1984	2,448	5.00	617	1,710	300	169		958	348	1,047	1,216	593	
1985	2,512	5.17			269	136		969	455	1,040	1,235	629	Child Abduction (NI) Order 1985
1986	2,577					174		1,093			1,296		
1987	2,604				213			1,051	395	1,068	1,407	726	
1988			293										Criminal Justice (Evidence etc.) (NI) Order 1988
1989	2,783	6.0		1,962	168	337	95*	955	292	1,055	1,540	750	
1990	2,850	6.0		1,839	141	328	94*	1,033	262	895	1,602	645	
1991	2,876	6.2		1,867	111	345		1,058	262	970	1,647	728	Child Support (NI) Order 1991
1992	2,660	5.7		1,918	93	399		908	137	1,033	1,621	585	
1993	2,658	5.8		1,621	84	398	128*	1,067	149	1,127	1,515	595	
1994	2,660	5.7		1,584				1,224	121	1,245	1,611	6,213	Children's Evidence (NI) Order 1995
1995	2,624	5.6		1,425	73	387	154*	1,210	92	1,220	1,660	491	Children (NI) Order 1995

* Applications only.

APPENDIX 4

Useful Agencies

BAR LIBRARY   Tel: 01 232 241 523
Royal Courts of Justice, Chicester St, Belfast BT1 3JF

BARNARDOS   Tel: 01 232 672 366
542 Upper Newtownards Road, Belfast 4

BELFAST LAW CENTRE   Tel: 01 232 321 307
7 University Road, Belfast BT7 1NA

CENTRE FOR CHILD CARE RESEARCH   Tel: 01 232 335 401
The Director QUB, 14A Lennoxvale, Malone Road, Belfast BT9 5BY

CENTRAL SERVICES AGENCY FOR H&PSS   Tel: 01 232 324 431
27 Adelaide Street, Belfast 1

CHILD CARE (NI)   Tel: 01 232 234 499
11 University Street, Belfast BT7 1FY

CHILD CARE LEGISLATION UNIT   Tel: 01 232 520 500
Room 511, Dundonald House Upper Newtownards Road, Belfast BT4 3SF

CHILD SUPPORT AGENCY   Tel: 01 232 896 896
Great Northern Tower, 17 Great Victoria Street, Belfast BT2 7AD

CHILD SUPPORT APPEAL TRIBUNAL   Tel: 01 232 539 900
3 Donegall Square North, Belfast

CITIZENS ADVICE BUREAU   Tel: 01 232 231 120 11
Upper Crescent, Belfast BT7 1NT

COMMISSIONER FOR COMPLAINTS   Tel: 01 232 233 821
Progressive House, 33 Wellington Place, Belfast BT1 6HN

COMMUNITY RELATIONS COUNCIL   Tel: 01 232 439 953
6 Murray Street, Belfast 1

CORONER'S OFFICE   Tel: 01 232 743 040
The Courthouse, Crumlin Road, Belfast 14

CROWN SOLICITOR'S OFFICE   Tel: 01 232 542 555
Centre House, Chichester House, Belfast

DEPARTMENT OF EDUCATION (DENI)   Tel: 01 247 279 279
Rathgael House, Balloo Road, Bangor, Co Down BT19 7PR

DEPARTMENT OF HEALTH AND SOCIAL SERVICES (DHSS)   Tel: 01 232 520 500
Castle Buildings, Stormont, Belfast BT4 3UD

DEPARTMENT OF DIRECTOR OF PUBLIC PROSECUTIONS (DPP)   Tel: 01 232 542 444
Royal Courts of Justice, Chichester Street, Belfast BT1 3JF

ENFORCEMENT OF JUDGMENTS OFFICE   Tel: 01 232 245 081
7th Floor, Bedford House, Bedford Street, Belfast BT2 7DS

EQUAL OPPORTUNITIES COMMISSION   Tel: 01 232 242 752
Chamber of Commerce House, 22 Great Victoria Street, Belfast BT2 7BA

FAMILY LAW ASSOCIATION (SOLS)   Tel: 01 849 461 509
The Secretary, 18A Church Street, Antrim

FAMILY MEDIATION SERVICE   Tel: 01 232 322 914
76 Dublin Road, Belfast BT2 7HP

FAMILY PLANNING ASSOCIATION   Tel: 01 232 325 488
113 University Street, Belfast BT7 1HP

GENERAL REGISTER OFFICE   Tel: 01 232 252 030
49–55 Chichester Street, Belfast BT1 4HL

GINGERBREAD   Tel: 01 232 231 417
169 University Street, Belfast BT7 1HR

INCORPORATED LAW SOCIETY OF NORTHERN IRELAND   Tel: 01 232 235 111
Legal Aid Department, Law Courts Building, Belfast

INSTITUTE FOR PROFESSIONAL LEGAL STUDIES   Tel: 01 232 335 567
QUB 10 Lennoxvale, Malone Road, Belfast BT9 5BY

LAND REGISTRY   Tel: 01 232 251 555
Lincoln Buildings, Great Victoria Street, Belfast 1

LAW REFORM ADVISORY COMMITTEE FOR NORTHERN IRELAND   Tel: 01 232 327 661
Permanent House, 21–3 Arthur Street, Belfast BT1 4JL

LAW SCHOOL   Tel: 01 232 245 133
QUB, 21 University Square, Belfast BT7 1NN

LAW SOCIETY OF NORTHERN IRELAND   Tel: 01 232 231614
90 Victoria Street, Belfast 1

LEGAL AID ASSESSMENT OFFICE   Tel: 01 504 319
500 Asylum Road, Londonderry

LEGAL AID DEPARTMENT   Tel: 01 232 246 441
Bedford House, 16–22 Bedford Street, Belfast BT2 7FL

NORTHERN IRELAND CHILDMINDING ASSOCIATION   Tel: 01 247 811 015
17A Court Street, Newtownards

NORTHERN IRELAND COUNCIL FOR VOLUNTARY ACTION (NICVA)   Tel: 01 232 321 224
127 Ormeau Road, Belfast 7

Northern Ireland Court Service   Tel: 01 232 328 594
Windsor House, 9–15 Bedford Street, Belfast BT2 7LT

Northern Ireland Guardian ad Litem Agency (NIGALA)   Tel: 01 232 316 550
Centre House, 79 Chichester Street, Belfast BT14 JE

Northern Ireland Pre-School Playgroup Association (NIPPA)
Tel: 01 232 662 825
Unit 3, Boucher Crescent, Belfast BT 12 6HU

National Society for Prevention of Cruelty to Children (NSPCC)
Tel: 01 232 240 311
16 Rosemary Street, Belfast BT1 1QD

Office of Care & Protection   Tel: 01 232 235 111
Royal Courts of Justice, PO Box 410, Chicester Street, Belfast BT1 3JF

Official Solicitor to the Supreme Court   Tel: 01 232 235 111
Royal Courts of Justice PO Box 410, Chicester Street, Belfast BT1 3JF

Parents Advice Centre   Tel: 01 232 238 800
Bryson House, 28 Bedford Street, Belfast BT2 7FE

Probate Office   Tel: 01 232 235 111
Royal Courts of Justice, PO Box 410, Chicester Street, Belfast BT1 3JF

Probation Board (NI)   Tel: 01 232 262 400
80 North Street, Belfast 1

Public Record Office   Tel: 01 232 251318
66 Balmoral Ave, Belfast BT9 6NY

Rape Crisis Centre   Tel: 01 232 249 696
29 Donegall Street, Belfast BT1 2FG

Regional Information Branch (DHSS)   Tel: 01 232 522 521
DHSS, Annexe 2, Castle Buildings, Stormont, Belfast BT4 3UD

Registry of Deeds   Tel: 01 232 251 777
Lincoln Buildings, Great Victoria Street, Belfast BT29 AG

Relate Counselling Services   Tel: 01 232 323 454
76 Dublin Road, Belfast BT2 7HP

Royal Ulster Constabulary (RUC)   Tel: 01 232 650 222
Headquarters, Knock Road, Belfast 5

Social Security Commissioners Office Tel: 01 232 332 344
Lancashire House, 5 Linenhall Street, Belfast 2

Voice of Young People in Care (VOYPIC)   Tel: 01 232 244 888
Albany House, 73 Great Victoria Street, Belfast BT29 AG

Index

ABDUCTION
  all ports alert 201
  children in care 204
  Conventions
    administration/procedure 198, 209
    European Convention 198
      registration of custody order 214
      restrictions of application 213
    Hague Convention 197, 206
      habitual residence 207
      rights of custody 208
      wrongful removal/detention 206
    policy 198
    prompt return 210
      exceptions to, 210–12
  criminal law 201
    kidnapping 203
    persons connected with child 202
    other persons 203
  definition 195
  family, by 195
  habitual residence 196
  jurisdiction 204–06
  Non-Convention cases 215
    paramountcy principles, application of 216
  preventative court orders
    necessity for order 200
    Parental Responsibility Order 199
    Prohibited Steps Order 199
    Residence Order 199
    surrender of passport 199
    Wardship Order 199–200, 455
  offense 195
  stranger, by 196
ABORTION 56, 63
  consent 58
  doctor/patient relationship 60
  for disturbed adolescents in care 150
  suicide risk 58, 59, 150
  unlawfully 57, 94
ADOPTION 69
  agreement of natural parents 121, 122
  application, lodging of 118
  bodies 100
  child should not be married 97
  consent to 41, 107, 123, 125
    unreasonable withholding 112, 113, 120, 124
  consequences
    adopters, for 134
    child, for 132
    natural parents, for 133
  declaration of no further involvement 106
  eligibility of adopters 99, 121, 124, 125
  Freeing Order 87, 104, 108, 109, 110, 119, 122, 127, 128, 387
    application for revocation 106
    consent to 41, 105
    revocation 111
    use of 111, 113
    vested in agency 107
    without parental 127
  guardian ad litem 78, 118
  hearing 121
  information
    child 132
    natural parents 133
  jurisdiction 95
  Order 87, 103, 125, 126, 127, 128, 387
    conditions attached to 129, 130, 131
  overseas children, and 63, 125
  parental misconduct 124
  partial order 132

party to
  unmarried father 50, 56, 122, 123
  placement 125, 127
    agency 116, 118, 119
    illegal 448
    private 115
    supervision 117
    Trust, by 119
    with parental agreement 102, 111, 119
  Registrar General 102
  surrogacy arrangement 73
  welfare principle 96, 97, 102, 108, 110, 114, 121, 125, 126
ADULTERY
  divorce and 176–7
APPEALS 127
  Case stated lxiii
  Court of Appeal lxii, lxiii, 72
  House of Lords lxii
  Point of law lxiii
ARTICLE 8 lxiii, 62, 67, 74, 88, 91, 124
  child abduction 201
  child, definition 250
  conditions attached to 171
  contact order 319, 376
    definition 254
    duration 257
    effect 255
    refused by child 257
    refused by parent 256
  court order 144, 158, 315
    except for child in care 156
    Trust application 316
  domestic violence 171
  private family law orders, contested arrangements
    flexibility of 250–51
    situations available in 248
  Prohibited Steps Order 259, 317
    Trust with leave of court 319
  Residence Order 250, 317
    child in care 317
    conditions 251
    consent by 318
    duration 254
    effects of 251
  Specific Issue Order 257–8
    Trust with leave of court 320
  third parties 128
ASSISTED PARENTHOOD 63
  Human Fertilisation and Embryology Act 1990 66–75
    child of surrogate arrangement 72
    consent 71
    of section 30 order 73
    genetic link 72
    information 74–5
    mother, definition of 67
    father/ donor father, definition of 68
    parent, legal status of 72
  medically 64
  Surrogacy Arrangements Act 1985 66
    commercial surrogacy 70
    mother, definition of 67
    enforceability of arrangement 69, 70
    locus standi
      birth parent, of 70
      genetically linked commissioning parent, of 69, 71

CHILD
  access 145
  Black Report 225–6, 263–4,
  best interest in surrogacy arrangement 70
  care law
    legislation 228
    reform in England and Wales 223–5
    reform in Northern Ireland 225–7
  care plan, under 372
  care proceedings 147
  Contact
    child in care 373, 378
    unmarried father 56
  Custody 145, 152
    parental fitness 153
    unmarried father 50
  day care 263
  discipline of child in care 378

CHILD (*contd.*)
    permissible restraint 379
    unacceptable 379
  education of 40
  eligibility of, for adoption 97
  filius nullius 64
  guardian *ad litem* 41
  in care
    parental access 116
  legitimacy 125
    common law 47
    legal significance of 42
    reform by 1995 Act 228
    void marriages, child of 48
    voidable marriages, child of 49
  legitimated
    statutory provisions 48
    subsequent marriage, by 48, 87
  legitimation 48–9
  medical treatment of 40, 41
    ability of child to give consent 40
  parental responsibility. *See* **PARENTAL RESPONSIBILITY**
  protected 118
  religious upbringing 41, 122, 129, 148
  removal from jurisdiction of 41
  rights of child, UN Convention 63
  separate legal interest 34
  UN Convention on the Rights of the Child 265, 370, 380
    influence on legislation 417, 438–9
  welfare 35, 38, 42, 43, 123, 145
    best interest of child, proceedings 35, 150
    conflict of interest 378
    duty of Trust 370
    factors 151
    harm, suffering, at risk of 147, 149, 152
    principle 228
    under Children (NI) Order 221

CHILD ABUSE
  abuse 114, 147, 323
  definition of 324
  emotional 330
  media reports of 224, 322
  neglect 325
  physical abuse 326
  sexual abuse 327
    corroboration 445
    hearsay evidence 444
    standard of proof 328–9
  significant harm threshold 324

CHILD PROTECTION
  agencies 331–3
  authority to conduct inquiry
    court, by 334
    RUC by 335
    Trust, by 336
  case conference 338
  Child Assessment Order 345
    effect of 347
    limitations of 348
    procedure 346
  child protection register 338–40
    effect of registration 340
    review 341
  criminal law 39
  Emergency Protection Order 348
    appeal from 354
    effect of 352
    limitations of 353
    procedural 351
    significant harm test 350
    urgency requirement 349
  Part VI of Children (NI) Order 1995 342–4
  police protection order 356–7
  professional enquiries into 337
    options of Trust 341
  Recovery Order 354–6

CHILDREN (NI) ORDER 1995
  application for directions 231
  article 8 orders. *see also* **ARTICLE 8** 231
  checklist considerations 236–41
    capability of parent / person meeting child's needs 240
    child's age and gender 238
    child's physical, emotional and educational needs 237

effect on child of change in circumstance 238
harm or ill-treatment suffered or at risk of 239
public law application 296, 297
wishes of child 237
child care and supervision
  beyond parental control 294–5
  coercive intervention 284, 298
  ill-treatment 293
  jurisdiction 287
  not a child of the State 286–7
  Orders, grounds for 300, 306, 312
  parties 288–9
  shared responsibility 287
  significant harm threshold 284, 286
    definition 292–5
divorce, separation, nullity proceedings
  contested arrangements for child 243, 250
  uncontested arrangements for child 244
courts, changes in
  appeals 234
  proceedings 233
  system 232–3
discretionary authority of judiciary 241
family assistance order 260
financial relief order 262
guardian of child, appointment of 262
guardian ad litem, role under 231
new concepts in 235–6
  limiting litigation 236
  no-delay principle 235, 297
  no-order presumption 236, 296
parental responsibility. *See also*
  PARENTAL RESPONSIBILITY
Parental Responsibility Order 261
Public Law Orders 298
  Care Order 298–303
  difference between care and supervision orders 299
  distinction between judicial and legislative authority 299
  education supervision order 310–15
  interim orders 306–08
  supervision order 299–304
private law
  checklist considerations 248
  no-delay principle 246
  no-order presumption 247
  paramountcy principle 245–6
policy for state intervention 229
recorded findings 231
unifying principles 230
wardship proceedings 250
welfare of child, paramountcy of 229, 235
  order directing investigation into child's circumstance 261
private law, in 245
CO-HABITATION 52
bankruptcy 54
contract 53
death or injury 55
domestic violence 52, 54
income support 54
property rights 54
public housing 54
reasons for 52
United Nations Convention on Rights of 223
COMPETENT
Gillick 13, 43, 59, 60, 126
  care proceedings 150, 157
  consent 422, 428
  House of Lords ruling 225, 237, 454
  separate level of interest for child 418, 420, 433
COUNTY COURT xxii, 66
  Care Centres xxii
  Domestic Proceedings Court xxii

DEATH
partner of, right to compensation 518
presumption of and dissolution of marriage
  decree of 44
  termination of marriage by 44

DIVORCE 14
  a mensa et thoro 174
  ancillary relief 550
    definition of 554
    delayed application for 567
    eligibility for 551
    factors court takes into consideration 561–5
    financial provision 555–8
    liability 553
    maintenance pending suit 554
    property adjustment order 558–61
    order for sale 561
  appeals from 192–3
  bars to
    connivance 185
    time bar 184–5
  clean break 566–72
    court application of 570–72
    fixed term periodical payments 568
    inappropriate 569
  children
    arrangements for 190
      refusal to grant until 191
    court's role 190
  conciliation/mediation 189
  decree absolute 43
    grant of 189
    legal effect 193
    refusal, lack of financial agreement 185
  decree *nisi* 14, 30, 176, 183
    gift made under a will, effect on 45
    grant of 189
  foreign divorces 191–2
  grounds for 29
    adultery 174, 176–8
    cruelty 174
    desertion 174, 180–82
    incurable insanity 174
    five years' separation 183
      grave financial hardship 183–4, 185
    two years' separation 182
    unreasonable behaviour 178–80
  guardianship 85

  irretrievable breakdown 175, 177
  legal aid 193
  pensions 194
  procedure
    certificate of readiness 188
    decree, grant of 186
    jurisdiction 186
    notice 187
    oral testimony 188
    petition 186
      cross petition 187–8
      lodging with supporting documents 187
  property arrangements 191
  will, effect on 193
DOMESTIC VIOLENCE 164
  children and 167
  cohabitees, law relating to 169
  criminal proceedings 165
  duration of orders 170
  emergency procedure 170
  Exclusion Order 168, 171
  inherent jurisdiction 172–3
  law reform report 170
  ouster orders 169
  Personal Protection Order 166–8
  remedies 165–6
DOMICILE
  adopted child of 97
  applicant for adoption/freeing order 99, 101
  Public law requirements of marriage 7
  change of 11
  of origin retained by wife 26

EC TREATY 72
ENGAGEMENT 5
  contractual agreement 5
  engagement ring 479
  gifts between fiancées 479
  pre-nuptial agreement 479
  property 477–8

FAMILY PROCEEDINGS COURT xxii
FOSTER CARE 365
  arrangement for placement of children 366

foster parents 365
  rights of 367
general responsibilities of
  duties 275–9
  employment 271
judicial review of 154
home placement 368
  under 1995 Order 369
loco parentis 149
paramountcy principle 285, 296
powers 148
post 1995 155, 157
private arrangements for fostering children 269–70
regulations 367
refuges for children at risk of harm 357
residential care placement 363
  under 1995 order 364

GREEN FORM SCHEME lxiv
GUARDIAN AD LITEM 124, 158
  adoption. see also Adoption 100, 120, 448, 454
  agency 291
  appointment 289
  conflict of views 460
  disclosure of information to 457
  duties of 457
  Human Fertilisation and Embryology 67
  instructions from, to solicitor 292, 459
  mental illness, petition for nullity 21
  Official Solicitor as 84, 157, 459
  panel 290
  representation of child 456
  wardship 143
GUARDIANSHIP 76
  appointment 80
    by court 79
    by parent 80
  family proceedings 79
  effect of 80–81
  grounds for 79–80
  historical 36, 37, 77
  1995 Order 84

HABEAS CORPUS 37
HAGUE CONVENTION ON INTER-COUNTRY ADOPTION 1993 265
HIGH COURT xxi, 66
  Family Division lxi
HOMOSEXUAL RELATIONSHIP 52
HUMAN RIGHTS
  European Commission of 140
  European Convention for protection of 15, 87, 141, 370
    effect on family law 222, 256
    decrees of 237
  European Court 15, 52, 63, 87, 265
    adoption, unmarried fathers 106, 123
    parenthood and chastisement 326
HYBRID ORDERS 321

INTER-COUNTRY ADOPTIONS
  Hague Convention on 103
INTESTATE SUCCESSION
  beneficiaries 593
  entitlement of
    marital family 595–8
    non-marital family 598–9
  hotchpot 594
  intestacy, definition of 593
  judicial determination of 600–603
    cohabitee 603
  statute law 594
  surviving spouse, rights of matrimonial home 45

JUDICIAL SEPARATION 160
  decree, effects of 161
  divorce proceedings following 161
  eligibility 160
  grounds for 161
  inheritance rights 162
  property adjustment 162, 164
  separation agreement 160, 163
JUVENILE COURT xxiii
JUVENILE JUSTICE SYSTEM
  Black Report 389, 397
  bodies 393–4
  committal proceedings 399–402

JUVENILE JUSTICE SYSTEM (*contd.*)
    arrest 399
    bail 400, 411
    juvenile court 401
    magistrates court 402
  DPP 391
  disposal options 403
    judicial 405
      community order 406–07
      custodial order 408
      non-treatment order 405
    non-judicial 404
  doli incapax 392
  jurisdiction 390
    courts 395
  policy 394
    twin track approach 395
  preventative powers 397–8
  remand 409–11
  terrorist offences 402–03
  treatment of offenders
    community 411
    custodial 412
      detention in secure accommodation 414
      detention in young offenders' centre 414
      training school 413

LAW COMMISSION RECOMMENDATION
  Custody of Children – Jurisdiction and Enforcement within the UK 204

LAW COMMISSION REPORT
  Breach of Promise of Marriage 6
  Distribution on Intestacy 594
  Domestic Violence and Occupation of the Family Home 172
  Family Law, Review of Child Law: Guardianship 76
  Financial Consequences of Divorce 566
  Grounds for Divorce 160
  Guardianship 65
  Guardianship and Custody 1988 243
  Illegitimacy 1979 65
  Illegitimacy 1982 52
  Illegitimacy 1986 52

LAW REPORTS lxiv
LEGAL AID lxiv
LEGAL AID BOARD
  duty of solicitor to 449
LEGAL INTEREST OF CHILD 416
  age and understanding 420
  legal interest
    public family law 424
      duties of court 424
      duties of others 426–7
      duties of Trust 425, 431
      paramountcy principle, court bound by 430
    medical treatment of child in care 428–429
    private family law 432
      duty of court 434
  statutory duty 418–420
  views of child 417
    consent 422–3
    definition 421

MAINTENANCE 62
  agreement private 538
    courts' involvement in 539–42
  appeal 532
  assessment 531
  child support scheme 52
    administrative framework 525–7
    child for whom liability owed 530–31
    considerations of agency 527–9
    jurisdiction 523–5
    maintenance assessment 534
    means tested benefit 534
    parent liable 529
  collection 532
  enforcement 533
  financial provision for children 536
  legislation 519
  of non-marital child, by father 50, 55, 88
  principles 520–22
  spouse's duty 537

Index 619

statute under
  Child Support/Care legislation 547–9
  Domestic Proceedings (NI) Order 1980 545–7
  Matrimonial Causes (NI) Order 1978 543–5
MAGISTRATES COURT xxii, 109
  alleged offence under Surrogacy Act 66
MARRIAGE 5
  adultery 30, 31, 62
  annulment 14, 15, 23
    decree for dissolution 43
  arranged 17
  bankruptcy 27
  bigamy 13
    decree of presumption of death, defence to 44
  capacity to marry 12
  ceremony
    civil marriage 18
    religious, postponement of 18
  citizenship 26
  civil marriages 7
    declaration, no known impediment to marriage 7
    signatures 8
    solemn vows 7
    Superintendent registrar's certificate 7
    witnesses 8
    written notice 7
  cohabitation
    consortium right to. *see* CONSORTIUM 28
    length of 18
  consent to 16
    capacity of 19, 21
    minor, of 13, 41
  consortium
    co-habitation, duty to 28
    criminal conversation 30
    loss of 30
    marital confidences 30
    meaning of 28
    right to 28
    restitution of conjugal rights 29
    sexual relations 29
  consummation of 14, 16
    infertility 17
    impotence 18, 22
    pre-marital intercourse 17
    wilful refusal to 18
  Church of Ireland 7
    Common License 8
    Publication of the Bans 8
    Register 8
    Special License 8
  contract
    capacity to 16, 27
    no presumption of 28
    criminal law 26, 29
  defects 13
    procedural 12
  desertion 11
  financial support 32
  foreign marriage 9
  formalities of marriage 7
  gender
    biological criteria 16
    surgically assisted change 15
  gift in contemplation of 6
  habitual residence 26
  Jewish 9
  lex celebrationis 10
  lex domiclii 10, 12
  lex loci celebrationis 16
  Licences 8
  maintenance of child 40
  marital name 26
  marital parenthood
    custody 33, 37, 40
    forfeit by father 34
    guardianship 33
    parental rights 32, 36, 40
  marital property 31
    effect on ownership 31
    third parties 32
  marriage of convenience 6, 19
  monogamy 6, 10
  matrimonial home

MARRIAGE (*contd.*)
   bankruptcy 27
   Non-Church of Ireland 9
   nullity 11, 15
      decree absolute 23
      decree of 18, 23
      duress 17, 19
      guardian ad litem 21
   polygamous 9, 10, 15
   pre-marital agreement 18
   Quaker 9
   rape within 29
   relationship prohibited degrees of 12
      affinity 12
      consanguinity 12
   spouses
      legal identity of wife 25
   status 26
   taxation 32
   termination of
      death, by 44
      divorce by. *see* DIVORCE 43
   valid consent 6
   void. *see* VOID MARRIAGE 5, 12, 14
   voidable *see* VOIDABLE MARRIAGE 5, 14, 17
   wills
      in contemplation of 28
MEDIATION 3

OFFICIAL SOLICITOR 83, 157
   appointment 447–8
   duties 447

PARENT
   cohabitee 55
   definition 39
   genetic 55
   non-cohabiting 62
   responsibility to child 39
   sexual orientation of 240
PARENTAL RESPONSIBILITY 79, 86, 96, 122, 123
   accommodation by Trust under 282
   by agreement 89
   by appointment 89
   court application by father 87, 88
   guardian of child's estate 85
   loss of 90
   medical treatment 157, 258
   neglect of child 325
   order of discharge 88
   residence order 253
   unmarried mother 47
   unmarried father 56
   under Children (NI) Order 1995 221, 241–2
PATERNITY
   blood tests 62, 529
   proof of 50
   samples, refusal to provide 51
   tests 51
PERJURY 13
PROPERTY
   cohabiting relationship 505
      acquiring the beneficial interest 508–12
      agreement between parties 507
      bankruptcy 517
      business 513
      finance 517
      matrimonial home 514–17
      presumption of advancement 514
      realisation of separate legal interests 506
      rights under trust 507
      tax 518
   constructive trusts 473, 477
      indirect contribution 484
      referable detriment 485–6
   implied trusts 472
   marital property 469
      common intention 481
      criteria applied by court 489
      historical 470–71
      property 480–81
      right to 479
   matrimonial home 475, 476
      charges 503–04
      creditors 498
      direct contributions 482–83

dispute between spouse and third parties 491–98
mortgages 502
order 490
right of occupation of 489
unmarried parent 514
presumption of advancement 473
indirect contributions and 487
proprietary estoppel 475
resulting trusts 472

RAPE
date 177
marital 165
sexual abuse 328, 330
REGISTRATION OF BIRTHS AND DEATHS 60–62
REPRESENTATION OF CHILD
audi alteram partem 435, 438
Black Report 435
civil proceedings 436
  guardian ad Litem 437
  next friend 436
complaints service provision by Trust 461–3
evidence
  children, on oath 442
  expert witnesses 446
  hearsay rule 443
  privilege against self incrimination 446
  unsworn evidence 443
  video 444–5
expert witness 449–51
guardian ad litem. *see also* **GUARDIAN AD LITEM**
family proceedings
  judgment against 442
  jurisdiction 438–9
  status of child 440
  sufficient understanding 441
official solicitor. *see* also **OFFICIAL SOLICITOR**
proceedings initiated by child 460
  leave of court 461
public proceedings 455–6

self representation 452
tests, to instruct a solicitor 453
solicitor 448
Trust social worker 454
RESIDENCE ORDER 88, 118, 124
foster-parent 128
grandparents 91

SECURE ACCOMMODATION 382
court role of 383
paramountcy principle 384
Trust's responsibility 384
SINGLE PARENT FAMILY 62
STEP PARENTS 92–3
SUCCESSION
rights of cohabitees 54
SURNAME
child's 253
cohabiting couple, use by 53
wife assuming husband's 26
SURROGACY 64
ethics 65

TRUST, HSS 265
accommodation by 280–83
  appointment of solicitor 291
  child's wishes 283
  legal status 360
  looked after 359
  after care by 387
care order. *see also* **CHILDREN ORDER** 103, 116, 137
  effect 377
  revival of 111
  review of 379
    representation 381
    statutory duty to review 380
  statutory 109
  legal standing of parent 362
care plan 371–2
child minding/day care 267, 279–80
  registration 268
child in care, decision making
  by court 376
  by Trust 374
children in need 266, 273–5, 281

child's wishes, duty to respect 371
consensual intervention 284
contact
   arrangements 373
   order 375
court directs investigation by 318
discharge from care 385
   age 387
   application for 385
   by making/substituting order 386
   duty to provide services of 388

VOID MARRIAGE
children status of 23, 48
decree of nullity 23
doctrine of estoppel 23

VOIDABLE MARRIAGE
bars to relief
   injustice to respondent 22
   petitioner's conduct 21
   time 22
children of 49
decree absolute 24
decree of nullity 23
grounds rendering voidable
   invalid consent 19
      duress 19
      mistake 20
      mental disorder 21
   pregnancy *per alium* 21
   unsoundness of mind 20
   venereal disease 21
non-consummation 17
rights under statutes 24
   wilful refusal to 18, 22

WARDSHIP 104, 108, 120, 309
abuse of child 147
   sexual 147, 154
applicant 141, 145
   private 158, 159
application 135
consent to adoption withheld 149
defendant 141

High Court 135, 136, 137, 138, 142
   judicial review 153–4
   jurisdiction 229
   powers to protect welfare of ward 146
   restricted post 1995 155
'important steps' 140
inherent jurisdiction
   leave by Trust 155–7, 320–21
   emergency 'stop and hold' powers 159
   supplement statutory powers 157, 158
jurisdiction 107, 126, 135, 144
last resort 146
order 116, 135, 139, 140
paramountcy principle 138, 139, 145, 151, 157
statutory arena, in 229
parens patriae 136, 156, 158
pre 1995 144, 358
procedure 143
Prohibited Steps Order 171
subject 141

WIFE
common law wife 55, 518

WILL
administration of 582–4
alterations to 578
contents of 574
contested 584–5
   children 589–91
   co-habitees 591–2
   spouses 586–9
   two-stage test 585
effect of
   divorce 581
   marriage 580
exempted disposition 574
formalities 575–7
dissolution of marriage, effect of 45
mutual testation 581
revocation 578–9
statute 573
testamentary guardian 78
testator 579